New Perspectives on

Microsoft®

Office 97
Professional

ENHANCED

The New Perspectives Series

The New Perspectives Series consists of texts and technology that teach computer concepts and microcomputer applications (listed below). You can order these New Perspectives texts in many different lengths, software releases, custom-bound combinations, CourseKits™ and Custom Editions®. Contact your Course Technology sales representative or customer service representative for the most up-to-date details.

The New Perspectives Series

Computer Concepts

Borland® dBASE®

Borland® Paradox®

Corel® Presentations™

Corel® Quattro Pro®

Corel® WordPerfect®

DOS

HTML

Lotus® 1-2-3®

Microsoft® Access

Microsoft® Excel

Microsoft® FrontPage 98

Microsoft® Internet Explorer

Microsoft® Office Professional

Microsoft® PowerPoint®

Microsoft® Windows® 3.1

Microsoft® Windows® 95

Microsoft® Windows® 98

Microsoft® Windows NT® Server 4.0

Microsoft® Windows NT® Workstation 4.0

Microsoft® Word

Microsoft® Works

Microsoft® Visual Basic® 4 and 5

Netscape Communicator™

Netscape Navigator™

Netscape Navigator™ Gold

New Perspectives on
Microsoft®
Office 97
Professional

ENHANCED

June Jamrich Parsons

Dan Oja

Stephanie Low
The College of Charleston

Roy Ageloff
University of Rhode Island

Beverly B. Zimmerman
Brigham Young University

S. Scott Zimmerman
Brigham Young University

Nancy Acree
University of Puget Sound

Joseph Adamski
Grand Valley State University

Sandra E. Poindexter
Northern Michigan University

Joan Carey
Carey Associates, Inc

Kathleen Finnegan

Ann Shaffer

A Susan Solomon Book

COURSE
TECHNOLOGY

ONE MAIN STREET, CAMBRIDGE, MA 02142

an International Thomson Publishing company I(T)P®

Cambridge • Albany • Bonn • Boston • Cincinnati • London • Madrid • Melbourne • Mexico City
New York • Paris • San Francisco • Singapore • Tokyo • Toronto • Washington

New Perspectives on Microsoft® Office 97 Professional—Enhanced is published by Course Technology.

Associate Publisher	Mac Mendelsohn
Series Consulting Editor	Susan Solomon
Product Managers	Mark Reimold, Donna Gridley, Rachel Crapser
Developmental Editors	Barbara Clemens, Kim Crowley, Terry Ann Kremer, Sasha Vodnik, Joan Carey, Robin Geller, Janice Jutras, Jessica Evans
Production Editors	Daphne Barbas, Roxanne Alexander, Nancy Ray, Melissa Lima
Text and Cover Designer	Ella Hanna
Cover Illustrator	Douglas Goodman

For more information contact:

Course Technology
One Main Street
Cambridge, MA 02142

ITP Europe
Berkshire House 168-173
High Holborn
London WCIV 7AA
England

Nelson ITP, Australia
102 Dodds Street
South Melbourne, 3205
Victoria, Australia

ITP Nelson Canada
1120 Birchmount Road
Scarborough, Ontario
Canada M1K 5G4

International Thomson Editores
Seneca, 53
Colonia Polanco
11560 Mexico D.F. Mexico

ITP GmbH
Königswinterer Strasse 418
53227 Bonn
Germany

ITP Asia
60 Albert Street, #15-01
Albert Complex
Singapore 189969

ITP Japan
Hirakawacho Kyowa Building, 3F
2-2-1 Hirakawacho
Chiyoda-ku, Tokyo 102
Japan

ISBN 0-7600-5798-2

Printed in the United States of America

10 9 8 7 6 5 4 3 2 1 BM 02 01 00 99 98

At Course Technology we have one foot in education and the other in technology. We believe that technology is transforming the way people teach and learn, and we are excited about providing instructors and students with materials that use technology to teach about technology.

Our development process is unparalleled in the higher education publishing industry. Every product we create goes through an exacting process of design, development, review, and testing.

Reviewers give us direction and insight that shape our manuscripts and bring them up to the latest standards. Every manuscript is quality tested. Students whose backgrounds match the intended audience work through every keystroke, carefully checking for clarity and pointing out errors in logic and sequence. Together with our own technical reviewers, these testers help us ensure that everything that carries our name is error-free and easy to use.

We show both how and why technology is critical to solving problems in college and in whatever field you choose to teach or pursue. Our time-tested, step-by-step instructions provide unparalleled clarity. Examples and applications are chosen and crafted to motivate students.

As the New Perspectives Series team at Course Technology, our goal is to produce the most timely, accurate, creative, and technologically sound product in the entire college publishing industry. We strive for consistent high quality. This takes a lot of communication, coordination, and hard work. But we love what we do. We are determined to be the best. Write to us and let us know what you think. You can also e-mail us at newperspectives@course.com.

The New Perspectives Series Team

Joseph J. Adamski	Jessica Evans	Scott MacDonald
Judy Adamski	Dean Fossella	Mac Mendelsohn
Roy Ageloff	Marilyn Freedman	William Newman
Tim Ashe	Kathy Finnegan	Dan Oja
David Auer	Robin Geller	David Paradice
Daphne Barbas	Kate Habib	June Parsons
Dirk Baldwin	Donna Gridley	Harry Phillips
Rachel Bunin	Roger Hayen	Sandra Poindexter
Joan Carey	Cindy Johnson	Mark Reimold
Patrick Carey	Charles Hommel	Ann Shaffer
Sharon Caswell	Janice Jutras	Karen Shortill
Barbara Clemens	Chris Kelly	Susan Solomon
Rachel Crapser	Mary Kemper	Susanne Walker
Kim Crowley	Stacy Klein	John Zeanchock
Melissa Dezotell	Terry Ann Kremer	Beverly Zimmerman
Michael Ekedahl	John Leschke	Scott Zimmerman

Preface The New Perspectives Series

What is the New Perspectives Series?

Course Technology's **New Perspectives Series** is an integrated system of instruction that combines text and technology products to teach computer concepts and microcomputer applications. Users consistently praise this series for innovative pedagogy, creativity, supportive and engaging style, accuracy, and use of interactive technology. The first New Perspectives text was published in January of 1993. Since then, the series has grown to more than 100 titles and has become the best-selling series on computer concepts and microcomputer applications. Others have imitated the New Perspectives features, design, and technologies, but none have replicated its quality and its ability to consistently anticipate and meet the needs of instructors and students.

What is the Integrated System of Instruction?

New Perspectives textbooks are part of a truly Integrated System of Instruction: text, graphics, video, sound, animation, and simulations that are linked and that provide a flexible, unified, and interactive system to help you teach and help your students learn. Specifically, the *New Perspectives Integrated System of Instruction* includes a Course Technology textbook in addition to some or all of the following items: Course Labs, Course Test Manager, Online Companions, and Course Presenter. These components—shown in the graphic on the back cover of this book—have been developed to work together to provide a complete, integrative teaching and learning experience.

How is the New Perspectives Series different from other microcomputer concepts and applications series?

The **New Perspectives Series** distinguishes itself from other series in at least four substantial ways: sound instructional design, consistent quality, innovative technology, and proven pedagogy. The applications texts in this series consist of two or more tutorials, which are based on sound instructional design. Each tutorial is motivated by a realistic case that is meaningful to students. Rather than learn a laundry list of features, students learn the features in the context of solving a problem. This process motivates all concepts and skills by demonstrating to students *why* they would want to know them.

Instructors and students have come to rely on the high quality of the **New Perspectives Series** and to consistently praise its accuracy. This accuracy is a result of Course Technology's unique multi-step quality assurance process that incorporates student testing at at least two stages of development, using hardware and software configurations appropriate to the product. All solutions, test questions, and other supplements are tested using similar procedures. Instructors who adopt this series report that students can work through the tutorials independently with minimum intervention or "damage control" by instructors or staff. This consistent quality has meant that if instructors are pleased with one product from the series, they can rely on the same quality with any other New Perspectives product.

The **New Perspectives Series** also distinguishes itself by its innovative technology. This series innovated Course Labs, truly *interactive* learning applications. These have set the standard for interactive learning.

How do I know that the New Perspectives Series will work?

Some instructors who use this series report a significant difference between how much their students learn and retain with this series as compared to other series. With other series, instructors often find that students can work through the book and do well on homework and tests, but still not demonstrate competency when asked to perform particular tasks outside the context of the text's sample case or project. With the **New Perspectives Series**, however, instructors report that students have a complete, integrative learning experience that stays with them. They credit this high retention and competency to the fact that this series incorporates critical thinking and problem-solving with computer skills mastery.

How does this book I'm holding fit into the New Perspectives Series?

New Perspectives applications books are available in the following categories:

Brief books are typically about 150 pages long, contain two to four tutorials, and are intended to teach the basics of an application.

Introductory books are typically about 300 pages long and consist of four to seven tutorials that go beyond the basics. These books often build out of the Brief editions by providing two or three additional tutorials.

Comprehensive books are typically about 600 pages long and consist of all of the tutorials in the Introductory books, plus a few more tutorials covering higher-level topics. Comprehensive books typically also include two Windows tutorials and three or four Additional Cases.

Advanced books cover topics similar to those in the Comprehensive books, but go into more depth. Advanced books present the most high-level coverage in the series.

Office suite books are typically 800 pages long and include coverage of each of the major components of the Office suite. These books often include tutorials introducing the suite, exploring the operating system, and integrating the programs in the suite. The book you are holding is an Office suite text.

Custom Books The New Perspectives Series offers you two ways to customize a New Perspectives text to fit your course exactly: *CourseKits*™, two or more texts packaged together in a box, and *Custom Editions*®, your choice of books bound together. Custom Editions offer you unparalleled flexibility in designing your concepts and applications courses. You can build your own book by ordering a combination of titles bound together to cover only the topics you want. Your students save because they buy only the materials they need. There is no minimum order, and books are spiral bound. Both CourseKits and Custom Editions offer significant price discounts. Contact your Course Technology sales representative for more information.

New Perspectives Series Microcomputer Applications				
■ **Brief Titles or Modules**	■ **Introductory Titles or Modules**	■ **Intermediate Tutorials**	■ **Advanced Titles or Modules**	☐ **Other Modules**
Brief	**Introductory**	**Comprehensive**	**Advanced**	**Custom Editions**
2 to 4 tutorials	6 or 7 tutorials, or Brief + 2 or 3 more tutorials	Introductory + 4 or 5 more tutorials. Includes Brief Windows tutorials and Additional Cases	Quick Review of basics + in-depth, high-level coverage	Choose from any of the above to build your own Custom Editions® or CourseKits™

What Makes this Book Enhanced?

This edition of New Perspectives on Microsoft Office 97 Professional has been significantly enhanced through updating and adding to the existing content.

Essential Computer Concepts We've completely updated the Essential Computer Concepts chapter to reflect the most recent developments in the computer industry. The same major topics are included, but we've also added new coverage of multimedia and expanded our coverage of the Internet and Networks. In addition, we've provided a new lab covering Multimedia applications.

Multimedia

Windows 98 Preview These enhancements for currency continues throughout the text. Following the Brief Windows 95 tutorials, students are presented with a brief explanation of what to expect with Windows 98. This introductory tour explains some of the new features of the operating system by comparing them to the Windows 95 system. Students are encouraged to look critically at these new features in order to decide whether to upgrade their systems.

I E 4

Internet Explorer This introduction to Web browsing has been updated to work with both Internet Explorer versions 3.0 and 4.0. Students can complete the steps using either browser. Notes in the margins and separate sets of steps are provided for users of version 3.0 when the steps or screens in the version 4.0 steps differ.

Web Page Creation/HTML Lab Another new lab featuring Web page creation has been added to the Creating Web Pages with Office 97 tutorial. This fully interactive lab introduces students to HTML coding, and allows them to explore making their own Web page.

Web Page Creation

Internet Assignments This text includes additional assignments that integrate the World Wide Web with the word processing, spreadsheet, database, and presentation graphics skills students learn in the tutorials. To complete these assignments, students will need to search the Web and follow the links from the *New Perspectives on Microsoft Office 97* home page. The Microsoft Office 97 home page is accessible through the Student Online Companion link found on the Course Technology home page at www.course.com. Please refer to the Read This Before You Begin page in the Internet Assignments portion of this text for more information.

In what kind of course could I use this book?

This book can be used in any course in which you want students to learn all of the most important topics of Microsoft Office 97 Professional. No prior computer experience is assumed. Students are first presented with a recently updated overview of computer concepts, followed by a quick introduction to Windows 95. This Enhanced text features a preview of what to expect from Windows 98 and a discussion of what kinds of questions to consider when upgrading. Once they are comfortable with the basics of computing and operating systems, they are briefly introduced to Internet concepts and World Wide Web browsing skills in a tutorial on Microsoft Internet Explorer, which can be completed using either version 3.0 or 4.0. Next, they receive a quick overview of the Office 97 programs, followed by four sets of tutorials that teach the basics of Word 97, Excel 97, Access 97, and PowerPoint 97. Students learn how to use Object Linking and Embedding (OLE) to create integrated Office documents in two tutorials that follow the Excel and PowerPoint sections. The book also includes a tutorial in which students learn how simple it is to create online and Word Wide Web documents using Office 97. Finally, students are able to integrate the skills they have learned in all applications with their web-browsing skills by using the Internet Assignments.

Please note that a unit on Microsoft Outlook 97, an integrated desktop information management program included in Office 97, is provided in the Instructor's Resource Kit that accompanies this textbook. For more information, see "Microsoft Outlook 97 Unit and Simulation Program" later in this preface.

How do the Windows 95 editions differ from the Windows 3.1 editions?

Sessions We've divided the tutorials into sessions. Each session is designed to be completed in about 45 minutes to an hour (depending, of course, upon student needs and the speed of your lab equipment). With sessions, learning is broken up into more easily assimilated portions. You can more accurately allocate time in your syllabus, and students can better manage the available lab time. Each session begins with a "session box," which quickly describes the skills students will learn in the session. Furthermore, each session is numbered, which makes it easier for you and your students to navigate and communicate about the tutorial. Look on page W 1.5 for the session box that opens Session 1.1 of Word 97.

Quick Check *Quick Checks* Each session concludes with meaningful, conceptual Quick Check questions that test students' understanding of what they learned in the session. For example, you can find the answers to the Word 97 Quick Check questions on pages W 4.31 through W 4.35.

New Design We have retained the best of the old design to help students differentiate between what they are to *do* and what they are to *read*. The steps are clearly identified by their shaded background and numbered steps. Furthermore, this new design presents steps and screen shots in a larger, easier to read format. This text also features easier to follow page numbering and colored tabs, so students always can find their place in the text. Some good examples of our new design are pages W 1.20 and W 1.21.

What features are retained in the Windows 95 editions of the New Perspectives Series?

"Read This Before You Begin" Page This page is consistent with Course Technology's unequaled commitment to helping instructors introduce technology into the classroom. Technical considerations and assumptions about software are listed to help instructors save time and eliminate unnecessary aggravation. Refer to page W 1.2 to see the Word 97 "Read This Before You Begin" page.

Tutorial Case Each tutorial begins with a problem presented in a case that is meaningful to students. The problem turns the task of learning how to use an application into a problem-solving process. The problems increase in complexity with each tutorial. These cases touch on multicultural, international, and ethical issues—so important to today's business curriculum. See page W 1.3 for the case that begins the first tutorial of Word 97.

Step-by-Step Methodology This unique Course Technology methodology keeps students on track. They enter data, click buttons, or press keys always within the context of solving the problem posed in the tutorial case. The text constantly guides students, letting them know where they are in the course of solving the problem. In addition, the numerous screen shots include labels that direct students' attention to what they should look at on the screen. On almost every page in this book, you can find an example of how steps, screen shots, and labels work together.

TROUBLE?

TROUBLE? Paragraphs These paragraphs anticipate the mistakes or problems that students are likely to have and help them recover and continue with the tutorial. By putting these paragraphs in the book, rather than in the Instructor's Manual, we facilitate independent learning and free the instructor to focus on substantive conceptual issues rather than on common procedural errors. Some representative examples of TROUBLE? paragraphs appear on page W 2.22.

Reference Windows Reference Windows appear throughout the text. They are succinct summaries of the most important tasks covered in the tutorials. Reference Windows are specially designed and written so students can refer to them when doing the Tutorial Assignments and Case Problems, and after completing the course. Page W 3.11 contains the Reference Window for Attaching a Template to a Document.

Task Reference The Task Reference contains a summary of how to perform common tasks using the most efficient method, as well as references to pages where the task is discussed in more detail. It appears as a table at the end of the book.

Tutorial Assignments, Case Problems, and Lab Assignments Each tutorial concludes with Tutorial Assignments, which provide students with additional hands-on practice of the skills they learned in the tutorial. See page W 3.30 for examples of Tutorial Assignments. The Tutorial Assignments are followed by four Case Problems that have approximately the same scope as the tutorial case. In the Windows 95 applications texts, the last Case Problem of each tutorial typically requires students to solve the problem independently, either "from scratch" or with minimum guidance. See page W 3.32 for examples of Case Problems. Finally, if a Course Lab accompanies a tutorial, Lab Assignments are included after the Case Problems. See page W 1.31 for examples of Lab Assignments.

Exploration Exercises The Windows environment allows students to learn by exploring and discovering what they can do. Exploration Exercises can be Tutorial Assignments or Case Problems that challenge students, encourage them to explore the capabilities of the program they are using, and extend their knowledge using the Help facility and other reference materials. Page W 3.30 contains Exploration Exercises for Tutorial 3 of Word 97.

What supplements are available with this textbook?

Course Labs: Now, Concepts Come to Life Computer skills and concepts come to life with the New Perspectives Course Labs—highly-interactive tutorials that combine illustrations, animations, digital images, and simulations. The Labs guide students step-by-step, present them with Quick Check questions, let them explore on their own, test their comprehension, and provide printed feedback. Lab icons at the beginning of the tutorial and in the tutorial margins indicate when a topic has a corresponding Lab. Lab Assignments are included at the end of each relevant tutorial. The Labs available with this book and the tutorials in which they appear are:

Essential Computer Concepts

Peripheral Devices

Essential Computer Concepts

User Interfaces

Essential Computer Concepts

Multimedia

Tutorial 1 Windows 95

Using a Keyboard

Tutorial 1
Windows 95

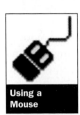

Using a
Mouse

Tutorial 2
Windows 95

Using Files

Internet Explorer,
Essential Concepts,
Internet Assignments

The Internet
World Wide Web

Tutorial 1
Word 97

Word
Processing

Tutorial 1
Excel 97

Spreadsheets

Tutorial 1
Access 97

Databases

Creating Web
Pages

Web Page
Creation

Internet
Assignments

E-Mail

Course Test Manager: Testing and Practice at the Computer or on Paper
Course Test Manager is a powerful testing and assessment package that enables instructors to create and print tests from Testbanks designed specifically for Course Technology titles. In addition, instructors with access to a networked computer lab (LAN) can administer, grade, and track tests on-line. Students can also take on-line practice tests, which generate customized study guides that indicate where in the text students can find more information on each question.

Skills Assessment Manager (SAM) This ground-breaking new assessment tool tests students' ability to perform real-world tasks live in the Microsoft Office 97 applications. Designed to be administered over a network, SAM tracks every action students perform in Microsoft Office 97 as they work through an exam. Upon completion of an exam, SAM assesses not only the *results* of students' work, but also the *way* students arrived at each answer and *how efficiently* they worked. Instructors may use SAM to create their own custom exams, or they may select from a library of pre-made exams, including exams that map to the content in this text as well as the Microsoft Office User Specialist certification program. SAM is available to test students who have purchased this text. Instructors interested in using SAM to test students out of a course, or to place them into a course, should contact their Course Technology sales representative.

Figures on CD-ROM This lecture presentation tool allows instructors to create electronic slide shows or traditional overhead transparencies using the figure files from the book. Instructors can customize, edit, save, and display figures from the text in order to illustrate key topics or concepts in class.

Microsoft Outlook 97 Unit and Simulation Program Microsoft Outlook is an integrated desktop information management program included in Office 97 that lets you manage your personal and business information and communicate with others. This unit focuses on the electronic mail features of Microsoft Outlook and has students work with a program called Learning Outlook E-mail, which looks and feels like Microsoft Outlook, but is actually a simulation. Instructors are granted a license to make a copy of the Getting Started with Microsoft Outlook unit and the Learning Outlook E-mail simulation program for any student who has purchased this book.

Online Companions: Dedicated to Keeping You and Your Students Up-To-Date
When you use a New Perspectives product, you can access Course Technology's faculty sites and student sites on the World Wide Web. You can browse this text's password-protected Faculty Online Companion to obtain an online Instructor's Manual, Solution Files, Student Files, and more by visiting Course Technology's Online Resource Center at http://www.course.com. Please see your Instructor's Resource Kit or call your Course Technology customer service representative for more information. Students can access this text's Student Online Companion, which contains Internet Assignments (see next paragraph) and other useful links, through the Online Resource Center.

Instructor's Manual New Perspectives Series Instructor's Manuals contain instructor's notes and solutions for each tutorial. Instructor's notes typically provide tutorial overviews and outlines, technical notes, lecture notes, and extra Case Problems. Solutions include answers to Tutorial Assignments, Case Problems, Internet Assignments, and Lab Assignments.

Student Files Student Files contain all of the data that students will use to complete the tutorials, Tutorial Assignments, and Case Problems. A Readme or Help file includes technical tips for lab management. See the inside covers of this book and the "Read This Before You Begin" pages for more information on Student Files.

Solution Files Solution Files contain the files students are asked to create or modify in the tutorials, Tutorial Assignments, Internet Assignments, and Case Problems.

The following supplements are included in the Instructor's Resource Kit that accompanies this textbook:

- electronic Instructor's Manual
- Solution Files
- Student Files
- Course Labs
- Course Test Manager Testbanks
- Course Test Manager Engine
- Figures on CD-ROM
- Microsoft Outlook 97 Unit and E-mail Simulation Program

Some of the supplements listed above are also available over the World Wide Web through Course Technology's password-protected Faculty Online Companion for this text. Please see your Instructor's Resource Kit or call your Course Technology customer service representative for more information.

Table of **Contents**

TUTORIAL 2
Creating a Worksheet

TUTORIAL 3
Developing a Professional-Looking Worksheet

Essential Computer Concepts

TUTORIAL

Credits

Essential Computer Concepts

CASE

International ComAir

Today Tenzing Lu begins her first job. She just graduated with a degree in business, and she is now a trainee in International ComAir's management development program. Her main responsibility is to work on special projects for the Vice-President of Operations, Ms. Thompson.

When Tenzing meets with Ms. Thompson to discuss her first project, Ms. Thompson explains that she is concerned that International ComAir might not be using computers as effectively as it could. She mentions that the company has large computers to handle reservations, but handles other operations manually. She also observes that recent graduates beginning their careers at International ComAir are out-producing some veteran employees. She thinks one of the reasons for this very welcome boost in productivity has been the everyday use of personal computers.

Ms. Thompson asks Tenzing to investigate how the average employee at International ComAir could benefit from the use of personal computers. Tenzing is to research this matter and recommend to management what the average employee should have for hardware and software.

Tenzing is most enthusiastic about her new assignment. Although she knows that she is not an expert on computing, she did have an excellent introductory course on computers in college that she thinks will be very useful for this assignment. Because she knows computers are constantly changing, she decides to evaluate the type of computing tools currently available that fit the company's needs. Tenzing decides to use the company library and the World Wide Web to fulfill this task. She has asked you to help her.

The ad in Figure 1 lists the specifications for a typical computer. To decide whether to recommend this computer, Tenzing and you need more information. This chapter will help you make a recommendation by developing your understanding of computer technology and terminology.

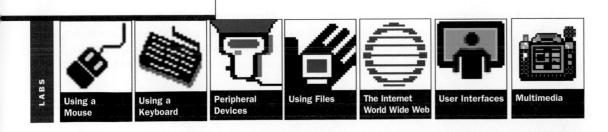

| LABS | Using a Mouse | Using a Keyboard | Peripheral Devices | Using Files | The Internet World Wide Web | User Interfaces | Multimedia |

Figure 1
MicroPlus
computer ad

What Is a Computer?

Computers have become essential tools in almost every type of activity in virtually every type of business. A **computer** is defined as an electronic device that accepts input, processes data, stores data, and produces output. It is a versatile tool with the potential to perform many different tasks.

A **computer system** includes a computer, **peripheral devices**, and **software**. The physical components of a computer are referred to as **hardware**. The design and construction of a particular computer is referred to as its **architecture**, or **configuration**. The technical details about each component are called **specifications**. For example, a computer system might be *configured* to include a printer; a *specification* for that printer might be a print speed of eight pages per minute or the capacity to print in color. The computer itself takes care of the processing function, but it needs additional components, called **peripherals**, to accomplish its input, output, and storage functions. In this chapter, you will learn more about the hardware that performs these basic computer functions.

Software refers to the intangible components of a computer system, particularly the **programs**, or lists of instructions, that the computer needs to perform a specific task. Software is the key to a computer's versatility. When your computer is using word processing software—for example, the Microsoft Word program—you can type memos, letters, and reports. When your computer is using accounting software, such as the Intuit QuickBooks accounting program, you can maintain information about what your customers owe you and display a graph showing the timing of customer payments.

The hardware and the software of a computer system work together to process data—the words, figures, sounds, and graphics that describe people, events, things, and ideas.

Tenzing knows that software is an important factor in making her recommendations about buying computers, so she makes a note to ask Ms. Thompson what software International ComAir is already using. This is important because the computers Tenzing recommends must be compatible with, or capable of using, that software. Figure 2 shows how you, the computer, the data, and the software interact to get work done. Suppose that you want to write a report. First, you instruct the computer to use the word processing program. After activating the word processing program, you begin to type the text of your report. What you type into the computer is called **input**. You might also need to issue commands that tell the computer exactly how to process your input. Perhaps you want to center the title and double-space the text. You use an input device, such as a keyboard or a mouse, to input data and issue commands.

Figure 2 ◀
Data is input,
processed,
stored, and
output

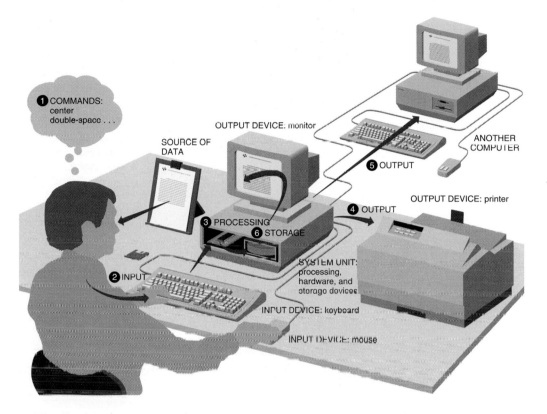

The computer processes the report according to your commands and the instructions contained in the software—the title becomes centered and all the text double-spaced. **Processing** changes the data you have input, for example, by moving text, sorting lists, or performing calculations. Or, you might choose to import from another computer an illustration, text, or numeric data such as stock prices. This processing takes place on the **main circuit board** of the computer, also referred to as the **motherboard**, which contains the computer's major electronic components. The electronic components of the main circuit board are referred to as **processing hardware**.

Using a computer to type your report has several advantages. The first is the speed at which you can perform the task. Second, the capability of storing the answer and using it over and over again, in so many different ways, makes using a computer the most effective way to perform many personal and clerical tasks. Finally, an important advantage is sharing data and output with others. You make a note to find out whether International ComAir employees will need to share their data.

Types of Computers

In her research, Tenzing finds that personal computers are not the only way to compute; there are other types of computers, which are classified by their size, speed, and cost. **Microcomputers**, also called **personal computers** (PCs), are the computers typically used by a single user, usually at home or at the office. They come in many shapes and sizes, as you can see in Figure 3.

Figure 3 ◄
Microcomputers

A standard desktop microcomputer fits on a desk and runs on power from an electrical wall outlet. The display screen is usually placed on top of the horizontal desktop case.

A microcomputer with a tower case contains the same basic components as a standard desktop microcomputer, but the vertically-oriented case is large and allows more room for expansion. The tower unit can be placed on the floor to save desk space.

A notebook computer is small and light, giving it the advantage of portability that standard desktop computers do not have. A notebook computer can run on power from an electrical outlet or batteries.

A personal digital assistant (PDA), or palm-top computer achieves even more portabillity than a notebook computer by shrinking or eliminating some standard components, such as the keyboard. On a keyboardless PDA, a touch-sensitive screen accepts characters drawn with your finger. PDAs easily connect to desktop computers to exchange and update information.

A **desktop** or **tower** microcomputer usually costs about $2,000. A **notebook** computer with similar capability is usually twice as expensive. The **personal digital assistant** (PDA) has limited capability, and not always a lower price.

Tenzing assumes that her recommendation to Ms. Thompson will include microcomputers because most daily tasks can be performed very efficiently using them. However, she wonders whether some employees might need the portability of notebook computers, and whether others might need a PDA. You suggest that Tenzing add these notes to her list of questions to ask Ms. Thompson.

Small and large businesses use microcomputers extensively. But some businesses, government agencies, and other institutions also use larger and faster types of computers: **minicomputers, mainframes**, and **supercomputers**. Unlike most microcomputers, these can have multiple input and output devices so that more than one user can work simultaneously.

Minicomputers, like the one in Figure 4, are somewhat larger than microcomputers. Physical size, however, is not the deciding factor when buying a minicomputer. The computing capability of a microcomputer may be more than a minicomputer, and a fairly typical minicomputer may cost between $20,000 and $250,000. Usually, a company decides to purchase a minicomputer when it must carry out the processing tasks for many users, especially when the users share large amounts of data. Each user inputs processing requests and views output through a terminal. A **terminal** is a device with a keyboard and screen used for input and output, but is not capable of processing on its own.

Figure 4 ◀
A typical minicomputer handles processing tasks for multiple users

Terminals act as each user's main input and output device. The terminal has a keyboard for input and a display screen for output, but it does not process the user's data. Instead, processing requests must be transmitted from the terminal to the minicomputer.

The minicomputer stores data for all the users in one centralized location.

Mainframe computers, like the one shown in Figure 5, are larger and more powerful than minicomputers. As with a minicomputer, one mainframe computer performs processing tasks for multiple users on terminals. However, the mainframe can handle many more users than a minicomputer. Mainframes are typically used to provide centralized storage, processing, and management for large amounts of data. The price of a typical mainframe computer can be several hundred thousand dollars.

Figure 5 ◀
The closet-sized system unit for the IBM S/390 G4 mainframe computer contains the processing unit, memory, and circuitry to support multiple terminals

The largest and fastest computers, called **supercomputers**, were first developed for high-volume computing tasks such as weather prediction. Supercomputers like the one shown in Figure 6 are also being used by large corporations when the tremendous volume of data would seriously delay processing on a mainframe computer. Although its cost can be several million dollars, a supercomputer's processing speed is so much faster than that of microcomputers, minicomputers, and mainframes that the investment can be worthwhile.

Figure 6 ◀
A Cray
supercomputer

processing hardware

How would Tenzing classify the computer in the advertisement shown in Figure 1 at the beginning of the chapter? If your answer is a desktop microcomputer, you are correct. The computer in that ad fits on a desk, is not portable, and probably costs $2,000 to $2,500.

Based on what you have learned about the computing process and types of computers, you and Tenzing decide to recommend that International ComAir purchase some microcomputers. When you look at the ad, however, you realize that there are several specifications that you still do not understand. Your recommendation will have to explain what each listed component does, and why it is important. The remainder of this chapter will focus on microcomputer hardware and software in more detail, so you can learn what you need to make a better recommendation.

Computer Hardware

As you've already learned, computer hardware can be defined as the physical components of a computer. Now look at the hardware you might use in a typical microcomputer system.

Input Devices

Using a Mouse

Using a Keyboard

Peripheral Devices

You input data and commands by using an input device such as a keyboard or a mouse. The computer can also receive input from a storage device. This section takes a closer look at the input devices you might use. Output and storage devices are covered in later sections.

The most frequently used input device is a keyboard. Figure 7 shows a standard 101-key keyboard. Newer keyboards are **ergonomic**, which means that they have been designed to fit the natural placement of your hands and should reduce your risk of repetitive-motion injuries. All keyboards consist of three major parts: the main keyboard, the keypads, and the function keys.

Figure 7 ◀
Traditional 101-
key keyboard

function keys

main keyboard

editing keypad

numeric keypad

All microcomputers also should be equipped with a pointing device. The most popular is a mouse such as the one in Figure 8, but your computer might be equipped with one of the other options pictured in Figure 9.

Figure 8 ◀
A mouse

Figure 9 ◀
Notebook
pointing
devices

Track point

Track ball

Touch pad

A **track point** is a small eraser-like device embedded among the typing keys. To control the on-screen pointer, you push the track point up, left, right or down. Buttons for clicking and double-clicking are located in front of the spacebar.

A **track ball** is like an upside-down mouse. By rolling the ball with your fingers, you control the on-screen pointer. Buttons for clicking are often located above or to the side of the track ball.

A **touch pad** is a touch-sensitive device. By dragging your finger over the surface, you control the on-screen pointer. Two buttons equivalent to mouse buttons are located in front of the touch pad.

The pointing device controls a **pointer** on the display screen. Using a pointing device is an important skill because most microcomputers depend on such devices to select commands and manipulate text or graphics on the screen. Computers that input from terminals do not normally use pointing devices.

Now that you have read about input devices, refer back to the computer advertisement shown in Figure 1 at the beginning of the chapter. Can you list the input devices included with the advertised system? A mouse and a keyboard are considered essential peripheral devices, so advertisements do not always list them. Unless the ad specifies some other input device, such as a track ball, you can safely assume the computer comes equipped with a traditional keyboard and mouse.

Output Devices

Output is the result of processing data; output devices show you those results. The most commonly used output devices are monitors and printers. A **monitor** is the TV-like device that displays the output from a computer, as shown in Figure 10.

Figure 10 ◀
A color monitor

Factors that influence the quality of a monitor are screen size, resolution, and dot pitch. **Screen size** is the diagonal measurement in inches from one corner of the screen to the other. 14", 15", and 17" are common measurements for today's monitors. The first microcomputer monitors and many terminals still in use today are character-based. A **character-based display** divides the screen into a grid of rectangles, one for each typed character. A monitor that is capable of displaying graphics, called a **graphics display**, divides the screen into a matrix of small dots called **pixels**. **Resolution** is the maximum number of pixels the monitor can display. Standard resolutions are 640 × 480, 800 × 600, 1,024 × 768, 1,280 × 1,024, and 1,600 × 1,200. Most newer monitors are capable of 1,280 × 1,024 resolution, but the objects on the screen are too small, so users prefer 640 × 480 or 800 × 600 resolutions. Resolution is easy to adjust on most monitors. **Dot pitch** measures the distance between pixels, so a smaller dot pitch means a sharper image. A .28 or .26 dot pitch (dp) is typical for today's monitors.

A computer display system consists of a monitor and a **graphics card**, also called a **video display adapter** or **video card**. This card is installed inside the computer, and controls the signals the computer sends to the monitor. If you plan to display a lot of images on the monitor, you may also need a **graphics accelerator card** to speed up the computer's ability to display them. When purchasing a monitor, you must be sure that it comes with a video card that is compatible with your computer.

Notebook computers use a different display technology because monitors are too bulky and heavy. Instead, they use a **liquid crystal display** (LCD) similar to a digital watch or the time display on a microwave oven. The size of these screens is also measured diagonally, typically 11.3" to 12.1" across. An **active matrix screen** updates rapidly and provides resolution similar to that of a monitor. If you want to display a lot of images, especially video, on a notebook computer, it should have an active matrix screen.

Refer back to the computer ad in Figure 1. Does this microcomputer include a monitor and video card? The correct answer is yes, both are included. What are the size and resolution of the monitor? The monitor is a 17" 1,600 × 1,200 .26 dp color monitor.

A **printer** produces a paper copy of the text or graphics processed by the computer. A paper or acetate transparency copy of computer output is called **hard copy**, because it is more tangible than the electronic or magnetic copies found on a disk, in the computer memory, or on the monitor. There are three popular categories of printers, and each has special capabilities.

The most popular printers for business use are **laser** printers, like the one shown in Figure 11, because they use the same technology as duplicating machines. A temporary laser image is transferred onto paper with a powdery substance called **toner**. This produces high-quality output quickly and efficiently. The speed of laser printers is measured in **pages per minute** (ppm). Color laser printers use several toner cartridges to apply color to the page. Non-color laser printers are less expensive than color laser printers.

Figure 11 ◀
A laser printer

A less expensive alternative is to use a color **ink-jet** printer such as the one shown in Figure 12. These printers carefully spray ink onto paper. The quality of the ink-jet output is almost comparable to a laser printer's output, but it is produced much more slowly. Ink-jet printers, with and without color capabilities, are very popular printers for home use.

Figure 12 ◀
An ink-jet
printer

Figure 13 shows a **dot matrix** printer, an example of the oldest technology currently found on the computer market. These printers transfer ink to the paper by striking a ribbon with pins. Using more pins controls the quality of the print, so a 24-pin dot matrix printer produces better quality print than a 9-pin. Dot matrix printers are most often used when a large number of pages need to be printed fairly quickly. The speed of dot matrix printers is measured in **characters per second** (cps). Some examples of their usefulness are the printing of grade reports, bank statements, or payroll checks. Also, they are the only type of printer that can print on multipart forms, so they continue to be useful to all kinds of businesses.

Figure 13 ◀
A dot matrix
printer

Tenzing and you are not sure if Ms. Thompson needs you to consider the purchase of printers to go with the recommended microcomputers. You notice that the computer ad in Figure 1 does not include a printer, so you make a note to ask if your recommendation should include one. If so, you decide to recommend both a color laser printer to print correspondence, advertisements, and brochures, and a high-speed dot matrix printer for clerical tasks.

Multimedia devices are another, relatively new category of peripheral devices. **Multimedia** is an integrated collection of computer-based media including text, graphics, sound, animation, and even video. Most microcomputers come equipped with a sound card and speakers that can play digital sounds. The sound card converts sounds so that they can be broadcast through speakers.

The computer advertised in Figure 1 includes a sound card and speakers. These are also output devices that you need to mention in your recommendation. You wonder what purpose these devices might serve at International ComAir. Tenzing suggests that Ms. Thompson might conduct teleconferences attended by employees in widespread locations, or record announcements that employees can play back at their convenience. Later in this chapter, you will learn how business users are sharing a variety of data resources, including digital sound.

Using Files

Processing Hardware

The most important computer function is processing data. Before you can understand this function and the hardware that executes it, you first need to learn how the computer represents and stores data.

Data representation

The characters used in human language are meaningless to a computer because it is an electronic device. Like a light bulb, the computer must interpret every signal as either "on" or "off." To do so, a microcomputer represents data as distinct or separate numbers. Specifically, it represents "on" with a 1 and "off" with a 0. These numbers are referred to as **binary digits**, or **bits**.

Microcomputers commonly use the **ASCII** code to represent character data. ASCII (pronounced "ASK-ee") stands for **American Standard Code for Information Interchange**.

A series of eight bits is called a **byte**. As Figure 14 shows, the byte that represents the integer value 0 is 00000000, with all eight bits "off" or set to 0. The byte that represents the integer value 1 is 00000001, and the byte that represents 255 is 11111111.

Figure 14
Binary representation of the numbers 0 through 255

Number	Binary Representation
0	00000000
1	00000001
2	00000010
3	00000011
4	00000100
5	00000101
6	00000110
7	00000111
8	00001000
⋮	⋮
253	11111101
254	11111110
255	11111111

Each byte represents a unique character such as the number 8, the letter *A*, or the symbol $. For example, Figure 15 shows that ASCII code represents the letter *A* by the byte 1000001, and the lowercase *a* by 1100001. The symbol $ is represented by 0100100. Even a space has its own unique value: 0100000. The phrase "Thank you!" is represented by 10 bytes. Each of the eight letters requires one byte, and the space and the exclamation point also require one byte each.

Figure 15
Sample ASCII code representing letters and symbols

Character	ASCII
(space)	0100000
$	0100100
A	1000001
B	1000010
a	1100001
b	1100010

As a computer user, you don't have to know the binary representations of numbers, characters, and instructions, because the computer handles all the necessary conversions internally. However, because the amount of memory in a computer and its storage capacity are expressed in bytes, you should be aware of how data is represented. **Storage** and **memory capacity** is the amount of data, or number of characters, that the device can handle at any given time. A **kilobyte** (KB) is 1,024 bytes, or approximately one thousand bytes. A **megabyte** (MB) is 1,048,576 bytes, or about one million bytes. A **gigabyte** (GB) is 1,073,741,824 bytes, or about one billion bytes. You will see the symbols KB, MB, and GB refer to both processing and storage hardware.

The Microprocessor

The two most important components of microcomputer hardware are the **microprocessor**, a silicon chip designed to manipulate data, and the **memory**, which stores instructions and data. The type of microprocessor and the memory capacity are two factors that directly affect the price and performance of a computer.

The **microprocessor**, such as the one shown in Figure 16, is an integrated circuit (an electronic component called a **chip**) which is located on the main circuit board inside the computer.

Figure 16 ◀
An Intel
Pentium micro-
processor,
found in many
IBM-compatible
computers

The terms **processor** and **central processing unit** (CPU) also refer to this device that is responsible for executing instructions to process data.

The speed of a microprocessor is determined by its clock speed, word size, and cache size. Think of the **clock speed** as the pulse of the processor. It is measured in millions of cycles per second, or **megahertz** (MHz), a measurement of electrical impulses. The microprocessor in the first IBM PC models operated at 4.77 MHz. Today's microprocessors are capable of speeds over 300 MHz.

Word size refers to the number of bits that are processed at one time. A computer with a large word size can process faster than a computer with a small word size. The earliest microcomputers had an 8-bit word size, but now a 32-bit or 64-bit word size is common.

Cache, sometimes called **RAM cache** or **cache memory**, is special high-speed memory reserved for the microprocessor's use. It speeds up the processing function by accessing data the computer anticipates you will request soon, while you are still working on something else.

Take another look at the computer advertised in Figure 1. What is the type and speed of its microprocessor? Your answer should be that it has a Pentium II microprocessor that can operate at 266 MHz and has 512 KB cache.

Memory

Computer **memory** is a set of storage locations on the main circuit board. Your computer has four types of memory: random access memory, virtual memory, read-only memory, and complementary metal oxide semiconductor (CMOS) memory.

Random access memory (RAM) is active during the processing function. It consists of electronic circuits on the motherboard that temporarily hold programs and data while the computer is on. Each circuit has an address that is used by the microprocessor to transmit and store data. Figure 17 illustrates how each byte of data is stored in a separate RAM address.

Figure 17
The microprocessor and RAM are active during the processing function

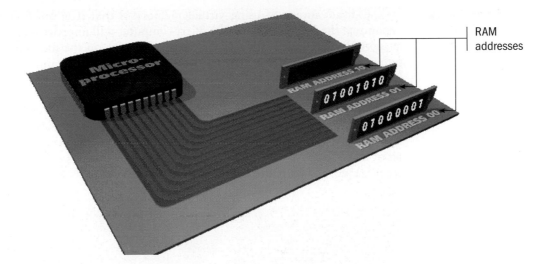

RAM addresses

RAM is constantly changing as long as the computer is on. The microprocessor is constantly using RAM to store and retrieve instructions and data as they are needed. The term **volatile** is used to describe this constantly changing state of RAM.

For example, if you are writing a paper, the word processing program that you are using is temporarily copied into RAM so the microprocessor can quickly access the instructions that you will need as you type and format your paper. As you type, the characters are also stored in RAM, along with the many fonts, special characters, graphics, and other objects that you might use to enhance the paper. How much you can include in your paper depends on the RAM capacity of the computer you are using.

Look at the computer ad in Figure 1. Notice that this computer has 32 MB of RAM. In other words, it has the capacity to temporarily store over 32 million characters at any one time. Although your paper might not be that long, the computer uses a lot of that available memory for programs and other data it needs to process your paper. The notation "expandable to 128 MB" tells you that you can add more RAM to this computer. Expandability is an important feature of any computer; you need to be able to change your computer's capability as your needs change. You don't have to worry about running out of RAM, however. Today's microcomputer software uses space on your computer's storage devices to simulate RAM if more is needed. This extra memory is called **virtual memory**. Figure 18 explains how it works.

Figure 18
How virtual memory works

1. Your computer is running a word processing program that takes up most of the program area in RAM, but you want to run a spreadsheet program at the same time.

2. The operating system moves the least-used segment of the word processing program into virtual memory on disk.

3. The spreadsheet program can now be loaded into the RAM vacated by the least-used segment of the word processing program.

4. If the least-used segment of the word processing program is later needed, it is copied from virtual memory back into RAM. To make room, some other infrequently used segment of a program will need to be transferred into virtual memory.

The disadvantage of using virtual memory is that it is much slower than RAM, so expanding the RAM capacity of a microcomputer will improve its performance. **Read-only memory** (ROM) is another set of electronic circuits on the motherboard inside the computer. Although you can expand your RAM capacity, you cannot add to ROM capacity. In fact, the manufacturer of the computer permanently installs ROM. It is the permanent storage location for a set of instructions that the computer uses when you turn it on.

The events that occur between the moment you turn on the computer and the moment you can actually begin to use the computer are called the **boot process**, as shown in Figure 19. When the computer is off, RAM is empty. When the computer is turned on, the set of instructions in ROM checks all the computer system's components to make sure they are working, and activates the essential software that controls the processing function.

Figure 19 ◀
ROM boot
program
activated

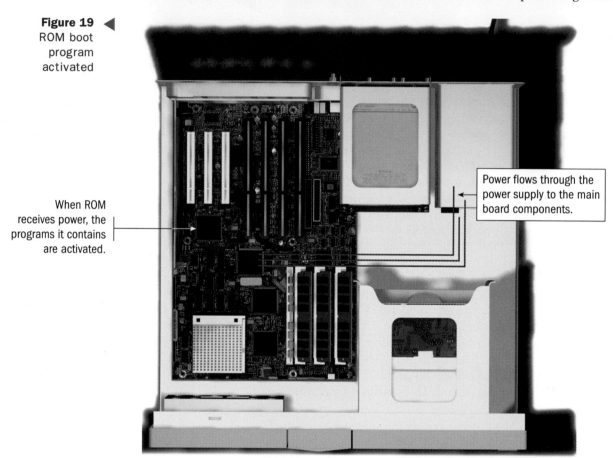

When ROM
receives power, the
programs it contains
are activated.

Power flows through the
power supply to the main
board components.

Complementary metal oxide semiconductor (CMOS) memory (pronounced "SEE-Moss") is another chip that is installed on the motherboard. It is also activated during the boot process and contains information about where the essential software is stored. A small rechargeable battery powers CMOS so its contents will be saved in between computer uses. Unlike ROM, which cannot be changed, CMOS must be changed every time you add or remove hardware to your computer system. Thus, CMOS is often referred to as semipermanent memory, ROM as permanent memory, and RAM as temporary memory.

Storage Devices and Media

Because RAM retains data only while the power is on, your computer must have a more permanent storage option. As Figure 20 shows, a storage device receives data from RAM and writes it on a storage medium, such as a disk. Later the data can be read and sent back to RAM to use again.

Figure 20 ◄
A storage device receives information from RAM, writes it on the storage medium, and reads and sends it back to RAM

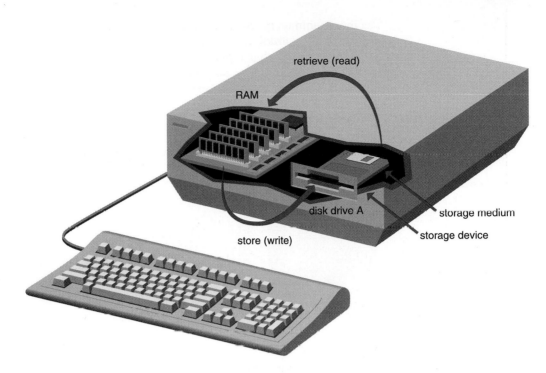

Before you can understand the hardware that stores data, you need to know how data is stored. All data and programs are stored as files. A computer **file** is a named collection of related bits that exists on a storage medium. There are two categories of files: executable files and data files. An **executable file** contains the instructions that tell a computer how to perform a specific task. The files that are used during the boot process, for instance, are executable. Users create **data files**, usually with software. For instance, your paper that you write with a word processing program is data, and must be saved as a data file if you want to use it again.

The storage devices where computer files are kept can be categorized by the method they use to store files. **Magnetic storage devices** use oxide-coated plastic storage media called mylar. Figure 21 illustrates the process of storing data on magnetic media.

Figure 21 ◄
Storing data on magnetic media

Before the data is stored, the particles in the magnetic surface of the disk are scattered in random patterns.

The read-write head magnetizes the particles. The positive poles of the magnetized particles point toward the negative pole of the read-write head.

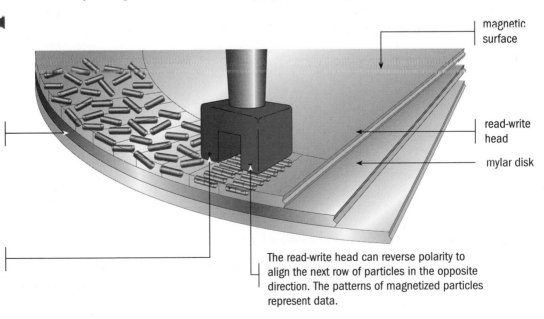

The read-write head can reverse polarity to align the next row of particles in the opposite direction. The patterns of magnetized particles represent data.

The most common magnetic storage devices are floppy disk drives, hard disk drives, and tape drives. **Floppy disks**, sometimes called **diskettes**, are flat circles of iron oxide-coated plastic enclosed in a hard plastic case. The most common size of floppy disks for microcomputers is 3.5". You may also see floppy disks in other sizes. For instance, 5.25" and 8" are used in older microcomputers. However, physical size is not the best way to describe floppy disks. Instead, the capacity of the disk is more important. The floppy disk in Figure 22 is a **high-density** disk, which means it has the capacity to store 1.44 MB. In contrast, a **low-density** disk of the same physical size can store only 720 KB. As a user, you need to know what capacity of floppy disk your microcomputer can accept.

Figure 22 ◀
3.5" disk

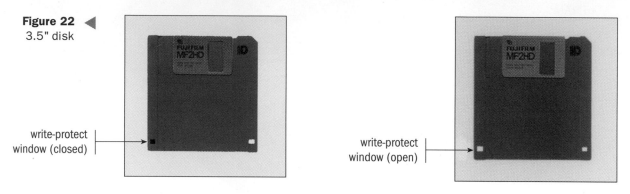

write-protect
window (closed)

write-protect
window (open)

Write protection prevents additional files from being stored on the disk, and any file from being erased from the disk. To write protect a 3.5" floppy disk, you open the write-protect window, as shown in Figure 22.

The other most common magnetic storage device is a **hard disk drive**, such as the one shown in Figure 23. This drive contains several iron oxide-covered metal platters that are usually sealed inside the computer. Hard disk storage has two advantages over floppy disk storage: speed and capacity.

Figure 23 ◀
Hard disk drive
opened to
illustrate
internal
components

The speed of a disk drive is measured by its **access time**, the time required to read or write one record of data. Access time is measured in **milliseconds** (ms), one-thousandth of a second. The hard disk drive included in Figure 1, for instance, has 10 ms access time. Its capacity is 6.4 GB; that is, it can store 6,871,947,673 characters. Although this seems like a very high number, a Windows-based microcomputer fully loaded with typical software can use up to 1 GB, and the addition of data files can quickly add up to several gigabytes.

Another magnetic storage device is a **tape drive** that provides inexpensive archival storage for large quantities of data. Tape storage is much too slow to be used for day-to-day computer tasks; therefore, tapes are used to make backup copies of data stored on hard disks. If a hard disk fails, data from the backup tape can be reloaded on a new hard disk with minimal interruption of operations. Some microcomputers include a **Zip drive**, a special high capacity floppy disk drive manufactured by Iomega Corporation. Zip drives can make copies of data, and transport large amounts of data from one computer to another.

Figure 24 shows the typical storage configuration of a microcomputer. It includes a **CD-ROM** drive, which stands for **Compact Disk Read Only Memory**. **Optical storage devices** use laser technology to read and write data on compact discs (CDs). CD-ROM drives have become standard components on microcomputers because of their high capacity and portability. One CD can store up to 680 MB, equivalent to more than 450 floppy disks.

Figure 24 ◄
Typical
microcomputer
storage
configurations

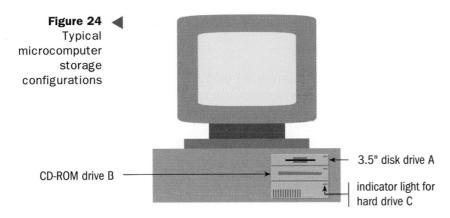

CD-ROM drive B

3.5" disk drive A

indicator light for
hard drive C

Like your audio CDs, this technology writes data on the surface of the CD by stamping it as a series of pits. Figure 25 shows how data is stored on optical media. The disadvantage of CD-ROM technology is that the surface of the CD is not rewriteable like magnetic media. Once the laser cuts a pit in its surface, the pit cannot be recut, so the data stored there cannot be changed. The most common uses of CD-ROMs are for software distribution and storing large data files such as graphics, animation, and video.

Figure 25 ◄
Storing data on
an optical disk

Areas that are
not pits have a
reflective surface.

When a CD-ROM disk
is manufactured, a
laser bums **pits** into
a reflective surface.
These pits become
dark, non-reflective
areas of the disk.

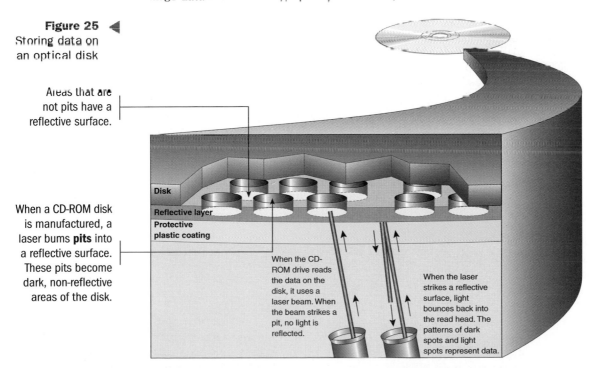

Disk

Reflective layer

Protective
plastic coating

When the CD-ROM drive reads the data on the disk, it uses a laser beam. When the beam strikes a pit, no light is reflected.

When the laser strikes a reflective surface, light bounces back into the read head. The patterns of dark spots and light spots represent data.

The original CD-ROM drive had a relatively slow access time: 600 ms. As the technology has improved, that access time has increased to less than 200 ms. A lower number means faster access. Also consider the drive's data transfer rate, measured in kilobits per second (Kbps), to classify it as 1X (the original with 150 Kbps per second), 2X (twice the original), 3X, and so on.

Look at Figure 1 again, and notice that this computer comes with a 16X variable CD-ROM drive. That means that the drive has an access time of around 100 to 180 ms, and a data transfer rate of 2.4 MB per second. To help you keep this in perspective, a 10X would designate 135 to 180 ms access time, with 1.6 MB per second data transfer rate.

Tenzing and you decide that your recommendation should include microcomputers with CD-ROM drives because most software is distributed in that format. As you use the computer, the storage devices fill up quickly with software and data, so it's a good idea to purchase as much storage capacity as your budget allows. Your recommendation will include high-capacity hard disk drives, and tape or Zip drives to use for backup copies. Most microcomputers come equipped with 3.5" 1.44 MB floppy disk drives, so you will include them, too.

Data Communications

The transmission of text, numeric, voice, or video data from one machine to another is called **data communications**. This broad-based definition encompasses many critical business activities, from sending a letter to the printer upstairs to sending an electronic mail (e-mail) message to the company office around the globe.

The four essential components of data communications are a sender, a receiver, a channel, and a protocol. The computer that originates the message is the **sender**. The message is sent over some type of **channel**, such as telephone or coaxial cable, a microwave signal, or optical fibers. The computer at the message's destination is called the **receiver**. The rules that establish an orderly transfer of data between the sender and the receiver are called **protocols**. Communication software and hardware establish these protocols at the beginning of the transmission, and both computers follow them strictly to guarantee an accurate transfer of data.

Data Bus

Peripherals are devices that can be added to a computer system to enhance its usefulness. Starting at the microprocessor, and passing through a continuous channel, the data travels out to the appropriate device. From an input device back to the microprocessor, the path is reversed. This communication between the microprocessor, RAM, and the peripherals is called the **data bus**.

An external peripheral device must have a corresponding **port** and **cable** that connect it to the back of the computer. Inside the computer, each port connects to a **controller card**, sometimes called an **expansion** or **interface card**. These cards, which provide an electrical connection to a variety of peripheral devices, plug into electrical connectors on the main board called slots or **expansion slots**. Figure 26 shows the data path that connects a printer to a computer. An internal peripheral device such as a hard disk drive may plug directly into the motherboard, or it may have an attached controller card. The transmission protocol is handled by a **device driver**, a computer program that can establish communication because it contains information about the characteristics of your computer and of the device.

Figure 26 ◀
The components necessary to connect a printer to a computer

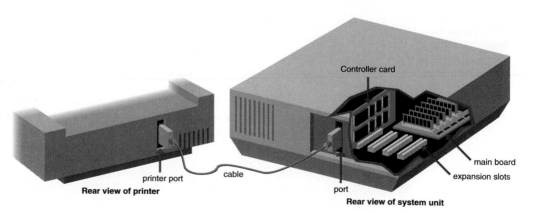

Microcomputers can have several types of ports, including parallel, serial, SCSI, and MIDI. Figure 27 diagrams how the ports on a desktop microcomputer might appear.

Figure 27
Microcomputer
expansion
ports

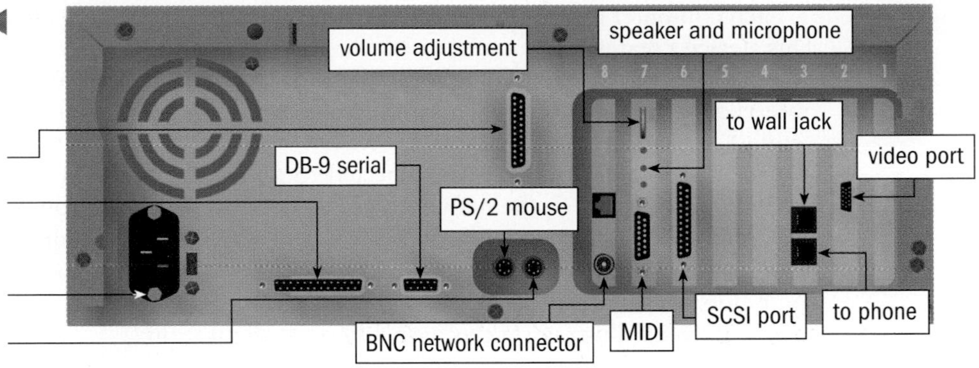

parallel

DB-25 serial

power

keyboard port

volume adjustment

DB-9 serial

PS/2 mouse

speaker and microphone

to wall jack

video port

BNC network connector

MIDI

SCSI port

to phone

A **parallel port** transmits data eight bits at a time. Parallel transmissions are relatively fast, but increase the risk for interference, so they are typically used to connect a printer that is near the computer. A **serial port** transmits data one bit at a time. Typically, a mouse, keyboard, and modem are connected with serial interfaces.

SCSI (pronounced "scuzzy") stands for **small computer system interface**. One SCSI port provides an interface for one or more peripheral devices. The first is connected directly to the computer through the port, and the second device is plugged into a similar port on the first device. SCSI connections can allow many devices to use the same port. They are particularly popular on Macintosh computers and notebook computers.

Figure 27 shows some other ports for telephone cables to connect a modem, a video port to connect a monitor, and a network connection. The interface to a sound card usually includes jacks for speakers, a microphone, and a **musical instrument digital interface** (MIDI), which is pronounced "middy." MIDI ports are used to connect computers to electronic instruments and recording devices.

Notebook computers may also include a **Personal Computer Memory Card International Association** (PCMCIA) slot. PCMCIA devices are credit-card-sized circuit boards that plug directly into the PCMCIA slot, and can contain additional memory, a modem, or a hard disk drive.

Look at Figure 1 at the beginning of the chapter. Does this computer include any of the ports illustrated in Figure 27? It mentions RS-232 and USB, which are types of serial ports, and parallel ports. You assure Tenzing that ports for speakers, a monitor, the mouse, and a modem are also probably included, since the advertisement lists those devices.

Networks

One of the most important types of data communications in the business world is a network connection. A **network** connects one computer to other computers and peripheral devices, enabling you to share data and resources with your coworkers. There are a variety of network configurations, too many to discuss thoroughly here. However, any type of network has some basic characteristics and requirements that you should know.

In a **local area network** (LAN), computers and peripheral devices are located relatively close to each other, generally in the same building. If you are using such a network, it is useful to know three things: the location of the data, the type of network card in your computer, and the communication software that manages protocols and network functions.

Some networks have one or more computers, called **file servers**, that act as the central storage location for programs and that provide mass storage for most of the data used on the network. A network with a file server is called a **client/server** network. These networks are dependent on the file server because it contains most of the data and software. When a network does not have a file server, all the computers essentially are equal, and programs and data are distributed among them. This is called a **peer-to-peer network**.

Each computer that is part of the network must have a **network interface card** installed. This device creates a communication channel between the computer and the network. **Network software** is also essential, establishing the communications protocols that will be observed on the network and controlling the "traffic flow" as data travels throughout the network.

A microcomputer that is not connected to a network is called a **standalone computer**. When it is connected to the network, it becomes a **workstation**. You have already learned that a **terminal** is a device with a keyboard and screen used for input and output, but is not capable of processing on its own. A terminal is connected to a network that uses minicomputers and mainframes as servers. Any device connected to the network is called a **node**. Figure 28 illustrates a typical network configuration.

Figure 28 ◀
Network nodes include workstations, printers, and servers

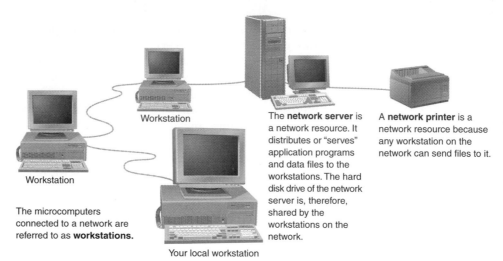

Workstation

Workstation

The microcomputers connected to a network are referred to as **workstations.**

Your local workstation

The **network server** is a network resource. It distributes or "serves" application programs and data files to the workstations. The hard disk drive of the network server is, therefore, shared by the workstations on the network.

A **network printer** is a network resource because any workstation on the network can send files to it.

Look at the computer ad in Figure 1. Is this computer networked? Can it be networked? Why or why not? Your answer should be that the computer is not currently part of a network and is not shipped with a network card. However, it should be possible to connect this computer to a network with the appropriate network card and software, which would have to be purchased separately.

Telecommunications

Telecommunications means communicating over a comparatively long distance. When it is not possible to connect users on one network, then telecommunications allows you to send and receive data over the telephone lines. To make this connection, you must use a communications device called a **modem**. A modem, which stands for *modulator-demodulator*, is a device that connects your computer to a standard telephone jack. The modem converts the **digital**, or stop-start, signals your computer outputs into **analog**, or continuous wave, signals (sound waves) that can traverse ordinary phone lines. Figure 29 shows the telecommunications process, in which a modem converts digital signals to analog signals at the sending site (modulates) and a second modem converts the analog signals back into digital signals at the receiving site (demodulates).

Figure 29 ◀
Using modems to send and receive a memo

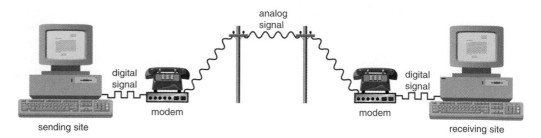

analog signal

digital signal

modem

digital signal

modem

sending site

receiving site

Look again at Figure 1. Although this computer ad doesn't list a network interface card, it does include a 33.6 bps fax/modem. The number 33.6 represents the modem's capability to send and receive 33,600 **bits per second** (bps). This speed is adequate for International ComAir employees to connect to their offices at other locations around the world.

The Internet
World Wide Web

The Internet

In the mid-1990s, the expansion of the Internet greatly enhanced the possibility of connecting to your global offices. The Internet was originally developed for the government to connect researchers around the world who needed to share data. Today, the Internet is the largest network in the world, connecting millions of people in almost 200 countries. It has become an invaluable communications channel for individuals, businesses, and governments around the world.

The first Internet experience most people have is to use **electronic mail**, more commonly called **e-mail**. This is the capability to send a message from one user's computer to another user's computer where it is stored until the receiver opens it. The vast network of networks that make up the Internet pass the message along through electronic links called **gateways**. E-mail has become such an integral part of business that you and Tenzing know that you must recommend it to International ComAir. Your recommendation will list its advantages: lower postage costs, lower long-distance charges, and increased worker productivity.

The newest commercial benefit of using the Internet is the emergence of the **World Wide Web**, sometimes referred to simply as the **Web**. The Web is a huge database of information that is stored on network servers in places that allow public access. The information is stored as text files called **Web pages** that can include text, graphics, sound, animation, and video. Figure 30 shows a sample web page.

Figure 30
A home page
on the World
Wide Web

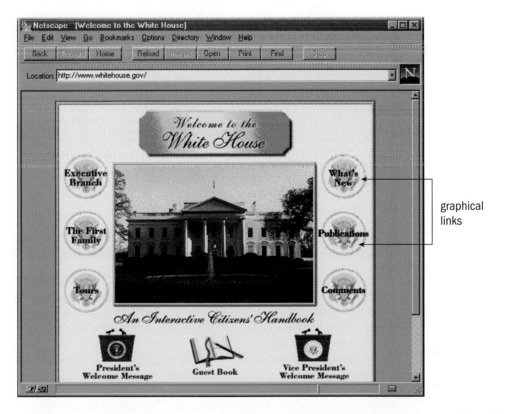

graphical
links

The evolution of multimedia and Internet technologies has made the World Wide Web the perfect communication tool for marketing business services and products. Hyperlinks are the primary resource for making the Web possible. A **hyperlink** is a place on a computer screen that is programmed to connect to a particular file on the same network server, or even on a network server on the other side of the globe. The communications software that helps you navigate the World Wide Web is called **Web browsing** software, or a **Web browser**. Tenzing and you decide to include the benefits of Internet and World Wide Web access in your recommendation to Ms. Thompson. In particular, you plan to convince her that International ComAir could allow individuals to make reservations and check flight status through the company's web pages.

Computer Software

Just as a tape player or CD player is worthless without tapes or CDs, computer hardware is useless without software. Many people think the word *software* applies to any part of the computer system that is not hardware, but that is not an accurate definition. We define **software** as the instructions and associated data that direct the computer to accomplish a task. Sometimes the term *software* refers to a single program, but often the term refers to a collection of programs and data that are packaged together, as shown in Figure 31. The software you use determines what type of computer you can use and what you can do with the computer.

Figure 31 ◀
A software
product

A **software package** contains disks or a CD-ROM and a reference manual.

The CD-ROM contains one or more **programs**, and possibly some data. For example, the Microsoft Office 97 software includes programs that help you draw graphics, write documents, and make calculations. The software also includes some data, such as a thesaurus of words and their synonyms.

User Interfaces

Software can be divided into two major categories: system software and application software. **System software** helps the computer carry out its basic operating tasks. **Application software** helps the user carry out a variety of tasks.

System Software

System software manages the fundamental operations of your computer, such as loading programs and data into memory, executing programs, saving data to disks, displaying information on the monitor, and transmitting data through a port to a peripheral device. There are four types of system software: operating systems, utilities, device drivers, and programming languages.

An **operating system** controls basic input and output, allocates system resources, manages storage space, maintains security, and detects equipment failure. You have already learned the importance of data communications, both inside a standalone computer and from a workstation to other users on a network. The flow of data from the microprocessor to memory to peripherals and back again is called basic **I/O**, or **input/output**. The operating system controls this flow of data like an air-traffic controller manages airport traffic.

A system resource is any part of the computer system, including memory, storage devices, and the microprocessor, that can be used by a computer program. The operating system allocates system resources so programs run properly. Most of today's computers are capable of **multitasking**—opening and running more than one program at a time—because the operating system is allocating memory and processing time to make multitasking possible. An example of multitasking is producing a document in your word processing program while you check a resource on the Internet. Both the word processing program and the web browsing program are allowed to use parts of the computer's resources, so you can look at the resource periodically while you are writing about it in your paper. The operating system is also responsible for managing the files on your storage devices. Not only does it open and save files, but it also keeps track of every part of every file for you and lets you know if any part is missing. This activity is like a filing clerk who puts files away when they are not being used, and gets them for you when you need them again. Figure 32 illustrates how the operating system assists word processing software to print a document.

Figure 32 ◀
The operating system: a liaison between the computer hardware and application software

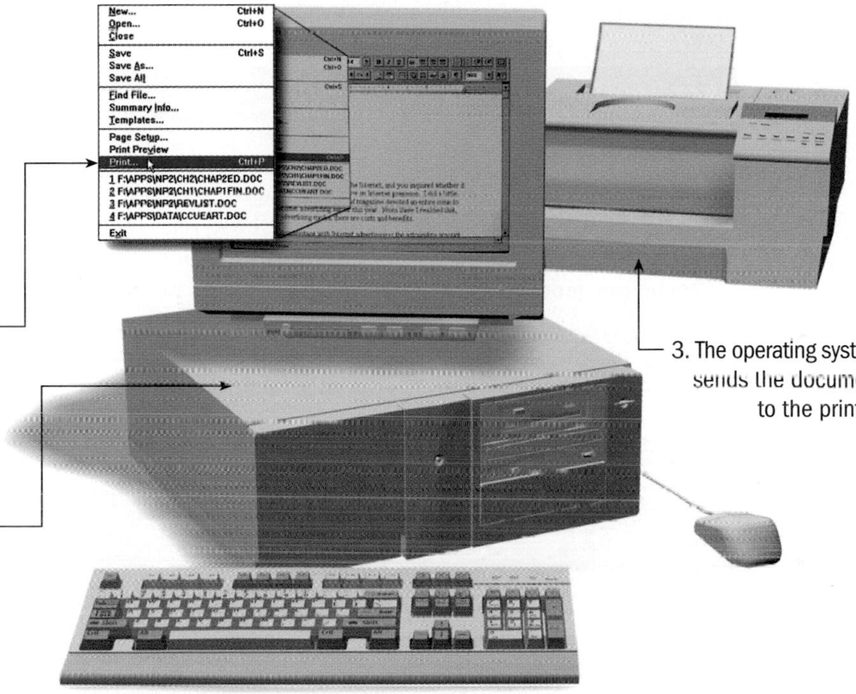

1. The user tells the word processing application to print the document.

2. The word processing application signals the operating system that a document must be sent to the printer.

3. The operating system sends the document to the printer.

While you are working on the computer, the operating system is constantly guarding against equipment failure. Each electronic circuit is checked periodically, and the moment a problem is detected, the user is notified with a warning message on the screen.

The operating system's responsibility to maintain security may include requiring a user-name and password or checking the computer for virus infection. Unscrupulous programmers deliberately construct harmful programs, called **viruses**, which instruct your computer to perform destructive activities, such as erasing a disk drive. Most viruses are more annoying than destructive, but computer users should protect themselves using virus protection software. **Virus protection software** searches executable files for the sequences of characters that may cause harm and disinfects the files by erasing or disabling those commands.

Microsoft Windows is referred to as an **operating environment** because it provides a **graphical user interface** (GUI, pronounced "goo-ey") that acts as a liaison between the user and all of the computer's hardware and software. In addition to the operating system, Windows also includes utilities, device drivers, and some application programs that perform common tasks. Since the mid-1980s, Windows has become one of the most popular operating environments because its graphics and menus make it easy to learn and quick to use.

Utilities are another category of system software that augment the operating system by taking over some of its responsibility for allocating hardware resources. There are many utilities that come with the operating system, but some independent software developers offer utilities for sale separately. For example, Norton Utilities, published by Symantec, is a very popular collection of utility software.

Each peripheral device requires a **device driver**, system software that helps the computer communicate with that particular device. When you add a device to an existing computer, part of its installation includes adding its device driver to the computer's configuration.

The last type of system software is **computer programming languages**, which a programmer uses to write computer instructions. The instructions are translated into electrical signals that the computer can manipulate and process. Some examples of popular programming languages are BASIC, Visual Basic, C, C++, COBOL, Ada, FORTRAN, Java, JavaScript, CGI, and Perl.

As you and Tenzing get ready to make your recommendations to International ComAir, you realize that the primary factor in deciding the computer specifications you choose to purchase is the software Ms. Thompson's employees will be using. Tenzing finds out that the majority of current computers are using Windows software and that employees will need to produce a variety of documents and perform some statistical analysis of reservations and flight data.

Multimedia

Application Software

Application software enables you to perform specific computer tasks. In the business world, some examples of tasks that are accomplished with application software are document production, spreadsheet, and database management. In addition, businesses may sometimes use graphics and presentation software, including multimedia applications.

Document production software includes word processing software, desktop publishing software, e-mail editors, and Web authoring software. All of these production tools have a variety of features that assist you in writing and formatting documents. Most offer **spell checking** to help you avoid typographical and spelling errors, as shown in Figure 33.

Figure 33 ◀
In-line
spell check

A wiggly red line
indicates a possible
spelling error.

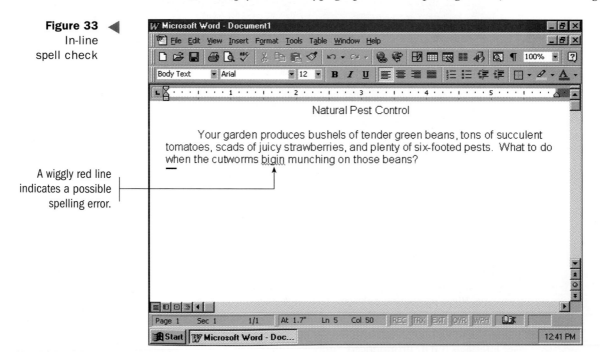

Many also assist you with **grammar-checking** and **thesaurus** tools to improve your writing by offering suggestions and alternatives. Most document production software allows you to perform **block operations**, an editing tool that quickly reorganizes your words after they have been typed. Block operations may also be called **copy-and-paste** or **cut-and-paste**, which is exactly what they allow you to do: copy or move words around. Document production software may also include **search** or **replace** features that allow you to look for a sequence of characters and substitute new text.

A **document template** is a preformatted document into which you type your text. A template might include format settings such as margins, line spacing, **font** (the style of type), and font size. Templates makes it easier to produce consistent documents, such as letterhead or business cards that make a business familiar. Figure 34 shows some of the document templates available with Microsoft Word, a popular word processing software package.

Figure 34 ◄
Document templates

Template categories include letters, memos, reports, and publications.

Within each category you can choose from several different templates.

The Preview shows you an example of a document created using the selected template.

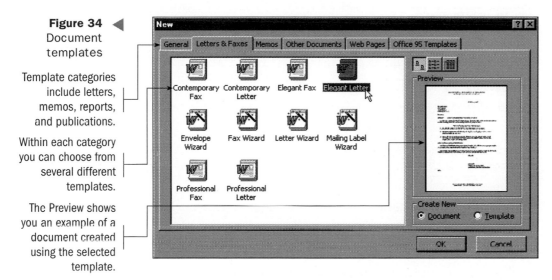

Desktop publishing software is a variation of word processing software that focuses on the format or printed appearance of documents. It is particularly useful for the design of brochures, posters, newsletters, and other documents that are printed in special sizes and formats. Desktop publishing features, such as automatic page numbering and the use of styles, facilitate the development of multiple-page documents. A **style** is a collection of formatting options that are given a name and used repeatedly throughout a document to maintain consistency. Modern word processing software now includes many desktop publishing features such as the automatic generation of a table of contents or index and the ability to insert graphics.

Data communications has opened up a new dimension of document production referred to as **electronic publishing**. Instead of printing and distributing documents in the traditional ways, many businesses and individuals are transmitting them electronically by including them in e-mail messages, posting them to the World Wide Web, or participating in electronic conferences where participants can view documents simultaneously. **Web authoring software** transforms word processing documents into a format that can be viewed electronically on remote computers.

Spreadsheet software is a numerical analysis tool that both businesses and individuals use extensively. You can use spreadsheet software, for example, to maintain your checkbook register. Most people use a calculator to keep track of their bank accounts, but using a spreadsheet has several advantages. Spreadsheet software creates a **worksheet**, composed of a grid of columns and rows. Each column is lettered, and each row is numbered. The intersection of a column and row is a **cell**, and each cell has a unique address, called its **cell reference**. Figure 35 shows a typical worksheet that includes a simple calculation.

Figure 35
A typical worksheet displays numbers and text in a grid of rows and columns. Cell B6 contains the result of a calculation performed by the spreadsheet software.

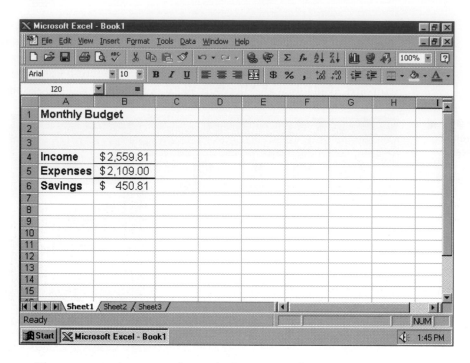

You type numbers into the grid, then create formulas that perform calculations using these numbers. In many ways, a spreadsheet is the ultimate calculator. Once your numbers are on the screen, you don't have to reenter them when you want to redo a calculation with revised or corrected numbers. As an additional benefit, spreadsheet software provides you with excellent printouts of the raw data or of graphs created from the data.

With the appropriate data and formulas, you can use an electronic spreadsheet to prepare financial reports, analyze investment portfolios, calculate amortization tables, examine alternative bid proposals, and project income, as well as perform many other tasks involved in making informed business decisions.

Graphs provide a quick, visual summary of data. With spreadsheet software it is simple to create attractive graphs. Because they are so easy to produce, you have to be careful that the way you are presenting your data is a visual representation of the truth. Figure 36 shows how changing the shape of a graph can dramatically change the visual summary it provides. Although the data in these two graphs is the same, the graph on the right makes it look as if sales are climbing at a faster rate than the other graph does.

Figure 36
Graphs can "stretch the truth"

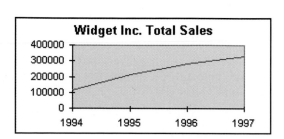

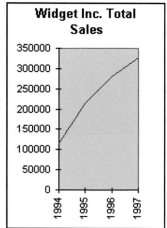

One of the most common types of application software is **database management** software. A **database** is a collection of information stored on one or more computers. The explosion of information in our society is primarily organized and managed in databases. A **structured database** is organized in a uniform format of records and fields. A familiar example of a structured database is the library card catalog, such as the one represented in Figure 37.

Figure 37
A structured database

one record →

fields →

data →

database →

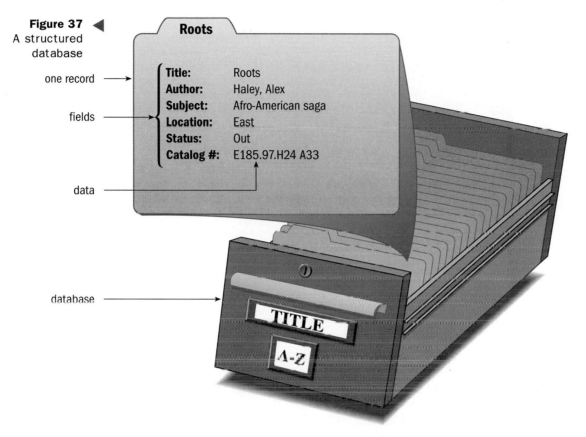

Structured databases typically store data that describes a collection of similar entities. Some other examples are student academic records, medical records, a warehouse inventory, or an address book.

A **free-form database** is a loosely structured collection of information, usually stored as documents rather than as records. The collection of word processing documents you have created and stored on your computer is an example of a free-form database. Another example is an encyclopedia stored on a CD-ROM containing documents, photographs, and even video clips. The most familiar example of a free-form database in our society is the World Wide Web with its millions of documents stored worldwide.

Graphics and presentation software allow you to create illustrations, diagrams, graphs, and charts that can be projected before a group, printed out for quick reference, or transmitted to remote computers. Most application software allows you to include graphics that you can create yourself using graphics software, such as Microsoft Paint or Adobe PhotoShop. You can also use **clip art**, simple drawings that are included as collections with many software packages. Microsoft PowerPoint is popular presentation software that allows you to create colorful presentations and transparencies. A Microsoft PowerPoint screen is shown in Figure 38.

Figure 38
A PowerPoint
for Windows 95
screen

Multimedia authoring software allows you to record digital sound files, video files, and animations that can be included in presentations and other documents. Macromedia Director and MicroMedium Digital Trainer Professional are two examples of software that you can use to create files that include multimedia. You can sequence and format the screens into tutorials or presentations. Like Web authoring software, multimedia authoring software also uses hypertext to link documents so that the reader can jump from one to another. Most modern application software allows users to integrate these multimedia elements into other types of files.

In the 1990s, one of the most powerful developments in computer use was the ability of users to use data created in one application in a document created by another application. For instance, it has become so easy to add a graphic to your word processing document that you forget the graphic was created and saved by someone using graphics software.

Applications that were designed for the Windows environment have added a new dimension to this merging capability. **Object linking and embedding** (OLE) refers to the ability to use data from another file, called the *source*. Embedding occurs when you copy and paste the source data in the new file. Think of embedding as taking a snapshot of the original. No matter what happens to the original, you still have the copy, as it appeared when you first copied it. Linking allows you to create a connection between the source data and the copy in the new file. The link updates the copy every time a change is made to the source data. The seamless nature of OLE among some applications is referred to as **integration,** and the ability to integrate data from all of your applications has become an important skill in business.

Tenzing and you are now ready to make your recommendation to Ms. Thompson including microcomputer hardware, network access, and software. Look back at Figure 1 to be sure that you understand each specification listed. Also consider the software options you should recommend. What will you include? The computer ad already lists Microsoft Windows, so your recommendation should include document production, spreadsheet, and database management software that is compatible with Microsoft Windows. You might also recommend e-mail and network communication software, including Web browsing and Web authoring software. Here's hoping that Ms. Thompson approves your recommendations. Good luck!

Review Questions

1. What is the key to a computer's versatility?
   a. software
   b. hardware
   c. price
   d. peripherals

2. Which one of the following would not be considered a microcomputer?
   a. desktop
   b. notebook
   c. mainframe
   d. personal digital assistant

3. Keyboards, monitors, hard disk drives, printers, and motherboards are all examples of which of the following?
   a. input devices
   b. output devices
   c. peripherals
   d. hardware

4. The selection of components that make up a particular computer system is referred to as the _____.
   a. configuration
   b. specification
   c. protocol
   d. device driver

5. Moving text, sorting lists, and performing calculations are examples of which of the following?
   a. input
   b. output
   c. processing
   d. storage

6. What do you call each 1 or 0 used in the representation of computer data?
   a. a bit
   b. a byte
   c. an ASCII
   d. a pixel

7. What usually represents one character of data?
   a. a bit
   b. a byte
   c. an integer
   d. a pixel

8. What is a megabyte?
   a. 10 kilobytes
   b. about a million bytes
   c. one-half a gigabyte
   d. about a million bits

9. Which one of the following microprocessors is fastest?
   a. 200 MHz Pentium
   b. 166 MHz Pentium Pro
   c. 200 MHz Pentium with MMX
   d. 233 MHz Pentium II

10. Which of the following temporarily stores data and programs while you are using them?
    a. ROM
    b. a floppy disk
    c. RAM
    d. a hard disk

11. What do you call a collection of data stored on a disk under a name that you assign it?
    a. a file
    b. the operating system
    c. a protocol
    d. a pixel

12. Which of the following storage media does not allow you to recycle by writing over old data?
    a. hard disk
    b. floppy disk
    c. CD
    d. tape

13. What connects a monitor to a computer?
    a. a parallel port
    b. a network card
    c. a graphics adapter
    d. new letter-quality mode

14. A microcomputer that is attached to a network is called a

    _____.

    a. desktop
    b. workstation
    c. terminal
    d. PDA

15. What telecommunications hardware is needed to convert digital signals to analog signals?
    a. mouse
    b. device driver
    c. modem
    d. slot

16. Which one of the following is system software?
    a. Microsoft Excel
    b. Microsoft Windows
    c. Microsoft Paint
    d. Microsoft Word

17. Which of the following is not a function of an operating system?
    a. controls basic input and output
    b. allocates system resources
    c. manages storage space
    d. carries out a specific task for the user

18. Random access memory (RAM) is measured in _____.

19. Disk access time is measured in _____.

20. The clock speed of a microprocessor is measured in _____.

21. _____ is the maximum number of pixels a monitor can display.

22. The transmission of text, numeric, voice, or video data from one computer to another is called _____.

23. Connecting a microcomputer to peripheral devices is called _____.

24. The capability to send a text message from one user to another user's account where it is stored until the receiver opens it, is called _____.

25. The _____ is a huge database of information that is stored on network servers around the world, and which users access by using browser software.

26. For each of the following data items, indicate how many bytes of storage would be required:

Data Item	Number of Bytes
North	
U.S.A.	
General Ledger	

27. Read the following requirements for using Microsoft Office 97 Professional Edition (taken from the documentation that accompanies the software). Then turn back to the computer advertisement shown in Figure 1 at the beginning of the chapter and determine if the computer specifications listed in the ad are sufficient to run Office 97.

To use Microsoft Office 97, you need:

- A personal or multimedia computer with a 486 or higher processor

- Microsoft Windows 95 operating system or Microsoft Windows NT 3.51 Service Pack 5 or later (will not run on earlier versions)

- 8 MB of memory required to run applications individually (12 MB required to run Microsoft Access); more memory may be required to run additional applications simultaneously

- 73–191 MB hard disk space required; approximately 121 MB required for typical installation, depending on configuration

- CD-ROM drive

- VGA or higher-resolution video adapter (Super VGA, 256-color recommended)

- Microsoft Mouse, Microsoft IntelliMouse, or compatible pointing device

Additional items or services required to use certain features include:

- 9,600 bps or higher modem (14.4 recommended)

- Multimedia computer required to access sound and other multimedia effects

- Microsoft Mail, Microsoft Exchange, Internet SMTP/POP3, or other MAPI-compliant messaging software required to use e-mail

- Some Internet functionality may require Internet access and payment of a separate fee to a service provider

28. Using the system requirements listed in Question 27, look through a recent computer magazine and find the least expensive computer that will run the Microsoft Office 97 Professional Edition software. Make a photocopy of the ad showing the specifications, price, and vendor. Write the name of the magazine and the issue date at the top of the photocopied ad. Write a two-page paper that supports your selection.

29. In this chapter, you learned that the use of multimedia requires special hardware and software. Look for current prices and specifications of multimedia hardware in advertisements in magazines or in your local newspaper. What are the highest priced devices, and why are they so expensive? In the following chart, add specifications and price for the most expensive examples of these devices that you can find. Look at the computer advertisement shown in Figure 1 at the beginning of the chapter and determine if the computer specifications listed in the ad are sufficient to run multimedia. If not, write a statement that justifies adding the cost of the higher-quality device you listed here.

Multimedia Device	Specifications	Price
CD-ROM drive		
Speakers		
Headphones		
Large, high-resolution monitor		

Lab Assignments

The following Lab Assignments are designed to accompany the interactive Course Labs. To start each Course Lab, click the Start button on the Windows 95 taskbar, point to Programs, point to Course Labs, point to New Perspectives Applications, and click the name of the Lab (for example, Using a Mouse). If you do not see Course Labs on your Program menu, see your instructor or technical support person.

Using a Mouse A mouse is a standard input device on most of today's computers. You need to know how to use a mouse to manipulate graphical user interfaces and to use the rest of the Labs.

1. The Steps for the Using a Mouse Lab show you how to click, double-click, and drag objects using the mouse. Click the Steps button and begin the Steps. As you work through the Steps, answer all of the Quick Check questions that appear. When you complete the Steps, you will see a Summary Report that summarizes your performance on the Quick Checks. Follow the directions on the screen to print the Summary Report.

2. In Explore, demonstrate your ability to use a mouse and to control a Windows program by creating a poster. To create a poster for an upcoming sports event, select a graphic, type the caption for the poster, then select a font, font styles, and a border. Print your completed poster.

Using a Keyboard To become an effective computer user, you must be familiar with your primary input device—the keyboard.

1. The Steps for the Using a Keyboard Lab provide you with a structured introduction to the keyboard layout and the function of special computer keys. Click the Steps button and begin the Steps. As you work through the Steps, answer all of the Quick Check questions that appear. When you complete the Steps, you will see a Summary Report that summarizes your performance on the Quick Checks. Follow the directions on the screen to print the Summary Report.

2. In Explore, start the typing tutor. You can develop your typing skills using the typing tutor in Explore. Take the typing test and print out your results.

3. In Explore, try to improve your typing speed by 10 words per minute. For example, if you currently type 20 words per minute, your goal would be 30 words per minute. Practice each typing lesson until you see a message that indicates you can proceed to the next lesson. Create a Practice Report as shown here to keep track of how much you practice. When you have reached your goal, print out the results of a typing test to verify your results.

Practice Record

Name: _____

Section: _____

Start Date: _____ Start Typing Speed: _____ wpm

End Date: _____ End Typing Speed: _____ wpm

Lesson #: _____ Date Practiced/Time Practiced _____

Peripheral Devices A wide variety of peripheral devices provide expandability for computer systems and provide users with the equipment necessary to accomplish tasks efficiently. In the Peripheral Devices Lab, you will use an online product catalog of peripheral devices.

1. Click the Steps button and begin the Steps. Complete the Steps to find out how to use the online product catalog. As you work through the Steps, answer all of the Quick Check questions that appear. When you complete the Steps, you will see a Summary Report that summarizes your performance on the Quick Checks. Follow the directions on the screen to print the Summary Report.

2. After you know how to use the product catalog to look up products, features, and prices, use the catalog to do the following:
   a. List the characteristics that differentiate printers.
   b. List the factors that differentiate monitors.
   c. Describe the factors that determine the appropriate type of scanner for a task.
   d. List the peripheral devices in the catalog that are specially designed for notebook computers.

3. Suppose that the company that produces the peripheral devices catalog selected your name from its list of customers for a free scanner. You can select any one of the scanners in the catalog. Assume that you own a notebook computer to which you could attach any one of the scanners. Click the Explore button and use the catalog to help you write a one-page paper explaining which scanner you would select, why you would select it, and how you would use it.

4. Suppose you are in charge of a new college computing lab. The lab will include 25 computers that are used by students from all departments at the college. You have a $3,000 budget for printers. Use the product catalog to decide which printers you would purchase for the lab. Write a one-page memo to your boss that justifies your choice.

5. Suppose you own a desktop microcomputer system, such as the one in Figure 3 of this chapter. You have an idea that you can earn the money for your college tuition by using your computer to help other students produce spiffy reports with color graphs and scanned images. Your parents have agreed to "loan" you $1,000 to get started. Click the Explore button and look through the online peripheral devices catalog. List any of the devices that might help you with this business venture. Write a one-page paper explaining how you would spend your $1,000 to get the equipment you need to start the business.

Using Files In this Lab you manipulate a simulated computer to view what happens in memory and on disk when you create, save, open, revise, and delete files. Understanding what goes on "inside the box" will help you quickly grasp how to perform basic file operations with most application software.

1. Click the Steps button to learn how to use the simulated computer to view the contents of memory and disk when you perform basic file operations. As you proceed through the Steps, answer all of the Quick Check questions that appear. After you complete the Steps, you will see a Quick Check Summary Report. Follow the instructions on the screen to print this report.

2. Click the Explore button and use the simulated computer to perform the following tasks:
   a. Create a document containing your name and the city in which you were born. Save this document as NAME.
   b. Create another document containing two of your favorite foods. Save this document as FOODS.
   c. Create another file containing your two favorite classes. Call this file CLASSES.
   d. Open the FOOD file and add another one of your favorite foods. Save this file without changing its name.
   e. Open the NAME file. Change this document so it contains your name and the name of your school. Save this as a new document called SCHOOL.
   f. Write down how many files are on the simulated disk and the exact contents of each file.
   g. Delete all the files.

3. In Explore, use the simulated computer to perform the following tasks:
   a. Create a file called MUSIC that contains the name of your favorite CD.
   b. Create another document that contains eight numbers and call this file LOTTERY.
   c. You don't win the lottery this week. Revise the contents of the LOTTERY file, but save the revision as LOTTERY2.
   d. Revise the MUSIC file so it also contains the name of your favorite musician or composer, and save this file as MUSIC2.
   e. Delete the MUSIC file.
   f. Write down how many files are on the simulated disk, and the exact contents of each file.

The Internet: World Wide Web One of the most popular services on the Internet is the World Wide Web. This Lab is a Web simulator that teaches you how to use Web browser software to find information. You can use this Lab whether or not your school provides you with Internet access.

1. Click the Steps button to learn how to use Web browser software. As you proceed through the Steps, answer all of the Quick Check questions that appear. After you complete the Steps, you will see a Quick Check Summary Report. Follow the instructions on the screen to print this report.

2. Click the Explore button on the Welcome screen. Use the Web browser to locate a weather map of the Caribbean Virgin Islands. What is its URL?

3. Enter the URL **http://www.atour.com**. A SCUBA diver named Wadson Lachouffe has been searching for the fabled treasure of Greybeard the pirate. A link from the Adventure Travel Web site leads to Wadson's Web page called "Hidden Treasure." In Explore, locate the Hidden Treasure page and answer the following questions:
   a. What was the name of Greybeard's ship?
   b. What was Greybeard's favorite food?
   c. What does Wadson think happened to Greybeard's ship?

4. In the Steps, you found a graphic of Jupiter from the photo archives of the Jet Propulsion Laboratory. In the Explore section of the Lab, you can also find a graphic of Saturn. Suppose one of your friends wants a picture of Saturn for an astronomy report. Make a list of the blue, underlined links your friend must click to find the Saturn graphic. Assume that your friend will begin at the Web Trainer home page.

5. Jump back to the Adventure Travel Web site. Write a one-page description of this site. In your, paper include a description of the information at the site, the number of pages the site contains, and a diagram of the links it contains.

6. Chris Thomson is a student at UVI and has his own Web pages. In Explore, look at the information Chris has included on his pages. Suppose you could create your own Web page. What would you include? Use word processing software to design your own Web pages. Make sure you indicate the graphics and links you would use.

User Interfaces You have learned that the hardware and software for a user interface determine how you interact and communicate with the computer. In the User Interfaces Lab, you will try five different user interfaces to accomplish the same task—creating a graph.

1. Click the Steps button to find out how each interface works. As you work through the Steps, answer all of the Quick Check questions. When you complete the Steps, you will see a Summary Report that summarizes your performance on the Quick Checks. Follow the directions on the screen to print the Summary Report.

2. In Explore, use each interface to make a 3-D pie graph using data set 1. Title your graphs "Cycle City Sales." Use the percent style to show the percent of each slice of the pie. Print each of the five graphs (one for each interface).

3. In Explore, select one of the user interfaces. Write a step-by-step set of instructions for producing a line graph using data set 2. This line graph should show lines and symbols, and have the title "Widget Production."

4. Using the user interface terminology you learned in this Lab and in this chapter, write a description of each of the interfaces you used in the Lab. Then suppose you work for a software publisher and you are going to create a software package for producing line, bar, column, and pie graphs. Which user interface would you use for the software? Why?

Multimedia Multimedia brings together text, graphics, sound, animation, video, and photo images. In this Lab you will learn how to apply multimedia and then have the chance to see what it might be like to design some aspects of multimedia projects.

1. Click the Steps button to learn about multimedia development. As you work through the Steps, answer all of the Quick Check questions that appear. After you complete the Steps, you will see a Quick Check Report. Follow the instructions on the screen to print this report.

2. How many videos are included in the Multimedia Mission Log? The image on the Mission Profile page is a vector drawing. What happens when you enlarge it?

3. Listen to the sound track on Day 4. Is this a WAV file or a MIDI file? Why do you think so? Is this a synthesized sound or a digitized sound? Listen to the sound track on the first page. Can you tell if this is a WAV file or a MIDI file?

4. Suppose you were hired as a multimedia designer for a multimedia series on targeting fourth- and fifth-grade students. Describe the changes you would make to the Multimedia Mission Log so it would be suitable for these students. Also, include a sketch showing a screen from your revised design.

5. The Multimedia Mission Log does not contain any hyperlinks. Suppose that you were hired to revise the design of this product to add hyperlinks. Provide a list of five specific instances where you would use hyperlinks and indicate what sort of information each would link to.

6. Multimedia can be effectively applied to projects such as encyclopedias, atlases, and animated storybooks; to computer-based training for foreign languages, first aid, or software applications; for games and sports simulations; for business presentations; for personal albums, scrapbooks, and baby books; for product catalogs and Web pages.

   Suppose you were hired to create one of these projects. Write a one-paragraph description of the project you would be creating. Describe some of the multimedia elements you would include. For each of the elements, indicate its source and whether you would need to obtain permission for its use. Finally, sketch a screen or two showing your completed project.

Index

New Perspectives on

Microsoft®
Windows® 95

BRIEF

TUTORIALS

Read This **Before You Begin**

STUDENT DISKS

To complete the tutorials and Tutorial Assignments, you need a Student Disk. Your instructor will either provide you with a Student Disk or ask you to make your own.

If you are supposed to make your own Student Disk, you will need a blank, formatted high-density disk. Follow the instructions in the section called "Creating Your Student Disk" in Tutorial 2 to use the Make Student Disk program to create your own Student Disk. See the inside front or inside back cover of this book for more information on Student Disk files, or ask your instructor or technical support person for assistance.

COURSE LABS

This book features three interactive Course Labs to help you understand Windows concepts. There are Lab Assignments at the end of each tutorial that relate to these Labs. To start a Lab, click the Start button on the Windows 95 taskbar, point to Programs, point to CTI Windows 95 Applications, point to Windows 95 New Perspectives Brief, and click the name of the Lab you want to use.

USING YOUR OWN COMPUTER

If you are going to work through this book using your own computer, you need:

■ **Computer System** Windows 95 must be installed on your computer. This book assumes a complete installation of Windows 95.

■ **Student Disk** Ask your instructor or lab manager for details on how to get the Student Disk. You will not be able to complete the tutorials or exercises in this book using your own computer until you have the Student Disk. The student files may also be obtained electronically over the Internet. See the inside front or inside back cover of this book for more details.

■ **Course Labs** See your instructor or technical support person to obtain the Course Lab software for use on your own computer.

To complete the tutorials and Tutorial Assignments in this book, your students must use a set of files on a Student Disk. The Instructor's Resource Kit for this book includes either two Student Files Setup Disks or a CD-ROM containing the student disk setup program. Follow the instructions on the disk label or in the Readme file to install the Make Student Disk program onto your server or standalone computers. Your students can then use the Windows 95 Start menu to run the program that will create their Student Disk. Tutorial 2 contains steps that instruct your students on how to generate student disks.

If you prefer to provide Student Disks rather than letting students generate them, you can run the Make Student Disk program yourself following the instructions in Tutorial 2.

COURSE LAB SOFTWARE

This book features three online, interactive Course Labs that introduce basic Windows concepts. The Instructor's Resource Kit for this book contains the Lab software either on four Course Labs Setup Disks or on a CD-ROM. Follow the instructions on the disk label or in the Readme file to install the Lab software on your server or standalone computers. Refer also to the Readme file for essential technical notes related to running the labs in a multiuser environment.
Once you have installed the Course Lab software, your students can start the Labs from the Windows 95 desktop by clicking the Start button on the Windows 95 taskbar, pointing to Programs, pointing to CTI Windows 95 Applications, pointing to Windows 95 New Perspectives Brief, and then clicking the name of the Lab they want to use.

CT LAB SOFTWARE AND STUDENT FILES

You are granted a license to copy the Student Files and Course Labs to any computer or computer network used by students who have purchased this book.

Exploring the Basics

Investigating the Windows 95 Operating System in the Computer Lab

OBJECTIVES

In this tutorial you will learn to:

- Identify the controls on the Windows 95 desktop

- Use the Windows 95 Start button to run software programs

- Identify and use the controls in a window

- Switch between programs using the taskbar

- Use Windows 95 controls such as menus, toolbars, list boxes, scroll bars, radio buttons, tabs, and check boxes

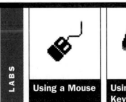

LABS

Using a Mouse   **Using a Keyboard**

CASE

Your First Day in the Lab

You walk into the computer lab and sit down at a desk. There's a computer in front of you, and you find yourself staring dubiously at the stack of software manuals. Where to start? As if in answer to your question, your friend Steve Laslow appears.

Gesturing to the stack of manuals, you tell Steve that you were just wondering where to start.

"You start with the operating system," says Steve. Noticing your slightly puzzled look, Steve explains that the **operating system** is software that helps the computer carry out basic operating tasks such as displaying information on the computer screen and saving data on your disks. Your computer uses the **Microsoft Windows 95** operating system—Windows 95, for short.

Steve tells you that Windows 95 has a "gooey" or **graphical user interface (GUI)**, which uses pictures of familiar objects, such as file folders and documents, to represent a desktop on your screen. Microsoft Windows 95 gets its name from the rectangular-shaped work areas, called "windows," that appear on your screen.

Steve continues to talk as he sorts through the stack of manuals on your desk. He says there are two things he really likes about Windows 95. First, lots of software is available for computers that have the Windows 95 operating system and all this software has a standard graphical user interface. That means once you have learned how to use one Windows software package, such as word-processing software, you are well on your way to understanding how to use other Windows software. Second, Windows 95 lets you use more than one software package at a time, so you can easily switch between your word-processing software and your appointment book software, for example. All in all, Windows 95 makes your computer an effective and easy-to-use productivity tool.

Steve recommends that you get started right away by using some tutorials that will teach you the skills essential for using Microsoft Windows 95. He hands you a book and assures you that everything on your computer system is set up and ready to go.

You mention that last summer you worked in an advertising agency where the employees used something called Windows 3.1. Steve explains that Windows 3.1 is an earlier version of the Windows operating system. Windows 95 and Windows 3.1 are similar, but Windows 95 is more powerful and easier to use. Steve says that as you work through the tutorials you will see notes that point out the important differences between Windows 95 and Windows 3.1.

Steve has a class, but he says he'll check back later to see how you are doing.

Using the Tutorials Effectively

These tutorials will help you learn about Windows 95. The tutorials are designed to be used at a computer. Each tutorial is divided into sessions. Watch for the session headings, such as Session 1.1 and Session 1.2. Each session is designed to be completed in about 45 minutes, but take as much time as you need. It's also a good idea to take a break between sessions.

Before you begin, read the following questions and answers. They are designed to help you use the tutorials effectively.

Where do I start?

Each tutorial begins with a case, which sets the scene for the tutorial and gives you background information to help you understand what you will be doing in the tutorial. Read the case before you go to the lab. In the lab, begin with the first session of the tutorial.

How do I know what to do on the computer?

Each session contains steps that you will perform on the computer to learn how to use Windows 95. Read the text that introduces each series of steps. The steps you need to do at a computer are numbered and are set against a color background. Read each step carefully and completely before you try it.

How do I know if I did the step correctly?

As you work, compare your computer screen with the corresponding figure in the tutorial. Don't worry if your screen display is somewhat different from the figure. The important parts of the screen display are labeled in each figure. Check to make sure these parts are on your screen.

What if I make a mistake?

Don't worry about making mistakes—they are part of the learning process. Paragraphs labeled "**TROUBLE?**" identify common problems and explain how to get back on track. Follow the steps in a **TROUBLE?** paragraph *only* if you are having the problem described. If you run into other problems:

- Carefully consider the current state of your system, the position of the pointer, and any messages on the screen.

- Complete the sentence, "Now I want to...." Be specific, because you are identifying your goal.

- Develop a plan for accomplishing your goal, and put your plan into action.

How do I use the Reference Windows?

Reference Windows summarize the procedures you learn in the tutorial steps. Do not complete the actions in the Reference Windows when you are working through the tutorial. Instead, refer to the Reference Windows while you are working on the assignments at the end of the tutorial.

How can I test my understanding of the material I learned in the tutorial?

At the end of each session, you can answer the Quick Check questions. The answers for the Quick Checks are at the end of the book.

After you have completed the entire tutorial, you should complete the Tutorial Assignments. The Tutorial Assignments are carefully structured so you will review what you have learned and then apply your knowledge to new situations.

What if I can't remember how to do something?

You should refer to the Task Reference at the end of the book; it summarizes how to accomplish commonly performed tasks.

What are the 3.1 Notes?

The 3.1 Notes are helpful if you have used Windows 3.1. The notes point out the key similarities and differences between Windows 3.1 and Windows 95.

What are the Interactive Labs, and how should I use them?

Interactive Labs help you review concepts and practice skills that you learn in the tutorial. Lab icons at the beginning of each tutorial and in the margins of the tutorials indicate topics that have corresponding Labs. The Lab Assignments section includes instructions for how to use each Lab.

Now that you understand how to use the tutorials effectively, you are ready to begin.

SESSION

1.1

In this session, in addition to learning basic Windows terminology, you will learn how to use a mouse, to start and stop a program, and to use more than one program at a time. With the skills you learn in this session, you will be able to use Windows 95 to start software programs.

Using a Keyboard

Starting Windows 95

Windows 95 automatically starts when you turn on the computer. Depending on the way your computer is set up, you might be asked to enter your user name and password. If prompted to do so, type your assigned user name and press the Enter key. Then type your password and press the Enter key to continue.

To start Windows 95:

1. Turn on your computer.

   TROUBLE? If the Welcome to Windows 95 box appears on your screen, press the Enter key to close it.

The Windows 95 Desktop

In Windows terminology, the screen represents a **desktop**—a workspace for projects and the tools needed to manipulate those projects. Look at your screen display and locate the objects labeled in Figure 1-1 on the following page.

Because it is easy to customize the Windows environment, your screen might not look exactly the same as Figure 1-1. You should, however, be able to locate objects on your screen similar to those in Figure 1-1.

Icons are small pictures that represent objects such as your computer, your computer network, a specific computer program, or a document. Your desktop probably contains several icons, such as My Computer, Network Neighborhood, and the Recycle Bin. You'll use these icons in later tutorials to work with files stored on your computer or on other computers on the network.

Figure 1-1 ◀
The Windows 95 desktop

The **desktop** is your workspace on the screen.

The **Start** button is one of the most important controls in Windows 95. You use the Start button to access essential Windows 95 functions, programs, and documents.

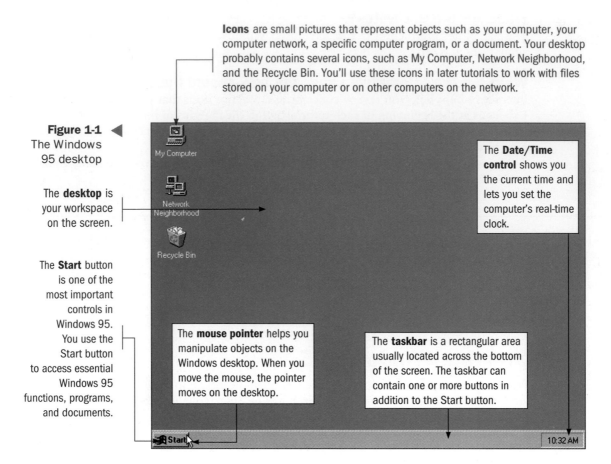

The **Date/Time control** shows you the current time and lets you set the computer's real-time clock.

The **mouse pointer** helps you manipulate objects on the Windows desktop. When you move the mouse, the pointer moves on the desktop.

The **taskbar** is a rectangular area usually located across the bottom of the screen. The taskbar can contain one or more buttons in addition to the Start button.

TROUBLE? If the screen goes blank or starts to display a moving design, press any key to restore the image.

Using the Mouse

Using a Mouse

A **mouse**, like those shown in Figure 1-2, is a pointing device that helps you interact with objects on the screen. In Windows 95 you need to know how to use the mouse to point, click, and drag. In this session you will learn about pointing and clicking. In Session 1.2 you will learn how to use the mouse to drag objects.

You can also interact with objects by using the keyboard; however, the mouse is much more convenient for most tasks, so the tutorials in this book assume you are using one.

Pointing

The **pointer**, or **mouse pointer**, is a small object that moves on the screen when you move the mouse. The pointer is usually shaped like an arrow. As you move the mouse on a flat surface, the pointer on the screen moves in the direction corresponding to the movement of the mouse. The pointer sometimes changes shape depending on where it is on the screen or the action the computer is completing.

Find the arrow-shaped pointer on your screen. If you do not see the pointer, move your mouse until the pointer comes into view.

Figure 1-2 ◄
The mouse

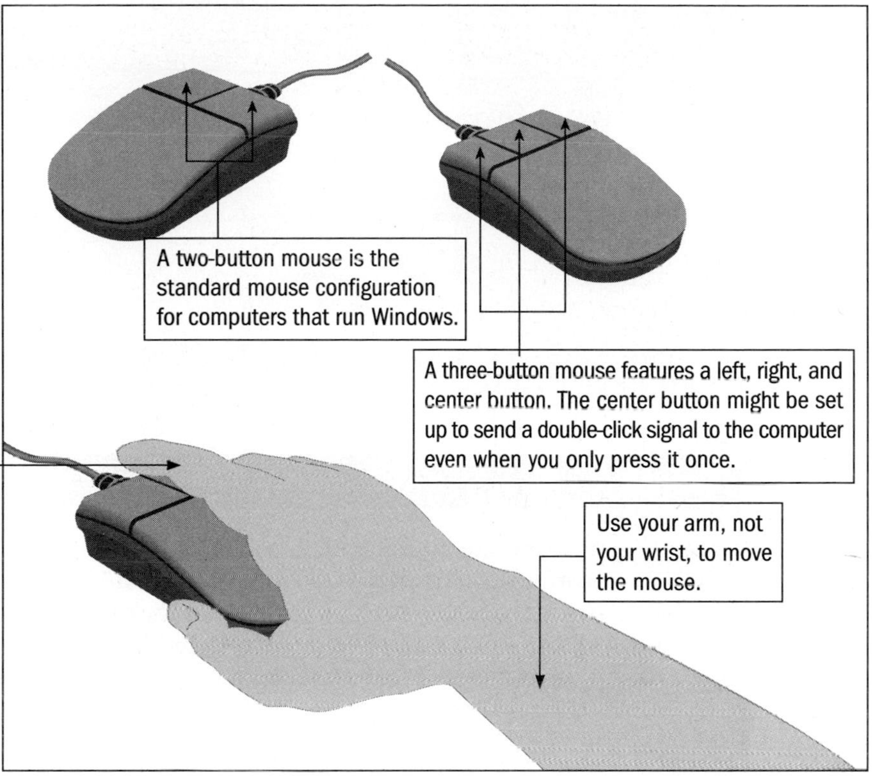

A two-button mouse is the standard mouse configuration for computers that run Windows.

A three-button mouse features a left, right, and center button. The center button might be set up to send a double-click signal to the computer even when you only press it once.

Use your arm, not your wrist, to move the mouse.

To hold the mouse, place your forefinger over the left mouse button. Place your thumb on the left side of the mouse. Your ring and small fingers should be on the right side of the mouse.

Basic "mousing" skills depend on your ability to position the pointer. You begin most Windows operations by positioning the pointer over a specific part of the screen. This is called **pointing**.

To move the pointer:

1. Position your right index finger over the left mouse button, as shown in Figure 1-2. Lightly grasp the sides of the mouse with your thumb and little finger.

   TROUBLE? If you want to use the mouse with your left hand, ask your instructor or technical support person to help you use the Control Panel to change the mouse settings to swap the left and right mouse buttons. Be sure you find out how to change back to the right-handed mouse setting, so you can reset the mouse each time you are finished in the lab.

2. Locate the arrow-shaped pointer on the screen.

3. Move the mouse and watch the movement of the pointer.

If you run out of room to move your mouse, lift the mouse and move it to a clear area on your desk, then place the mouse back on the desk. Notice that the pointer does not move when the mouse is not in contact with the desk.

When you position the mouse pointer over certain objects, such as the objects on the taskbar, a "tip" appears. These "tips" are called **ToolTips**, and they tell you the purpose or function of an object.

To view ToolTips:

1. Use the mouse to point to the **Start** button [Start]. After a few seconds, you see the tip "Click here to begin" as shown in Figure 1-3 on the following page.

Figure 1-3 ◀
Viewing ToolTips

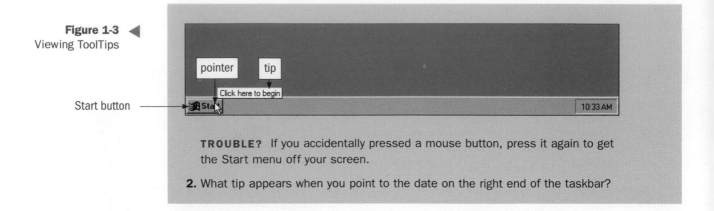

Figure 1-3 ◀
Viewing ToolTips

Start button

pointer   tip

Click here to begin

Start   10:33 AM

TROUBLE? If you accidentally pressed a mouse button, press it again to get the Start menu off your screen.

2. What tip appears when you point to the date on the right end of the taskbar?

3.1 NOTE

Windows 3.1 users frequently double-click the mouse to accomplish tasks. Double-clicking means pressing the mouse button twice in rapid succession. Many people had trouble learning how to double-click, so Windows 95 does not require double-clicking.

Clicking

When you press a mouse button and immediately release it, it is called **clicking**. Clicking the mouse selects an object on the desktop. *You usually click the left mouse button, so* unless the instructions tell you otherwise, always click the left mouse button.

Windows 95 shows you which object is selected by highlighting it, usually by changing the object's color, putting a box around it, or making the object appear to be pushed in, as shown in Figure 1-4.

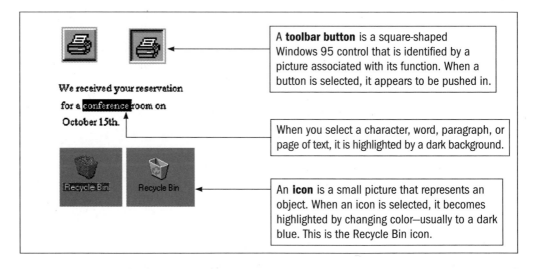

Figure 1-4 ◀
Selected objects

We received your reservation
for a conference room on
October 15th.

Recycle Bin   Recycle Bin

A **toolbar button** is a square-shaped Windows 95 control that is identified by a picture associated with its function. When a button is selected, it appears to be pushed in.

When you select a character, word, paragraph, or page of text, it is highlighted by a dark background.

An **icon** is a small picture that represents an object. When an icon is selected, it becomes highlighted by changing color—usually to a dark blue. This is the Recycle Bin icon.

To select the Recycle Bin icon:

1. Position the pointer over the **Recycle Bin** icon.

2. Click the mouse button and notice how the color of the icon changes to show that it is selected.

Starting and Closing a Program

The software you use is sometimes referred to as a program or an application. To use a program, such as a word-processing program, you must first start it. With Windows 95 you start a program by clicking the Start button. The Start button displays a menu.

A **menu** is a list of options. Windows 95 has a **Start menu** that provides you with access to programs, data, and configuration options. One of the Start menu's most important functions is to let you start a program.

The Reference Window below explains how to start a program. Don't do the steps in the Reference Window now; they are for your later reference.

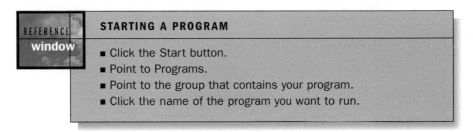

REFERENCE **window**

STARTING A PROGRAM

- Click the Start button.
- Point to Programs.
- Point to the group that contains your program.
- Click the name of the program you want to run.

3.1 NOTE

WordPad is similar to Write in Windows 3.1.

Windows 95 includes an easy-to-use word-processing program called WordPad. Suppose you want to start the WordPad program and use it to write a letter or report.

To start the WordPad program from the Start menu:

1. Click the **Start** button 🅰Start as shown in Figure 1-5. A menu appears.

Figure 1-5 ◀
Starting the
WordPad program

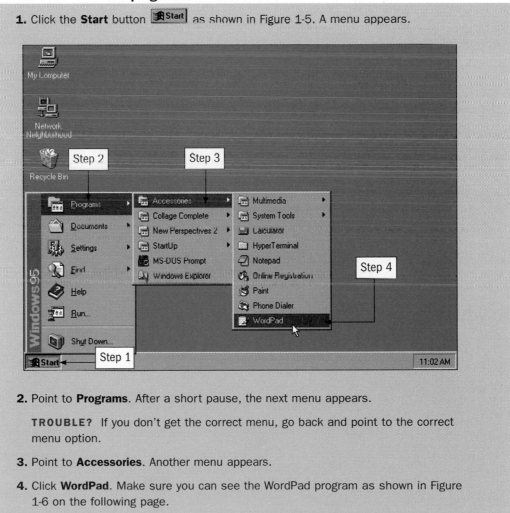

2. Point to **Programs**. After a short pause, the next menu appears.

   TROUBLE? If you don't get the correct menu, go back and point to the correct menu option.

3. Point to **Accessories**. Another menu appears.

4. Click **WordPad**. Make sure you can see the WordPad program as shown in Figure 1-6 on the following page.

Figure 1-6
The WordPad
program

WordPad program
window

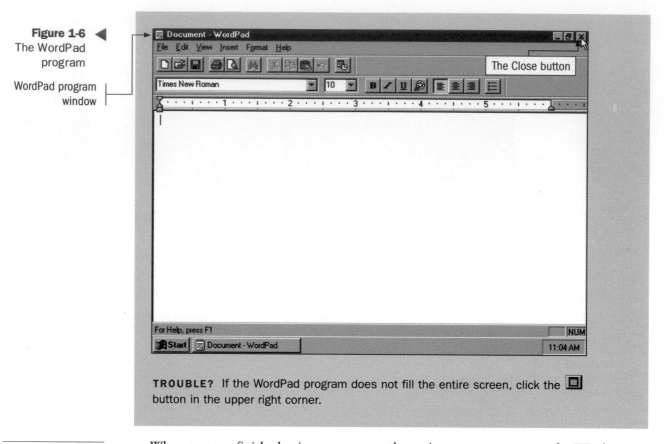

TROUBLE? If the WordPad program does not fill the entire screen, click the ▣ button in the upper right corner.

3.I NOTE

As with Windows 3.1, in Windows 95 you can also exit a program using the Exit option from the File menu.

When you are finished using a program, the easiest way to return to the Windows 95 desktop is to click the Close button ✖.

To exit the WordPad program:

1. Click the **Close** button ✖. See Figure 1-6. You will be returned to the Windows 95 desktop.

Running More than One Program at the Same Time

3.I NOTE

Paint in Windows 95 is similar to Paintbrush in WIndows 3.1.

One of the most useful features of Windows 95 is its ability to run multiple programs at the same time. This feature, known as **multi-tasking**, allows you to work on more than one task at a time and to quickly switch between tasks. For example, you can start WordPad and leave it running while you then start the Paint program.

To run WordPad and Paint at the same time:

1. Start WordPad.

TROUBLE? You learned how to start WordPad earlier in the tutorial: Click the Start button, point to Programs, point to Accessories, and then click WordPad.

2. Now you can start the Paint program. Click the **Start** button ▦Start again.

3. Point to **Programs**.

4. Point to **Accessories**.

5. Click **Paint**. The Paint program appears as shown in Figure 1-7. Now two programs are running at the same time.

TROUBLE? If the Paint program does not fill the entire screen, click the ▢ button in the upper right corner.

Figure 1-7 ◀
The Paint
Program

Paint program
window

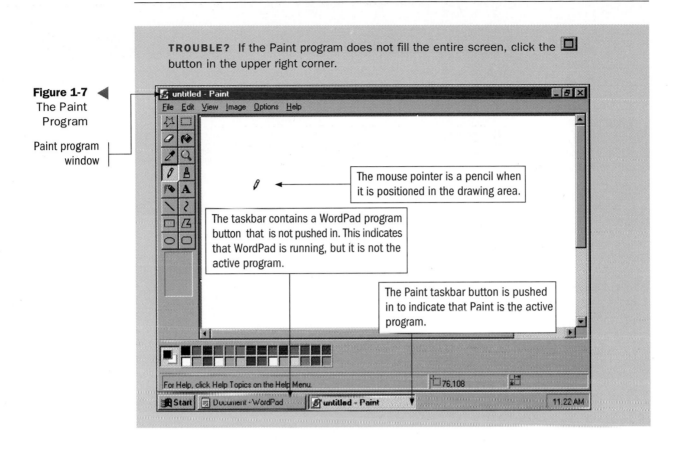

The mouse pointer is a pencil when it is positioned in the drawing area.

The taskbar contains a WordPad program button that is not pushed in. This indicates that WordPad is running, but it is not the active program.

The Paint taskbar button is pushed in to indicate that Paint is the active program.

3.1 NOTE

With Windows 3.1, some users had difficulty finding program windows on the desktop. The buttons on the Windows 95 taskbar make it much easier to keep track of which programs are running.

What happened to WordPad? The WordPad button is still on the taskbar, so even if you can't see it, WordPad is still running. You can imagine that it is stacked behind the Paint program, as shown in Figure 1-8.

Other projects might be hidden under the project you are working on. For example, you might have worked on a letter earlier, but it is now under the picture you are currently drawing.

You might keep other projects handy on your desk. Anytime you want to work with one of them, you bring it to the center of your desk.

Figure 1-8 ◀
Programs
stacked on top
of a desk

Think of your screen
as the main work
area of your desk.

The project with which you are currently working is in your main work area. This project might be a multi-page document.

Switching Between Programs

3.1 NOTE

In Windows 95, you can still use Alt-Tab to switch between programs. You can also click any open window to switch to it.

Although Windows 95 allows you to run more than one program, only one program at a time is active. The **active** program is the program with which you are currently working. The easiest way to switch between programs is to use the buttons on the taskbar.

REFERENCE window	**SWITCHING BETWEEN PROGRAMS**
	■ Click the taskbar button that contains the name of the program to which you want to switch.

To switch between WordPad and Paint:

1. Click the button labeled **Document - WordPad** on the taskbar. The Document - WordPad button now looks like it has been pushed in to indicate it is the active program.

2. Next, click the button labeled **untitled - Paint** on the taskbar to switch to the Paint program.

Closing WordPad and Paint

It is good practice to close each program when you are finished using it. Each program uses computer resources such as memory, so Windows 95 works more efficiently when only the programs you need are open.

To close WordPad and Paint:

1. Click the **Close** button ⊠ for the Paint program. The button labeled "untitled - Paint" disappears from the taskbar.

2. Click the **Close** button ⊠ for the WordPad program. The WordPad button disappears from the taskbar, and you return to the Windows 95 desktop.

Shutting Down Windows 95

It is very important to shut down Windows 95 before you turn off the computer. If you turn off your computer without correctly shutting down, you might lose data and damage your files.

To shut down Windows 95:

1. Click the **Start** button 🏁Start on the taskbar to display the Start menu.

2. Click the **Shut Down** menu option to display the Shut Down Windows dialog box.

3. Make sure the **Shut down the computer?** option is selected.

4. Click the **Yes** button.

5. Wait until you see a message indicating it is safe to turn off your computer, then switch off your computer.

You should typically use the option "Shut down the computer?" when you want to turn off your computer. However, other shut-down options are available. For example, your school might prefer that you select the option to "Close all programs and log on as a different user." This option logs you out of Windows 95, leaves the computer turned on, and allows another user to log on without restarting the computer. Check with your instructor or technical support person for the preferred method for your school's computer lab.

Quick Check

1. Label the components of the Windows 95 desktop in the figure below:

Figure 1-9 ◀

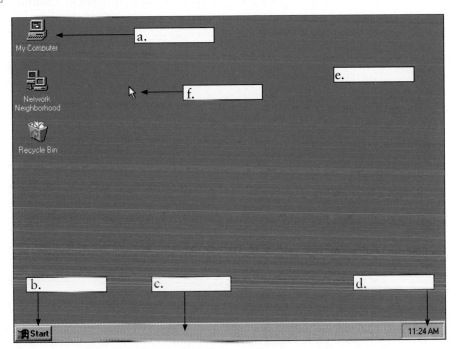

2. The _____ feature of Windows 95 allows you to run more than one program at a time.

3. The _____ is a list of options that provides you with access to programs, data, and configuration options.

4. What should you do if you are trying to move the pointer to the left edge of your screen, but your mouse runs into the keyboard?

5. Windows 95 shows you that an icon is selected by _____ it.

6. Even if you can't see a program, it might be running. How can you tell if a program is running?

7. Why is it good practice to close each program when you are finished using it?

8. Why do you need to shut down Windows 95 before you turn off your computer?

SESSION

1.2

In this session you will learn how to use many of the Windows 95 controls to manipulate windows and programs. You will learn how to change the size and shape of a window and to move a window so that you can customize your screen-based workspace. You will also learn how to use menus, dialog boxes, tabs, buttons, and lists to specify how you want a program to carry out a task.

Anatomy of a Window

When you run a program in Windows 95, it appears in a window. A **window** is a rectangular area of the screen that contains a program or data. A window also contains controls for manipulating the window and using the program. WordPad is a good example of how a window works.

Windows, spelled with an uppercase "W," is the name of the Microsoft operating system. The word "window" with a lowercase "w" refers to one of the rectangular windows on the screen.

To look at window controls:

1. Make sure Windows 95 is running and you are at the Windows 95 desktop screen.

2. Start WordPad.

   TROUBLE? To start WordPad, click the Start button, point to Programs, point to Accessories, and then click WordPad.

3. Make sure WordPad takes up the entire screen.

   TROUBLE? If WordPad does not take up the entire screen, click the ▢ button in the upper right corner.

4. On your screen, identify the controls labeled in Figure 1-10.

Figure 1-10 ◀
Window
controls

The **menu bar**
contains the
titles of menus,
such as File,
Edit, and Help.

The **toolbar**
contains buttons
that provide
you with a
shortcut to the
commands listed
on the menus.

The **status
bar** provides
you with
abbreviated
help relevant to
the task you
are doing.

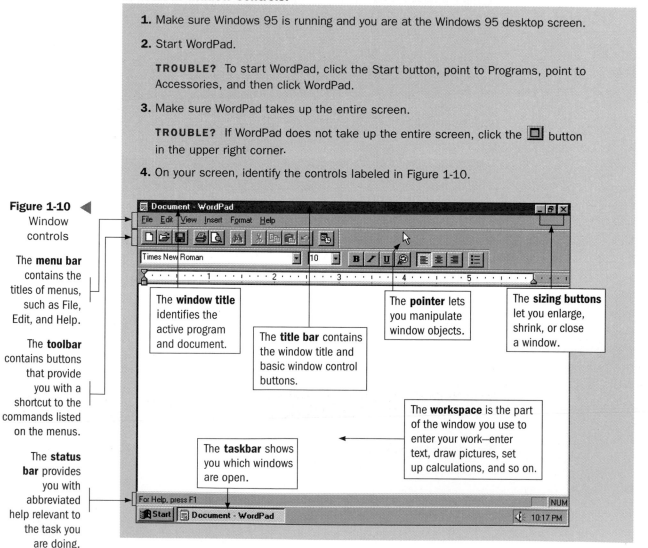

The **window title** identifies the active program and document.

The **title bar** contains the window title and basic window control buttons.

The **pointer** lets you manipulate window objects.

The **sizing buttons** let you enlarge, shrink, or close a window.

The **workspace** is the part of the window you use to enter your work—enter text, draw pictures, set up calculations, and so on.

The **taskbar** shows you which windows are open.

Manipulating a Window

There are three buttons located on the right side of the title bar. You are already familiar with the Close button. The Minimize button hides the window. The other button either maximizes the window or restores it to a predefined size. Figure 1-11 shows how these buttons work.

Figure 1-11 ◀
Minimize,
Maximize and
Restore buttons

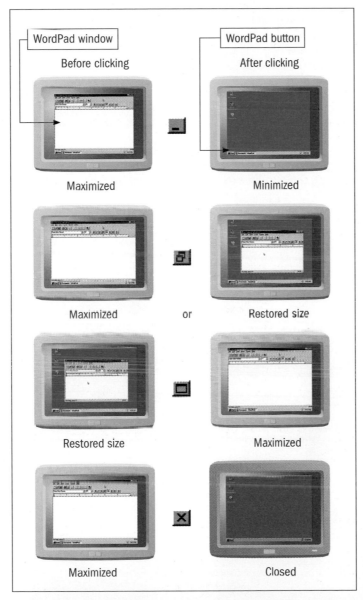

WordPad window
Before clicking

WordPad button
After clicking

Maximized

Minimized

The **Minimize button** 🔲 shrinks the window, so you only see its button on the taskbar.

Maximized   or   Restored size

Restored size   Maximized

The middle button appears as a **Restore button** 🗗 or a **Maximize button.** 🔲 When the window is maximized, the Restore button appears. It can be used to reduce the size of the window to a predetermined or "normal" size. When the window does not fill the entire screen, the Maximize button appears. Clicking the Maximize button enlarges the window to fill the screen.

Maximized   Closed

The **Close button** 🗙 closes the window and removes its button from the taskbar at the bottom of the screen.

Minimizing a Window

The **Minimize button** 🔲 shrinks the current window so that only the button on the taskbar remains visible. You can use the Minimize button when you want to temporarily hide a window but keep the program running.

To minimize the WordPad window:

1. Click the **Minimize** button 🔲. The WordPad window shrinks so only the Document - WordPad button on the taskbar is visible.

   TROUBLE? If you accidentally clicked the Close button and closed the window, use the Start button to start WordPad again.

Redisplaying a Window

You can redisplay a minimized window by clicking the program's button on the taskbar. When you redisplay a window, it becomes the active window.

To redisplay the WordPad window:

1. Click the **Document - WordPad** button on the taskbar. The WordPad window is restored to its previous size. The Document - WordPad button looks pushed in as a visual clue that it is now the active window.

Restoring a Window

The **Restore** button 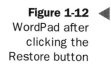 reduces the window so it is smaller than the entire screen. This is useful if you want to see more than one window at a time. Also, because of its small size, you can drag the window to another location on the screen or change its dimensions.

To restore a window:

1. Click the **Restore** button 🗗 on the WordPad title bar. The WordPad window will look similar to Figure 1-12, but the exact size of the window on your screen might be slightly different.

Figure 1-12 ◀
WordPad after clicking the Restore button

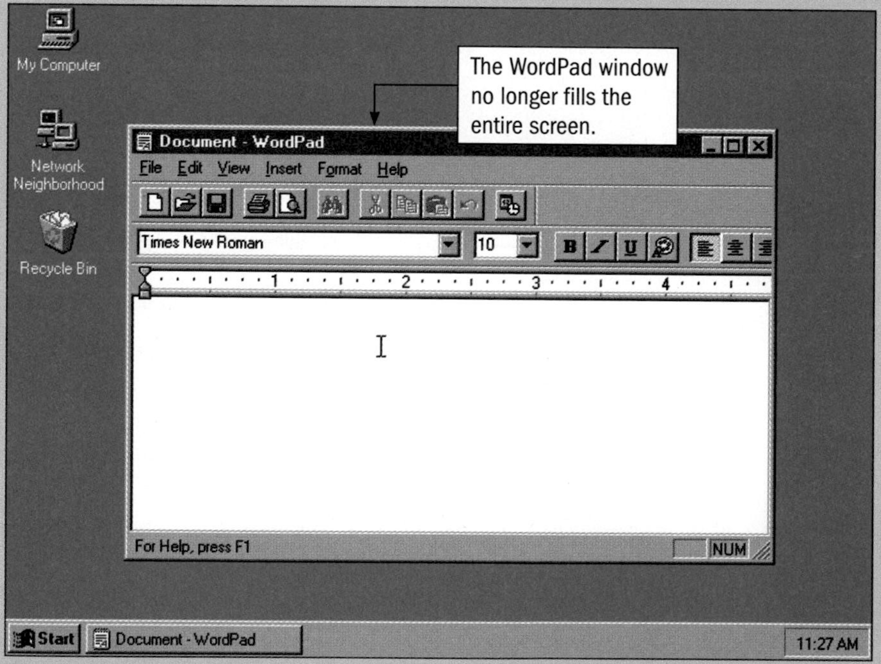

The WordPad window no longer fills the entire screen.

Moving a Window

You can use the mouse to **move** a window to a new position on the screen. When you hold down the mouse button while moving the mouse, it is called **dragging**. You can move objects on the screen by dragging them to a new location. If you want to move a window, you drag its title bar.

To drag the WordPad window to a new location:

1. Position the mouse pointer on the WordPad window title bar.

2. While you hold down the left mouse button, move the mouse to drag the window. A rectangle representing the window moves as you move the mouse.

3. Position the rectangle anywhere on the screen, then release the left mouse button. The WordPad window appears in the new location.

4. Now drag the WordPad window to the upper-left corner of the screen.

Changing the Size of a Window

3.I NOTE

You can also change the size of a window by dragging the top, bottom, sides, and corners of the window, as you did in Windows 3.1.

You can also use the mouse to change the size of a window. Notice the sizing handle at the lower right corner of the window. The **sizing handle** provides a visible control for changing the size of a current window.

To change the size of the WordPad window:

1. Position the pointer over the sizing handle. The pointer changes to a diagonal arrow.

2. While holding down the mouse button, drag the sizing handle down and to the right.

3. Release the mouse button. Now the window is larger.

4. Practice using the sizing handle to make the WordPad window larger or smaller.

Maximizing a Window

The **Maximize button** enlarges a window so that it fills the entire screen. You will probably do most of your work using maximized windows because you can see more of your program and data.

To maximize the WordPad window:

1. Click the **Maximize** button on the WordPad title bar.

Using Program Menus

Most Windows programs use menus to provide an easy way for you to select program commands. The **menu bar** is typically located at the top of the program window and shows the titles of menus such as File, Edit, and Help.

Windows menus are relatively standardized—most Windows programs include similar menu options. It's easy to learn new programs, because you can make a pretty good guess about which menu contains the command you want.

Selecting Commands from a Menu

When you click any menu title, choices for that menu appear below the menu bar. These choices are referred to as **menu options**. To select a menu option, you click it. For example, the File menu is a standard feature in most Windows programs and contains the options related to working with a file: creating, opening, saving, and printing a file or document.

To select Print Preview from the File menu:

1. Click **File** in the WordPad menu bar to display the File menu.

   TROUBLE? If you open a menu but decide not to select any of the menu options, you can close the menu by clicking its title again.

2. Click **Print Preview** to open the preview screen and view your document as it will appear when printed. This document is blank because you didn't enter any text.

3. After examining the screen, click the button labeled "Close" to return to your document.

Not all menu options immediately carry out an action—some show submenus or ask you for more information about what you want to do. The menu gives you hints about what to expect when you select an option. These hints are sometimes referred to as **menu conventions**. Study Figures 1-13a and 1-13b so you will recognize the Windows 95 menu conventions.

Figure 1-13a ◀
Menu
Conventions

Some menu options are toggle switches that can be either "on" or "off." When a feature is turned on, a **check mark** appears next to the menu option. When the feature is turned off, there is no check mark.

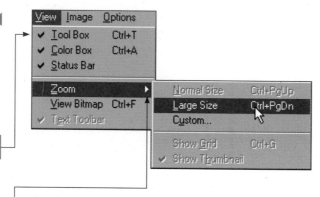

Certain menu selections lead you to an additional menu, called a **submenu**. A triangle on the right side of the menu choice indicates menu options that lead to submenus. When you move the pointer to a menu option with a triangle next to it, the submenu automatically appears.

Figure 1-13b ◀
Menu
conventions
(continued)

Some menu options are followed by a series of three dots, called an **ellipsis**. The dots indicate that you must make additional selections from a dialog box after you select that option. Options without dots do not require additional choices—they take effect as soon a you click them.

Sometimes certain menu options are unavailable. For example, a word-processing program might prevent you from trying to delete text if a document is blank. When a menu option is not available, it is usually **"grayed-out"** to provide you with a visual cue that the function is not available.

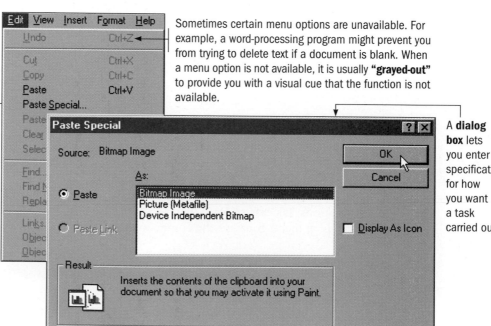

A **dialog box** lets you enter specification for how you want a task carried out.

Using Toolbars

A **toolbar** contains buttons that provide quick access to important program commands. Although you can usually perform all program commands using the menus, the toolbar provides convenient one-click access to frequently-used commands. For most Windows 95 functions, there is usually more than one way to accomplish a task. To simplify your introduction to Windows 95 in this tutorial, you will learn only one method for performing a task. As you become more accomplished using Windows 95, you can explore alternative methods.

In Session 1.1 you learned that Windows 95 programs include ToolTips that indicate the purpose and function of a tool. Now is a good time to explore the WordPad toolbar buttons by looking at their ToolTips.

To find out a toolbar button's function:

1. Position the pointer over any button on the toolbar, such as the Print Preview icon. After a short pause, the name of the button appears in a box and a description of the button appears in the status bar just above the Start button.

2. Move the pointer to each button on the toolbar to see its name and purpose.

You select a toolbar button by clicking it.

To select the Print Preview toolbar button:

1. Click the **Print Preview** button. The Print Preview dialog box appears. This is the same dialog box that appeared when you selected File, Print Preview from the menu bar.

2. Click Close to close the Print Preview dialog box.

Using List Boxes and Scroll Bars

As you might guess from the name, a **list box** displays a list of choices. In WordPad, date and time formats are shown in the Date/Time list box. List box controls include arrow buttons, a scroll bar, and a scroll box, as shown in Figure 1-14.

Figure 1-14 ◀
List box

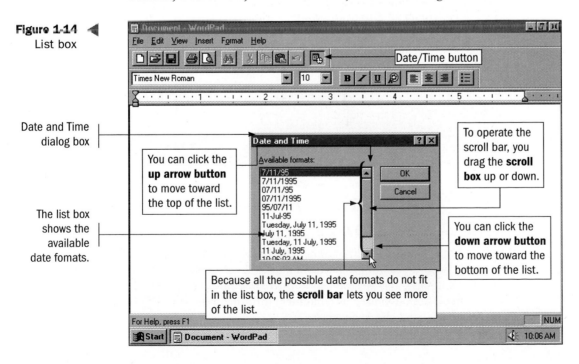

Date and Time dialog box

You can click the **up arrow button** to move toward the top of the list.

The list box shows the available date formats.

To operate the scroll bar, you drag the **scroll box** up or down.

You can click the **down arrow button** to move toward the bottom of the list.

Because all the possible date formats do not fit in the list box, the **scroll bar** lets you see more of the list.

To use the Date/Time list box:

1. Click the **Date/Time** button 🖼 to display the Date and Time dialog box. See Figure 1-14.

2. To scroll down the list, click the **down arrow** button 🔽. See Figure 1-14.

3. Find the scroll box on your screen. See Figure 1-14.

4. Drag the **scroll box** to the top of the scroll bar. Notice how the list scrolls back to the beginning.

5. Find a date format similar to "October 2, 1997." Click that date format to select it.

6. Click the **OK** button to close the Date and Time list box. This inserts the current date in your document.

A variation of the list box, called a **drop-down list box,** usually shows only one choice, but can expand down to display additional choices on the list.

To use the Font Size drop-down list:

1. Click the **down arrow** button 🔽 shown in Figure 1-15.

Figure 1-15 ◀
Type-size drop-down list box

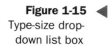

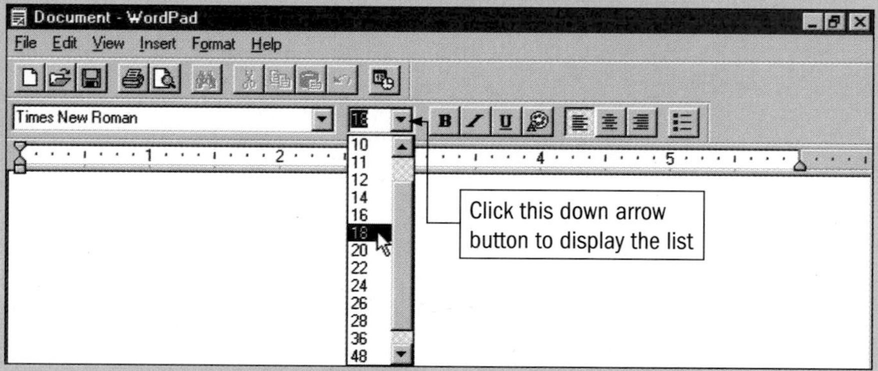

2. Click **18**. The drop-down list disappears and the font size you selected appears at the top of the pull-down list.

3. Type a few characters to test the new font size.

4. Click the **down arrow** button 🔽 in the Font Size drop-down list box again.

5. Click **12**.

6. Type a few characters to test this type size.

7. Click the **Close** button ❌ to close WordPad.

8. When you see the message "Save changes to Document?" click the **No** button.

Using Tab Controls, Radio Buttons, and Check Boxes

Dialog boxes often use tabs, radio buttons, or check boxes to collect information about how you want a program to perform a task. A **tab control** is patterned after the tabs on file folders. You click the appropriate tab to view different pages of information or choices. Tab controls are often used as containers for other Windows 95 controls such as list boxes, radio buttons, and check boxes.

Radio buttons, also called **option buttons**, allow you to select a single option from among one or more options. **Check boxes** allow you to select many options at the same time. Figure 1-16 explains how to use these controls.

Figure 1-16 ◀
Tabs, radio
buttons, and
check boxes

A **tab** indicates
an "index card"
that contains
information or
a group of
controls, usually
with related
functions. To look
at the functions
on an index
card, click the tab.

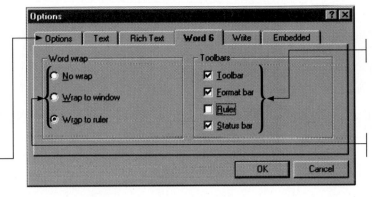

Check boxes allow you to
select one or more options
from a group. When you click
a check box, a check mark
appears in it. To remove a
check mark from a box,
click it again.

Radio buttons are round
and usually come in groups
of two or more. You can
select only one radio button
from a group. Your selection
is indicated by a black dot.

Using Help

Windows 95 **Help** provides on-screen information about the program you are using. Help for the Windows 95 operating system is available by clicking the Start button on the taskbar, then selecting Help from the Start menu. If you want Help for a program, such as WordPad, you must first start the program, then use the Help menu at the top of the screen.

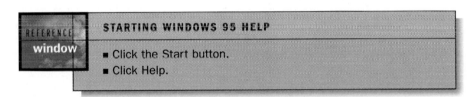

REFERENCE
window

STARTING WINDOWS 95 HELP

■ Click the Start button.
■ Click Help.

To start Windows 95 Help:

1. Click the **Start** button.

2. Click **Help.**

Help uses tabs for each section of Help. Windows 95 Help tabs include Contents, Index, and Find as shown in Figure 1-17 on the following page.

Figure 1-17 ◀
Windows 95
Help

Each section of
Help is divided
into "books."
To open a book,
you click the
book, then click
the Open button.

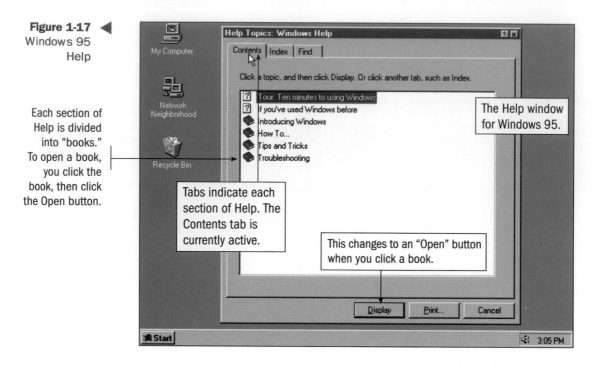

The Help window
for Windows 95.

Tabs indicate each
section of Help. The
Contents tab is
currently active.

This changes to an "Open" button
when you click a book.

The **Contents tab** groups Help topics into a series of books. You select a book, which then provides you with a list of related topics from which you can choose. The **Index tab** displays an alphabetical list of all the Help topics from which you can choose. The **Find tab** lets you search for any word or phrase in Help.

Suppose you're wondering if there is an alternative way to start programs. You can use the Contents tab to find the answer to your question.

3.1 NOTE

You can also double-click to select and open a topic in a single step.

To use the Contents tab:

1. Click the **Contents** tab to display the Contents window.

2. Click the **How To...** book title, then click the **Open** button. A list of related books appears below the book title. See. Figure 1-18.

Figure 1-18 ◀
Help window

Click this book,
then click the
Open button to
display a list of
related books.

Books related to
the "How To" topic.

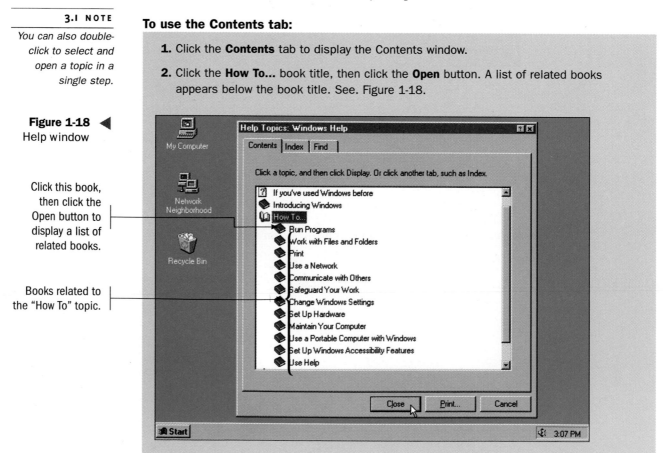

3. Click the **Run Programs** book, then click the **Open** button. The table of contents for this Help book is displayed.

4. Click the topic **Starting a Program**, then click the **Display** button. A Help window appears and explains how to start a program.

Help also provides you with definitions of technical terms. You can click any under-lined term to see its definition.

To see a definition of the term "taskbar":

1. Point to the underlined term, **taskbar** until the pointer changes to a hand. Then click.

2. After you have read the definition, click the definition to deselect it.

3. Click the **Close** button ⊠ on the Help window.

The **Index tab** allows you to jump to a Help topic by selecting a topic from an indexed list. For example, you can use the Index tab to learn how to arrange the open windows on your desktop.

To find a Help topic using the Index tab:

1. Click the **Start** button.

2. Click **Help**.

3. Click the **Index** tab.

4. A long list of indexed Help topics appears. Drag the scroll box down to view additional topics.

5. You can quickly jump to any part of the list by typing the first few characters of a word or phrase in the line above the Index list. Type **desktop** to display topics related to the Windows 95 desktop.

6. Click the topic **arranging open windows on** in the bottom window.

7. Click the **Display** button as shown in Figure 1-19.

Figure 1-19 ◄
Displaying a
Help Topic

Click here to type
words or phrases.

Index topics are
displayed here.
Click the topic to
select it.

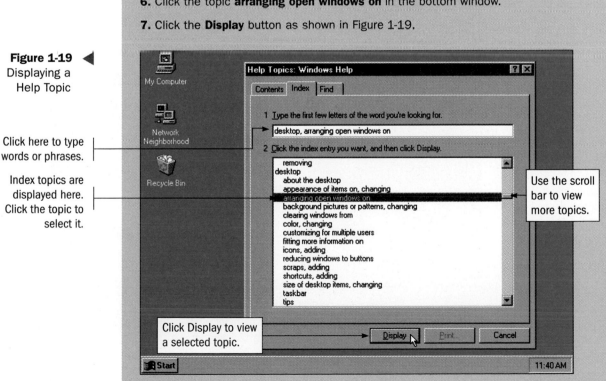

8. Click the **Close** button ☒ to close the Windows Help window.

The **Find tab** contains an index of all words in Windows 95 Help. You can use it to search for Help pages that contain a particular word or phrase. For example, suppose you heard that a screen saver blanks out your screen when you are not using it. You could use the Find tab to find out more about screen savers.

To find a Help topic using the Find tab:

1. Click the **Start** button [Start].

2. Click **Help**.

3. Click the **Find** tab.

> **TROUBLE?** If the Find index has not yet been created on your computer, the computer will prompt you through several steps to create the index. Continue with Step 4 below after the Find index is created.

4. Type **screen** to display a list of all topics that start with the letters "screen."

5. Click **screen-saver** in the middle window to display the topics that contain the word "screen-saver."

6. Click **Having your monitor automatically turn off**, then click the **Display** button.

7. Click the **Help window** button shown in Figure 1-20. The screen saver is shown on a simulated monitor.

> **TROUBLE?** If you see an error message, your lab does not allow students to modify screen savers. Click the OK button and go to Step 9.

Figure 1-20 ◀
Clicking a
Button in Help

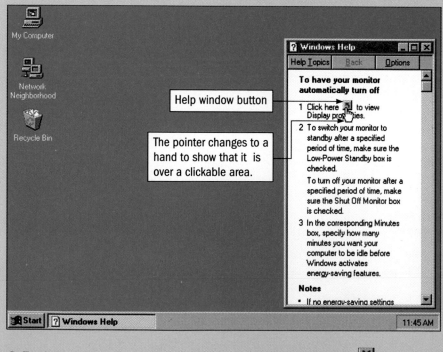

8. To close the Display properties window, click the **Close** button ☒ in the Display Properties window.

9. Click the **Close** button ☒ to close the Help window.

Now that you know how Windows 95 Help works, don't forget to use it! Use Help when you need to perform a new task or when you forget how to complete a procedure.

Quick Check

1 Label the parts of the window shown in Figure 1-21.

Figure 1-21 ◀

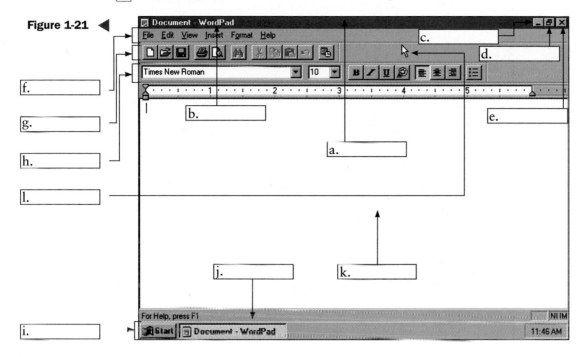

f.

g.

h.

l.

i.

2 Provide the name and purpose of each button:
   a. ▬
   b. ▢
   c. ▣
   d. ✖

3 Explain each of the following menu conventions:
   a. Ellipsis...
   b. Grayed out
   c. ▶
   d. ✔

4 A(n) _____ consists of a group of buttons, each of which provides one-click access to important program functions.

5 Label each part of the dialog box below:

Figure 1-22 ◀

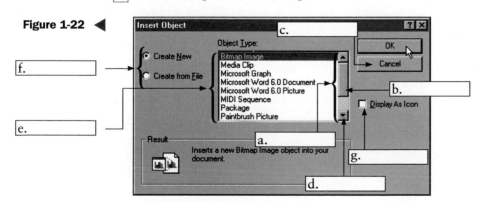

f.

e.

6 │ Radio buttons allow you to select _____ option(s) at a time, but _____ allow you to select one or more options.

7 │ It is a good idea to use _____ when you need to learn how to perform new tasks, simplify tedious procedures, and correct actions that did not turn out as you expected.

End Note

You've finished the tutorial, but Steve Laslow still hasn't returned. Take a moment to review what you have learned. You now know how to start a program using the Start button. You can run more than one program at a time and switch between programs using the buttons on the taskbar. You have learned the names and functions of window controls and Windows 95 menu conventions. You can now use toolbar buttons, list boxes, drop-down lists, radio buttons, check boxes, and scroll bars. Finally, you can use the Contents, Index, and Find tabs in Help to extend your knowledge of how to use Windows 95.

Tutorial Assignments

1. Running Two Programs and Switching Between Them In this tutorial you learned how to run more than one program at a time using WordPad and Paint. You can run other programs at the same time, too. Complete the following steps and write out your answers to questions b through f:

    a. Start the computer. Enter your user name and password if prompted to do so.
    b. Click the Start button. How many menu options are on the Start menu?
    c. Run the program Calculator program located on the Programs, Accessories menu. How many buttons are now on the taskbar?
    d. Run the Paint program and maximize the Paint window. How many application programs are running now?
    e. Switch to Calculator. What are the two visual clues that tell you that Calculator is the active program?
    f. Multiply 576 by 1457. What is the result?
    g. Close Calculator, then close Paint.

2. WordPad Help In Tutorial 1 you learned how to use Windows 95 Help. Just about every Windows 95 program has a help feature. Many computer users can learn to use a program just by using Help. To use Help, you would start the program, then click the Help menu at the top of the screen. Try using WordPad Help:

    a. Start WordPad.
    b. Click Help on the WordPad menu bar, then click Help Topics.
    c. Using WordPad help, write out your answers to questions 1 through 3.
        1. How do you create a bulleted list?
        2. How do you set the margins in a document?
        3. What happens if you hold down the Alt key and press the Print Screen key?
    d. Close WordPad.

3. Using Help to Explore Paint In this assignment, you will use the Paint Help to learn how to use the Paint program. Your goal is to create and print a picture that looks like the one in Figure 1-23.

Figure 1-23 ◀

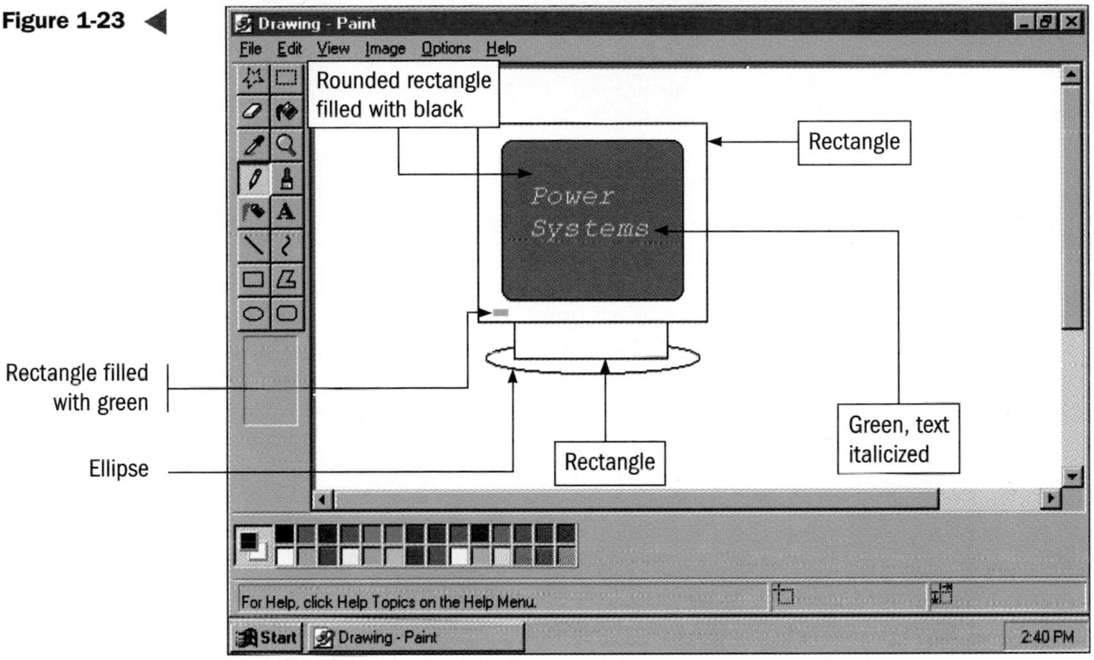

Rounded rectangle filled with black

Rectangle

Power Systems

Rectangle filled with green

Ellipse

Rectangle

Green, text italicized

a. Start Paint.

b. Click Help, then click Help Topics.

c. Use Paint Help to learn how to put text in a picture and how to draw rectangles and circles.

d. Draw a picture of a monitor using rectangles, circles, and text as shown in Figure 1-23.

e. Print your picture.

f. Close Paint.

4. The Windows 95 Tutorial Windows 95 includes a five part on-line tutorial. In Tutorial 1 you learned about starting programs, switching windows, and using Help. You can use the on-line Windows 95 Tutorial to review what you learned and pick up some new tips for using Windows 95. Complete the following steps and write out your answers to questions f, g, and h:

a. Click the Start button to display the Start menu.

b. Click Help to display Windows help.

c. Click the Contents tab.

d. From the Contents screen, click Tour: Ten minutes to using Windows.

e. Click the Display button. If an error message appears, the Tour is probably not loaded on your computer. You will not be able to complete this assignment. Click Cancel, then click OK to cancel and check with your instructor or technical support person.

f. Click Starting a Program and complete the tutorial. What are the names of the seven programs on the Accessories menu in the tutorial?

g. Click Switching Windows and complete the on-line tutorial. What does the Minimize button do?

h. Click Using Help and complete the tutorial. What is the purpose of the ❓ button?

i. Click the Exit button to close the Tour window.

j. Click the Exit Tour button to exit the Tour and return to the Windows 95 desktop.

Lab Assignments *not required*

Using a Keyboard

1. Learning to Use the Keyboard If you are not familiar with computer keyboards, you will find the Keyboard Lab helpful. This Lab will give you a structured introduction to special computer keys and their function in Windows 95. As you work through the Lab, you will be asked to answer Quick Check questions about what you have learned. At the end of the lab, you will see a summary report of your answers. If your instructor wants you to print out your answers to these questions, click the Print button on the summary report screen.

    a. Click the Start button.

    b. Point to Programs, then point to CTI Windows 95 Applications.

    c. Click Windows 95 New Perspectives Brief.

    d. Click Using a Keyboard. If you cannot find Windows 95 New Perspectives Brief or Using a Keyboard, ask for help from your instructor or technical support person.

Using a Mouse

2. Mouse Practice If you would like more practice using a mouse, you can complete the Mouse Lab. As you work through the Lab, you will be asked to answer Quick Check questions about what you have learned. At the end of the lab, the Quick Check Report shows you how you did. If your instructor wants you to print out your answers to these questions, click the Print button on the summary report screen.

    a. Click the Start button.

    b. Point to Programs, then point to CTI Windows 95.

    c. Point to Windows 95 New Perspectives Brief.

    d. Click Using a Mouse. If you cannot find Windows 95 New Perspectives Brief or Using a Mouse, ask for help from your instructor or technical support person.

Working with Files

OBJECTIVES

In this tutorial you will learn to:

- Format a disk

- Enter, select, insert, and delete text

- Create and save a file

- Open and edit a file

- Print a file

- Create a Student Disk

- View the list of files on your disk

- Move, copy, delete, and rename a file

- Make a backup of your floppy disk

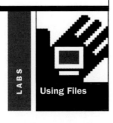

LABS

Using Files

CASE

Your First Day in the Lab—Continued

Steve Laslow is back from class, grinning. "I see you're making progress!"

"That's right," you reply. "I know how to run programs, control windows, and use Help. I guess I'm ready to work with my word-processing and spreadsheet software now."

Steve hesitates before he continues, "You could, but there are a few more things about Windows 95 that you should learn first."

Steve explains that most of the software you have on your computer—your word-processing, spreadsheet, scheduling, and graphing software—was created especially for the Windows 95 operating system. This software is referred to as **Windows 95 applications** or **Windows 95 programs**. You can also use software designed for Windows 3.1, but Windows 95 applications give you more flexibility. For example, when you name a document in a Windows 95 application, you can use descriptive filenames with up to 255 characters, whereas in Windows 3.1 you are limited to eight-character names.

You typically use Windows 95 applications to create files. A **file** is a collection of data that has a name and is stored in a computer. You typically create files that contain documents, pictures, and graphs when you use software packages. For example, you might use word-processing software to create a file containing a document. Once you create a file, you can open it, edit its contents, print it, and save it again—usually using the same application program you used to create it.

Another advantage of Windows 95 is that once you know how to save, open, and print files with one Windows 95 application, you can perform those same functions in *any* Windows 95 application. This is because Windows 95 applications have similar controls. For example, your word-processing and spreadsheet software will have identical menu commands to save, open, and print documents. Steve suggests that it would be worth a few minutes of your time to become familiar with these menus in Windows 95 applications.

You agree, but before you can get to work, Steve gives you one final suggestion: you should also learn how to keep track of the files on your disk. For instance, you might need to find a file you have not used for a while or you might want to delete a file if your disk is getting full. You will definitely want to make a backup copy of your disk in case something happens to the original. Steve's advice seems practical, and you're eager to explore these functions so you can get to work!

Tutorial 2 will help you learn how to work with Windows 95 applications and keep track of the files on your disk. When you've completed this tutorial, you'll be ready to tackle all kinds of Windows 95 software!

SESSION

2.1

In Session 2.1 you will learn how to format a disk so it can store files. You will create, save, open, and print a file. You will find out how the insertion point is different from the mouse pointer, and you will learn the basic skills for Windows 95 text entry, such as inserting, deleting, and selecting.
For this tutorial you will need two blank 3 ½-inch disks.

Formatting a Disk

Before you can save files on a disk, the disk must be formatted. When the computer **formats** a disk, the magnetic particles on the disk surface are arranged so data can be stored on the disk. Today, many disks are sold preformatted and can be used right out of the box. However, if you purchase an unformatted disk, or if you have an old disk that you want to completely erase and reuse, you can format the disk using the Windows 95 Format command.

The following steps tell you how to format a 3 ½-inch high-density disk using drive A. Your instructor will tell you how to revise the instructions given in these steps if the procedure is different for your lab equipment.

All data on the disk you format will be erased, so don't perform these steps using a disk that contains important files.

To format a disk:

1. Start Windows 95, if necessary.

2. Write your name on the label of a 3 ½-inch disk.

3. Insert your disk in drive A. See Figure 2-1.

Figure 2-1 ◀
Inserting a disk into the disk drive

edge with the notch goes into the drive first

edge with the label goes in last

floppy disk drive

TROUBLE? If your disk does not fit in drive A, put it in drive B and substitute drive B for drive A in all of the steps for the rest of the tutorial.

4. Click the **My Computer** icon to select it, then press the **Enter** key. Make sure you can see the My Computer window. See Figure 2-2.

TROUBLE? If you see a list instead of icons like those in Figure 2-2, click View. Then click Large Icon.

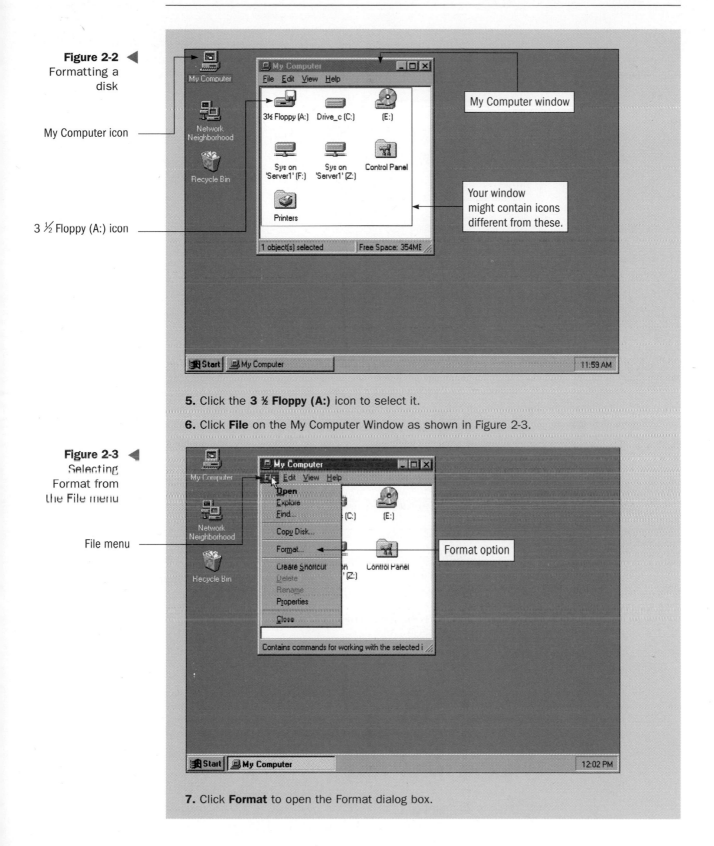

Figure 2-2
Formatting a
disk

My Computer icon

3 ½ Floppy (A:) icon

5. Click the **3 ½ Floppy (A:)** icon to select it.

6. Click **File** on the My Computer Window as shown in Figure 2-3.

Figure 2-3
Selecting
Format from
the File menu

File menu

7. Click **Format** to open the Format dialog box.

8. Make sure the dialog box settings on your screen match those in Figure 2-4.

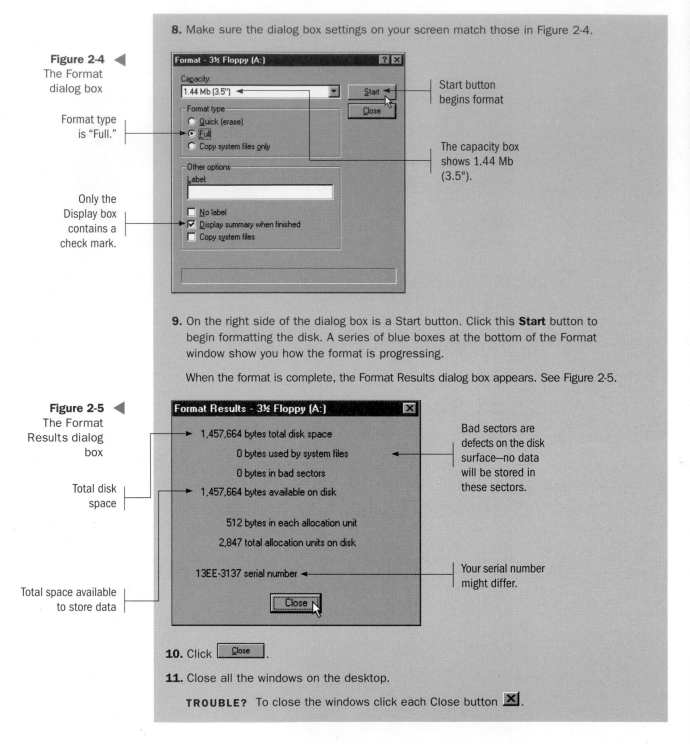

Figure 2-4 ◀
The Format
dialog box

Format type
is "Full."

Only the
Display box
contains a
check mark.

Start button
begins format

The capacity box
shows 1.44 Mb
(3.5").

Figure 2-5 ◀
The Format
Results dialog
box

Total disk
space

Total space available
to store data

Bad sectors are
defects on the disk
surface—no data
will be stored in
these sectors.

Your serial number
might differ.

9. On the right side of the dialog box is a Start button. Click this **Start** button to begin formatting the disk. A series of blue boxes at the bottom of the Format window show you how the format is progressing.

When the format is complete, the Format Results dialog box appears. See Figure 2-5.

10. Click | Close |.

11. Close all the windows on the desktop.

TROUBLE? To close the windows click each Close button ✖.

Working with Text

To accomplish many computing tasks, you need to type text in documents and text boxes. Windows 95 facilitates basic text entry by providing a text-entry area, by showing you where your text will appear on the screen, by helping you move around on the screen, and by providing insert and delete functions.

When you type sentences and paragraphs of text, do *not* press the Enter key when you reach the right margin. The software contains a feature called **word wrap** that automatically continues your text on the next line. Therefore, you should press Enter only when you have completed a paragraph.

If you type the wrong character, press the Backspace key to backup and delete the character. You can also use the Delete key. What's the difference between the Backspace and the Delete keys? The Backspace key deletes the character to left. The Delete key deletes the character to the right.

Now you will type some text using WordPad to learn about text entry.

To type text in WordPad:

1. Start WordPad.

   TROUBLE? If the WordPad window does not fill the screen, click the Maximize button ▢.

2. Notice the flashing vertical bar, called the **insertion point**, in the upper-left corner of the document window. The insertion point indicates where the characters you type will appear.

3. Type your name, using the Shift key to type uppercase letters and using the spacebar to type spaces, just like on a typewriter.

4. Press the **Enter** key to end the current paragraph and move the insertion point down to the next line.

5. As you type the following sentences, watch what happens when the insertion point reaches the right edge of the screen:

   This is a sample typed in WordPad. See what happens when the insertion point reaches the right edge of the screen.

   TROUBLE? If you make a mistake, delete the incorrect character(s) by pressing the Backspace key on your keyboard. Then type the correct character(s).

The Insertion Point versus the Pointer

The insertion point is not the same as the mouse pointer. When the mouse pointer is in the text-entry area, it is called the **I-beam pointer** and looks like I. Figure 2-6 explains the difference between the insertion point and the I-beam pointer.

Figure 2-6 ◀
The insertion point vs. the pointer

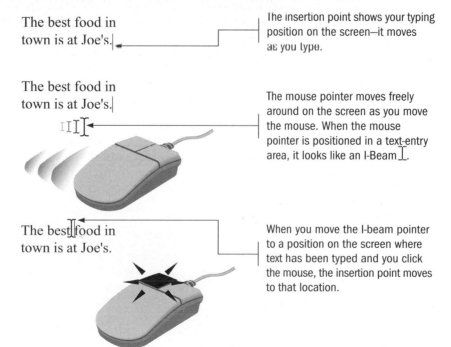

The insertion point shows your typing position on the screen—it moves as you type.

The mouse pointer moves freely around on the screen as you move the mouse. When the mouse pointer is positioned in a text-entry area, it looks like an I-Beam I.

When you move the I-beam pointer to a position on the screen where text has been typed and you click the mouse, the insertion point moves to that location.

To move the insertion point:

1. Check the location of the insertion point and the I-beam pointer. The insertion point should be at the end of the sentence you typed in the last set of steps.

   TROUBLE? If you don't see the I-beam pointer, move your mouse until you see it.

2. Use the mouse to move the I-beam pointer to the word "sample," then click the left mouse button. The insertion point jumps to the location of the I-beam pointer.

3. Move the I-beam pointer to a blank area near the bottom of the work space and click the left mouse button. *Notice that the insertion point does not jump to the location of the I-beam pointer.* Instead the insertion point jumps to the end of the last sentence. The insertion point can move only within existing text. It cannot be moved out of the existing text area.

Selecting Text

Many text operations are performed on a **block** of text, which is one or more consecutive words, sentences, or paragraphs. Once you select a block of text, you can delete it, move it, replace it, underline it, and so on. As you select a block of text, the computer highlights it. If you want to remove the highlighting, just click in the margin of your document.

Suppose you want to replace the phrase "See what happens" with "You can watch word wrap in action." You do not have to delete the text one character at a time. Instead you can highlight the entire phrase and begin to type the replacement text.

To select and replace a block of text:

1. Move the I-beam pointer just to the left of the word "See."

2. While holding down the left mouse button, drag the I-beam pointer over the text to the end of the word "happens." The phrase "See what happens" should now be highlighted. See Figure 2-7.

Figure 2-7 ◀
Highlighting
text

Position the
I-beam pointer here.

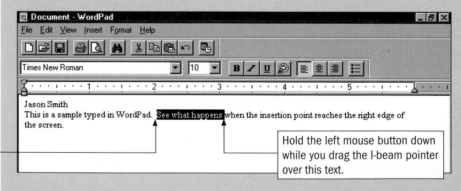

3. Release the left mouse button.

   TROUBLE? If the phrase is not highlighted correctly, repeat Steps 1 through 3.

4. Type: **You can watch word wrap in action**

   The text you typed replaces the highlighted text. Notice that you did not need to delete the highlighted text before you typed the replacement text.

Inserting a Character

Windows 95 programs usually operate in **insert mode**—when you type a new character, all characters to the right of the cursor are pushed over to make room.

Suppose you want to insert the word "sentence" before the word "typed."

To insert characters:

1. Position the I-beam pointer just before the word "typed," then click.

2. Type: **sentence**.

3. Press the **spacebar**.

3.1 NOTE

When you save a file with a long filename, Windows 95 also creates an eight-character filename that can be used by Windows 3.1 applications. The eight-character filename is created by using the first six non-space characters from the long filename, then adding a tilde (~) and a number. For example, the filename Car Sales for 1997 would be converted to Carsal~1.

Notice how the letters in the first line are pushed to the right to make room for the new characters. When a word gets pushed past the right margin, the word-wrap feature pushes it down to the beginning of the next line.

Saving a File

As you type text, it is held temporarily in the computer's memory. For permanent storage, you need to save your work on a disk. In the computer lab, you will probably save your work on a floppy disk in drive A.

When you save a file, you must give it a name. Windows 95 allows you to use filenames containing up to 255 characters, and you may use spaces and punctuation symbols. You cannot use the symbols \ ? : * " < > | in a filename, but other symbols such as &, -, and $ are allowed.

Most filenames have an extension. An **extension** is a suffix of up to three characters that is separated from the filename by a period, as shown in Figure 2-8.

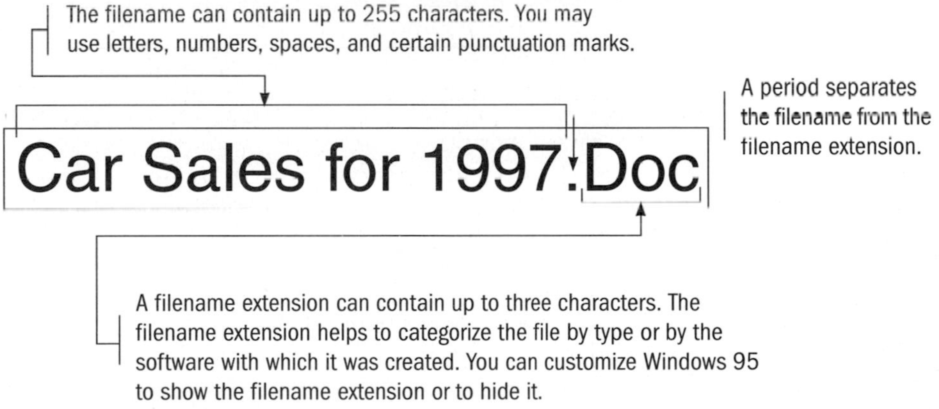

The filename can contain up to 255 characters. You may use letters, numbers, spaces, and certain punctuation marks.

A period separates the filename from the filename extension.

Figure 2-8
Filename and extension

Car Sales for 1997.Doc

A filename extension can contain up to three characters. The filename extension helps to categorize the file by type or by the software with which it was created. You can customize Windows 95 to show the filename extension or to hide it.

The file extension indicates which application you used to create the file. For example, files created with Microsoft Word software have a .Doc extension. In general, you will not add an extension to your filenames, because the application software automatically does this for you.

Windows 95 keeps track of file extensions, but does not always display them. The steps in these tutorials refer to files using the filename, but not its extension. So if you see the filename Sample Text in the steps, but "Sample Text.Doc" on your screen, don't worry—these are the same files.

Now you can save the document you typed.

To save a document:

1. Click the **Save** button 🖫 on the toolbar. Figure 2-9 shows the location of this button and the Save As dialog box that appears after you click it.

Figure 2-9 ◀
The Save button

Save button

Save As
dialog box
appears after
you click the
Save button

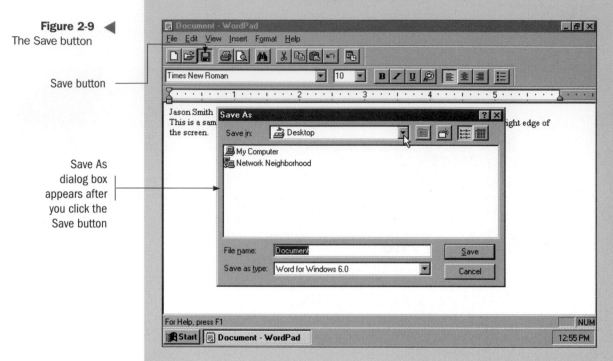

2. Click ▾ on the side of the Save in: box to display a list of drives. See Figure 2-10.

Figure 2-10 ◀
Selecting the
drive

3½ Floppy (A:)
drive menu
option

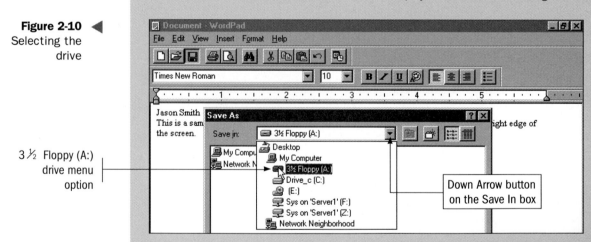

Down Arrow button
on the Save In box

3. Click **3½ Floppy (A:)**.

4. Select the text in the File Name box.

TROUBLE? To select the text, position the I-beam pointer at the beginning of the word "Document." While you hold down the mouse button, drag the I-beam pointer to the end of the word.

5. Type **Sample Text** in the File Name box.

6. Click the **Save** button. Your file is saved on your Student Disk and the document title, "Sample Text," appears on the WordPad title bar.

What if you tried to close WordPad *before* you saved your file? Windows 95 would display a message—"Save changes to Document?" If you answer "Yes," Windows displays the Save As dialog box so you can give the document a name. If you answer "No," Windows 95 closes WordPad without saving the document.

After you save a file, you can work on another document or close WordPad. Since you have already saved your Sample Text document, you should continue this tutorial by closing WordPad.

To close WordPad:

1. Click the **Close** button ☒ to close the WordPad window.

Opening a File

Suppose you save and close the Sample Text file, then later you want to revise it. To revise a file you must first open it. When you **open** a file, its contents are copied into the computer's memory. If you revise the file, you need to save the changes before you close the application or work on a different file. If you close a revised file without saving your changes, you will lose the revisions.

Typically, you would use one of two methods to open a file. You could select the file from the Documents list or the My Computer window, or you could start an application program and then use the Open button to open the file. Each method has advantages and disadvantages. You will have an opportunity to try both methods.

The first method for opening the Sample Text file simply requires you to select the file from the Documents list or the My Computer window. With this method the document, not the application program, is central to the task; hence this method is sometimes referred to as *document-centric*. You only need to remember the name of your document or file—you do not need to remember which application you used to create the document.

The Documents list contains the names of the last 15 documents used. You access this list from the Start menu. When you have your own computer, the Documents list is very handy. In a computer lab, however, the files other students use quickly replace yours on the list.

If your file is not in the Documents list, you can open the file by selecting it from the My Computer window. Windows 95 starts an application program that you can use to revise the file, then automatically opens the file. The advantage of this method is its simplicity. The disadvantage is that Windows 95 might not start the application you expect. For example, when you select Sample Text, you might expect Windows 95 to start WordPad because you used WordPad to type the text of the document. Depending on the software installed on your computer system, however, Windows 95 might start the Microsoft Word application instead. Usually this is not a problem. Although the application might not be the one you expect, you can still use it to revise your file.

> **3.1 NOTE**
>
> *Document-centric features are advertised as an advantage of Windows 95. But you can still successfully use the application-centric approach you used with Windows 3.1 by opening your application, then opening your document.*

To open the Sample Text file by selecting it from My Computer:

1. Click the **My Computer** icon. Press the **Enter** key. The My Computer window opens.

2. Click the **3½ Floppy (A:)** icon, then press the **Enter** key. The 3½ Floppy (A:) window opens.

   TROUBLE? If the My Computer window disappears when you open the 3½ floppy (A:) window, click View, click Options, then click the Folder tab, if necessary. Click the radio button labelled "Browse Folders using a separate window for each folder." Then click the OK button.

3. Click the **Sample Text** file icon, then press the **Enter** key. Windows 95 starts an application program, then automatically opens the Sample Text file.

   TROUBLE? If Windows 95 starts Microsoft Word instead of WordPad, don't worry. You can use Microsoft Word to revise the Sample Text document.

Now that Windows 95 has started an application and opened the Sample Text file, you could make revisions to the document. Instead, you should close all the windows on your desktop so you can try the other method for opening files.

To close all the windows on the desktop:

1. Click ☒ on each of the windows.

TROUBLE? If you see a message, "Save changes to Document?" click the No button.

The second method for opening the Sample Text file requires you to open WordPad, then use the Open button to select the Sample Text file. The advantage of this method is that you can specify the application program you want to use—WordPad in this case. This method, however, involves more steps than the method you tried previously.

To start WordPad and open the Sample Text file using the Open button:

1. Start WordPad.

2. Click the **Open** button 🗁 on the toolbar. Figure 2-11 shows the location of this button and the dialog box that appears after you click it.

Figure 2-11 ◀
The Open button
and dialog box

Open button

Open dialog box

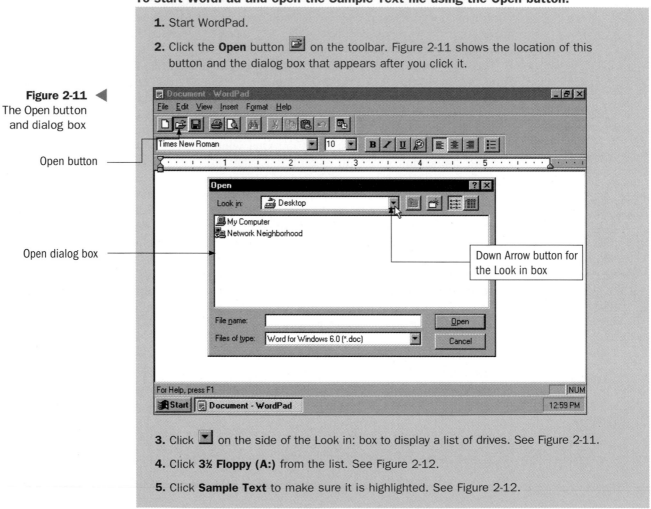

Down Arrow button for
the Look in box

3. Click ▼ on the side of the Look in: box to display a list of drives. See Figure 2-11.

4. Click **3½ Floppy (A:)** from the list. See Figure 2-12.

5. Click **Sample Text** to make sure it is highlighted. See Figure 2-12.

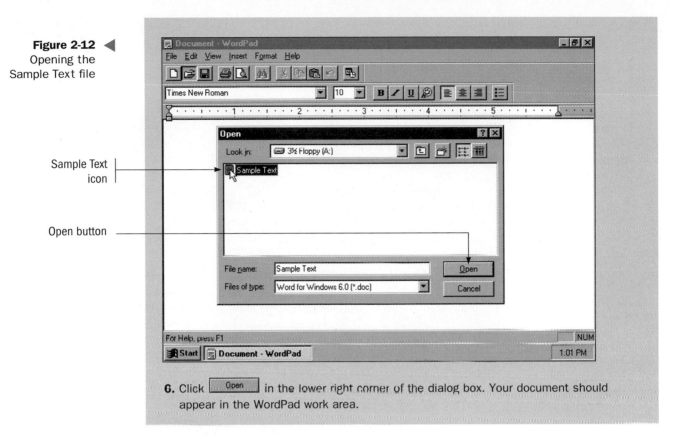

Figure 2-12 ◀
Opening the
Sample Text file

Sample Text
icon

Open button

6. Click [Open] in the lower right corner of the dialog box. Your document should appear in the WordPad work area.

Printing a File

Now that the Sample Text file is open, you can print it. It is a good idea to use Print Preview before you send your document to the printer. **Print Preview** shows on screen exactly how your document will appear on paper. You can check your page layout so you don't waste paper printing a document that is not quite the way you want it. Your instructor or technical support person might supply you with additional instructions for printing in your school's computer lab.

To preview, then print the Sample Text file:

1. Click the **Print Preview** button ▣ on the toolbar.

2. Look at your print preview. Before you print the document and use paper, you should make sure that the font, margins, and other document features look the way you want them to.

   TROUBLE? If you can't read the document text on screen, click the Zoom In button.

3. Click the **Print** button. A Print dialog box appears.

4. Study Figure 2-13 to familiarize yourself with the controls in the Print dialog box.

This is the name of the printer that Windows 95 will use for this printout. If you are using a network, you might have a choice of printers. If you need to select a different printer, ask your instructor or your technical support person for help.

The Properties button lets you modify the way your printer is set up. Do not change any of the settings on your school printer without the consent of your instructor or technical support person.

Figure 2-13 ◀
The Print
dialog box

In the Print range box, you specify how much of the document you want to print. If you want to print only part of a document, click the Pages radio button and then enter the starting and ending pages for the printout.

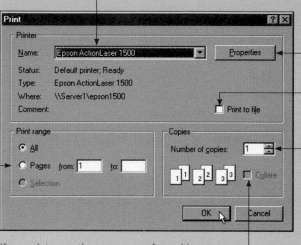

When you click this check box, your printout will go on your disk instead of to the printer.

You can specify how many copies you want by typing the number in this box. Alternatively, you can use the arrow buttons to increase or decrease the number in the box.

If you print more than one copy of a multi-page document, you can specify that you want the printout collated, so you don't have to collate the pages manually.

5. Make sure your screen shows the Print range set to "All" and the number of copies set to "1."

6. Click the **OK** button to print your document. If a message appears telling you printing is complete, click the **OK** button.

TROUBLE? If your document does not print, make sure the printer has paper and the printer on-line light is on. If your document still doesn't print, ask your instructor or technical support person for help.

7. Close WordPad.

TROUBLE? If you see the message "Save changes to Document?" click the "No" button.

Quick Check

1 A(n) _____ is a collection of data that has a name and is stored on a disk or other storage medium.

2 _____ erases all the data on a disk and arranges the magnetic particles on the disk surface so the disk can store data.

3 When you are working in a text box, the pointer shape changes to a(n) _____.

4 The _____ shows you where each character you type will appear.

5 _____ automatically moves text down to the beginning of the next line when you reach the right margin.

6 Explain how you select a block of text: _____.

7 Which of these characters are not allowed in Windows 95 file names: \ ? : * " < > | ! @ # $ % ^ & ; + - ( ) /

8   In the filename New Equipment.Doc, .Doc is a(n) ————————.

9   Suppose you created a graph using the Harvard Graphics software and then you stored the graph on your floppy disk under the name Projected 1997 Sales - Graph. The next day, you use Harvard Graphics to open the file and change the graph. If you want the new version of the file on your disk, you need to ————————.

10   You can save ———————— by using the Print Preview feature.

SESSION

2.2

In this session, you will learn how to manage the files on your disk—a skill that can prevent you from losing important documents. You will learn how to list information about the files on your disk; organize the files into folders; and move, delete, copy, and rename files.

Creating Your Student Disk

For this session of the tutorial, you must create a Student Disk that contains some sample files. *You can use the disk you formatted in the previous session.*

If you are using your own computer, the CTI Windows 95 Applications menu selection will not be available. Before you proceed, you must go to your school's computer lab and find a computer that has the CTI Windows 95 Applications installed. Once you have made your own Student Disk, you can use it to complete this tutorial on any computer you choose.

To add the sample files to your Student Disk:

1. Write "Windows 95 Student Disk" on the label of your formatted disk.

2. Place the disk in Drive A.

> **TROUBLE?** If your 3½-inch disk drive is B, place your formatted disk in that drive instead, and for the rest of this session substitute Drive B where ever you see Drive A.

3. Click the **Start** button [Start]. See Figure 2-14.

Figure 2-14 ◀
Making your
Student Disk

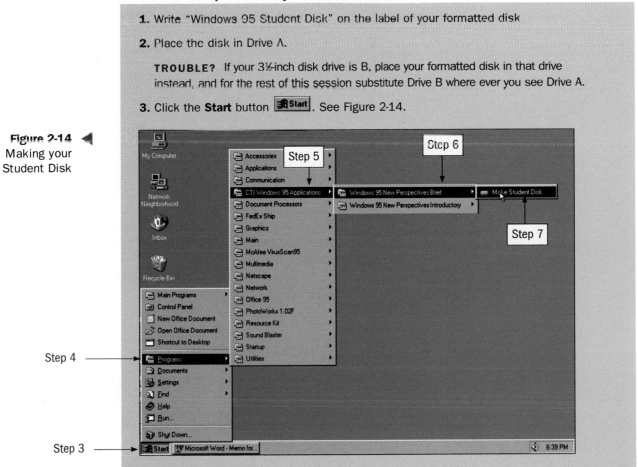

4. Point to **Programs**.

5. Point to **CTI Windows 95 Applications**.

TROUBLE? If CTI Windows 95 Applications is not listed, contact your instructor or technical support person.

6. Point to **Windows 95 New Perspectives Brief**.

7. Select **Make Student Disk**.

A dialog box opens, asking you to indicate the drive that contains your formatted disk.

8. If it is not already selected, click the Drive radio button that corresponds to the drive containing your student disk.

9. Click the **OK** button.

The sample files are copied to your formatted disk. A message tells you when all the files have been copied.

10. Click **OK.**

11. If necessary, close all the open windows on your screen.

Your Student Disk now contains sample files that you will use throughout the rest of this tutorial.

My Computer

The **My Computer** icon represents your computer, its storage devices, and its printers. The My Computer icon opens into the My Computer window, which contains an icon for each of the storage devices on your computer. On most computer systems the My Computer window also contains Control Panel and Printers folders, which help you add printers, control peripheral devices, and customize your Windows 95 work environment. Figure 2-15 on the following page explains more about the My Computer window.

You can use the My Computer window to keep track of where your files are stored and to organize your files. In this section of the tutorial you will move and delete files on your Student Disk in drive A. If you use your own computer at home or computer at work, you would probably store your files on drive C, instead of drive A. However, in a school lab environment you usually don't know which computer you will use, so you need to carry your files with you on a floppy disk that you use in drive A. In this session, therefore, you will learn how to work with the files on drive A. Most of what you learn will also work on your home or work computer when you use drive C.

In this session you will work with several icons, including My Computer. As a general procedure, when you want to open an icon, you click it and then press the Enter key.

Figure 2-15 ◄
Information
about My
Computer

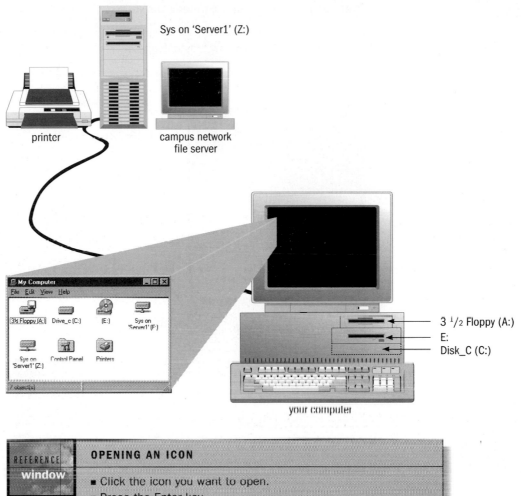

Sys on 'Server1' (Z:)

printer

campus network
file server

3 ¹/₂ Floppy (A:)
E:
Disk_C (C:)

your computer

REFERENCE window

OPENING AN ICON

■ Click the icon you want to open.
■ Press the Enter key.

Now you should open the My Computer icon.

To open the My Computer Icon:

1. Click the **My Computer** icon to select it.

2. Press the **Enter** key. The My Computer window opens.

Now that you have opened the My Computer window, you can find out what is on your Student Disk in drive A.

To find out what is on your Student Disk:

1. Open the **3½ Floppy (A:)** icon by clicking it, then pressing the **Enter** key. A window appears showing the contents of drive A:. See Figure 2-16.

Figure 2-16 ◀
Contents of
Student Disk

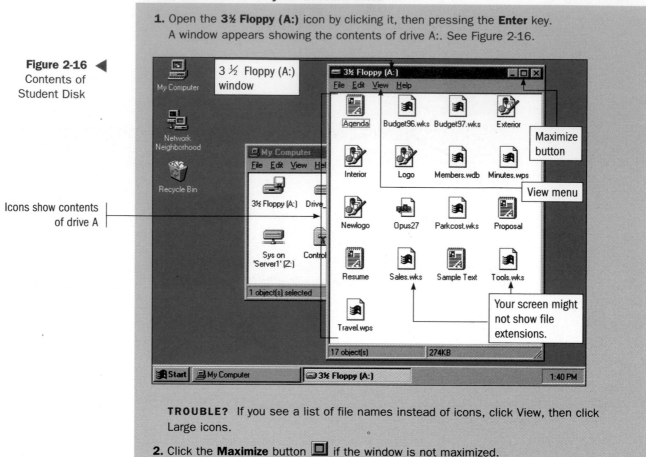

Icons show contents
of drive A

TROUBLE? If you see a list of file names instead of icons, click View, then click Large icons.

2. Click the **Maximize** button 🗖 if the window is not maximized.

Windows 95 provides four ways to view the contents of a disk—large icons, small icons, list, or details. The standard view, shown on your screen, displays a large icon and title for each file. The icon provides a visual cue to the type and contents of the file, as Figure 2-17 illustrates.

Figure 2-17 ◀
Program and
file icons

Text files that you can open and read using the WordPad or NotePad software are represented by notepad icons.

The icons for Windows programs usually depict an object related to the function of the program. For example, an icon that looks like a calculator signifies the Windows Calc program; an icon that looks like a computer signifies the Windows Explorer program.

Many of the files you create are represented by page icons. Here the page icon for the Circles file shows some graphics tools to indicate the file contains a graphic. The Page icon for the Access file contains the Windows logo, indicating that Windows does not know if the file contains a document, graphics, or data base.

Folders provide a way to group and organize files. A folder icon contains other icons for folders and files. Here, the System folder contains files used by the Windows operating system.

Non-Windows programs are represented by this icon of a blank window.

The **Details** view shows more information than the large icon, small icon, and list views. Details view shows the file icon, the filename, the file size, the application you used to create the file, and the date/time the file was created or last modified.

To view a detailed list of files:

1. Click **View** then click **Details** to display details for the files on your disk as shown in Figure 2-18.

Figure 2-18 ◄
Detailed file list

File icon ———

Filename ———

Your screen might not
show file extensions

Total number of
files and folders
in the window

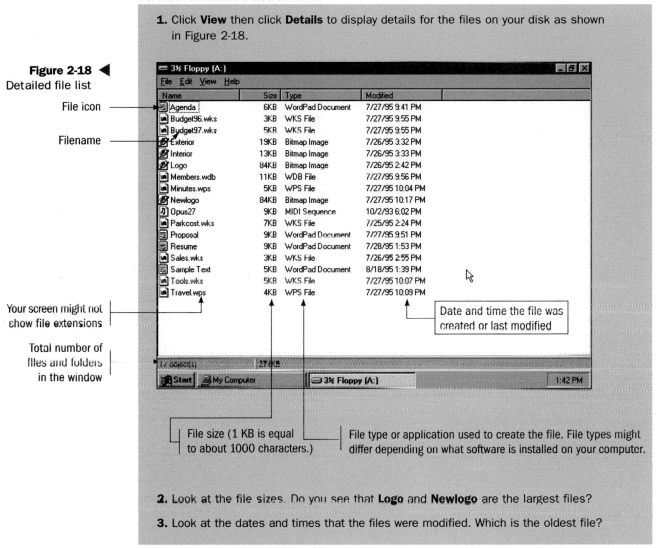

File size (1 KB is equal
to about 1000 characters.)

File type or application used to create the file. File types might
differ depending on what software is installed on your computer.

Date and time the file was
created or last modified

2. Look at the file sizes. Do you see that **Logo** and **Newlogo** are the largest files?

3. Look at the dates and times that the files were modified. Which is the oldest file?

Now that you have looked at the file details, switch back to the large icon view.

To switch to the large icon view:

1. Click **View** then click **Large Icons** to return to the large icon display.

Folders and Directories

A list of files is referred to as a **directory**. The main directory of a disk is sometimes called the **root directory**. The root directory is created when you format a disk and is shown in parentheses at the top of the window. For example, at the top of your screen you should see "3 ½ Floppy (A:)." The root directory is A:. In some situations, the root directory is indicated by a backslash after the drive letter and colon, such as A:\. All of the files on your Student Disk are currently in the root directory.

If too many files are stored in a directory, the directory list becomes very long and difficult to manage. A directory can be divided into **folders** (also called **subdirectories**), into which you group similar files. The directory of files for each folder then becomes much shorter and easier to manage. For example, you might create a folder for all the papers you write for an English 111 class as shown in Figure 2-19.

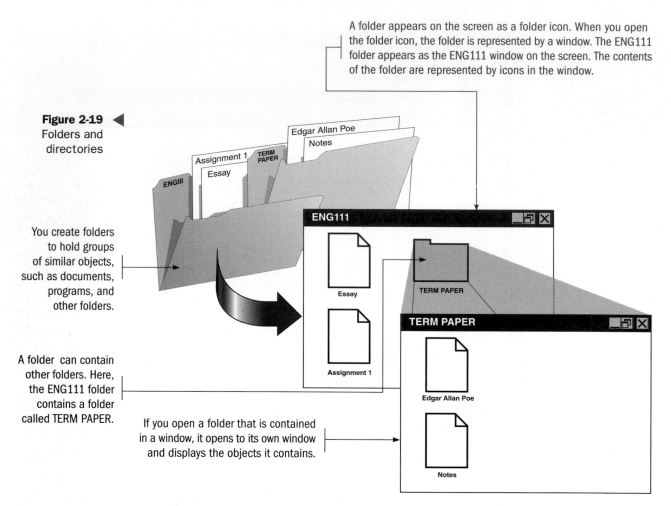

A folder appears on the screen as a folder icon. When you open the folder icon, the folder is represented by a window. The ENG111 folder appears as the ENG111 window on the screen. The contents of the folder are represented by icons in the window.

Figure 2-19 ◄
Folders and
directories

You create folders
to hold groups
of similar objects,
such as documents,
programs, and
other folders.

A folder can contain
other folders. Here,
the ENG111 folder
contains a folder
called TERM PAPER.

If you open a folder that is contained
in a window, it opens to its own window
and displays the objects it contains.

Now, you'll create a folder called My Documents to hold your document files.

To create a My Documents folder:

1. Click **File** then point to **New** to display the submenu.

2. Click **Folder**. A folder icon with the label "New Folder" appears.

3. Type **My Documents** as the name of the folder.

4. Press the **Enter** key.

When you first create a folder, it doesn't contain any files. In the next set of steps you will move a file from the root directory to the My Documents folder.

CREATING A NEW FOLDER

- Open the My Computer icon to display the My Computer window.
- Open the icon for the drive on which you want to create the folder.
- Click File then point to New.
- From the submenu click Folder.
- Type the name for the new folder.
- Press the Enter key.

Moving and Copying a File

You can move a file from one directory to another or from one disk to another. When you move a file it is copied to the new location you specify, then the version in the old location is erased. The move feature is handy for organizing or reorganizing the files on your disk by moving them into appropriate folders. The easiest way to move a file is to hold down the *right* mouse button and drag the file from the old location to the new location. A menu appears and you select Move Here.

You can also copy a file from one directory to another, or from one disk to another. When you copy a file, you create an exact duplicate of an existing file in whatever disk or folder you specify. To copy a file from one folder to another on your floppy disk, you use the same procedure as for moving a file, except that you select Copy Here from the menu.

Suppose you want to move the Minutes file from the root directory to the My Documents folder. Depending on the software applications installed on your computer, this file is either called Minutes or Minutes.wps. In the steps it is referred to simply as Minutes.

To move the Minutes file to the My Documents folder:

1. Click the **Minutes** icon to select it.

2. Press and hold the right mouse button while you drag the **Minutes** icon to the My Documents folder. See Figure 2-20.

Figure 2-20 ◀
Moving a file

Minutes file

My Documents folder

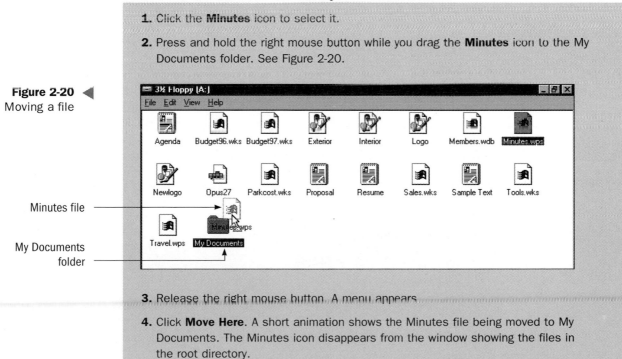

3. Release the right mouse button. A menu appears.

4. Click **Move Here**. A short animation shows the Minutes file being moved to My Documents. The Minutes icon disappears from the window showing the files in the root directory.

MOVING A FILE

- Open the My Computer icon to display the My Computer window.
- If the document you want to move is in a folder, open the folder.
- Hold down the *right* mouse button while you drag the file icon to its new folder or disk location.
- Click Move Here.
- If you want to move more than one file at a time, hold down the Ctrl key while you click the icons for all the files you want to move.

3.1 NOTE

Windows 3.1 users be careful! When you delete or move an icon in the Windows 95 My Computer window you are actually deleting or moving the file. This is quite different from the way the Windows 3.1 Program Manager worked.

Anything you do to an icon in the My Computer window is actually done to the file represented by that icon. If you move an icon, the file is moved; if you delete an icon, the file is deleted.

After you move a file, it is a good idea to make sure it was moved to the correct location. You can easily verify that a file is in its new folder by displaying the folder contents.

To verify that the Minutes file was moved to My Documents:

1. Click the **My Documents** folder, then press **Enter**. The My Documents window appears and it contains one file—Minutes.

2. Click the My Documents window **Close** button ✕.

   TROUBLE? If the My Computer window is no longer visible, click the My Computer icon, then press Enter. You might also need to open the 3 ½ Floppy (A:) icon.

Deleting a File

You delete a file or folder by deleting its icon. However, be careful when you delete a *folder*, because you also delete all the files it contains! When you delete a file from the hard drive, the filename is deleted from the directory but the file contents are held in the Recycle Bin. If you change your mind and want to retrieve the deleted file, you can recover it by clicking the Recycle Bin.

When you delete a file from a floppy disk, it does not go into the Recycle Bin. Instead it is deleted as soon as its icon disappears. Try deleting the file named Agenda from your Student Disk. Because this file is on the floppy disk and not on the hard disk, it will not go into the Recycle Bin.

To delete the file Agenda:

1. Click the icon for the file **Agenda**.

2. Press the **Delete** key.

3. If a message appears asking, "Are sure you want to delete Agenda?", click **Yes**. An animation, which might play too quickly to be seen, shows the file being deleted.

COPYING AN ENTIRE FLOPPY DISK

DELETING A FILE

- Click the icon for the file you want to delete.
- Press the Delete key.

Renaming a File

You can easily change the name of a file using the Rename option on the File menu or by using the file's label. Remember that when you choose a filename it can contain up to 255 characters, including spaces, but it cannot contain \ ? : " < > | characters.

Practice using this feature by renaming the Sales file to give it a more descriptive filename.

To rename Sales:

1. Click the **Sales** file to select it.

2. Click the label "Sales". After a short pause a solid box outlines the label and an insertion point appears.

3. Type **Preliminary Sales Summary** as the new filename.

4. Press the **Enter key**.

5. Click the **Close** button ☒ to close the 3 ½-inch Floppy (A:) window.

RENAMING A FILE

- Click the icon for the file you want to rename.
- Click the label of the icon.
- Type the new name for the file.
- Press the Enter key.

Copying an Entire Floppy Disk

You can have trouble accessing the data on your floppy disk if the disk gets damaged, exposed to magnetic fields, or picks up a computer virus. If the damaged disk contains important files, you will have to spend many hours to try to reconstruct those files. To avoid losing all your data, it is a good idea to make a copy of your floppy disk. This copy is called a **backup** copy.

If you wanted to make a copy of an audio cassette, your cassette player would need two cassette drives. You might wonder, therefore, how your computer can make a copy of your disk if you have only one disk drive. Figure 2-21 illustrates how the computer uses only one disk drive to make a copy of a disk.

Figure 2-21 ◀
Using one disk
drive to make a
copy of a disk

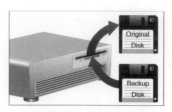

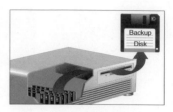

1. First, the computer
copies the data from your
original disk into memory.

2. Once the data is in
memory, you remove your
original disk from the drive
and replace it with your
backup disk.

3. The computer moves the
data from memory onto
your backup disk.

REFERENCE
window

MAKING A BACKUP OF YOUR FLOPPY DISK

- Click My Computer then press the Enter key.
- Insert the disk you want to copy in drive A.
- Click the 3 ½ Floppy (A:) icon ⌨ to select it.
  _{3½ Floppy (A:)}
- Click File then click Copy Disk to display the Copy Disk dialog box.
- Click Start to begin the copy process.
- When prompted, remove the disk you want to copy. Place your backup disk in drive A.
- Click OK.
- When the copy is complete, close the Copy Disk dialog box.
- Close the My Computer dialog box.

If you have two floppy disks, you can make a backup of your Student Disk now. Make sure you periodically follow the backup procedure, so your backup is up-to-date.

To back up your Student Disk:

1. Write your name and "Backup" on the label of your second disk. This will be your backup disk.

2. Make sure your Student Disk is in drive A.

3. Make sure the My Computer window is open. See Figure 2-22.

Figure 2-22 ◀
The My
Computer
window

4. Click the **3 ½ Floppy (A:)** icon  to select it.

   TROUBLE? If you mistakenly open the 3½ Floppy (A:) *window*, click ⊠.

5. Click **File**.

6. Click **Copy Disk** to display the Copy Disk dialog box as shown in Figure 2-23.

Figure 2-23 ◀
The Copy Disk
dialog box

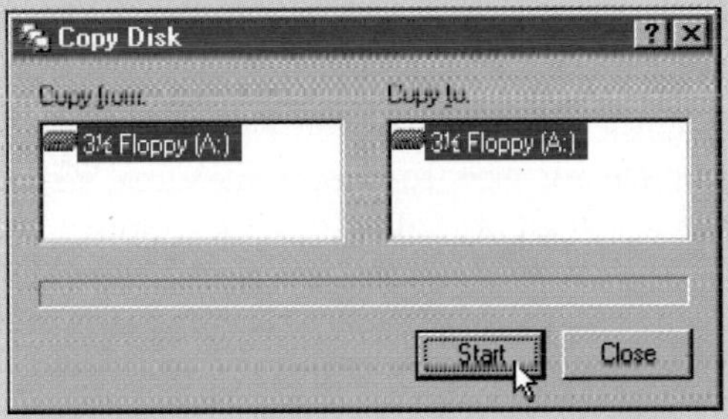

7. On the lower right side of the dialog box, you'll see a Start button. Click this **Start** button to begin the copy process.

8. When the message, "Insert the disk you want to copy from (source disk)..." appears, click the **OK** button.

9. When the message, "Insert the disk you want to copy to (destination disk)..." appears, insert your backup disk in drive A.

10. Click the **OK** button. When the copy is complete, you will see the message "Copy completed successfully."

11. After the data is copied to your backup disk, click ⊠ on the blue title bar of the Copy Disk dialog box.

12. Click ⊠ on the My Computer window to close the My Computer window.

13. Remove your disk from the drive.

Each time you make a backup, the data on your backup disk is erased, and replaced with the data from your updated Student Disk. Now that you know how to copy an entire disk, make a backup whenever you have completed a tutorial or you have spent a long time working on a file.

Quick Check

1. If you want to find out about the storage devices and printers connected to your computer, click the _____ icon.

2. If you have only one floppy disk drive on your computer, it is identified by the letter _____.

3. The letter C: is typically used for the _____ drive of a computer.

4. What are the five pieces of information that the Details view supplies about each of your files?

5. The main directory of a disk is referred to as the _____ directory.

6. You can divide a directory into _____.

7. If you delete the icon for a file, what happens to the file?

8. If you have one floppy disk drive, but you have two disks, can you copy a file from one floppy disk to another?

End Note

Just as you complete the Quick Check for Session 2.2, Steve appears. He asks how you are doing. You summarize what you remember from the tutorial, telling him that you learned how to insert, delete, and select text. You also learned how to work with files using Windows 95 software—you now know how to save, open, revise, and print a document. You tell him that you like the idea that these file operations are the same for almost all Windows 95 software. Steve agrees that this makes work a lot easier.

When Steve asks you if you have a supply of disks, you tell him you do, and that you just learned how to format a disk and view a list of files on your disk. Steve wants you to remember that you can use the Details view to see the filename, size, date, and time. You assure him that you remember that feature—and also how to move, delete, and rename a file.

Steve seems pleased with your progress and agrees that you're now ready to use software applications. But he can't resist giving you one last warning—don't forget to back up your files frequently!

Tutorial Assignments

1. Opening, Editing, and Printing a Document In this tutorial you learned how to create a document using WordPad. You also learned how to save, open, and print a document. Practice these skills by opening the document on your Student Disk called Resume, which is a résumé for Jamie Woods. Make the changes shown in Figure 2-24, and then print the document. After you print, save your revisions.

Figure 2-24 ◀

Change this to your name, address, and phone number. If you don't have an office number delete this.

Change this to the name of your university or college.

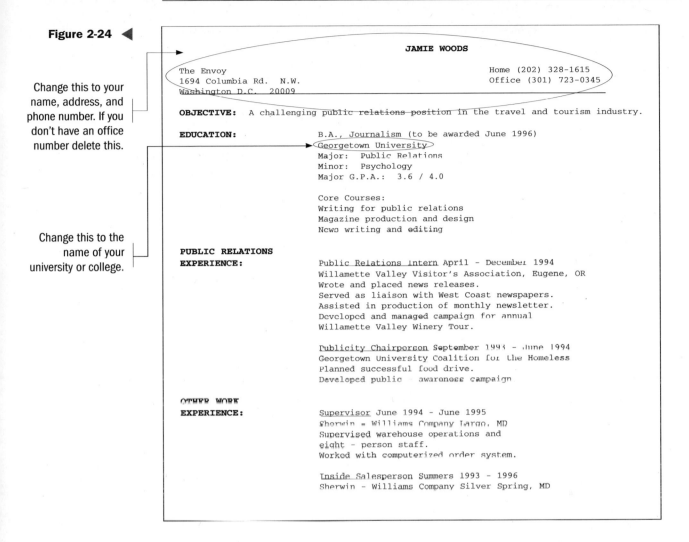

2. Creating, Saving, and Printing a Letter Use WordPad to write a one-page letter to a relative or a friend. Save the document in the My Documents folder with the name "Letter." Use the Print Preview feature to look at the format of your finished letter, then print it, and be sure you sign it.

3. Managing Files and Folders Earlier in this tutorial you created a folder and moved the file called Minutes into it. Now complete a through g below to practice your file management skills.

    a. Create a folder called Spreadsheets on your Student Disk.
    b. Move the files ParkCost, Budget96, Budget97, and Sales into the Spreadsheets folder.
    c. Create a folder called Park Project.
    d. Move the files Proposal, Members, Tools, Logo, and Newlogo into the Park Project folder.
    e. Move the ParkCost file from the Spreadsheets folder to the Park Project folder.
    f. Delete the file called Travel.
    g. Switch to the Details view and answer the following questions:

Write out your answers to questions a through e.

    a. What is the largest file in the Park Project folder?
    b. What is the newest file in the Spreadsheets folder?
    c. How many files are in the root directory?
    d. How are the Members and Resume icons different?
    e. What is the file with the most recent date on the entire disk?

4. More Practice with Files and Folders For this assignment, you will format your disk again and put a fresh version of the Student Disk files on it. Complete a through h below to practice your file management skills.

    a. Format a disk.

    b. Create a Student Disk. Refer to the section "Creating Your Student Disk" in Session 2.2.

    c. Create three folders on your new Student Disk: Documents, Budgets, and Graphics.

    d. Move the files Interior, Exterior, Logo, and Newlogo to the Graphics folder.

    e. Move the files Travel, Members and Minutes to the Documents folder.

    f. Move Budget96 and Budget97 to the Budgets folder.

    g. Switch to the Details view.

Answer questions a through f.

    a. What is the largest file in the Graphics folder?

    b. How many WordPad documents are in the root directory?

    c. What is the newest file in the root directory?

    d. How many files in all folders are 5KB in size?

    e. How many files in the Documents folder are WKS files?

    f. Do all the files in the Graphics folder have the same icon?

5. Finding a File Microsoft Windows 95 contains an on-line Tour that explains how to find files on a disk without looking through all the folders. Start the Windows 95 Tour (if you don't remember how, look at the instructions for Tutorial Assignment 1 in Tutorial 1), then click Finding a File, and answer the following questions:

    a. To display the Find dialog box, you must click the _____ button, then select _____ from the menu, and finally click _____ from the submenu.

    b. Do you need to type in the entire filename to find the file?

    c. When the computer has found your file, what are the steps you have to follow if you want to display the contents of the file?

6. Help with Files and Folders In Tutorial 2 you learned how to work with Windows 95 files and folders. What additional information on this topic does Windows 95 Help provide? Use the Start button to access Help. Use the Index tab to locate topics related to files and folders. Find at least two tips or procedures for working with files and folders that were not covered in the tutorial. Write out the tip in your own words and indicate the title of the Help screen that contains the information.

Lab Assignments

1. Using Files Lab In Tutorial 2 you learned how to create, save, open, and print files. The Using Files Lab will help you review what happens in the computer when you perform these file tasks. To start the Lab, follow these steps:

    a. Click the Start button.

    b. Point to Programs, then point to CTI Windows 95 Applications.

    c. Point to Windows 95 New Perspectives Brief.

    d. Click Using Files. If you can't find Windows 95 New Perspectives Brief or Using Files, ask for help from your instructor or technical support person.

Answer the Quick Check questions that appear as you work through the Lab. You can print your answers at the end of the Lab.

Answers to Quick Check Questions

SESSION 1.1

1 a. icon b. Start button c. taskbar d. Date/Time control e. desktop f. pointer

2 Multitasking

3 Start menu

4 Lift up the mouse, move it to the right, then put it down, and slide it left until the pointer reaches the left edge of the screen.

5 Highlighting

6 If a program is running, its button is displayed on the taskbar.

7 Each program that is running uses system resources, so Windows 95 runs more efficiently when only the programs you are using are open.

8 Answer: If you do not perform the shut down procedure, you might lose data.

SESSION 1.2

1 a. title bar b. program title c. Minimize button d. Restore button e. Close button f. menu bar g. toolbar h. formatting bar i. status bar j. taskbar k. workspace l. pointer

2 a. Minimize button—hides the program so only its button is showing on the taskbar.
   b. Maximize button—enlarges the program to fill the entire screen.
   c. Restore button—sets the program to a pre-defined size.
   d. Close button—stops the program and removes its button from the taskbar.

3 a. Ellipses—indicate a dialog box will appear.
   b. Grayed out—the menu option is not currently available.
   c. Submenu—indicates a submenu will appear.
   d. Check mark—indicates a menu option is currently in effect.

4 Toolbar

5 a. scroll bar b. scroll box c. Cancel button d. down arrow button e. list box f. radio button g. check box

6 one, check boxes

7 On-line Help

SESSION 2.1

1 file

2 formatting

3 I-beam

4 insertion point

5 word wrap

6 | You drag the I-beam pointer over the text to highlight it.

7 | \ ? : * < > | "

8 | extension

9 | save the file again

10 | paper

SESSION 2.2

1 | My Computer

2 | A (or A:)

3 | Hard (or hard disk)

4 | Filename, file type, file size, date, time

5 | Root

6 | Folders (or subdirectories)

7 | It is deleted from the disk.

8 | Yes

N E W
PERSPECTIVES
S E R I E S

Microsoft
Windows® 98
Preview

T U T O R I A L

Microsoft Windows 98 Preview

A Brief Comparison of the Windows 95 and Windows 98 Operating Systems

OBJECTIVES

In this tutorial, you will:

- Explore the differences between the Windows 95 and Windows 98 desktop

- Compare the Windows 95 and Windows 98 Start menus

- Compare mouse operations under Windows 95 and Windows 98

- Examine Active Desktop capabilities

- Explore Web view

- Preview additional Windows 98 features

Upgrading to a New Operating System

If you have worked with computers for very long, you already know that computer owners regularly face the decision to upgrade. **Upgrading** is the process of placing a more recent version of a product onto your computer. Upgrades to **hardware**, the physical components of a computer, occur when a computer user decides to purchase a newer computer or computer component that will add features, space, or speed to his or her computer system.

Upgrades to **software**, the set of instructions that make a computer perform a specific task, occur when a user decides to take advantage of improvements in a more recent version of a software product. Software developers produce new versions of software for a variety of reasons. Because hardware is constantly changing as new technology emerges, software developers need to ensure that their software takes full advantage of the latest hardware technology. For example, when it became cheaper and easier to expand the amount of memory on personal computers, many software companies developed their software to take advantage of extra memory. Another important reason for software revisions is usability. Developers are constantly trying to make their software easier to learn and use. For example, when it became clear that people found a graphical interface easy to work with, most software companies provided such an interface to their software. Software revisions also occur when a new software technology emerges. Developers update their products so they can compete against newer products that use newer technology. For example, with the recent explosion in popularity of the World Wide Web, many software companies hastened to include Web features in their products.

Microsoft Corporation's operating system revision from Windows 95 to Windows 98 is a response to these and other trends. For example, hardware now exists that makes it possible for you to run your computer through your television set, so Windows 98 includes a software accessory, TV Viewer, that lets you use this technology if you have the appropriate hardware. Windows 98 features such as automated disk maintenance are a response to the demand for ease of use. To take advantage of emerging software technology, Microsoft designed Windows 98 around features of the World Wide Web.

The decision to upgrade your operating system can be difficult to make. Upgrades can be expensive. To take full advantage of the Windows 98 upgrade, you might need to purchase new hardware, such as an Internet connection via a modem, a TV tuner card, or additional memory. Some revisions don't greatly affect how a software product is used, but other revisions change the interface so significantly that computer owners need to evaluate whether the advantages of upgrading are greater than the disadvantages of having to learn a practically new product. Users also consider the newness of the technology before they upgrade; some like to wait until the dust settles and the technology is tested and proven before they risk using it on their own computers.

In this tutorial, you'll examine how the upgrade to Windows 98 from Windows 95 affects what you see as you use the interface. This tutorial was developed using a prerelease version of Windows 98, so there might be slight differences between what you see in the figures and what you see in the final product. If you want more information about a feature that seems to be operating differently from what you see here, click the Start button and then click Help. Use the online Help system to learn more about the feature.

The Windows 98 Desktop

When you first turn on your computer, you might not notice much difference between the Windows 95 and Windows 98 desktops. Recall that the **desktop** is the workspace on your screen. Because it's easy to customize the desktop, someone might have changed your desktop so that it looks different from the one shown in the figures in this tutorial. You should, however, be able to locate objects similar to those in the figures. Figure 1 shows the Windows 95 desktop. Remember that you might see additional icons, and your screen might show a different background.

Figure 1 ◀
Windows 95
desktop

icons →

desktop →

Date/Time control;
you might see
additional controls

taskbar displays
program buttons
when programs are
running

Start button opens
the Start menu

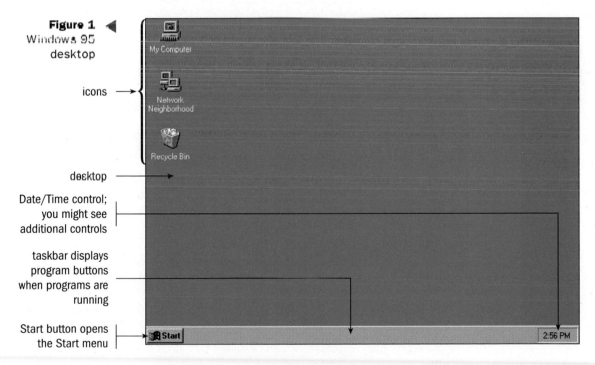

Figure 2 shows the Windows 98 desktop. Notice that the Start button, taskbar, Date/Time control, and icons all look the same as their Windows 95 counterparts. Your Windows 98 desktop might show additional objects; you'll learn more about these shortly.

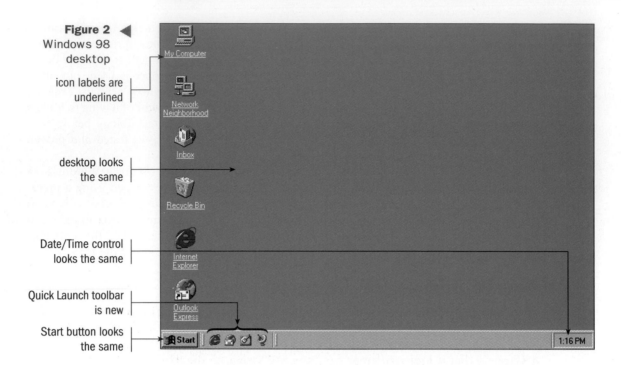

Figure 2 ◀
Windows 98
desktop

icon labels are
underlined

desktop looks
the same

Date/Time control
looks the same

Quick Launch toolbar
is new

Start button looks
the same

There are really only two visible differences between the basic Windows 95 and Windows 98 desktops:

- Windows 98 includes the Quick Launch toolbar.

- In Windows 98, icon names can appear underlined.

If you have access to the Internet and the Web, and if your desktop has been customized, it's possible you'll see additional desktop objects. Windows 98 makes it possible to integrate your Web experience into your desktop, as you'll see shortly.

Underlined Icon Names

The underlined icon names you see are evidence of Microsoft's attempt to make your experience with the Windows 98 desktop more like your experience with the Web. The **World Wide Web,** or just the **Web,** is a service on the Internet that allows you to view documents on computers around the world. Documents on the Web are called **Web pages.** Web pages contain elements known as **links** that you can select, usually by clicking a mouse, to move to another part of the document or another document altogether. A link can be a word, a phrase, or a graphic image. When a link consists of text, the text link usually appears underlined and in a different color.

To view Web pages, you use a program called a **browser.** When you click a link on a Web page in your browser, you jump to a different location—perhaps to a page stored on another computer, as shown in Figure 3.

Web page on
rock climbing

Figure 3 ◄
Clicking Web
page links

click this link
to jump to a
different document

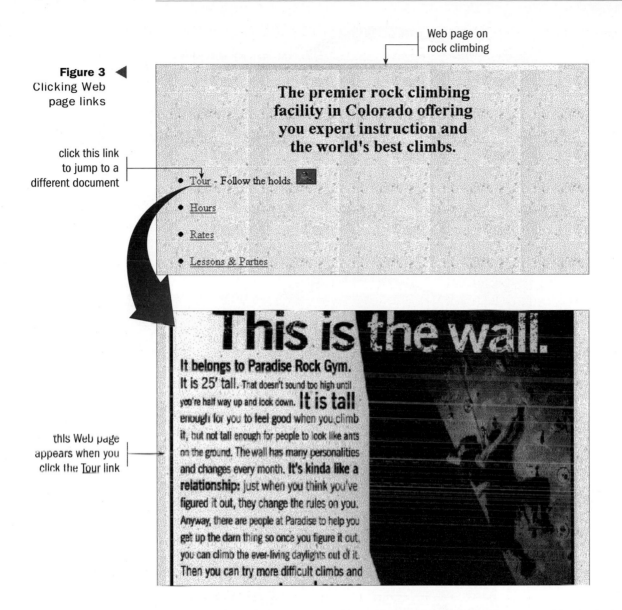

this Web page
appears when you
click the Tour link

On the Windows 98 desktop, icon labels are underlined to resemble the links you see on Web pages. By attempting to mimic the Web experience, Microsoft is trying to simplify how you interact with your computer. If the actions you take on the desktop are similar to those you take in your browser, you have to learn only one set of techniques.

Thus, when you click one of the icon labels on the Windows 98 desktop, you "jump" to that icon's destination. For example, in Windows 95, to open My Computer, you had to double-click its icon (or click its icon to select it and then press Enter). In Windows 98, however, the My Computer icon label is underlined just like a link. When you point at the icon label, the pointer changes from ⬚ to ⬚, just as it would if you pointed at a link in your browser. When you click the underlined icon label, you "jump" to the My Computer window. The result is the same: The My Computer window opens, but the Windows 98 technique is more like the technique you use on the Web. Figure 4 illustrates this difference.

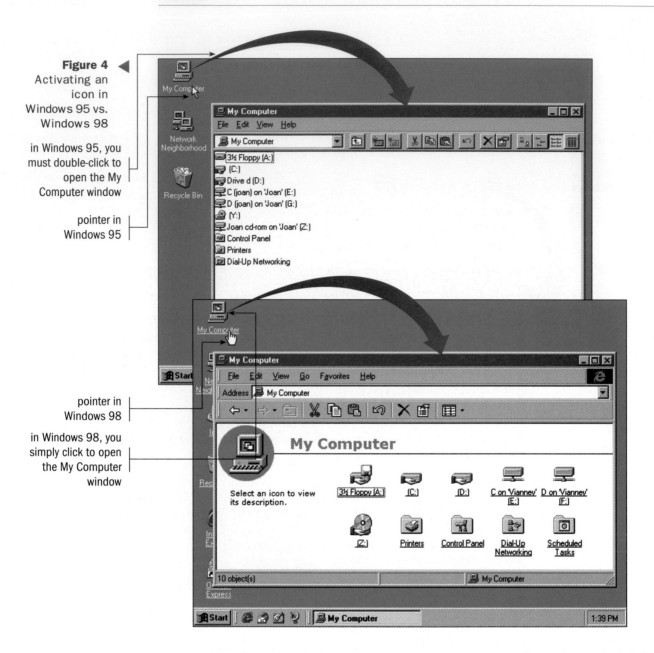

Figure 4 ◄
Activating an
icon in
Windows 95 vs.
Windows 98

in Windows 95, you
must double-click to
open the My
Computer window

pointer in
Windows 95

pointer in
Windows 98

in Windows 98, you
simply click to open
the My Computer
window

As you work with the Windows 98 operating system, you'll see that underlined text appears not just on the desktop but in numerous places—the My Computer window, the folder windows, and the Windows Explorer window, just to name a few. You can also display Windows 98 icons in the traditional Windows 95 manner: From My Computer, click View, click Folder Options, and then on the General tab, click the Classic style option button.

The Quick Launch Toolbar

The Windows 95 taskbar displays the Start button, buttons that correspond to active programs or open documents, and the tray area that includes the Date/Time control and any other active controls. The Windows 98 taskbar looks the same except for one difference: You can now display toolbars on the taskbar. Figure 5 shows the Windows 95 taskbar, and below it, the Windows 98 taskbar.

Figure 5 ◀
Taskbars in
Windows 95
and
Windows 98

Windows 95 taskbar ─

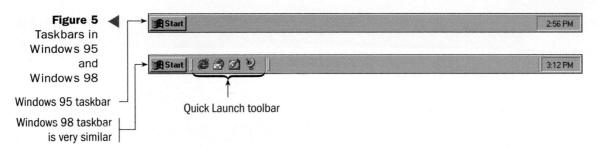

Windows 98 taskbar
is very similar

Quick Launch toolbar

Unless a user has customized his or her taskbar, only the Quick Launch toolbar appears on the Windows 98 taskbar, but you can also display three other taskbar toolbars. Like a toolbar in an application, the taskbar toolbars give you single-click access to common operations.

Figure 6 summarizes the Windows 98 taskbar toolbars.

Figure 6 ◀
Windows 98
taskbar
toolbars

Toolbar	Description
Address	As in a browser, allows you to select or enter an address, such as a URL, to open the browser to that location.
Links	As in a browser, displays buttons for popular Web pages, such as the Microsoft home page. When you click a button on the Links toolbar, your browser opens and displays the location you clicked.
Desktop	Displays a button for each desktop icon on the taskbar.
Quick Launch	Displays buttons for Internet services and for a direct route to the desktop.

The Quick Launch toolbar is the only toolbar to appear by default; the others you can enable by right-clicking the taskbar, pointing at the Toolbars menu option, and clicking the toolbar you want. Figure 7 shows a Windows 98 taskbar with the Address and Links toolbars visible in addition to the Quick Launch toolbar.

scroll arrow appears
when there are
additional objects
on a toolbar

Figure 7 ◀
Windows 98
taskbar with
multiple
toolbars

Quick Launch toolbar ──────

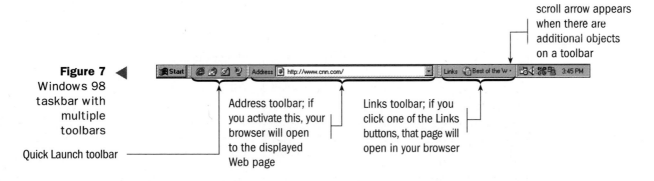

Address toolbar; if
you activate this, your
browser will open
to the displayed
Web page

Links toolbar; if you
click one of the Links
buttons, that page will
open in your browser

Figure 8 describes the default buttons on the Quick Launch toolbar.

Figure 8 ◀
Quick Launch
toolbar buttons

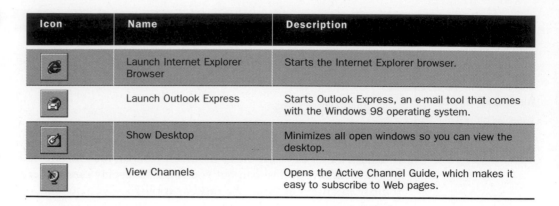

Icon	Name	Description
	Launch Internet Explorer Browser	Starts the Internet Explorer browser.
	Launch Outlook Express	Starts Outlook Express, an e-mail tool that comes with the Windows 98 operating system.
	Show Desktop	Minimizes all open windows so you can view the desktop.
	View Channels	Opens the Active Channel Guide, which makes it easy to subscribe to Web pages.

You can easily customize the taskbar toolbars by adding and removing buttons. Figure 9, for example, shows a taskbar whose Quick Launch toolbar includes buttons for popular applications.

Figure 9 ◀
Quick Launch
toolbar with
application
buttons

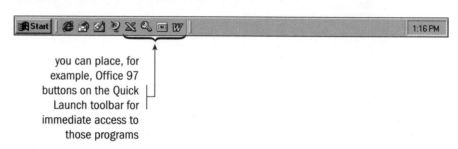

you can place, for
example, Office 97
buttons on the Quick
Launch toolbar for
immediate access to
those programs

To add a button to the Windows 98 Quick Launch toolbar, you simply drag the object you want to the toolbar.

The Start Menu

The Windows 98 Start menu looks similar to the Windows 95 Start menu. The only difference is that the Windows 98 Start menu includes a Favorites folder and a Windows Update link to Microsoft's Web site. Figure 10 shows the two Start menus. Again, since you can customize Start menus, yours might look different.

Figure 10 ◀
Windows 95
and
Windows 98
Start menus

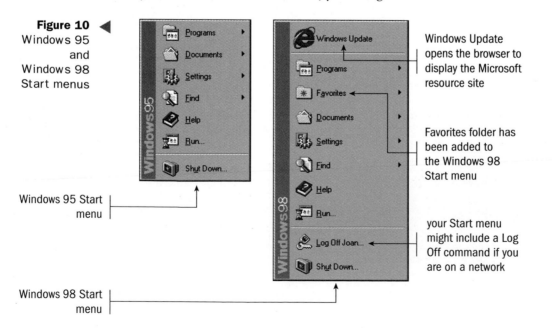

Windows Update
opens the browser to
display the Microsoft
resource site

Favorites folder has
been added to
the Windows 98
Start menu

your Start menu
might include a Log
Off command if you
are on a network

Windows 95 Start
menu

Windows 98 Start
menu

The Favorites folder that Microsoft has added to the Windows 98 Start menu duplicates the Favorites folder in your browser. In your browser, you create a Favorites folder by collecting and saving a list of favorite Web pages. Once a Web page is in your Favorites folder, you can return to it in your browser by simply selecting the page from the folder. By duplicating the browser's list of favorite Web pages on the Windows 98 Start menu, Microsoft allows you to reach your favorite Web pages without having to go through the interim steps of starting your browser and opening the Favorites folder. To view a favorite Web page in Windows 98, you simply click Start, point at the Favorites option, and then click the Web page you want. Your browser launches automatically and connects you directly to that page.

The Windows Update link that appears on the Windows 98 Start menu is a Microsoft resource site on the Web that you connect to by clicking Windows Update on the Start menu. Your browser displays the Windows Update page, which helps you ensure that your system is running the most recent and efficient system software possible.

You might notice one final difference between the Windows 95 and Windows 98 Start menus. If you have more items on your Start menu than can be displayed on the screen, Windows 95 doubles the width of the menu to display the entire list of Start menu objects. Windows 98, however, adds to the bottom of the Start menu an arrow to which you can point to see additional objects.

Mouse Operation

You won't notice a difference between how your mouse operates in Office 97 or your other Windows 95 applications when you run them under the Windows 98 operating system. But if you work with certain Windows 98 windows, such as My Computer or Windows Explorer, be aware that Microsoft has simplified the actions you need to take with the mouse.

You've already seen that the icons on your desktop now behave like links and are, therefore, activated with a single-click rather than a double-click. In fact, in Windows 98, single-clicking completely replaces double-clicking on the desktop. In Windows 95, you generally selected an object by clicking it, but in Windows 98, you select an object by simply pointing to it for a moment. Windows 98 uses the term **hover** to describe pointing to an object, such as an icon, long enough to select it. Passing the pointer over an icon does not select it; you need to hover the pointer over the object long enough for Windows 98 to realize that you mean to select it. Once you've practiced hovering, you'll find it easy. Figure 11 summarizes how mouse functions have changed from Windows 95 to Windows 98.

Figure 11 ◄
Comparing
mouse
functions

Task	Windows 95	Windows 98
Select	Click	Hover
Open or run	Double-click (or click and press Enter)	Click
Select multiple contiguous objects	Shift+click	Shift+hover
Select multiple noncontiguous objects	Ctrl+click	Ctrl+hover

Changes in mouse operation do not affect Windows 98 dialog boxes: They affect only the desktop, My Computer, Windows Explorer, and similar windows.

Active Desktop

In Windows 95, to experience the Web you generally must first start your browser (although new generations of Internet communications software products are now bypassing the browser and placing Web information directly on the desktop even without the Windows 98 operating system). Users with Web access will find Windows 98 **Active Desktop** technology brings Web content directly to the desktop, without requiring extra communications software, allowing your desktop to act like your personal Web page.

You can enable Active Desktop by right-clicking the desktop, pointing to Active Desktop, and then clicking View As Web Page. Active Desktop integrates your Web experience with the Windows 98 desktop in two primary ways: with background wallpaper and with Web components. You can use a Web page as the desktop's background, and you can place Web components (updateable information from the Web) on the desktop.

Using a Web Page as Background Wallpaper

If you've ever worked with the Desktop Properties dialog box in Windows 95 (which you access by right-clicking the desktop and then clicking Properties), you might have experimented with the look of your desktop by changing the color or pattern of the default background wallpaper.

Windows 95 limits you to using image files as your background wallpaper. Trying to create a desktop background that integrated text and images and other objects is impossible. Windows 98, however, extends your control over your desktop's background by allowing you to use Web pages as wallpaper. To write Web pages, you use a language called **HTML**, which stands for Hypertext Markup Language. HTML uses special codes to describe how the page should appear on the screen. A document created using the HTML language is called an **HTML file** and is saved with the htm or html extension.

Because Windows 98 enables you to use an HTML file as your background wallpaper, your Windows 98 desktop background can feature text, images, links, and multimedia objects. You can use Microsoft Word to save a document as an HTML file; also, you can use the HTML editor included with Windows 98, FrontPage Express, to create more complex and sophisticated HTML files. Alternatively, you can use the Internet Explorer browser to save an existing Web page as an HTML file that you can then use as your wallpaper. To use a Web page as your wallpaper, right-click the desktop, click Properties, click the Background tab, click the Browse button, locate and select the HTML file you want to use, then click the OK button.

The added control Windows 98 gives you over background wallpaper makes it possible to make the desktop a launch pad for your most important projects. A corporation, for example, might create an HTML file that contains important company information, an updateable company calendar, links to company documents, a sound clip welcoming new employees to the company, and so on.

Figure 12 shows a sample Windows 98 desktop that might appear on the computers of a gift shop chain's main headquarters.

Figure 12 ◀
Windows 98 desktop with a background HTML file

embedded updateable program

embedded image file

embedded video clip

This company created a wallpaper that includes links to product groups, information about the company, a video clip of a recent company outing, and links to current events, company protocols, and training procedures.

Web Components on the Desktop

In addition to using a Web page as a background, you can also add Web components to the Windows 98 desktop in resizable, movable windows. A **Web component** is an object on the desktop that you can set to update automatically via your Web connection. For example, you might place a weather map, an investor ticker, or a news component on your desktop. You can schedule when each component will update itself and the information will be delivered to your desktop without your having to look for it.

Windows 95 users can purchase separate software that performs a similar function, such as the Internet Explorer 4.0 browser, Netscape Communicator's Netcaster component, or a product such as PointCast. But with Windows 98, the ability to place update-able Web information on the desktop is actually *integrated* into the operating system.

Figure 13 shows a Windows 98 desktop with several such Web components.

Figure 13 ◄
Windows 98 desktop with Web components

CNN news

Wall Street Journal news

weather

investment ticker

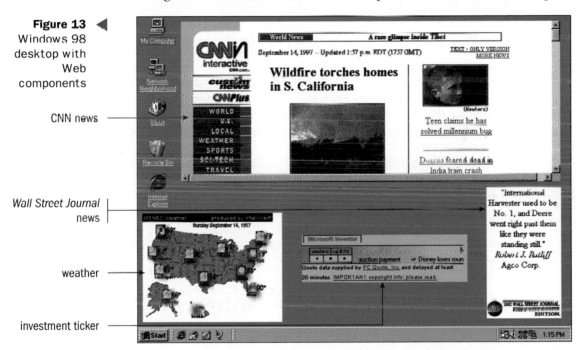

Every morning when this user checks her desktop, each component will have been automatically updated (if, that is, she has set the update schedules that way). The weather map will show the morning's weather instead of weather from the night before, her news service will display the most recent news, and the other Web components will update in a similar fashion. If she wants a more detailed look at, for example, the news, she can select and enlarge one of the Web component windows.

There are three ways to add Web components to the Windows 98 desktop:

■ The Active Desktop Gallery offers a small set of useful Web components, including the weather map, investment ticker, clock, and so on. To access the Active Desktop Gallery, right-click the desktop, point to Active Desktop, and then click Customize my Desktop. A list of current Web components appears on the Web tab of the Display Properties dialog box. To add new ones, click the New button and follow the prompts to locate the Active Desktop Gallery.

- The Channel Bar lists companies that have agreements with Microsoft to deliver information directly to the desktops of those who subscribe to the Active Channel service. (A site that offers regularly updated information that can be delivered to the desktop on a predetermined schedule is called a **channel**.) When you subscribe to a channel delivery service, you request that information be "broadcast" to you from that channel at whatever schedule you specify. To add a channel from the Channel Bar, you must first enable the Channel Bar from the Web tab of the Display Properties dialog box. Once you can see the Channel Bar, click the channel you want to add. Follow the prompts to add the channel to your list of channels.

- You can add your own components by connecting to channel sites not necessarily associated with Microsoft and then subscribing to those channels. In most cases, you do this by connecting to the site with your browser. Sites that support channel delivery include a link that asks if you want to subscribe to the site. Click the link and follow the prompts; they vary from site to site.

If any of these components are on your desktop, a rectangular block appears that seems to be a part of the background. When you select that component, however, a window border appears that you can resize and move.

Web View in Explorer Windows

In addition to the Web components that appear on the desktop, the Windows 98 Explorer windows also have changed to extend the Web experience to folder navigation. The term **Explorer windows** is a general term that applies to windows such as Windows Explorer, My Computer, the folder and drive windows, and the Printer window. In other words, any window that displays and allows you to navigate the object hierarchy of your computer is an Explorer window.

With Windows 98 Explorer windows, you can enable **Web view**, which does the following:

- Displays objects on your computer as links

- Allows single-click navigation

- Adds to the window an HTML document with customizable links and information

- Enables you to use the Explorer window as a browser

Figure 14 shows the My Computer window as it looks in Windows 95 and in Windows 98.

Windows 98

Figure 14 ◀
My Computer in
Windows 95
and
Windows 98

Windows 95 My
Computer window

Windows 98
My Computer window

toolbars are different

list of objects is the
same as in Windows
95, except labels are
underlined and
perform like links

Web view HTML
document contains
text and images that
you can customize

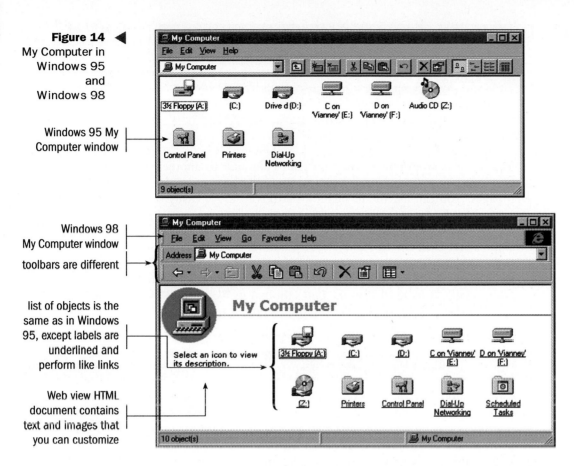

The Windows 95 window shows the familiar object list, but Windows 98 Explorer windows now have HTML documents in the background that you can customize. The ability to customize the Explorer windows by editing their background HTML page makes it easier than ever for you to work efficiently. For example, you could customize a network folder's HTML page so that anyone who accesses that Explorer window sees a description of the folder's contents, links to the most important objects in that window, and links to related objects. You might customize a network folder containing 1999 corporate reports so that it contains links to corporate reports for 1998 and 1997.

The objects that your computer displays look like the links you see on a Web page. As on the desktop, a single click suffices to open the object. For example, if you click the Floppy (A:) icon, the A: window opens. If you are used to thinking of a link as something that targets an object on the Web, you'll have to expand your vision. In Windows 98, links target any object accessible to your computer—not just Web pages, but also local drives, network folders, and files.

Web View Toolbars

In the Explorer windows, the Windows 95 Standard toolbar has been updated to include buttons that enable you to use the Explorer windows as browsers. The Address toolbar looks like the Address bar in a browser, and the Standard toolbar includes buttons that allow you to navigate through the hierarchy of drives and folders just as you would move through pages on the Web in your browser. Figure 15 first shows the Windows 95 Standard toolbar and then the Windows 98 Address and Standard toolbars on separate lines so you can see all the buttons.

Figure 15
My Computer
toolbars in
Windows 95
and
Windows 98

Windows 98 adds the
Address toolbar

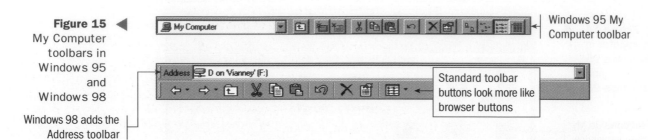

Windows 95 My
Computer toolbar

Standard toolbar
buttons look more like
browser buttons

As you move from one location on your computer to another, Windows 98 "remembers" where you've been, just as in your browser you can move back to previously viewed Web pages. You can use the navigation buttons to move easily through the hierarchy of your computer's objects.

Suppose you want to view the contents of a folder on drive A:. You could open My Computer and click the A: icon. The A: Explorer window would open. Then you could click the folder whose contents you want to view. The folder's Explorer window would open. To return to My Computer, you'd simply click the Back button twice.

Additionally, you can display the Links toolbar in Web view. When you click one of the buttons on the Links toolbar, the Explorer window functions just like your browser to display the page you selected.

Using Windows Explorer to Browse the Web

In both Windows 95 and Windows 98, Windows Explorer displays a hierarchy of objects on your computer. Windows 98 includes the Internet icon 🅔 as one of those objects. You might recognize this icon as the one that appears on the desktop in Windows 95; if you have an Internet service set up on your computer, double-clicking that icon on the Windows 95 desktop starts your browser. In Windows 98, however, when you click 🅔 in the Windows Explorer window, your browser's home page appears in the Exploring window. Figure 16 shows Windows Explorer with the object hierarchy on the left and a Web page off the Internet on the right.

Figure 16
Using Windows
Explorer as a
browser

current location is
a Web page

click to connect to
your home page

Explorer toolbars
resemble
browser toolbars

Web page displayed
directly in the
Windows Explorer
window

Notice that when you select a Web page in Windows Explorer, the standard Explorer toolbars and menus are replaced with toolbars and menus that are more browser-oriented. Indeed, you could use Windows Explorer as a Web-browsing tool.

Additional Windows 98 Features

This tutorial has focused primarily on how upgrading to Windows 98 affects the way you interact with the operating system. But Windows 98 offers many other features that replace or expand Windows 95 functions, as well as some completely new features. Figure 17 describes some of the most intriguing updated, expanded, or new features. You might not understand the technology behind all these features, but they should give you an idea of what you can do if you are running Windows 98 with the latest hardware.

Figure 17 ◀
Additional
Windows 98
features

Feature	Description
Digital Versatile Disc (DVD) support	The successor to CD-ROM disks, DVD stores many times the capacity of a CD-ROM, enough to store full-length digitized movies that you can then view on your monitor or TV screen if you have the appropriate hardware.
Disk space	The space available on your hard disk is limited by the type of file system you use. Windows 95 employs the FAT 16 file system. With Windows 98 FAT 32, you can store up to 30 percent more data on your disk, and you can work with drives that are much larger than those available to FAT 16. The FAT 32 converter utility also makes it easy to upgrade your file system.
Internet communications	Windows 98 ships with Internet Explorer, an Internet communications software suite that offers state-of-the-art integrated browsing, e-mail, newsgroup, Web page editing, and conferencing software—and much more!
Internet Connection Wizard	Establishing a connection to the Internet is much easier with this wizard, which works with your Internet service provider to configure your Internet connection properly.
On-line Help	Information about the Windows 98 operating system now appears as a Web page, and is continually updated by Microsoft. You can access the Windows 98 Help Desk to receive online technical support.
Peripheral device support	Windows 98 supports Universal serial bus (USB) technology, a hardware device that plugs into a single port from which you can run multiple peripheral devices.
Power management	If you own a new PC that supports OnNow hardware technology, your PC will start much more quickly, and you will consume less power if you take advantage of power-down features.
Speed	Windows 98 runs your applications faster, saving you time.
Tune-Up Wizard	In an effort to simplify and streamline your computer maintenance program, the Tune-Up Wizard analyzes your system and helps you schedule maintenance tasks such as defragmentation, disk scan, and backup. Most of the maintenance tools have also been improved.
TV Viewer	This accessory brings television to the PC—not just regular TV signals, but also content-rich broadcasts that provide interactivity on your TV. For example, a cooking show might include links to recipes that you could download over your TV satellite or cable connection.
Video playback	ActiveMovie expands the multimedia capabilities of your computer, featuring improved video playback.
Windows Update	Accessed directly from the Windows 98 Start menu, this Microsoft site features a service that scans your system and allows you to update it with the most recent software. This site also helps you troubleshoot problems.

When computer owners consider whether or not to upgrade, they review feature lists and comparisons such as the ones you've seen in this tutorial. They then assess their needs and budget to determine whether to make the upgrade.

Now that you've had a chance to explore how Windows 98 changes the operating system landscape, you can see why users must balance the advantages against the sometimes uncertain world of switching to a new operating system and a new way of working with computers. Many users believe, however, that Windows 98 raises personal computing to new heights, and the benefits far outweigh the challenges.

Tutorial Assignments

1. Based on what you've read in this tutorial, if you were a Windows 95 user, would you make the upgrade to Windows 98? Write a one-page essay that answers this question. In your essay, you'll need to define your computing needs, address how Windows 95 fulfills those needs, and evaluate the degree to which Windows 98 could better meet those needs. Be sure to itemize the features that influence you the most —both pro and con.

2. Using the resources available to you, either online or through your library, locate information about the release of Windows 98. Computing trade magazines, both hard copy and online, are an excellent source of information about software. Read several articles about Windows 98 and then write a one-page essay that discusses the features that seem most important to the people who evaluated the software. If you find reviews of the software, mention the features that reviewers had the strongest reaction to, pro or con.

3. Write a single-page essay defending or refuting the following proposition: "Software developers upgrade their software only to make money."

4. Interview two people you know who are well-informed computer users. Ask them how they decide when to upgrade a software product. If they are using a PC with the Windows 3.X, 95, or 98 operating system, ask them why they did or did not upgrade to Windows 98. Write a single-page essay summarizing what you learned from these interviews about making the decision to upgrade.

5. Based on what you learned about Windows 98 in this tutorial, what Windows 98 features interest you the most? The least? Write two paragraphs describing those features and explaining why you do or do not find them interesting.

6. How has Windows 98 changed the concept of the "home computer"? Research the Windows 98 features that might benefit home users, such as its TV and appliance capabilities, and write two paragraphs summarizing those features and assessing how they could impact home life.

Microsoft® Internet Explorer

TUTORIAL

Read This **Before You Begin**

TO THE STUDENT

TO THE STUDENT

You can complete this tutorial using either Internet Explorer 3 or Internet Explorer 4, though the figures show the version 4 window. Notes in the margin alert version 3 users to differences in the figures or functions. In most cases the two versions function similarly, but when the Steps you take with version 3 differ significantly from those you take with version 4, a separate set of Steps is provided. Follow the Steps preceded by 🔵 if you are using version 3, and follow those preceded by 🔵 if you are using version 4. If no icon precedes a set of Steps, users of both versions can follow those Steps. You can discover the version you are using by clicking Help and then clicking About Internet Explorer.

STUDENT DISK

To complete this tutorial and the end-of-tutorial assignments in this book, you need one Student Disk. Your instructor will either provide you with a Student Disk or ask you to make your own.

If you are supposed to make your own Student Disk, you will need one blank, formatted high-density disk. You will need to copy a set of folders from a file server or standalone computer onto your disk. Your instructor will tell you which computer, drive letter, and folders contain the files you need. The following table shows you which folders go on your disk, so that you will have enough disk space to complete all the tutorials, Tutorial Assignments, and Case Problems:

Student Disk	Write this on the disk label	Put these folders on the disk
1	Student Disk: Internet Explorer	Tutorial.01

See the inside front or inside back cover of this book for more information on Student Disk files, or ask your instructor or technical support person for assistance.

COURSE LABS

This tutorial features an interactive Course Lab to help you understand Internet concepts. There are Lab Assignments at the end of the tutorial that relate to this Lab. To start the Lab, click the Start button on the Windows taskbar, point to Programs, point to Course Labs, point to New Perspectives Applications, and click the Internet World Wide Web lab.

USING YOUR OWN COMPUTER

If you are going to work through this book using your own computer, you need:

- **Computer System**   Microsoft Internet Explorer version 3 or 4 must be installed on your computer. This book assumes a complete installation of Internet Explorer 3 or any installation of Internet Explorer 4.

- **Student Disk**   Ask your instructor or lab manager for details on how to get the Student Disk. You will not be able to complete this tutorial or the end-of-tutorial assignments using your own computer until you have a Student Disk. The Student Files may also be obtained electronically over the Internet. See the inside front or inside back cover of this book for more details.

- **Course Labs**   See your instructor or technical support person to obtain the Course Lab software for use on your own computer.

TO THE INSTRUCTOR

To complete this tutorial and the end-of-tutorial assignments in this book, your students must use a set of files on a Student Disk. These files are included in the Instructor's Resource Kit, and they may also be obtained electronically over the Internet. See the inside front or inside back cover of this book for more details. Follow the instructions in the Readme or Help file to copy the files to your server or standalone computer. You can view the Readme file using WordPad.

Once the files are copied, you can make Student Disks for the students yourself, or you can tell students where to find the files so they can make their own Student Disk. Make sure the files get correctly copied onto the Student Disks by following the instructions in the Student Disk section above, which will ensure that students have enough disk space to complete all the tutorials and end-of-tutorial assignments.

COURSE LAB SOFTWARE

The Course Lab software is distributed on a CD-ROM included in the Instructor's Resource Kit. To install the Course Lab software, follow the setup instructions in the Readme file on the CD-ROM. Refer also to the Readme file for essential technical notes related to running the Labs in a multi-user environment. Once you have installed the Course Lab software, your students can start the Labs from the Windows desktop by following the instructions in the Course Labs section above.

COURSE TECHNOLOGY STUDENT FILES AND LAB SOFTWARE

You are granted a license to copy the Student Files and Course Lab software to any computer or computer network used by students who have purchased this book.

Navigating the Web with Internet Explorer

Conducting Teacher Workshops at Northern University

OBJECTIVES

In this tutorial you will:

- Understand the structure of the Internet and the World Wide Web

- Identify Internet Explorer components

- Start and exit Internet Explorer and view and hide Explorer toolbars

- Open a Web page from your Student Disk

- Navigate links and frames

- Open a Web page with its URL

- Move among Web pages

- Load images

- Print a Web page

- Get online help

LABS

**The Internet
World Wide Web**

CASE

Northern University

Michelle Pine, an education student at Northern University, is researching the use of the Internet as a teaching tool in the classroom and as an aid for preparing class lessons. She uses the Northern University Internet connection regularly to keep in contact with her friends and professors. She also uses an online service at home to communicate with her family, who live in New Mexico.

Michelle has been amazed at the wealth and variety of information she has found freely available on the Internet, especially the amount geared toward educators. At forums, educators can share ideas, advice, and encouragement. Teachers can find current information about every subject that can be incorporated into the curriculum. Geography and history, for example, come alive with multimedia travel through various time periods and lands. Science is no longer limited by physical equipment, and students can conduct experiments in virtual labs that would be impossible in many classrooms. Humanity studies become more vibrant through tours of world-famous museums, music, and video clips from particular artists, styles, or times. The more Michelle looks, the more resources she finds. What's more, she has discovered that information is updated and added daily.

As a special project for one of her education courses, Michelle is planning a two-hour workshop for teachers on Internet basics and Internet Explorer. The 25 educators enrolled in the workshop have little working knowledge of the Internet and Internet Explorer but are interested in its possibilities.

Michelle asks you to help her facilitate the workshop. She'd like to give the talk while you help out at the computer keyboard. Michelle wants to begin by giving the educators an overview of the Internet and the World Wide Web. Then she'll teach them Internet Explorer basics using a presentation she created especially for the workshop. Finally, she'll demonstrate how to connect to and navigate through pages on the Web.

Using the Tutorial Effectively

This tutorial will help you learn about Internet Explorer. It is designed to be used at a computer. The tutorial is divided into sessions, each of which is designed to be completed in about 45 minutes, but take as much time as you need. When you've completed a session, it's a good idea to exit the program and take a break.

Before you begin, read the following questions and answers, which are designed to help you use the tutorials effectively.

Where do I start?

Each tutorial begins with a case, which sets the scene and gives you background information to clarify what you will be doing in the tutorial. Ideally, you should read the case before you go to the lab. In the lab, begin with the first session.

How do I know what to do on the computer?

Each session contains steps that you will perform on a computer to learn how to use Internet Explorer. Read the text that introduces each series of steps. The steps you need to perform at a computer are numbered and set against a colored background. Read each step carefully and completely before you try it.

How do I know if I did the step correctly?

As you work, compare your computer screen with the corresponding figure in the tutorial. Don't worry if your screen display is somewhat different from the figure. The important parts of the screen display are labeled in each figure. Check to make sure these parts are on your screen.

What if I make a mistake?

Don't worry about making mistakes; they are part of the learning process. Paragraphs labeled "**TROUBLE?**" identify common problems and explain how to get back on track. Follow the steps in a **TROUBLE?** paragraph only if you are having the problem described. If you run into other problems:

- Carefully consider the current state of your system, the position of the pointer, and any messages on the screen.

- Complete the sentence, "Now I want to... ." Be specific, because you are identifying your goal.

- Develop a plan for accomplishing your goal, then put your plan into action.

What if I am using a different version of Internet Explorer?

You can complete this tutorial using Internet Explorer 3 or Internet Explorer 4, though the figures show the version 4 window. Notes in the margin alert version 3 users to differences in the figures or functions. In most cases, the two versions function similarly; but when the Steps you take with version 3 differ significantly from those you take with version 4, a separate set of Steps is provided. Follow the Steps preceded by **IE3** if you are using version 3, and follow those preceded by **IE4** if you are using version 4. If no icon precedes a set of Steps, users of both versions can follow those Steps. You can check which version you are using by clicking Help and then clicking About Internet Explorer.

How do I use the Reference Windows?

Reference Windows summarize the procedures you learn in the tutorial steps. Do not complete the actions in the Reference Windows when you are working through each tutorial. Instead, refer to the Reference Windows while you are working on the assignments at the end of the tutorial.

How can I test my understanding of the material I learned in the tutorial?

At the end of each session, answer the Quick Check questions. The answers for the Quick Check questions appear on page 47.

After you have completed the entire tutorial, complete the Tutorial Assignments and Case Problems. They are carefully structured so you will review what you have learned and then apply your knowledge to new situations.

What if I can't remember how to do something?

Refer to the Task Reference at the end of the book; it summarizes how to accomplish tasks using the mouse, the menus, and the keyboard.

What is the Internet World Wide Web Course Lab, and how should I use it?

This interactive Lab helps you review concepts and practice skills that you learn in the tutorial. The Lab Assignments section at the end of the tutorial includes instructions for how to use the Lab.

Now that you've seen how to use this tutorial effectively, you are ready to begin.

SESSION

1

In this session, you will learn about the Internet, the World Wide Web, and Internet Explorer. You will also learn how to start and exit Internet Explorer, identify components of the Internet Explorer window, work with Internet Explorer toolbars, view Web pages, activate and abort a link, and work with frames.

The Internet
World Wide Web

The Internet

Michelle wants to begin her talk by giving an overview of the technology that makes it possible for people to communicate with each other using their computers. She also wants to familiarize her audience with common network terms that will make it possible for them to understand how the Internet operates.

When two or more computers are linked together so that they can exchange information and resources, they create a structure known as a **network**. Networks facilitate the sharing of data and resources among multiple users. Some computers, called **servers**, provide specific resources to the network, such as print capabilities or stored files. Figure 1 shows a small network consisting of a single server, a shared printer, and a handful of computers.

Figure 1 ◀
Small network

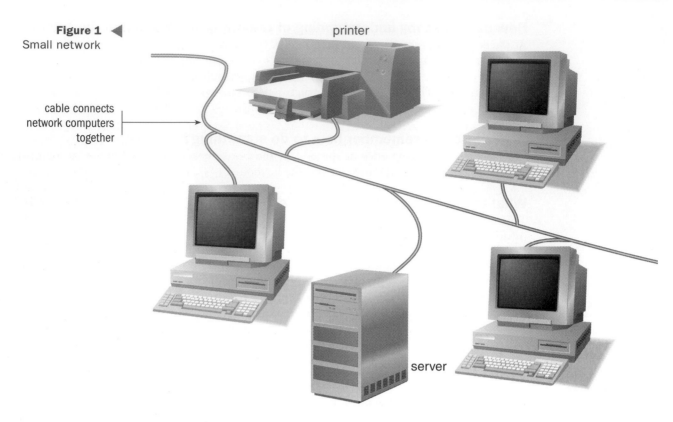

printer

cable connects
network computers
together

server

Networks can also be connected to each other to allow information to be shared between computers on different networks. The **Internet**, the largest and most famous example of a "network of networks," is made up of millions of computers linked to networks all over the world. Computers and networks on the Internet are connected by fiber-optic cables, satellites, phone lines, and other communication systems, as shown in Figure 2.

Figure 2 ◀
Structure of
the Internet

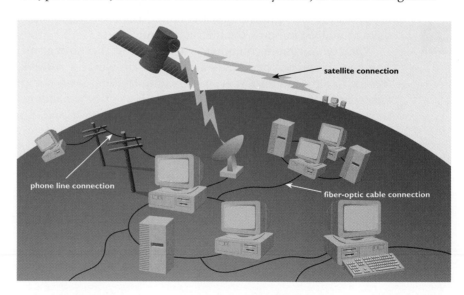

satellite connection

phone line connection

fiber-optic cable connection

Computers on a network are often called **hosts**, and thus a computer with Internet access is sometimes called an **Internet host**.

The Internet, by design, is a decentralized structure. There is no Internet "company." Instead, the Internet is a collection of different organizations, such as universities and companies, that organize their own information. There are no rules about where information is stored, and no one regulates the quality of information available on the Internet. Even though the lack of central control can make it hard for beginners to find their way through the resources on the Internet, there are some advantages. The Internet is open to innovation and rapid growth as different organizations and individuals have the freedom to test new products and services and make them quickly available to a global audience. One such service developed in recent years is the **World Wide Web**, an Internet service that makes finding information and moving around the Internet easy.

The World Wide Web

The foundation of the World Wide Web was laid in 1989 by Timothy Berners-Lee and other researchers at the CERN research facility near Geneva, Switzerland. They wanted to make it easy for researchers to share data with a minimum of training and support. They created a system of **hypertext documents**—electronic files that contain elements known as **links**, which you can select, usually by clicking a mouse, to move to another part of the document or another document altogether. A link can be a word or phrase or a graphic image.

The system of hypertext documents developed at CERN proved to be easily adaptable to other information sources on the Internet. Within the space of a few years, hypertext documents were being created by numerous organizations for a large variety of topics. Because it was easy to link these different hypertext documents together, a single user could jump from one set of hypertext documents to another without much effort. This interconnected structure of hypertext documents became known as the World Wide Web or simply the Web.

Each hypertext document on the Web is called a **Web page** and is stored on a computer on the Internet called a **Web server**. A Web page can contain links to other Web pages located anywhere on the Internet—on the same computer as the original Web page or on an entirely different computer halfway across the world. The ability to cross-reference other Web pages with links is one of the most important features of the Web.

Figure 3 shows how when you click a link on one Web page you move to another Web page.

Web page on
rock climbing

Figure 3 ◀
Link in one
hypertext
document
opens another

click this link
to jump to a
different document

The premier rock climbing
facility in Colorado offering
you expert instruction and
the world's best climbs.

- Tour - Follow the holds.

- Hours

- Rates

- Lessons & Parties

this Web page
appears when you
click the Tour link

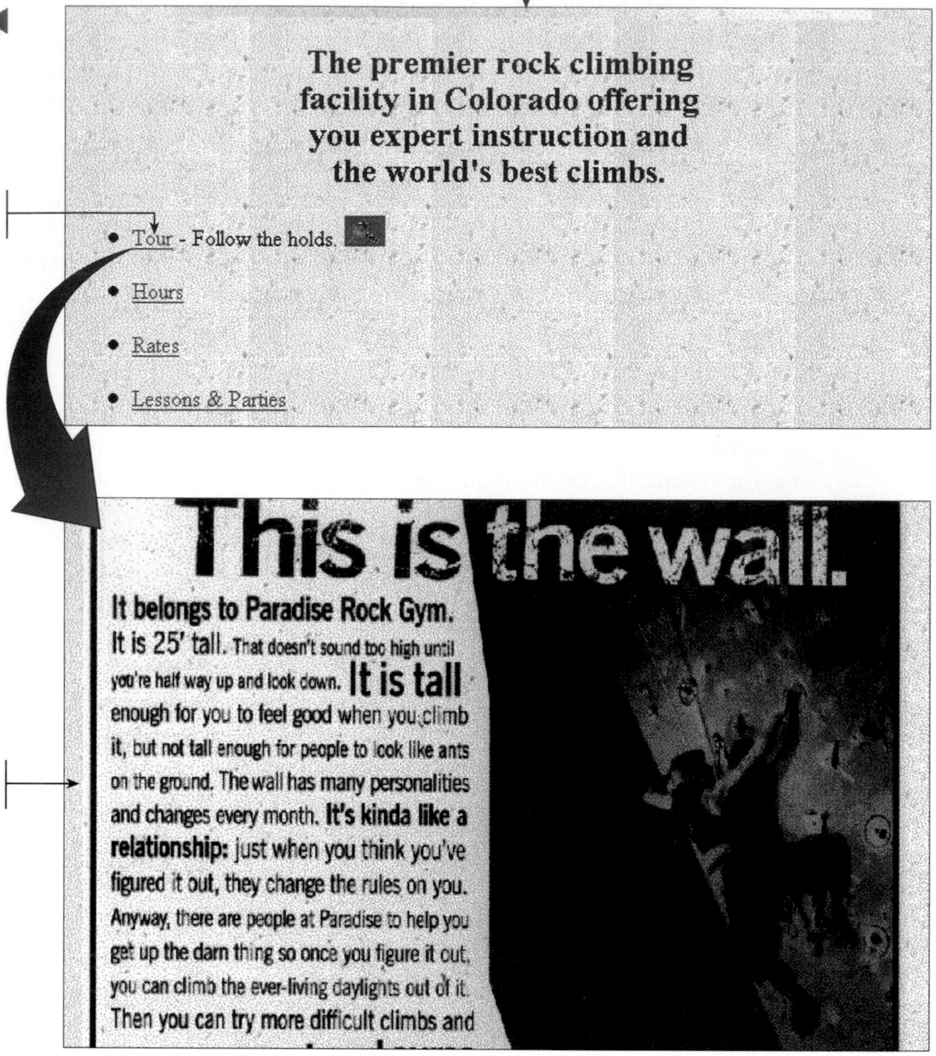

This is the wall.

It belongs to Paradise Rock Gym.
It is 25′ tall. That doesn't sound too high until
you're half way up and look down. **It is tall**
enough for you to feel good when you climb
it, but not tall enough for people to look like ants
on the ground. The wall has many personalities
and changes every month. **It's kinda like a**
relationship: just when you think you've
figured it out, they change the rules on you.
Anyway, there are people at Paradise to help you
get up the darn thing so once you figure it out,
you can climb the ever-living daylights out of it.
Then you can try more difficult climbs and

When you click a link, you can also connect to other file types, including scanned photographs, graphic images, film clips, sounds, and computer programs. A link could lead you into a discussion group called a **forum** or **newsgroup** where users share information on topics of common interest. Another link might point to the e-mail address of an individual (should you want to send a message).

Navigating Web pages using hypertext is an efficient way of accessing information. Michelle points out that when you read a book you follow a linear progression, reading one page after another. With hypertext, you progress through the pages in whatever order you want. Hypertext allows you to skip from one topic to another, following the information path that interests you, as shown in Figure 4.

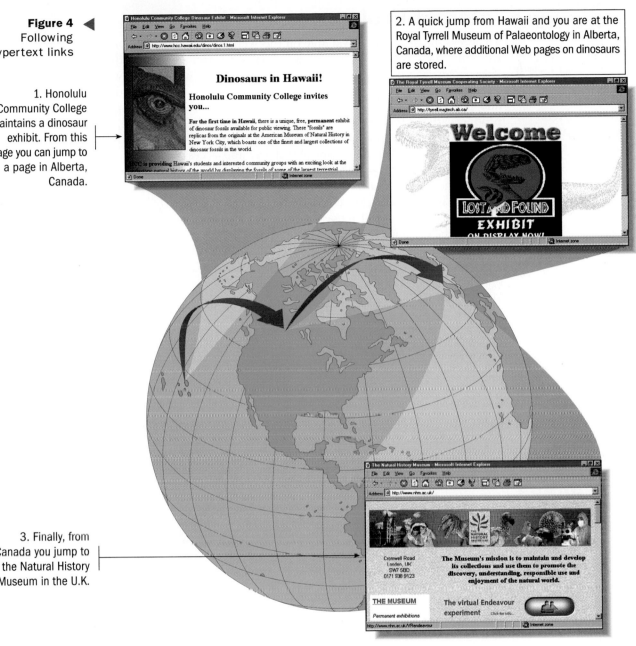

Figure 4
Following hypertext links

1. Honolulu Community College maintains a dinosaur exhibit. From this page you can jump to a page in Alberta, Canada.

2. A quick jump from Hawaii and you are at the Royal Tyrrell Museum of Palaeontology in Alberta, Canada, where additional Web pages on dinosaurs are stored.

3. Finally, from Canada you jump to the Natural History Museum in the U.K.

Hypertext has great appeal because a single Internet user can jump from one set of hypertext documents to another set without much effort. Perhaps the greatest source of the Web's popularity, however, lies in the ease with which users can create their own Web pages. All you need is an account on a computer connected to the Internet that allows you to store your Web page and make it available for others to read. Many companies that sell access to the Internet, called **Internet Service Providers** or **ISPs**, include Web pages as part of their service.

Internet Explorer

INTERNET EXPLORER 3

Internet Explorer 3 is a standalone browser and does not include any of the suite components that come with the Internet Explorer 4 suite. Version 3 is, however, designed to work with other Microsoft products, including Microsoft Outlook for e-mail, Microsoft Word for Web page editing, and Internet News for newsgroups.

INTERNET EXPLORER 3

Internet Explorer 3 offers only the browser installation. This tutorial assumes a complete installation of version 3.

To access the documents available on the Web, to communicate with others, and to publish your own Web page, you need special software. Until recently, you needed to purchase one program, called a **browser**, to view and work with Web pages, another to communicate with e-mail or participate in group discussions, and yet another to create and publish a Web page. Software developers are now producing **suites**, or groups of products, that allow you to be active on the Web with a single, seamlessly integrated package. **Internet Explorer** is Microsoft Corporation's Web software suite. It provides all the tools you need to communicate, share, and access information on the World Wide Web, and for this reason it is Northern University's product of choice. Michelle plans to use Internet Explorer at the workshop because it is easy to use and understand.

A note in the margin, like this one, is an example of a note for users of Internet Explorer 3. These margin notes will appear throughout this tutorial whenever there are differences between the versions.

Michelle provides the following overview of the tools available in various installations and versions of Internet Explorer. She emphasizes that you shouldn't worry if you don't understand the functions of each component right now. You'll learn more about the individual Internet Explorer tools later.

You can obtain either the Browser Only, Standard, or Full installation of Internet Explorer. The Browser Only installation features browsing capabilities. The Standard installation adds e-mail and newsgroup capabilities. The Full installation adds conferencing, presentation, Web page creation, and additional functions to the Standard installation. This book assumes a Full installation. Figure 5 lists the most significant services Internet Explorer provides for each installation.

Figure 5 ◄
Internet Explorer 4 components

INTERNET EXPLORER 3

Figure 5 applies only to Internet Explorer 4.

Service	Description
Browser Only	
Internet Explorer	Browser that retrieves, displays, and organizes documents. These documents are retrieved from Web servers and displayed on your computer.
Standard adds the following:	
Outlook Express	E-mail and newsgroup manager that allows you to send, receive, compose, edit, search, and sort e-mail. **E-mail**, or electronic mail, is a note you write and send across the Internet. Outlook Express can handle e-mail containing practically any file type—graphics, sounds, videos and so on. Outlook Express also functions as a newsgroup manager that helps you participate in a discussion group.
Full adds the following:	
NetMeeting	Video, audio, and data conferencing software that allows you to meet and collaborate with others in real time.
NetShow	Online application software that helps you integrate audio and video into online presentations.
FrontPage Express	Web page editor that you use to create and edit Web pages.

You can also obtain additional components, useful **add-ons**, or software programs that extend the capabilities of the Internet Explorer suite, from Microsoft's Web site. You install add-ons using instructions that come with them; once an add-on is installed, Internet Explorer uses the add-on's capabilities just like other built-in Internet Explorer features.

Michelle wants to keep the workshop simple, focusing only on navigating the Web rather than on e-mail, newsgroups, and Web page publishing. Thus, she will use only the browser component of Internet Explorer in her presentation.

What Is Internet Explorer?

With Internet Explorer, you can visit sites around the world; view multimedia documents; transfer files, images, and sounds to your computer; conduct searches for specific topics; and run software on other computers. Underneath the surface, Internet Explorer is running a variety of Internet services, but because Internet Explorer handles the commands for you, you can be blissfully unaware of the complexity of what really happens when you navigate the Web.

When a user tries to view a Web page, the user's browser, in this case Internet Explorer, locates and retrieves the document from the Web server and displays its contents on the user's computer. As shown in Figure 6, the server stores the Web page in one location, and browsers anywhere in the world can view it.

Figure 6 ◀
Using a
browser to
view a Web
page on a
server

Internet
Explorer browser

browser in California
locates and displays
document stored on
server in Florida

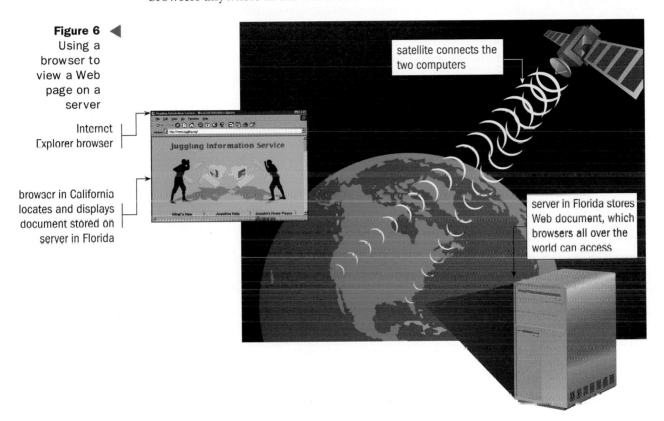

Here, a browser in California is accessing a document stored on a Web server in Florida. You might retrieve such a page without knowing or caring on which Web server it is stored. The wonder of the World Wide Web is that you can view a document stored on a Web server across the room or across the world using the same technique. Information stored on a server in Cairo is just as accessible as is one in Cleveland. Is there any doubt why the Web has been called the "Information Superhighway"?

Starting Internet Explorer

Before you can start using Internet Explorer to explore the Web, you must have an Internet connection. In a university setting your connection might come from the campus network on which you have an account. If you are working on a home computer, your connection might come over the phone line from an account with an Internet Service Provider. How you connect to the Internet depends on what service you have, but at a university you will most likely already be connected to the Internet and can start Internet Explorer and immediately begin to browse the Web.

Michelle explains that, unlike many other software applications, Internet Explorer does not open with a standard start-up screen. Instead, you see a document called the **home page**—the Web page that appears when you start Internet Explorer. Internet

Explorer allows each computer installation to specify what home page users will see when they start Internet Explorer. When you launch Internet Explorer, you might see:

- The Microsoft Corporation home page
- Your school's or institution's home page
- A page your technical support person sets as the default
- A blank page

A home page can also refer to the Web page that a person, organization, or business has created to give information about itself. A home page might include information about the host, links to other sites, or relevant graphics and sounds. When Michelle starts Internet Explorer from home, she connects to the Microsoft Corporation home page, which provides fundamental information about Microsoft and its software. When she starts it in the university's lab, she sees Northern University's home page, stored on a Web server at Northern University.

REFERENCE window

STARTING INTERNET EXPLORER

- Click the Start button, point to Programs, point to the Internet Explorer program group, then click Internet Explorer.

or

- If your desktop displays an Internet icon that starts Internet Explorer, click or double-click that icon, depending on your operating system's configuration.

or

- If the Quick Launch toolbar appears on your taskbar with icons for different Internet Explorer components, click the Internet Explorer button right from your taskbar to launch Internet Explorer.

INTERNET EXPLORER 3

Depending on your operating system configuration, this third option might not be available to you with Internet Explorer 3.

These instructions show you how to start Internet Explorer from the Start menu. There are two sets of Steps: one for Internet Explorer 3 and one for Internet Explorer 4. Internet Explorer 3 Steps are preceded by 🅸🅴3 and Internet Explorer 4 Steps by 🅸🅴4. If you are using Internet Explorer 3, follow the Steps marked with 🅸🅴3. If you are using Internet Explorer 4, follow the Steps marked with 🅸🅴4. Steps not marked with either icon can safely be followed by users of both versions, though Internet Explorer 3 users should take special note of marginal notes denoting slight differences. If you aren't sure whether you are using version 3 or 4, click Help, click About Internet Explorer, and note the version number. (If you see additional digits after your version number, such as version 3.02, disregard them.)

To start Internet Explorer 3:

IE 3

1. If necessary, connect to your Internet account.

   TROUBLE? If you are in a university setting, you are probably already connected and can skip Step 1. If you don't know how to connect to your Internet account, ask your technical support person for help or call your Internet Service Provider's technical support line.

2. Click the **Start** button 🏁Start on the Windows taskbar.

3. Point at **Programs** with the mouse pointer. After a short pause, the Programs menu opens with a list of the programs available on your computer, including Internet Explorer. See Figure 7.

Figure 7
Start menu
for Internet
Explorer 3

your menus and
desktop might look
different

point here to open
Programs menu

click to start
Internet Explorer 3

Start button

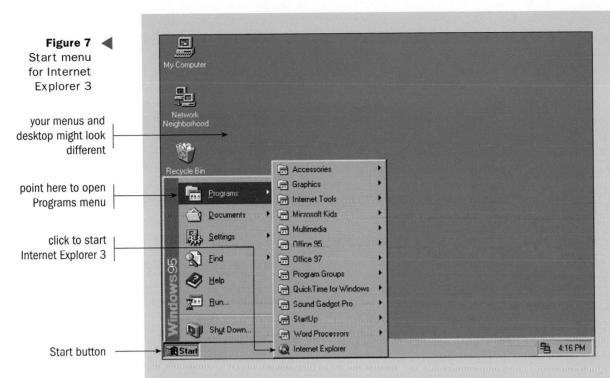

TROUBLE? If you don't see Internet Explorer on the Programs menu, it might be located on a submenu, such as Internet Tools. If you still can't find the Internet Explorer option after searching the most likely submenus, ask your instructor or technical support person for assistance. If you are using your own computer, make sure Internet Explorer is installed.

4. Click **Internet Explorer** to start Internet Explorer. The home page specified by your site's installation will open.

TROUBLE? If this is the first time Internet Explorer has been used on your computer, you might be prompted to establish a connection or to set other settings. If you are using a computer that is not your own, ask your technical support person for assistance. If you are using your own computer, read the instructions, proceed through the dialog boxes that appear, providing information where requested, then click Next when you finish each step. If you reach a dialog box that you don't understand, you might need to call your Internet Service Provider's technical support line for assistance.

5. Click the **Maximize** button ⬜ in the upper-right corner of the Microsoft Internet Explorer window if the window is not already maximized. See Figure 8, which shows the Microsoft Corporation home page.

TROUBLE? If your screen shows a different home page, don't worry.

TROUBLE? If your window looks different, don't worry. You'll soon learn how to customize the Internet Explorer window so that it matches the figures.

Figure 8
Internet
Explorer 3
window

title bar

menu bar

Standard toolbar

Address bar

status bar

activity indicator

Links toolbar; your toolbars might be arranged differently

scroll bar

document window; yours will be different

To start Internet Explorer 4:

IE 4

1. If necessary, connect to your Internet account.

TROUBLE? If you are in a university setting you are probably already connected and can skip Step 1. If you don't know how to connect to your Internet account, ask your technical support person for help or call your Internet Service Provider's technical support line.

2. Click the **Start** button [Start] on the Windows taskbar.

3. Point at **Programs** with the mouse pointer. After a short pause, the Programs menu opens with a list of the programs available on your computer.

4. Point at **Internet Explorer** on the Programs menu, then point at **Internet Explorer** on the Internet Explorer menu. See Figure 9.

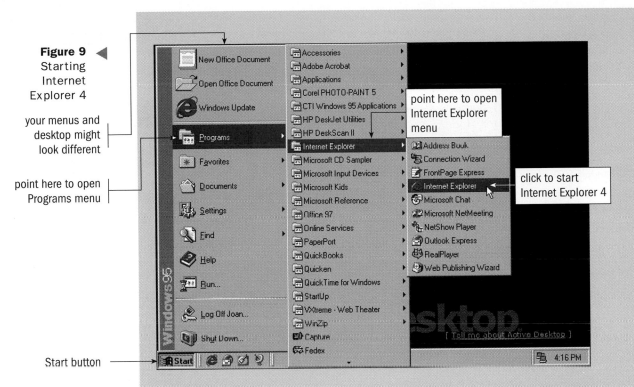

Figure 9 ◀
Starting
Internet
Explorer 4

your menus and
desktop might
look different

point here to open
Programs menu

Start button

TROUBLE? If you don't see Internet Explorer on the Programs menu, ask your instructor or technical support person for assistance. If you are using your own computer, make sure Internet Explorer is installed.

TROUBLE? If you are running a browser-only installation of Internet Explorer 4, you will not see all of the Internet Explorer components shown in Figure 9.

TROUBLE? If your Internet Explorer menu shows different entries, don't worry. You just have a different version of Internet Explorer.

5. Click **Internet Explorer** to start Internet Explorer. The home page specified by your site's installation will open.

TROUBLE? If this is the first time Internet Explorer has been used on your computer, you might be prompted to establish a connection or to set other **settings**. If you are using a computer that is not your own, ask your technical support person for assistance. If you are using your own computer, read the instructions, proceed through the dialog boxes that appear, providing information where requested (such as your e-mail address), then click Next when you finish each step. If you reach a dialog box that you don't understand, you might need to call your Internet Service Provider's technical support line for assistance.

6. Click the **Maximize** button ▢ in the upper-right corner of the Microsoft Internet Explorer window if the window is not already maximized. See Figure 10, which shows the Microsoft Corporation home page.

TROUBLE? If your screen shows a different home page, don't worry.

TROUBLE? If your window looks different, don't worry. You'll soon learn how to customize the Internet Explorer window so that it matches the figures.

Figure 10 ◀
Internet
Explorer 4
window

title bar

menu bar

Standard toolbar

Address bar

document window;
yours will be different

Quick Launch bar

status bar

Regardless of which page appears when you first start Internet Explorer—the Microsoft home page, your university's home page, or a different home page—your window should share some common components with the one in Figure 10. Michelle points out the most important parts of the Internet Explorer window, shown in Figure 11. Don't worry if you don't see all these components. You'll soon learn how to make them appear.

Figure 11 ◀
Internet
Explorer window
components

Window component	Description
Title bar	Identifies the active Web page.
Menu bar	Groups Internet Explorer commands by menu name. You click a menu name to open a menu, and then click the command you want.
Standard toolbar	Offers single-click access to the more common menu commands.
Address bar	Identifies the address of the active Web page—the one currently displayed in the Internet Explorer document window. The address of a Web page is called its **uniform resource locator**, or **URL**. You'll learn more about URLs in the next session.
Links toolbar	Displays buttons that you can click to jump immediately to individual Web pages. You can add buttons for your personal favorites.
Quick Launch bar	Displays buttons that you can click to access different components of Internet Explorer.
Document window	Displays the active Web page.
Scroll bars	Allows you to move through the active page content. Click the up and down arrows on the vertical scroll bar to move the page up and down, or less frequently, the left and right arrows on the horizontal scroll bar to move the page left and right. You can also drag the scroll box or click above and below it to move through a page.
Activity indicator	Displays the Internet Explorer logo, which appears as a rotating globe [image] when a page is loading and [image] when the browser is idle. If the activity indicator is idle but the page doesn't seem to have been successfully retrieved, you know there is a problem with the connection.
Status bar	Indicates the status of the document you are retrieving from the Web server.

INTERNET EXPLORER 3

The Quick Launch toolbar will probably not appear for Internet Explorer 3 users (unless you are running Internet Explorer 3 on a Windows 98 computer and have added an Internet Explorer 3 icon).

Controlling the Internet Explorer Display

The Internet Explorer window looks different depending on what objects are displayed, such as the Address or Links bars, Standard toolbar, or an Explorer bar. You can easily drag toolbars to different locations so that more of the document window is available, or you can hide toolbars if you aren't likely to use them. You can also display the buttons with only icons instead of icons with Text Labels—again, to make more space available in the document window. For now, you want to display only the Standard toolbar with icons (not Text Labels) and the Address bar.

To control the Internet Explorer display for version 3:

IE 3

1. Click **View**, click **Options**, and then, if necessary, click the **General** tab. First, you'll experiment with displaying and moving the Links toolbar.

2. Make sure all five checkboxes are checked in the Toolbar area, as shown in Figure 12. If any checkboxes are not checked, click them to select them.

Figure 12 ◀
Checking
Internet
Explorer 3
display options

General tab is
selected

these options might
be unavailable on
your computer

make sure all five
check boxes are
selected

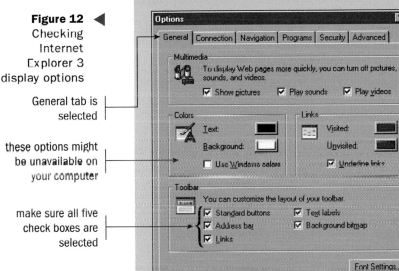

3. Click the **OK** button.

4. Click **View** to open the View menu. Notice the Toolbar and the Status Bar options. The presence of a checkmark indicates whether that object or feature is enabled. For example, if the second option in the View menu—Status Bar—has a checkmark next to it, the status bar is visible.

5. If Toolbar is not preceded by a checkmark, click **Toolbar**. Then reopen the View menu. If Status Bar is not preceded by a checkmark, click **Status Bar**. Click **View** one last time to ensure that both Toolbar and Status Bar are preceded by a checkmark.

   TROUBLE? If either option is not preceded by a checkmark when you click View one last time, click the option that is not checked. Then repeat Steps 4 and 5.

6. Now practice dragging the Links toolbar to a new location. To drag a toolbar, you will use the vertical bar that precedes it, as shown in Figure 13. Point at the vertical bar in front of the Links toolbar. The pointer changes from ↕ to ↔. Now drag the Links toolbar below the Address bar.

   TROUBLE? If the Links toolbar is already below the Address bar, drag it above the Address bar.

7. Drag the Links toolbar to the right of the Address bar.

8. Now resize the Links toolbar. Point at the vertical bar preceding the Links toolbar. Drag the vertical bar to the left. The Links toolbar is enlarged. The Address bar shrinks.

9. Now hide the Links toolbar, because you don't need it in this tutorial. Click **View**, click **Options**, and then click the **General** tab. Click the **Links** check box and the **Text labels** check box to deselect these options. Click the **OK** button. The Links toolbar disappears, the Address bar enlarges to the entire width of the window, and the text labels disappear from the Standard toolbar buttons. Compare your screen to Figure 13.

Figure 13
Final Internet Explorer 3 display

vertical bar allows you to move and resize toolbar

only Standard toolbar and Address bar are visible

buttons show only icons, not text labels

To control the Internet Explorer display for version 4:

IE 4

1. Click **View** to open the View menu and then point to **Toolbars**. The commands you see control the presence or absence of objects and their features in the Internet Explorer window. The presence of a checkmark indicates whether that object or feature is enabled. For example, if the second command in the View menu, Status Bar, has a checkmark next to it, the status bar is visible. Figure 14 shows a screen whose status bar is visible, whose Standard, Address, and Links toolbars are all visible, and whose buttons show text labels. Notice on the menu that all these commands have checkmarks next to them.

   TROUBLE? If fewer toolbars are displayed on your screen or if they are organized differently, don't worry. You'll learn to control the position of the toolbars in the next steps.

Internet
Explorer

Figure 14
Viewing status
of Internet
Explorer 4
display

Standard toolbar
is visible, with
Text Labels

Address bar is visible

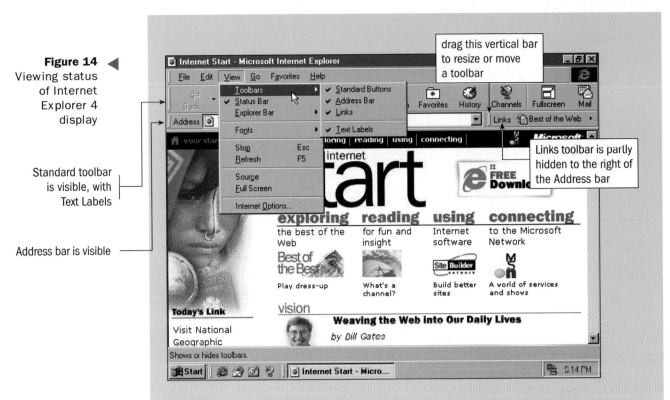

drag this vertical bar
to resize or move
a toolbar

Links toolbar is partly
hidden to the right of
the Address bar

2. Now you'll experiment with hiding a toolbar. Look at the Toolbars submenu, which should still be open and note whether Links has a checkmark next to it. If it does, click **Links**. The Links toolbar disappears.

3. Click **View**, point at **Toolbars**, and then click **Links**, which should not have a checkmark next to it, again. The Links toolbar reappears in its previous position.

4. Now practice dragging the Links toolbar to a new location. To drag a toolbar, drag the vertical bar that precedes it, as shown in Figure 14. Point at the vertical bar in front of the Links toolbar. The pointer changes from ⬚ to ↔. Now drag the Links toolbar below the Address bar. As you drag, the pointer changes to ⬚.

   TROUBLE? If the Links toolbar is already below the Address bar, drag it above the Address bar.

   TROUBLE? If your Address bar isn't visible, click View, point to Toolbars, click Address Bar, and then repeat Step 4.

5. Drag the Links toolbar to the right of the Address bar.

6. Now resize the Links toolbar. Point at the vertical bar preceding the Links toolbar. Drag the vertical bar to the left. The Links toolbar is enlarged. The Address bar shrinks.

7. Now hide the Links toolbar, because you don't need it in this tutorial. Click **View**, point to **Toolbars**, and then click **Links**. The Links toolbar disappears and the Address bar enlarges to the entire width of the window.

8. Click **View** and then point to **Toolbars**. If there is a checkmark next to the Text Labels command in the Toolbar submenu, click **Text Labels** to remove the checkmark. The toolbar buttons now appear without Text Labels.

9. Click **View** once more, point to **Explorer Bar**, and click **None** to ensure no Explorer bars are visible. Compare your screen to Figure 15.

The components of your Internet Explorer window should now match the figures. Michelle can now begin demonstrating how to navigate the Web.

Navigating the Web

Once you are connected to the Internet and you have started the Internet Explorer browser, you can view Web pages using several different methods. If you have a Web page in the form of a file on a disk, you can simply open that page in your browser. If you are currently viewing a page with links, you can also click a link to activate it and jump to that page. You'll practice both methods now.

Opening a Web Page

Michelle has prepared a Web page that she will use at the workshop because she wants to be able to start from the same point from any computer, regardless of what home page appears in the document window. Michelle's Web page file is provided on your Student Disk. You'll open it in the Internet Explorer browser, and then you will be viewing the same page shown in the figures and you will be able to navigate the same links.

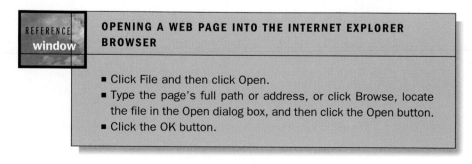

REFERENCE window

OPENING A WEB PAGE INTO THE INTERNET EXPLORER BROWSER

- Click File and then click Open.
- Type the page's full path or address, or click Browse, locate the file in the Open dialog box, and then click the Open button.
- Click the OK button.

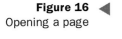

Keep in mind that you are opening Michelle's file off your Student Disk, not off the Web. You can use the Internet Explorer browser to view Web page files on your Student Disk, on your computer's other drives, and on Web servers around the world. You'll learn how to view a file on the Web in Session 1.2.

To open a specific Web page:

1. Place your Student Disk in drive A. See the "Read This Before You Begin" page to make sure you are using the correct disk for this tutorial.

   TROUBLE? If you are using drive B, place your Student Disk in that drive instead, and for the rest of these tutorials substitute drive B wherever you see drive A.

2. Click **File** and then click **Open**.

3. Type **a:\Tutorial.01\michelle.htm** as shown in Figure 16.

   TROUBLE? If you are using drive B, type b:\Tutorial.01\Michelle.htm instead.

Figure 16 ◄
Opening a page

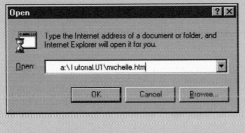

4. Click the **OK** button. The Web page Michelle has prepared for the workshop opens. See Figure 17.

Figure 17 ◄
Michelle's
workshop page

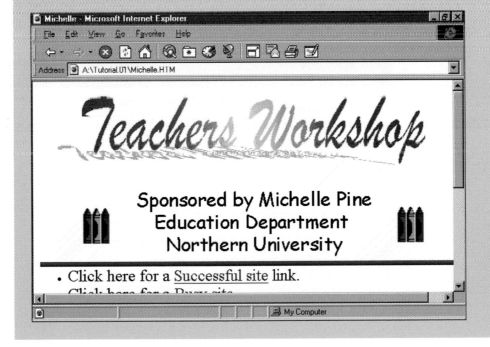

A hypertext link on the Web, like a link in a chain, is a connector between two points. Links can appear in two ways: as text that you click or as a graphic that you click. A **text link** is a word or phrase that is underlined and often boldfaced or colored differently. A graphic link is a graphic image that you click to jump to another location. When you aren't sure whether a graphic image is a link, point to it with the mouse pointer. When you move the mouse pointer over a link—text or graphic—it changes shape from ⌖ to ⌧. The ⌧ pointer indicates that when you click, you will activate that link and jump to the new location. The destination of the link appears in the status bar, and for some graphic links a small identification box appears next to your pointer.

As you'll see, Michelle's workshop pages contain both text and graphic links. The text links are underlined and in color. Each link gives Internet Explorer the information it needs to locate the page. When you activate a link, you jump to a new location, called the **target** of the link, which can be another location on the active Web page (for example, often the bottom of a Web page contains a link that jumps you up to the top), a different document or file, or a Web page stored on a remote Web server anywhere in the world.

When you activate a link, there are three possible outcomes:

1. You successfully reach the target of the link. Internet Explorer contacts the site (host) you want, connects into the site, transfers the data from the host to your computer, and displays the data on your screen.

2. The link's target is busy, perhaps because the server storing the link's target is overwhelmed with too many requests. You'll have to try a different link, or try this link later.

3. The link points to a target that doesn't exist. Documents are often removed from Web servers as they become obsolete, or they are moved to new locations, and links that point to those documents are not updated.

The amount of time it takes to complete a link, called the **response time**, can vary, depending upon the number of people trying to connect to the same site, the number of people on the Internet at that time, and the site design.

Activating a Link

Activating a link starts a multi-step process. Although Internet Explorer does the work for you, it is important to follow the sequence of events so you can recognize problems when they occur and understand how to resolve them.

Figure 18 illustrates the string of events that occur when you link to a site. When you point to a link, the status bar displays a message that it is connecting to the address of the link's target, called its **Uniform Resource Locator** or **URL**. When you click a link the activity indicator animates. The status bar displays a series of messages indicating that Internet Explorer is opening the host (or site) you want to visit and is waiting for a reply, is transferring data, and finally, is done.

Figure 18
Activating
a link

progress bar
begins to fill in

status bar message
shows part of URL

each pass fills in
more detail

progress bar
continues to expand

status bar continues
to display progress

page is complete

document is done

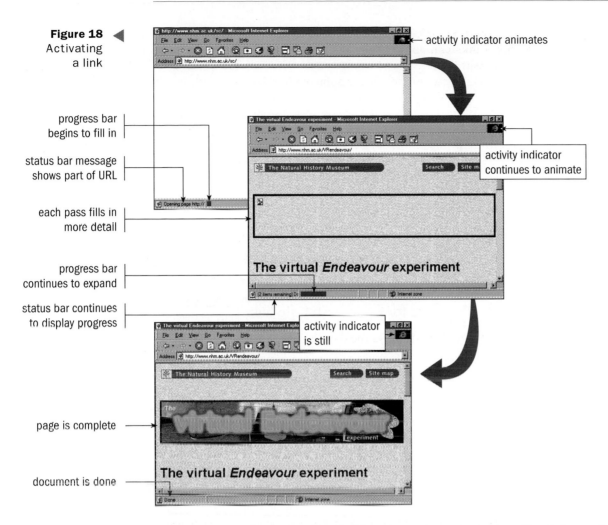

activity indicator animates

activity indicator
continues to animate

activity indicator
is still

You can see the Web page build as Internet Explorer transfers information to your screen in multiple passes. The first wave brings a few pieces to the page, and with each subsequent pass, Internet Explorer fills in more detail until the material is complete. The progress bar fills in to indicate how much of the Web page has transferred. The vertical scroll box scrolls up as Internet Explorer adds more information and detail to the page. You don't have to wait until the page is complete before scrolling or clicking another link, but it might be difficult to determine links and other information until the page is mostly filled in.

Michelle's page contains links that let you experience each of the three outcomes mentioned earlier. First, you'll successfully activate a link.

To initiate a link to a Web page:

1. If necessary, scroll through Michelle's page until you find the "Click here for a Successful site link" sentence.

2. Point at the **Successful site** link. Notice that the pointer changes shape from ↖ to 🖑, indicating that you are pointing to a hypertext link. The status bar shows the URL for that link. See Figure 19.

Figure 19 ◄
Pointing to
a link

link's target appears
in status bar

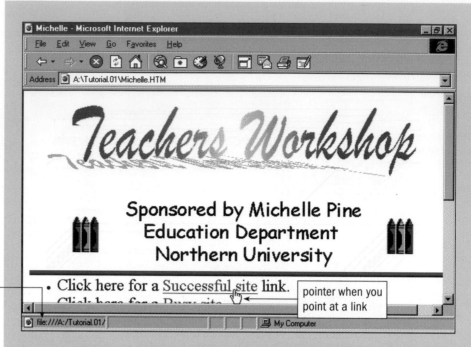

TROUBLE? If the status message area does not contain a URL, slowly move your pointer over the underlined words. When you see the URL in the status message area, the pointer is positioned correctly.

3. Click the **Successful site** link to activate the link. The status bar notes the progress of the link. When the status bar displays, "Done," the link is complete and the Web page that is the target of the link appears. See Figure 20.

TROUBLE? If a message dialog box opens, the link was not successful. Click the OK button to close the dialog box, and repeat Steps 1 through 3. After you click the hypertext link, make sure you do not click anywhere else on the page until the link is complete.

Figure 20 ◄
Completed
link

graphic link

text link

status bar indicates
link is complete

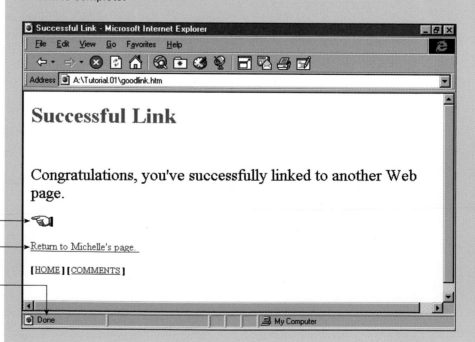

4. Move the pointer over the graphic image of a pointing hand. The pointer changes to ☝ and the URL of Michelle's page appears in the status bar. This is a graphic link; to return to Michelle's page you could click it or the text link below it.

5. Click the **pointing hand** graphic link to return to Michelle's page.

You connected to a Web page with a single click, and then you used the graphic link in that page to return to Michelle's page. Using hypertext links is a simple way to move from one Web page to another. Notice that the Successful site link on Michelle's page has changed color (you might need to scroll down to see this). Internet Explorer displays text links you've already activated in a different color so you know which links you've already tried.

Aborting a Busy Link

Sometimes when you try to connect to a site, the link is not successful. Much like an expressway, the Internet can become so congested that the paths cannot support the number of users at peak times. When this happens, traffic backs up and slows to a halt, in effect closing the road. At these peak times, the load is too heavy for the Internet.

Aborting, or interrupting, a link is like taking the next exit ramp on the Internet. When the response time to a link seems too slow (longer than a few minutes) or nothing seems to be happening, you have no way of knowing how long it will take to complete a link. You can tell that a link is stalled when one of the following situations occurs:

1. the status message area does not change, but

2. the Stop button 🔘 on the toolbar is active, and

3. the activity indicator is animated 🔲

Rather than waiting for a site that has a long queue or is so busy it can't even respond to your request, you can abort the link.

Michelle wants to show the workshop how to stop an unsuccessful link. There is one site that she has tried to visit many times but has been unsuccessful. She asks you to try to link to that site.

To abort a delayed link:

1. Scroll down until you see the list of Busy site links on Michelle's page. The Busy site links target sites that are often busy—though they might not be when you perform Step 2.

2. Click the **Busy site** link to initiate the link. Watch the status message area; if the site is busy, it comes to a halt, although the activity indicator remains animated and the Stop button active. The link is stalled. See Figure 21. The line to visit this site might be very long, or many people might be using the Internet and you just can't get to the site. Either way, you'll want to abort the link rather than wait an interminable amount of time.

Figure 21
Stalled link

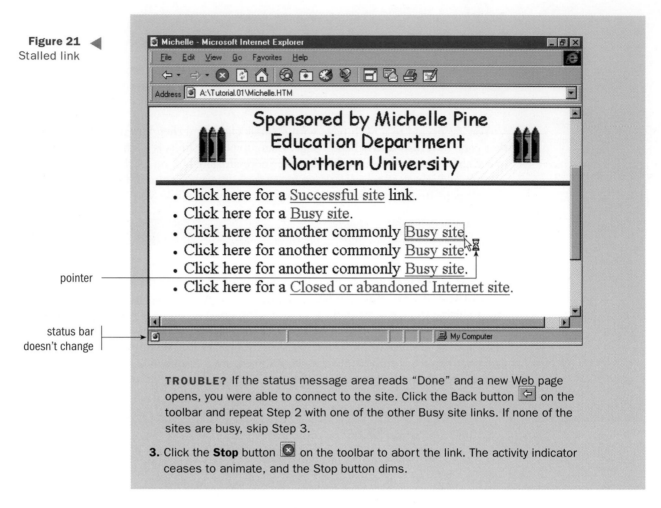

pointer

status bar
doesn't change

TROUBLE? If the status message area reads "Done" and a new Web page opens, you were able to connect to the site. Click the Back button [⇐] on the toolbar and repeat Step 2 with one of the other Busy site links. If none of the sites are busy, skip Step 3.

3. Click the **Stop** button [⊗] on the toolbar to abort the link. The activity indicator ceases to animate, and the Stop button dims.

Now try a link that no longer exists.

Activating a Defunct Link

Michelle wants to show the workshop that a link not only might complete successfully or stall, but that it might also be aborted by Internet Explorer. She explains that Internet Explorer terminates a link and displays an error message indicating the site was not found because:

■ The URL specified by the hypertext link might no longer be active.

■ The URL might be typed incorrectly.

■ The server could not reach the site within the server's programmed wait time (for example, 90 seconds).

When such a message dialog box appears, you have no choice but to acknowledge the message and give up.

To end an Internet Explorer–terminated link:

1. If necessary, scroll down the page, then click the **Closed or abandoned Internet site** link to initiate a link to a nonexistent site. A message dialog box opens. See Figure 22. The dialog box indicates that Internet Explorer is unable to locate the server containing the target of the link.

Figure 22 ◀
Terminated link

INTERNET EXPLORER 3

Don't worry if the message dialog box in Internet Explorer 3 looks slightly different.

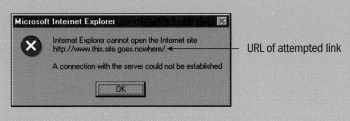

URL of attempted link

2. Click the **OK** button to close the dialog box.

In this case, Internet Explorer aborted the link because it could not establish a connection with the server. The server supposedly storing the target of the link does not have a proper domain name. Every host is part of a **domain**, or group, that has a unique name, similar to a family surname. Just as family members can share a surname yet live in separate households both nearby and far away, a domain contains one or more hosts that might be at the same physical location or spread great distances apart. Some domains are small and contain just a few hosts. Others are very large and contain hundreds of hosts. An educational institution or a government agency might each have its own domain name.

Each host can have a domain name registered with the **Domain Name Server (DNS)**. When you link to a site, Internet Explorer checks to see if the domain in its URL is registered with the DNS. If the site is not registered (similar to an unlisted telephone number in the phone book), Internet Explorer opens the message dialog box. Unless you know the correct URL for that site, you cannot link to it.

Working with Frames

Michelle wants to illustrate one more navigational concept. Web page designers often divide their pages into parts, called frames, to organize their information more effectively. A **frame** is a section of the document window. Each frame can have its own set of scroll bars and can display the contents of a different location. Many Web sites today employ frames because they allow the user to see different areas of information simultaneously. When you scroll through the contents of one frame, you do not affect the other frame or frames.

Michelle wants you to demonstrate frames using a page that she is designing for Northern University and the Education Department, listing available degree programs. She's included a link for this page on her main page.

To scroll through a frame:

1. Scroll to the bottom of Michelle's page until you see the "Click here to see how frames work" sentence.

2. Click the **frames** link. Figure 23 shows the page that opens. It contains three frames. The top frame identifies the page as that of the Education Department. The frame on the left identifies the two types of undergraduate programs—certification and noncertification—and the right frame displays information about the programs.

Figure 23
Web page
with frames

Fullscreen button

top frame
identifies page

left frame
contains links

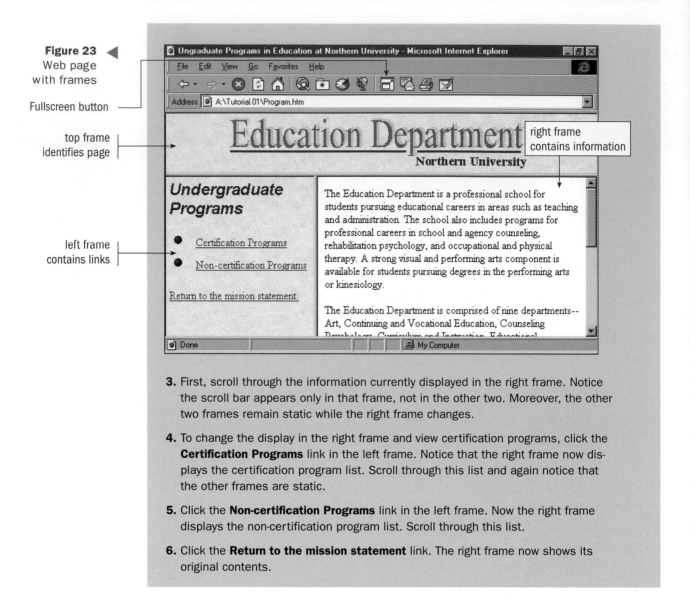

3. First, scroll through the information currently displayed in the right frame. Notice the scroll bar appears only in that frame, not in the other two. Moreover, the other two frames remain static while the right frame changes.

4. To change the display in the right frame and view certification programs, click the **Certification Programs** link in the left frame. Notice that the right frame now displays the certification program list. Scroll through this list and again notice that the other frames are static.

5. Click the **Non-certification Programs** link in the left frame. Now the right frame displays the non-certification program list. Scroll through this list.

6. Click the **Return to the mission statement** link. The right frame now shows its original contents.

INTERNET EXPLORER 3

There is no Fullscreen button in Internet Explorer 3. You can hide the toolbars and status bar to view more of the Web page in version 3. Skip the following steps if you are using Version 3.

By using frames, Michelle has made it possible for users to examine only the information they are interested in. Knowing how to recognize and navigate frames is increasingly important because many Web pages now use them.

Pages with frames often contain a great deal of information, and you might want to display more of it on your screen. Internet Explorer offers a Fullscreen button on the Standard toolbar, which you can click, to make the active Web page take up the maximum amount of space on your screen.

To view the Education Department Web page at full screen capacity:

1. Click the **Fullscreen** button ⊟. The title, status, and menu bars disappear, the toolbars collapse, and you see as much of the Web page as possible.

2. Click ⊟ to restore the display.

Exiting Internet Explorer

Michelle decides to take a break in the workshop. Before you leave the computer, you need to close Internet Explorer. The next time you start Internet Explorer, the window will show the home page designated for your installation. To return to a site you visited in this session, you will need to reopen the Web page and link to the sites you want to see.

To exit Internet Explorer:

1. Click **File**.

2. Click **Close**. The Internet Explorer window closes.

You have completed Session 1.1. You have opened Internet Explorer, opened a Web page in the Internet Explorer browser, linked to a site successfully, aborted a stalled link, had Internet Explorer terminate a link for you, and experimented with frames.

Quick Check

[1] True or False: When you start Internet Explorer, you will always see the same screen, no matter what computer you are using.

[2] What is a home page?

[3] The address of a Web page is called a(n) _____.

[4] How does Internet Explorer display a text link that you've already activated?

[5] When you try to link to a Web site but the page you want does not immediately appear, you might need to _____ the link because of congestion on the Internet.

[6] What does Internet Explorer mean when it tells you, "The server does not have a DNS entry"?

SESSION

2

In this session, you will learn more about URLs and how to open a Web page using its URL, how to navigate the Web with Internet Explorer using toolbar buttons, how to speed up things by viewing images on demand, how to print Web pages, and how to use the online Help feature.

Opening a Location with a URL

Michelle now wants to show the instructors how to locate specific Web pages and how to use them in their classes. Some of the educators mention that they've read journal articles about integrating the Internet into the curricula for all age groups. These articles usually supply Internet addresses for helpful online resources. Michelle explains how to access these sites.

Clicking a hypertext link is just one way of jumping to a Web page. Clicking links, often called "surfing," is an easy way to navigate the Web when you don't have a specific destination in mind and just want to follow content links. Often, however, you want to visit a particular site. In order to get to that site, you need to know its address, which must be in a certain form. Entering the Uniform Resource Locator (URL) for a Web page is a direct route to get to a specific site.

A URL is composed of a protocol identifier, a server address, and a file pathname. For example, when Michelle saves the undergraduate program list she is creating for the Education Department, it will have the following URL:

http://www.northern.edu/education/program.html

protocol   server address   file pathname

Computers use standardized procedures, called **protocols**, to transmit files. Web documents travel between sites using **HyperText Transfer Protocol** or **HTTP**, so every URL for a Web page begins with "http://" to identify its type. Another common protocol you might see is **File Transfer Protocol**, or **FTP**, a protocol that facilitates transferring files over the Web.

The server address contains the domain name and tells the exact location of the Internet server and the type of organization that owns and operates it. For example, in the domain name "www.northern.edu" the "www" indicates that the server is on the World Wide Web, "northern" indicates the name of the organization that owns the server (Northern University), and "edu" indicates that it's an educational site. The entire domain name tells you that Northern is an educational site on the Web. Figure 24 lists common domain name types. Outside the United States, domain name types include a two-letter country code. For example, "fi" indicates that the server is located in Finland.

Figure 24 ◀
Domain name
types

Domain	Description	Domain	Description	Domain	Description
au	Australia	fr	France	net	Networking organizations
ca	Canada	gov	Government agencies	org	Nonprofit organizations
com	Commercial sites	int	International organizations	uk	United Kingdom
de	Germany	jp	Japan		
edu	Educational institutions	mil	Military sites		

All files stored on a network server must have a unique pathname just as files on a disk do. The pathname includes the folder or folders the file is stored in, plus the filename and its extension. The filename and extension are always the last item in the pathname. The filename extension for Web pages is usually html (or just htm), which stands for hypertext markup language. Michelle's Education Department programs file, for example, is named program.html and is located in the education folder on the Northern server.

Sometimes when you try to go to a specific site, you might see an error message such as the one shown in Figure 25. If you see such an error message, you should check the URL in the Address box on the Address bar and make sure every character is typed correctly, then try again.

Figure 25 ◀
URL Not Found
error message

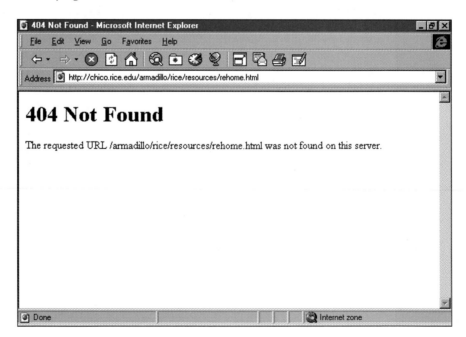

Remembering two important facts about a URL will make it significantly easier to use a URL to access an Internet site:

- Domain names in a URL are case-sensitive. A URL must be typed with the same capitalization shown. The URL http://www.Mysite.com is different from http://WWW.mysite.com. Unless the server can interpret case-sensitive addresses, you will get an error message when a URL doesn't exist with the exact name and capitalization entered. Whether you copy a URL from a magazine article or get it from a friend, make sure you copy the characters and their cases exactly.

- Internet sites continuously undergo name and address changes. A network server might have changed names, the file might be stored in a different folder, or the page you want might no longer be available. Remember, no one person or organization controls the Internet. Organizations and individuals can add files, rename them, and delete them at will. Often when a URL changes, you can find the forwarding address (URL) at the old URL. Other times, a site will simply vanish from a server, with no forwarding information.

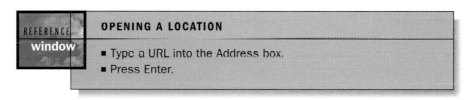

REFERENCE
window

OPENING A LOCATION

- Type a URL into the Address box.
- Press Enter.

Lyle Sanchez, one of the educators, wants to find an interesting site that he can show his students as an "in class field trip." He asks you to help him. You are going to use a set of Web pages designed by the publisher of this book for this tutorial. The URL for the Web page you need is http://www.course.com/downloads/NewPerspectives/msie4. You can type this URL directly in the Address box on the Address bar.

To open a location:

1. Launch Internet Explorer and make sure Standard and Address toolbars are visible and the buttons display icons without Text Labels.

   TROUBLE? If you need help starting Internet Explorer or setting the options, refer to the appropriate sections earlier in this tutorial.

2. Click the **Address** box to highlight the current entry, which should be the URL for your home page.

   TROUBLE? If the current entry is not highlighted, highlight it manually by dragging the mouse from the far left to the far right of the URL. The entire entry must be highlighted so that the new URL you type replaces the current entry.

3. Type **http://www.course.com/downloads/NewPerspectives/msie4** in the Address box. Make sure you type the URL exactly as shown. Notice the two slashes after the protocol identifier; the protocol identifier is always followed by the two slashes. See Figure 26.

Figure 26 ◀
Opening a Web
page with
its URL

4. Press **Enter**. Internet Explorer will follow the same steps as it did when you clicked hypertext to link to a site and will connect you to the selected Web page. See Figure 27.

   TROUBLE? If you receive a Not Found error message, the URL might not be typed correctly. Repeat Steps 2 through 4, making sure that the URL in the Address box matches the one shown in Figure 26. You can correct a minor error by double-clicking in the Address box, using the arrow keys to move to the error, and then making the correction. If the URL matches Figure 26 exactly, or if you see a different error message, press the Enter key to try connecting to the Web page again. If you see the same error message, ask your instructor or technical support person for help.

Figure 27 ◀
Opened
Web page

URL of current
Web page

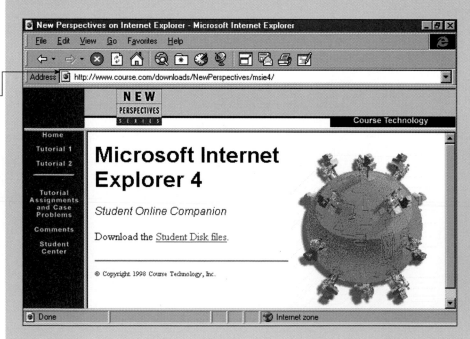

The Web page shown in Figure 27 was designed for Internet Explorer 4, but both Internet Explorer 4 and Internet Explorer 3 users will work with it in this tutorial.

Moving Among Web Pages

In Internet Explorer, you can flip among Web pages you've visited in a session as though they were pages in a magazine that you have held with a finger. Rather than memorizing and retyping URLs of places you have visited, you can use toolbar buttons to move back one page at a time through the pages, move forward again one page at a time, or return to the "front cover" of your home page. Internet Explorer "remembers" which pages you've been to during your current Web session, and it provides navigation buttons on the Standard toolbar so that you can easily move through those pages. See Figure 28.

Figure 28 ◄
Navigation buttons in Internet Explorer

INTERNET EXPLORER 3

In Internet Explorer 3, the Home button is called the Start Page button, though it uses the same icon.

Button	Icon	Description
Back	←	Returns you to the Web page you were most recently viewing. If you click it twice, it returns you to the page you were viewing before that, and so on, until you reach the first page you viewed in the current session. This button is active only when you have viewed more than one Web page in the current session.
Forward	→	Reverses the effect of the Back button, sending you forward to the page from which you just clicked the Back button. This button is active only when you have used the Back button.
Home	⌂	Retrieves your home page, the first page that Internet Explorer displays when you begin a session.

To visit and then move among visited Web pages:

1. Click the **Tutorial 1** link in the left frame of the Web page to open the Learning to Navigate page. This Web page contains hypertext links to educational resource sites available on the Internet. Lyle wants to look at the Field Trips/Museums link.

2. Click the **Field Trips/Museums** link in the Subject Areas list to see the list of sites available from this Web page. See Figure 29.

Figure 29 ◄
Field Trips/Museums list

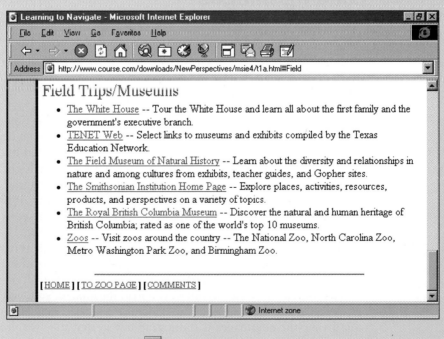

3. Click the **Back** button ← (the button label appears as "Back to Learning to Navigate"; when possible the label identifies the page to which you will return). The Learning to Navigate page reappears on your screen.

INTERNET EXPLORER 3

There is no small arrow to the right of the Back button in Internet Explorer 3, so you won't have this problem.

INTERNET EXPLORER 3

The icon in Step 6, 🏠, labeled Home in Internet Explorer 4, is labeled Start Page in Internet Explorer 3. When the Steps tell you to click the Home button, substitute the Start Page button.

TROUBLE? If you click the small arrow to the right of the Back button, a list opens. Click the arrow again to close the list, and repeat Step 3. This time make sure you click ⬅.

4. Click ⬅ until you return to your home page. Notice that the Back button dims, indicating that you have reached the first page you viewed since you started Internet Explorer; you can move back only as far as the home page.

TROUBLE? If your Back button is already dimmed after you return to the Learning to Navigate page, then you are at your starting point, and your Internet Explorer installation does not have a home page that appears upon startup. Just continue with Step 5.

5. You have moved backward through the earlier pages and now want to return to the Field Trips/Museums list. Click the **Forward** button ➡ until the Field Trips/Museums list appears. Notice that the Forward button is dimmed again, indicating that you are looking at the last page you visited.

TROUBLE? If your Forward button is not dimmed, you have linked from the Learning to Navigate page to another Web page. Continue clicking the Forward button until it is dimmed; this is your furthest point of travel.

6. Click the **Home** button 🏠 to return to your home page.

TROUBLE? If the Home button is dimmed, your Internet Explorer installation does not designate a home page location, and the initial page content area when you started Internet Explorer was blank. Just continue with the tutorial.

You've seen that it's simple to navigate through Web pages, but sometimes the pages take quite a while to load. Michelle tells the workshop participants that pages load more quickly when they don't contain images.

Loading Images

Images, the graphics and pictures such as drawings or photographs that accompany a Web page, make Internet documents more attractive and informative and can enhance comprehension. For example, if you're studying modern history, you can find up-to-date information on the Internet about the geography and current events of warring countries. Because the countries' borders change so quickly, maps that accompany these articles may be more current than any printed atlas.

The use of graphics, however, significantly increases the time a Web page takes to load. A page that contains only text loads in seconds whereas one containing elaborate images can take minutes. Clearly, a trade-off exists between speed and quality. Deciding which factor to favor depends on the situation. When you have a lot of time or enjoy the richness of images, you might want to automatically load the images for every page. When you want to look at a large number of pages in a short amount of time, you probably want to load just text. With Internet Explorer, you can switch between these two options as frequently as you want.

If you opt to hide images, a graphic image on a Web page is represented with an icon similar to 🖼. Although this option offers speed, the advantage of loading images automatically is that you can see and use all the links that are on the page. Remember that images can also be links to other Web pages. Unless you load the images, you won't be able to see these links.

Michelle asks you to find sites that the teachers might want to use in their classes. You'll view the next pages without graphics so that they will load faster.

INTERNET EXPLORER 3

To locate the Show pictures check box in Internet Explorer 3, click View, click Options, and then click the General tab.

VIEWING IMAGES ON DEMAND

- Click View, then click Internet Options.
- Click the Advanced tab.
- In the Multimedia section, click the Show pictures check box to deselect it.
- Click the OK button.

To view Web pages without images:

1. Click **View**, then click **Internet Options**.

2. Click the **Advanced** tab.

3. Scroll down to the Multimedia section, then click the **Show pictures** check box to deselect it. See Figure 30.

Figure 30 ◀
Setting image preferences

options for Internet Explorer 3

deselect this checkbox

INTERNET EXPLORER 3

In place of Step 1, click View, and then click Options. In place of Step 2, click the General tab. The Show pictures checkbox is in the Multimedia area. Figure 30 shows the dialog boxes for Internet Explorer versions 3 and 4.

options for Internet Explorer 4

deselect this checkbox

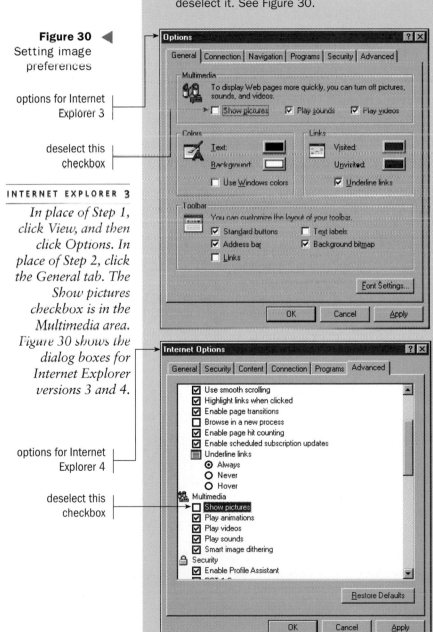

INTERNET EXPLORER 3

In Internet Explorer 3, the image icons might look slightly different.

4. Click the **OK** button. The images still appear on the page because you already loaded images for your home page. On the next link you activate, the images will be hidden.

5. Click the **Back** button until you see Field Trips/Museums.

6. Click the **Zoos** link to open the Zoos page, which contains links to several national zoos. Notice that you connect very quickly, and icons replace the images. See Figure 31.

Figure 31 ◀
Zoos page with image icons

icons replace images —

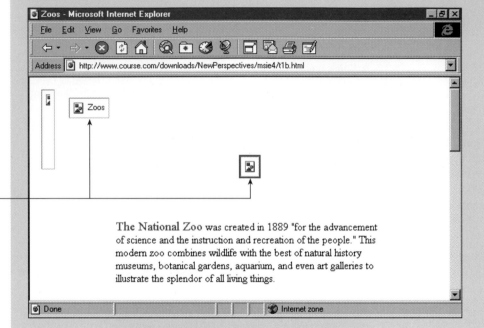

7. Scroll through the **Zoos** page and read the descriptions. Notice there are no hypertext links.

You suspect that the images on this Web page might be links to other pages that the teachers might want to see because none of the text contains links. When you are viewing pages without pictures, you can still examine an individual picture using the picture's **shortcut menu**, a menu that opens when you click an object on the screen with the right mouse button; this is called **right-clicking**. Shortcut menus display commands relevant to the object you right-click. You decide to view the large image with the blue outline.

INTERNET EXPLORER 3

In Internet Explorer 3, the icon you need to right-click does not have a blue border.

To view an individual image when images aren't loading automatically:

1. Point at the large image with the blue border and notice that the pointer changes from ▷ to ⬆. This indicates that the graphic contains links.

2. Right-click the image with the blue border. See Figure 32.

Figure 32
Opening an
image icon's
shortcut menu

click this icon with
right mouse button to
open shortcut menu

shortcut menu

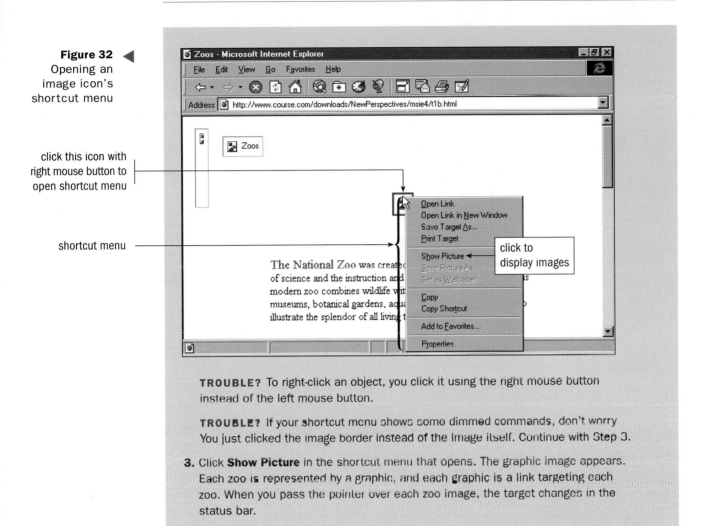

TROUBLE? To right-click an object, you click it using the right mouse button instead of the left mouse button.

TROUBLE? If your shortcut menu shows some dimmed commands, don't worry. You just clicked the image border instead of the image itself. Continue with Step 3.

3. Click **Show Picture** in the shortcut menu that opens. The graphic image appears. Each zoo is represented by a graphic, and each graphic is a link targeting each zoo. When you pass the pointer over each zoo image, the target changes in the status bar.

Graphics can contain important information and links, so unless you are in a hurry, it's best to view Web pages with graphics intact. You decide to reset Internet Explorer so that graphics are shown automatically. When you change settings for a page (or when the page changes for some other reason), you can use the Refresh button ⟳ to reload the page.

INTERNET EXPLORER 3

In place of Step 1, click View, and then click Options. In place of Step 2, click the General tab. The Show pictures checkbox is in the Multimedia area.

To load the images:

1. Click **View**, then click **Internet Options**.

2. Click the **Advanced** tab.

3. Scroll down to the Multimedia section, then click the **Show pictures** checkbox to select it.

4. Click the **OK** button.

5. Click the **Refresh** button ⟳. The page reloads from top to bottom with the images. When it's completely loaded, your page should look like Figure 33. The page is much more interesting to view this way and contains other links you couldn't see with the icons.

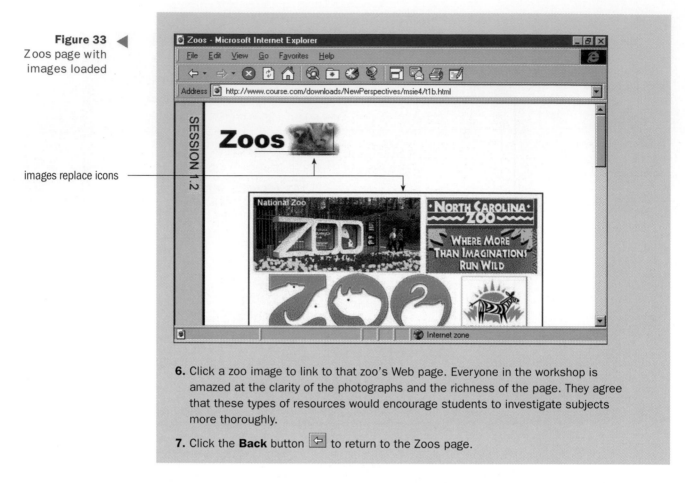

Figure 33
Zoos page with
images loaded

images replace icons

6. Click a zoo image to link to that zoo's Web page. Everyone in the workshop is amazed at the clarity of the photographs and the richness of the page. They agree that these types of resources would encourage students to investigate subjects more thoroughly.

7. Click the **Back** button to return to the Zoos page.

Because your settings now specify showing pictures, any new page you connect to will show pictures. When, however, you are in a hurry and don't need to see pictures, deselecting the Show pictures option can save you time, because a page loads more quickly when the browser doesn't have to display graphic images.

Printing a Web Page

Although reducing paper consumption is an advantage of browsing information online, sometimes you'll find it useful to print a Web page. For example, you might want to refer to the information later when you don't have computer access, or you might want to give a copy of the Web page to someone who doesn't have access to a computer or to the Internet.

Although Web pages can be any size, printers tend to use 8-1/2 x 11-inch sheets of paper. When you print, Internet Explorer automatically reformats the text of the Web page to fit the page dimension. Because lines might break at different places or text size might be altered, the printed Web page might be longer than you expect. You can specify the number of pages you want to print in the Print dialog box.

You decide that the directory of zoos is a good handout for the teachers in the workshop, so you decide to print out a copy. Michelle suggests that you print just the first page for the teachers. If the teachers want other information, they can return to the site and see the material online.

To print a Web page:

1. Click **File**, then click **Print**.

2. If necessary, click the **Pages** option button, type **1** in the from box, press the **Tab** key to move to the to box, and then type **1**. This indicates that you want to print only the page range 1–1 of the document, or just the first page of the document. Your completed dialog box should look similar to Figure 34.

Figure 34
Print dialog box

your printer might
be different

select page
range to print

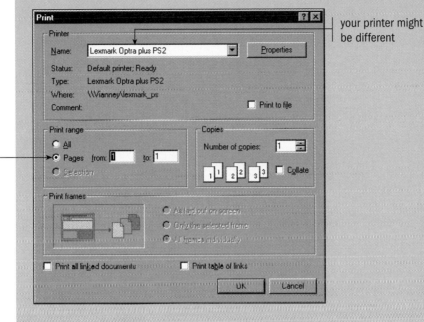

TROUBLE? If your Print dialog box looks somewhat different from Figure 34, don't worry. The Print dialog box changes to reflect the options available for the printer you are using. Just continue with Step 3.

3. Click the **OK** button to print the first page of the Web page.

Getting Online Help

INTERNET EXPLORER 3

The Help system for Internet Explorer 3 is a local reference, but there are links on the Help menu that connect you to useful Microsoft sites.

Charlotte DuMont, another instructor at the workshop, has been taking notes about how to use Internet Explorer, but she wants to know what to do if she needs help and no one familiar with Internet Explorer is around.

One of the best sources of information and help is always available when you're using any of the Internet Explorer components. Internet Explorer's Help system is an online reference created and maintained by Microsoft for use with its software; you can open the Help window from the Help menu or by clicking the Help buttons found in certain dialog boxes. The Help system provides a Table of Contents window, an Index, and a Search feature that helps you locate topics by keyword.

Even though the workshop members just saw how to load pages without pictures, Charlotte isn't sure she remembers the precise steps. She asks you to help her find information about this option. You suggest looking up the word "pictures" in the Index.

To get online Help in Internet Explorer 3:

1. Click **Help**, then click **Help Topics**. The Help window opens.

2. Click the **Index** tab. See Figure 35.

IE3

Figure 35
Help Topics
Index in
Internet
Explorer 3

Index tab

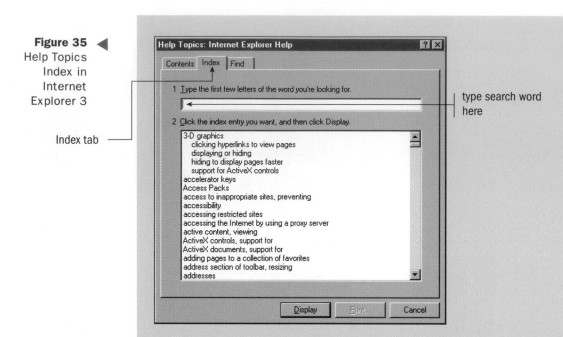

type search word
here

3. Type **pictures** in the box and wait until the word "pictures" is highlighted in the Index list.

4. Scroll down the Index list to view the pictures entries.

5. Click the entry **hiding to display pages faster**, then click the **Display** button. The information you need appears in its own window. Read the text to review how to display pages without pictures. See Figure 36.

Figure 36
Information on
displaying
pages without
pictures

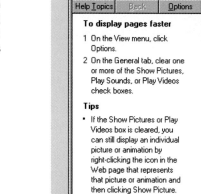

6. Click the **Close** button to close the Help window.

7. Click **File**, then click **Close** to close Internet Explorer.

To get online Help in Internet Explorer 4:

IE4

1. Click **Help**, then click **Contents and Index**. The Help window opens.

2. Click the **Index** tab. See Figure 37.

Figure 37 ◀
Help window
Index in
Internet
Explorer 4

Index tab ──

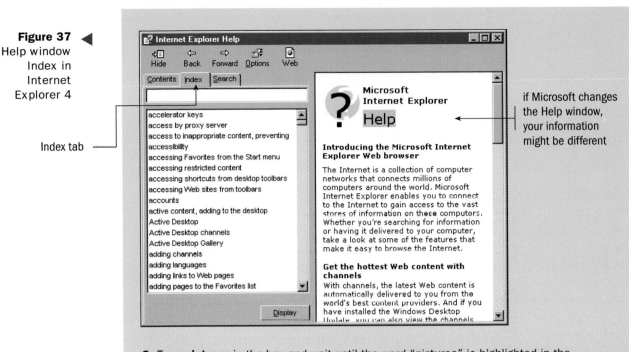

if Microsoft changes
the Help window,
your information
might be different

3. Type **pictures** in the box and wait until the word "pictures" is highlighted in the Index list.

4. Scroll down the Index list to view the pictures entries.

5. Click the entry **hiding to display pages faster**, then click the **Display** button. The information you need appears in the Index pane on the right side of the Help window. Read the text to review how to display pages without pictures. See Figure 38.

Figure 38 ◀
Graphics
entries

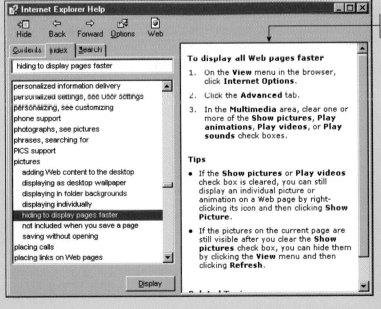

Help now shows
information on
displaying pictures

6. Click the **Close** button to close the Help window.

7. Click **File**, then click **Close** to close Internet Explorer.

Michelle ends the workshop with comments from the educators about incorporating the Internet in their classes. Lyle suggests that the information superhighway might bridge some of the gaps between metropolitan and rural schools as well as between wealthy and disadvantaged districts by providing common, equally accessible resources to all. As technology costs decrease and states encourage network connections in their public schools, distinctions such as these will begin to fade.

Quick Check

1. Someone has given you the URL of an interesting Web page. How can you view that Web page?

2. In the URL http://www.irs.ustreas.gov/prod/cover.html, what is the protocol? What is the server address? What is the name of the Web page file? In which folder is it located?

3. Is the Web page located at the URL http://www.CTI.COM/HOME.html the same as the Web page located at URL http://www.cti.com/home.html? Why or why not?

4. What is FTP?

5. When you see a URL with ".edu" in it, what do you know about that site's Web server?

6. You can easily flip through Web pages using the _____, _____, and _____ toolbar buttons.

7. Why might you want to load text only and not pictures?

8. True or False: A printed Web page cannot contain any graphics or special formatting.

Tutorial Assignments

Michelle wants to gear her next workshop for college-level educators. She needs to find out how much the Internet is being used for educational purposes in higher education, what types of sites and information are available, and who is involved with this new approach to education.

She asks you to look at trends in the Internet and answer the following questions: How is the Internet affecting higher education? Do you think the overall trends will be positive? What are some of the possible negative side-effects?

Michelle suggested a few Web pages from which you can begin looking for answers. Do the following:

1. If necessary, launch Internet Explorer.

2. Open the Web page at the URL http://www.course.com/downloads/NewPerspectives/msie4.

3. Click the Tutorial Assignments and Case Problems link.

4. Scroll down until you see the Tutorial 1 Tutorial Assignments section.

5. Connect to the World Lecture Hall link in the "Universities Around the World" section.

6. Follow one of the links that interests you and see if you can find any information you can use to answer Michelle's questions. If you try any busy or defunct sites, follow a different link path.

7. Print the first page of the World Lecture Hall page you linked to.

8. Return to the Tutorial Assignments and Case Problems page.

9. Connect to the Distance Education on the WWW link in the Tutorial 1 Tutorial Assignments section.

10. Scroll through the page. Navigate links as necessary to answer these questions: What are four main kinds of services? What is the relevance of the WWW to distance education?

11. Print just the first two pages of this Web page.

12. Submit to your instructor the printout and the answers to Michelle's questions based on the information you found in Step 6 and your answers to Step 10.

Case Problems

1. University Informational Pages Karla Marletti, director of admissions at Southern University, noticed that an increasing number of universities are placing Web pages on the Internet. She wants her university to remain current in its use of technology and decides that the school should put a Web page on the Web. She is not sure what layout or design would be most appealing for the page or what type of information should be included. She asks you to find a couple of Web pages that you think have attractive and effective designs with interesting and helpful content.

If necessary, start Internet Explorer, then do the following:

1. Open the Web page at the URL "http://www.course.com/downloads/NewPerspectives/msie4."

2. Click the Tutorial Assignments and Case Problems link.

3. Scroll down until you see the Tutorial 1 Case Problems section.

4. Connect to the University Informational Pages link to find a listing of universities with Web pages.

5. Visit three Web pages for universities within the United States and then visit two Web pages for universities outside the United States.

6. Choose Web pages for two universities that you think have an unusual or attractive layout and interesting and relevant content.

7. Print the first page of your two favorite university Web pages. On the hard copy, explain what you liked about that Web page and submit your explanation to your instructor.

2. The Fresno Daily Helen Wu, a staff journalist for *The Fresno Daily*, a newspaper serving the community of Fresno, California, just received an assignment to write a feature article on how the Internet is changing the way people spend their leisure time. As part of her article, Helen wants to discuss the current size of the Internet and its rate of growth. She asks you to find statistics on the current number of Internet domains, the current number of Internet hosts, the current number of Web sites, and the percentage that these figures have grown since they were counted last.

If necessary, launch Internet Explorer, then do the following:

1. Open the Web page at the URL "http://www.course.com/downloads/NewPerspectives/msie4."

2. Click the Tutorial Assignments and Case Problems link.

3. Scroll down until you see the Tutorial 1 Case Problems section.

4. Connect to one of the two *Fresno Daily* links to find a listing of relevant Web pages.

5. Navigate through the Web pages to look for the statistics Helen needs.

6. When you find a Web page that contains a relevant statistic, print the information you need.

7. When you have all the information, write a short report about your findings on the back of the printout.

8. Circle the URL of each page you used. *Hint*: When you print a Web page, Internet Explorer inserts a header and footer that include the page name, page number, URL, and date. Check the footer of the printed Web page.

3. The Carpet Shoppe The Carpet Shoppe imports and sells handwoven rugs from Thailand, Burma, and India. Four times each year, Al Sanchez, the owner, travels to these countries to replenish his inventory of new carpets.

Al has decided that it's time to convert to computerized inventory and accounting systems. Al isn't sure whether to purchase a Macintosh or an IBM-compatible system. He wants a portable computer that he could bring on his buying trips. With a laptop computer, not only will he have the most current figures at his fingertips, but he will also be able to communicate with his employees at home without worrying about the time difference or the cost of international phone calls. He wants a top-of-the-line notebook computer that won't become obsolete quickly. The more RAM, the bigger the disk storage space, and the faster the modem, the better.

He asks you to find information such as the model name, model number, and features about different brands of computers. Most of the bigger computer manufacturers place Web pages on the Internet with their latest computer models and prices, so you can begin looking there.

If necessary, launch Internet Explorer, then do the following:

1. Open the Web page at the URL "http://www.course.com/downloads/NewPerspectives/msie4."

2. Click the Tutorial Assignments and Case Problems link.

3. Scroll down until you see the Tutorial 1 Case Problems section.

4. Find information about a top-of-the line notebook computer from Apple.

5. Print any Web pages that contain relevant information.

6. Find information about a top-of-the line notebook computer from IBM.

7. Print any Web pages that contain relevant information.

8. Write a summary report of the information you found, and make a recommendation regarding which notebook computer you think Al should buy.

4. Marketing 305 Consumer Behavior The students of Marketing 305 (MK305) have prepared a survey to study consumer behavior in online environments. They plan to compile a report that discusses what consumers think about two malls available on the Internet, how products' prices compare to their local malls, and what percentage of people are willing to shop online.

If necessary, launch Internet Explorer, then do the following:

1. Open the Web page at the URL "http://www.course.com/downloads/NewPerspectives/msie4."

2. Click the Tutorial Assignments and Case Problems link.

3. Scroll down until you see the Tutorial 1 Case Problems section.

4. Navigate through two online shopping malls looking at various products.

5. Print one sample product description from each mall.

6. Compare a similar product available at each mall. See how information about the product is presented as well as its price.

7. Return to the Tutorial Assignments and Case Problems page and locate the MK305 survey link.

8. Connect to the MK305 survey page.

9. Answer the survey questions. When you are done, click the Submit button. Global Marketers Inc. displays a completed survey.

10. Print the completed survey and submit it to your instructor.

Lab Assignments

This Lab Assignment is designed to accompany the interactive Course Lab called Internet World Wide Web. To start the Lab, click the Start button on the taskbar, point to Programs, point to Course Labs, point to New Perspectives Applications, then click Internet World Wide Web. If you do not see Course Labs on your Programs menu, see your instructor or technical support person.

The Internet World Wide Web One of the most popular services on the Internet is the World Wide Web. This lab is a Web simulator that teaches you how to use Web browser software to find information. You can use this lab whether or not your school provides you with Internet access.

1. Click the Steps button to learn how to use Web browser software. As you proceed through the steps, answer all of the Quick Check questions that appear. After you complete the steps, you will see a Quick Check Summary Report. Follow the instructions on the screen to print this report.

2. Click the Explore button on the Welcome screen. Use the Web browser to locate a weather map of the Caribbean Virgin Islands. What is its URL?

3. A SCUBA diver named Wadson Lachouffe has been searching for the fabled treasure of Greybeard the pirate. A link from the Adventure Travel Web site leads to a Wadson's Web page called "Hidden Treasure." Click the Explore button. Locate the Hidden Treasure page and answer the following questions:
   a. What was the name of Greybeard's ship?
   b. What was Greybeard's favorite food?
   c. What does Wadson think happened to Greybeard's ship?

4. In the steps, you found a graphic of Jupiter from the photo archives of the Jet Propulsion Laboratory. In the Explore section of the lab, you can also find a graphic of Saturn. Suppose one of your friends wanted a picture of Saturn for an astronomy report. Make a list of the blue, underlined links your friend must click to find the Saturn graphic. Assume that your friend will begin at the Web Trainer home page.

5. Enter the URL "http:\\www.atour.com" to jump to the Adventure Travel Web site. Write a one-page description of this site. In your paper include a description of the information at the site, the number of pages the site contains, and a diagram of the links it contains.

6. Chris Thomson is a student at UVI and has his own Web pages. In Explore, look at the information Chris has included on his pages. Suppose you could create your own Web page. What would you include? Use word processing software to design your own Web pages. Make sure you indicate the graphics and links you would use.

Answers to Quick Check Questions

SESSION 1.1

1 False

2 The Web page that appears when you start Internet Explorer or the page that a person, organization, or business has created to give information about itself.

3 URL

4 in a different color

5 abort

6 The domain in the URL is not registered with the Domain Name Server (DNS).

SESSION 1.2

1 Type it in the Address box, then press Enter.

2 protocol: http; server address: www.irs.ustreas.gov; filename: cover.html; folder: prod

3 No. URLs are case sensitive.

4 File Transfer Protocol, used to transfer files

5 It is an educational institution.

6 Back, Forward, and Home

7 Page loads faster without images.

8 False

INTERNET EXPLORER 3

In Internet Explorer 3, the Home button is called the Start Page button.

NEW PERSPECTIVES SERIES

Introducing
Microsoft® **Office 97**
Professional

TUTORIAL

Read This **Before You Begin**

To complete this tutorial, you need to use a computer on which Microsoft Windows 95 or Microsoft Windows NT Workstation 4.0 (or a later version) and Microsoft Office 97 Professional are installed. This tutorial assumes a custom installation of Microsoft Office 97 Professional that includes the Microsoft Office Shortcut Bar.

If the Microsoft Office Shortcut Bar is not installed on your system, you will not be able to complete some of the steps and assignments in this tutorial. If this is the case, you should read through the steps and assignments that include the Office Shortcut Bar without completing them.

Note that there are no Student Disks for this tutorial.

Introducing Microsoft Office 97 Professional

Preparing an Office 97 Training Seminar for Pet Provisions Employees

Office

Pet Provisions

CASE Pet Provisions, a company Manny Cordova founded in 1993, sells organic pet food and environmentally friendly pet supplies to stores around the world. During the first couple of years, company employees purchased the software programs they were most comfortable using. However, the company has expanded to the point where employees frequently need to share information. Manny has decided to standardize the computer programs all his employees use to make it easier to create consistent documents and reports from shared data. He has selected Microsoft Office 97 Professional. Although many employees already use individual Microsoft programs, few are aware of the power and flexibility of Microsoft Office 97 Professional. Manny asks you to prepare a company wide training seminar to demonstrate the potential of Microsoft Office to Pet Provisions employees.

Using Microsoft Office 97 Professional

Microsoft Office 97 is a collection of the most popular Microsoft software programs. It is available in two editions: Professional and Standard. Both versions include Word, Excel, PowerPoint, and Outlook, but only Office 97 Professional contains Access, a database program. These tutorials assume you are using Microsoft Office 97 Professional, or simply **Office**.

The programs that make up Office are designed to share many features, so once you've learned one program, it's easy to learn the others. Because each program is part of Office, you can share, or integrate, information between programs effortlessly, as shown in Figure 1. This saves you time, and ensures your information remains consistent and accurate.

Figure 1 ◀
Office 97
Professional
programs

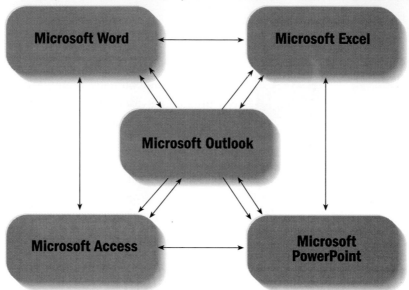

Each Office program contains valuable tools to help you accomplish many tasks, such as composing reports, analyzing data, preparing presentations, and compiling information. During your presentation, you'll give Pet Provisions a brief overview of each Office program.

Microsoft Word 97, or simply Word, is a **word-processing program** you use to create text documents. Word offers many special features that help you compose and update all types of documents ranging from letters and newsletters to reports and even books—all in attractive and readable formats. You also can use Word to create, insert, and position figures, tables, and other graphics to enhance the look of your documents. Figure 2 shows a business letter a Pet Provisions sales representative composed in Word to send information to a customer about the company's new products.

Figure 2 ◀
Pet Provisions
letter
composed in
Word

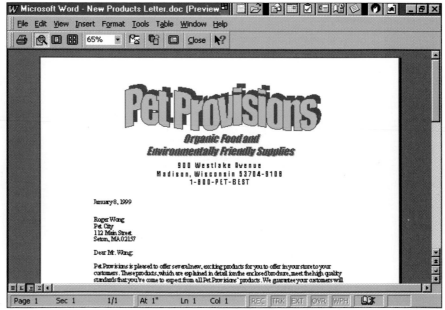

Microsoft Excel 97, or simply Excel, is a **spreadsheet program** you use to display, organize, and analyze numerical information. With Excel it is easy to perform calculations. Its graphic capabilities enable you to display data visually (for example, as pie charts or bar graphs) to help readers grasp the significance of and the connections between the information. Figure 3 shows an Excel worksheet that Pet Provisions' operations department uses to track the company's financial performance.

Figure 3 ◀
Excel
worksheet with
Pet Provisions
financial data

Excel chart ——

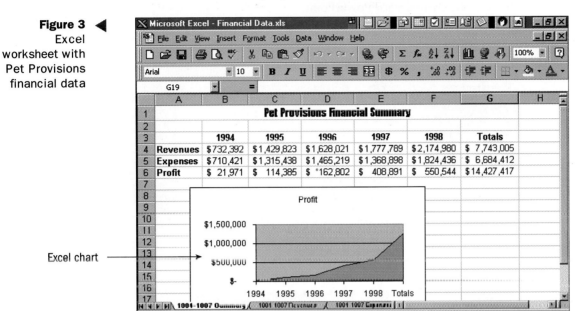

Microsoft Access 97, or simply Access, is a **database program** you use to enter, maintain, and retrieve related information. You can use Access to create entry forms to make data entry easier, customize how you organize and retrieve information, and create professional-looking reports to improve the readability of your data. Figure 4 shows an Access database listing customer names and addresses compiled by the Pet Provisions sales department; for each order a customer places, the database provides shipping information and invoicing data.

Figure 4 ◀
Access
database
listing Pet
Provisions
customers and
their addresses

Cust Num	Store Name	Street	City	State/Prov	Postal Code
201	Wonder of Pets	5480 Alpine Lane	Gardner	MA	01440
129	Acquatic World	95 North Bay Boulevard	Warwich	RI	02287
135	Pet Supplies Plus	2840 Cascade Road	Laconia	NH	03246
104	Pet House	Pond Hill Road	Millinocket	ME	04462
515	Pets Plus	8200 Baldwin Boulevard	Burlington	VT	05406
165	Pet Foods	1935 Snow Street SE	Nagatuck	CT	06770
423	Wonderful Pets	H. 1055	Budapest	Hungary	1/A
322	World of Pets	114 Lexington	Plattsburgh	NY	12901
136	Animal House	4090 Divison Street NW	Fort Lauderdale	FL	33302
131	Pets R Us	15365 Old Bedford Trail	Mishawaka	IN	46544
122	V.I. Pets	8404 E. Fletcher Road	Clare	MI	48617
163	Pets Unlimited	1366 36th Street	Roscommon	MI	48653
325	Pet Max	56 Four Mile Road	Grand Rapids	MI	49505
133	Supply Your Pets	2874 Western Avenue	Sioux Falls	SD	57057
107	Pamper Your Pets	82 Mix Avenue	Bonners Ferry	ID	83805
203	Animal Supplies	2159 Causewayside	Edinburgh	Scotland	EH9 1PH
202	Exotic Pets	2140 Edgewood Parkway	Thunder Bay	Ontario	L5B 1X2
407	Pets & More Ltd	44 Tower Lane	Leeds	England	LS12 3SD
128	Pets in the Northern Lights	37 Queens Highway	Moose Jaw	Saskatchewan	SON 1W0

Microsoft PowerPoint 97, or simply PowerPoint, is a **presentation graphics program** you use to create professional-looking and effective presentations. With PowerPoint, you have the flexibility to show presentations on your computer monitor, project them onto a screen as a slide show, or display them on the World Wide Web (WWW). You also can use PowerPoint to generate presentation-related documents such as audience handouts, outlines, and speaker's notes. Figure 5 shows a slide that the sales department at Pet Provisions created with PowerPoint.

Figure 5 ◄
PowerPoint
slide
announcing Pet
Provisions' new
product line

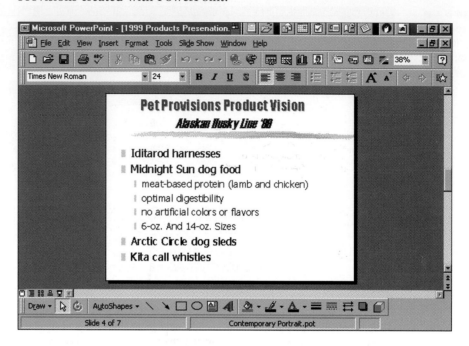

Microsoft Outlook 97, or simply Outlook, is a **desktop information management program** you use for a wide range of organizational tasks, such as planning your schedule, arranging meetings, sending and receiving e-mail, creating and organizing to-do and contact lists, and delegating tasks. You can also use Outlook to print schedules, task lists, or phone directories. Figure 6 shows how Pet Provisions manager Shondra Lewis uses Outlook to plan her schedule and create a to-do list.

Figure 6 ◄
Outlook
Calendar
window

additional
Outlook tools

daily schedule

personal
to-do list

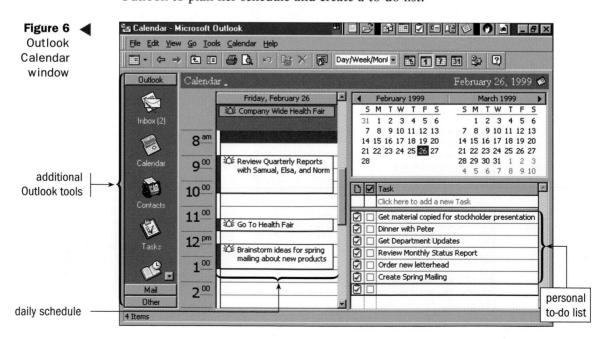

Office offers a number of additional tools that you can use within its programs. Figure 7 describes some primary Office tools and shows how Pet Provisions might use them in its daily business activities.

Figure 7 ◀
Office Tools

Office Tool	Example
Clip Gallery organizes clip art, sounds, movies, and pictures in one location, making it convenient and easy to create multimedia documents. **Clip art** images are illustrations you can insert in your documents and size as you choose. Office comes with more than 1,000 pieces of clip art. You can add your own images and sounds to the Clip Gallery. Pet Provisions might use Clip Gallery to illustrate a report.	
Office Art is a drawing tool that comes with all Office programs. You can use Office Art to create 3-D objects, flowcharts, text boxes, and **WordArt** (shaped text) enhanced with interesting combinations of shading, fills, colors, borders, and other effects such as rotations and changed dimensions. Pet Provisions might use Office Art to design a unique letterhead.	
Hyperlinks, borrowed from WWW technology, create a single-click connection between and within your documents and to Internet sites. The **Web toolbar** provides tools for navigating between hyperlinked documents. Pet Provisions might use a hyperlink to connect a Word report summarizing the company's financial status to the actual data in an Excel worksheet.	
All Office programs can be saved as **HTML** (HyperText Markup Language), the file format used on the WWW. After creating your document, you can use the Save As HTML command to activate the **Internet Assistant**, a program that converts your Office file into HTML format so you can post it on a Web site. Pet Provisions might convert a PowerPoint slide presentation about its newest product line into HTML format and then post it on the company's Web site so customers can learn about upcoming products.	
The **Office Binder** is a program that you use to organize, save, and print related files created in different Office programs. For example, Manny uses the Office Binder to save a series of documents about reducing company expenses, including a memo to department managers created in Word, a letter to all employees created in Word, and profit and expense data compiled in Excel.	
Microsoft IntelliMouse provides a simple way to navigate long documents. You can use the wheel between the two mouse buttons to scroll, zoom, pan quickly, or even switch to a reading mode, where the document scrolls automatically. Pet Provisions plans to purchase the IntelliMouse for its employees in the near future.	

Integrating Programs

One of the main advantages of Office is its ability to integrate information between programs. In other words, with Office you can move information from one program to another, share information between program files, and share files and information with other Office users. Integration ensures consistency and saves time because you don't have to reenter the same information in several Office programs. The staff at Pet Provisions will be able to use integration on a daily basis. Some examples include:

■ An Excel chart created by the accounting department can compare this year's and last year's fourth-quarter results. This Excel chart could also appear in a quarterly financial report created in Word. A hyperlink from the Word report to the Excel worksheet could allow employees reading the report on-screen to access the original chart data in Excel. See Figure 8.

■ An Excel chart showing the five-year sales growth of Pet Provisions can be duplicated onto a PowerPoint slide. The slide is part of the human resources department's presentation to potential employees. See Figure 9.

■ An Access database or an Outlook contact list containing the names and addresses of customers can be combined with a form letter the Pet Provisions marketing department creates in Word to produce a mailing promoting the company's newest product. See Figure 10.

Figure 8 ◄
Integrating an Excel chart into a Word document

profitability chart integrated into financial report

hyperlink to original data

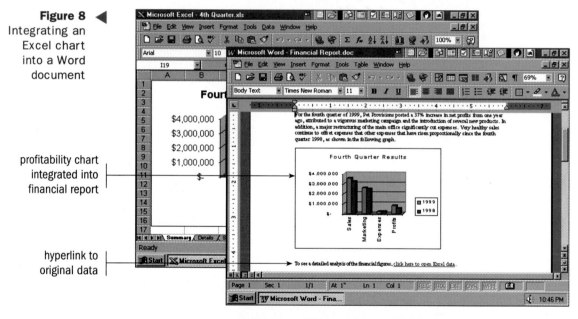

Figure 9 ◄
Integrating an Excel chart into a PowerPoint presentation

sales growth chart integrated into a presentation slide

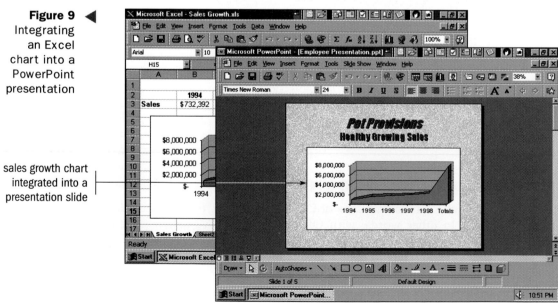

Figure 10 ◀
Integrating
Access data
or Outlook
contacts
into a Word
form letter

Access data

Word form letter

merged information

Outlook contacts

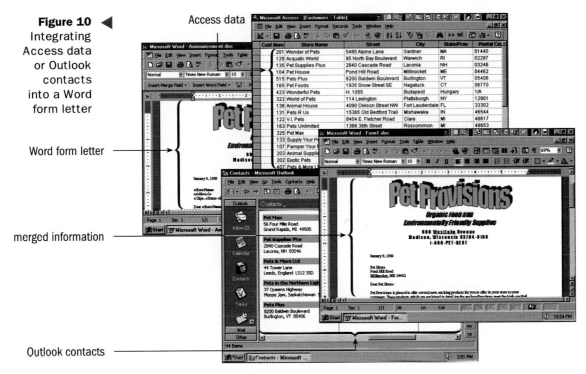

These few examples show how you can take information from one Office program and effectively integrate it into another. Now that you are familiar with the programs and tools available with Office, you're ready to explore some of its other features, which you will present at the Pet Provisions training seminar.

Displaying and Moving the Office Shortcut Bar

Once you purchase and install Office, you might see the Office Shortcut Bar, similar to the one shown in Figure 11, displayed on your screen. The **Office Shortcut Bar** is a toolbar containing buttons for starting programs installed on your computer. It is also used to perform common tasks, such as opening new and existing Office documents.

Figure 11 ◀
Docked Office
Shortcut Bar

Office Shortcut
Bar displayed on
Windows 95 desktop

If the Office Shortcut Bar does not appear on your Windows 95 desktop, either it is not installed or it is not displayed. Because the Office Shortcut Bar is *not* included in the "Typical" Office installation, you might need to ask your instructor or technical support person for assistance. Without the Office Shortcut Bar installed on your system, you will not be able to complete some of the steps in this tutorial. In this case, you will simply read rather than complete the steps that include the Office Shortcut Bar.

Because using the Office Shortcut Bar is an efficient way to navigate Office programs and documents, you plan to show Pet Provisions employees how to display the Office Shortcut Bar during your presentation. If the Office Shortcut Bar already appears on your screen, skip to the next set of steps, "To reposition the Office Shortcut Bar."

To display the Office Shortcut Bar:

1. Make sure Windows 95 is running on your computer and the Windows 95 desktop appears on your screen.

   TROUBLE? If you are running Windows NT Workstation 4.0 (or later) on your computer or network, don't worry. Although the figures in these tutorials were created while running Windows 95, Windows NT 4.0 and Windows 95 share the same interface, and Microsoft Office runs equally well using either operating system.

2. Click the **Start** button on the taskbar to display the Start menu, and then point to **Programs** to display the Programs menu.

3. Point to **StartUp** on the Programs menu, and then point to **Microsoft Office Shortcut Bar**. See Figure 12. Depending on how your computer is set up, your desktop and menu might contain different icons and commands.

Figure 12 ◀
Displaying the
Microsoft
Office
Shortcut Bar

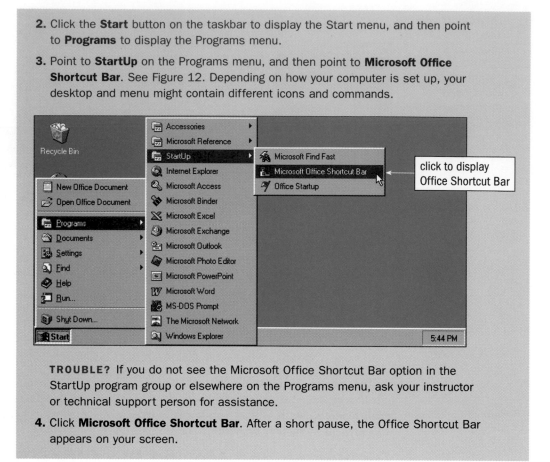

TROUBLE? If you do not see the Microsoft Office Shortcut Bar option in the StartUp program group or elsewhere on the Programs menu, ask your instructor or technical support person for assistance.

4. Click **Microsoft Office Shortcut Bar**. After a short pause, the Office Shortcut Bar appears on your screen.

Now that the Office Shortcut Bar appears on your screen, you can change its location, if necessary. The Office Shortcut Bar, like any toolbar, can be either docked or floating. A **docked** toolbar is attached to one of the edges of the screen, while a **floating** toolbar is not attached to any edge of the screen.

Although the default location of the Office Shortcut Bar is docked along the right side of your screen, the most practical location to dock it is near the upper-right corner of your screen where it won't cover other screen elements. To move the entire Office Shortcut Bar, use the click-drag method. **Click-drag** is a way to move an object with your mouse to a new location on your desktop.

To reposition the Office Shortcut Bar:

1. Place your pointer anywhere on the **Office Shortcut Bar** except on a button.

2. Press and hold the left mouse button while you drag the mouse to the upper-right corner of the screen. Notice that an outline of the Office Shortcut Bar corresponds with the movement of your mouse.

   TROUBLE? If your Office Shortcut Bar is already docked at the top of your screen, drag the mouse down to the center of the screen, and then release the mouse button. Repeat Steps 1 and 2.

   TROUBLE? If an outline of the Office Shortcut Bar does not appear, or if a dialog box or program window opens, your pointer was probably not situated on a blank portion of the Office Shortcut Bar. Click the Close button ☒ for that dialog box or window, and then repeat Steps 1 and 2.

3. Release the left mouse button when the outline of the Office Shortcut Bar stretches partially across the top of your screen. This is the docked position as shown in Figure 11.

TROUBLE? If the Office Shortcut Bar stretches across the entire top edge of your screen, then your Office Shortcut Bar is not set to AutoFit into the Title Bar area. Right-click anywhere on the Office Shortcut Bar except on a button, click Customize, click the View tab, click the AutoFit into Title Bar area check box to select it, and then click the OK button.

You also can drag the Office Shortcut Bar to other positions on your screen, such as docked to the left or right edge or floating in the center. The Office Shortcut Bar remains wherever you position it, regardless of the programs, windows, and dialog boxes you open.

Customizing the Office Shortcut Bar

In addition to moving the Office Shortcut Bar, you can customize its contents to match your task requirements. You can change the Office Shortcut Bar to fit the way you work. For example, you can add a toolbar that contains buttons for programs you work with frequently or you can hide a particular toolbar button that you don't use often.

By default, the Office Shortcut Bar displays only the Office toolbar. However, you can easily add other toolbars, such as the Programs or Favorites toolbar, to the existing Office Shortcut Bar. The **Programs toolbar** buttons (shortcuts for opening and switching between programs) represent the programs installed on your computer, while the **Favorites toolbar** buttons provide access to the programs and documents you use most frequently. As you become familiar with Office and its programs, you also can create your own toolbars to add to the Office Shortcut Bar.

If the Office Shortcut Bar contains more than one toolbar, you'll be able to only view one toolbar at a time even though the titles or buttons for each of the other toolbars appear. Because Pet Provisions employees will often need the flexibility of additional toolbars on the Office Shortcut Bar, you'll demonstrate at your presentation how to add the Programs toolbar to the Office Shortcut Bar. However, you might not need all of the buttons displayed on the various Office Shortcut Bar toolbars. In those instances, you can remove individual buttons from any toolbar, leaving only those programs and tasks you use most frequently. Because Pet Provisions does not use MS-DOS, you will show the employees how to remove that button from the Programs toolbar.

To customize the Office Shortcut Bar:

1. Right-click anywhere (except on a button) on the Office Shortcut Bar to open a menu, and then click **Customize** to open the Customize dialog box.

2. Click the **Toolbars** tab to select it, and then click the **Programs** check box to select it. The Programs toolbar appears on the Office Shortcut Bar. See Figure 13. Notice that although you can see the contents of the Programs toolbar, you can see only the buttons for the Office toolbar. Depending on the programs installed on your computer, your Programs toolbar might contain different buttons than those shown in Figure 13.

Figure 13 ◀
Office Shortcut
Bar with
Programs
toolbar

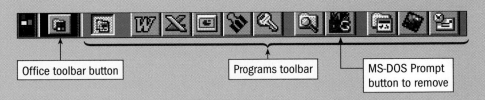

Office toolbar button   Programs toolbar   MS-DOS Prompt
                                                     button to remove

Next, you'll remove a button from the toolbar.

3. Click the **Buttons** tab, scroll down in the Show these Files as Buttons list box, and, if necessary, click the **MS-DOS Prompt** check box to deselect it. See Figure 14. The MS-DOS Prompt button disappears from the Programs toolbar on the Office Shortcut Bar.

Figure 14 ◀
Customize
dialog box

deselected check box
removes button from
Office Shortcut Bar

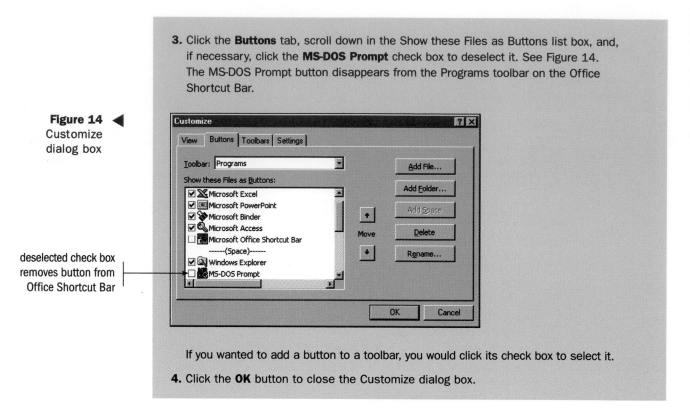

If you wanted to add a button to a toolbar, you would click its check box to select it.

4. Click the **OK** button to close the Customize dialog box.

You can customize all the toolbars and menus within each Office program just as easily as you did the Office Shortcut Bar. Once Pet Provisions employees have learned to display and customize the Office Shortcut Bar, you will show them the ease with which they can open more than one program and switch between them.

Opening and Switching Between Programs

In Office, you can perform common tasks several ways. For example, there are several ways to open a program. You can click the Start button on the taskbar and then use the Programs menu to open any program you have installed. Also, you can click the New Office Document button 🖼 or Open Office Document button 🗁 on the Office Shortcut Bar (or click the same commands on the Start menu) to open new or existing documents and their associated programs. Alternatively, you can open a specific program from the Programs toolbar on the Office Shortcut Bar. The method you choose depends on your personal preference.

If you open two or more programs, you can quickly switch from one program to another either by clicking the appropriate program button on the taskbar or by clicking the Programs toolbar on the Office Shortcut Bar. Because Pet Provisions employees often work in two or three programs at a time, you'll show them different ways to open programs and then switch between them.

To open and then switch between programs:

1. Click the **Start** button on the taskbar, and then click **New Office Document** (or click the **New Office Document** button 🖼 on the Office toolbar on the Office Shortcut Bar). The New Office Document dialog box opens. See Figure 15.

Figure 15 ◀
New Office
Document
dialog box

tabs contain
blank files for all
Office programs

click to open blank
Word document

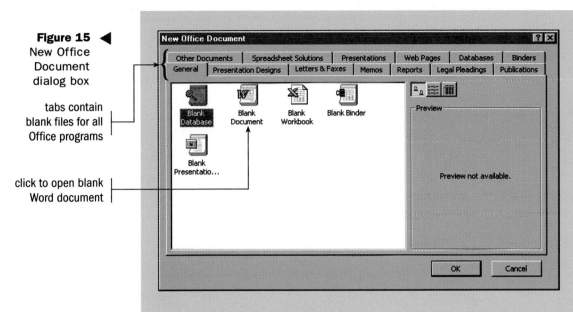

2. If necessary, click the **General** tab, click the **Blank Document** icon, and then click the **OK** button. Microsoft Word opens with a new, blank document.

3. If necessary, click the **Programs** button 🖼 on the Office Shortcut Bar, and then click the **Microsoft Excel** button ⊠ to start Excel and open a new, blank worksheet.

   TROUBLE? If you don't see the Microsoft Excel button on the Programs toolbar, click the Start button, point to Programs, and then click Microsoft Excel. If you don't see the Microsoft Excel option on the Programs menu, ask your instructor or technical support person for assistance.

4. To switch from Excel to Word without closing Excel, click the **Word** button 🔳 on the Office Shortcut Bar. See Figure 16.

Figure 16 ◀
Word and Excel
programs
opened

Office Assistant
(might not appear
on your screen)

click to switch
back to Excel

taskbar

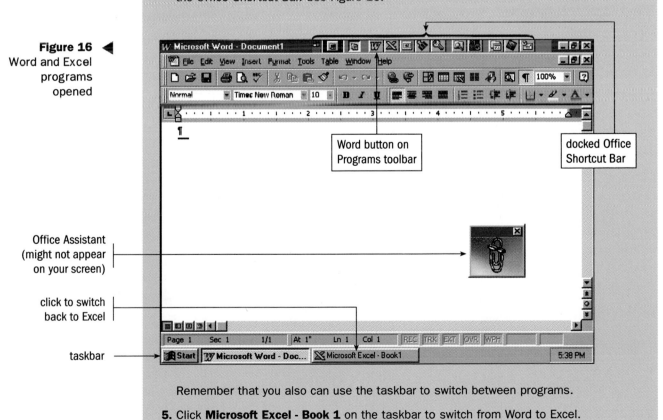

Word button on
Programs toolbar

docked Office
Shortcut Bar

Remember that you also can use the taskbar to switch between programs.

5. Click **Microsoft Excel - Book 1** on the taskbar to switch from Word to Excel.

As you can see, you can open programs and switch between them in seconds using Office and Windows 95. Getting help is just as easy.

Getting Help

Like all Microsoft programs, Office comes with an extensive Help system, which you can access through the Help menu. You can look up any particular task or topic you need help with by clicking the Contents and Index option on the Help menu to open the Help Topics dialog box. You can also click the What's This? option on the Help menu and then click any toolbar button, menu command, dialog box option, or other item in your window to display a brief description of that item. If you would like to know the name of a button, you can position the mouse pointer over a button to view its **ScreenTip**, a yellow box containing the button's name. Because you plan to show the Pet Provisions employees how to use the ScreenTip feature, you decide to try it now.

To display a ScreenTip:

1. Position your pointer on the **Office Assistant** button on the Standard toolbar. The ScreenTip "Office Assistant" should appear on your screen.

TROUBLE? If a ScreenTip does not appear, your pointer might not be directly on the button. Be sure to position the tip of the pointer in the middle of the Office Assistant button.

2. Move your pointer away from the Office Assistant button to hide the ScreenTip.

ScreenTips are a fast and easy way to determine the function of a particular toolbar button. You think the staff at Pet Provisions should find the ScreenTip feature helpful.

For more in-depth help, you can use the Office Assistant. The **Office Assistant** is an interactive guide to finding information in the Office Help system. Using the Office Assistant is just like having a technical expert at your side to answer any questions or help you solve any problems you encounter while working in Office. You simply specify what task you want to perform or what topic you need assistance with in the Office Assistant text box. Then the Office Assistant steps you through a specific procedure or explains a difficult concept in clear, everyday language. For example, you might ask the Office Assistant how to format a worksheet cell in Excel. In addition, the Office Assistant appears as you begin to perform a common task, such as writing a letter, and asks if you want any help. Sometimes as you work, a light bulb appears in the Office Assistant button or window. This indicates that the Assistant has a tip for completing your task more efficiently. For example, a light bulb might appear when you select a menu command instead of clicking the corresponding toolbar button.

REFERENCE window

GETTING HELP FROM THE OFFICE ASSISTANT

- Open any Office program.
- Click the Office Assistant button on the Standard toolbar.
- Type a question or topic in the text box, and then click the Search button.
- Click the button next to the topic you want.
- When you are finished, click the Close button in the upper-right corner of the window.

When you present Office to the Pet Provisions employees, you want to make sure they understand all the various ways they can access help while working in Office. You'll show them how to use the Office Assistant to get help and find information.

To get help using the Office Assistant:

1. Click the **Office Assistant** button on the Standard toolbar to open the Office Assistant. If necessary, click in the text box, and then type **get help**. See Figure 17.

Figure 17 ◀
Office
Assistant
in Excel

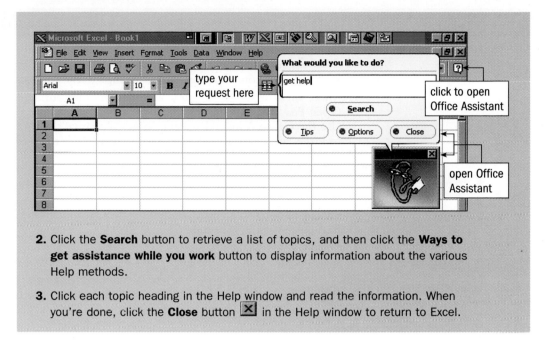

2. Click the **Search** button to retrieve a list of topics, and then click the **Ways to get assistance while you work** button to display information about the various Help methods.

3. Click each topic heading in the Help window and read the information. When you're done, click the **Close** button ☒ in the Help window to return to Excel.

The Office Assistant will enable the staff at Pet Provisions to get answers to any questions they might have after your presentation or to find further information about a topic.

Exiting Programs

Whenever you finish working with an Office program, you should close it. You can exit a program with a button or from a menu. You'll use both methods to close Word and Excel.

To exit a program:

> **1.** Click the **Close** button ☒ in the upper-right corner of the window to exit Excel. The Word window appears on your screen.
>
> **2.** Click **File** on the menu bar, and then click **Exit**. The Word program closes.

Now that you've mastered the basics of Office and learned about its power and flexibility, you tell Manny that you're ready to present the training seminar about Office 97 Professional to Pet Provisions employees.

Quick Check

1. What are two benefits of using Office?
2. Match the following software programs to their descriptions:

    ____ Word a. Enters, maintains, and retrieves information

    ____ Excel b. Provides e-mail, scheduling, and file-sharing capabilities

    ____ PowerPoint c. Displays, organizes, and analyzes numerical data

    ____ Access d. Creates effective presentations

    ____ Outlook e. Creates a variety of text documents

3. A(n) _____ toolbar is one that is attached to an edge of your screen.
4. What are two ways you can customize the Office Shortcut Bar?
5. What are three ways to open Office programs?
6. The _____ is an interactive guide to finding information in the Help system.

Tutorial Assignments

At your training seminar on Office 97 Professional for the employees of Pet Provisions, you will show the attendees some of the more common procedures. Before the seminar, you decide to practice your demonstration. Complete the following:

1. Make sure the Office Shortcut Bar appears on your screen.
2. Open PowerPoint.
3. Use the Office Assistant to learn how to change the toolbar buttons from small to large, and then do it. Use the same procedure to change the buttons back to regular size.
4. Close the Office Assistant.
5. Add the MS-DOS button back to the Office Shortcut Bar.
6. Open Access.
7. Switch to the PowerPoint window, and then switch back to the Access window.
8. Exit Access using a button.
9. Exit PowerPoint using a menu command.
10. Remove the Programs toolbar from the Office Shortcut Bar.

Answers to Quick Check Questions

1 integration and data-sharing capabilities; ability to switch easily between programs

2 e, c, d, a, b

3 docked

4 add and remove toolbars, add and remove buttons

5 click Start, point to Programs, and then click any program command; click any program button on the Programs toolbar of the Office Shortcut Bar; or click the New Office Document or Open Office Document icons on the Start menu or Office Shortcut Bar

6 Office Assistant

Introducing Microsoft Office 97 **Index**

NEW
PERSPECTIVES
SERIES

Microsoft®
Word 97

LEVEL I

TUTORIALS

Read This **Before You Begin**

STUDENT DISK

To complete Word 97 Tutorials 1-4, you need a Student Disk. Your instructor will either provide you with a Student Disk or ask you to make your own.

If you are supposed to make your own Student Disk, you will need one blank, formatted, high-density disk. You will need to copy a set of folders from a file server or standalone computer onto your disk. Your instructor will tell you which computer, drive letter, and folders contain the files you need. The following table shows you which folders go on your disk:

Student Disk	Write this on the disk label	Put these folders on the disk
1	Student Disk 1: Word 97 Tutorials 1-4	Tutorial.01, Tutorial.02, Tutorial.03, Tutorial.04

See the inside front or inside back cover of this book for more information on Student Disk files, or ask your instructor or technical support person for assistance.

COURSE LAB

Tutorial 1 features an interactive Course Lab to help you understand word processing concepts. There are Lab Assignments at the end of the tutorial that relate to this Lab. To start the Lab, click the Start button on the Windows 95 Taskbar, point to Programs, point to Course Labs, point to New Perspectives Applications, and click Word Processing.

USING YOUR OWN COMPUTER

If you are going to work through this book using your own computer, you need:

■ **Computer System** Microsoft Windows 95 or Microsoft Windows NT Workstation 4.0 (or a later version) and Microsoft Word 97 must be installed on your computer. This book assumes a typical installation of Microsoft Word 97.

■ **Student Disk** Ask your instructor or lab manager for details on how to get the Student Disk. You will not be able to complete the tutorials or end-of-tutorial assignments in this book using your own computer until you have a Student Disk. The Student Files may also be obtained electronically over the Internet. See the inside front or inside back cover of this book for more details.

■ **Course Lab** See your instructor or technical support person to obtain the Course Lab software for use on your own computer.

To complete Word 97 Tutorials 1-4, your students must use a set of files on a Student Disk. These files are included in the Instructor's Resource Kit, and they may also be obtained electronically over the Internet. See the inside front or inside back cover of this book for more details. Follow the instructions in the Readme file to copy the files to your server or standalone computer. You can view the Readme file using WordPad. Once the files are copied, you can make Student Disks for the students yourself, or you can tell students where to find the files so they can make their own Student Disks.

COURSE LAB SOFTWARE

The Course Lab software is distributed on a CD-ROM included in the Instructor's Resource Kit. To install the Course Lab software, follow the setup instructions in the Readme file on the CD-ROM. Refer also to the Readme file for essential technical notes related to running the Lab in a multi-user environment. Once you have installed the Course Lab software, your students can start the Lab from the Windows 95 desktop by following the instructions in the Course Labs section above.

COURSE TECHNOLOGY STUDENT FILES AND LAB SOFTWARE

You are granted a license to copy the Student Files and Lab software to any computer or computer network used by students who have purchased this book.

Creating a Document

Writing a Business Letter for Crossroads

LABS

Word Processing

CASE

Crossroads

Karen Liu is executive director of Crossroads, a small, non-profit organization in Tacoma, Washington. Crossroads distributes business clothing to low-income clients who are returning to the job market or starting new careers. To make potential clients in the community more aware of their services, Crossroads reserves an exhibit booth each year at a local job fair sponsored by the Tacoma Chamber of Commerce. Crossroads needs to find out the date and location of this year's fair, as well as some other logistical information, before they can reserve a booth. Karen asks you to write a letter requesting this information from the Tacoma Chamber of Commerce.

In this tutorial you will create Karen's letter using Microsoft Word 97, a popular word-processing program. Before you begin typing the letter, you will learn to start the Word program, identify and use the elements of the Word screen, and adjust some Word settings. You will then go on to create a new Word document, type in the text of the Crossroads letter, save the letter, and then print the letter for Karen. In the process of entering the text, you'll learn several ways of correcting typing errors. You'll also learn how to use the Word Help system, which allows you to quickly find answers to your questions about the program.

Using the Tutorials Effectively

These tutorials are designed to be used at a computer. Each tutorial is divided into sessions. Watch for the session headings, such as "Session 1.1" and "Session 1.2." Each session is designed to be completed in about 45 minutes, but take as much time as you need. When you've completed a session, it's a good idea to exit the program and take a break. You can exit Microsoft Word by clicking the Close button in the top-right corner of the program window.

Before you begin, read the following questions and answers. They are designed to help you use the tutorials effectively.

Where do I start?

Each tutorial begins with a case, which sets the scene for the tutorial and gives you background information to help you understand what you will be doing in the tutorial. Read the case before you go to the lab. In the lab, begin with the first session of the tutorial.

How do I know what to do on the computer?

Each session contains steps that you will perform on the computer to learn how to use Microsoft Word. The steps are numbered and are set against a colored background. Read the text that introduces each series of steps, and read each step carefully and completely before you try it.

How do I know if I did the step correctly?

As you work, compare your computer screen with the corresponding figure in the tutorial. Don't worry if your screen display is somewhat different from the figure. The important parts of the screen display are labeled in each figure. Check to make sure these parts are on your screen.

What if I make a mistake?

Don't worry about making mistakes—they are part of the learning process. Paragraphs labeled "TROUBLE?" identify common problems and explain how to get back on track. Follow the steps in a TROUBLE? paragraph *only* if you are having the problem described. If you run into other problems, carefully consider the current state of your system, the position of the pointer, and any messages on the screen.

How do I use the Reference Windows?

Reference Windows summarize the procedures you learn in the tutorial steps. Do not complete the actions in the Reference Windows when you are working through the tutorial. Instead, refer to the Reference Windows while you are working on the assignments at the end of the tutorial.

How can I test my understanding of the material I learned in the tutorial?

At the end of each session, you can answer the Quick Check questions. If necessary, refer to the Answers to Quick Check Questions to check your work.

After you have completed the entire tutorial, you should complete the Tutorial Assignments and Case Problems. These exercises are carefully structured so you will review what you have learned and then apply your knowledge to new situations.

What if I can't remember how to do something?

You should refer to the Task Reference at the end of the book; it summarizes how to accomplish commonly performed tasks.

What is the Word Processing Course Lab, and how should I use it?

This interactive Lab helps you review word processing concepts and practice skills that you learn in Tutorial 1. The Lab Assignments section at the end of Tutorial 1 includes instructions for using the Lab.

Now that you've seen how to use the tutorials effectively, you are ready to begin.

SESSION 1.1	*In this session you will learn how to start Word, how to identify and use the parts of the Word screen, and how to adjust some Word settings. With the skills you learn in this session, you'll be prepared to use Word to create a variety of documents, such as letters, reports, and memos.*

Four Steps to a Professional Document

Word helps you produce quality work in minimal time. Not only can you type a document, you can quickly make editing changes and corrections, adjust margins and spacing, create columns and tables, and add graphics to your documents. The most efficient way to produce a document is to follow these four steps: 1) planning and creating, 2) editing, 3) formatting, and 4) printing.

In the long run, *planning* saves you time and effort. First, you should determine what you want to say. State your purpose clearly and include enough information to achieve that purpose without overwhelming or boring your reader. Be sure to *organize* your ideas logically. Also, decide how you want your document to look—its *presentation*. In this case, your letter to the Tacoma Chamber of Commerce will take the form of a standard business letter. Karen has given you a handwritten note with all her questions for the Tacoma Chamber of Commerce, as shown in Figure 1-1.

Figure 1-1 ◀
Karen's questions about the job fair

> Please write the Tacoma Chamber of Commerce and find out the following:
>
> What are the location and dates for this year's job fair?
>
> Is a map of the exhibit area available? What size booths are available and how can we reserve a booth?
>
> Who do we contact about what physical facilities are available at each booth?
>
> Send the letter to the Chamber's president. The address is 210 Shoreline Vista, Suite 1103, Tacoma WA 98402.

After you've planned your document, you can go ahead and *create* it using Word. The next step, *editing*, consists of reading through the document you've created, then correcting your errors, and finally adding or deleting text to make the document easy to read.

Once your document is error-free, you can *format* it to make it visually appealing. As you'll learn in Tutorial 2, formatting features, such as white space (blank areas of a page), line spacing, boldface, and italics can help make your document easier to read. *Printing* is the final phase in creating an effective document. In this tutorial, you will preview your document before you spend time and resources to print it.

Starting Word

Before you can apply these four steps to produce the letter using Word, you need to start Word and learn about the general organization of the Word screen. You'll do that now.

To start Microsoft Word:

1. Make sure Windows 95 is running on your computer and the Windows 95 desktop appears on your screen.

   TROUBLE? If you're running Windows NT Workstation 4.0 (or a later version) on your computer or network, don't worry. Although the figures in this book were created while running Windows 95, Windows NT 4.0 and Windows 95 share the same interface, and Word 97 runs equally well under either operating system.

2. Click the **Start** button on the taskbar to display the Start menu, and then point to **Programs** to display the Programs menu.

3. Point to **Microsoft Word** on the Programs menu. See Figure 1-2.

Figure 1-2 ◄
Starting
Microsoft Word

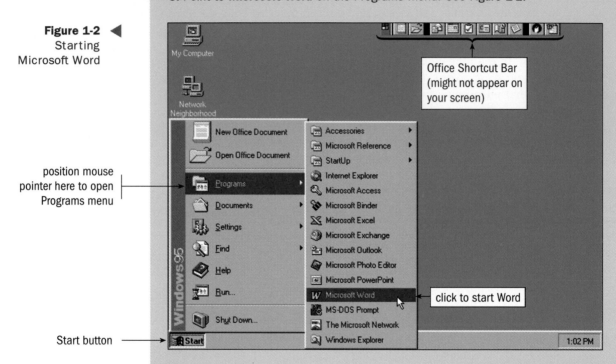

position mouse
pointer here to open
Programs menu

Start button

   TROUBLE? If you don't see the Microsoft Word option on the Programs menu, ask your instructor or technical support person for help.

   TROUBLE? The Office Shortcut Bar, which appears along the top border of the desktop in Figure 1-2, might look different on your screen, or it might not appear at all, depending on how your system is set up. Since the Office Shortcut Bar is not required to complete these tutorials, it has been omitted from the remaining figures in this text.

4. Click **Microsoft Word**. After a short pause, the Microsoft Word copyright information appears in a message box and remains on the screen until the Word program window, containing a blank Word document, is displayed. See Figure 1-3.

Word

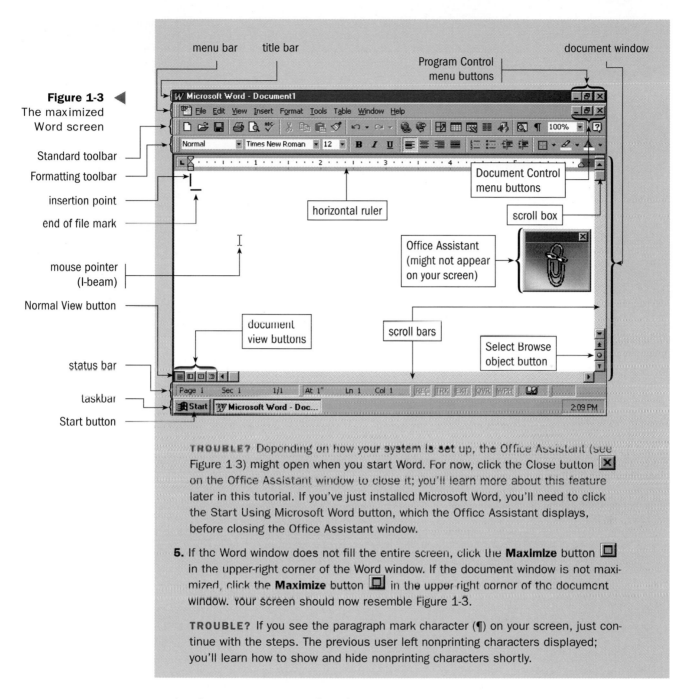

Figure 1-3
The maximized
Word screen

menu bar   title bar   document window

Program Control
menu buttons

Standard toolbar

Formatting toolbar

insertion point

end of file mark

horizontal ruler

Document Control
menu buttons

scroll box

Office Assistant
(might not appear
on your screen)

mouse pointer
(I-beam)

Normal View button

document
view buttons

scroll bars

Select Browse
object button

status bar

taskbar

Start button

TROUBLE? Depending on how your system is set up, the Office Assistant (see Figure 1-3) might open when you start Word. For now, click the Close button ☒ on the Office Assistant window to close it; you'll learn more about this feature later in this tutorial. If you've just installed Microsoft Word, you'll need to click the Start Using Microsoft Word button, which the Office Assistant displays, before closing the Office Assistant window.

5. If the Word window does not fill the entire screen, click the **Maximize** button ☐ in the upper-right corner of the Word window. If the document window is not maximized, click the **Maximize** button ☐ in the upper-right corner of the document window. Your screen should now resemble Figure 1-3.

TROUBLE? If you see the paragraph mark character (¶) on your screen, just continue with the steps. The previous user left nonprinting characters displayed; you'll learn how to show and hide nonprinting characters shortly.

Word is now running and ready to use.

The Word Screen

The Word screen is made up of both a program window and a document window. The **program window**, also called the Word window, opens automatically when you start Word and contains all the toolbars and menus. The **document window**, which opens within the Word window, is where you type and edit documents.

Figure 1-3 shows the Word screen with both windows maximized. If your screen doesn't look exactly like Figure 1-3, just continue for now. Figure 1-4 lists each element of the Word screen and summarizes its function. You are already familiar with some of these elements, such as the menu bar, title bar, and status bar, because they are common to all Windows screens.

Figure 1-4 ◀
Summary
of functions of
Word screen

Screen Element	Function
Title bar	Identifies the current application (i.e., Microsoft Word); shows the filename of the current document
Control menu buttons	Program Control menu buttons size and close the Word window; Document Control menu buttons size and close the current document window
Menu bar	Contains lists or menus of all the Word commands
Standard toolbar	Contains buttons to activate frequently used commands
Formatting toolbar	Contains buttons to activate common font and paragraph formatting commands
Select Browse object button	Displays buttons that allow you to move quickly through the document
Horizontal ruler	Adjusts margins, tabs, and column widths; vertical ruler appears in page layout view
Document window	Area where you enter text and graphics
Document view buttons	Show document in four different views: normal view, online layout view, page layout view, and outline view
Status bar	Provides information regarding the location of the insertion point
Taskbar	Shows programs that are running and allows you to switch quickly from one program to another
Mouse pointer	Changes shape depending on its location on the screen (i.e., I-beam pointer in text area; arrow in nontext areas)
Insertion point	Indicates location where characters will be inserted or deleted
Scroll bars	Shift text vertically and horizontally on the screen so you can see different parts of the document
Scroll box	Helps you move quickly to other pages of your document
Start button	Starts a program, opens a document, provides quick access to Windows 95 Help

If at any time you would like to check the name of a Word toolbar button, just position the mouse pointer over the button without clicking. A **ScreenTip**, a small yellow box with the name of the button, will appear.

Checking the Screen Before You Begin Each Tutorial

Word provides a set of standard settings, called **default settings**, that are appropriate for most documents. The setup of your Word document might have different default settings from those shown in the figures. This often happens when you share a computer and another user changes the appearance of the Word screen. The rest of this section explains what your screen should look like and how to make it match those in the tutorials.

Word

Setting the Document View to Normal

You can view your document in one of four ways—normal, online layout, page layout, or outline. **Online layout** and **outline view** are designed for special situations that you don't need to worry about now. You will, however, learn more about **page layout view**—which allows you to see a page's design and format—in later tutorials. In most cases you'll want to use **normal view** when completing these tutorials. Depending on the document view selected by the last person who used Word, you might need to change the document back to normal view.

To make sure the document window is in normal view:

1. Click the **Normal View** button 📧 to the left of the horizontal scroll bar. See Figure 1-5. If your document window was not in normal view, it changes to normal view now.

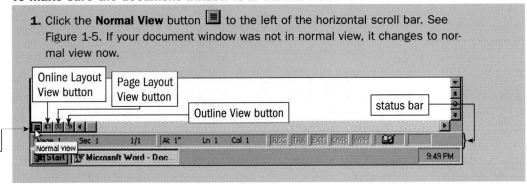

Figure 1-5 ◀
Changing to normal view

Normal View button

Online Layout View button

Page Layout View button

Outline View button

status bar

Displaying the Toolbars and Ruler

These tutorials frequently use the Standard toolbar and the Formatting toolbar to help you work more efficiently. Each time you start Word, check to make sure both toolbars appear on your screen. If either toolbar is missing, or if other toolbars are displayed, perform the steps below.

To display or hide a toolbar:

1. Position the pointer over any visible toolbar and click the right mouse button. A shortcut menu appears. The menu lists all available toolbars, and displays a check mark next to those currently displayed.

2. If the Standard or Formatting toolbar is not visible, click its name on the shortcut menu to place a check mark next to it. If any toolbars besides the Formatting and Standard toolbars have checkmarks, click each one to remove the check mark and hide the toolbar.

As you complete these tutorials, the ruler should also be visible to help you place items precisely. If your ruler is not visible, perform the next step.

To display the ruler:

1. Click **View** on the menu bar, and then click **Ruler** to place a check mark next to it.

Setting the Font and Font Size

A **font** is a set of characters that has a certain design, shape, and appearance. Each font has a name, such as Courier, Times New Roman, or Arial. The **font size** is the actual height of a character, measured in points, where one point equals $\frac{1}{72}$ of an inch in height. You'll learn more about fonts and font sizes in Tutorial 2, but for now simply keep in mind that most of the documents you'll create will use the Times New Roman font in a font size of 12 points. Word usually uses a default setting of 10-point font size in new documents. This font size, however, is not as easy to read as the larger 12-point font. If your font setting is not Times New Roman 12 point, you should change the default setting now. You'll use the menu bar to choose the desired commands.

To change the default font and font size:

1. Click **Format** on the menu bar, and then click **Font** to open the Font dialog box. If necessary, click the Font tab. See Figure 1-6.

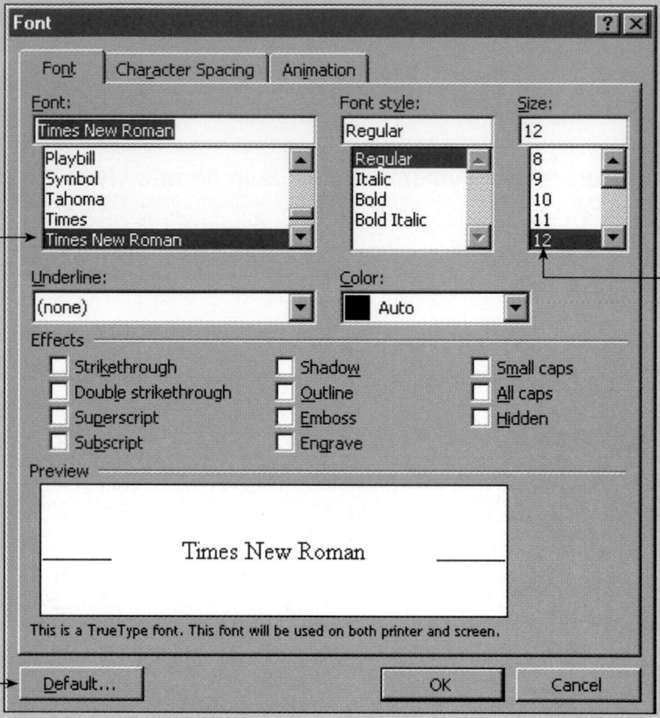

Figure 1-6 ◀
Font dialog box

use this font →

use this point size

click to make selected font settings the defaults

2. In the Size list box, click **12** to change the font to 12 point.

3. Click **Times New Roman** to make sure that it is listed in the Font text box.

4. Click the **Default** button to make Times New Roman and 12 point the default settings. Word displays a message asking you to verify that you want to make 12 point Times New Roman the default font.

5. Click the **Yes** button.

Displaying Nonprinting Characters

Nonprinting characters are symbols that can be displayed on the screen but that do not show up when you print your document. You can display them when you are working on the appearance, or **format**, of your document. For example, one nonprinting character marks the end of a paragraph (¶), while another marks the space between words (•). It's sometimes helpful to display nonprinting characters so you can actually see whether you've typed an extra space, ended a paragraph, typed spaces instead of tabs, and so on. In general, in these tutorials, you will display nonprinting characters only when you are formatting a document. You'll display them now, though, so you can use them as guides when typing your first letter.

To display nonprinting characters:

1. Click the **Show/Hide ¶** button 🔳 on the Standard toolbar to display the nonprinting characters. A paragraph mark (¶) appears at the top of the document window. See Figure 1-7.

Figure 1-7 ◀
Nonprinting
characters
activated

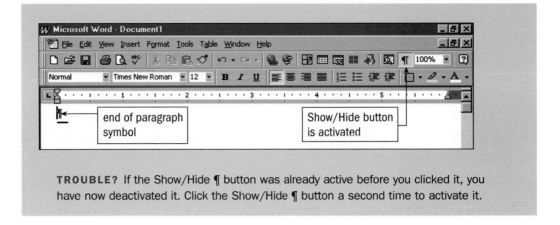

TROUBLE? If the Show/Hide ¶ button was already active before you clicked it, you
have now deactivated it. Click the Show/Hide ¶ button a second time to activate it.

To make sure your screen always matches the figures in this book, remember to complete the checklist in Figure 1-8 each time you sit down at the computer.

Figure 1-8 ◀
Word screen
session
checklist

Screen Element	Setting	Check
Document view	Normal	
Program and document windows	Maximized	
Standard toolbar	Displayed	
Formatting toolbar	Displayed	
Other toolbars	Hidden	
Nonprinting characters	Hidden	
Font	Times New Roman	
Point size	12 point	
Ruler	Displayed	

Quick Check

1. In your own words, list and describe the steps in creating a document.
2. How do you start Word from the Windows 95 desktop?
3. Define each of the following in your own words:
   a. Standard toolbar
   b. ruler
   c. insertion point
   d. font
   e. default settings
4. How do you change the default font size?
5. How do you display or hide the Standard toolbar?
6. How do you display or hide nonprinting characters?

Now that you have planned a document, opened the Word program, identified screen elements, and adjusted settings, you are ready to create a new document. In the next session, you will create Karen's letter to the Tacoma Chamber of Commerce.

SESSION 1.2

In this session you will create a one-page document using Word. You'll learn how to correct errors and scroll through your document. You'll also learn how to name, save, preview, and print the document, and how to use the Word Help system.

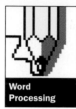

Word Processing

Typing a Letter

You're ready to type Karen's letter to the Tacoma Chamber of Commerce. Figure 1-9 shows the completed letter printed on the company letterhead. You'll begin by opening a new blank page (in case you accidentally typed something in the current page). Then you'll move the insertion point to about 2½ inches from the top margin of the paper to allow space for the Crossroads letterhead.

Figure 1-9 ◀
Job fair letter

1414 East Bellingham S.W.
Suite 318
Tacoma, WA 98402

February 21, 1998

Deborah Brown, President
Tacoma Chamber of Commerce
210 Shoreline Vista, Suite 1103
Tacoma, WA 98402

Dear Deborah:

Recently, you contacted our staff about the Chamber's decision to sponsor a job fair again this year. We are interested in participating as we have done in the past.

Please send us information about the dates and location for this year's fair. If a map of the exhibit area is available, we would appreciate receiving a copy of it. Also, please send us the name and address of someone we can contact regarding the on-site physical facilities. Specifically, we need to know what size the exhibit booths are and how we can reserve one.

Thank you for your help in this matter. We look forward to participating in the job fair and hope to hear from you soon.

Sincerely yours,

Karen Liu
Executive Director

To open a new document:

1. If you took a break after the last session, make sure the Word program is running, that nonprinting characters are displayed, and that the font settings in the Formatting toolbar are set to 12 point Times New Roman.

2. Click the **New** button 🗋 on the Standard toolbar to open a new, blank document.

3. Press the **Enter** key eight times. Each time you press the Enter key, a nonprinting paragraph mark appears. In the status bar (at the bottom of the document window) you should see the setting "At 2.5"", indicating that the insertion point is 2½ inches from the top of the page. Another setting in the status bar should read "Ln 9", indicating the insertion point is in line 9 of the document. See Figure 1-10.

Figure 1-10 ◀
Document window after inserting blank lines

insertion point at 2.5 inches

line number

vertical location

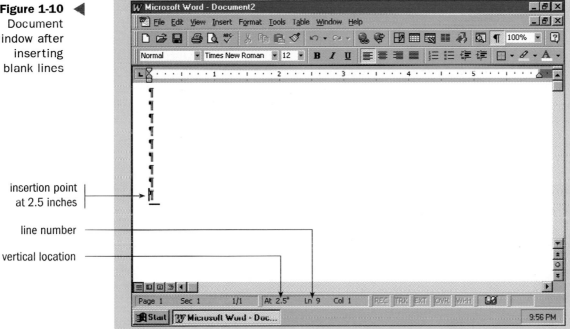

TROUBLE? If the paragraph mark doesn't appear each time you press the Enter key, the nonprinting characters might be hidden. To show the nonprinting characters, click the Show/Hide ¶ button 🔲.

TROUBLE? If you pressed the Enter key too many times, just press the Backspace key to delete each extra line and paragraph mark. If you're on line 9 but the At number is not 2.5", don't worry. Different fonts and monitors produce slightly different measurements when you press the Enter key.

Using AutoText Tips

Now you're ready to type the date. As you do it, you'll take advantage of Word's **AutoText** feature, which automatically types dates and other regularly used words and text for you.

To insert the date using an AutoText tip:

1. Type **Febr** (the first four letters of February). An AutoText tip appears above the line, as shown in Figure 1-11.

Figure 1-11 ◀
AutoText tip

tip shows the
rest of the word

press the Enter key to insert the rest of
the word, or keep typing to ignore tip

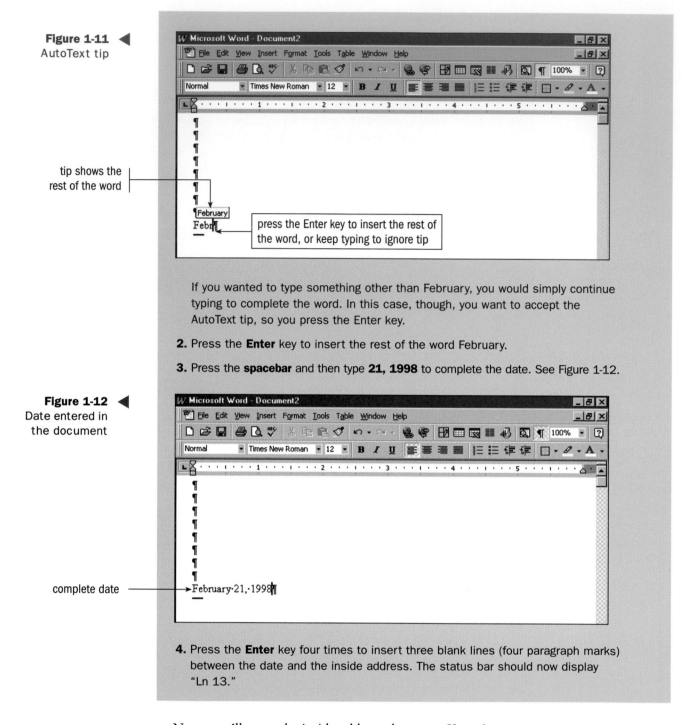

If you wanted to type something other than February, you would simply continue typing to complete the word. In this case, though, you want to accept the AutoText tip, so you press the Enter key.

2. Press the **Enter** key to insert the rest of the word February.

3. Press the **spacebar** and then type **21, 1998** to complete the date. See Figure 1-12.

Figure 1-12 ◀
Date entered in
the document

complete date

4. Press the **Enter** key four times to insert three blank lines (four paragraph marks) between the date and the inside address. The status bar should now display "Ln 13."

Next, you'll enter the inside address shown on Karen's note.

Entering Text

You'll enter the inside address by typing it. If you type a wrong character, simply press the Backspace key to delete the mistake and then retype it.

To type the inside address:

1. Type **Deborah Brown, President** and press the **Enter** key. As you type, the non-printing character (•) appears between words to indicate a space.

Word

TROUBLE? If a wavy red or green line appears beneath a word, check to make sure you typed the text correctly. If you did not, use the Backspace key to remove the error, and then retype the text correctly.

2. Type the following text, pressing the **Enter** key after each line to enter the inside address.

Tacoma Chamber of Commerce
210 Shoreline Vista, Suite 1103
Tacoma, WA 98402

3. Press the **Enter** key again to add a blank line between the inside address and the salutation. See Figure 1-13.

Figure 1-13 ◀
Document
window
showing inside
address

inside address ——

extra blank line ——

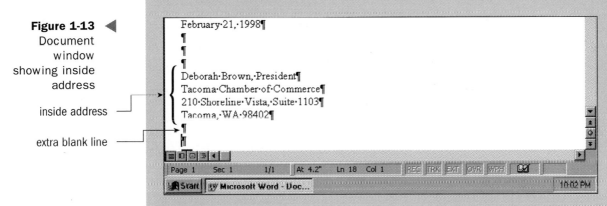

4. Type **Dear Deborah:** and press the **Enter** key twice to double space between the salutation and the body of the letter.

When you press the Enter key the first time, the Office Assistant appears and asks if you would like help writing your letter. See Figure 1-14.

Figure 1-14 ◀
Office
Assistant

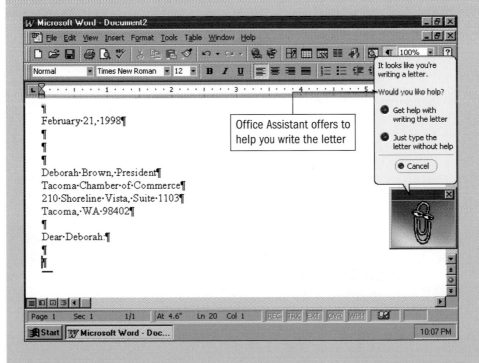

The Office Assistant is a special feature that sometimes appears to offer help on routine tasks. In this case, you could click the "Get help with writing the letter button" and have the Office Assistant lead you through a series of dialog boxes designed to set up the basic elements of your letter automatically. You'll learn more about the

Office Assistant later in this tutorial. Then, in the Tutorial Assignments, you'll have a chance to create a letter with the help of the Office Assistant. For now, though, you'll close the Office Assistant and continue writing your letter.

5. Click the **Just type the letter without help** button to close the Office Assistant.

You have completed the date, the inside address, and the salutation of Karen's letter, using a standard business letter format. You're ready to complete the letter. Before you do, however, you should save what you have typed so far.

Saving a Document

The letter on which you are working is stored only in the computer's memory, not on a disk. If you were to exit Word, turn off your computer, or experience an accidental power failure, the part of Karen's letter that you just typed would be lost. You should get in the habit of frequently saving your document to a disk.

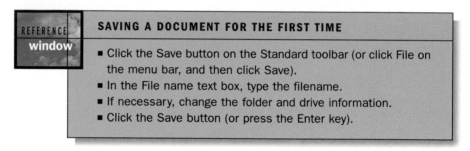

REFERENCE window

SAVING A DOCUMENT FOR THE FIRST TIME

- Click the Save button on the Standard toolbar (or click File on the menu bar, and then click Save).
- In the File name text box, type the filename.
- If necessary, change the folder and drive information.
- Click the Save button (or press the Enter key).

After you name your document, Word automatically appends the .doc filename extension to identify the file as a Microsoft Word document. However, depending on how Windows 95 is set up (or configured) on your computer, you might not actually see .doc extension. These tutorials assume that filename extensions are hidden.

To save the document:

1. Place your Student Disk in the appropriate disk drive.

    TROUBLE? If you don't have a Student Disk, you need to get one before you can proceed. Your instructor or technical support person will either give you one or ask you to make your own by following the instructions on the "Read This Before You Begin" page at the beginning of this tutorial. See your instructor or technical support person for more information.

2. Click the **Save** button 🖫 on the Standard toolbar. The Save As dialog box opens. See Figure 1-15.

Figure 1-15 ◀
Save As
dialog box

change folder to
Tutorial.01

type filename here

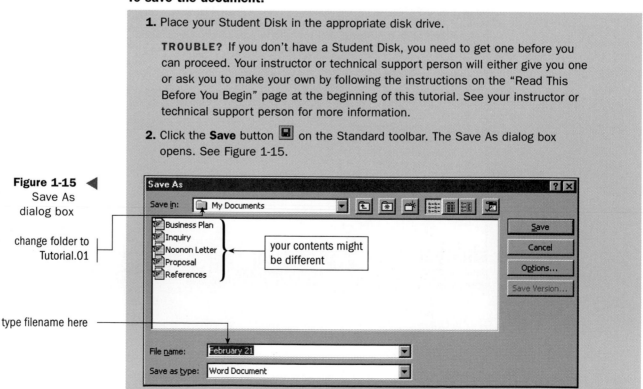

3. Type **Tacoma Job Fair Letter** in the File name text box.

4. Click the **Save in** list arrow, click the drive containing your Student Disk, and then double-click the **Tutorial.01** folder. The Tutorial.01 folder is now open for saving the file. See Figure 1-16.

Figure 1-16 ◀
Save As dialog
box with
Tutorial.01
folder open

folder on
Student Disk

filename

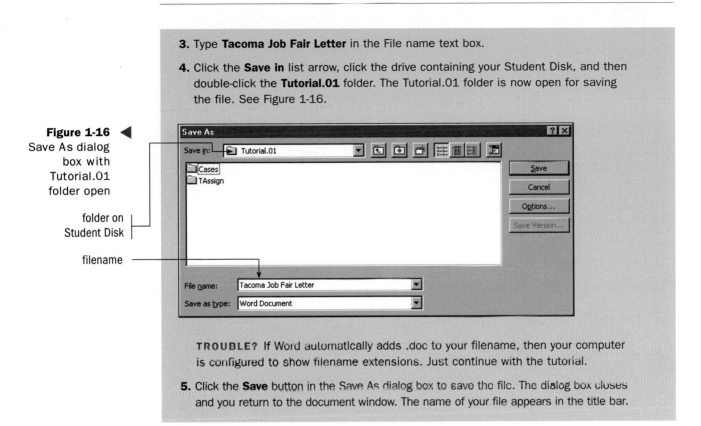

TROUBLE? If Word automatically adds .doc to your filename, then your computer is configured to show filename extensions. Just continue with the tutorial.

5. Click the **Save** button in the Save As dialog box to save the file. The dialog box closes and you return to the document window. The name of your file appears in the title bar.

Word Wrap

With your document saved, you're ready to complete Karen's letter. As you type the body of the letter, do not press the Enter key at the end of each line. When you type a word that extends into the right margin, both the insertion point and the word move automatically to the next line. This automatic text line breaking is called **word wrap**. You'll see how word wrap works as you type the body of Karen's letter.

To observe word wrap while typing a paragraph:

1. Make sure the insertion point is at Ln 20 Col 1 (according to the settings in the status bar). If it's not, move it to that location by pressing the arrow keys.

2. Type the following sentence slowly and watch when the insertion point automatically jumps to the next line: **Recently, you contacted our staff about the Chamber's decision to sponsor a job fair again this year.** Notice how Word automatically moves the last few words to a new line. See Figure 1-17.

Figure 1-17 ◀
Word wrapping
text

beginning of first
paragraph

word wrapped
to new line

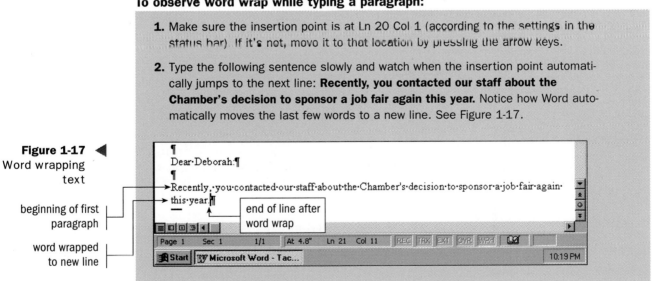

TROUBLE? If your screen does not match Figure 1-17 exactly, don't be concerned. The word or letter at which word wrap occurred in your document and the status bar values might be different from Figure 1-17 because fonts have varying letter widths and produce slightly different measurements on monitors. Continue with Step 3. If you see any other AutoText tips as you type, ignore them.

3. Press the **spacebar** twice, and type **We are interested in participating as we have done in the past.** (including the period) to enter the rest of the first paragraph of the letter.

4. Press the **Enter** key to end the first paragraph, and then press the **Enter** key again to double space between the first and second paragraphs.

Scrolling

After you finish the last set of steps, the insertion point will probably be at the bottom of your document window. It might seem that no room is left in the document window to type the rest of Karen's letter. However, as you continue to add text at the end of your document, the text that you typed earlier will scroll (or shift up) and disappear from the top of the document window. You'll see how scrolling works as you enter the final text of Karen's letter.

To observe scrolling while you're entering text:

1. Make sure the insertion point is at the bottom of the screen, to the left of the second paragraph mark in the body of the letter.

2. Type the second paragraph, as shown in Figure 1-18, and then press the **Enter** key twice to insert a blank line. Notice that as you type the paragraph, the top of the letter scrolls off the top of the document window. Don't worry if you make a mistake in your typing. You'll learn a number of ways to correct errors in the next section.

Figure 1-18 ◀
Text scrolled
off the screen

date and inside
address scrolled
off the screen

second paragraph

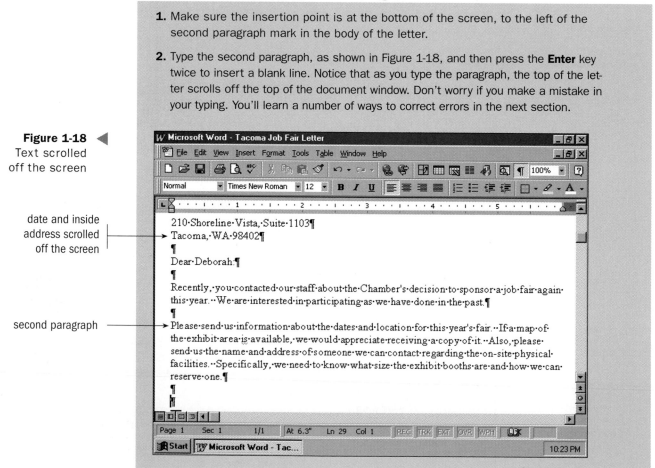

Correcting Errors

Have you made any typing mistakes yet? If so, don't worry. The advantage of using a word processor is that you can correct mistakes quickly and efficiently. Word provides several ways to correct errors when you're entering text.

If you discover a typing error as soon as you make it, you can press the Backspace key to erase the characters and spaces to the left of the insertion point one at a time. Backspacing will erase both printing and nonprinting characters. After you erase the error, you can type the correct characters.

Word also provides a feature, called **AutoCorrect**, that checks for errors in your document as you type and automatically corrects common typing errors, such as "adn" for "and." If the spelling of a particular word doesn't appear as it would in the Word electronic dictionary or isn't in the dictionary (for example, a person's name), a wavy *red* line appears beneath the word. If you accidentally type an extra space between words or make a grammatical error (such as typing "he walk" instead of "he walks"), a wavy *green* line appears beneath the error. You'll see how AutoCorrect works when you intentionally make some typing errors.

To find common typing errors:

1. Carefully and slowly type the following sentence exactly as it is shown, including the spelling errors and the extra space between the last two words: **Word corects teh common typing misTakes you make.** Press the **Enter** key when you are finished typing. Notice that as you press the spacebar after the words "corects" and "misTakes," a wavy red line appears on the screen beneath each word, indicating that the word might be misspelled. Notice also that when you pressed the spacebar after the word "teh," Word automatically corrected the spelling to "the." After you pressed the Enter key, a wavy green line appeared under the last two words, alerting you to the extra space. See Figure 1-19.

Figure 1-19 ◀
Document
window
showing
typing errors

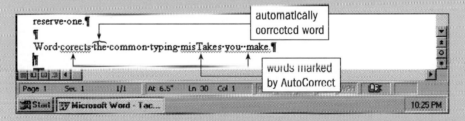

TROUBLE? If red and green wavy lines do not appear beneath mistakes, Word is probably not set to automatically check spelling and grammar as you type. Click Tools on the menu bar, and then click Options to open the Options dialog box. Click the Spelling and Grammar tab. Make sure there are check marks in the Check spelling as you type and the Check grammar as you type check boxes, and click OK. If Word does not automatically correct the incorrect spelling of "the," click Tools on the menu bar, click AutoCorrect, and make sure that all five boxes at the top of the AutoCorrect tab have check marks. Then scroll down the AutoCorrect list to make sure that there is an entry that changes "teh" to "the," and click OK.

TROUBLE? If the Office Assistant appears with a tip on correcting errors, you can close the Office Assistant window by clicking its Close button ▣.

2. Position the pointer ⌶ over the word "corects" and click the right mouse button. A list box appears with suggested spellings. See Figure 1-20.

Figure 1-20 ◀
List box
showing
AutoCorrect
suggested
spellings

click to replace
misspelled word

insertion point after
right-clicking
misspelled word

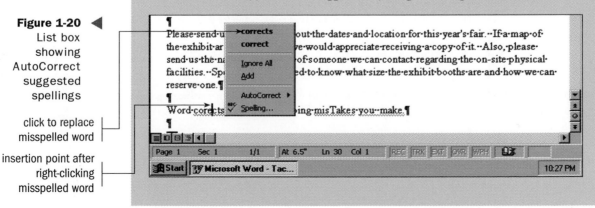

TROUBLE? If the list box doesn't appear, repeat Step 2 making sure you click the right mouse button, not the left one.

3. Click **corrects** in the list box. The list box disappears and the correct spelling appears in your document. Notice that the wavy red line disappears after you correct the error.

4. Position the pointer I directly over the word "misTakes" and click the right mouse button. A list box appears with suggested spellings.

5. Click **mistakes** in the list box. The list box disappears and the correct spelling appears in your document.

6. Press the → key until the insertion point is to the right of the letter "u" in the word "you." Press the **Delete** key to delete the extra space.

You can see how quick and easy it is to correct common typing errors with AutoCorrect. Use it or the Backspace or Delete keys now to correct mistakes you might have made when typing the first part of the letter. Before you continue typing Karen's letter, you'll need to delete your practice sentence.

To delete the practice sentence:

1. Click between the period and the paragraph mark at the end of the sentence.

2. Press and hold the **Backspace** key until the entire sentence is deleted. Then press the **Delete** key to delete the extra paragraph mark.

3. Make sure the insertion point is in line 29. There should be one nonprinting paragraph mark between the second paragraph and the paragraph you will type next.

Finishing the Letter

You're ready to complete the rest of the letter. As you type, you can use any of the techniques you learned in the previous section to correct mistakes.

To complete the letter:

1. Type the final paragraph of the body of the letter, as shown in Figure 1-21, and then press the **Enter** key twice. Accept or ignore AutoText tips as necessary. Your screen should look like Figure 1-21. Notice that the date and the inside address now scroll off the top of the document window.

Figure 1-21 ◀
Final paragraph

third paragraph ──────▶

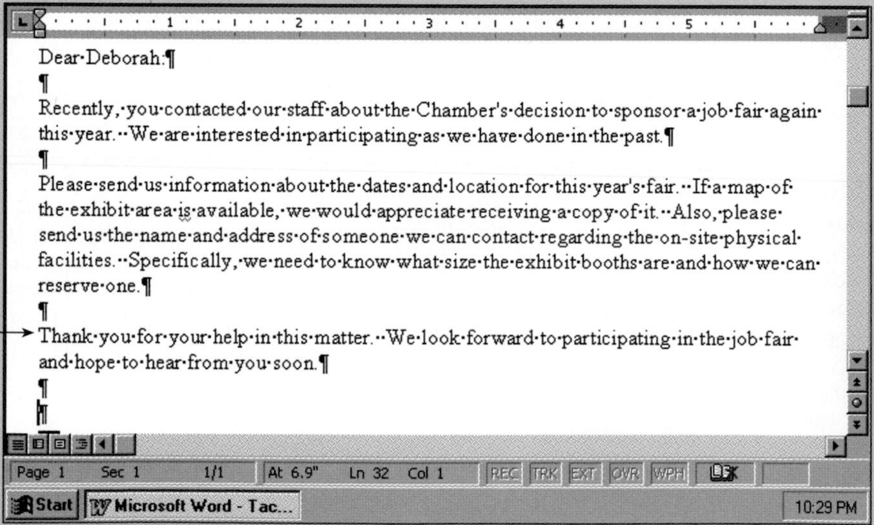

> **TROUBLE?** If your screen does not match Figure 1-21 exactly, don't be concerned. Because of variations in font sizes and monitors, more or less text might have scrolled off your screen. Just continue with Step 2.
>
> 2. Type **Sincerely yours,** (including the comma) to enter the complimentary close.
>
> 3. Press the **Enter** key four times to allow space for Karen's signature.
>
> 4. Type **Karen Liu**, press the **Enter** key, and then type **Executive Director** to complete your letter. See Figure 1-22.

Figure 1-22 ◀
Complimentary
closing of letter

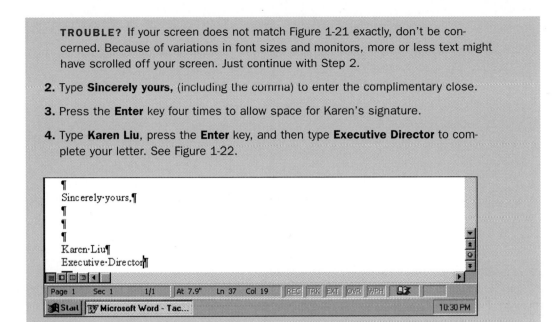

In the last set of steps, you watched the text at the top of your document move off your screen. You can scroll this hidden text back into view so you can read the beginning of the letter. When you do, the text at the bottom of the screen will scroll out of view.

To scroll the text using the scroll bar:

> 1. Position the mouse pointer on the up arrow on the vertical scroll bar. Press and hold the mouse button to scroll the text. When the text stops scrolling, you have reached the top of the document and can see the beginning of the letter.

Now that you have completed the letter, you'll save the completed document.

Saving the Completed Letter

Although you saved the letter earlier, the text that you typed since then exists only in the computer's memory. That means you need to save your document again. It's especially important to save your document before printing. Then, if you experience problems that cause your computer to stop working while you are printing, you will still have a copy of the document containing your most recent additions and changes on your disk.

To save the completed letter:

> 1. Make sure your Student Disk is still in the appropriate disk drive.
>
> 2. Click the **Save** button 🔲 on the Standard toolbar. Because you named and saved this file earlier, you can save the document without being prompted for information. Word saves your letter with the same name you gave it earlier.

Previewing and Printing a Document

The current document window displays the text, but you cannot see an entire page without scrolling. To see how the page will look when printed, you need to use the Print Preview window.

To preview the document:

1. Click the **Print Preview** button 📄 on the Standard toolbar. The Print Preview window opens and displays a full-page version of your letter, as shown in Figure 1-23. This shows how the letter will fit on the printed page.

Figure 1-23 ◀
Print preview version of the letter

one page button

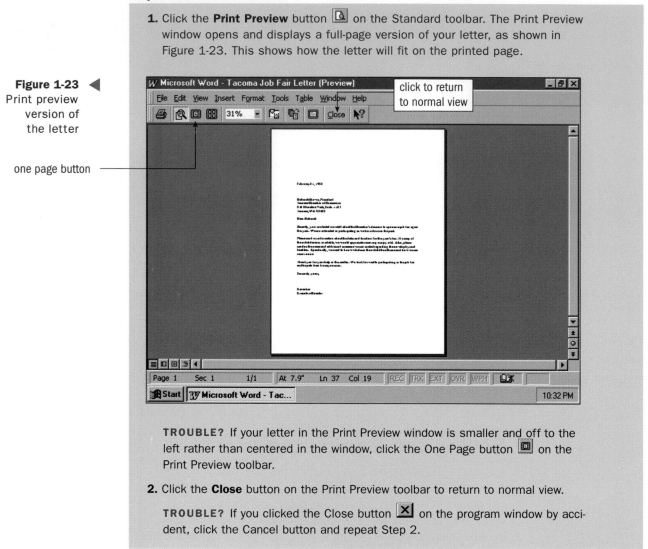

    TROUBLE? If your letter in the Print Preview window is smaller and off to the left rather than centered in the window, click the One Page button 🔲 on the Print Preview toolbar.

2. Click the **Close** button on the Print Preview toolbar to return to normal view.

    TROUBLE? If you clicked the Close button ✕ on the program window by accident, click the Cancel button and repeat Step 2.

You've seen how the letter will appear on the printed page. The text looks well-spaced and the letterhead will fit at the top of the page. You're ready to print the letter.

In each session, the first time you print from a shared computer, you should check the settings in the Print dialog box and make sure the number of copies is set to one. After that, you can *use* the Print button on the Standard toolbar to send your document directly to the printer without displaying the Print dialog box.

To print a document:

1. Make sure your printer is turned on and paper is in the printer.

2. Click **File** on the menu bar, and then click **Print**. The Print dialog box opens. See Figure 1-24.

Figure 1-24 ◀
Print dialog box

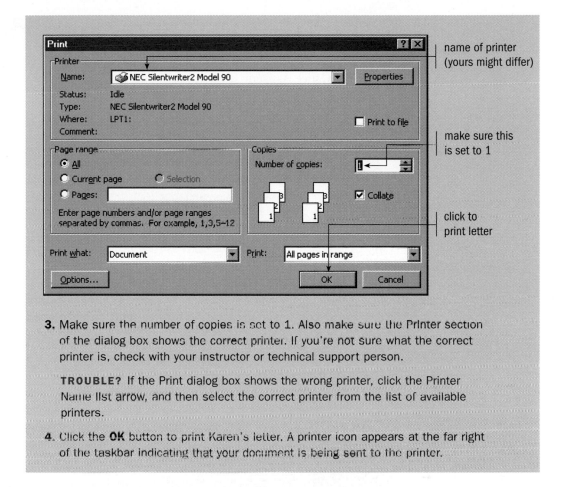

3. Make sure the number of copies is set to 1. Also make sure the Printer section of the dialog box shows the correct printer. If you're not sure what the correct printer is, check with your instructor or technical support person.

TROUBLE? If the Print dialog box shows the wrong printer, click the Printer Name list arrow, and then select the correct printer from the list of available printers.

4. Click the **OK** button to print Karen's letter. A printer icon appears at the far right of the taskbar indicating that your document is being sent to the printer.

Your printed letter should look similar to Figure 1-9 only without the Crossroads letterhead. The word wraps, or line breaks, might not appear in the same places on your letter because the size and spacing of characters vary slightly from one printer to the next.

Karen also needs an envelope to mail her letter in. Printing an envelope is an easy task in Word. You'll have a chance to try it in the Tutorial Assignments at the end of this tutorial. If you wanted to learn how to print an envelope yourself, you could use the Word Help system, which you'll learn about in the next section.

Getting Help

The Word Help system provides quick access to information about commands, features, and screen elements. The Contents and Index command on the Help menu displays the Help Topics window, which offers several options. You can look up a specific entry on the Index tab, search by general topics on the Contents tab, or search for information on a specific topic using the Find tab.

The What's This? command on the Help menu provides context-sensitive Help information. When you choose this command, the pointer changes to the Help pointer ▷**?**, which you can then use to click any object or option on the screen to see a description of the object.

You've already encountered another form of help, the Office Assistant, an animated figure that automatically offers advice on current tasks. You'll learn how to use the Office Assistant in the next section.

Getting Help with the Office Assistant

The **Office Assistant** is an interactive guide to finding information on the Help system. You can ask the Office Assistant a question, and it will look through the Help system to find an answer.

REFERENCE window	**USING THE OFFICE ASSISTANT**
	■ Click the Office Assistant button on the Standard toolbar (or choose Microsoft Word Help from the Help menu).
	■ Type your question and then click the Search button.
	■ Click a topic from the list of topics displayed.
	■ To hide the Office Assistant, click its Close button.

You'll use the Office Assistant now to learn how to print an envelope.

To use the Office Assistant to learn how to print an envelope:

1. Click the **Office Assistant** button 🔲 on the Standard toolbar. The Office Assistant opens, offering help on topics related to the task you most recently performed (if any), and asking what you'd like to do. See Figure 1-25.

Figure 1-25 ◀
Office
Assistant

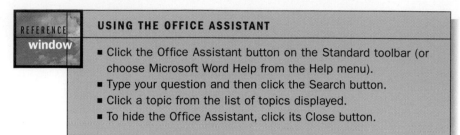

2. Type **How do I print an envelope?** and then click the **Search** button.

3. Another dialog box opens, with more specific print topics. Click the **Print an address on an envelope** button to display information on that topic. See Figure 1-26.

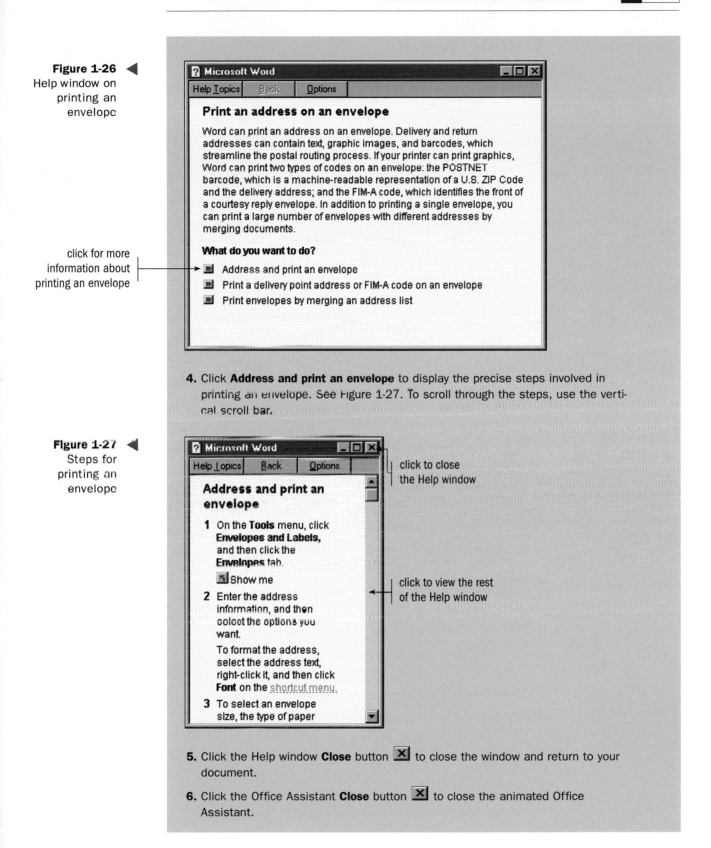

Figure 1-26
Help window on printing an envelope

click for more information about printing an envelope

4. Click **Address and print an envelope** to display the precise steps involved in printing an envelope. See Figure 1-27. To scroll through the steps, use the vertical scroll bar.

Figure 1-27
Steps for printing an envelope

click to close the Help window

click to view the rest of the Help window

5. Click the Help window **Close** button ✕ to close the window and return to your document.

6. Click the Office Assistant **Close** button ✕ to close the animated Office Assistant.

Some Help windows have different formats than those you've just seen. However, they all provide the information you need to complete any task in Word.

Exiting Word

You have now finished typing and printing the letter to the Tacoma Chamber of Commerce, and you are ready to **exit**, or quit, Word to close the program.

REFERENCE window	**EXITING WORD**
	■ Click the Close button in the upper-right corner of the Word window (or click File on the menu bar, and then click Exit).
	■ If you're prompted to save changes to the document, click the Yes button; then, if necessary, type a name of the document and click the OK button.

Because you've completed the first draft of Karen's letter, you can close the document window and exit Word now.

To exit Word:

1. Click the **Close** button ☒ on the document window to close the letter.

TROUBLE? If you see a dialog box with the message "Do you want to save changes to Tacoma Job Fair Letter?", you have made changes to the document since the last time you saved it. Click the Yes button to save the current version and close it.

2. Click the **Close** button ☒ in the upper-right corner of the Word window. Word closes and you return to the Windows 95 desktop.

TROUBLE? If you see a dialog box with the message "Do you want to save changes to Document1?", click the No button.

You give the letter for the Tacoma Chamber of Commerce to Karen for her to review.

Quick Check

1. Why should you save a document to your disk several times, even if you haven't finished typing it?

2. How do you save a document for the first time?

3. How do you see the portion of the document that has scrolled from sight?

4. What is Print Preview and when should you use it?

5. In your own words, define each of the following:

   a. scrolling

   b. word wrap

   c. AutoCorrect

   d. Office Assistant

6. How do you exit Word?

Now that you have created and saved Karen's letter, you are ready to learn about editing and formatting a document in the next tutorial.

Tutorial Assignments

Karen received a response from the Chamber of Commerce containing the information she requested about the job fair, and Crossroads has firmed up its plans to participate as exhibitors. Karen now needs to staff the booth with Crossroads employees for each day of the five-day fair. She sends a memo to employees asking them to commit to a date. Create the memo shown in Figure 1-28 by completing the following:

1. If necessary, start Word and make sure your Student Disk is in the appropriate disk drive, and check your screen to make sure your settings match those in the tutorials.

2. Click the New button on the Standard toolbar to display a new, blank document.

3. Press the Caps Lock key and type "MEMORANDUM" (without the quotation marks) in capital letters and then press the Caps Lock key again.

4. Press the Enter key twice, type "Date:" (without the quotation marks), press the Tab key, and then insert today's date from your computer clock by clicking Insert on the menu bar, clicking Date and Time, and then clicking the date format that corresponds to February 21, 1998.

5. Continue typing the rest of the memo exactly as shown in Figure 1-28, including any misspellings and extra words. (This will give you a chance to practice correcting errors in Step 7.) Instead of Karen Liu's name after "From", however, type your own. Press the Tab key after "To:" "From:", and "RE:" to align the memo heading evenly. If the Office Assistant appears, close it by clicking its Close button.

Figure 1-28 ◀
Sample memo

MEMORANDUM

Date: February 21, 1998

To: Staff Members

From: Karen Liu

RE: Dates for 1998 Job Fair

The the 1998 Job Fair sponsored by the Tacoma Chamber of Commerce will be held September 15-20 from 10:00 a.m. to 5:30 p.m.. This fiar provvides us with an oportunity to inform Tacoma residents about our services. In the past, we have each spent one day helping at the exhibit. Please let me know by tomorrow which day you would prefer this year.

Thanks.

6. Save your work as Fair Date Memo in the TAssign folder for Tutorial 1.

7. Correct the misspelled words, indicated by the wavy red lines. To ignore an AutoCorrect suggestion, click Ignore All. Then correct any grammatical or other errors indicated by wavy green lines. Use the Backspace key to delete any extra words.

8. Scroll to the beginning of the letter. Click at the beginning of the first line and insert room for the letterhead by pressing the Enter key until the first line is at about line 14.

9. Save your most recent changes.

10. Preview and print the memo.

11. Use the Office Assistant to find the steps necessary for printing an address on an envelope. On a piece of paper, write down the necessary steps.

12. Print an envelope by following the steps you discovered in step 11. (Check with your instructor or technical support person to make sure you can print envelopes. If not, print on an 8½ × 11-inch sheet of paper.)

13. Close the document without saving your most recent changes.

14. Click the New button on the Standard toolbar to open a new, blank document.

15. Write a letter to Deborah Brown at the Tacoma Chamber of Commerce, asking for information about food service at the job fair. Enter the date, the inside address, and the salutation as you did in the tutorial. Press the Enter key, and, when the Office Assistant opens, click the Get Help with writing the letter button. Following the Office Assistant's instructions, choose the desired options in the Letter Wizard dialog boxes. Click the Next button to move from one dialog box to the next. Type the text of your letter in the document window. Save the letter as Food Service in the TAssign folder for Tutorial 1, and print it.

16. Use the What's This? feature to learn about the program's ability to count the words in your document. Click Help on the menu bar, and then click What's This? The mouse pointer changes to an arrow with a question mark. Click Tools on the menu bar, click Word Count, and then read the text box contents. When you are finished reading, click the text box to close it.

Case Problems

1. Letter to Confirm a Conference Date As convention director for the Tallahassee Convention and Visitors Bureau, you are responsible for promoting and scheduling the convention center. The Southern Georgia chapter of the National Purchasing Management Association has reserved the convention center for their annual conference on October 24–25, 1998 and has requested a written confirmation of their reservation.

Create the letter using the skills you learned in the tutorial. Remember to include today's date, the inside address, the salutation, the date of the reservation, the complimentary close, and your name and title. If the instructions show quotation marks around text you type, do not include the quotation marks in your letter. To complete the letter, do the following:

1. If necessary, start Word, make sure your Student Disk in the appropriate disk drive, and check your screen to make sure your settings match those in the tutorials.

2. Open a new blank page, and press the Enter key six times to insert enough space for a letterhead.

3. Use AutoText to type today's date at the insertion point.

4. Insert three blank lines after the date, and, using the proper business letter format, type the inside address: "Danetta Blackwelder, 618 Live Oak Plantation Road, Valdosta, GA 31355."

5. Insert a blank line after the inside address, type the salutation "Dear Ms. Blackwelder:", and then insert another blank line. If the Office Assistant appears click the Cancel button.

6. Write one paragraph confirming the reservation for October 24–25, 1998.

7. Insert a blank line and type the complimentary close "Sincerely," (include the comma).

8. Add four blank lines to leave room for the signature, and then type your name and title.

9. Use Word's Contents and Index command on the Help menu to find out how to center a line of text. Then center your name and title.

10. Save the letter as Confirmation Letter in the Cases folder for Tutorial 1.

11. Reread your letter carefully and correct any errors.

12. Save any new changes.

13. Preview the letter using the Print Preview button on the Standard toolbar.

14. Print the letter.

15. Close the document.

2. Letter to Request Information About a "Learning to Fly" Franchise You are the manager of the UpTown Sports Mall and are interested in obtaining a franchise for "Learning to Fly," a free-fall bungee jumping venture marketed by Ultimate Sports, Inc. After reading an advertisement for the franchise, you decide to write for more information.
Create the letter by doing the following:

1. If necessary, start Word, make sure your Student Disk in the appropriate disk drive, and check your screen to make sure your settings match those in the tutorials.

2. Open a new, blank document, and press the Enter key six times to insert sufficient space for a letterhead.

3. Use AutoText to type today's date at the insertion point.

4. Insert three blank lines after the date, and, using the proper business letter format, type the inside address: "Ultimate Sports, Inc., 4161 Comanche Drive, Colorado Springs, CO 80906."

5. Insert a blank line after the inside address, type the salutation "Dear Franchise Representative:", and then insert another blank line. Close the Office Assistant if necessary.

6. Type the first paragraph as follows: "I'm interested in learning more about the Learning to Fly bungee jumping franchise. As manager of UpTown Sports Mall, I've had success with similar programs, including both rock climbing and snowboarding franchises."(Do not include the quotation marks.)

7. Save your work as Bungee Request Letter in the Cases folder for Tutorial 1.

8. Insert one blank line, and type the following: "Please answer the following questions:". Then press the Enter key and type these questions on separate lines: "How much does your franchise cost?" "Does the price include the cost for installing the 70-foot tower illustrated in your advertisement?" "Does the price include the cost for purchasing the ropes and harnesses?" Then use the Office Assistant to find out how to add bullets, and, following its instructions, insert a bullet in front of each question.

9. Correct any typing errors indicated by wavy lines. (*Hint:* Because "bungee" is spelled correctly, click Ignore All on the AutoCorrect menu to remove the red line under "bungee.")

10. Insert another blank line, and type the complimentary close "Sincerely," (include the comma).

11. Insert three blank lines to leave room for the signature, and type your full name and title. Then press the Enter key and type "UpTown Sports Mall."

12. Save the letter with changes.

13. Preview the letter using the Print Preview button.

14. Print the letter.

15. Close the document.

3. Memo of Congratulations Glenna Zumbrennen is owner, founder, and president of Cuisine Unlimited. She was recently recognized as the 1998 New Hampshire Woman Business Owner of the Year by the National Association of Women Business Owners. She was also named to the 1998 Small Business Administration Advisory Council. Do the following:

1. If necessary, start Word, make sure your Student Disk in the appropriate disk drive, and check your screen to make sure your settings match those in the tutorials.

2. Write a brief memo congratulating Glenna on receiving these awards. Remember to use the four-part planning process. You should plan the content, organization, and style of the memo, and use a standard memo format similar to the one shown in Figure 1-28.

3. Save the document as Awards Memo in the Cases folder for Tutorial 1.

4. Preview the memo using the Print Preview button.

5. Print the memo.

6. Close the document.

4. Writing a Personal Letter with the Letter Template Word provides templates, which are models with predefined formatting, to help you create documents quickly and effectively. For example, the Letter template helps you create letters with professional-looking letterheads and with various letter formats. Do the following:

1. If necessary, start Word, make sure your Student Disk in the appropriate disk drive, and check your screen to make sure your settings match those in the tutorials.

2. Click File on the menu bar, and then click New. The New dialog box opens.

3. Click the Letters & Faxes tab, click Contemporary Letter, and then click the OK button.

4. Follow the instructions given in the document window. You might be asked to type personal information such as your name and address.

5. For the inside (recipient's) name and address, type a real or fictitious name and address.

6. In the body of the letter, include a sentence or two explaining that you're using the Word Letter template to create this letter.

7. After typing the letter, make sure that you're listed as the person sending the letter. (Someone else's name might be listed if you're not using your own computer or the personal information is already entered into Word.)

8. Save the letter as My Template Letter (in the Cases folder for Tutorial 1) and then print it.

9. If you completed Step 11 in the Tutorial Assignments, create an envelope for this letter and print it (if necessary, on an 8½ x 11 inch sheet of paper).

10. Close the document.

Lab Assignments

These Lab Assignments are designed to accompany the interactive Course Lab called Word Processing. To start the Word Processing Lab, click the Start button on the Windows 95 taskbar, point to Programs, point to Course Labs, point to New Perspectives Applications, and click Word Processing. If you do not see Course Labs on your Programs menu, see your instructor or technical support person.

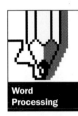

Word Processing Word processing software is the most popular computerized productivity tool. In this Lab you will learn how word processing software works.

1. Click the Steps button to learn how word processing software works. As you proceed through the Steps, answer all of the Quick Check questions that appear. After you complete the Steps, you will see a Quick Check summary report. Follow the instructions on the screen to print this report.

2. Click the Explore button to begin. Click File on the menu bar, and then click Open to display the Open dialog box. Click the file TIMBER.TEX, and then press the Enter key to open the letter to Northern Timber Company. Make the following modifications to the letter, and then print it. You do not need to save the letter.
   a. In the first and last lines of the letter, change "Jason Kidder" to your name.
   b. Change the date to today's date.
   c. Select the second paragraph, which begins "Your proposal did not include. . ." Move this paragraph so it is the last paragraph in the text of the letter.
   d. Change the cost of a permanent bridge to $20,000.
   e. Spell check the letter.

3. Using Explore, open the file STARS.TEX. Make the following modifications to the document, and then print it. You do not need to save the document.
   a. Center and bold the title.
   b. Change the title font to 16 point Arial.
   c. Bold DATE, SHOWER, and LOCATION.
   d. Move the January 2–3 line to the top of the list.
   e. Number the items in the list 1., 2., 3., and so on.
   f. Add or delete tabs to realign the columns.
   g. Double space the entire document.

4. Using Explore, compose a one-page, double-spaced letter to your parents or to a friend. Make sure you date and spell check the letter. Print the letter and sign it. You do not need to save your letter.

Editing and Formatting a Document

Preparing an Annuity Plan Description for Right-Hand Solutions

OBJECTIVES

In this tutorial you will:

- Open, rename, and save a previously saved document

- Move the insertion point around the document

- Delete text

- Reverse edits using the Undo and Redo commands

- Move text within the document

- Find and replace text

- Change margins, alignment, and paragraph indents

- Copy formatting with the Format Painter

- Emphasize points with bullets, numbering, boldface, underlining, and italics

- Change fonts and adjust font sizes

CASE

Right-Hand Solutions

Reginald Thomson is a contract specialist for Right-Hand Solutions, a company that provides small businesses with financial and administrative services. Right-Hand Solutions contracts with independent insurance companies to prepare insurance plans and investment opportunities for these small businesses. Brandi Paxman, vice president of administrative services, asked Reginald to plan and write a document that describes the tax-deferred annuity plan for their clients' employee handbooks. Now that Brandi has commented on and corrected the draft, Reginald asks you to make the necessary changes and print the document.

In this tutorial, you will edit the annuity plan description according to Brandi's comments. You will open a draft of the annuity plan, resave it, and delete a phrase. You'll move text using two different methods, and find and replace one version of the company name with another.

You will also change the overall look of the document by changing margins, indenting and justifying paragraphs, and copying formatting from one paragraph to another. You'll create a bulleted list to emphasize the types of financial needs the annuity plan will cover and a numbered list for the conditions under which employees can receive funds. Then you'll make the title more prominent by centering it, changing its font, and enlarging it. You'll italicize the questions within the plan to set them off from the rest of the text, and underline an added note about how to get further information to give it emphasis. Finally, you will print a copy of the plan so you can proofread it.

SESSION

2.1

In this session you will edit Reginald's document by deleting words and by moving text within the document. Then you'll find and replace text throughout the document.

Opening the Document

Brandi's editing marks and notes on the first draft are shown in Figure 2-1. You'll begin by opening the first draft of the description, which has the filename Annuity.

Figure 2-1 ◀
Draft of annuity
plan showing
Brandi's edits
(page 1)

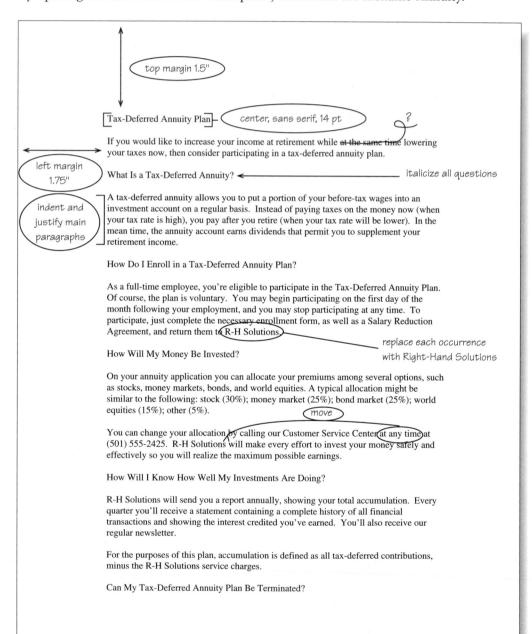

Word

Figure 2-1 ◀
Draft of annuity
plan showing
Brandi's edits
(page 2)

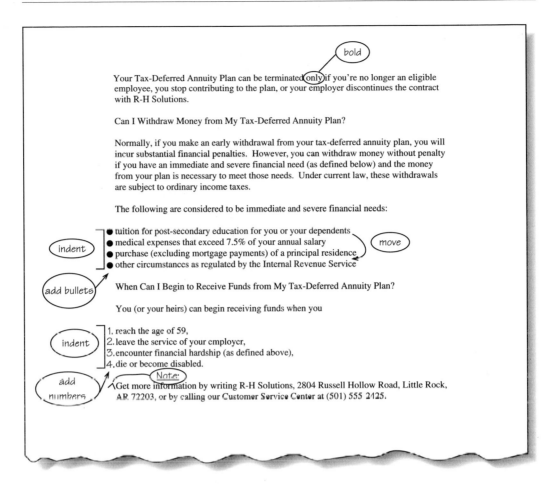

To open the document:

1. Place your Student Disk into the appropriate disk drive.

2. Start Word as usual.

3. Click the **Open** button 📂 on the Standard toolbar to display the Open dialog box, shown in Figure 2-2.

Figure 2-2 ◀
The open
document

names and files
specified here

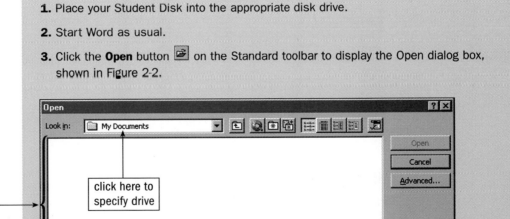

4. Click the **Look in** list arrow. The list of drives and files appears.

5. Click the drive that contains your Student Disk.

6. Double-click the **Tutorial.02** folder.

7. Click **Annuity** to select the file.

> **TROUBLE?** If you see "Annuity.doc" in the folder, Windows 95 might be configured so that the filename extension is displayed. Click Annuity.doc and continue with Step 8. If you can't find the file with or without the filename extension, make sure you're looking in the Tutorial.02 folder and on the drive that contains your Student Disk, and check to make sure the Files of type text box displays Word Documents or All Files. If you still can't locate the file, ask your instructor or technical support person for help.

8. Click the **Open** button. The document opens, with the insertion point at the beginning of the document. See Figure 2-3.

Figure 2-3 ◀
The open
document

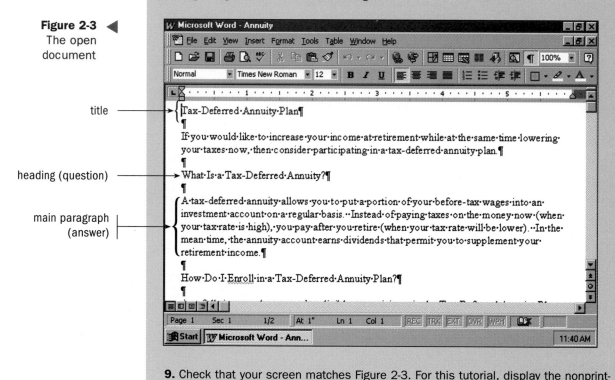

title

heading (question)

main paragraph
(answer)

9. Check that your screen matches Figure 2-3. For this tutorial, display the nonprinting characters so that the formatting elements (tabs, paragraph marks, and so forth) are visible and easier to change.

Renaming the Document

To avoid altering the original file Annuity, you will save the document using the filename RHS Annuity Plan. Saving the document with another filename creates a copy of the file and leaves the original file unchanged in case you want to work through the tutorial again.

To save the document with a new name:

1. Click **File** on the menu bar, and then click **Save As**. The Save As dialog box opens with the current filename highlighted in the File name text box.

2. Click to the left of "Annuity" in the File name text box, type **RHS**, and then press the **spacebar**. Press the → key to move the insertion point to the right of the letter "y" in "Annuity," press the **spacebar**, and then type **Plan**. The filename changes to RHS Annuity Plan.

3. Click the **Save** button to save the document with the new filename.

Now you can edit the document. To make all of Brandi's edits, you'll need to learn how to quickly move the insertion point to any location in the document.

Moving the Insertion Point Around the Document

The arrow keys on your keyboard, ←, →, ↑, and ↓, allow you to move the insertion point one character at a time to the left or right, or one line at a time up or down. If you want to move more than one character or one line at a time, you can point and click in other parts of a line or the document. You can also press a combination of keys to move the insertion point. As you become more experienced with Word, you'll decide for yourself which method you prefer.

To see how quickly you can move through the document, you'll use keystrokes to move the insertion point to the beginning of the second page and to the end of the document.

To move the insertion point with keystrokes:

1. Press and hold down the **Ctrl** key while you press the **Page Down** key to move the insertion point to the beginning of the next page. Notice that the status bar indicates that the insertion point is now on page 2.

2. Press the ↑ key twice to move to the previous paragraph. Notice the automatic page break, a dotted line that Word inserts automatically to mark the beginning of the new page. See Figure 2-4. As you insert and delete text or change formatting in a document, the location of the automatic page breaks in your document continually adjust to account for the edits.

Figure 2-4 ◀
Automatic
page break

insertion point at
the end of page 1

automatic
page break

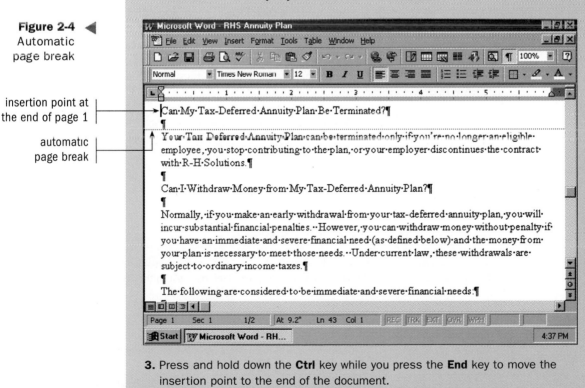

3. Press and hold down the **Ctrl** key while you press the **End** key to move the insertion point to the end of the document.

4. Press and hold down the **Ctrl** key while you press the **Home** key to move the insertion point back to the beginning of the document.

Figure 2-5 summarizes the keystrokes you can use to move the insertion point around the document.

Figure 2-5 ◀
Key strokes for
moving the
insertion point

Press	To Move Insertion Point
← or →	Left or right one character at a time
↑ or ↓	Up or down one line at a time
Ctrl + ← or Ctrl + →	Left or right one word at a time
Ctrl + ↑ or Ctrl + ↓	Up or down one paragraph at a time
Home or End	To the beginning or to the end of the current line
Ctrl + Home or Ctrl + End	To the beginning or to the end of the document
PageUp or PageDown	To the previous screen or to the next screen
Alt + Ctrl + PageUp or Alt + Ctrl + PageDown	To the top or to the bottom of the document window
Ctrl + PageUp or Ctrl + PageDown	To the beginning of the previous page or the next page

Using Select, Then Do

One of the most powerful editing features in Word is the "select, then do" feature. It allows you to select (highlight) a block of text and then do something to that text such as deleting, moving, or formatting it. You can select text using either the mouse or the keyboard; however, the mouse is usually the easier and more efficient way. You can quickly select a line or paragraph by clicking on the **selection bar**, which is the blank space in the left margin area of the document window. Figure 2-6 summarizes methods for selecting text with the mouse.

Figure 2-6 ◀
Methods for
selecting text
with the mouse

To Select	Do This
A word	Double-click the word
A line	Click in the selection bar next to the line
A sentence	Press and hold down the Ctrl key and click within the sentence
Multiple lines	Click and drag in the selection bar next to the lines
A paragraph	Double-click in the selection bar next to the paragraph, or triple-click within the paragraph
Multiple paragraphs	Click and drag in the selection bar next to the paragraphs, or triple-click and drag
The entire document	Press and hold down the Ctrl key and click in the selection bar, or triple-click in the selection bar
A block of text	Click at the beginning of a block, press and hold down the Shift key and click at the end of the block; highlights all the words in the block

Deleting Text

Brandi wants you to delete the phrase "at the same time" in the first paragraph of the document. You'll use the "select, then do" feature to delete the phrase now.

To select and delete a phrase from the text:

1. Click and drag ⌶ over the phrase "at the same time" located in the first line of the first paragraph. The phrase and the space following it are highlighted, as shown in Figure 2-7. Notice that dragging the pointer over the second and successive words automatically selects the entire words and the spaces following them. This makes it much easier to select words and phrases than selecting them one character at a time.

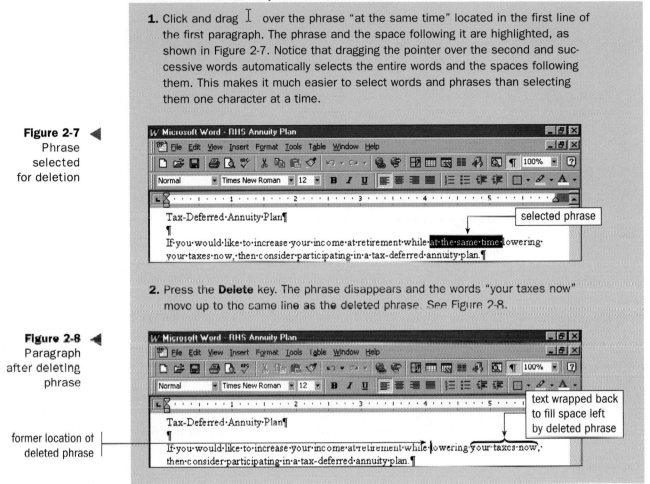

Figure 2-7 ◀
Phrase
selected
for deletion

Figure 2-8 ◀
Paragraph
after deleting
phrase

former location of
deleted phrase

2. Press the **Delete** key. The phrase disappears and the words "your taxes now" move up to the same line as the deleted phrase. See Figure 2-8.

After rereading the paragraph, Reginald decides the phrase shouldn't have been deleted after all. He checks with Brandi and she agrees. You could retype the text, but there's an easier way to restore the phrase.

Using the Undo and Redo Commands

To undo (or reverse) the very last thing you did, simply click the Undo button on the Standard toolbar. If you want to reinstate your original change, the Redo button reverses the action of the Undo button (or redoes the undo). To undo anything more than your last action, you can click the Undo list arrow on the Standard toolbar. This list shows your most recent actions. Undo reverses the action only at its original location. You can't delete a word or phrase and then undo it at a different location.

USING UNDO AND REDO

- Click the Undo button on the Standard toolbar (or click Edit on the menu bar, and then click Undo) to reverse the very last thing you did.
- To reverse several previous actions, click the Undo list arrow on the Standard toolbar. Click an action on the list to reverse all actions up to and including the one you click.
- To undo your previous actions one-by-one, in the reverse order in which you performed them, click the Undo button one time for every action you want to reverse.
- If you undo an action by mistake, click the Redo button on the Standard toolbar (or click Edit on the menu bar, and then click Repeat) to reverse the undo.

Reginald suggested that you reverse your previous deletion, but left the final decision up to you. You decide to make the change to see how the sentence reads. Rather than retyping the phrase, you will reverse the edit using the Undo button.

To undo the deletion:

1. Click the **Undo** button on the Standard toolbar to undo your deletion. The phrase "at the same time" reappears in your document and is highlighted.

   TROUBLE? If the phrase doesn't reappear in your document and something else changes in your document, you probably made another edit or change to the document (such as pressing the Backspace key) between the deletion and the undo. Click the Undo button on the Standard toolbar until the phrase reappears in your document.

2. Click within the paragraph to deselect the phrase.

   As you read the sentence, you decide that it reads better without the phrase. Instead of selecting and deleting it again, you'll redo the undo.

3. Click the **Redo** button on the Standard toolbar.

   The phrase "at the same time" disappears from your document again.

4. Click the **Save** button on the Standard toolbar to save your changes to the document.

You have edited the document by deleting the text that Brandi marked for deletion. Now you are ready to make the rest of the edits she suggested.

Moving Text Within a Document

One of the most important uses of "select, then do" is moving text. For example, Brandi wants to reorder the four points Reginald made in the section "Can I Withdraw Money from My Tax-Deferred Annuity Plan?" on page 2 of his draft. You could reorder the list by deleting the sentence and then retyping it at the new location, but a much more efficient approach is to select and then move the sentence. Word has several ways to move text: drag and drop, cut and paste, and copy and paste.

Dragging and Dropping Text

The easiest way to move text within a document is called drag and drop. With **drag and drop,** you select the text you want to move, press and hold down the mouse button while you drag the pointer to a new location, and then release the mouse button.

DRAGGING AND DROPPING TEXT

- Select the text to be moved.
- Press and hold down the mouse button until the drag-and-drop pointer appears, and then drag the selected text to its new location.
- Use the dashed insertion point as a guide to determine the precise spot where the text will be inserted.
- Release the mouse button to drop the text at the new location.

Brandi requested a change in the order of the items in the bulleted list on page 2 of Reginald's draft, so you'll use the drag-and-drop method to reorder the items. At the same time, you'll get some practice using the selection bar to highlight a line of text.

To move text using drag and drop:

1. Scroll through the document until you see "tuition for post-secondary education...", the first in the list of "immediate and severe financial needs:", which begins in the middle of page 2.

2. Click ✍ in the selection bar to the left of the line beginning "tuition..." to select that line of text, including the return character. See Figure 2-9.

Figure 2-9
Selected
text to
drag and drop

pointer in
selection bar

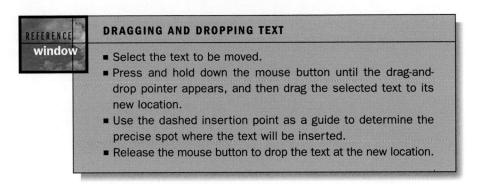

3. Position the pointer over the selected text. The shape of the pointer changes to ⬉ .

4. Press and hold down the mouse button until the drag-and-drop pointer ⬉, which has a dashed insertion point, an arrow, and a small square called a move box, appears.

5. Drag the selected text down three lines until the dashed insertion point appears to the left of the word "other." Make sure you use the dashed insertion point to guide the text to its new location rather than the mouse pointer or the move box; the dashed insertion point marks the precise location of the drop. See Figure 2-10.

Figure 2-10 ◀
Moving text
with drag-and-
drop pointer

selected text
to be moved

dashed
insertion point

drag-and-drop pointer

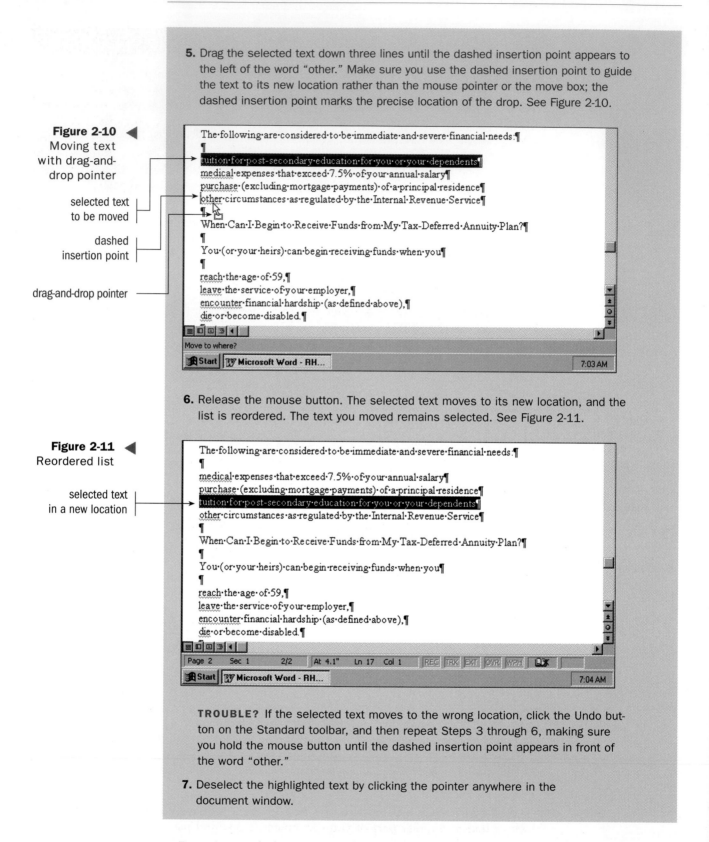

6. Release the mouse button. The selected text moves to its new location, and the list is reordered. The text you moved remains selected. See Figure 2-11.

Figure 2-11 ◀
Reordered list

selected text
in a new location

TROUBLE? If the selected text moves to the wrong location, click the Undo button on the Standard toolbar, and then repeat Steps 3 through 6, making sure you hold the mouse button until the dashed insertion point appears in front of the word "other."

7. Deselect the highlighted text by clicking the pointer anywhere in the document window.

Dragging and dropping works well if you're moving text a short distance in a document; however, Word provides another method, called cut and paste, that works well for moving text either a short distance or beyond the current screen.

Word

Cutting or Copying and Pasting Text

To **cut** means to remove text from the document and place it on the Windows Clipboard. The Clipboard stores only one item at a time; when you cut a new piece of text or a graphic, it replaces what was on the Clipboard. To **paste** means to transfer a copy of the text from the clipboard into the document at the insertion point. To perform a cut-and-paste operation, you select the text you want to move, cut (remove) it from the document, and then paste (restore) it into the document in a new location. If you don't want to remove the text from its original location, you can copy it (rather than cutting it) and then paste the copy in a new location. This procedure is known as "copy and paste."

REFERENCE
window

CUTTING OR COPYING AND PASTING TEXT

- Select (highlight) the text you want to move.
- Click the Cut button on the Standard toolbar. (Or if you only want to make a copy, click the Copy button instead.)
- Move the insertion point to the target location in the document.
- Click the Paste button on the Standard toolbar.

Brandi suggested moving the phrase "at any time" (in the paragraph beginning "You can change your allocation...") to a new location. You'll use cut and paste to move this phrase.

To move text using cut and paste:

1. Scroll the document up until you can see the paragraph just above the heading "How Will I Know...." on page 1.

2. Click and drag the mouse to highlight the complete phrase "at any time." See Figure 2-12.

Figure 2-12 ◀
Text to move using cut and paste

new location for text ——

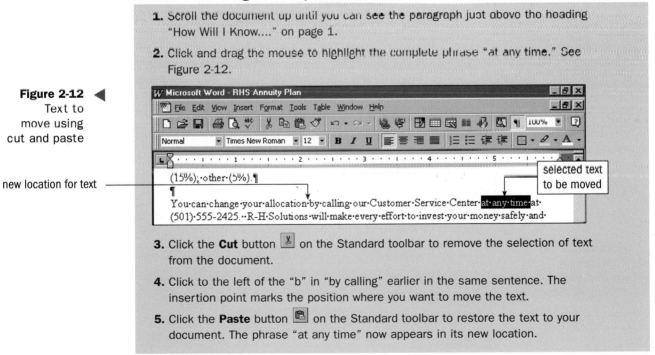

selected text to be moved

3. Click the **Cut** button 🔏 on the Standard toolbar to remove the selection of text from the document.

4. Click to the left of the "b" in "by calling" earlier in the same sentence. The insertion point marks the position where you want to move the text.

5. Click the **Paste** button 📋 on the Standard toolbar to restore the text to your document. The phrase "at any time" now appears in its new location.

Keep in mind that you can also use the copy-and-paste method to move a copy of a block of text to another part of your document. Copy and paste works much the same way as cut and paste.

Finding and Replacing Text

When you're working with a longer document, the quickest and easiest way to locate a particular word or phrase is to use the Find command. If you want to replace characters or a phrase with something else, you can use the Replace command, which combines the Find command with a substitution feature. The Replace command searches through a document and substitutes the text you're searching for with the replacement text you specify. As Word performs the search, it will stop and highlight each occurrence of the search text and let you determine whether to substitute the replacement text by clicking the Replace button. If you want to substitute every occurrence of the search text with the replacement text, you can click the Replace All button.

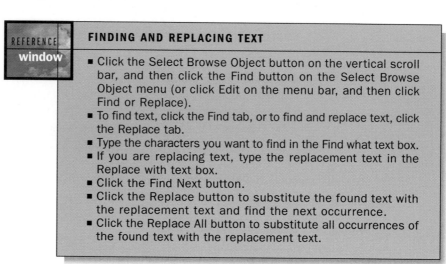

REFERENCE window

FINDING AND REPLACING TEXT

- Click the Select Browse Object button on the vertical scroll bar, and then click the Find button on the Select Browse Object menu (or click Edit on the menu bar, and then click Find or Replace).
- To find text, click the Find tab, or to find and replace text, click the Replace tab.
- Type the characters you want to find in the Find what text box.
- If you are replacing text, type the replacement text in the Replace with text box.
- Click the Find Next button.
- Click the Replace button to substitute the found text with the replacement text and find the next occurrence.
- Click the Replace All button to substitute all occurrences of the found text with the replacement text.

Brandi wants the shortened version of the company name, "R-H Solutions," to be spelled out as "Right-Hand Solutions" every time it appears in the text.

To replace "R-H Solutions" with "Right-Hand Solutions:

1. Click the **Select Browse Object** button 🔘 on the vertical scroll bar.

2. Click the **Find** button 🔍 on the Select Browse Object menu. The Find and Replace dialog box appears.

3. Click the **Replace** tab.

4. Type **R-H Solutions** in the Find what text box, press the **Tab** key, and type **Right-Hand Solutions** in the Replace with text box. See Figure 2-13.

Figure 2-13 ◀
Find and
Replace
dialog box

type search text here ⎯

type replacement
text here ⎯

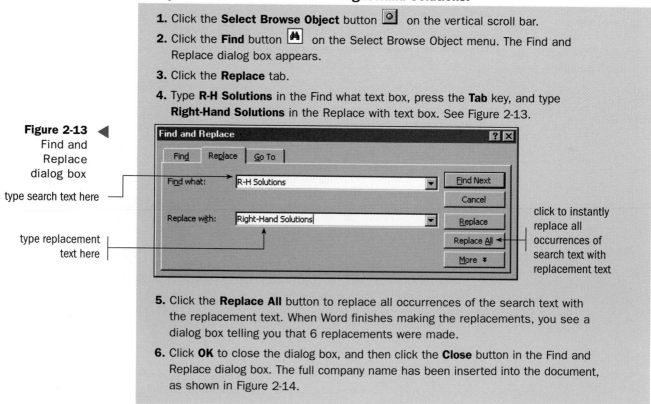

click to instantly
replace all
occurrences of
search text with
replacement text

5. Click the **Replace All** button to replace all occurrences of the search text with the replacement text. When Word finishes making the replacements, you see a dialog box telling you that 6 replacements were made.

6. Click **OK** to close the dialog box, and then click the **Close** button in the Find and Replace dialog box. The full company name has been inserted into the document, as shown in Figure 2-14.

Figure 2-14 ◀
The name
"Right-Hand
Solutions"
inserted into
the document

replacement text ——————

replacement text ——————

replacement text ——————

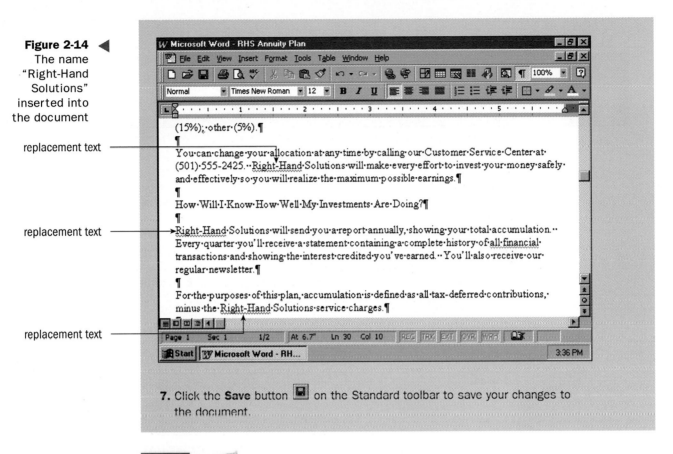

7. Click the **Save** button 🖫 on the Standard toolbar to save your changes to the document.

Quick Check

1. How do you open a document and save a copy of it with a new name?

2. Which key(s) do you press to move the insertion point to the following places:
   a. end of the document
   b. beginning of the document
   c. beginning of the next page

3. Explain how to delete text from a document.

4. Define the following terms in your own words:
   a. select, then do
   b. selection bar
   c. drag and drop

5. Explain how to select a phrase in the middle of a paragraph. Explain how to select a complete line of text.

6. What is the purpose of the Undo command? What is the purpose of the Redo command?

7. True or False: You can use the Undo command to restore deleted text at a new location in your document.

8. What is the difference between cut and paste, and copy and paste?

9. When you use the drag-and-drop method to move text, how do you know where the text will be positioned when it is dropped?

10. Explain how to find and replace text using the Select Browse Object button.

You have completed the content changes Brandi suggested, but she has some more changes for you that will improve the plan's appearance. In the next session, you'll enhance the Annuity Plan by changing the width, spacing, and alignment of text.

SESSION 2.2

In this session you will make the formatting changes Brandi suggested. You'll use a variety of formatting commands to change the margins, spacing, and tabs, and to justify and align the text. You'll also learn how to use the Format Painter, how to create bulleted and numbered lists, and how to change fonts, font sizes, and sizes.

Changing the Margins

In general, it's best to begin formatting by making the changes that affect the overall appearance of the document. In this case, you need to adjust the margin settings of the annuity plan summary.

Word uses default margins of 1.25 inches for the left and right margins, and 1 inch for the top and bottom margins. The numbers on the ruler (displayed below the Formatting toolbar) indicate the distance in inches from the left margin, not from the left edge of the paper. Unless you specify otherwise, changes you make to the margins will affect the entire document, not just the current paragraph or page.

REFERENCE window

CHANGING MARGINS FOR THE ENTIRE DOCUMENT

- With the insertion point anywhere in your document and no text selected, click File on the menu bar, then click Page Setup.
- If necessary, click the Margins tab to display the margin settings.
- Click the margins arrows to change each setting, or type a new margin value in each text box.
- Make sure the Apply to list box displays Whole document.
- Click the OK button.

You need to change the top margin to 1.5 inches and the left margin to 1.75 inches, as suggested by Brandi. The left margin needs to be wider than usual to allow space for making holes so that the document can be added to a three-ring binder. In the next set of steps, you'll change the margins with the Page Setup command. You can also change margins in page layout view; you'll practice that method in the Tutorial Assignments.

To change the margins in the annuity plan summary:

1. If you took a break after the last lesson, make sure Word is running, that the RHS Annuity Plan document is open, and that nonprinting characters are displayed.

2. Click once anywhere in the document to make sure no text is selected.

3. Click **File** on the menu bar, and then click **Page Setup** to open the Page Setup dialog box.

4. If necessary, click the **Margins** tab to display the margin settings. See Figure 2-15.

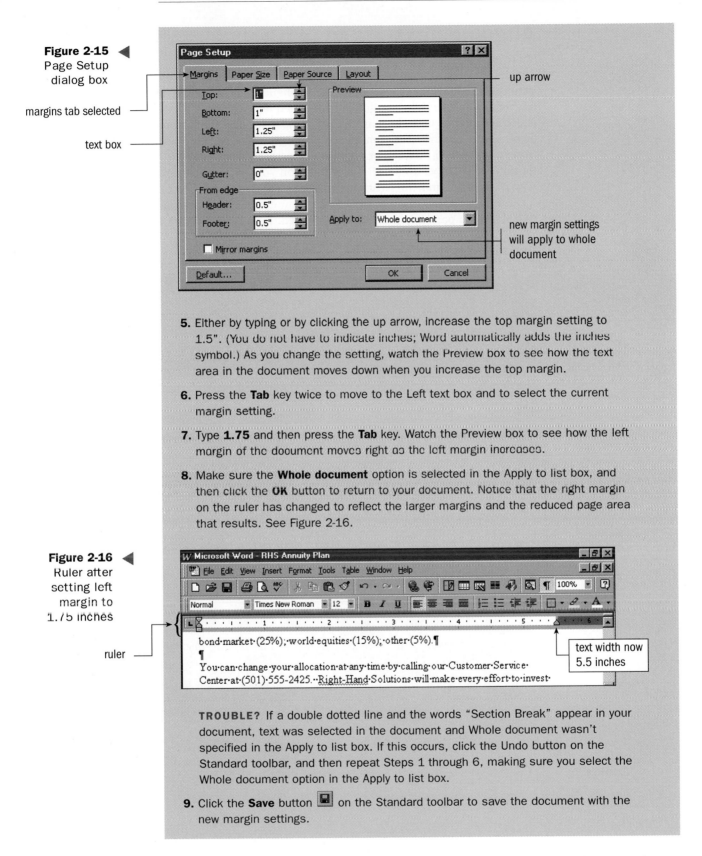

Figure 2-15 ◀
Page Setup
dialog box

margins tab selected

text box

up arrow

new margin settings
will apply to whole
document

5. Either by typing or by clicking the up arrow, increase the top margin setting to 1.5". (You do not have to indicate inches; Word automatically adds the inches symbol.) As you change the setting, watch the Preview box to see how the text area in the document moves down when you increase the top margin.

6. Press the **Tab** key twice to move to the Left text box and to select the current margin setting.

7. Type **1.75** and then press the **Tab** key. Watch the Preview box to see how the left margin of the document moves right as the left margin increases.

8. Make sure the **Whole document** option is selected in the Apply to list box, and then click the **OK** button to return to your document. Notice that the right margin on the ruler has changed to reflect the larger margins and the reduced page area that results. See Figure 2-16.

Figure 2-16 ◀
Ruler after
setting left
margin to
1.75 inches

ruler

text width now
5.5 inches

TROUBLE? If a double dotted line and the words "Section Break" appear in your document, text was selected in the document and Whole document wasn't specified in the Apply to list box. If this occurs, click the Undo button on the Standard toolbar, and then repeat Steps 1 through 6, making sure you select the Whole document option in the Apply to list box.

9. Click the **Save** button 🖫 on the Standard toolbar to save the document with the new margin settings.

Now you are ready to make formatting changes that affect individual paragraphs.

Aligning Text

Word defines a paragraph as any text that ends with a paragraph mark symbol (¶). The alignment of a paragraph or document refers to how the text lines up horizontally between the margins. By default, text is aligned along the left margin but is ragged, or uneven, along the right margin. This is called **left alignment**. With **right alignment**, the text is aligned along the right margin and is ragged along the left margin. With **center alignment**, text is centered between the left and right margins. With **justified alignment**, full lines of text are spaced between or aligned along both the left and the right margins (similar to that in a newspaper column). The paragraph you are reading now is justified. The easiest way to apply alignment settings is by clicking buttons on the Formatting toolbar.

Brandi indicated that the title of the annuity plan description should be centered and that the main paragraphs should be justified. First, you'll center the title.

To center align the title:

1. Click anywhere in the title "Tax-Deferred Annuity Plan" at the beginning of the document.

2. Click the **Center** button ▤ on the Formatting toolbar. The text centers between the left and right margins. See Figure 2-17.

Figure 2-17 ◀
Title centered

centered title ──────

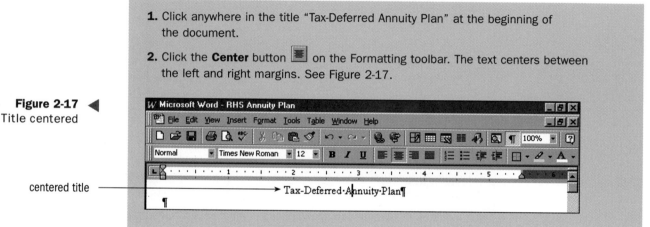

Now you'll use the Justify button to justify the text in the first two main paragraphs.

To justify the first two paragraphs using the Formatting toolbar:

1. Click anywhere in the first paragraph, which begins "If you would like to increase...", and click the Justify button ▤ on the Formatting toolbar. The justification would be easier to see if the paragraph had more lines of text. You'll see the effects more clearly after you justify the second paragraph in the document.

2. Move the insertion point to the second main paragraph, which begins "A tax-deferred annuity allows...".

3. Click ▤ again. The text is evenly spaced between the left and right margins. See Figure 2-18.

Figure 2-18
Text justified
using the
Formatting
toolbar

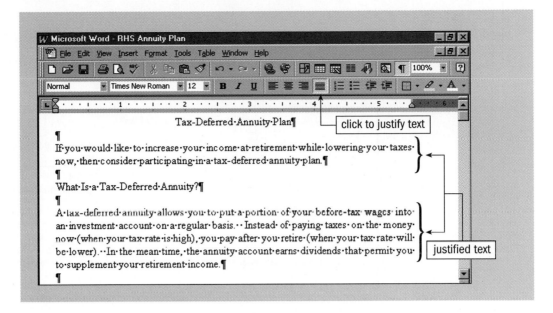

You'll justify the other paragraphs later. Now that you've learned how to change the paragraph alignment, you can turn your attention to indenting paragraphs.

Indenting a Paragraph

When you become a more experienced Word user, you might want to use some special forms of paragraph formatting, such as a hanging indent (where the first line of the paragraph extends into the left margin) or a right indent (where all lines of the paragraph are indented from the right margin). In this document, though, you'll only need to indent the main paragraphs 0.5 inches from the left margin. This is a simple kind of paragraph indent, requiring only a quick click on the Formatting toolbar's Increase Indent button. According to Brandi's notes, you need to indent all of the main paragraphs, starting with the second paragraph.

To Indent a paragraph using the Increase Indent button:

1. Make sure the insertion point is still located anywhere within the second paragraph, which begins "A tax deferred annuity allows…".

2. Click the **Increase Indent** button on the Formatting toolbar twice. (Don't click the Decrease Indent button by mistake.) The entire paragraph moves right .5" each time you click the Increase Indent button. The paragraph is indented 1", .5" more than Brandi wants.

3. Click the **Decrease Indent** button on the Formatting toolbar to move the paragraph left .5". The paragraph is now indented 0.5 inches from the left margin, as shown in Figure 2-19.

Figure 2-19 ◀
Indented
paragraph

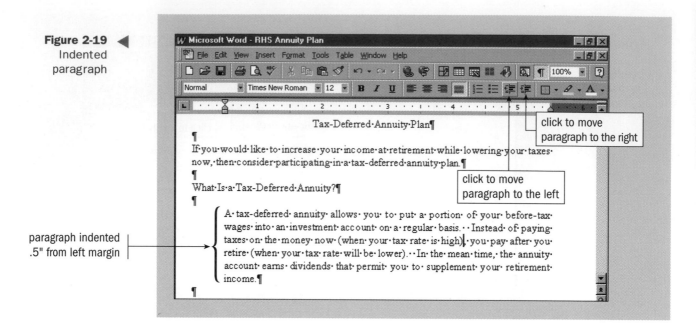

paragraph indented
.5" from left margin

You could continue to indent, and then justify, each paragraph individually, but there's an easier way—the Format Painter command. The Format Painter allows you to copy both the indentation and alignment changes to all the other main paragraphs in the document.

In addition to changing the horizontal alignment of text on the page, you can also change the vertical spacing, called **line spacing**. You can easily make the text double-spaced or, if you want the lines a little closer together, one-and-a-half spaced. You'll practice this in an Exploration Exercise in the Tutorial Assignment at the end of the tutorial.

Using Format Painter

The Format Painter makes it easy to copy all the formatting features of one paragraph to one or more other paragraphs. You'll use the Format Painter now to copy the formatting of the second paragraph to other main paragraphs. You'll begin by highlighting the paragraph whose format you want to copy. (Notice that you can't simply move the insertion point to that paragraph.)

To copy paragraph formatting with the Format Painter:

1. Double-click in the selection bar to select the second paragraph, which is indented and justified and begins "A tax-deferred annuity...".

2. Double-click the **Format Painter** button 🖌 on the Standard toolbar. Notice that the Format Painter button stays pressed. When you move the pointer over text it changes to 🖌 to indicate that the format of the selected paragraph can be painted (or copied) onto another paragraph.

3. Scroll down, and then click anywhere in the third paragraph, which begins "As a full-time employee...". The format of the third paragraph shifts to match the format of the selected paragraph. See Figure 2-20. As you can see, both paragraphs are now indented and justified. The pointer remains as the Format Painter pointer.

Figure 2-20
Formats copied
with Format
Painter

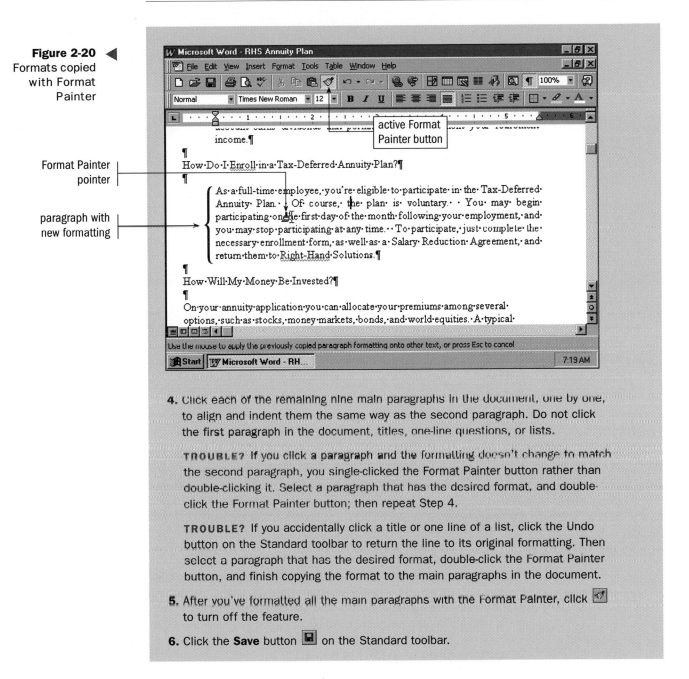

Format Painter
pointer

paragraph with
new formatting

4. Click each of the remaining nine main paragraphs in the document, one by one, to align and indent them the same way as the second paragraph. Do not click the first paragraph in the document, titles, one-line questions, or lists.

TROUBLE? If you click a paragraph and the formatting doesn't change to match the second paragraph, you single-clicked the Format Painter button rather than double-clicking it. Select a paragraph that has the desired format, and double-click the Format Painter button; then repeat Step 4.

TROUBLE? If you accidentally click a title or one line of a list, click the Undo button on the Standard toolbar to return the line to its original formatting. Then select a paragraph that has the desired format, double-click the Format Painter button, and finish copying the format to the main paragraphs in the document.

5. After you've formatted all the main paragraphs with the Format Painter, click to turn off the feature.

6. Click the **Save** button on the Standard toolbar.

All the main paragraphs in the document are formatted with the correct indentation and alignment. Your next job is to make the lists easier to read by adding bullets and numbers.

Adding Bullets and Numbers

Bullets (•) or numbers are useful whenever you need to emphasize a particular list of items. Brandi requested that you add bullets to the list of financial needs on page 2 to make them stand out.

To apply bullets to a list of items:

1. Scroll the document until you see the list of financial needs below the sentence "The following are considered to be immediate and severe financial needs:".

2. Select the four items that appear in the middle of page 2 (from "Medical expenses" to "Internal Revenue Service"). The text doesn't need to be fully highlighted; as long as you select a single character in a line, you can apply bullets to the paragraph.

3. Click the **Bullets** button 📋 on the Formatting toolbar to activate the Bullets feature. A rounded bullet, a special character, appears in front of each item, and each line indents to make room for the bullet.

4. Click the **Increase Indent** button 🔳 to align the bullet text at the one-half inch mark, just below the left edge of the paragraphs above them.

TROUBLE? If the bullets in your document are already indented, you probably indented the list when you indented the main paragraphs earlier; don't click the Increase Indent button. If the bulleted list is now indented too much, click the Decrease Indent button until the bullet text is at the .5" mark on the ruler.

5. Click anywhere within the document window to deselect the text. Figure 2-21 shows the indented bulleted list. Note that the text itself, not the bullets, is indented.

Figure 2-21 ◀
Indented
bulleted list

bulleted list ⟶

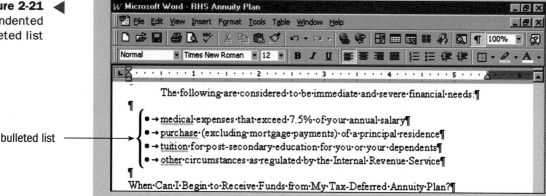

Next, you need to add numbers to the list that identifies when benefits can be received in the section below the bulleted list. For this you'll use the Numbering button, which automatically numbers the selected paragraphs with consecutive numbers and aligns them. If you insert a new paragraph, delete a paragraph, or reorder the paragraphs, Word automatically adjusts the numbers to make sure they remain consecutive.

To apply numbers to the list of items:

1. Scroll down to the next section, and then select the list that begins "Reach the age..." and ends with "...become disabled."

2. Click the **Increase Indent** button 🔳 on the Formatting toolbar to indent the paragraph one-half inch. Notice that you can indent paragraphs before or after adding bullets or numbers. The order doesn't matter.

3. Click the **Numbering** button 📋 on the Formatting toolbar. Consecutive numbers appear in front of each item in the indented list.

4. Click anywhere in the document to deselect the text. Figure 2-22 shows the indented and numbered list.

Figure 2-22 ◄
Indented
numbered list

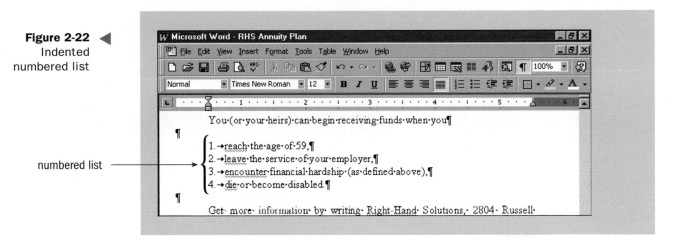

numbered list ────────►

The text of the document is now properly aligned and indented. The bullets and numbers make the lists easy to read and give readers visual clues as to what type of information they contain. Next, you need to adjust the formatting of individual words.

Changing the Font and Font Size

All of Brandi's remaining changes have to do with changing fonts, adjusting font sizes, and emphasizing text with font styles. The first step is to change the font of the title from 12-point Times New Roman to a 14-point bold Arial. This will make the title stand out from the rest of the text.

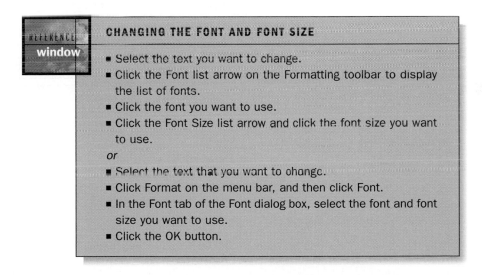

REFERENCE window

CHANGING THE FONT AND FONT SIZE

- Select the text you want to change.
- Click the Font list arrow on the Formatting toolbar to display the list of fonts.
- Click the font you want to use.
- Click the Font Size list arrow and click the font size you want to use.

or

- Select the text that you want to change.
- Click Format on the menu bar, and then click Font.
- In the Font tab of the Font dialog box, select the font and font size you want to use.
- Click the OK button.

Brandi wants you to change not only the font of the title, but also its size and style. To do this, you'll use the Formatting toolbar. She wants you to use a **sans serif** font, which is a font that does not have the small horizontal lines at the tops and bottoms of the letters. Sans serif fonts are often used in titles so they contrast with the body text. Times New Roman is a serif font, and Arial is a sans serif font. The text you are reading now is a serif font, and the text in the steps below is a sans serif font.

To change the attributes of the title using the Font command:

1. Press **Ctrl + Home** to move to the beginning of the document, and then select the title.

2. Click the **Font** list arrow on the Formatting toolbar. A list of available fonts appears in alphabetical order, with the name of the current font highlighted in the font list and in the Font text box. See Figure 2-23. Your list of fonts might be different from those shown in the figure. Fonts that have been used recently appear above the double line.

Figure 2-23 ◀
Font list

current font

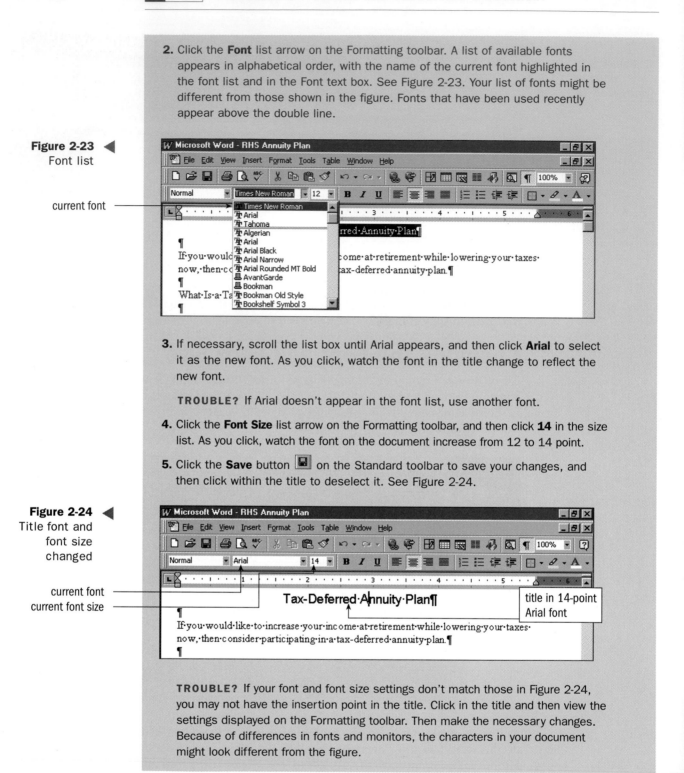

3. If necessary, scroll the list box until Arial appears, and then click **Arial** to select it as the new font. As you click, watch the font in the title change to reflect the new font.

TROUBLE? If Arial doesn't appear in the font list, use another font.

4. Click the **Font Size** list arrow on the Formatting toolbar, and then click **14** in the size list. As you click, watch the font on the document increase from 12 to 14 point.

5. Click the **Save** button 🖫 on the Standard toolbar to save your changes, and then click within the title to deselect it. See Figure 2-24.

Figure 2-24 ◀
Title font and
font size
changed

current font
current font size

title in 14-point
Arial font

TROUBLE? If your font and font size settings don't match those in Figure 2-24, you may not have the insertion point in the title. Click in the title and then view the settings displayed on the Formatting toolbar. Then make the necessary changes. Because of differences in fonts and monitors, the characters in your document might look different from the figure.

Emphasizing Text with Boldface, Underlining, and Italics

You can emphasize words in your document with boldface, underlining, or italics. These styles help you make specific thoughts, ideas, words, or phrases stand out. Brandi marked a few words on Reginald's draft that need this kind of special emphasis.

Bolding Text

Brandi wants to make sure that clients' employees see that the tax-deferred annuity plan can be terminated only under certain conditions. You will do this by bolding the word "only."

To change the font style to boldface:

1. Scroll down so you can view the first line of the paragraph beneath the question "Can My Tax-Deferred Annuity Plan Be Terminated?" on page 2.

2. Select the word "only" (immediately after the word "terminated").

3. Click the **Bold** button [B] on the Formatting toolbar, and then click anywhere in the document to deselect the text. The word appears in bold, as shown in Figure 2-25.

Figure 2-25 ◀
Word in
boldface

Bold button ────

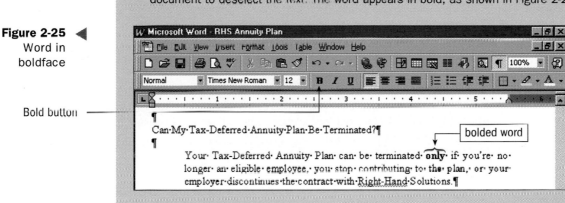

Underlining Text

The Underline command works in the same way as the Bold command. Brandi's edits indicate that the word "Note" should be inserted and underlined at the beginning of the final paragraph. You'll make both of these changes at once using the Underline command.

To underline text:

1. Press **Ctrl** + **End** to move the insertion point to the end of the document. Then move the insertion point to the left of the word "Get" in the first line of the final paragraph.

2. Click the **Underline** button [U] on the Formatting toolbar to turn on underlining. Notice that the Underline button remains pressed. Now, whatever text you type will be underlined on your screen and in your printed document.

3. Type **Note** and then click [U] to turn off underlining. Notice that the Underline button is no longer pressed, and the word "Note" is underlined.

4. Type **:** (a colon) and then press the **spacebar** twice. See Figure 2-26.

Figure 2-26 ◀
Word typed
with underline

underlined word ────

Underline button ────

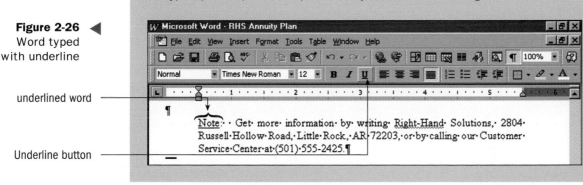

Italicizing Text

Next, you'll make annuity plan document conform with the other documents that Right-Hand Solutions produces by changing each question (heading) in the document to italics. This makes the document easier to read by clearly separating the sections. You'll begin with the first heading.

To italicize the question headings:

1. Press **Ctrl** + **Home** to return to the beginning of the document, and then select the text of the first heading, "What Is a Tax-Deferred Annuity?", by triple-clicking the text.

2. Click the **Italic** button *I* on the Formatting toolbar. The heading changes from regular to italic text.

3. Repeat Steps 1 and 2 to italicize the next heading. Now try a shorter way to italicize the text by repeating the formatting you just applied.

4. Select the next heading and then press the **F4** key. Repeat for each of the remaining five questions (headings) in the document. The italicized headings stand out from the rest of the text and help give the document a visual structure.

5. Click the **Save** button 🖫 on the Standard toolbar to save your work.

You have made all the editing and formatting changes that Brandi requested for the annuity plan description. You are ready to print a copy of the document. You don't need to change any print settings, so you can use the Print button on the Standard toolbar.

To preview and print the document:

1. Click the **Print Preview** button 🔍 on the Standard toolbar, and examine the document's appearance.

2. Click the **Print** button 🖨 on the Print Preview toolbar. After a pause, the document prints.

3. Click the **Close** button on the Print Preview toolbar, then click the **Close** button ☒ on the program window to close your document and exit Word.

You now have a hard copy of the final annuity plan description, as shown in Figure 2-27.

Figure 2-27
Final version of
RHS annuity
plan (page 1)

Tax-Deferred Annuity Plan

If you would like to increase your income at retirement while lowering your taxes now, then consider participating in a tax-deferred annuity plan.

What Is a Tax-Deferred Annuity?

A tax-deferred annuity allows you to put a portion of your before-tax wages into an investment account on a regular basis. Instead of paying taxes on the money now (when your tax rate is high), you pay after you retire (when your tax rate will be lower). In the mean time, the annuity account earns dividends that permit you to supplement your retirement income.

How Do I Enroll in a Tax-Deferred Annuity Plan?

As a full-time employee, you're eligible to participate in the Tax-Deferred Annuity Plan. Of course, the plan is voluntary. You may begin participating on the first day of the month following your employment, and you may stop participating at any time. To participate, just complete the necessary enrollment form, as well as a Salary Reduction Agreement, and return them to Right-Hand Solutions.

How Will My Money Be Invested?

On your annuity application you can allocate your premiums among several options, such as stocks, money markets, bonds, and world equities. A typical allocation might be similar to the following: stock (30%); money market (25%); bond market (25%); world equities (15%); other (5%).

You can change your allocation at any time by calling our Customer Service Center at (501) 555-2425. Right-Hand Solutions will make every effort to invest your money safely and effectively so you will realize the maximum possible earnings.

How Will I Know How Well My Investments Are Doing?

Right-Hand Solutions will send you a report annually, showing your total accumulation. Every quarter you'll receive a statement containing a complete history of all financial transactions and showing the interest credited you've earned. You'll also receive our regular newsletter.

Figure 2-27 ◀
Final version of
RHS annuity
plan (page 2)

For the purposes of this plan, accumulation is defined as all tax-deferred contributions, minus the Right-Hand Solutions service charges.

Can My Tax-Deferred Annuity Plan Be Terminated?

Your Tax-Deferred Annuity Plan can be terminated **only** if you're no longer an eligible employee, you stop contributing to the plan, or your employer discontinues the contract with Right-Hand Solutions.

Can I Withdraw Money from My Tax-Deferred Annuity Plan?

Normally, if you make an early withdrawal from your tax-deferred annuity plan, you will incur substantial financial penalties. However, you can withdraw money without penalty if you have an immediate and severe financial need (as defined below) and the money from your plan is necessary to meet those needs. Under current law, these withdrawals are subject to ordinary income taxes.

The following are considered to be immediate and severe financial needs:

- medical expenses that exceed 7.5% of your annual salary
- purchase (excluding mortgage payments) of a principal residence
- tuition for post-secondary education for you or your dependents
- other circumstances as regulated by the Internal Revenue Service

When Can I Begin to Receive Funds from My Tax-Deferred Annuity Plan?

You (or your heirs) can begin receiving funds when you

1. reach the age of 59,
2. leave the service of your employer,
3. encounter financial hardship (as defined above),
4. die or become disabled.

Note: Get more information by writing Right-Hand Solutions, 2804 Russell Hollow Road, Little Rock, AR 72203, or by calling our Customer Service Center at (501) 555-2425.

Quick Check

1. Name and describe the four types of text alignment or justification, and how to align and justify text using Word.

2. What is the purpose of the Format Painter and how does it work?

3. Explain how to indent a paragraph 0.5 inches or more from the left margin.

4. True or False: The larger the point size, the smaller the font that will be displayed and printed.

5. How do you apply bullets to a list of items?

6. Describe the steps necessary to bold a word or phrase.

7. Describe the steps necessary to change the font of a word or phrase.

8. Explain how to find the word "strategy" in a long document and replace every occurrence with the word "plan."

9. Explain how to change a document's margins.

In this tutorial, you have helped Reginald plan, edit, and format the annuity plan that will appear in the employee handbooks of Right-Hand Solutions' clients. Now that you have fine-tuned the content, adjusted the text appearance and alignment, and added a bulleted list and a numbered list, the plan is visually appealing and easy to read.

You give the hard copy to Reginald, who makes two photocopies—one for Brandi and one for the copy center, which copies and distributes the document to all clients of Right-Hand Solutions.

Tutorial Assignments

Now that Reginald has completed the description of the annuity plan, Brandi tells him that she also wants to include a sample quarterly statement and a sample contract change notice in the client's employee handbooks to show employees how easy the statements are to read. You'll open and format this document now.

1. If necessary, start Word, make sure your Student Disk is in the appropriate disk drive, and check your screen to make sure your settings match those in the tutorial.

2. Open the file RHSQuart from the TAssign folder for Tutorial 2 on your Student Disk, and save the document as RHS Quarterly Report.

3. Make all edits and formatting changes marked on Figure 2-28. However, when you substitute Right-Hand Solutions in place of We in the first paragraph, use copy and paste, copying the company name from the top of the letter (without the paragraph mark) before you bold it.

Figure 2-28 ◀

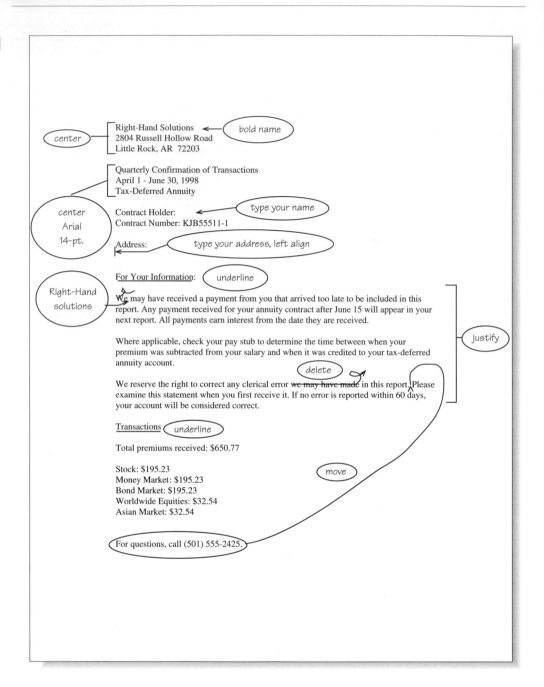

4. Save the document and print it.

5. Close the document.

6. Open the file RHSPort from the TAssign folder on your Student Disk, and save the file as RHS Portfolio Changes.

7. Make all the edits and formatting changes marked on Figure 2-29. However, instead of using the Formatting toolbar to change Current Allocation Accounts to bold 14 point, click Format on the menu bar, and then click Font to open the Font dialog box. Click the appropriate selections in the Font style and Size list boxes.

Figure 2-29 ◀

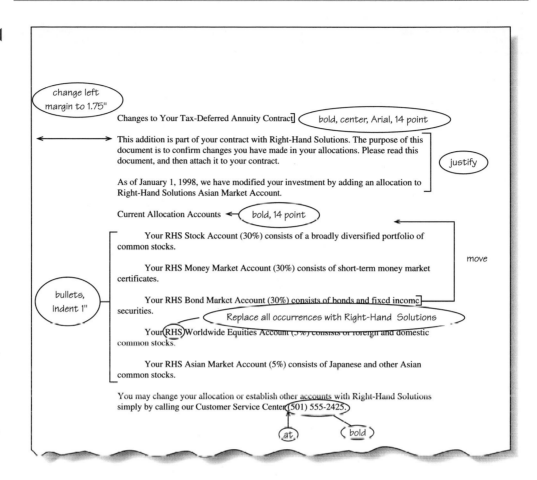

8. Change the margins using the ruler in page layout view:
   a. Click the Page Layout View button.
   b. Select all the text in the document by pressing Ctrl + A.
   c. Position the pointer on the ruler at the right margin, which is indicated by a change from white to gray background, and then press and hold down the mouse button. The pointer changes to a two-headed arrow, which allows you to adjust the right margin. Drag the margin left to the 5″ mark on the ruler, and then release the mouse button. Save the document.

9. Change the line spacing of the text.
   a. Make sure all the text in the document is selected.
   b. Click Format on the menu bar, and then click Paragraph to open the Paragraph dialog box.
   c. Click the Indents and Spacing tab.
   d. Click the Line spacing list arrow, and then click 1.5 lines.
   e. Click the OK button.

10. Click the Print Preview button on the Standard toolbar to check your work.

11. Use the Print command on the File menu to open the Print dialog box. Print two copies of the document by changing the Number of copies setting in the Print dialog box.

12. You can find out the number of words in your documents by using the Word Count command on the Tools menu. Use this command to determine the number of words in the document, and then write that number in the upper-right corner of one of the printouts.

13. Save and close the document.

Case Problems

1. Raleigh Rentals Michele Stafford manages Raleigh Rentals, a storage facility in Huntsville, Alabama. She has written the draft of a tenant information sheet outlining Raleigh Rental's policies for new customers. She asks you to edit and format the document for her.

1. If neccessary, start Word, make sure your Student Disk is in the appropriate disk drive, and check your screen to make sure your settings match those in the tutorials.

2. Open the file Raleigh from the Tutorial 2 Cases folder on your Student Disk, and save it as Raleigh Rental Policies.

3. Delete the word "general" from the first sentence of the first full paragraph. (Remember to use the Undo and Redo buttons to correct any editing mistakes as you work.)

4. Delete the sentence at the end of the second paragraph that begins "If you renew your contract...".

5. Insert the bolded sentence "A bill will not be sent to you." after the first sentence under the heading "Rental Payments".

6. Delete the second paragraph under the heading "Rental Payments".

7. Move the heading "Fees" and the sentence below it so that they appear after the "Rental Charges" section, not before it.

8. Delete the phrase "not negotiable, and are" from the first sentence under the heading "Rental Charges".

9. Change all of the margins (top, bottom, left, and right) to 1.5 inches.

10. For each paragraph following a heading, indent the paragraph 0.5 inch and set the alignment to justify. (*Hint:* Format the first paragraph and then use the Format Painter to format each successive paragraph.)

11. Use the Find tab in the Find and Replace dialog box to find the phrase "in writing" in the last sentence under the heading "Termination" and italicize it.

12. Create bullets for the list under the heading "Delinquent Accounts," and indent the list 0.5 inch.

13. Change both lines of the title to 16-point Arial (or another font of your choice).

14. Center and bold both lines of the title.

15. Bold all of the headings.

16. Replace the misspelling "sub-let" with "sublet" wherever it appears in the document.

17. Save, preview, and print the rental information sheet, and close the document.

2. Synergy Synergy provides productivity training for large companies across the country. Matt Patterson is Synergy's marketing director for the Northeast region. Matt wants to provide interested clients with a one-page summary of Synergy's productivity training.

1. If neccessary, start Word, make sure your Student Disk is in the appropriate disk drive, and check your screen to make sure your settings match those in the tutorials.

2. Open the file Synergy from the Tutorial 2 Cases folder on your Student Disk, and save it as Synergy Training Summary.

3. Change the title at the beginning of the document to a 14-point sans serif font. Be sure to pick a font that looks professional and is easy to read. (Remember to use the Undo and Redo buttons to correct any editing mistakes as you work.)

4. Center and bold the title.

5. Delete the word "main" from the second sentence of the first paragraph after the document title.

6. Create bullets for the list of training components following the first paragraph.

7. Under the heading "Personal Productivity Training Seminar" delete the second sentence from the first paragraph.

8. Under the heading "Personal Productivity Training Seminar" delete the phrase "in attendance at the seminar" from the first sentence in the second paragraph.

9. In the first paragraph under the heading "Management Productivity Training," move the second sentence beginning with "As a result" to the end of the paragraph.

10. Switch the order of the paragraphs under the "Field Services Technology and Training" heading.

11. Change the top margin to 1.5 inches.

12. Change the left margin to 1.75 inches.

13. Bold each of the headings.

14. Bold both occurrences of the word "free" in the second paragraph under the "Field Services Technology and Training" heading.

15. Save, preview, and print Synergy Training Summary, and then close the file.

3. Rec-Tech Ralph Dysktra is vice president of sales and marketing at Rec-Tech, an outdoor and sporting gear store in Conshohocken, Pennsylvania. Each quarter, Ralph and his staff mail a description of new products to Rec-Tech's regular customers. Ralph has asked you to edit and format the first few pages of this quarter's new products description.

1. If neccessary, start Word, make sure your Student Disk is in the appropriate disk drive, and check your screen to make sure your settings match those in the tutorials.

2. Open the file Backpack from the Tutorial 2 Cases folder on your Student Disk, and save it as Backpacker's Guide.

3. Delete the word "much" from the first sentence of the paragraph below the heading "Snuggle Up to These Prices". (Remember to use the Undo and Redo buttons to correct any editing mistakes as you work.)

4. Reverse the order of the last two paragraphs under the heading "You'll Eat Up the Prices of This Camp Cooking Gear!"

5. Move the last sentence at the end of the document to the end of the first full paragraph.

6. Reorder the items under the "RecTech Gear Up Ideas" heading by moving the first two product ideas to the end of the list.

7. Add bullets to the gear up product ideas.

8. Change the top margin to 2 inches.

9. Change the left margin to 1.75 inches.

10. Justify all the paragraphs in the document. (*Hint:* To select all paragraphs in the document at one time, click Edit on the menu bar, and then click Select All.)

11. Replace all occurrences of "RecTech" with "Rec-Tech."

12. Apply a 14-point sans serif font to each of the headings. Be sure to pick a font that looks professional and is easy to read.

13. Change the title's font to the same font you used for the headings, except set the size to 16 point.

14. Center and bold both lines of the title.

15. Bold the names and prices for all of the brand-name products in the Backpackers Guide.

16. Save, preview, and print the document, and then close the file.

4. Movie Review Your student newspaper has asked you to review four films currently showing in your area.

1. If neccessary, start Word, make sure your Student Disk is in the appropriate disk drive, and check your screen to make sure your settings match those in the tutorials.

2. Write a brief summary (1–2 paragraphs) for each movie and provide a rating for each movie. Correct any spelling errors. Save the document as Movie Review in the Tutorial 2 Cases folder on your Student Disk and print it.

Edit and format the document by doing the following:

3. Rearrange the order in which you discuss the movies to alphabetical order. (Remember to use the Undo and Redo buttons to correct any editing mistakes as you work.)

4. Change the top margin to 2 inches.

5. Set the left margin to 1.75 inches.

6. Add a title to your review, and then center and bold it.

7. Set the paragraph alignment to justify.

8. Italicize the title of each movie.

9. Save the edited document as Edited Movie Review.

10. Print the document.

11. Save and close your document.

Creating a Multiple-Page Report

Writing a Recommendation Report for AgriTechnology

OBJECTIVES

In this tutorial you will:

- Divide a document into sections
- Center a page between the top and bottom margins
- Create a header
- Number the pages in a document
- Attach a template and apply styles
- Create a table
- Add rows and shading to a table
- Widen table columns and align table text

CASE

AgriTechnology

Brittany Jones works for AgriTechnology, a biotechnology company that develops genetically engineered food products. Recently, AgriTechnology began shipping the EverRipe tomato to supermarkets. The EverRipe tomato is genetically engineered to stay ripe and fresh nearly twice as long as other varieties. Because of its longer shelf life and vine-ripened taste, supermarkets are eager to stock the new tomato, and the demand has been high. Unfortunately, the EverRipe tomato is also more susceptible to bruising than the usual varieties. Nearly 20 percent of the first year's crop was unmarketable because of damage sustained during shipping and handling. AgriTechnology's vice president, Ramon Espinoza, appointed Brittany to head a task force to determine how to increase the profitability of the EverRipe. The task force is ready to present the results of their study in the form of a report with an accompanying table. Brittany asks you to help prepare the report.

In this tutorial, you will format the report's title page so that it has a different layout from the rest of the report. The title page will contain only the title and subtitle, and will not have page numbers like the rest of the report. You will give the report a professional appearance quickly by applying a set of predefined formats that come with the Word program. You will also add a table to the AgriTechnology report that summarizes the task force's recommendations.

In this session you will review the task force's recommendation report. You will then learn how to divide a document into sections; center a page between the top and bottom margins; create a header; and number the pages in a document. Finally, you will learn how to attach a template and apply styles.

Planning the Document

As head of the task force, Brittany divided the responsibility for the report among the members of the group. Each person gathered information about one aspect of the problem and wrote the appropriate section of the report. Now Brittany must compile all the findings into a coherent and unified report. In addition, she must also follow the company's style guidelines for the content, organization, style, and format.

The report content includes the results of the study—obtained from interviews with other employees and visits to the packaging and distribution plant, trucking company, etc.—and recommendations for action.

Because Brittany knows some executives will not have time to read the entire report, she organized the report so it begins with an executive summary. The body of the report provides an in-depth statement of the problem and recommendations for solving that problem. At the end of the report, she summarizes the cost of the improvements.

The report's style follows established standards of business writing, emphasizing clarity, simplicity, and directness.

In accordance with AgriTechnology's style guide, Brittany's report will begin with a title page, with the text centered between the top and bottom margins. Every page except the title page will include a line of text at the top, giving a descriptive name for the report, as well as the page number. The text and headings will be formatted to look like all AgriTechnology's reports, following company guidelines for layout and text style.

At the end of the report, there will be a table that summarizes the costs of the proposed changes.

Opening the Draft of the Report

Brittany has already combined the individual sections into a draft of the report. You'll open the document and perform the formatting tasks indicated in Figure 3-1.

Figure 3-1 ◀
Initial draft of
task force's
report with
edits
(page 1)

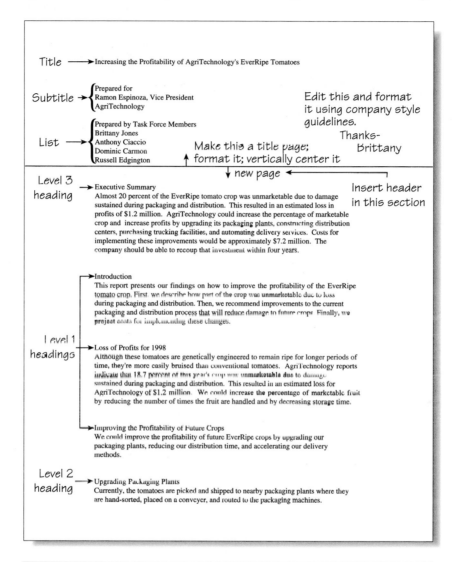

Figure 3-1 ◀
Initial draft of
task force's
report with
edits
(page 2)

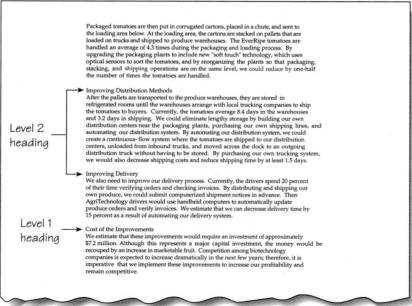

To open the document:

1. Start Word and place your Student Disk in the appropriate drive. Make sure your screen matches the figures in this tutorial. Because you'll be making large-scale formatting changes in this session, there is no need to display the nonprinting characters.

2. Open the file **EverRipe** from the **Tutorial.03** folder on your Student Disk.

3. To avoid altering the original file, save the document as **EverRipe Report** in the same folder.

Your first step is to change the layout of the title page.

Formatting the Document in Sections

According to the company guidelines, the title page of the report should be centered between the top and bottom margins of the page. In order to format the title page differently from the rest of the report, you need to divide the document into sections. A **section** is a unit or part of a document that can have its own page orientation, margins, headers, footers, and vertical alignment. Each section, in other words, is like a mini-document within a document.

To divide a document into sections, you insert a **section break**, a dotted line with the words "End of Section" that marks the point at which one section ends and another begins. Sections can start on a new page or continue on the same page. The easiest way to insert a section break is to use the Break command on the Insert menu.

To insert a section break after the title:

1. Position the insertion point immediately to the left of the "E" in the heading "Executive Summary." You want the text above this heading to be on a separate title page and the executive summary to begin the second page of the report.

2. Click **Insert** on the menu bar, and then click **Break** to open the Break dialog box. See Figure 3-2.

Figure 3-2 ◀
Break
dialog box

click here ——

You can use this dialog box to insert several types of breaks into your document, including a page break, which places the text after it onto a new page. Instead of inserting a page break, however, you will insert a section break that indicates both a new section and a new page.

3. Click the **Next page** option button in the Section breaks area, and then click the **OK** button. A double-dotted line and the words "Section Break (Next Page)" appear before the heading "Executive Summary," indicating that you have inserted a section break. The status bar indicates that the insertion point is on page 2, section 2. See Figure 3-3.

Figure 3-3 ◀
End of
section break

insertion point
in section 2

section number

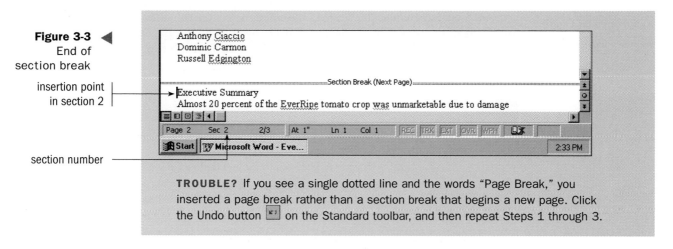

TROUBLE? If you see a single dotted line and the words "Page Break," you
inserted a page break rather than a section break that begins a new page. Click
the Undo button ⬚ on the Standard toolbar, and then repeat Steps 1 through 3.

Now that the title page is a separate section and page from the rest of the report, you
can make changes affecting only that section, leaving the rest of the document intact.

Changing the Vertical Alignment of a Section

You're ready to center the title text vertically on the title page. But first you want to look
at the layout of the report pages. To do this, you'll switch to the Print Preview window
which shows the general layout of the report.

To see the document in Print Preview:

1. Click the **Print Preview** button ⬚ on the Standard toolbar to open the Print
   Preview window.

2. If you only see one or two pages, click the **Multiple Pages** button ⬚ on the
   Print Preview toolbar, and then click and drag across the top three pages in the
   drop-down box to select "1 × 3 Pages." The three pages of the report are
   reduced in size and appear side-by-side. See Figure 3-4. Although you cannot
   read the text on the pages, you can see their general layout.

Figure 3-4 ◀
Print Preview
of report

Print Preview toolbar

unformatted
title page

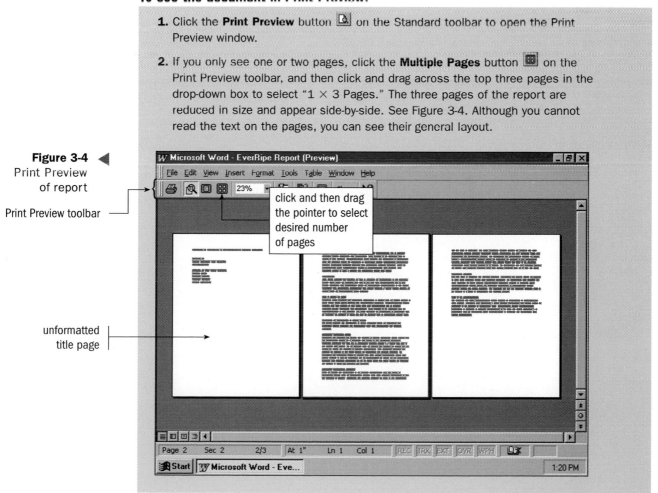

Now you can change the vertical alignment to center the lines of text between the top and bottom margins. The **vertical alignment** specifies how a page of text is positioned on the page between the top and bottom margins—flush at the top, flush at the bottom, or centered between the top and bottom margins.

REFERENCE
window

VERTICALLY ALIGNING A SECTION

- Insert a section break to create a separate section for the page you want to align.
- Move the insertion point within the section you want to align.
- Click File on the menu bar, click Page Setup, click the Layout tab, and then select the alignment option you want.
- Make sure the Apply to list box displays the This section option.
- Click the OK button.

You'll center the title page text from within the Print Preview window.

To change the vertical alignment of the title page:

1. If the Magnifier button is selected, click it once to deselect it.

2. Click the leftmost page in the Print Preview window to make sure the current page is page 1 (the title page). The status bar in the Print Preview window indicates the current page.

3. Click **File** on the menu bar, and then click **Page Setup** to open the Page Setup dialog box.

4. Click the **Layout** tab if it is not already selected. In the Apply to list box, click **This section** if it is not already selected so that the layout change affects only the first section, not both sections, of your document.

5. Click the **Vertical alignment** list arrow, and then click **Center** to center the pages of the current section—in this case just page 1—vertically between the top and bottom margins.

6. Click the **OK** button to return to the Print Preview window. The text of the title page is centered vertically, as shown in Figure 3-5.

Word

Figure 3-5 ◀
Title page
vertically
centered

text centered
between top and
bottom margins

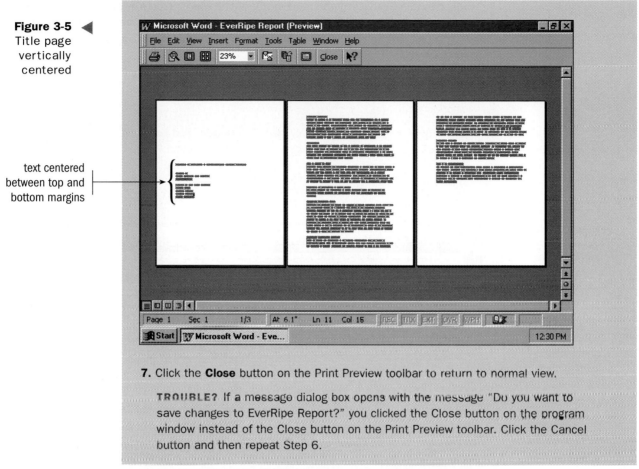

7. Click the **Close** button on the Print Preview toolbar to return to normal view.

TROUBLE? If a message dialog box opens with the message "Do you want to save changes to EverRipe Report?" you clicked the Close button on the program window instead of the Close button on the Print Preview toolbar. Click the Cancel button and then repeat Step 6.

You have successfully centered the title page text. Next, you turn your attention to placing a descriptive name for the report and the page number at the top of every page.

Adding Headers

The AgriTechnology report guidelines require a short report title and the page number to be printed at the top of every page except the title page. Text that is printed at the top of every page is called a **header**. For example, the section name, tutorial number, and page number printed at the top of the page you are reading is a header. Similarly, a **footer** is text that is printed at the bottom of every page. (You'll have a chance to work with footers in the Tutorial Assignments at the end of this tutorial.)

When you insert a header or footer into a document, you switch to Header and Footer view. The Header and Footer toolbar is displayed and the insertion point moves to the top of the document, where the header will appear. The main text is dimmed, indicating that it cannot be edited until you return to normal or page layout view.

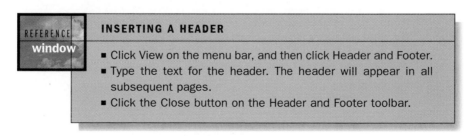

REFERENCE
window

INSERTING A HEADER

- Click View on the menu bar, and then click Header and Footer.
- Type the text for the header. The header will appear in all subsequent pages.
- Click the Close button on the Header and Footer toolbar.

You'll create a header for the main body of the report (section 2) that prints "EverRipe Recommendation Report" at the left margin and the page number at the right margin.

To insert a header for section 2:

1. Make sure the insertion point is anywhere after the heading "Executive Summary" on page 2 so that the insertion point is in section 2 and not in section 1.

2. Click **View** on the menu bar, and then click **Header and Footer**. The screen changes to Header and Footer view, and the Header and Footer toolbar appears in the document window. The header area appears in the top margin of your document surrounded by a dashed line and displays the words "Header -Section 2-." See Figure 3-6.

Figure 3-6 ◄
Creating
a header

header area ——

Header and
Footer toolbar ——►

Same as Previous
button pressed ——

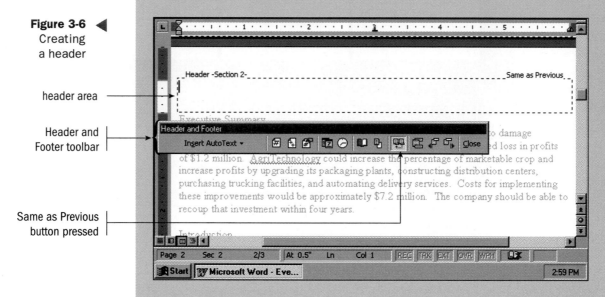

TROUBLE? If the header area displays "Header -Section 1-," click the Show Next button on the Header and Footer toolbar until the header area displays "Header -Section 2-."

TROUBLE? If the main text of the document doesn't appear on the screen, click the Show/Hide Document Text button on the Header and Footer toolbar, and continue with Step 3.

TROUBLE? If the Header and Footer toolbar covers the header area, drag the toolbar below the header area, similar to the position shown in Figure 3-6.

3. Click the **Same as Previous** button on the Header and Footer toolbar so that the button is not pressed. This ensures that the text of the current header will apply only to the current section (section 2), not to the previous section (section 1) also.

4. Type **EverRipe Recommendation Report**. The title is automatically aligned on the left. See Figure 3-7.

Figure 3-7 ◀
Text of header

report title

deselect so header
text prints only in
section 2

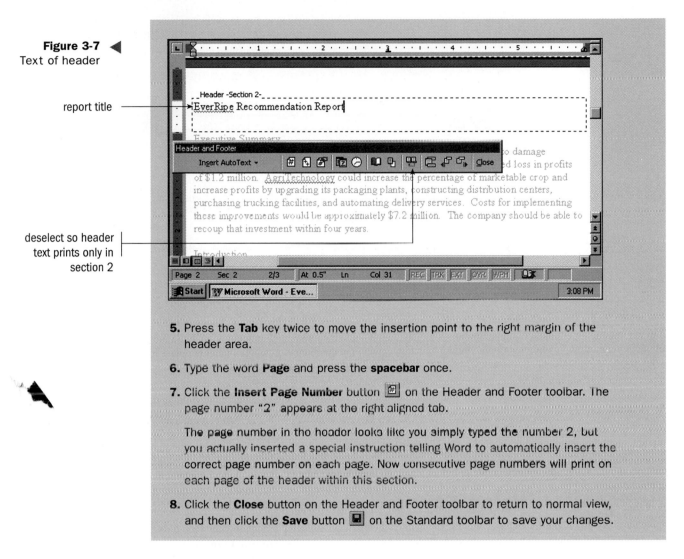

5. Press the **Tab** key twice to move the insertion point to the right margin of the header area.

6. Type the word **Page** and press the **spacebar** once.

7. Click the **Insert Page Number** button ▣ on the Header and Footer toolbar. The page number "2" appears at the right aligned tab.

The page number in the header looks like you simply typed the number 2, but you actually inserted a special instruction telling Word to automatically insert the correct page number on each page. Now consecutive page numbers will print on each page of the header within this section.

8. Click the **Close** button on the Header and Footer toolbar to return to normal view, and then click the **Save** button ▣ on the Standard toolbar to save your changes.

Notice that you can't see the header in normal view. To see exactly how the header will appear on the printed page, you can switch to page layout view, which lets you read the headers and footers as well as see the margins.

To view the header and margins in page layout view:

1. Click the **Page Layout View** button ▣.

2. Click the **Zoom Control** list arrow on the Standard toolbar, and then click **75%**. You can now see the header and the page margins. Next, you'll use the browse buttons to examine each page.

3. Click the **Select Browse Object** button ▣ below the vertical scroll bar and click the Browse by Page button ▢. The cursor moves to the top of the third page.

4. Click the **Previous Page** button ▣ (just below the vertical scroll bar) twice to move to page 1.

5. Click the **Next Page** button ▣ to move to the top of the second page.

6. Click the **Next Page** button ▣ again to move to the top of the third page. Notice that the header appears on pages 2 and 3 but not the title page. See Figure 3-8.

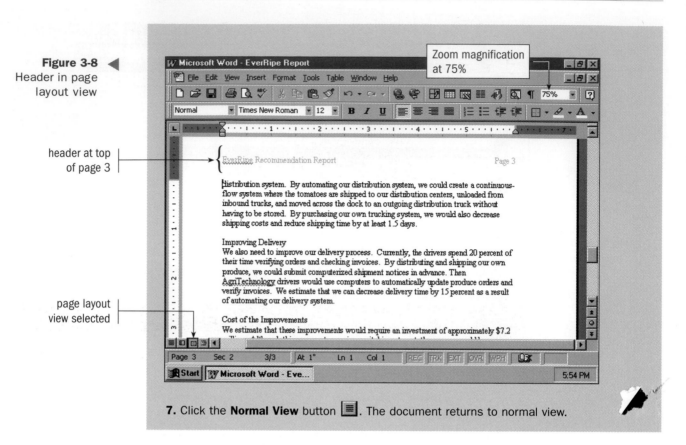

Figure 3-8 ◀
Header in page
layout view

header at top
of page 3

page layout
view selected

7. Click the **Normal View** button ▤. The document returns to normal view.

The recommendation report now has the required header. Your next job is to make style changes throughout the document.

Using Styles

As you know, it's often helpful to use the Format Painter to copy formatting from one paragraph to another. However, when you are working on a longer document, you'll find it easier to use a set of formats known as a **style**. Every Word document opens with a set of predefined styles which include: Normal (the default style for paragraphs in a Word document), Heading 1, Heading 2, and Heading 3. Word's default Normal style is defined as 10 point Times New Roman, left alignment, with single-line spacing. You can modify any of the predefined styles to suit the needs of your document, as you did when you changed the font size to 12 point at the beginning of the first tutorial.

The style of the current paragraph (the paragraph where the cursor is located) appears in the Style list box on the Formatting toolbar. All available styles are listed in the Style list, as shown in Figure 3-9. Styles affecting individual characters appear with a letter "a" in the gray box to the right of the style name (for example, the Page Number style in Figure 3-9); paragraph styles appear with the paragraph icon in the gray box (for example, the Heading 1 style in Figure 3-9). The font size of each style is also displayed. For example, the Page Number style is 10 point. All styles in the list appear with the formatting characteristics applied so you can see what they look like before choosing one.

Figure 3-9
List of available
default styles

click to display
list of styles

current style

font size

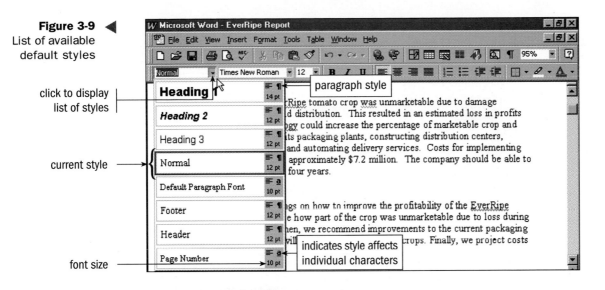

Attaching a Template to a Document

You can change the available styles by using a different template. A **template** is a set of predefined styles designed for a specific type of document. For example, Word provides templates for formatting reports, brochures, memos, letters, or resumes, among others. Word's default template, the Normal template, contains the Normal paragraph style described earlier.

There are two steps to using a template. First you need to attach the template to the document. Then you need to apply the template's styles to the various parts of the document. You'll begin by attaching a new template to the EverRipe Report document.

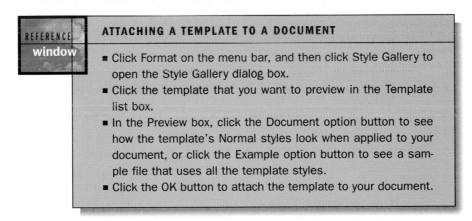

REFERENCE
window

ATTACHING A TEMPLATE TO A DOCUMENT

- Click Format on the menu bar, and then click Style Gallery to open the Style Gallery dialog box.
- Click the template that you want to preview in the Template list box.
- In the Preview box, click the Document option button to see how the template's Normal styles look when applied to your document, or click the Example option button to see a sample file that uses all the template styles.
- Click the OK button to attach the template to your document.

Brittany tells you that all reports produced at the company use Word's predefined Professional Report template. She suggests you preview the template to see what it looks like, and then attach it to the recommendation report. You'll use the Style Gallery to do this.

To preview and attach the Professional Report template to your document:

1. Click **Format** on the menu bar, and then click **Style Gallery** to open the Style Gallery dialog box. The recommendation report appears in the Preview of window and "(current)" appears in the Template list box. The report appears formatted the same way as it is in the document window.

2. Scroll to and then click **Professional Report** in the Template list box to select the template. In the Preview of Report window, the text of your document changes to reflect the new Normal style for the Professional Report template. See Figure 3-10.

Figure 3-10 ◀
Style Gallery
with preview of
Professional
Report
template

selected template ——

click to see
sample document

preview of document ——

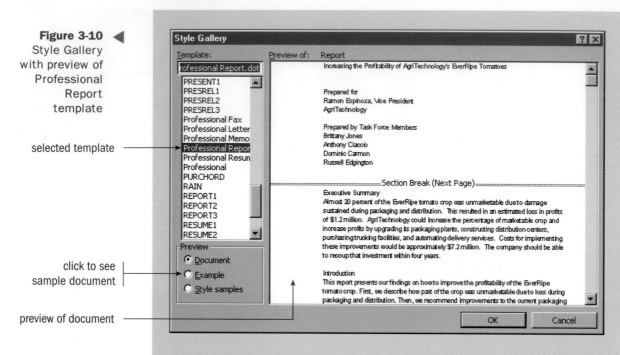

3. In the Preview box, click the **Example** option button to see a sample document that uses all the Professional Report template styles. Scroll through the sample document to preview all the styles that are available to you in this template.

4. Click the **OK** button to attach the template to the report and return to the document window. The template's default font (10-point Arial) and paragraph indentation are applied to the entire document, because the text in the document has been formatted with the Normal style, and because no other styles, such as a Heading style, have been applied to the text at this point. You'll see the Professional Report template styles when you apply them in the next section.

5. Click the **Style** list arrow on the Formatting toolbar. Scroll through the style list to verify that the styles of the Professional Report template are now available in this document, and then click the **Style** list arrow again to close the style list.

At this point, the only apparent change in the text is that the font changed from 12 point Times New Roman to 10 point Arial and that the paragraphs are left-indented 0.75 inch. (On some computers, the 10 point Arial is also condensed so that the font is actually Arial Narrow.) Now that the Professional Report template is attached to the report, you can begin applying its styles to the document.

Applying Styles

The best way to apply a template's styles to a document is to highlight individual parts of the document, and then select the appropriate style from the Style list on the Formatting toolbar. For example, to format the report title, you would highlight "Increasing the Profitability of AgriTechnology's EverRipe Tomatoes" on the title page, and then select the Title Cover style from the Style list.

You'll apply the Professional Report template styles now, beginning with the report title.

To apply styles to the report document:

1. Scroll to the title page, and then drag the pointer to select the title **Increasing the Profitability of AgriTechnology's EverRipe Tomatoes**.

Word

2. Click the **Style** list arrow on the Formatting toolbar to open the Style list. Scroll down the list, and then click **Title Cover**. Word applies the style to the selected text. Notice that the font of the Title Cover style is 32 point Arial Black.

3. Deselect the text. See Figure 3-11. Notice that the Title Cover style dramatically emphasizes the title. You'll get a better idea of its positioning on the page when you preview and print the document.

Figure 3-11 ◀
Title formatted
with Title
Cover style

formatted text →

unformatted text →

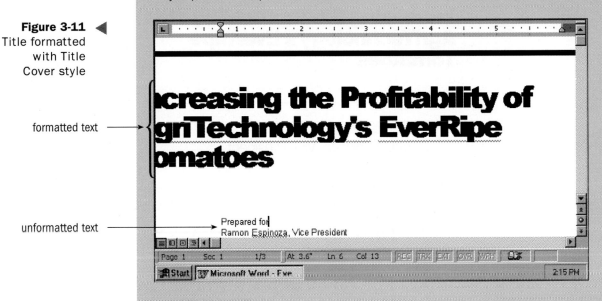

4. Continue formatting the rest of the document by coloring text and applying the styles indicated in Figure 3-12. Keep in mind that you do not have to apply a new style to any text not labeled in Figure 3-12, because Word already applied the Normal style for the Professional template when you attached it to the document. Be careful to choose List 2 when formatting the name list; there are several list and list continuation styles in this template, each with a different indent. Use the Undo button to undo any mistakes. To repeat applying a style you just applied, press the F4 key. When you are finished, your document should look similar to Figure 3-12. You might not be able to see the gray background of the Block Quotation style until you print the document.

Figure 3-12 ◀
Formatted
version of
recommenda-
tion report
(title page)

Subtitle Cover ──────→

List 2 ──────→

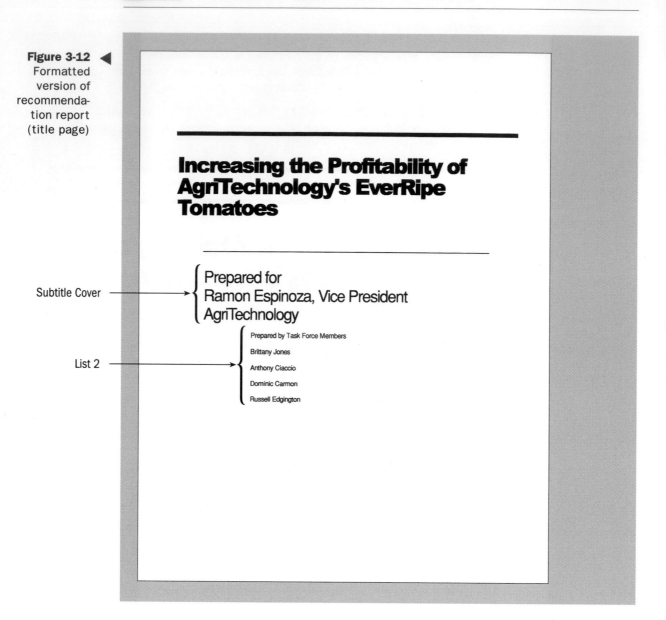

Word

Figure 3-12 ◄
Formatted
version of
recommenda-
tion report
(page 2)

Heading 3 ─────────

Block Quotation ────

Heading 1 ─────────

Heading 1 ─────────

Heading 1 ─────────

Heading 2 ─────────

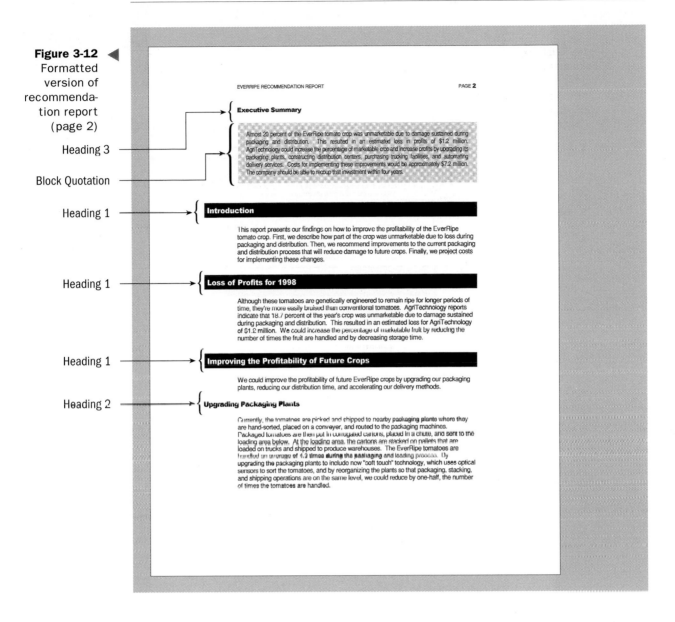

EVERRIPE RECOMMENDATION REPORT   PAGE **2**

Executive Summary

Almost 20 percent of the EverRipe tomato crop was unmarketable due to damage sustained during packaging and distribution. This resulted in an estimated loss in profits of $1.2 million. AgriTechnology could increase the percentage of marketable crop and increase profits by upgrading its packaging plants, constructing distribution centers, purchasing trucking facilities, and automating delivery services. Costs for implementing these improvements would be approximately $7.2 million. The company should be able to recoup that investment within four years.

Introduction

This report presents our findings on how to improve the profitability of the EverRipe tomato crop. First, we describe how part of the crop was unmarketable due to loss during packaging and distribution. Then, we recommend improvements to the current packaging and distribution process that will reduce damage to future crops. Finally, we project costs for implementing these changes.

Loss of Profits for 1998

Although these tomatoes are genetically engineered to remain ripe for longer periods of time, they're more easily bruised than conventional tomatoes. AgriTechnology reports indicate that 18.7 percent of this year's crop was unmarketable due to damage sustained during packaging and distribution. This resulted in an estimated loss for AgriTechnology of $1.2 million. We could increase the percentage of marketable fruit by reducing the number of times the fruit are handled and by decreasing storage time.

Improving the Profitability of Future Crops

We could improve the profitability of future EverRipe crops by upgrading our packaging plants, reducing our distribution time, and accelerating our delivery methods.

Upgrading Packaging Plants

Currently, the tomatoes are picked and shipped to nearby packaging plants where they are hand-sorted, placed on a conveyer, and routed to the packaging machines. Packaged tomatoes are then put in corrugated cartons, placed in a chute, and sent to the loading area below. At the loading area, the cartons are stacked on pallets that are loaded on trucks and shipped to produce warehouses. The EverRipe tomatoes are handled an average of 4.2 times during the packaging and loading process. By upgrading the packaging plants to include new "soft touch" technology, which uses optical sensors to sort the tomatoes, and by reorganizing the plants so that packaging, stacking, and shipping operations are on the same level, we could reduce by one-half, the number of times the tomatoes are handled.

Figure 3-12 ◄
Formatted
version of
recommenda-
tion report
(page 3)

Heading 2

Heading 2

Heading 1

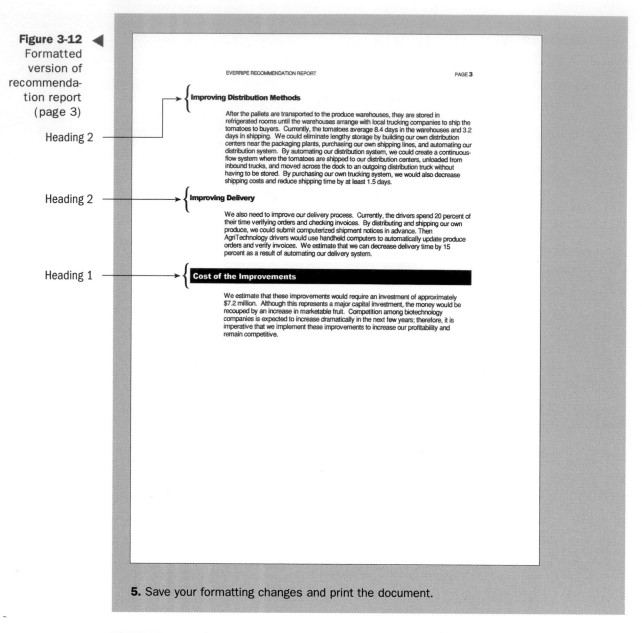

5. Save your formatting changes and print the document.

Quick Check

1. Define the following in your own words:
   a. style
   b. template
   c. Style list
   d. section (of a document)
   e. vertical alignment
   f. header

2. Why would you need to insert a section break into a document?

3. Explain how to center the title page vertically between the top and bottom margins.

4. What is the difference between a header and a footer?

5. How do you insert the page number in a header?

6. What are the two steps involved in using a new template?

7 How do you attach a template to a document?

8 Explain how you applied styles to the EverRipe Report document.

You have planned, formatted, and printed Brittany's recommendation report so that the results are professional-looking, clearly presented, and easy to read. You have done this using the Word features that quickly add formatting to an entire section of a document: headers, templates, and styles. Next you will add and format a table that summarizes the costs and benefits of the task force's recommendations.

SESSION

3.2

In this session you will learn how to add a table to the report. Then you'll add rows to the table, widen the columns in the table, and align the text in the table. Finally you'll add shading to make the table look more professional.

Inserting Tables

The Word Table feature allows you to quickly organize data and to arrange text in an easy-to-read format of columns and rows. Figure 3-13 summarizes the elements of a Word table.

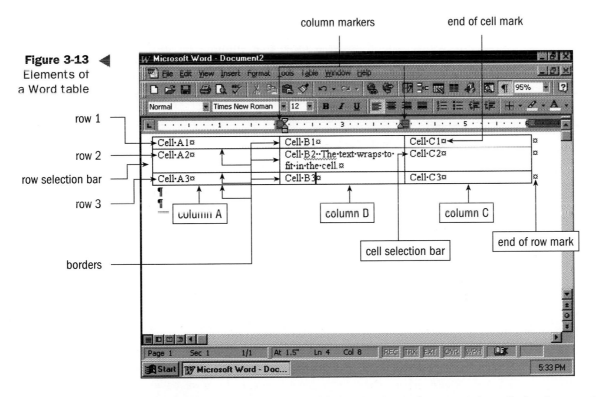

Figure 3-13
Elements of
a Word table

A **table** is information arranged in horizontal rows and vertical columns. As you can see by looking through this book, a table is an efficient way of communicating a lot of information in an easy-to-read format. It's convenient to refer to table rows as if they were labeled with numbers (row 1 at the top, row 2 below row 1, and so forth), and each column as a letter (column A on the far left, column B to the right of column A, and so forth). However, you do not see row and column numbers on the screen.

The area where a row and column intersect is called a **cell**. Each cell is identified by a column and row label. For example, the cell in the upper-left corner of a table is cell A1 (column A, row 1), the cell to the right of that is cell B1, the cell below cell A1 is A2, and so forth. The table's structure is indicated by **borders**, which are lines that outline the rows and columns. With Word's Table feature, you can create a blank table and then insert information into it, or you can convert existing text into a table. You'll begin with a blank table in the next section. In the Tutorial Assignments at the end of this tutorial, you'll have a chance to convert text into a table.

Creating a Table Using the Insert Table Button

The easiest way to create a table is by moving the insertion point to the location in your document where you want a table, clicking the Insert Table button on the Standard toolbar, and then specifying the number of rows and columns you need in your table. Word inserts a blank table structure with the number of rows and columns you specified.

REFERENCE window	**CREATING A BLANK TABLE USING THE INSERT TABLE BUTTON**
	▪ Place the insertion point where you want the table to appear in the document.
	▪ Click the Insert Table button on the Standard toolbar to display a drop-down grid.
	▪ Drag the pointer to select the desired number of rows and columns, and then release the mouse button.

Brittany wants you to create a table that summarizes information in the EverRipe report, which you formatted in the previous session. Figure 3-14 shows a sketch of what Brittany wants the table to look like. The table will allow AgriTechnology's executives to see at a glance the cost and benefits of each improvement.

Figure 3-14
Sketch of
EverRipe table

Projected Improvement	Initial Cost	Percent of Total Cost	Benefit
Upgrade packaging plants	$2,500,000	35%	Reduce by one-half the number of times tomatoes are handled
Improve distribution methods	$3,700,000	51%	Decrease shipping costs and reduce shipping time by 1.5 days
Automate delivery paperwork	$1,000,000	14%	Decrease delivery time by 15%
Total	$7,200,000		

You'll use the Insert Table button to create the table.

To create a blank table using the Insert Table button:

1. If you took a break after the last session, make sure Word is running and that the EverRipe Report document is open. Because you will be working with table formatting elements in this session, make sure the nonprinting characters are displayed.

2. Position the insertion point at the end of the last paragraph in the report, and press the **Enter** key twice to insert a space between the text and the table. Word inserts the table at the location of the insertion point.

3. Click the **Insert Table** button on the Standard toolbar. A drop-down grid resembling a miniature table appears below the Insert Table button. The grid initially has four rows and five columns. You can drag the pointer to extend the grid to as many rows and columns as you need. In this case, you need only four rows and four columns.

4. Position the pointer in the upper-left cell of the grid, and then click and drag the pointer down and across the grid until you highlight four rows and four columns. As you drag the pointer across the grid, Word indicates the size of the table (rows by columns) at the bottom of the grid. See Figure 3-15.

Figure 3-15 ◀
Insert
Table grid

click to insert table

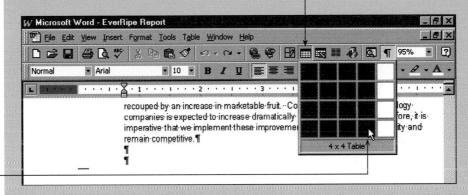

drag to select
table size

5. Release the mouse button. An empty table, four rows by four columns, appears in your document with the insertion point blinking in the upper-left corner (cell A1).

The table is outlined with borders, and the four columns are of equal width. The column widths are indicated by **column markers** on the ruler. Each cell contains an end-of-cell mark, and each row contains an end-of-row mark.

TROUBLE? If you don't see the end-of-cell and end-of-row marks, you need to show nonprinting characters. Click the Show/Hide ¶ button ⧉ on the Standard toolbar to show nonprinting characters.

Now that you've created the table, you are ready to enter text and numbers summarizing the EverRipe report.

Entering Text in a Table

You can enter text in a table by moving the insertion point to a cell and typing. If the text takes up more than one line in the cell, Word automatically wraps the text to the next line and increases the height of that cell and all the cells in that row. To move the insertion point to the next cell to the right, you can either click in that cell or press the Tab key. If you want to return to the previous cell, you can press and hold down the Shift key while you press the Tab key. Figure 3-16 summarizes the keystrokes for moving within a table.

Figure 3-16 ◀
Keystrokes for
moving around
a table

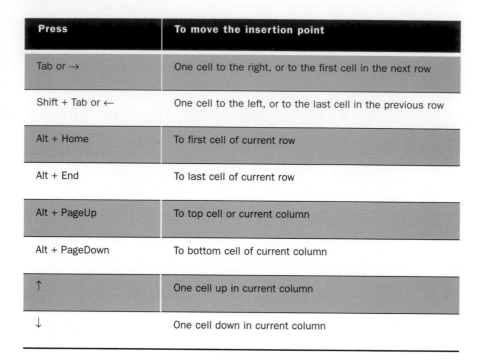

Press	To move the insertion point
Tab or →	One cell to the right, or to the first cell in the next row
Shift + Tab or ←	One cell to the left, or to the last cell in the previous row
Alt + Home	To first cell of current row
Alt + End	To last cell of current row
Alt + PageUp	To top cell or current column
Alt + PageDown	To bottom cell of current column
↑	One cell up in current column
↓	One cell down in current column

Now you are ready to insert information into the table.

To insert data into the table:

1. Make sure the insertion point is in cell A1 of the table.

2. Type **Projected Improvement**. Watch the end-of-cell mark move to the right as you type.

3. Press the **Tab** key to move to cell B1. See Figure 3-17.

Figure 3-17 ◀
Adding text
to the table

end-of-cell mark ——

new text ——

insertion point
in cell B1

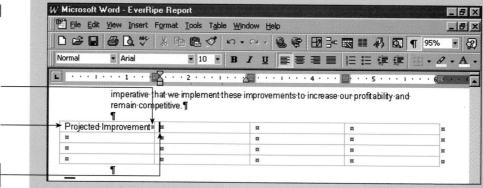

TROUBLE? If you accidentally pressed the Enter key instead of the Tab key, Word created a new paragraph within cell A1 rather than moving the insertion point to cell B1. Press the Backspace key to remove the paragraph mark, and then press the Tab key to move to cell B1.

4. Type **Initial Cost** and then press the **Tab** key to move to cell C1.

5. Type **Percent of Total Cost** and then press the **Tab** key to move to cell D1.

6. Type **Benefit** and then press the **Tab** key to move the insertion point from cell D1 to cell A2. Notice that when you press the Tab key in the last column of the table, the insertion point moves to the first column in the next row.

You have entered the **heading row**, the row that identifies the information in each column.

7. Type the remaining information for the table, as shown in Figure 3-18, pressing the Tab key to move from cell to cell.

Figure 3-18
Table with completed information

heading row

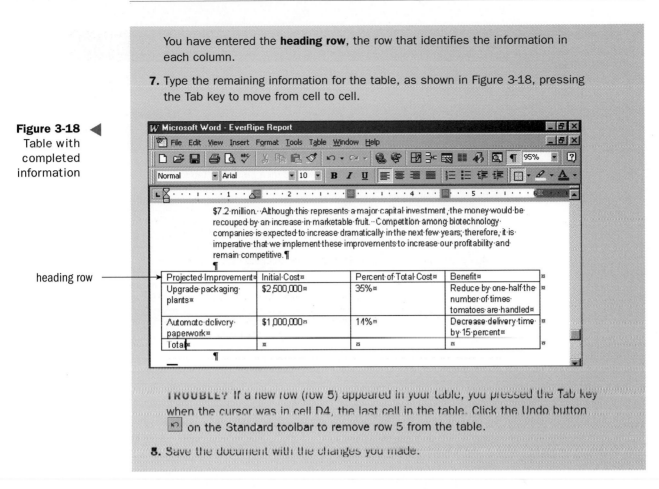

TROUBLE? If a new row (row 5) appeared in your table, you pressed the Tab key when the cursor was in cell D4, the last cell in the table. Click the Undo button on the Standard toolbar to remove row 5 from the table.

8. Save the document with the changes you made.

Keep in mind that many of the methods you've used to edit a document, such as the Backspace key, the copy-and-paste feature, the Undo button, and the AutoCorrect feature, work the same way in a table. Just like in a paragraph, you must select text within a table in order to edit it.

Inserting Additional Rows

When creating a table, you might be unsure about how many rows or columns you will actually need. You might need to delete extra rows and columns, or, as in this case, you might need to add them. Either way, you can easily modify an existing table's structure. Figure 3-19 summarizes ways to insert or delete rows and columns in a table.

Figure 3-19 ◀
Ways to insert
or delete table
rows and
columns

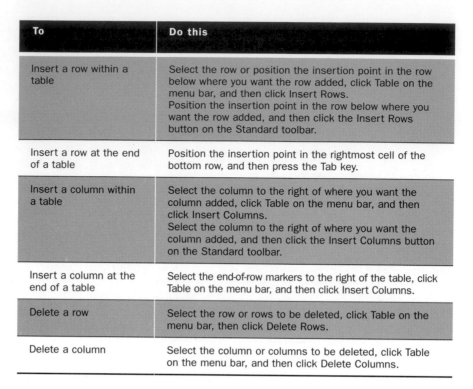

To	Do this
Insert a row within a table	Select the row or position the insertion point in the row below where you want the row added, click Table on the menu bar, and then click Insert Rows. Position the insertion point in the row below where you want the row added, and then click the Insert Rows button on the Standard toolbar.
Insert a row at the end of a table	Position the insertion point in the rightmost cell of the bottom row, and then press the Tab key.
Insert a column within a table	Select the column to the right of where you want the column added, click Table on the menu bar, and then click Insert Columns. Select the column to the right of where you want the column added, and then click the Insert Columns button on the Standard toolbar.
Insert a column at the end of a table	Select the end-of-row markers to the right of the table, click Table on the menu bar, and then click Insert Columns.
Delete a row	Select the row or rows to be deleted, click Table on the menu bar, then click Delete Rows.
Delete a column	Select the column or columns to be deleted, click Table on the menu bar, and then click Delete Columns.

Word allows you to insert additional rows either within or at the end of a table. You can insert a row or rows within the table with the Insert Rows command on the Table menu. To insert a row at the end of the table, you simply place the insertion point in the last cell of the last row and press the Tab key.

After looking over the EverRipe table, you see that you forgot to include a row on improving distribution methods. You'll insert that row and the relevant data now using the Insert Rows command, which inserts a row above the current row. To insert a row above the "Automate delivery paperwork" row (row 3), you begin by selecting that row. You will insert the new row using the Table shortcut menu, which contains frequently used table commands.

To insert a row within the table:

1. Position the pointer in the margin next to cell A3 (which contains the text "Automate delivery paperwork"). This area is called the row **selection bar**. The pointer changes to ⟡ .

2. Click to select row 3.

3. With the pointer ⟢ positioned anywhere over the selected row, click the right mouse button. The Table shortcut menu opens. Notice that the shortcut menu includes a Delete Rows command, which you could use if you needed to delete the selected row. In this case, however, you want to insert a row. See Figure 3-20.

Figure 3-20 ◀
Table shortcut
menu

click to insert
a new row

click to delete the
selected row

click here to
select row

right-click over
highlighted
row to display
shortcut menu

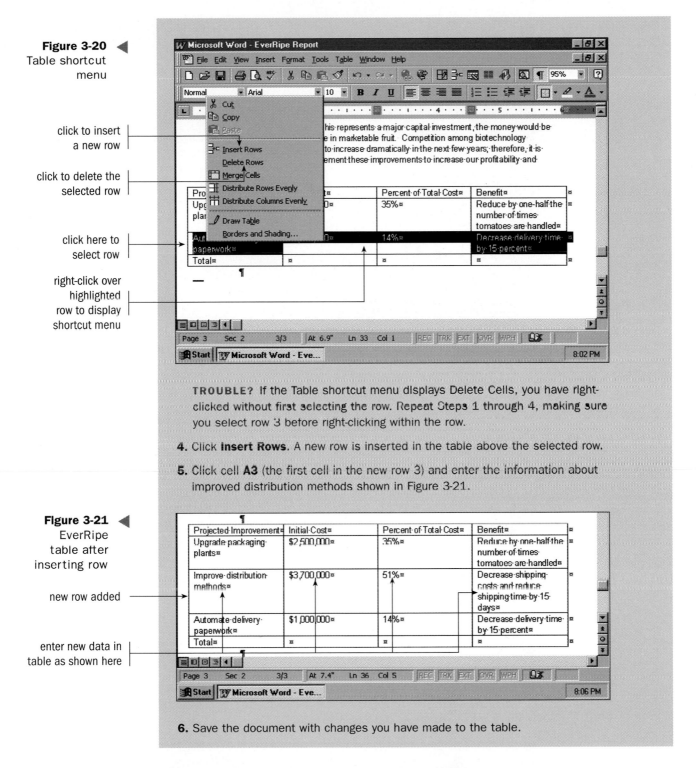

TROUBLE? If the Table shortcut menu displays Delete Cells, you have right-clicked without first selecting the row. Repeat Steps 1 through 4, making sure you select row 3 before right-clicking within the row.

4. Click **Insert Rows**. A new row is inserted in the table above the selected row.

5. Click cell **A3** (the first cell in the new row 3) and enter the information about improved distribution methods shown in Figure 3-21.

Figure 3-21 ◀
EverRipe
table after
inserting row

new row added

enter new data in
table as shown here

Projected·Improvement¤	Initial·Cost¤	Percent·of·Total·Cost¤	Benefit¤	¤
Upgrade·packaging·plants¤	$2,500,000¤	35%¤	Reduce·by·one-half·the·number·of·times·tomatoes·are·handled¤	¤
Improve·distribution·methods¤	$3,700,000¤	51%¤	Decrease·shipping·costs·and·reduce·shipping·time·by·15·days¤	¤
Automate·delivery·paperwork¤	$1,000,000¤	14%¤	Decrease·delivery·time·by·15·percent¤	¤
Total¤	¤	¤	¤	¤

6. Save the document with changes you have made to the table.

Using AutoSum to Total a Table Column

Rather than calculating column totals by hand and entering them, you can easily have Word compute the totals of numeric columns in a table.

To total the values in the Cost column:

1. Click cell **B5**, the last call in the Initial Cost column.

2. Click the **Tables and Borders** button ⊞ on the Standard toolbar. The Tables and Borders toolbar appears and the document automatically changes to page layout view.

TROUBLE? If the Office Assistant opens, displaying a hint on working with this window, just click the Cancel button to close the Office Assistant.

3. Click the **AutoSum** button Σ on the Tables and Borders toolbar. The total of the column appears in cell B5 formatted with a dollar sign and two decimal places. You want it to match the numbers above it, so you'll delete the decimal point and the two zeroes.

4. Click **Table** on the menu bar, and then click **Formula**.

5. Click the **Number Format** list arrow, and select the only format with a dollar sign.

6. In the Number Format text box, click to the right of the format and press the **Backspace** key until only $#, ##0 remains, as shown in Figure 3-22.

Figure 3-22 ◀
Formula dialog box after adjusting number format

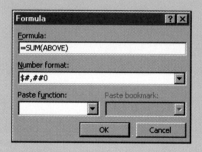

7. Click **OK**. The Initial Cost total is now formatted like the numbers above it.

8. Click the **Close** button ✕ on the Tables and Borders toolbar. If it is docked below the Formatting toolbar, and does not have a Close button, right click the toolbar and click Tables and Borders to remove the checkmark next to it.

9. Click the **Normal View** button ▤.

You have finished creating the tables and entering data. Now you can concentrate on improving the table's appearance.

Formatting Tables

Word provides a variety of ways to enhance the appearance of the tables you create: you can alter the width of the columns and the height of the rows, or change the alignment of text within the cells or the alignment of the table between the left and right margins.

After reviewing your work, Brittany decides the EverRipe table needs formatting to make it more attractive and easier to read.

Changing Column Width and Height

Sometimes you'll want to adjust the column widths in a table in order to make the text easier to read. If you want to specify an exact width for a column, you should use the Cell Height and Width command on the Table menu. However, it's usually easiest simply to drag the column's right-hand border to a new position.

The Initial Cost column (column B) and the Percent of Total Cost column (column C) are too wide for the information they contain and should be decreased. Also, the Benefit column (column D) would be easier to read if it was a little wider. You'll change these widths by dragging the column borders, using the ruler as a guide. Keep in mind that to change the width of a column, you need to drag the column's rightmost border.

To change the width of columns by dragging the borders:

1. Position the insertion point anywhere in the EverRipe table. Make sure you do not select any cells.

2. Move the pointer over the border between columns B and C (in other words, over the rightmost border of column B). The pointer changes to ✛ .

3. Click and drag the pointer to the left until the border reaches 2.5 inches on the ruler, and then release the mouse button. Notice that as the second column decreases in width, the width of column C increases, but the overall width of the table does not change. See Figure 3-23.

Figure 3-23 ◄
Table after
decreasing
the width of
column B

drag this pointer
to change the
column width

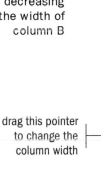

4. Click and drag the right border of column C to the left until it reaches about 3.5 inches on the ruler. Notice that Word automatically adjusted column D to compensate for the changes in columns B and C. Instead of being crowded onto several short lines, the text in column D is stretched out into one or two longer, easier-to-read lines. This means you don't have to worry about widening the last column.

You can change the height of rows by dragging a row border, just as you changed column widths by dragging a column border. You'll make row 1 taller to make it more prominent. To do this you have to change to page layout view.

To change the height of row 1:

1. Click the **Page Layout View** button ▣ .

2. Position the pointer over the bottom border of the heading row. The pointer changes to ⬥ .

3. Drag the row border downward about ¼".

4. Click the **Normal View** button ▤ .

The EverRipe table now looks much better with its new column widths and row height. Next you'll align the text to make the table even more attractive.

Aligning Text Within Cells

Aligning the text within the cells of a table makes the information easier to read. For example, aligning numbers and percentages along the right margin helps the reader to quickly compare the values. Centering the headings makes the columns more visually appealing. You can align text within the cells the same way you do other text—with the alignment buttons on the Formatting toolbar.

The dollar and percentage amounts in columns B and C would be much easier to read if you were to align the numbers on the right side of the cells. The table would also look better with the headings centered.

To right-align the numerical data and center the headings:

1. Drag the pointer to select cells **B2** through **C5**. See Figure 3-24.

Figure 3-24 ◀
Selected data

selected cells are
currently left-aligned

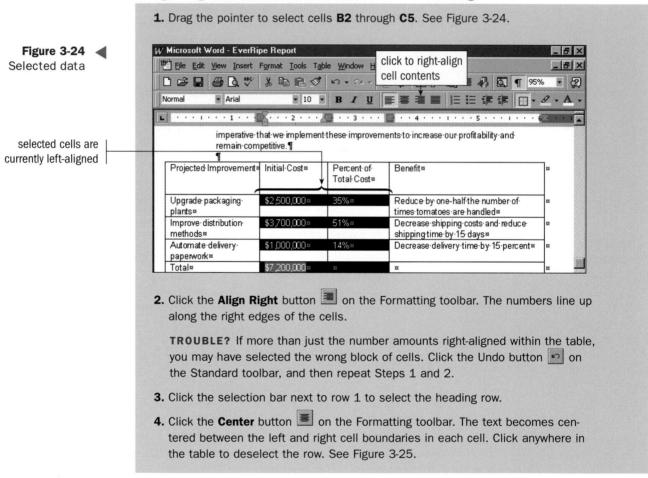

2. Click the **Align Right** button on the Formatting toolbar. The numbers line up along the right edges of the cells.

    TROUBLE? If more than just the number amounts right-aligned within the table, you may have selected the wrong block of cells. Click the Undo button on the Standard toolbar, and then repeat Steps 1 and 2.

3. Click the selection bar next to row 1 to select the heading row.

4. Click the **Center** button on the Formatting toolbar. The text becomes centered between the left and right cell boundaries in each cell. Click anywhere in the table to deselect the row. See Figure 3-25.

Figure 3-25 ◀
Table
with newly
aligned text

headings are
now centered
horizontally

dollar values and
percentages are
now right-aligned

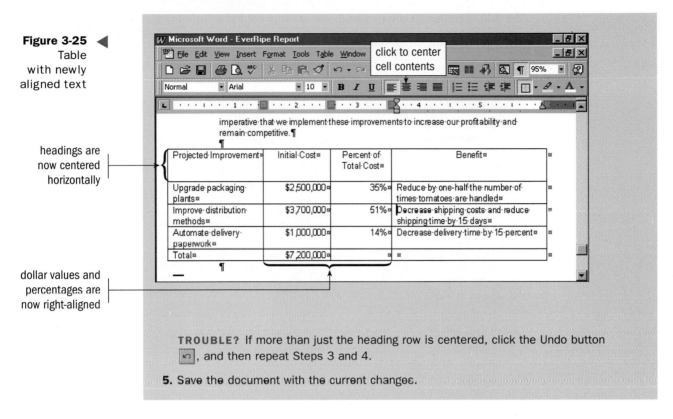

TROUBLE? If more than just the heading row is centered, click the Undo button, and then repeat Steps 3 and 4.

5. Save the document with the current changes.

The tables look better with the headings centered and the numbers right-aligned. Now you'll vertically align the text in the heading row so that it is centered between the top and bottom lines.

To align the text in the heading row vertically:

1. Click to the left of row 1 to select the heading row of the table.

2. Click the **Tables and Borders** button on the Standard toolbar.

3. Click the **Center Vertically** button on the Tables and Borders toolbar. The text becomes vertically centered in the row.

4. Close the Tables and Borders toolbar, and then click anywhere in the document to deselect the row.

5. Click the **Normal View** button.

You'll finish formatting the table by adding shading to the cells containing the headings.

Adding Shading

With the Borders and Shading dialog box, adding **shading** (a gray or colored background) to any text in a document is a simple task. Shading is especially useful in tables when you want to emphasize headings, totals, or other important items. In most cases, when you add shading to a table, you'll also need to bold the shaded text to make it easier to read.

You'll add a light gray shading to the heading row. You'll also bold the headings. As with most formatting tasks, you'll begin by selecting the row you want to format, and then you'll open the Borders and Shading dialog box, which is a good way to make several formatting changes at once.

To add shading to the heading row and to bold the headings:

1. Click to the left of row 1 to select the heading row of the table.

2. Click **Format** on the menu bar, and then click **Borders and Shading**. The Borders and Shading dialog box opens.

3. Click the **Shading** tab to display a list of shading options. The Fill section displays the available colors and shades of gray that you can use to shade the heading row.

4. Click the **top right square**. The label Gray-12.5% appears to the right of the color selections, and the Preview section on the right shows a sample. See Figure 3-26.

Figure 3-26 ◀
Shading tab

click this 12.5% gray ─────

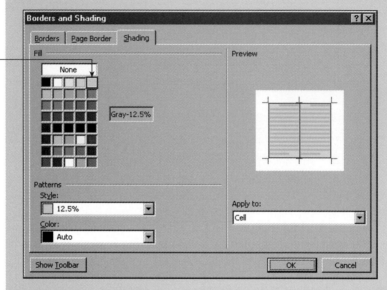

5. Click the **OK** button. A light gray background appears in the heading row. Now you need to bold the text to make the headings stand out from the shading.

6. Click the **Bold** button **B** on the Formatting toolbar to bold the headings.

   TROUBLE? If any of the headings break incorrectly (for example, if the "t" in "Cost" moves to its own line), you might need to widen columns to accommodate the bolded letters. Drag the column borders as necessary to adjust the column widths so that all the column headings are displayed correctly.

7. Click in the selection bar next to the last row to select the Total row.

8. Click the **Bold** button on the formatting toolbar to bold the total.

9. Click anywhere outside the total row to deselect it and then save your changes. Your completed table should look like Figure 3-27.

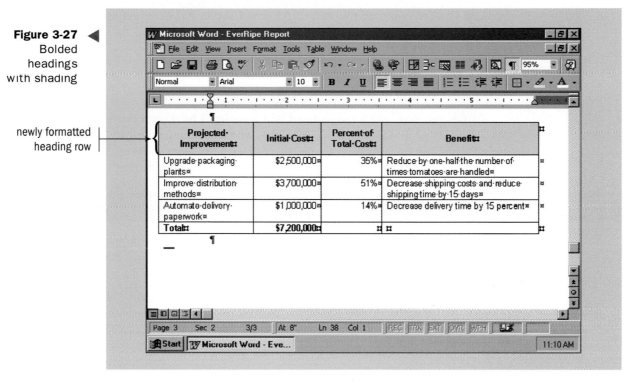

Figure 3-27
Bolded
headings
with shading

newly formatted
heading row

Now that you're finished with the EverRipe table, you print a copy of the full report to give to Brittany. You'll preview the report first to make sure the table fits on the third page.

To preview the table:

1. Click the **Print Preview** button [icon] on the Standard toolbar to open the Print Preview window.

2. Make sure the Magnifier button [icon] is selected and then click the table. The table looks fine, so you decide to print the report.

3. Click the **Print** button [icon] on the Print Preview toolbar to print the report; then close the document and exit Word.

You now have a hard copy of the EverRipe report including the table, which summarizes the report text. Brittany is pleased with your work.

Quick Check

1. Explain how to insert a blank table structure into a document.

2. How do you adjust the width of the columns in a table?

3. Why would you usually right-align numbers in a table?
   a. to quickly see the place value of the numbers
   b. to make the table look more attractive
   c. to make the table easier to understand
   d. all of the above

4. Define the following terms in your own words:
   a. table
   b. cell
   c. shading

5 List two ways to move from cell A1 to cell A2 in a table, then list two ways to move from cell B7 to cell B6.

6 Explain how to total a column of numbers in a table.

7 Explain how to insert a new row into a table.

In this tutorial, you have planned and formatted Brittany's recommendation report, and have added a table to summarize the report recommendations. As a result, the report information is readily available to readers who want to skim for the most important points, as well as to those who want more detailed information.

Tutorial Assignments

AgriTechnology adopted the recommendations the task force made in the EverRipe report. It is now two years later and the task force is issuing a report on the progress of the new packaging, distribution, and delivery policies. You'll format this report now.

1. If necessary, start Word and make sure your Student Disk is in the appropriate disk drive, and check your screen to make sure your settings match those in the tutorial. Display nonprinting characters as necessary

2. Open the file StatRep from the TAssign folder for Tutorial 3 on your Student Disk, and then save it as AgTech Status Report.

3. Divide the document into two sections. Insert a section break after the names of the task force members, and begin the executive summary on a new page.

4. Vertically align the first section of the document using the Justified alignment option in the Page Setup dialog box, and view the results in Print Preview.

5. Move the insertion point to section 2. Click View on the menu bar, and then click Header and Footer. Use the Word online Help system to learn the functions of the buttons on the Header and Footer toolbar. Then, on the Header and Footer toolbar, click the Switch Between Header and Footer button to move to the footer area of the document. Using the same techniques you used to create a header in the tutorial, create a footer for section 2 that reads "EverRipe Status Report" at the left margin, centers the page number preceded by the word "Page," and prints in 9-point bold Arial. (*Hint:* To center the page number, use the second tab stop.)

6. Create a header for this section that aligns your name at the left margin and the date at the right margin. (*Hint:* Use the Insert Date button on the Header and Footer toolbar to insert the date.) Close the Header and Footer toolbar.

7. Attach the Professional Report template to the document using the Style Gallery command on the Format menu, and preview how the report will look with sample text.

8. AutoFormat automatically formats selected text based on the options available in the attached template. Try using AutoFormat now by selecting the text of the title page, clicking Format on the menu bar, and then clicking AutoFormat on the Format menu. In the AutoFormat dialog box, make sure the AutoFormat now option button is selected, then click the OK button. Do you like the look of the formatted page? Why or why not?

9. Select the heading and text of the executive summary, and apply the Block Quotation style.

10. Apply the Heading 1 style to the heading "Introduction."

11. Apply the Heading 2 style to the headings "Loss of Profits for the EverRipe Crop," "Efforts to Improve Profitability," "Cost of the Improvements," and "Other Factors Influencing Profitability." Notice that the Heading 2 style does not insert space above the heading, so insert a return before each one.

12. Apply the Heading 3 style to the headings "Upgraded Packaging Plants," "Improved Distribution Methods," and "Improved Delivery." Insert a paragraph return before each Heading 3.

13. Save the document.

14. Preview and print the document, and then close it.

Open the file ZonReq from the TAssign folder for Tutorial 3 on your Student Disk, save the document as Zoning Request, and then complete the following:

15. Divide the document into two sections. End the first section after the words "Chicago, Illinois"; begin the second section on a new page.

16. Vertically align the first section of the document using the Top alignment option in the Page Setup dialog box.

17. Create a header for section 2 that prints "Zoning Request" at the left margin and has a right-aligned page number preceded by the word "Page."

18. On the Header and Footer toolbar, click the Switch Between Header and Footer button to move to the footer area of the document. Using the same techniques you used to create a header in the tutorial, create a footer for section 2 that aligns your name at the left margin and the date on the right margin.

19. Attach the Contemporary Report template to the document.

20. Using the styles you think most appropriate, format section 1. Preview the title page to make sure it fits on one page, and make any necessary adjustments.

21. Apply the Heading 1 style to the headings "Expansion Plans," "Benefits to the Community," and "Request for Zoning Changes." (*Hint:* After applying the style once, use the F4 key to apply it subsequent times.)

22. Apply the Heading 2 style to the headings "Plans to Expand Our Current Packaging Plant" and "Plans to Build a Distribution Center."

23. Apply the Block Quotation style to the "Summary" heading and paragraph text.

24. Save the document; then preview and print it.

Create a table before the Summary summarizing the Zoning Request report by completing the following:

25. Use the Insert Table button on the Standard toolbar to insert a 6-by-3 table. (In other words, a table with six rows and three columns.)

26. Type the headings "Project," "Cost" and "Jobs Added" in row 1.

27. In row 2, type "Expand Packaging Plant," "$1,200,000," and "150" in the appropriate cells.

28. In row 3, type "Build Distribution Center," "$1,300,000," and "150" in the appropriate cells.

29. Skip two rows, and then in the last row type "Total".

30. Use the AutoSum button on the Tables and Borders toolbar to total the Cost and Jobs Added column. Format the Cost total without decimal points using the Formula command on the Table menu.

31. Use the same techniques you learned for inserting rows to delete the blank row 4. Begin by selecting the row, and then right-clicking to open the Table shortcut menu. Then click Delete Rows. Repeat these steps to delete the remaining blank row.

32. Drag the right border of column B to the left until the border reaches 3 inches on the ruler. Drag the right border of column C (the Jobs Added column) to the left until the border reaches 4.25 inches on the ruler. Continue adjusting columns as necessary until the columns appear correctly formatted.

33. Right-align the numbers in the table and center the headings.

34. Format the heading row by adding a light gray shading and by bolding the headings as well. This time use the Tables and Borders toolbar. Click the Tables and Borders button to display the toolbar. Click the Shading Color arrow, and then click the light gray color of your choice.

35. Increase the height of the heading row, and then center the headings vertically in the row.

36. Center the table on the page by selecting all the table rows, and clicking the center button on the Formatting toolbar.

37. Preview, print and close the document.

Word will automatically convert text separated by commas, paragraph marks or tabs into a table. To try this feature now, open the file Members from the TAssign folder for Tutorial 3 on your Student Disk, and save it as Task Force Members. Then complete the following:

38. Select the list of task force members (including the heading), click Table on the menu bar, and then click Convert Text to Table. In the Convert Text to Table dialog box, make sure the settings indicate that the table should have 2 columns and that the text is currently separated by commas. Then click the OK button. Word automatically converts the list of task force members into a table.

39. Format the table appropriately, using the techniques you learned in the tutorial.

40. Save the document, and then preview and print it.

Case Problems

1. Ocean Breeze Bookstore Annual Report As manager of Ocean Breeze Bookstore in San Diego, California, Reed L. Paige must submit an annual report to the Board of Directors.

1. If necessary, start Word, make sure your Student Disk is in the appropriate drive, and check your screen to make sure your settings match those in the tutorials.

2. Open the file OceanRep from the Cases folder for Tutorial 3 on your Student Disk, and save it as Ocean Breeze Report. Then complete the following:

3. Divide the document into two sections. End the first section after the phrase "Ocean Breeze Bookstore"; begin section 2 on a new page.

4. Move the insertion point to section 2. Create a header for the entire document that aligns "Ocean Breeze Annual Report" on the left margin and the date on the right margin. To make the header appear in both sections, select the Same as Previous button on the Header and Footer toolbar.

5. Attach the Elegant Report template to the document.

6. Apply the Part Label style to the title page text, and then vertically align the first section of the document using the Center alignment option in the Page Setup dialog box.

7. Select the heading and text of the summary and apply the Block Quotation style.

8. Apply the Heading 2 style to the headings "Introduction," "Mission Statement," "Company Philosophy," and "Organization." (*Hint:* Use the F4 key to apply the style the second and subsequent times.)

9. Apply the Heading 1 style to the headings "Children's Story Hour," "Summer Reading Contest," and "Home Delivery."

10. Apply the Heading 3 style to the headings "Board of Directors," "Store Management and Personnel," and "Autograph Signings."

11. Preview and save the document.

12. Scroll to the end of the document and insert one blank line. Then insert a 2-column by 8-row table listing first the members of the board of directors and then the managers. Use the headings "Name" and "Title." You'll find the names and titles listed in the report.

13. Adjust the table column widths as necessary.

14. Increase the height of the heading row, center the column headings horizontally and vertically, and then bold them.

15. Insert a row and add your name to the list of board of directors members.

16. Format the heading row with a light gray shading.

17. Save, preview, print, and close the document.

2. Ultimate Travel's "Europe on a Budget" Report As director of Ultimate Travel's "Europe on a Budget" tour, Bronwyn Bates is required to write a report summarizing this year's tour.

1. If necessary, start Word, make sure your Student Disk is in the appropriate drive, and check your screen to make sure your settings match those in the tutorials.

2. Open the file Europe from the Cases folder for Tutorial 3 on your Student Disk, and save it as Europe Tour Report.

3. Divide the document into two sections. End the first section with the phrase "Tour Director"; begin the second section on a new page.

4. Vertically align the first section using the Center alignment option in the Page Setup dialog box.

5. Create a header for section 2 that contains the text "Ultimate Travel," centered. (*Hint:* To center text in the header, use the second tab stop.)

6. On the Header and Footer toolbar, click the Switch Between Header and Footer button to move to the footer area of the document. Using the same techniques you used to create a header in the tutorial, create a footer for section 2 that aligns "Evaluation Report" on the left margin and the date on the right margin.

7. Attach the Professional Report template to the document.

8. Apply the Heading 1 style to all the headings.

9. In the table, adjust column widths as necessary.

10. Bold the text in column A (the left-hand column) and then center it horizontally.

11. Use the same techniques you learned for inserting rows to delete the blank row 2: select the row, right-click to open the Table shortcut menu, and then click Delete Rows.

12. Format column A (the left-hand column) with a light gray shading.

13. Save, preview, print, and close the document.

3. Advisory Letter on a Tuition Increase Your school wants to raise tuition beginning next term. As head of the Student Advisory Board, you must submit a letter to the school's president about the increase.

1. If necessary, start Word, make sure your Student Disk is in the appropriate drive, and check your screen to make sure your settings match those in the tutorials.

2. Write a one-page letter explaining the following issues: what the current tuition or fees are at your school, what the new current tuition and fees will be, and three reasons why the school should wait for another year to increase tuition. Include a return address, inside address, date, salutation, and closing.

3. Save your document as Tuition Letter in the Cases folder for Tutorial 3 on your Student Disk.

4. Correct spelling and punctuation as necessary.

5. Attach the Professional Letter template.

6. AutoFormat automatically formats selected text based on the options available in the attached template. Try using AutoFormat now by clicking Format on the menu bar, and then clicking AutoFormat. In the AutoFormat dialog box, click the AutoFormat and review each change option button, and then click the OK button. Do you like the look of the formatted letter? Why or why not? Accept the AutoFormat changes, or reject them and choose another format.

7. What are the font and paragraph attributes for the inside address and closing for the Professional Letter template? Apply new styles as necessary.

8. Print your letter.

9. Attach the Contemporary Letter template.

10. Use the Style list on the Formatting toolbar to apply new styles to each part of your letter.

11. Print your letter with the Contemporary Letter template styles.

12. Attach the Elegant Letter template.

13. What are the font and paragraph attributes for the date and body text for the Elegant Letter template?

14. Use either the Style list box or AutoFormat to apply new styles to each part of your letter.

15. Print your letter with the Elegant Letter template styles.

16. Save the current version of your letter using the filename Tuition Letter 2, and then close the document.

4. Monthly Menu Deciding what to cook each night can be difficult when it's dinnertime and you're hungry. To avoid making spaghetti every night next month, you'll plan next month's dinner menu now.

1. If necessary, start Word, make sure your Student Disk is in the appropriate drive, and check your screen to make sure your settings match those in the tutorials.

2. Open a new document and create a table (7 rows by 7 columns).

3. In row 2 of the table, type the days of the week in 12-point font of your choice.

4. Adjust the right column borders so that the name of each day of the week is on one line.

5. Bold the days of the week headings and center them horizontally in the cells. Add a light gray shading. Adjust column widths as necessary.

6. Type the number of each day of the month in a cell, and press the Enter key to place the number on its own line; then press the Tab key to move to the next cell. For example, if September 1 is a Tuesday, type "1" in cell C3, press the Enter key, and then press the Tab key. Repeat for the remaining days of the month.

7. Type the name of a main dish in the second line of each cell of the table for the first two weeks of the month.

8. Use a variation of drag and drop to copy each menu item from the first two weeks into the cells of the second two weeks. Highlight the first menu item (not including the date), and then press and hold down the Ctrl key and drag the menu item to the first day of the third week.

9. Fill in the remaining cells by copying menu items for the rest of the month.

10. Save the menu document as Monthly Menu in the Cases folder for Tutorial 3 on your Student Disk.

11. Preview and print the document. Then close the document.

Desktop Publishing a Newsletter

Creating a Newsletter for FastFad Manufacturing Company

OBJECTIVES

In this tutorial you will:

- Identify desktop publishing features

- Create a title with WordArt

- Create newspaper-style columns

- Insert clip art

- Wrap text around a graphic

- Incorporate drop caps

- Use typographic characters

- Add a page border and shaded background

FastFad Manufacturing Company

CASE

Gerrit Polansky works for FastFad Manufacturing Company, which designs and manufactures plastic figures (action figures, vehicles, and other toys) for promotional sales and giveaways in the fast-food and cereal industries. It is Gerrit's job to keep FastFad's sales staff informed about new products. He does this by producing and distributing a monthly newsletter that contains brief descriptions of these new items and ideas for marketing them. Recently, FastFad added MiniMovers, which are small plastic cars, trucks, and other vehicles, to its line of plastic toys. Gerrit needs to get the information about these products to the sales staff quickly—so the company can market the toys to FastFad's clients while the toys are still the fad. He has asked you to help him create the newsletter.

The newsletter needs to be eye-catching because the sales reps get a lot of printed product material and it's sometimes difficult for them to focus on any one product. Gerrit also wants you to create a newsletter that is neat, organized, and professional-looking. He wants it to contain headings so the sales reps can scan it quickly for the major points, as well as graphics that will give the newsletter a distinctive "look" that the reps will remember. He wants you to include a picture that will reinforce the newsletter content and help the reps remember the product. All of these tasks are easy in Word, especially with the Microsoft Clip Gallery, which lets you choose from a large collection of predesigned images that you can insert in your documents.

In this tutorial, you'll plan the layout of the newsletter, keeping in mind the audience (the sales representatives). Then you'll get acquainted with the desktop publishing features and elements you'll need to use to create the newsletter you want, and you'll learn how desktop publishing differs from other word processing tasks. You'll format the title using an eye-catching design and divide the document into newspaper-like columns to make it easier for the sales reps to read. You'll include a piece of predesigned art that adds interest and focus to the text. You'll then fine-tune the newsletter layout, give it a more professional appearance with typographic characters, and put a border around the page and a shaded background behind the text to give the newsletter a finished look.

SESSION

4.1

In this session, you will see how Gerrit planned his newsletter, and learn about desktop publishing features and elements. Then you will create the newsletter title using WordArt, modify the title's appearance, and then format the text of the newsletter into newspaper-style columns.

Planning the Document

The newsletter will provide a brief overview of the new FastFad products, followed by a short explanation of what the MiniMovers are and why children will like them. Like most newsletters, it will be written in an informal style that conveys information quickly. The newsletter title will be eye-catching and will help readers quickly identify the document. The newsletter text will be split into two columns to make it easier to read, and headings will help readers scan the information quickly. A picture will add interest and illustrate the newsletter content. Drop caps and other desktop publishing elements will help draw readers' attention to certain information, make the newsletter design attractive, and give it a professional appearance.

Features of Desktop Publishing

Desktop publishing is the production of commercial-quality printed material using a desktop computer system from which you can enter and edit text, create graphics, compose or lay out pages, and print documents. The following features are commonly associated with desktop publishing:

- **High-quality printing.** A laser printer or high-resolution inkjet printer produces high-quality final output.

- **Multiple fonts.** Two or three font types and sizes provide visual interest, guide the reader through the text, and convey the tone of the document.

- **Graphics.** Graphics, such as horizontal or vertical lines (called **rules**), boxes, electronic art, and digitized photographs help illustrate a concept or product, draw a reader's attention to the document, and make the text visually appealing.

- **Typographic characters.** Typographic characters such as typographic long dashes, called **em dashes** (—), in place of double hyphens (--) separate dependent clauses; typographic medium-width dashes, called **en dashes** (–), are used in place of hyphens (-) as minus signs and in ranges of numbers; and typographic bullets (•) signal items in a list to make the text professional-looking.

- **Columns and other formatting features.** Columns of text, **pull quotes** (small portions of text pulled out of the main text and enlarged), shaded areas and other special formatting features that you don't frequently see in letters and other documents distinguish desktop-published documents.

You'll incorporate many of these desktop publishing features into the FastFad newsletter for Gerrit.

Elements of a Desktop-Published Newsletter

Successful desktop publishing requires that you first know what elements professionals use to desktop publish a document. Figure 4-1 defines the desktop publishing elements that you have not yet used in the preceding tutorials. Gerrit wants you to incorporate these elements to produce the final copy of the newsletter shown in Figure 4-2. The newsletter includes some of the typical desktop publishing elements that you can add to a document using Word.

Figure 4-1
Desktop
publishing
elements

Element	Description
Columns	Two or more vertical blocks of text that fit on one page
WordArt	Text modified with special effects, such as rotated, curved, bent, shadowed, or shaded letters
Clip art	Prepared graphic images that are ready to be inserted into a document
Drop cap	Oversized first letter of word beginning a paragraph that extends vertically into two or more lines of the paragraph
Typographical symbols	Special characters that are not part of the standard keyboard, such as em dashes (—), copyright symbols (©), or curly quotation marks (")

Figure 4-2
FastFad
newsletter

title created in WordArt

different font types, sizes, and styles

typographic symbol

clip art graphic

drop cap

border

two columns

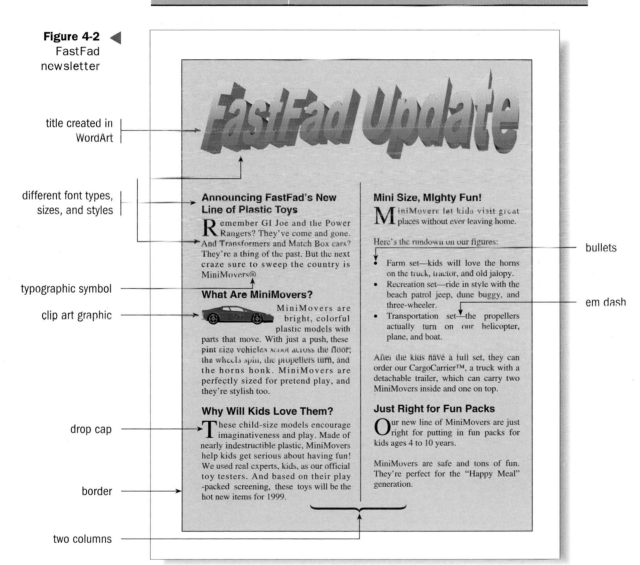

bullets

em dash

Your first step is to create the newsletter's title.

Using WordArt to Create the Newsletter Title

Gerrit wants the title of the newsletter, "FastFad Update," to be eye-catching and dramatic, as shown in Figure 4-2. The Microsoft Office WordArt feature, available from Word as well as from other Microsoft Office 97 programs, provides great flexibility in designing text with special effects that expresses the image or mood you want to convey in your printed documents. With WordArt you can apply color and shading, as well as alter the shape and size of the text. You can easily "wrap" the document text around WordArt shapes.

You begin creating a WordArt image by choosing a text design from the WordArt Gallery. Then you type in the text you want to enhance, and format it.

When you create a WordArt image, Word automatically switches to page layout view. When the document is in normal view, WordArt images are not visible. Page layout view is the most appropriate view to use when you are desktop publishing with Word, because it shows you exactly how the text and graphics fit on the page, and the vertical ruler that appears in page layout view helps you to position graphical elements more precisely.

REFERENCE window	CREATING SPECIAL TEXT EFFECTS USING WORDART
	■ Click the Drawing button on the Standard toolbar to display the Drawing toolbar. ■ Click the Insert WordArt button on the Drawing toolbar. ■ Click the style of text you want to insert, and then click the OK button. ■ Type the text you want in the Edit WordArt Text dialog box. ■ Click the Font and Size list arrows to select the font and font size you want. ■ If you want, click the Bold or Italic button, or both. ■ Click the OK button. ■ With the WordArt selected, drag any handle to reshape and resize it. To keep the text in the same proportions as the original, press and hold down the Shift key while you drag a handle.

To begin, you'll open the file that contains Gerrit's text, often called **copy**, and then you'll use WordArt to create the newsletter title. Gerrit wants the title formatted in the Arial font, since the headings in the rest of the document are in Arial.

To create the title of the newsletter using WordArt:

1. Start Word, and insert your Student Disk in the appropriate drive. Make sure your screen matches the figures in this tutorial, and make sure you display the nonprinting characters so you can see more accurately where to insert text and graphics.

2. Open the file **MiniInfo** from the **Tutorial.04** folder on your Student Disk, and then save it as **FastFad Newsletter**.

3. With the insertion point at the beginning of the document, press the **Enter** key to insert a new, blank line, and press the ↑ key to return the insertion point to the new, blank line. Then apply the **Normal** style using the Style list on the Formatting toolbar.

4. With the insertion point at the beginning of the document, click the **Drawing** button 🔲 on the Standard toolbar to display the Drawing toolbar, which appears at the bottom of the screen.

5. Click the **Insert WordArt** button 🔲 on the Drawing toolbar. The WordArt Gallery dialog box opens, displaying the 30 WordArt styles available.

6. Click the **WordArt style** in the bottom row, the fourth column from the left, as shown in Figure 4-3.

Figure 4-3 ◄
WordArt
Gallery styles

click this style ──────────

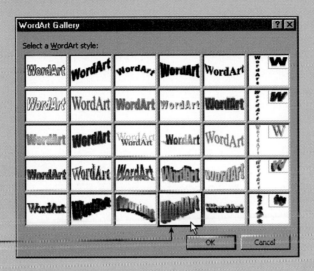

7. Click the **OK** button. The Edit WordArt Text dialog box opens, displaying "Your Text Here," the default text, which you will replace with Gerrit's newsletter title.

8. Type **FastFad Update**. Make sure you make "FastFad" one word, no space.

9. Click the **OK** button.

The WordArt image appears as the newsletter title at the top of the newsletter, the WordArt toolbar appears on the screen, and the document changes to page layout view. Don't worry that the image partially covers the newsletter text or if it's below the first paragraph. You'll fix that later.

The WordArt image you have created is considered a Word **drawing object**. This means that you can modify its appearance (color, shape, size, alignment, etc.) using the buttons on the Drawing toolbar or the WordArt toolbar. Although the object looks like text, Word does not treat it like text. The object will not appear in normal view, and Word will not spell check it, as it does regular text. Think of it as a piece of art rather than as text.

The WordArt object is selected, indicated by the eight small squares called **resize handles** surrounding it, and the small yellow diamond called an **adjustment handle**. The resize and adjustment handles let you change the size and shape of the selected object. Before you change the size of the object, you'll first change its font size and formatting. The default font for this WordArt style is Impact, but Gerrit wants you to change it to match the font of the newsletter headings.

To change the font and formatting of the WordArt object:

1. Double-click the **WordArt object**. The Edit WordArt Text dialog box opens.

2. Click the Font list arrow, scroll to and then click **Arial Black**. The text in the preview box changes to Arial Black. Black indicates a thicker version of the Arial font, not its color. Now change the font size and style.

   TROUBLE? If you do not have Arial Black on your font menu, choose Arial or another sans serif font.

3. Click the **Size** list arrow, scroll to and then click **40**, and then click the **Italic** button [*I*]. The text in the preview box enlarges to 40 points italic.

4. Click the **OK** button. The newsletter title changes to 40-point, italic Arial Black.

The default shape of the WordArt style you selected is an upward slanting shape called Cascade Up. Gerrit wants something a little more symmetrical. In WordArt, you can easily change the shape of any object to any of the 40 shapes that Word supplies.

To change the shape of the WordArt object:

1. Click the **WordArt Shape** button [Abc] on the WordArt toolbar. The palette of shapes appears, with the Cascade Up shape selected.

2. Click the **Deflate** shape (fourth row, second column from the left), as shown in Figure 4-4.

Figure 4-4 ◀
WordArt
shapes

Deflate shape ──────

WordArt toolbar ──────

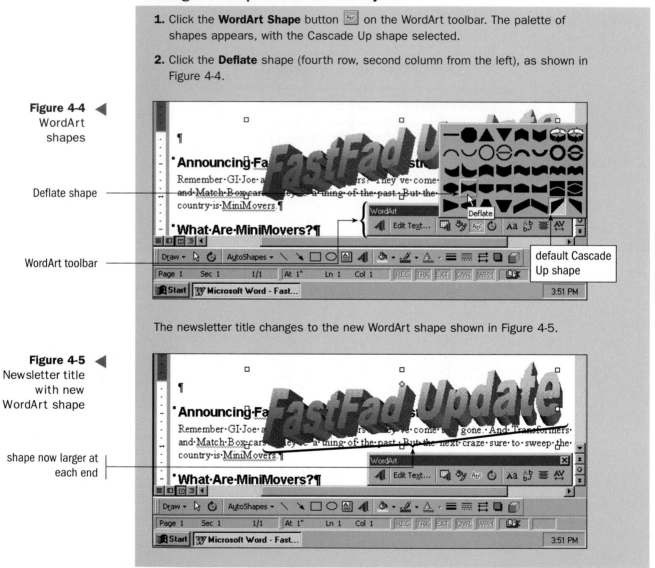

The newsletter title changes to the new WordArt shape shown in Figure 4-5.

Figure 4-5 ◀
Newsletter title
with new
WordArt shape

shape now larger at
each end

Editing a WordArt Object

Now that the newsletter title is the font and shape you want, you'll move the title above the text and insert space between the WordArt object and the newsletter text. You'll do this using the text wrapping feature in the Format WordArt dialog box. This dialog box gives you the option of changing many WordArt features at once. For now, however, you'll just use it to separate the object from the text.

To insert space between the WordArt object and the newsletter text:

1. With the WordArt object selected, click the **Format WordArt** button [image] on the WordArt toolbar to open the Format WordArt dialog box.

2. Click the **Wrapping** tab.

3. In the Wrapping style section, click the **Top & bottom** icon. See Figure 4-6.

Figure 4-6 ◄
Settings to separate WordArt object from text

Wrapping tab ————

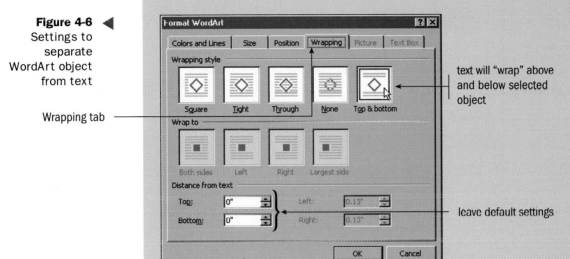

text will "wrap" above and below selected object

leave default settings

You could use the settings at the bottom of the dialog box to insert space between the object and the text, but the title object has enough space around it, so you don't need to change these settings now.

4. Click the **OK** button. The newsletter title is now above the text.

TROUBLE? If the title is not above the text, drag it there now.

Now you only need to position the title and widen it proportionally so it fits neatly within the newsletter margins. The position of the WordArt object in the text is indicated by a small anchor symbol in the left margin. You can widen any WordArt object by dragging its resize handle. To keep the object the same proportion as the original, you hold down the Shift key as you drag the resize handle, which will prevent "stretching" the object more in one direction than the other. Then you'll rotate it a little so it looks more balanced.

To position, enlarge, and rotate the WordArt object:

1. Drag the WordArt object to the left until the lower-left corner of the first "F" in the word "FastFad" is aligned with the left margin and then release the mouse button. Since you can only see the text outline (not the text itself) as you drag the object, you might need to repeat the procedure. Use the left edge of the text or the left margin in the ruler as a guide.

2. With the WordArt object still selected, position the pointer over its lower-right resize handle. The pointer changes to ↘.

3. Press and hold the **Shift** key and drag the resize handle to the right margin, using the horizontal ruler as a guide. See Figure 4-7. As you drag the handle, the pointer changes to +. If necessary, repeat the procedure to make the rightmost edge of the "e" in the word "Update" line up with the right margin. Now you'll lower the right side of the WordArt object.

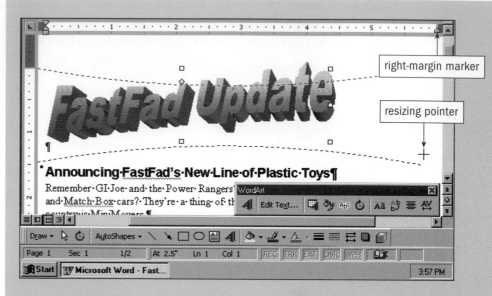

4. With the WordArt object still selected, click the **Free Rotate** button [icon] on the WordArt toolbar. Small green rotation handles surround the object.

5. Move the pointer over the document. The pointer changes to [icon].

6. Position the pointer over the green circle on the lower-right corner of the object, and then drag the rotation handle down about a half inch, or until the title text appears to be horizontal. See Figure 4-8.

lower the right side of
the image

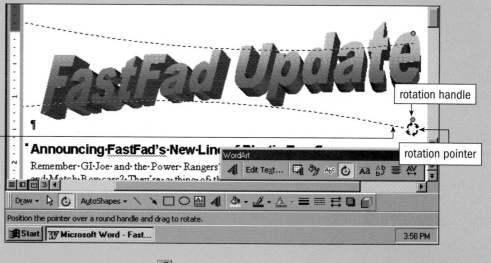

7. Click the **Drawing** button [icon] on the Standard toolbar to close the Drawing toolbar, and then click anywhere in the newsletter text to deselect the WordArt object. See Figure 4-9.

Figure 4-9
Newsletter
after enlarging
and rotating
the WordArt
object

title aligned between
left and right margins

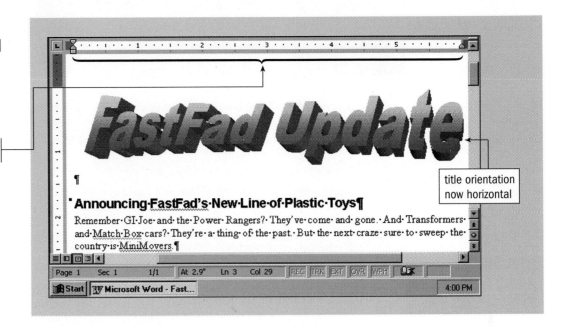

Announcing·FastFad's·New·Line·of·Plastic·Toys¶

Remember·GI·Joe· and· the·Power·Rangers?·They've·come· and· gone.·And·Transformers·
and·Match·Box·cars?·They're·a·thing·of·the·past.·But·the·next·craze·sure·to·sweep·the·
country·is·MiniMovers.¶

title orientation
now horizontal

You have inserted and formatted a WordArt object that will draw the attention of the
sales reps to the newsletter as they review this document among all the other product
literature they have to read.

Formatting Text into Newspaper-Style Columns

Because newsletters are meant for quick reading, they usually are laid out in newspaper-
style columns. In **newspaper-style columns**, a page is divided into two or more vertical
blocks or columns. Text flows down one column, continues at the top of the next column,
flows down that column, and so forth. Newspaper-style columns are easier to read
because the columns tend to be narrow and the type size a bit smaller than the text in a
letter. This enables the eye to see more text in one glance than when text is set in longer
line lengths and in a larger font size.

If you want some of your text to be in columns and other text to be in full line lengths,
you must insert section breaks into your document and apply the column format only to
those sections you want in columns. In this case, Gerrit wants only the text below the title
to be divided into two columns. You could select this text and use the Columns button on
the Standard toolbar to automatically insert a section break and divide the text into
columns, but Gerrit also wants you to add a vertical line between the columns. So you'll
use the Columns command on the Format menu, which lets you both divide the text into
columns with a line between them and insert a section break in the location you specify.
Without the section break, the line between the columns would extend up through the title.

REFERENCE window

FORMATTING TEXT INTO NEWSPAPER-STYLE COLUMNS

- Select the text you want to divide into columns, or don't select any text if you want the entire document divided into columns.
- Click the Columns button on the Standard toolbar, and highlight the number of columns you want to divide the text into. or
- Move the insertion point to the location where you want the columns to begin.
- Click Format on the menu bar, and then click Columns to open the Columns dialog box.
- Select the column style in the Presets section, and type the number of columns you want in the Number of columns text box.
- If necessary, click the Equal column width check box to deselect it, and then set the width of each column in the Width and spacing section.
- Click the Apply to list arrow, and select the This point forward or Whole document option.
- If you want a vertical rule between the columns, click the Line between check box and click the OK button.

To apply newspaper-style columns to the body of the newsletter:

1. Position the insertion point to the left of the word "Announcing" just below the title.

2. Click **Format** on the menu bar, and then click **Columns**. The Columns dialog box opens.

3. In the Presets section, click the **Two** icon.

4. If necessary, click the **Line between** check box to select it. The text in the Preview box changes to a two-column format with a vertical rule between the columns.

   You want these changes to affect only the text after the title, so you'll need to insert a section break and apply the column formatting to the text after the insertion point.

5. Click the **Apply to** list arrow, and then click **This point forward** to have Word automatically insert a section break at the insertion point. See Figure 4-10.

Figure 4-10 ◀
Completed columns dialog box

creates two columns of the same width

adds section break at insertion point location

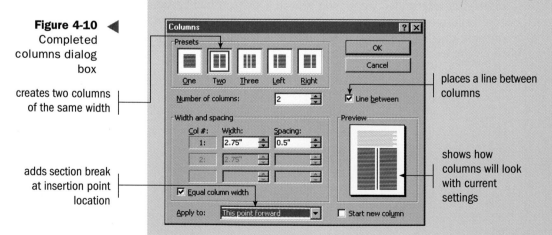

places a line between columns

shows how columns will look with current settings

6. Click the **OK** button to close the dialog box and return to the document window. A section break appears, and the insertion point is now positioned in section 2.

TROUBLE? You might need to move the WordArt object so it is above the section break. If necessary, drag the WordArt object above the section break. The section break moves down and the two-column text begins just after it. If necessary, drag the WordArt object again to adjust its position. When an object is selected, you can also use the arrow keys on the keyboard to adjust its position.

7. Click anywhere in the newsletter text to deselect the WordArt object.

Viewing the Whole Page

As you lay out a document for desktop publishing, you should periodically look at the whole page, so you can see how the layout looks. The best way to do this is in page layout view using Zoom Control.

To zoom out and view the whole page:

1. Click the **Zoom Control** list arrow 100% ▾ on the Standard toolbar, and then click **Whole Page**. Word displays the entire page of the newsletter so you can see how the two-column format looks on the page. See Figure 4-11.

Figure 4-11 ◀
Page layout
view showing
the two
columns

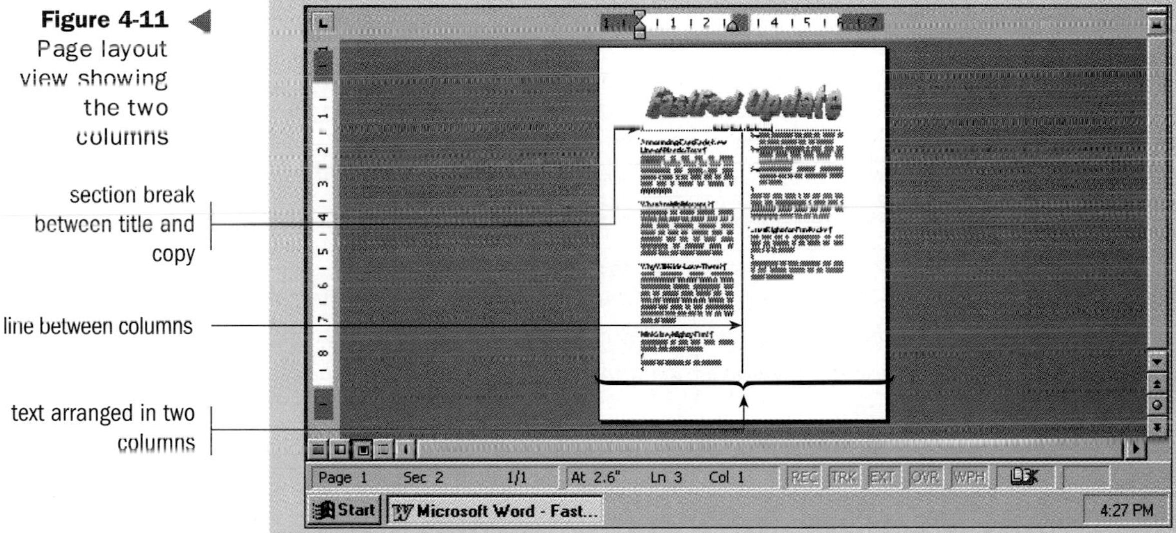

section break
between title and
copy

line between columns

text arranged in two
columns

TROUBLE? Your columns may break at a slightly different line than those shown in the figure. This is not a problem; just continue with the tutorial.

The newsletter title, now with a horizontal orientation, is centered on the page and the copy is in a two-column format. The text fills the left column but not the right column, and the top of the right column is higher than the left. You'll fix this later, after you add a graphic and format some of the text.

2. Click the **Zoom Control** list arrow again, and then click **100%**. Word returns to the full-size page layout view.

3. Save the document.

Quick Check

1 In your own words, explain three features commonly associated with desktop publishing.

2 In your own words, define the following terms:
   a. WordArt
   b. resize handle
   c. newspaper-style columns

3 List the steps for creating a WordArt object in a Word document.

4 How do you change the size of a WordArt object after you have inserted it into a Word document?

5 What is the purpose of the WordArt Shape button on the WordArt toolbar?

6 True or False: Normal view shows how text will fit into newspaper-style columns.

7 To format text into newspaper-like columns, you use the _____ command on the _____ menu.

8 If you want one part of your document to be in two columns and another part to be in full width, you must insert a _____ between the two sections.

9 True or False: Formatting a document into newspaper-like columns will automatically make the columns of equal length.

You have set up an eye-catching title for Gerrit's FastFad newsletter and formatted the text in newspaper style columns to make it easier to read. Now Gerrit wants you to insert a graphic that is appropriate to the newsletter content, possibly some type of car to represent the MiniMover product. As you will see, the Microsoft Clip Gallery, available from Word as well as other Microsoft Office programs, contains graphics that you can use with many different types of documents. After you add clip art, you'll add more graphic interest by formatting some of the text. Then you'll give the newsletter a finished look by making the columns equal in length, and give the page some depth by adding a shaded background.

SESSION 4.2

In this session you will insert, resize, and crop clip art, and change the way the text wraps around the clip art. Then you'll create drop caps, insert typographic symbols, balance columns, place a border around the newsletter, add a shaded background, and print the newsletter.

Inserting Clip Art

Graphics, which can include artwork, photographs, charts, tables, designs, or even designed text like WordArt, add variety to documents and are especially appropriate for newsletters. Word enables you to include many types of graphics in your documents. You can create a graphic in another Windows program and insert it into your document using the Picture command on the Insert menu. You can also insert a picture, as well as sounds and videos, from the Microsoft Clip Gallery, a collection of **clip art** images, or existing artwork that you can insert into documents, which is part of Microsoft Office 97. You will insert an existing piece of clip art into the newsletter. Gerrit wants you to use a graphic that reflects the newsletter content.

REFERENCE window

INSERTING CLIP ART

- Move the insertion point to the location in your document where you want the graphic image to appear.
- Click Insert on the menu bar, point to Picture, and then click Clip Art to open the Microsoft Clip Gallery 3.0 dialog box.
- Click the Clip Art tab.
- Click the category that best represents the type of art you need.
- Click the image you want to use.
- Click the Insert button.

To insert the clip art image of a car into the newsletter:

1. If you took a break after the last session, make sure Word is running, the FastFad Newsletter is open, the document is in page layout view, and the non-printing characters are displayed.

2. Position the insertion point to the left of the word "MiniMovers" in the second paragraph of the newsletter just below the heading.

3. Click **Insert** on the menu bar, point to **Picture**, and then click **Clip Art**. The Microsoft Clip Gallery 3.0 dialog box opens.

   TROUBLE? If you see a dialog box informing you that additional clips are available on the Microsoft Office CD-ROM, click the OK button.

4. If necessary, click the **Clip Art** tab to display the clip art options, and then click the **Transportation** category.

5. Click the **red sports car image** in the upper-left corner of the preview window. See Figure 4-12.

Figure 4-12 ◄
Clip Art tab of the Microsoft Clip Gallery 3.0 dialog box

selected sports car image will be inserted

only images in the transporation category are displayed

images shown here reflect selected category

click to insert selected image into document

click here to see enlarged preview

6. Click the **Insert** button to insert the image of the red sports car in the newsletter at the insertion point, and then save the newsletter.

   The sports car clip art extends across both columns. Like the WordArt object you worked with earlier, the clip art image is a graphic object with resize handles that you can use to change its size. Word inserts an anchor symbol in the left margin, indicating the object's position relative to the text. The Picture toolbar appears whenever the clip art object is selected. See Figure 4-13.

Figure 4-13 ◄
The newsletter
with the clip art
object inserted

resize handles

object inserted at
insertion point
between heading
and text

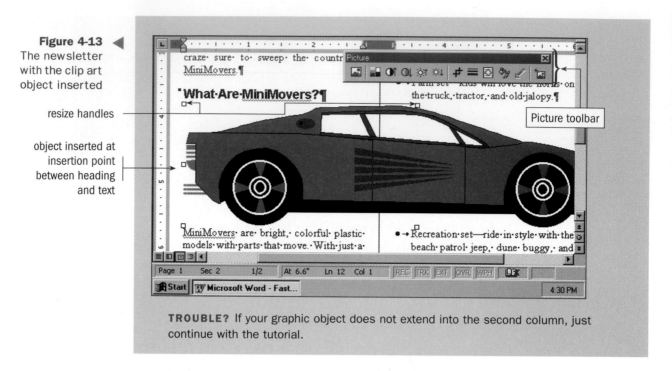

TROUBLE? If your graphic object does not extend into the second column, just continue with the tutorial.

Gerrit would like the image to be smaller so it doesn't distract attention from the text.

Resizing a Graphic

Often, you need to change the size of a graphic so that it fits into your document better. This is called **scaling** the image. You can resize a graphic by either dragging its resize handles or, for more precise control, by using the Format Picture dialog box.

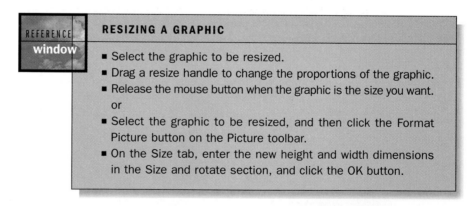

REFERENCE
window

RESIZING A GRAPHIC

- Select the graphic to be resized.
- Drag a resize handle to change the proportions of the graphic.
- Release the mouse button when the graphic is the size you want.
  or
- Select the graphic to be resized, and then click the Format Picture button on the Picture toolbar.
- On the Size tab, enter the new height and width dimensions in the Size and rotate section, and click the OK button.

For Gerrit's newsletter, the dragging technique will work fine.

To resize the clip art graphic:

1. Make sure the clip art graphic is selected, and scroll to the right so you can see the lower-right resize handle of the object.

2. Drag the lower-right resize handle up and to the left, so the front of the car extends only about halfway into the first column. You don't have to hold down the Shift key, as you do with WordArt, to resize it proportionally. See Figure 4-14.

Figure 4-14
Resizing the
sports car
graphic

anchor symbol
indicates position
relative to text

dotted line box
indicates new size

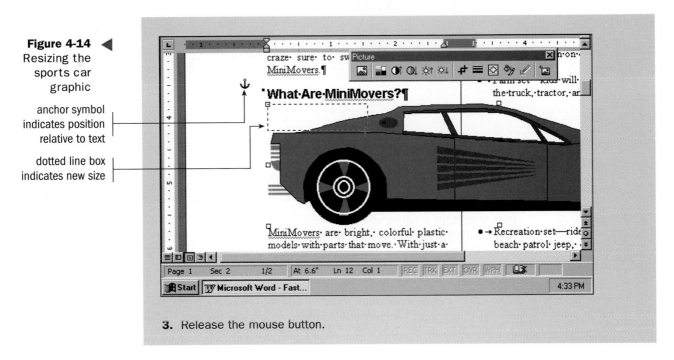

3. Release the mouse button.

Gerrit wonders if the sports car image would look better if you cut off the back end and showed only the front half.

Cropping a Graphic

You can **crop** the graphic, that is, cut off one or more of its edges, using either the Crop button on the Picture toolbar or the Format Picture dialog box. Once you crop a graphic, the part you crop off becomes hidden from view, but still remains a part of the graphic image, so you can always change your mind and restore a cropped graphic to it original form.

To crop the sports car graphic:

1. If necessary, click the clip art to select it. The resize handles appear.

2. Click the **Crop** button 🔲 on the Picture toolbar.

3. Position the pointer directly over the left-middle resize handle of the object. The pointer changes to ⌖ .

4. Press and hold down the mouse button and drag the handle to the right so that only the front door and hood are visible. and then release the mouse button. See Figure 4-15.

Figure 4-15
Cropping the
sports car
graphic

cropping tool

left half of image
hidden from view

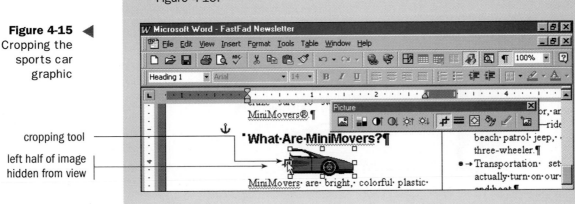

Gerrit decides he prefers you to display the whole sports car, so he asks you to return to the original image.

5. Click the **Undo** button 🔄 on the Standard toolbar. The cropping action is reversed, and the full image of the sports car reappears.

Now Gerrit wants you to make the text to wrap (or flow) to the right of the graphic, making the car look as if it's driving into the text.

Wrapping Text Around a Graphic

Text wrapping is often used in newsletters to add interest and to prevent excessive open areas, called **white space**, from appearing on the page. You can wrap text around objects many different ways in Word. You can have the text wrap above and below the graphic, through it, or wrap the text to follow the shape of the object, even if the graphic has an irregular shape. To wrap text you can use the Text Wrapping button on the Picture toolbar or the options available on the Wrapping tab of the Format Picture dialog box. You'll use the dialog box because you're going to change not only how the text will wrap, but also the amount of space above and below the graphic.

To wrap text around the car graphic:

1. If necessary, click the clip art to select it.

2. Click the **Format Picture** button 🖼️ on the Picture toolbar. The Format Picture dialog box opens.

3. Click the **Wrapping** tab.

4. In the Wrapping style section, click the **Tight** icon, the second icon from the left.

5. In the Wrap to section, click the **Right** icon.

6. In the Distance from text section, click the **Right** up arrow once to display **.2"**. Don't worry about the Left setting, since the text will wrap only around the right side. Now you'll add space above the graphic so it is separated from the section heading.

7. Click the **Position** tab, and click the **Vertical** arrows until the text box displays **.5"**.

8. Click the **OK** button. The text wraps around the car, following its shape.

9. Click anywhere in the text to deselect the graphic, and then save the newsletter. Your screen should look similar to Figure 4-16.

Figure 4-16 ◀
Text wrapped
around graphic

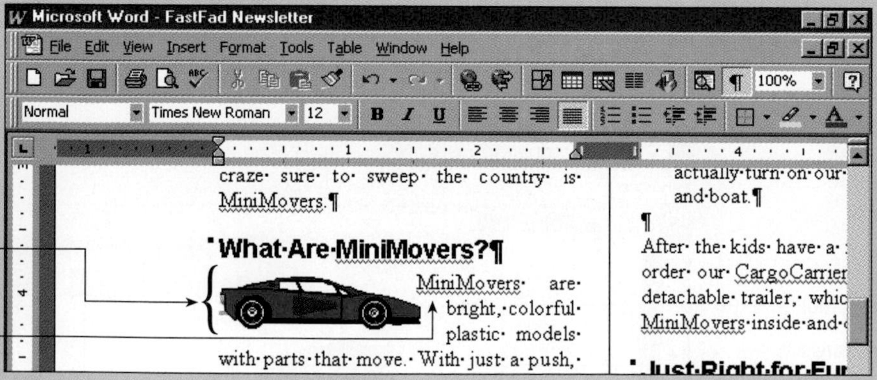

graphic separated
from text above
and below

text fits around
irregular shape

The image of the sports car draws the reader's attention to the beginning of the newsletter, but the rest of the text looks somewhat plain. Gerrit suggests adding a drop cap at the beginning of each section.

Inserting Drop Caps

A **drop cap** is a large, uppercase (capital) letter that highlights the beginning of the text of a newsletter, chapter, or some other document section. The drop cap usually extends from the top of the first line of the paragraph down two or three succeeding lines of the paragraph. The text of the paragraph wraps around the drop cap. Word allows you to create a drop cap for the first letter of the first word of a paragraph.

You will create a drop cap for the first paragraph following each heading in the newsletter (except for the first heading, where the clip art image is located). The drop cap will extend two lines into the paragraph.

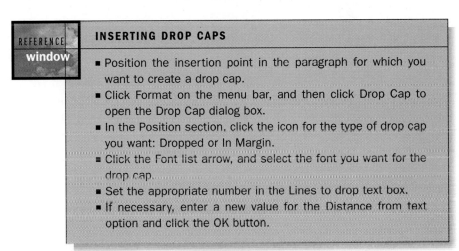

REFERENCE window

INSERTING DROP CAPS

- Position the insertion point in the paragraph for which you want to create a drop cap.
- Click Format on the menu bar, and then click Drop Cap to open the Drop Cap dialog box.
- In the Position section, click the icon for the type of drop cap you want: Dropped or In Margin.
- Click the Font list arrow, and select the font you want for the drop cap.
- Set the appropriate number in the Lines to drop text box.
- If necessary, enter a new value for the Distance from text option and click the OK button.

To insert drop caps in the newsletter:

1. Position the insertion point in the paragraph following the first heading, just to the left of the word "Remember."

2. Click **Format** on the menu bar, and then click **Drop Cap**. The Drop Cap dialog box opens.

3. In the Position section, click the **Dropped** icon.

4. Click the **Lines to drop** down arrow once to display **2**. You won't need to change the default distance from the text. See Figure 4-17.

Figure 4-17 ◄
Drop Cap
dialog box

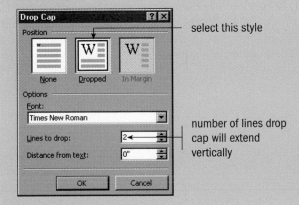

5. Click the **OK** button to close the dialog box. Word automatically formats the first character of the paragraph as a drop cap. See Figure 4-18.

Figure 4-18 ◀
Drop cap
begins the
paragraph

text wraps around
drop cap

drop cap selected

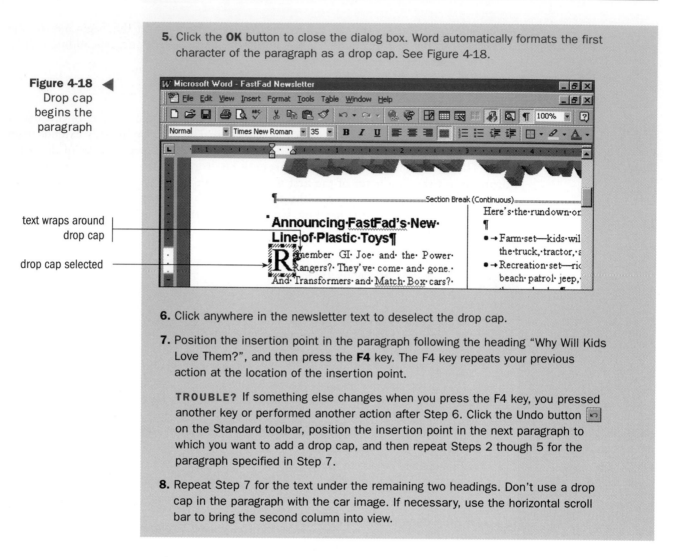

6. Click anywhere in the newsletter text to deselect the drop cap.

7. Position the insertion point in the paragraph following the heading "Why Will Kids Love Them?", and then press the **F4** key. The F4 key repeats your previous action at the location of the insertion point.

> **TROUBLE?** If something else changes when you press the F4 key, you pressed another key or performed another action after Step 6. Click the Undo button 🔄 on the Standard toolbar, position the insertion point in the next paragraph to which you want to add a drop cap, and then repeat Steps 2 though 5 for the paragraph specified in Step 7.

8. Repeat Step 7 for the text under the remaining two headings. Don't use a drop cap in the paragraph with the car image. If necessary, use the horizontal scroll bar to bring the second column into view.

The newsletter looks more lively with the drop caps. Next, you turn your attention to the issue of inserting a registered trademark symbol beside the trademark names.

Inserting Symbols and Special Characters

Gerrit used standard word-processing characters rather than **typographic characters** (special symbols and punctuation marks) when he typed the newsletter copy. For example, he typed straight quotation marks instead of curly quotation marks and he typed two dashes in place of an em dash. However, Word automatically converted some of the standard characters (such as the dashes and the quotation marks) into the more polished looking typographic characters. Figure 4-19 lists some the characters that Word converts to symbols automatically.

Word

Figure 4-19 ◀
Common
typographical
symbols

To insert this symbol or character	Type	Word converts it to
em dash	word- -word	word—word
quotation marks	"word"	"word"
copyright symbol	(c)	©
registered trademark symbol	(r)	®
trademark symbol	(tm)	™
ordinal numbers	1st, 2nd, 3rd, etc.	1st, 2nd, 3rd, etc.
fractions	1/2, 1/4	½, ¼
arrows	--> or <--	→ or ←

To insert typographic characters into a finished document after you've finished typing it, it's easiest to use the Symbol command on the Insert menu. In order to make the newsletter look professionally formatted, you'll insert a special character now—namely, a registered trademark symbol—at the appropriate places.

FastFad protects the names of its products by registering the names as trademarks. You'll indicate that in the newsletter by inserting the registered trademark symbol (®) at the first occurrence of the trademark names "MiniMovers" and a trademark symbol (™) for the first occurrence of "CargoCarrier."

REFERENCE window

INSERTING SYMBOLS AND SPECIAL CHARACTERS

- Move the insertion point to the location where you want to insert a particular symbol or special character.
- Click Insert on the menu bar, and then click Symbol to open the Symbol dialog box.
- Click the appropriate symbol from those shown in the symbol character set on the Symbols tab, or click the name from the list on the Special Characters tab.
- Click the Insert button.
- Click the Close button.

To insert the registered trademark symbol:

1. Position the insertion point at the end of the word "MiniMovers" in the first paragraph, just before the period.

2. Click **Insert** on the menu bar, and then click **Symbol** to open the Symbol dialog box.

3. If necessary, click the **Special Characters** tab. See Figure 4-20.

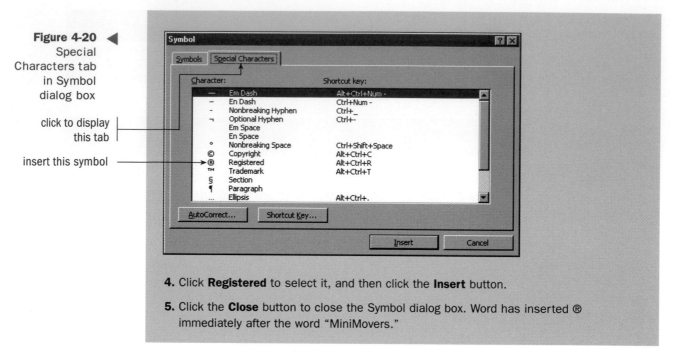

4. Click **Registered** to select it, and then click the **Insert** button.

5. Click the **Close** button to close the Symbol dialog box. Word has inserted ®
immediately after the word "MiniMovers."

If you have to insert symbols repeatedly, or if you want to insert them quickly as you type,
it's often easier to use the Word AutoCorrect feature to insert them. You'll use AutoCorrect
now to insert the trademark symbol (™) after the first occurrence of CargoCarrier. First,
you'll look in the AutoCorrect settings to make sure the correct entry is there.

To enter a symbol using AutoCorrect:

1. Click **Tools** on the menu bar, and then click **AutoCorrect**. In the Replace column
on the left side of the dialog box, you see (tm), which means that any occurrence
of (tm) in the document will automatically be corrected to the trademark symbol.

2. Click the **Cancel** button.

3. Position the insertion point just after the word "CargoCarrier" in the second column, in the paragraph above the heading "Just Right for Fun Packs."

4. Type **(tm)**. Word automatically converts your typed characters into the trademark
symbol.

The trademark symbols help make the newsletter look more professional. Next, you
decide to adjust the columns of text so they are approximately the same length.

Balancing the Columns

You could shift text from one column to another by adding blank paragraphs to move the
text into the next column or by deleting blank paragraphs to shorten the text so it will fit
into one column. Instead, Word can automatically **balance** the columns, or make them of
equal length, for you.

To balance the columns:

1. Position the insertion point at the end of the text in the right column, just after
period following the word "generation." Now change the zoom control to Whole
Page so you can see the full effect of the change.

2. Click the **Zoom Control** list arrow on the Standard toolbar, and then click
Whole Page.

3. Click **Insert** on the menu bar, and then click **Break**. The Break dialog box opens.

4. In the Section breaks section, click the **Continuous** option button.

5. Click the **OK** button. Word inserts a continuous section break at the end of the text, which, along with the first section break you inserted earlier, defines the area in which it should balance the columns.

As you can see, Word automatically balances the text between the two section breaks.

The balanced columns make the layout look much more professional. However, notice that the top margin is narrower than the bottom margin. The newsletter would look better if it had the same amount of space above and below the content. You can do this by enlarging the document's top margin.

To increase the top margin of the newsletter:

1. Click **File** on the menu bar, and then click **Page Setup**. The Page Setup dialog box opens.

2. If necessary, click the **Margins** tab to select it.

3. Click the **Top** up arrow four times to increase the setting to **1.4"**.

4. In the **Apply to** list box in the lower-right portion of the dialog box, select **Whole Document**.

5. Click the **OK** button. The entire content of the newsletter moves down, creating a similar amount of space above and below it. See Figure 4-21.

Figure 4-21 ◄
The newsletter
with balanced
columns and
vertical
placement

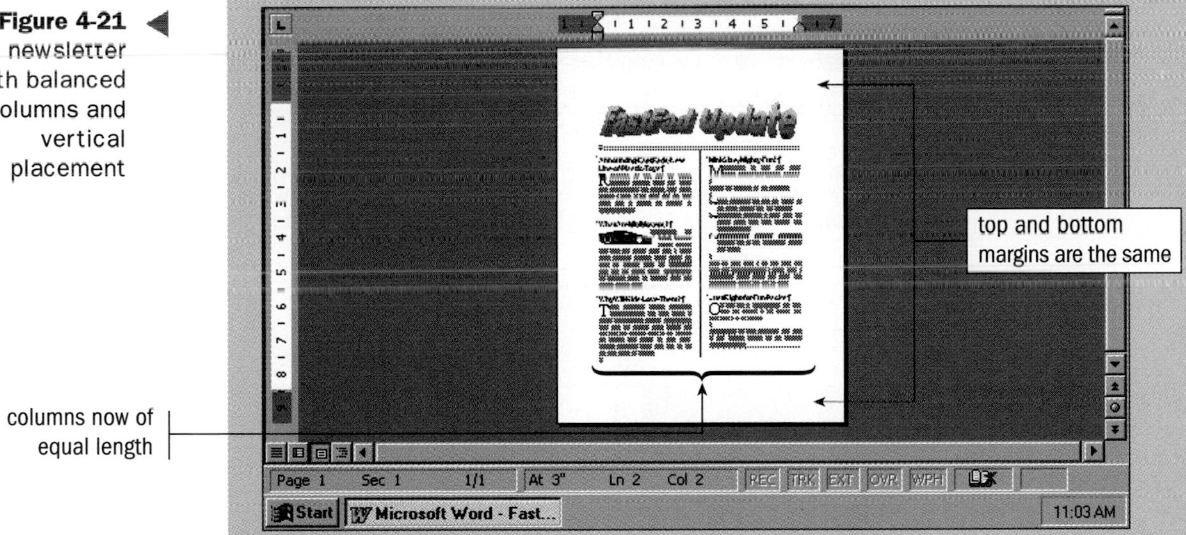

top and bottom
margins are the same

columns now of
equal length

TROUBLE? Depending on the size of the WordArt object, the placement of your newsletter content may differ from that shown in the figure. Adjust the size of the WordArt object and the top margin until the newsletter is centered vertically on the page.

Drawing a Border Around the Page

Gerrit wants to give the newsletter a little more pizzazz. He suggests adding a border around the newsletter, and adding a shaded background. In the steps that follow, you'll create a page border and background using the Word Drawing toolbar. You'll also learn how to move an object—in this case, a shaded box—behind text and other objects. In the Tutorial Assignments, you'll learn how to insert a page border using another, more automated method—the Page Border command.

To draw a border around the newsletter:

1. Make sure the document is in page layout view and that the zoom control setting is set to Whole Page, so you can see the entire newsletter.

2. Click the **Drawing** button 🔲 on the Standard toolbar. The Drawing toolbar appears at the bottom of the document window.

3. Click the **Rectangle** button 🔲 on the Drawing toolbar.

4. Position the pointer slightly higher than and to the left of the first "F" in the "FastFad" title near the upper-left corner of the newsletter. The pointer changes to + when positioned over the document.

5. Click and drag the pointer to the lower-right corner of the newsletter to surround the newsletter with a box. See Figure 4-22.

Figure 4-22 ◄
Drawing a border around the newsletter

drawing pointer

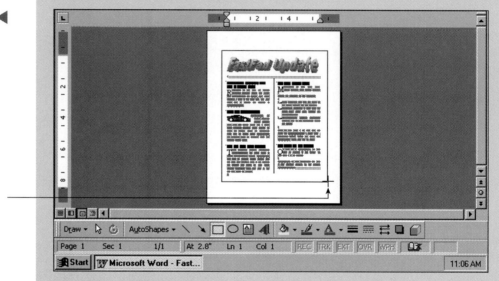

6. Release the mouse button.

   When you release the mouse button, a white rectangle covers the newsletter text. You'll fix this in a minute.

7. Click the **Line Style** button ▤ on the Drawing toolbar to display a list of line style options. See Figure 4-23.

Figure 4-23 ◄
Line styles on the Drawing toolbar

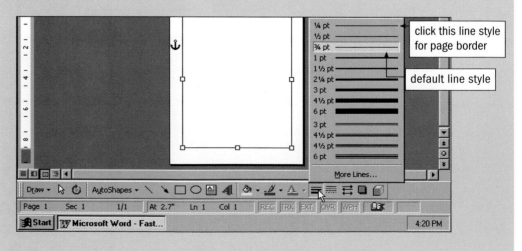

click this line style for page border

default line style

8. Click **1/4 pt** at the top of the list to select this line style option.

9. Click the list arrow next to the **Fill Color** button 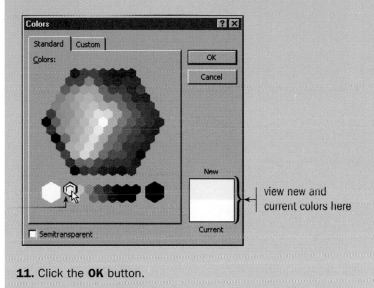 on the Drawing toolbar, and then click More Fill Colors to open the Colors dialog box. Here you can select or customize the color you want for the shaded background.

10. Click the **first gray color tile** in the second row from the bottom. A preview of the color you have selected appears in the top half of the preview square on the right side of the dialog box. See Figure 4-24.

Figure 4-24 ◀
Selecting a
fill color

select this tile

view new and
current colors here

11. Click the **OK** button.

The fill color covers the text, but you want it to be a background shading. You'll need to send the filled rectangle to the back or bring the text to the front in order to see the text over the fill, which you'll do in the next section.

Document Layers

When you add shading or lines around text, you are creating layers. Think of printing your document on two sheets of clear plastic. One sheet contains the text of your document, the other sheet contains borders and shading. When you place one sheet on top of the other, or layer them, the sheets' contents combine to create the complete document. If you place the sheet with shading and borders over the text, you cannot see the text through it. If you place the sheet with the text over the shading and borders, the shading and borders are visible around the text.

Right now the background shading is positioned as the top layer of the document. You need to send that layer to the back of the text layer so the shading is visible behind the text instead of obscuring it.

To move the shading to the back and print the final newsletter:

1. Click the **Draw** button on the Drawing toolbar.

2. Point to **Order**, and then click **Send to Back**. The shaded box moves to the layer behind the WordArt and ClipArt objects.

3. Click the **Draw** button again, point to **Order**, and then click **Send Behind Text**. The shaded box moves to the layer behind the text.

4. Click anywhere in the newsletter text to deselect the border. The text layer and the graphics appear on top of the shading layer. See Figure 4-25.

Figure 4-25 ◀
Completed
newsletter

filled rectangle is now
behind newsletter
copy and graphics

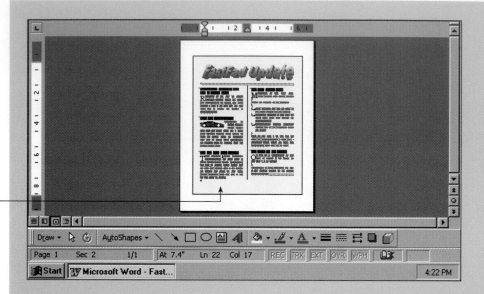

TROUBLE? If the sports car disappears from the newsletter, you selected Send Behind Text, instead of Send to Back in Step 2. To correct this, select the shaded rectangle, and then repeat Steps 1 and 2, making sure you select Send to Back from the Order menu.

5. Save the completed newsletter.

6. Click the **Print Preview** button on the Standard toolbar. Preview the newsletter.

7. Click the **Print** button on the Print Preview toolbar to print the newsletter. If you have a black-and-white printer, the orange and yellow letters of the title and the red car appear in shades of gray.

TROUBLE? If you see an error message when you try to print, your printer might not have enough memory to print the newsletter with the background shading. Return to page layout view. Click the border to select it, click the Fill Color list arrow on the Drawing toolbar, click No Fill as the color to remove the background shading, and then try to print again. If you still have problems, ask your instructor or technical support person for assistance.

8. If necessary, click the **Close** button on the Print Preview toolbar to return to page layout view.

9. Close the newsletter and exit Word.

Quick Check

1 Define the following in your own words:
 a. clip art
 b. typographic characters
 c. drop cap
 d. crop

2 Describe the procedure for inserting a clip art graphic in Word.

3 In your own words, explain the difference between resizing and cropping a graphic.

4 Describe the procedure for creating a drop cap.

5 How do you insert the registered trademark symbol in a document? What are two other symbols or special characters that you can add to a document with Word?

6 Besides the Symbol command on the Insert menu, what is another way of entering typographic symbols?

7 Describe the process for drawing a border around text and adding background shading.

8 Describe the procedure for balancing columns in Word.

You give the printed newsletter to Gerrit, along with a copy on disk. He thinks it looks great and thanks you for your help. He'll print it later on a color printer (in order to make the most of the colors in the WordArt title and the sports car clip art) and distribute the newsletter to FastFad's sales staff.

Tutorial Assignments

Gerrit's FastFad newsletter was a success; the sales representatives all seemed to have good product knowledge, and the sales for MiniMovers were brisk. The sales reps themselves have asked Gerrit for a product information sheet, similar to the newsletter, about another product, FastFad Sports Figures. The sales reps want to be able to print it and send it directly to their clients. You'll produce that newsletter now.

1. If necessary, start Word and make sure your Student Disk is in the appropriate disk drive. Check your screen to make sure your settings match those in the tutorial and that the nonprinting characters and Drawing toolbar are displayed.

2. Open the file FigSpecs from the TAssign folder for Tutorial 4 on your Student Disk, and then save it as Sports Figures.

3. Insert a new, blank line at the top of the document, format in Normal style, and then click the Insert WordArt button on the Drawing toolbar.

4. Choose the WordArt style in the lower-left corner of the WordArt Gallery dialog box.

5. Type "FastFad Figures" in the Enter WordArt Text dialog box, click OK, and then drag the WordArt above the first heading.

6. Use the WordArt Shape button on the WordArt toolbar to apply the Deflate shape (fourth row, second column from left), and change the font to 24 point Arial bold.

7. Use the Format WordArt dialog box Wrapping tab to apply the Top & bottom wrapping style.

8. Drag the lower-right and then the lower-left resize handles to enlarge the image to the entire width between the left and right margins.

9. Save the document.

10. Position the insertion point to the left of the first word in the first heading, and then format the text into two columns using the Columns dialog box. Insert a section break so that the columns appear from this point forward. Do not insert a line between columns.

11. View the whole newsletter in page layout view, using the Whole Page zoom control setting, and make any necessary adjustments.

12. Return to 100% zoom control in page layout view, and then position the insertion point immediately after the first paragraph (on the same line). Click Insert on the menu bar, point to Picture, and then click **Clip Art** to open the Microsoft Clip Gallery dialog box.

13. Insert the tennis player clip art image from the Sports & Leisure category.

14. Select and resize the sports image so it fits in the left half of the first column.

15. Crop the graphic to remove the tennis racket from the left side of the image, and then move the graphic left using the keyboard arrow keys.

16. Select the clip art object, click the Format Picture button on the Picture toolbar, and click the Wrapping tab. Set the Wrapping style to Tight, and wrap the text around the right side of the image for the Dropped position.

17. Format a drop cap for the first paragraph following the "Five Sets of Figures" heading, using the default settings for the Dropped position.

18. Insert the trademark symbol after the first occurrence of "FastFad Sports Figures," using either of the techniques you used in the tutorial.

 19. As you might have noticed, Word automatically justifies text in newspaper columns. To try changing the alignment now: Select both columns of text by clicking before the first word of text, pressing and holding down the Shift key, and then clicking at the end of the text. Use the Align Left button on the Formatting toolbar to change the columns' text alignment to left alignment.

20. Make the columns of equal length by balancing the columns. Position the insertion point at the end of the document, click Insert on the menu bar, and then click Break. In the Section breaks section, click the Continuous option button, and then click the OK button.

 21. A pull quote is a phrase or quotation taken from the text that summarizes a key point. To insert a pull quote now: Select the words "FastFad: We take play seriously" (at the end of the second column) and then click the Cut button on the Standard toolbar. Click the Text Box button on the Drawing toolbar, and then below the two columns, drag the pointer to draw a text box that spans the width of the page. With the insertion point located in the text box, click the Paste button on the Standard toolbar. Select the text in the text box, and then use the Font command on the Format menu to format the text in the box as 16 point Arial italic. Click the Center button on the Formatting toolbar to center the text in the box. Use the Fill Color list arrow on the Drawing toolbar to fill the selected text box with a light turquoise color.

 22. Sometimes you may want to use the Replace command to replace standard word processing characters with typographic characters. To replace every occurrence of -- (two dashes) with — (em dash): Position the insertion point at the beginning of the first paragraph of text. Click Edit on the menu bar, and then click Replace. In the Find what text box type "--" (two dashes), and then press the Tab key to move the insertion point to the Replace with text box. Click the More button to display more options, and then click the Special button at the bottom of the dialog box. Click Em Dash in the list to display Word's special code for em dashes in the Replace with text box. Click the Replace All button. When the operation is complete, click the OK button, and then click the Close button.

 23. Add a border to the page using the Page Border command. Click Format on the menu bar, and then click Borders and Shading. In the Borders and Shading toolbox, click the Page Border tab. You can use this tab to customize the border type, line style, color, and width. Select the following options—Setting: Box, Width: 1pt., Apply to: Whole document—and then click OK.

24. Look at the newsletter border in page layout view, using the Whole Page zoom control setting. Center the newsletter contents vertically by adjusting the top margin for the whole document in the Page Layout dialog box.

25. Preview, save, and print the document.

Case Problems

1. City of San Antonio, Texas Blas Rodriguez is the manager of information systems for the city of San Antonio. He and his staff, along with the city manager, have just decided to convert all city computers from the DOS/Windows 3.1 operating system to Windows 95 and to standardize applications software on Microsoft Office 97. Blas writes a monthly newsletter on computer operations and training, so this month he decides to devote the newsletter to the conversion to Windows 95 and to Microsoft Office 97.

1. If necessary, start Word, make sure your Student Disk is in the appropriate drive, and check your screen to make sure your settings match those in the tutorials.

2. Open the file CityComp from the Cases folder for Tutorial 4 on your Student Disk, and then save the file as Computer.

3. Cut the text of the newsletter title, "Focus on Computers." Click the Insert WordArt button on the Drawing toolbar, and then choose the WordArt style in the fourth row, first column. Paste the text (using the Ctrl + V shortcut keys) into the Edit WordArt Text dialog box.

4. In Edit WordArt Text dialog box, set the font to 32 point Arial bold, and apply the Triangle Up shape (top row, third button from the left).

5. Drag the WordArt to the top of the newsletter, and set the wrapping style to Top & bottom in the Format WordArt dialog box.

6. Experiment with changing the shape of the WordArt object by dragging the yellow adjustment handle.

7. Resize the WordArt object so that it spans the width of the page from left margin to right margin and so that its maximum height is about 1 inch. (*Hint:* Use the resize handles while watching the horizontal and vertical rulers in page layout view to adjust the object to the appropriate size.)

8. Center and italicize the subtitle of the newsletter, "Newsletter from the Information Management Office."

9. Insert a continuous section break before the subtitle.

10. To highlight the paragraph with the city name, center the text and then insert a border around all four sides. (*Hint:* Use the Borders button on the Formatting toolbar.)

11. Format the body of the newsletter into two newspaper-style columns, and set the format of the columns so that no vertical rule appears between the columns.

12. Position the insertion point at the beginning of the first paragraph under the heading "Training on MS Office 97," and insert the clip art image from the People at Work category that shows a person talking in front of a group.

13. Resize the picture so that it is 35 percent of its normal size. Instead of dragging the resize handles as you did in the tutorial, use the Size tab in the Format Picture dialog box to scale the image. Adjust the Height and Width settings to 35 percent in the Scale section, and then make sure the Lock aspect ratio check box is selected.

14. Drag the graphic horizontally to the center of the newsletter, and in the Wrapping tab of the Format Picture dialog box, set the wrapping style to Tight, and Wrap to option to Both sides. Make the Left and Right Distance from text .2.

15. Replace any double hyphens with typographic em dashes.

16. Make sure the newsletter fits on one page; if necessary decrease the height of the WordArt title until the newsletter fits on one page.

17. Draw a rectangular border around the entire page of the newsletter. Fill it with a color of your choice, and then use the Draw button on the Drawing toolbar to layer it at the back.

18. If necessary, balance the columns and adjust the newsletter's position on the page.

19. Save and print the newsletter, and then close the file.

2. Federal Van Lines Corporation Martin Lott is the executive secretary to Whitney Kremer, director of personnel for Federal Van Lines (FVL) Corporation, a national moving company with headquarters in Minneapolis, Minnesota. Whitney assigned Martin the task of preparing the monthly newsletter People on the Move, which provides news about FVL employees. Although Martin and others before him have been preparing the newsletter for several years, Martin decides it's time to change the layout and wants to use Word's desktop publishing capabilities to design the newsletter. You will use text assembled by other FVL employees for the body of the newsletter.

1. If necessary, start Word, make sure your Student Disk is in the appropriate drive, and check your screen to make sure your settings match those in the tutorials.

2. Open the file FVL_News from the Cases folder for Tutorial 4 on your Student Disk, and then save it as FVL Newsletter.

3. Change the top and bottom margins to 0.75 inches, and the right and left margin to 1.0 inch. Then insert a blank line at the beginning of the newsletter and apply the normal style to it.

4. Create a WordArt title for the newsletter "People on the Move"; set the font to 24 point Arial bold. Apply the WordArt style in the third row, fourth column from the left, and set the shape of the text to Wave 2 (third row, sixth column from the left).

5. Drag the WordArt title to the top of the newsletter, and set the wrapping style to Top & bottom.

6. Resize the WordArt proportionally so that the title spans the width of the page from left margin to right margin and so that the height of the title is about 1 inch. (*Hint:* Use the resize handles while watching the horizontal and vertical rulers in page layout view to adjust the object to the appropriate size.)

7. Format the body of the newsletter into three newspaper-style columns of equal width and place a vertical rule between the columns. (Remember to use three columns, and not two as you did in the tutorial.) Make sure the rules do not extend through the title object.

8. Position the insertion point at the beginning of the paragraph below the heading "FLV Chess Team Takes Third," and insert the image called "Knight" from the Cases folder for Tutorial 4 on your Student Disk. (*Hint:* Use the same method as you would to insert a clip art image, except instead of selecting Clip Art from the Insert Picture menu, select From File. In the Insert Picture dialog box, go to the location of the file on your Student Disk, select the filename, and then click the Insert button.)

9. Scale the height and the width of the picture to 60 percent of its normal size. (*Hint:* To scale the size, use the Format Picture command, and then set the Scale values on the Size tab, making sure the Lock aspect ratio check box is selected.)

10. Crop 0.3, 0.4, 0.2, and 0.4 inches from the left, right, top, and bottom of the picture, respectively. Use the Picture tab in the Format Picture dialog box, and insert the values in the Crop from text boxes.

11. Drag the clip art to the right side of the center column about 2 inches below the heading. (*Hint:* Select the clip art, and then drag it from the center.)

12. Wrap the text around the clip art.

13. Format drop caps in the first paragraph after each heading. Use the default settings for number of lines, but change the font of the drop cap to Arial.

14. If necessary, decrease the height of the WordArt title until the entire newsletter fits onto one page and so each column starts with a heading.

15. Add a rectangular border around the entire page of the newsletter using the Page Border command. See the Tutorial Assignments, step 23, for instructions.

16. Save the newsletter, preview, and then print the newsletter. Close the file.

3. Riverside Wellness Clinic The Riverside Wellness Clinic, located in Vicksburg, Mississippi, is a private company that contracts with small and large businesses to promote health and fitness among their employees. MaryAnne Logan, an exercise physiologist, is director of health and fitness at the clinic. As part of her job, she writes and desktop publishes a newsletter for the employees of the companies with which the clinic contracts. She's ready to prepare the newsletter for the October 1998 issue.

1. If necessary, start Word, make sure your Student Disk is in the appropriate drive, and check your screen to make sure your settings match those in the tutorials.

2. Open the file Wellness from the Cases folder for Tutorial 4 on your Student Disk, and then save it as Wellness Newsletter.

3. Change the top and bottom margins to 0.5 inches and the left and right margins to 0.75 inches.

4. At the beginning of the newsletter, create a WordArt title "To Your Health." Choose any WordArt style that you feel would be appropriate to the newsletter content, and set the font to Arial bold, 24 point.

5. Set the shape of the text to any option that looks appropriate to the subject matter.

6. Move the title to the top of the document.

7. Add a shadow to the WordArt title (or adjust the existing one) by clicking the Shadow button on the Drawing toolbar. Select a Shadow option, and then use the Shadow Settings option on the Shadows menu to select a good color for the shadow. Close the Shadow settings menu. For the purpose of this exercise, choose a shadow style that is behind the text, not in front of it.

8. Rotate the WordArt 90 degrees. (*Hint:* In the Format WordArt dialog box, click the Size tab and set the Rotation option to 90 degrees.)

9. Resize the WordArt graphic box so that the WordArt object spans the height of the page from the top margin to the bottom margin, and so that the width of the object is about 1 inch. (*Hint:* Use the resize handles while watching the horizontal and vertical rulers in page layout view to adjust the object to the appropriate size.)

10. Drag the WordArt object to the left edge of the page.

11. Set the Wrapping style to Square, set the Wrap to option to Right, and then change the Right setting under Distance from text to .2".

12. At the top of the page, to the right of the title, italicize the subtitle and the line that contains the issue volume and number of the newsletter.

13. Format the body of the newsletter into two newspaper-style columns with a vertical rule between the columns. (*Hint:* The columns' widths will be uneven because the WordArt title takes up part of the first column space.)

14. To the right of each of the words "NordicTrack" and "HealthRider," insert a registered trademark symbol (®), and then change the font size of the symbol to 8 points. (*Hint:* Highlight the symbol and change the font size.)

15. Balance the columns and if necessary adjust the top margin to center the newsletter vertically on the page.

16. Add a rectangular border around the page using the Page Border command. To do this, follow the instructions in the Tutorial Assignments, step 23.

17. Save the newsletter, preview, and then print it. Close the document.

4. Holiday Greetings Newsletter As a way of keeping in touch with family and friends, a friend suggests that you send out a New Year's greeting newsletter. In the one-page newsletter, you'll include articles about you and your family or friends, recent activities, favorite hobbies, movies, books, and future plans. You'll desktop publish the copy into a professional-looking newsletter.

1. If necessary, start Word, make sure your Student Disk is in the appropriate drive, and check your screen to make sure your settings match those in the tutorials.

2. Write two articles to include in the newsletter; save each article in a separate file.

3. Plan the general layout of your newsletter.

4. Create a title ("New Year's News") for your newsletter with WordArt.

5. Save the document as "New Years News."

6. Insert the current date and your name as editor below the title.

7. Insert the articles you wrote into your newsletter. Open the first article file, select all of the text, copy it, click in the newsletter file at the location where you want it to appear, then paste it. Repeat the procedure for the second article.

8. Format your newsletter with multiple columns.

9. Insert a clip art picture into your newsletter, and wrap text around it.

10. Format at least two drop caps in the newsletter.

11. Create a colored background for the newsletter. Center the contents vertically by adjusting the top margin.

12. Save and print the newsletter.

13. Close the document.

Answers to Quick Check Questions

SESSION 1.1

1   Determine what you want to write about; organize ideas logically; determine how you'll say what you want to say; create your document with Word; edit your document; format your document; print your document.

2   Click Start, point to Programs, click Microsoft Word on the Programs menu or point to Microsoft Office on the Programs menu and click Microsoft Word.

3   a. a ribbon of icons providing menu shortcuts;
    b. bar displaying grid marks every 1/4 inch;
    c. blinking vertical bar indicating where typed characters will appear;
    d. set of characters of a certain shape;
    e. set of standard format settings.

4   Click Format, click Font, select the desired font size, click Default, click Yes.

5   Click View, point to Toolbars, click Standard.

6   Click the Show/Hide ¶ button on the Standard toolbar.

SESSION 1.2

1   You should save a document several times so you don't lose your work in the event of a power failure or other computer problem.

2   Click the Save button on the Standard toolbar. Specify the correct folder and directory in the Save in list box, type the file name in the File name text box, click Save.

3   To display a portion of the document that has scrolled from sight, click the up or down scroll arrows on the vertical scroll bar.

4   Print Preview allows you to see what the printed document will look like. You should use it before printing a document that you have made changes to or when printing a document for the first time.

5   a. shifting or moving the text in the document window to see the entire document one screen at a time;
    b. automatic breaking of a line of text at the right margin;
    c. feature that automatically corrects common misspellings and typing errors;
    d. Help feature that answers questions about current tasks; sometimes appears automatically.

6   Click the Word window Close button.

SESSION 2.1

1   Click the Open button on the Standard toolbar, or click File, click Open, and double-click the file. Click File, click Save As, select the location, type the new filename, click OK.

2   a. Ctrl + End
    b. Ctrl + Home
    c. Ctrl + PageDown

3   Select the text to delete, press Delete.

4   a. The process of first selecting the text to be modified, and then performing operations such as moving, formatting, or deleting on it.
    b. The blank space in the left margin area of the document window, which allows you to easily select entire lines or large blocks of text.
    c. The process of moving text by first selecting the text, then pressing and holding the mouse button while moving the text to its new location in the document, and finally releasing the mouse button.

5   Position the pointer at the beginning of the phrase, press and hold down the mouse button, drag the mouse pointer to the end of the phrase, and then release the mouse button.

    Click in the selection bar next to the line of text you want to select.

6   The Undo command allows you to reverse the last action or set of actions you performed.

    The Redo command allows you to restore a change you reversed using Undo.

7   False.

8   When you use cut and paste, the text is removed from its original location and inserted at a new location in the document.

    When you use copy and paste, the text remains in its original location, and a copy of it is also inserted in a new location in the document.

9   The text will be inserted at the location of the dashed insertion point.

10 Click the Select Browse Object button, click the Find button, click the Replace tab, type the search text in the Find what text box, type the replacement text in the Replace with text box, click Find Next or click Replace All.

SESSION 2.2

1   Align left: each line flush left, ragged right; align right: each line flush right, ragged left; center: each line centered, both ends ragged; justify: each line flush left and flush right; select the text to be aligned or justified, click the appropriate button on the Formatting toolbar.

2   The Format Painter allows you to easily apply the formatting from one block of text to other text.

    Select the text whose format you want to copy, double-click the Format Painter button on the Standard toolbar, click in each paragraph you want to format. When you are done, click the Format Painter button to turn it off.

3   Make sure the insertion point is located in the paragraph you want to indent, and then click the Increase Indent button on the Formatting toolbar once for each half-inch you want to indent.

4   False.

5   Select all the items you wish to bullet, and then click the Bullets button on the Formatting toolbar.

6   Select the text you wish to make bold, and then click the Bold button on the Formatting toolbar.

7 Select the text whose font you wish to change, click the Font list arrow on the Formatting toolbar, and then click the name of the new font on the list.

8 Click the Select Browse Object button, click the Find button, click the Replace tab, type "strategy" in the Find what text box, type "plan" in the Replace with text box, click Replace All.

9 With no text selected, click File, click Page Setup, click the Margins tab, type the new values in the text boxes or click the spin arrows to change the settings. Make sure the Apply to text box displays Whole document, and then click OK.

SESSION 3.1

1 a. a set of formats that can include font, size, and attributes such as bold and italic;
b. a set of predefined styles designed for a specific type of document;
c. a list, accessible from the Formatting toolbar, that allows you to apply a style to selected text;
d. a unit or part of a document that can have its own page orientation, margins, headers, footers, and vertical alignment;
e. the position of the text between the top and bottom margins;
f. text that is printed at the top of every page

2 A section break allows you to format different parts of the document in different ways. In the tutorial, the section break you inserted allowed you to create a header that was printed only on pages 2 and 3, and it allowed you to vertically center the text on the first page only.

3 Insert a section break, move the insertion point within the section you want to align, click File, click Page Setup, click the Layout tab, select the center in the Vertical Alignment list box, make sure This section is selected in the Apply to list box, click OK.

4 A header appears at the top of a page, while a footer appears at the bottom of a page.

5 Click the Insert Page Number button on the Header and Footer toolbar.

6 First, attach the template to the document. Then apply the template's styles to the various parts of the document.

7 Click Format, click Style Gallery, click the template you want to preview, verify that you have selected the template you want, click OK.

8 You selected text, clicked the Style list arrow on the Formatting toolbar, clicked the name of the style to apply to the text.

SESSION 3.2

1 Click the place in the document where you want to insert the table. Click the Insert Table button on the Header and Footer toolbar, click and drag to select the numbers of rows and columns you want in your table, release the mouse button.

2 Position the pointer over the border between two columns, click and drag the pointer until the column is the width you want, release the mouse button.

3 d.

4 a. information arranged in horizontal rows and vertical columns; b. the area where a row and column intersect; c. a gray or colored background

5 Click cell A2 or press the Tab key; click cell B6 or press the ↑ key.

6 Click the cell below the column, click the Tables and Borders button on the Standard toolbar, and then click the AutoSum button on the Tables and Borders toolbar.

7 Click in the selection bar to select the row above which you want to insert a row, right-click the selected row, click Insert Rows.

SESSION 4.1

1 (list 3) The printing is high-quality; the document uses multiple fonts; the document incorporates graphics; the document uses typographic characters; the document makes use of columns and other special formatting features.

2 a. a Microsoft Office feature that allows you to design text with special effects;
   b. a square handle you can use to change the size of a graphic;
   c. an arrangement of text using narrow columns that read top to bottom and consecutively from left to right

3 Position the insertion point at the location where you want to create WordArt, click the Drawing button on the Standard toolbar, click the Insert WordArt button on the Drawing toolbar, click the style of text you want to insert, click OK, type the text you want and make formatting selections, click OK.

4 To resize a WordArt object, select the object, drag the resize handles; to resize proportionally, press and hold the Shift key while dragging a handle.

5 The WordArt Shape button allows you to choose the basic shape of a WordArt object.

6 True. Normal view shows each column in its own section; only page layout view, however, shows how the columns appear in the final document.

7 To format text into newspaper-like columns, you use the <u>Columns</u> command on the <u>Format</u> menu.

8 If you want one part of your document to be in two columns, and another part to be in full width, you must insert a <u>section break</u> between the two sections.

9 False. Column formatting will automatically justify the text on each line, but not the lengths of the columns.

SESSION 4.2

1 a. existing artwork that you can insert into your document;
   b. special symbols and punctuation marks that distinguish desktop-published documents;
   c. a large, uppercase letter that highlights the beginning of the text of a newsletter, chapter, or some other document section;
   d. to cut off one or more of the edges of a graphic

2 Position the insertion point at the location where you want to insert the image, click Insert, point to Picture, click Clip Art, click the Clip Art tab, click the category you want to use, click the image you want to insert, click Insert.

3 Resizing leaves the graphic intact but changes its dimensions. Cropping actually removes part of the graphic from view.

4 Click in the paragraph that you want to begin with a drop cap, click Format, click Drop Cap, click the icon for the type of drop cap to insert, select the font, set the appropriate number in the Lines to drop text box, click OK.

5 Click where you want to insert the symbol in the document, click Insert, click Symbol, select the symbol to insert, click Insert.

   ™, ©

6 Make sure that the AutoCorrect feature is set up to replace typing with special symbols; then type text that Word will convert to the symbol you want to insert.

7 Click the Drawing button on the Standard toolbar, click the Rectangle button on the Drawing toolbar, drag to create the rectangle you want to insert, click the Line Style button and select the appropriate style, click the Fill Color list arrow and select the fill color you want to use, click OK.

8 Position the insertion point at the end of the last column you want to balance, click the Zoom Control list arrow on the Standard toolbar, click Whole Page, click Insert, click Break, click the Continuous option button in the Section breaks section, click OK.

NEW
PERSPECTIVES
SERIES

Microsoft®
Excel 97

LEVEL I

TUTORIALS

Read This **Before You Begin**

STUDENT DISK

To complete Excel 97 Tutorials 1-4, you need two Student Disks. Your instructor will either provide you with Student Disks or ask you to make your own.

If you are supposed to make your own Student Disks, you will need **two** blank, formatted high-density disks. You will need to copy a set of folders from a file server or standalone computer onto your disks. Your instructor will tell you which computer, drive letter, and folders contain the files you need. The following table shows you which folders go on your disks:

Student Disk	Write this on the disk label	Put these folders on the disk
1	Student Disk 1: Excel 97 Tutorials 1-3	Tutorial.01, Tutorial.02, Tutorial.03
2	Student Disk 2: Excel 97 Tutorial 4	Tutorial.04

See the inside front or inside back cover of this book for more information on Student Disk files, or ask your instructor or technical support person for assistance.

COURSE LAB

Tutorial 1 features an interactive Course Lab to help you understand spreadsheet concepts. There are Lab Assignments at the end of the tutorial that relate to this Lab. To start the Lab, click the Start button on the Windows 95 Taskbar, point to Programs, point to Course Labs, point to New Perspectives Applications, and click Spreadsheets.

USING YOUR OWN COMPUTER

If you are going to work through this book using your own computer, you need:

■ **Computer System** Microsoft Excel 97 and Windows 95 or Windows NT Workstation 4.0 must be installed on your computer. This book assumes a typical installation of Microsoft Excel 97.

■ **Student Disks** Ask your instructor or technical support person for details on how to get the Student Disks. You will not be able to complete the tutorials or exercises in this book using your own computer until you have Student Disks. The Student Files may also be obtained electronically over the Internet. See the inside front or inside back cover of this book for more details.

■ **Course Lab** See your instructor or technical support person to obtain the Course Lab software for use on your own computer.

To complete Excel 97 Tutorials 1-4, your students must use a set of student files on two Student Disks. These files are included in the Instructor's Resource Kit, and they may also be obtained electronically over the Internet. See the inside front or inside back cover of this book for more details. Follow the instructions in the Readme file to copy the files to your server or standalone computer. You can view the Readme file using WordPad. Once the files are copied, you can make Student Disks for the students yourself, or you can tell students where to find the files so they can make their own Student Disks.

COURSE LAB SOFTWARE

The Course Lab software is distributed on a CD-ROM included in the Instructor's Resource Kit. To install the Course Lab software, follow the setup instructions in the Readme file on the CD-ROM. Refer also to the Readme file for essential technical notes related to running the Lab in a multi-user environment. Once you have installed the Course Lab software, your students can start the Lab from the Windows 95 desktop by following the instructions in the Course Lab section above.

COURSE TECHNOLOGY STUDENT FILES AND COURSE LAB SOFTWARE

You are granted a license to copy the Student Files and Lab software to any computer or computer network used by students who have purchased this book.

TUTORIAL 1

Using Worksheets to Make Business Decisions

Evaluating Sites for an Inwood Design Group Golf Course

OBJECTIVES

In this tutorial you will:

- Start and exit Excel

- Discover how Excel is used in business

- Identify the major components of the Excel window

- Navigate an Excel workbook and worksheet

- Open, save, print, and close a worksheet

- Enter text, numbers, formulas, and functions

- Correct mistakes

- Perform what if analysis

- Clear contents of cells

- Use the Excel Help system

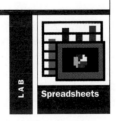

LAB
Spreadsheets

CASE

Inwood Design Group

In Japan, golf is big business. Spurred by the Japanese passion for the sport, golf enjoys unprecedented popularity. But because Japan is a small, mountainous country, the 12 million golfers have fewer than 2,000 courses from which to choose. Fees for 18 holes on a public course average between $200 and $300; golf club memberships are bought and sold like stock shares. The market potential is phenomenal, but building a golf course in Japan is expensive because of inflated property values, difficult terrain, and strict environmental regulations.

Inwood Design Group plans to build a world-class golf course, and one of the four sites under consideration is Chiba Prefecture, Japan. Other possible sites are Kauai, Hawaii; Edmonton, Canada; and Scottsdale, Arizona. You and Mike Nagochi are members of the site selection team for Inwood Design Group. The team is responsible for collecting information on the sites, evaluating that information, and recommending the best site for the new golf course.

Your team identified five factors likely to determine the success of a golf course: climate, competition, market size, topography, and transportation. The team has already collected information on these factors for three of the four potential golf course sites. Mike has just returned from visiting the last site in Scottsdale, Arizona.

Using Microsoft Excel 97 for Windows 95, Mike has created a worksheet that the team can use to evaluate the four sites. He needs to complete the worksheet by entering the data for the Scottsdale site. He then plans to bring the worksheet to the group's next meeting so that the team can analyze the information and recommend a site to management.

In this tutorial you will learn how to use Excel as you work with Mike to complete the Inwood site selection worksheet and work with the Inwood team to select the best site for the golf course.

Excel

Using the Tutorials Effectively

These tutorials are designed to be used at a computer. Each tutorial is divided into sessions. Watch for the session headings, such as "Session 1.1" and "Session 1.2." Each session is designed to be completed in about 45 minutes, but take as much time as you need. When you've completed a session, it's a good idea to exit the program and take a break. You can exit Microsoft Excel by clicking the Close button in the top-right corner of the program window.

Before you begin, read the following questions and answers. They are designed to help you use the tutorials effectively.

Where do I start?

Each tutorial begins with a case, which sets the scene for the tutorial and gives you background information to help you understand what you will be doing in the tutorial. Read the case before you go to the lab. In the lab, begin with the first session of the tutorial.

How do I know what to do on the computer?

Each session contains steps that you will perform on the computer to learn how to use Microsoft Excel. The steps are numbered and are set against a colored background. Read the text that introduces each series of steps, and read each step carefully and completely before you try it.

How do I know if I did the step correctly?

As you work, compare your computer screen with the corresponding figure in the tutorial. Don't worry if your screen display is somewhat different from the figure. The important parts of the screen display are labeled in each figure. Check to make sure these parts are on your screen.

What if I make a mistake?

Don't worry about making mistakes—they are part of the learning process. Paragraphs labeled **TROUBLE?** identify common problems and explain how to get back on track. Follow the steps in a **TROUBLE?** paragraph *only* if you are having the problem described. If you run into other problems, carefully consider the current state of your system, the position of the pointer, and any messages on the screen.

How do I use the Reference Windows?

Reference Windows summarize the procedures you learn in the tutorial steps. Do not complete the actions in the Reference Windows when you are working through the tutorial. Instead, refer to the Reference Windows while you are working on the assignments at the end of the tutorial.

How can I test my understanding of the material I learned in the tutorial?

At the end of each session, you can answer the Quick Check Questions. If necessary, refer to the Answers to Quick Check Questions to check your work.

After you have completed the entire tutorial, you should complete the Tutorial Assignments and Case Problems. These exercises are carefully structured so you will review what you have learned and then apply your knowledge to new situations.

What if I can't remember how to do something?

You should refer to the Task Reference at the end of the book; it summarizes how to accomplish commonly performed tasks.

What is the Spreadsheets Course Lab, and how should I use it?

This interactive Lab helps you review spreadsheet concepts and practice skills that you learn in Tutorial 1. The Lab Assignments section at the end of Tutorial 1 includes instructions for using the Lab.

Now that you've seen how to use the tutorials effectively, you are ready to begin.

> **SESSION**
> # 1.1
>
> *In this session you will learn what a spreadsheet is and how it is used in business. You will learn what Excel is and about the Excel window and its elements, how to move around a worksheet using the keyboard and the mouse, and how to open a workbook.*

Spreadsheets

What Is Excel?

Excel is a computerized spreadsheet. A **spreadsheet** is an important business tool that helps you analyze and evaluate information. Spreadsheets are often used for cash flow analysis, budgeting, decision making, cost estimating, inventory management, and financial reporting. For example, an accountant might use a spreadsheet like the one in Figure 1-1 for a budget.

Figure 1-1 ◀
Budget
spreadsheet

Cash Budget Forecast

	January Estimated	January Actual
Cash in Bank (Start of Month)	$1,400.00	$1,400.00
Cash in Register (Start of Month)	100.00	100.00
Total Cash	$1,500.00	$1,500.00
Expected Cash Sales	$1,200.00	$1,420.00
Expected Collections	400.00	380.00
Other Money Expected	100.00	52.00
Total Income	$1,700.00	$1,852.00
Total Cash and Income	$3,200.00	$3,352.00
All Expenses (for Month)	$1,200.00	$1,192.00
Cash Balance at End of Month	$2,000.00	$2,160.00

To produce the spreadsheet in Figure 1-1, you could manually calculate the totals and then type your results, or you could use a computer and spreadsheet program to perform the calculations and print the results. Spreadsheet programs are also referred to as electronic spreadsheets, computerized spreadsheets, or just spreadsheets.

In Excel 97, the document you create is called a **workbook**. Each workbook is made up of individual worksheets, or **sheets**, just as a spiral-bound notebook is made up of sheets of paper. You will learn more about using multiple sheets later in this tutorial. For now, just keep in mind that the terms *worksheet* and *sheet* are often used interchangeably.

Starting Excel

Mike arrives at his office early because he needs to work with you to finish the worksheet and get ready for your meeting with the design team.

Start Excel and complete the worksheet that Mike will use to help the design team decide about the golf course site.

To start Microsoft Excel:

1. Make sure Windows 95 is running on your computer and the Windows 95 desktop appears on your screen.

TROUBLE? If you're running Windows NT Workstation 4.0 (or a later version) on your computer or network, don't worry. Although the figures in this book were created while running Windows 95, Windows NT 4.0 and Windows 95 share the same interface, and Microsoft Excel 97 runs equally well under either systems.

2. Click the **Start** button on the taskbar to display the Start menu, and then point to **Programs** to display the Programs menu.

3. Point to **Microsoft Excel** on the Programs menu. See Figure 1-2.

Figure 1-2 ◀
Starting
Microsoft Excel

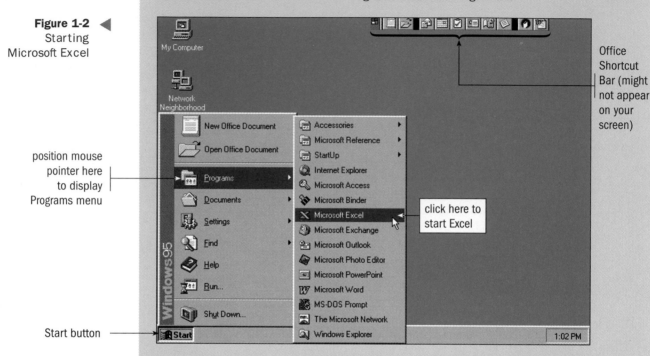

position mouse
pointer here
to display
Programs menu

Start button

Office
Shortcut
Bar (might
not appear
on your
screen)

click here to
start Excel

TROUBLE? If you don't see the Microsoft Excel option on the Programs menu, ask your instructor or technical support person for assistance.

TROUBLE? The Office Shortcut Bar, which appears along the top border of the desktop in Figure 1-2, might look different on your screen or it might not appear at all, depending on how your system is set up. The steps in these tutorials do not require that you use the Office Shortcut Bar; therefore, the remaining figures do not display the Office Shortcut Bar.

4. Click **Microsoft Excel**. After a short pause, the Microsoft Excel copyright information appears in a message box and remains on the screen until the Excel program window and a blank worksheet are displayed. See Figure 1-3.

TROUBLE? Depending on how your system is set up, the Office Assistant (see Figure 1-3) window might open when you start Excel. For now, click the Close button ☒ on the Office Assistant window to close it; you'll learn more about this feature later in this tutorial. If you've started Microsoft Excel immediately after installing it, you'll need to click the Start Using Microsoft Excel option, which the Office Assistant displays, before closing the Office Assistant window.

Figure 1-3 ◀
Excel Program
window
with blank
worksheet

title bar

Name box

active cell

mouse pointer

row headings

active sheet

status bar

sheet tab
scroll buttons

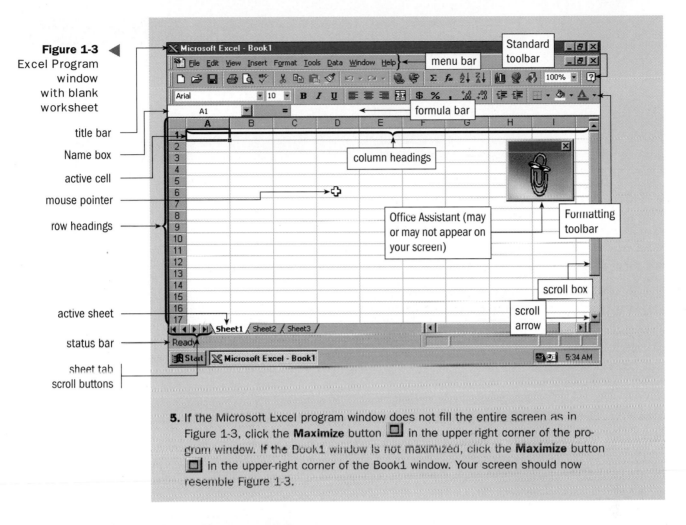

5. If the Microsoft Excel program window does not fill the entire screen as in Figure 1-3, click the **Maximize** button 🔲 in the upper right corner of the program window. If the Book1 window is not maximized, click the **Maximize** button 🔲 in the upper-right corner of the Book1 window. Your screen should now resemble Figure 1-3.

The Excel Window

The Excel window layout is consistent with the layout of other Windows programs. It contains many common features, such as the title bar, menu bar, scroll bars, and taskbar. Figure 1-3 shows these elements as well as the main components of the Excel window. Take a look at each of these Excel components so you know their location and purpose.

Toolbars

Toolbars allow you to organize the commands in Excel. The menu bar is a special toolbar at the top of the window that contains menus such as File, Edit, and View. The Standard toolbar and the Formatting toolbar are located below the menu bar. The **Standard** toolbar contains buttons corresponding to the most frequently used commands in Excel. The **Formatting** toolbar contains buttons corresponding to the commands most frequently used to improve the appearance of a worksheet.

Formula Bar

The **formula bar**, located immediately below the toolbars, displays the contents of the active cell. A **cell's contents** is the data you enter into it. As you type or edit data, the changes appear in the formula bar. At the left end of the formula bar is the **Name box.** This area displays the cell reference for the active cell.

Worksheet Window

The document window, usually called the **worksheet window** or **workbook window**, contains the sheet you are creating, editing, or using. Each worksheet consists of a series of columns identified by lettered column headings and a series of rows identified by numbered row headings. Columns are assigned alphabetic labels from A to IV (256 columns). Rows are assigned numeric labels from 1 to 65,536 (65,536 rows).

A **cell** is the rectangular area where a column and a row intersect. Each cell is identified by a **cell reference**, which is its column and row location. For example, the cell reference B6 indicates the cell where column B and row 6 intersect. The column letter is always first in the cell reference. B6 is a correct cell reference; 6B is not. The **active cell** is the cell in which you are currently working. Excel identifies the active cell with a dark border that outlines one cell. In Figure 1-3, cell A1 is the active cell. Notice that the cell reference for the active cell appears in the reference area of the formula bar. You can change the active cell when you want to work elsewhere in the worksheet.

Pointer

The **pointer** is the indicator that moves on your screen as you move your mouse. The pointer changes shape to reflect the type of task you can perform at a particular location. When you click a mouse button, something happens at the pointer's location. In Figure 1-3 the pointer looks like a white plus sign ✛.

Sheet Tabs

The **sheet tabs** let you move quickly between the sheets in a workbook; you can simply check the sheet tab of the sheet you want to move to. By default, a new workbook consists of three worksheets. If your workbook contains many worksheets, you can use the **sheet tab scroll buttons** to scroll through the sheet tabs that are not currently visible to find the sheet you want.

Moving Around a Worksheet

Before entering or editing the contents of a cell, you need to select that cell to make it the active cell. You can select a cell using either the keyboard or the mouse.

Using the Mouse

Using the mouse, you can quickly select a cell by placing the mouse pointer on the cell and clicking the mouse button. If you need to move to a cell that's not currently on the screen, use the vertical and horizontal scroll bars to display the area of the worksheet containing the cell you are interested in, and then select the cell.

Using the Keyboard

In addition to the mouse, Excel provides you with many keyboard options for moving to different cell locations within your worksheet. Figure 1-4 shows some of the keys you can use to select a cell within your worksheet.

Figure 1-4 ◀
Keys to move
around the
worksheet

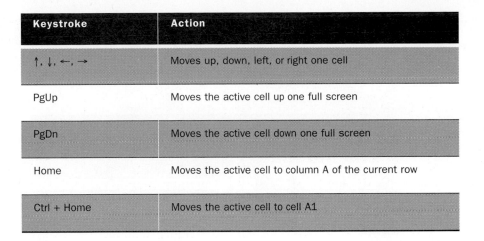

Keystroke	Action
↑, ↓, ←, →	Moves up, down, left, or right one cell
PgUp	Moves the active cell up one full screen
PgDn	Moves the active cell down one full screen
Home	Moves the active cell to column A of the current row
Ctrl + Home	Moves the active cell to cell A1

Now, try moving around the worksheet using your keyboard and mouse.

To move around the worksheet:

1. Position the mouse pointer ⟍ over cell E8, then click the **left mouse** button to make it the active cell. Notice that the cell is surrounded by a black border to indicate that it is the active cell and that the Name box on the formula bar displays E8.

2. Click cell D4 to make it the active cell.

3. Press the → key to make cell C4 the active cell.

4. Press the ↓ key to make cell C5 the active cell. See Figure 1-5.

Figure 1-5 ◀
Cell C5 as
active cell

active cell

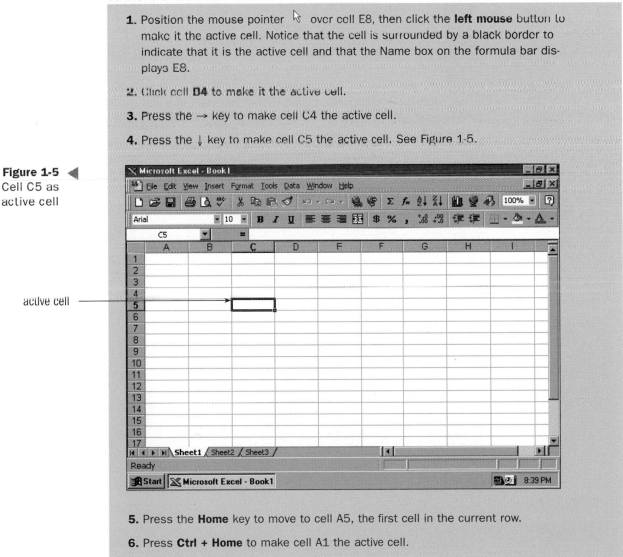

5. Press the **Home** key to move to cell A5, the first cell in the current row.

6. Press **Ctrl + Home** to make cell A1 the active cell.

So far you've moved around the portion of the worksheet you can see. Many worksheets can't be viewed entirely on one screen. Next, you'll use the keyboard and mouse to move beyond the worksheet window.

To move beyond the worksheet window:

1. Press the **Page Down** key to move the display down one screen. The active cell is now cell A17 (the active cell on your screen may be different). Notice that the row numbers on the left side of the worksheet indicate you have moved to a different area of the worksheet. See Figure 1-6.

Figure 1-6 ◀
Worksheet
screen after
moving to
different area
of worksheet

row headings
changed

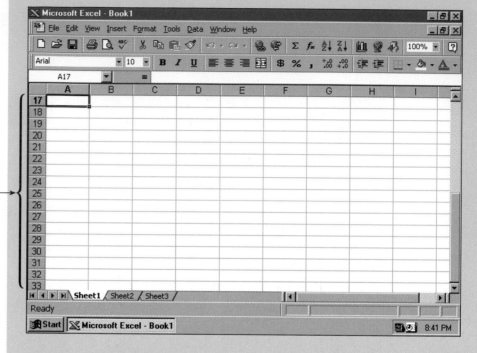

2. Press the **Page Down** key again to move the display down one screen. Notice that the row numbers indicate that you have moved to a different area of the worksheet.

3. Press the **Page Up** key to move the display up one screen. The active cell is now cell A17 (the active cell on your screen may be different).

4. Click the **vertical scroll bar arrow** until row 12 is visible. Notice that the active cell is still A17 (the active cell on your screen may be different). Using the scroll bar changes the portion of the screen you can view without changing the active cell.

5. Click cell **C12** to make it the active cell.

6. Click the blank area above the vertical scroll box to move up a full screen.

7. Click the blank area below the vertical scroll box to move down a full screen.

8. Click the **scroll box** and drag it to the top of the scroll area to again change the area of the screen you're viewing. Notice that the ScrollTip appears telling you where you will scroll to.

9. Click cell **E6** to make it the active cell.

As you know, a workbook can consist of one or more worksheets. Excel makes it easy to switch between them. Next, try moving from worksheet to worksheet.

Navigating in a Workbook

The sheet tabs let you move quickly between the different sheets in a workbook. If you can see the tab of the sheet you want, click the tab to activate the worksheet. You can also use the sheet tab scroll buttons to see sheet tabs hidden from view. Figure 1-7 describes the four tab scrolling buttons and their effects.

Figure 1-7 ◀
Sheet tab
scrolling
buttons

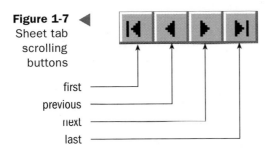

first

previous

next

last

Next, try moving to a new sheet.

To move to Sheet2:

1. Click the **Sheet2** tab. Sheet2, which is blank, appears in the worksheet window. Notice that the Sheet2 sheet tab is white and the name is bold, which means that Sheet2 is now the active sheet. Cell A1 is the active cell in Sheet2.

2. Click the **Sheet3** tab to make it the active sheet.

3. Click the **Sheet1** tab to make it the active sheet. Notice that cell E6 is the active cell.

Now that you have some basic skills navigating a worksheet and workbook, you can begin working with Mike to complete the golf site selection worksheet.

Opening a Workbook

When you want to use a workbook that you previously created, you must first open it. Opening a workbook transfers a copy of the workbook file from the hard drive or 3½-inch disk to the random access memory (RAM) of your computer and displays it on your screen. When the workbook is open, the file is both in RAM and on the disk.

After you open a workbook, you can view, edit, print, or save it again on your disk.

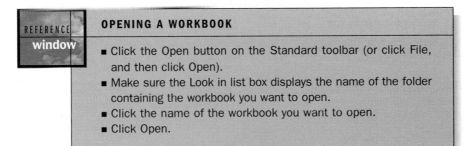

REFERENCE window	**OPENING A WORKBOOK**
	■ Click the Open button on the Standard toolbar (or click File, and then click Open). ■ Make sure the Look in list box displays the name of the folder containing the workbook you want to open. ■ Click the name of the workbook you want to open. ■ Click Open.

Mike created a workbook to help the site selection team evaluate the four potential locations for the golf course. The workbook, Inwood, is on your Student Disk.

To open an existing workbook:

1. Place your Excel Student Disk in the appropriate drive.

   TROUBLE? If you don't have a Student Disk, you need to get one before you can proceed. Your instructor or technical support person will either give you one or ask you to make your own by following the instructions on the "Read This Before You Begin" page before this tutorial. See your instructor or technical support person for information.

2. Click the **Open** button 🖻 on the Standard toolbar. The Open File dialog box opens. See Figure 1-8.

Figure 1-8 ◀
Open dialog box

names and files specified here (yours may differ)

click here to specify drive

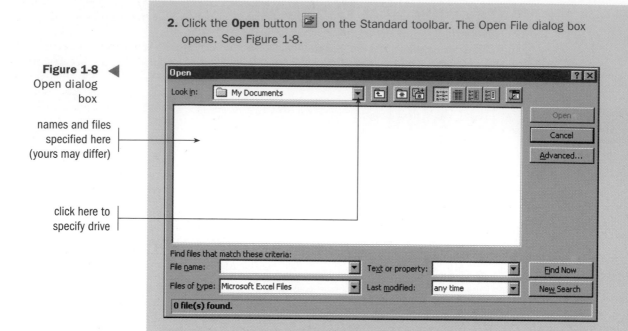

3. Click the **Look in** list arrow to display the list of available drives. Locate the drive containing your Student Disk. In this text, we assume your Student Disk is a 3½-inch floppy in drive A.

4. Click the drive that contains your Student Disk. A list of documents and folders on your Student Disk appears in the list box.

5. In the list of document and folder names, double-click **Tutorial.01** to display that folder in the Look in list box, then click **Inwood**.

6. Click the **Open** button. (You could also double-click the filename to open the file.) The Inwood workbook opens and the first sheet in the workbook, Title Sheet, appears. See Figure 1-9.

TROUBLE? If you do not see Inwood listed, use the scroll bar to see additional names.

Figure 1-9 ◀
Title Sheet sheet in Inwood workbook

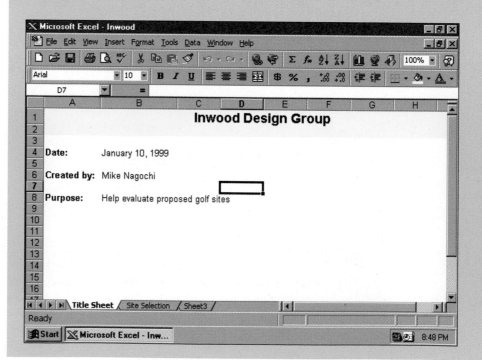

Layout of the Inwood Workbook

The first worksheet, Title Sheet, contains information about the workbook. The Title Sheet shows who created the workbook, the date when it was created, and its purpose.

Mike explains that whenever he creates a new workbook he makes sure he documents it carefully. This information is especially useful if he returns to a workbook after a long period of time (or if a new user opens it) because it provides a quick review of the workbook's purpose.

After reviewing the Title Sheet, Mike moves to the Site Selection worksheet.

To move to the Site Selection worksheet:

1. Click the **Site Selection** sheet tab to display the worksheet Mike is preparing for the site selection team. See Figure 1-10.

Figure 1-10 ◀
Site Selection
worksheet

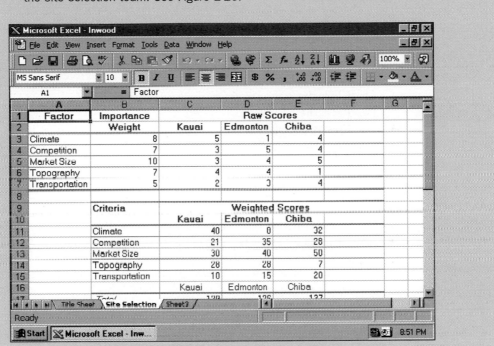

	Factor	Importance		Raw Scores			
		Weight	Kauai	Edmonton	Chiba		
3	Climate	8	5	1	4		
4	Competition	7	3	5	4		
5	Market Size	10	3	4	5		
6	Topography	7	4	4	1		
7	Transportation	5	2	3	4		
8							
9		Criteria		Weighted Scores			
10			Kauai	Edmonton	Chiba		
11		Climate	40	8	32		
12		Competition	21	35	28		
13		Market Size	30	40	50		
14		Topography	28	28	7		
15		Transportation	10	15	20		
16			Kauai	Edmonton	Chiba		
17		Total	129	126	137		

Mike explains the general layout of the Site Selection worksheet to you. He reminds you that to this point he has only entered data for three of the four sites. He will provide the missing Scottsdale information to you. Cells C2 through E2 list three of the four sites under consideration for which he has data. Cells A3 through A7 contain the five factors on which the team's decision will be based: Climate, Competition, Market Size, Topography, and Transportation. They assign scores for climate, competition, market size, topography, and transportation to each location. The team uses a scale of 1 to 5 to assign a raw score for each factor. Higher raw scores indicate strength; lower raw scores indicate weakness. Cells C3 through E7 contain the raw scores for the first three locations. For example, the raw score for Kauai's climate is 5; the two other locations have scores of 1 and 4, so Kauai, with its warm, sunny days all year, has the best climate for the golf course of the three sites visited so far. Edmonton, on the other hand, has cold weather and only received a climate raw score of 1.

The raw scores, however, do not provide enough information for the team to make a decision. Some factors are more important to the success of the golf course than others. The team members assigned an *importance weight* to each factor according to their knowledge of what factors contribute most to the success of a golf course. The importance weights are on a scale from 1 to 10, with 10 being most important. Mike entered the weights in cells B3 through B7. Market size, weighted 10, is the most important factor. The team believes the least important factor is transportation, so transportation is assigned a lower weight. Climate is important but the team considers market size most important. Therefore, they do not use the raw scores to make a final decision. Instead, they multiply each raw score by its importance weight to produce a weighted score. Which of the three sites already visited has the highest weighted score for any factor? If you look at the scores in cells C11 through E15, you see that Chiba's score of 50 for market size is the highest weighted score for any factor.

Cells C17 through E17 contain the total weighted scores for the three locations. With the current weighting and raw scores, Chiba is the most promising site, with a total score of 137.

Quick Check

1. A(n) _____ is the rectangular area where a column and a row intersect.

2. When you _____ a workbook, the computer copies it from your disk into RAM.

3. The cell reference _____ refers to the intersection of the fourth column and the second row.

4. To move the worksheet to the right one column:
   a. Press the Enter key
   b. Click the right arrow on the horizontal scroll bar
   c. Press the Escape key
   d. Press Ctrl + Home

5. To make Sheet2 the active worksheet, you would _____.

6. What key or keys do you press to make cell A1 the active cell?

You have now reviewed the layout of the worksheet. Now, Mike wants you to enter the data on Scottsdale. Based on his meeting with local investors and a visit to the Scottsdale site, he has assigned the following raw scores: Climate 5, Competition 2, Market Size 4, Topography 3, and Transportation 3. To complete the worksheet, you must enter the raw scores he has assigned to the Scottsdale site. You will do this in the next session.

SESSION 1.2

In this session you will learn how to enter text, values, formulas, and functions into a worksheet. You will use this data to perform what-if analysis using a worksheet. You'll also correct mistakes, and use the online Help system to determine how to clear the contents of cells. Finally, you'll learn how to print a worksheet, and how to close a worksheet and exit Excel.

Text, Values, Formulas, and Functions

As you have now observed, an Excel workbook can hold one or more worksheets, each containing a grid of 256 columns and 65,536 rows. The rectangular areas at the intersections of each column and row are called cells. A cell can contain a value, text, or a formula. To understand how the spreadsheet program works, you need to understand how Excel manipulates text, values, formulas, and functions.

Text

Text entries include any combination of letters, symbols, numbers, and spaces. Although text is sometimes used as data, it is more often used to describe the data contained in a worksheet. Text is often used to label columns and rows in a worksheet. For example, a projected monthly income statement contains the months of the year as column headings and income and expense categories as row labels. To enter text in a worksheet, you select the cell in which you want to enter the text by clicking the cell to select it, then typing the text. Excel automatically aligns the text on the left when it is displayed in a cell.

Mike's Site Selection worksheet contains a number of column heading labels. You need to enter the label for Scottsdale in the Raw Scores and Weighted Scores sections of the worksheet.

To enter a text label:

1. If you took a break after the last session, make sure Excel is running and make sure the Site Selection worksheet of the Inwood workbook is displayed.

2. Click cell **F2** to make it the active cell.

3. Type **Scottsdale**, then press the **Enter** key.

   TROUBLE? If you make a mistake while typing, you can correct the error with the Backspace key. If you realize you made an error after you press the Enter key, retype the entry by repeating Steps 2 and 3.

4. Click cell **F10** and type **S**. Excel completes the entry for you based on the entries already in the column. If your data involves repetitious text, this feature, known as **AutoComplete,** can make your data entry go more quickly.

5. Press the **Enter** key to complete the entry.

6. Click cell **F16**, type **S**, and press the **Enter** key to accept Scottsdale as the entry in the cell. See Figure 1-11.

Figure 1-11
Worksheet
after text
entered

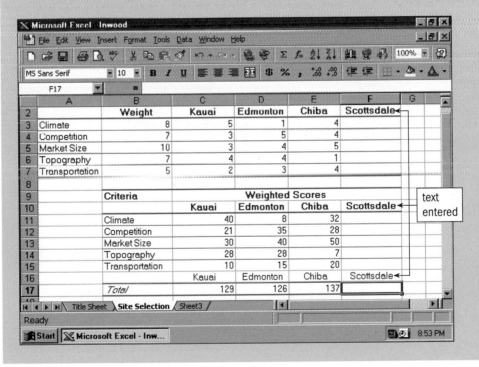

Next, you need to enter the raw scores Mike assigned to Scottsdale.

Values

Values are numbers that represent a quantity of some type: the number of units in inventory, stock price, an exam score, and so on. Examples of values are 378, 25.2, and -55. Values can also be dates (11/29/99) and times (4:40:31). As you type information in a cell, Excel determines whether the characters you're typing can be used as values. For example, if you type 456, Excel recognizes it as a value and it is right-justified when displayed in the cell. On the other hand, Excel treats some data commonly referred to as "numbers" as text. For example, Excel treats a telephone number (1-800-227-1240) or a social security number (372-70-9654) as text that cannot be used for calculations.

You need to enter the raw scores for Scottsdale.

To enter a value:

1. If necessary, click the scroll arrow so row 2 is visible. Click cell **F3**, type **5** and then press the **Enter** key. The cell pointer moves to cell F4.

2. With the cell pointer in cell F4, type **2** and press the **Enter** key.

3. Enter the value **4** for Market Size in cell F5, the value **3** for Topography in cell F6, and the value **3** for Transportation in cell F7. See Figure 1-12.

Figure 1-12 ◀
Worksheet
after numbers
entered

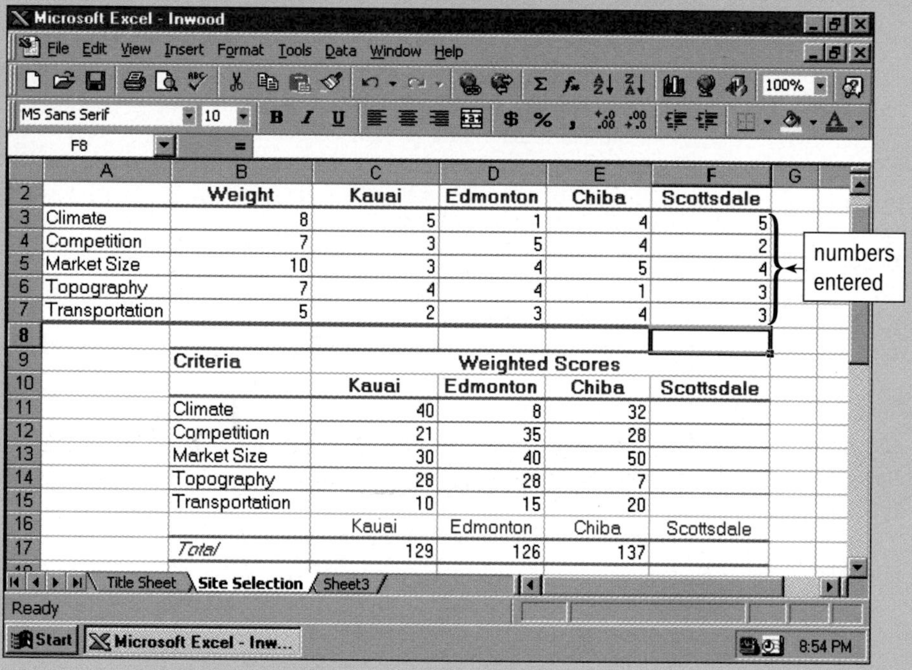

Next, you enter the formulas to calculate Scottsdale's weighted score in each category.

Formulas

When you need to perform a calculation in Excel you use a formula. A **formula** is the arithmetic used to calculate values displayed in a worksheet. You can take advantage of the power of Excel by using formulas in worksheets. If you change one number in a worksheet, Excel recalculates any formula affected by the change.

An Excel formula always begins with an equal sign (=). Formulas are created by combining numbers, cell references, arithmetic operators, and/or functions. An **arithmetic operator** indicates the desired arithmetic operations. Figure 1-13 shows the arithmetic operators used in Excel.

Figure 1-13 ◀
Arithmetic
operators used
in formulas

Arithmetic Operation	Arithmetic Operator	Example	Description
Addition	+	=10+A5	Adds 10 to the value in cell A5
Subtraction	–	=C9–B9	Subtracts the value in cell B9 from the value in cell C9
Multiplication	*	=C9*B9	Multiplies the value in cell B9 by the value in cell C9
Division	/	=C9/B9	Divides the value in cell C9 by the value in cell B9
Exponentiation	^	=10^B5	Raises 10 to the value stored in cell B5

The result of the formula is displayed in the cell where you entered the formula. To view the formula that has been entered in a cell, you must first select the cell, then look at the formula bar.

REFERENCE
window

ENTERING A FORMULA

- Click the cell where you want the result to appear.
- Type = and then type the rest of the formula.
- For formulas that include cell references, such as B2 or D78, you can type the cell reference or you can use the mouse or arrow keys to select each cell.
- When the formula is complete, press the Enter key.

You need to enter the formulas to compute the weighted scores for the Scottsdale site. The formula multiples the raw score for a factor by the importance weight assigned to the factor. Figure 1-14 displays the formulas you need to enter into the worksheet.

Figure 1-14 ◀
Formula to
calculate
Scottsdale's
weighted score

Cell	Formula	Explanation
F11	=B3*F3	Multiplies importance weight by raw score for climate
F12	=B4*F4	Multiplies importance weight by raw score for competition
F13	=B5*F5	Multiplies importance weight by raw score for market size
F14	=B6*F6	Multiplies importance weight by raw score for topography
F15	=B7*F7	Multiplies importance weight by raw score for transportation

To enter the formula to calculate each weighted score for the Scottsdale site:

1. Click cell **F11** to make it the active cell. Type **=B3*F3** to multiply the weight assigned to the climate category by the raw score assigned to Scottsdale for the climate category. Press the **Enter** key. The value 40 is displayed in cell F11.

   TROUBLE? If you make a mistake while typing, you can correct the error with the Backspace key. If you realize you made an error after you press the Enter key, repeat Step 1 to retype the entry.

2. Click cell **F12**, type **=B4*F4**, and then press the **Enter** key. This formula multiplies the weight assigned to competition (the contents of cell B4) by Scottsdale's raw score for competition (cell F4). The value 14 is displayed.

3. Enter the remaining formulas from Figure 1-14 into cells F13, F14, and F15. When completed, your worksheet will look like Figure 1-15.

Figure 1-15 ◄
Worksheet after entering formulas to calculate weighted score

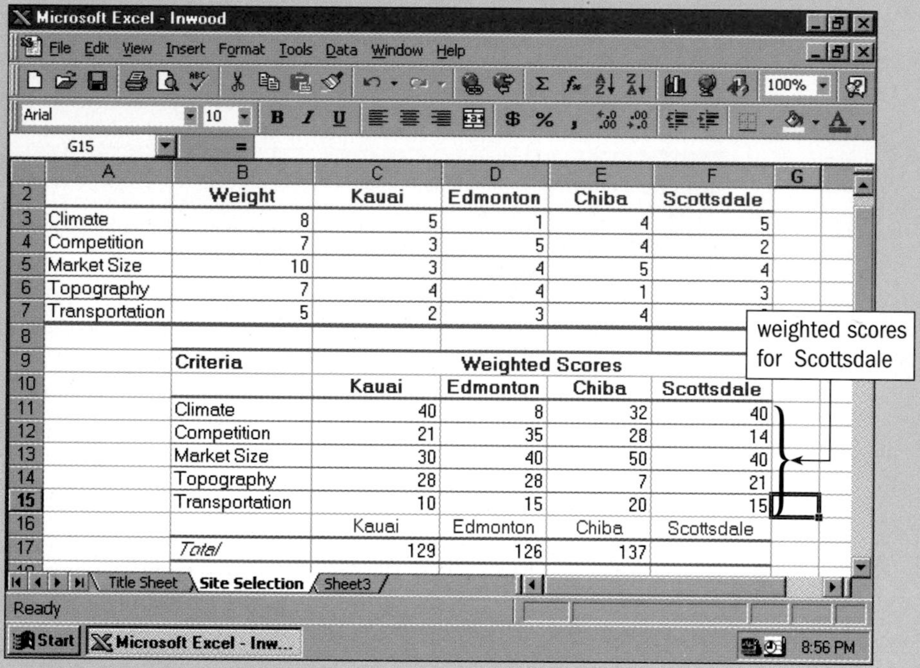

You now have to enter the formula to calculate the total weighted score for Scottsdale into the worksheet. You can use the formula =F11+F12+F13+F14+F15 to calculate the total score for the Scottsdale site. As an alternative, you can use a function to streamline this long formula.

Functions

A **function** is a special prewritten formula that's a shortcut for commonly used calculations. For example, the SUM function is a shortcut for entering formulas that total values in rows or columns. You can use the SUM function to create the formula =SUM(F11:F15) instead of typing the longer =F11+F12+F13+F14+F15. The SUM function in this example adds the range F11 through F15. A **range** can be a single cell or a rectangular block of cells, often rows or columns. The range reference in the function SUM(F11:F15) refers to the rectangular block of cells beginning at F11 and ending at F15. Figure 1-16 shows several examples of ranges.

Figure 1-16 ◀
Examples of
ranges

range D4:I4

range B3:B9

range D14:D14

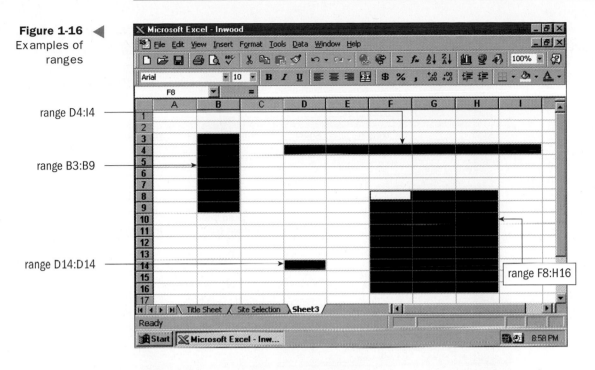

range F8:H16

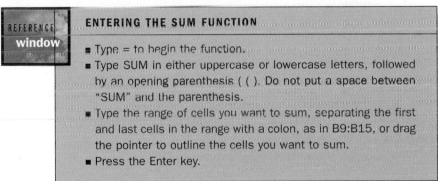

REFERENCE window

ENTERING THE SUM FUNCTION

- Type = to begin the function.
- Type SUM in either uppercase or lowercase letters, followed by an opening parenthesis ( ). Do not put a space between "SUM" and the parenthesis.
- Type the range of cells you want to sum, separating the first and last cells in the range with a colon, as in B9:B15, or drag the pointer to outline the cells you want to sum.
- Press the Enter key.

You use the SUM function to compute the total score for the Scottsdale site.

To enter the formula using a function:

1. Click cell **F17** to make it the active cell.

2. Type **=SUM(F11:F15)**. Notice that the formula appears in the cell and the formula bar as you enter it. See Figure 1-17.

Figure 1-17
Viewing
the SUM
function before
completing
the entry

SUM function
appears in
formula bar

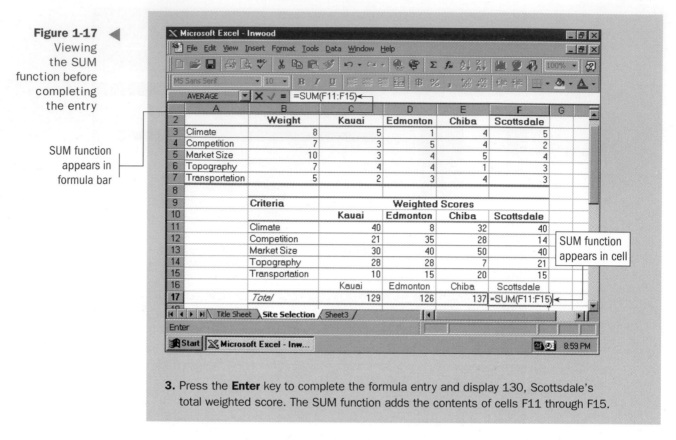

3. Press the **Enter** key to complete the formula entry and display 130, Scottsdale's total weighted score. The SUM function adds the contents of cells F11 through F15.

The worksheet for site selection is now complete. Mike's worksheet contains columns of information about the site selection and a chart displaying the weighted scores for each potential site. To see the chart you must scroll the worksheet.

To scroll the worksheet to view the chart:

1. Click the **scroll arrow** button on the vertical scroll bar until the section of the worksheet containing the chart is displayed. See Figure 1-18.

Figure 1-18
Scrolling the
worksheet to
view the chart

Chiba is leading site

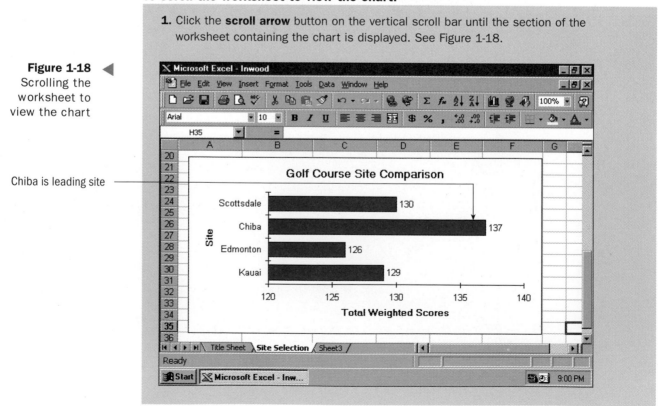

2. After you look at the chart, click and drag the **scroll box** to the top of the vertical scroll bar.

You have completed the worksheet; Mike decides to save it before showing it to the site selection team.

Saving the Workbook

To store a workbook permanently, so you can use it again without having to reenter the data and formulas, you must save it as a file on a disk. When you save a workbook, you copy it from RAM onto your disk. You'll use either the Save or the Save As command. The Save command copies the workbook onto a disk using its current filename. If a version of the file already exists, the new version replaces the old one. The Save As command asks for a filename before copying the workbook onto a disk. When you enter a new filename, you save the current file under that new name. The previous version of the file remains on the disk under its original name.

As a general rule, use the Save As command the first time you save a file or whenever you modify a file and want to save both the old and new versions. Use the Save command when you modify a file and want to save only the current version.

It is a good idea to save your file often. That way, if the power goes out or the computer stops working, you're less likely to lose your work. Because you use the Save command frequently, the Standard toolbar has a Save button , a single mouse-click shortcut for saving your workbook.

REFERENCE window

SAVING A WORKBOOK WITH A NEW FILENAME

- Click File and then click Save As.
- Change the workbook name as necessary.
- Make sure the Save in box displays the folder in which you want to save your workbook.
- Click the Save button.

Mike's workbook is named Inwood. On your screen is a version of Inwood that you modified during this work session. Save the modified workbook under the new name Inwood 2. This way if you want to start the tutorial from the beginning, you can open the Inwood file and start over.

To save the modified workbook under a new name:

1. Click **File** on the menu bar, and then click **Save As**. The Save As dialog box opens with the current workbook name in the File name text box.

2. Click at the end of the current workbook name, press the **spacebar**, and then type **2**. *(Do not press the Enter key.)*

Before you proceed, check the other dialog box specifications to ensure that you save the workbook on your Student Disk.

3. If necessary, click the **Save in** list arrow to display the list of available drives and folders. Click **Tutorial.01**.

4. Confirm that the Save as type text box specifies "Microsoft Excel Workbook."

5. When your Save As dialog box looks like the one in Figure 1-19, click the **Save** button to close the dialog box and save the workbook. Notice that the new workbook name, Inwood 2, now appears in the title bar.

Figure 1-19 ◀
Saving the
worksheet with
a new filename

new filename ——

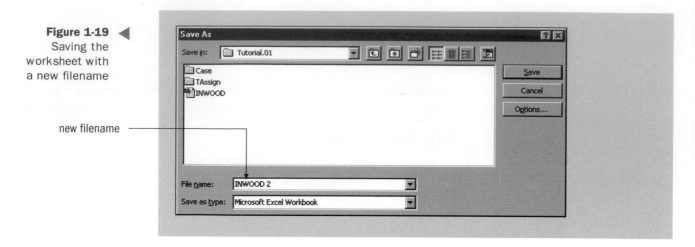

You now have two versions of the workbook: the original file—Inwood—and the modified workbook—Inwood 2.

Changing Values and Observing Results

The worksheet for site selection is now complete. Mike is ready to show it to the group. As the team examines the worksheet, you ask if the raw scores take into account recent news that a competing design group has announced plans to build a $325-million golf resort just 10 miles away from Inwood's proposed site in Chiba. Mike admits that he assigned the values before the announcement, so the raw scores do not reflect the increased competition in the Chiba market. You suggest revising the raw score for the competition factor to reflect this market change in Chiba.

When you change a value in a worksheet, Excel recalculates the worksheet and displays updated results. The recalculation feature makes Excel an extremely useful decision-making tool because it lets you quickly and easily factor in changing conditions. When you revise the contents of one or more cells in a worksheet and observe the effect this change has on all the other cells, you are performing a **what-if analysis**. In effect, you are saying, what if I change the value assigned to this factor? What effect will it have on the outcomes in the worksheet?

Since another development group has announced plans to construct a new golf course in the Chiba area, the team decides to lower Chiba's competition raw score from 4 to 2.

To change Chiba's competition raw score from 4 to 2:

1. Click cell **E4**. The black border around cell E4 indicates that it is the active cell. The current value of cell E4 is 4.

2. Type **2**. Notice that 2 appears in the cell and in the formula bar, along with a formula palette of three new buttons. The buttons shown in Figure 1-20—the Cancel button ⊠, the Enter button ☑, and the Edit Formula button ▣—offer alternatives for canceling, entering, and editing data and formulas.

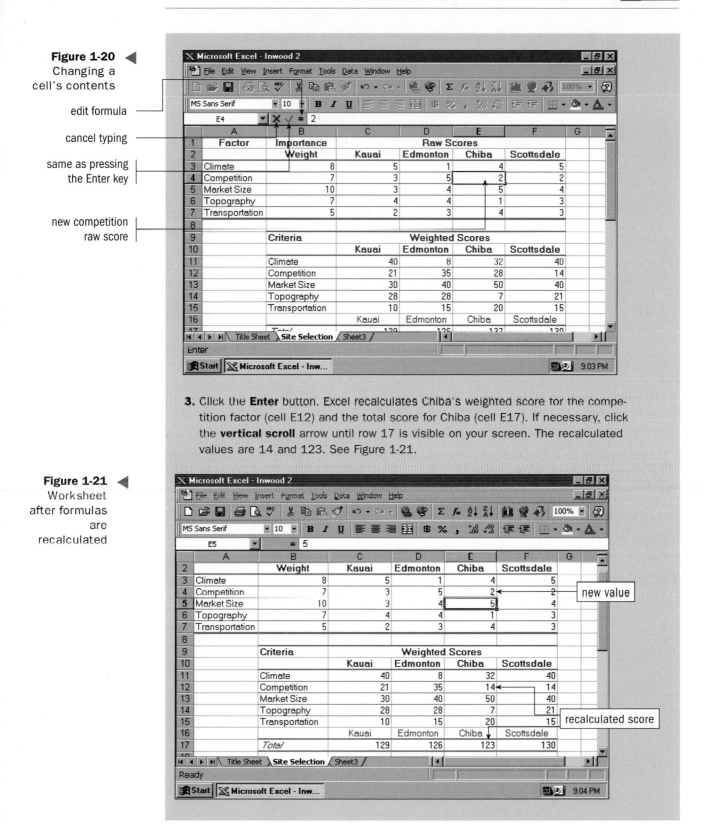

Figure 1-20 ◀
Changing a
cell's contents

edit formula ─────

cancel typing ─────

same as pressing
the Enter key ─────

new competition
raw score ─────

3. Click the **Enter** button. Excel recalculates Chiba's weighted score for the competition factor (cell E12) and the total score for Chiba (cell E17). If necessary, click the **vertical scroll** arrow until row 17 is visible on your screen. The recalculated values are 14 and 123. See Figure 1-21.

Figure 1-21 ◀
Worksheet
after formulas
are
recalculated

The team takes another look at the total weighted scores in row 17. Scottsdale is now the top-ranking site, with a total weighted score of 130. Chiba's total weighted score is now 123.

As the team continues to discuss the worksheet, several members express concern over the importance weight used for transportation. In the current worksheet, transportation is weighted 5 (cell B7). You remember that the group agreed to use an importance weight of 2 at a previous meeting. You ask Mike to change the importance weight for transportation.

To change the importance weight for transportation:

1. Click cell **B7** to make it the active cell.

2. Type **2** and press the **Enter** key. Cell B7 now contains the value 2 instead of 5. Cell B8 becomes the active cell. See Figure 1-22. Notice that the weighted scores for transportation (row 15) and the total weighted scores for each site (row 17) have all changed.

Figure 1-22 ◄
Worksheet after change made to the transportation importance weight

new value

all transportation scores recalculated

all total scores recalculated

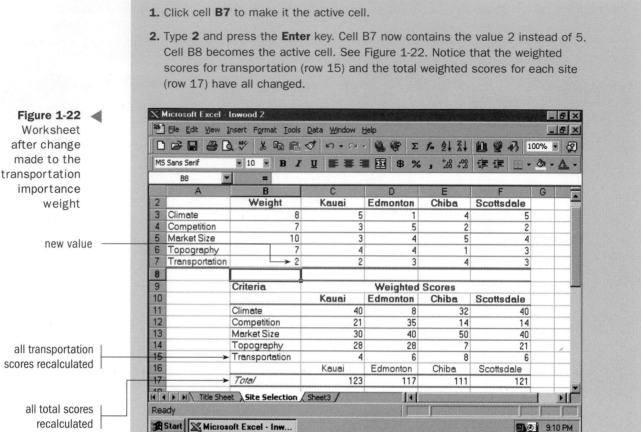

The change in the transportation importance weight puts Kauai ahead as the most favorable site, with a total weighted score of 123.

As you enter and edit a worksheet, there are many data entry errors that can occur. The most commonly made mistake on a worksheet is a typing error. Typing mistakes are easy to correct.

Correcting Mistakes

It is easy to correct a mistake as you are typing information in a cell, before you press the Enter key. If you need to correct a mistake as you are typing information in a cell, press the Backspace key to back up and delete one or more characters. When you are typing information in a cell, don't use the cursor arrow keys to edit because they move the cell pointer to another cell. One of the team members suggests changing the label "Criteria" in cell B9 to "Factors." The team members agree and you make the change to the cell.

To correct a mistake as you type:

1. Click cell **B9** to make it the active cell.

2. Type **Fak**, intentionally making an error, but don't press the Enter key.

3. Press the **Backspace** key to delete "k."

4. Type **ctors** and press the **Enter** key.

Now the word "Factors" is in cell B9. Mike suggests changing "Factors" to "Factor." The team agrees. To change a cell's contents after you press the Enter key, you use a different method. Double-clicking a cell or pressing the F2 key puts Excel into Edit mode, which lets you use the Backspace key, the ← and → keys, and the mouse to change the text in the formula bar.

REFERENCE window

CORRECTING MISTAKES USING EDIT MODE

- Double-click the cell you want to edit to begin Edit mode and display the contents of the cell in the formula bar (or click the cell you want to edit, then press F2).
- Use Backspace, Delete, ←, →, or the mouse to edit the cell's contents either in the cell or in the formula bar.
- Press the Enter key when you finish editing.

You use Edit mode to change "Factors" to "Factor" in cell B9.

To change the word "Factors" to "Factor" in cell B9:

1. Double-click cell **B9** to begin Edit mode. Note that "Edit" appears in the status bar, reminding you that Excel is currently in Edit mode.

2. Press the **End** key if necessary to move the cursor to the right of the word "Factors," then press the **Backspace** key to delete the "s."

3. Press the **Enter** key to complete the edit.

You ask if the team is ready to recommend a site. Mike believes that based on the best information they have, Kauai should be the recommended site and Scottsdale the alternative site. You ask for a vote, and the team unanimously agrees with Mike's recommendation.

Mike wants to have complete documentation to accompany the team's written recommendation to management, so he wants to print the worksheet.

As he reviews the worksheet one last time, he thinks that the labels in cells C16 through F16 (Kauai, Edmonton, Chiba, Scottsdale) are unnecessary and decides he wants you to delete them before printing the worksheet. You ask how you delete the contents of a cell or a group of cells. Mike is not sure, so he suggests using the Excel Help system to find the answer.

Getting Help

If you don't know how to perform a task or forget how to carry out a particular task, Excel provides an extensive Help system. The Excel Help system provides the same options as the Help system in other Windows programs—the Help Contents, the Help Index, and the Find feature. The Excel Help system also provides additional ways to get help as you work. One way to get help is to use the Office Assistant, which you may have seen on your screen when you first started Excel, and which you hid earlier in this tutorial. The Office Assistant, an animated object, pops up on the screen when you click the Office Assistant button on the Standard toolbar. The Office Assistant answers questions, offers tips, and provides help for a variety of Excel features. In addition to the Office Assistant, Figure 1-23 identifies several other ways you can get help.

Figure 1-23 ◀
Alternative ways
to get help

Action	Results in
On Help menu, click Contents and Index, click Contents tab	Displays an outline of topics and subtopics on which you can get information
On Help menu, click Contents and Index, click Index tab	Displays alphabetical listings of topics; enter first few letters in the box to scroll to an entry
On Help menu, click Contents and Index, click Find tab	Provides capability to find all topics that contain a particular word or words
Press F1	Activates the Office Assistant
On Help menu, click What's This?	Pointer changes to the Help pointer, which you use to click any object or option on the screen to see a description of the object

REFERENCE
window

USING THE OFFICE ASSISTANT

- Click the Office Assistant button on the Standard toolbar (or choose Microsoft Excel Help from the Help menu) to display the Office Assistant.
- Click Tips for information on using features more effectively.
  or
- Type an English-language question on an area where you need help, and then click Search.
- Click the suggested Help topic.
- To hide the Office Assistant, click its Close button.

Use the Office Assistant to get information on how to clear the contents of cells.

To get Help using the Office Assistant:

1. Click the Office Assistant ⊞ button to display an animated object and an information box. See Figure 1-24.

Figure 1-24 ◀
Office
Assistant with
information box

enter question here ——

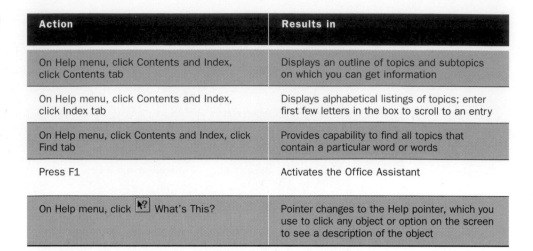

The Office Assistant can respond to an English-language question.

2. Type **how do I clear cells**, and then click **Search** to display several possible Help topics. See Figure 1-25.

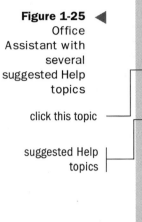

Figure 1-25 ◀
Office Assistant with several suggested Help topics

click this topic ―

suggested Help topics |

3. Click the first suggestion, **Clear contents, formats, or comments from cells**, to open a How To window on this topic. See Figure 1-26.

Figure 1-26 ◀
How To window on Clear contents, formats, or comments from cells

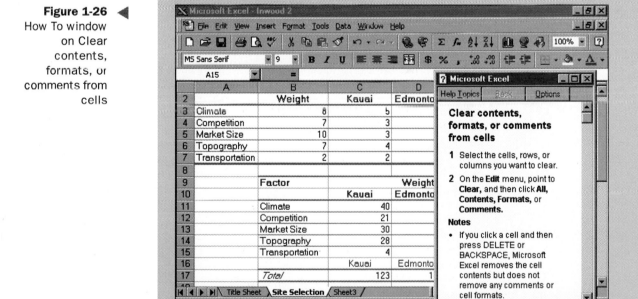

You can print the contents of the How To window, or you can click the Keep Help On Top command from the Options menu to keep the How To window on the screen where you can refer to it as you go through each step.

4. After reviewing the information, click the **Close** button ☒ on the How To window.

5. Click the **Close** button ☒ in the upper-right corner of the Office Assistant to hide the Assistant.

After reviewing the information from the Office Assistant, you are ready to remove the labels from the worksheet.

Clearing Cell Contents

As you are building or modifying your worksheet, you may occasionally find that you have entered a label, number, or formula in a cell that you want to be empty. To erase the contents of a cell, you use either the Delete key or the Clear command on the Edit menu. Removing the contents of a cell is known as clearing a cell. Do not press the spacebar to enter a blank character in an attempt to clear a cell's content. Excel treats a blank character as text, so even though the cell appears to be empty, it is not.

REFERENCE
window

CLEARING CELL CONTENTS

■ Click the cell you want to clear, or select a range of cells you want to clear.
■ Press the Delete key.
or
■ Click Edit, point to Clear, and then click Contents to erase only the contents of a cell, or click All to completely clear the cell contents, formatting, and notes.

You are ready to clear the labels from cells C16 through F16.

To clear the labels from cells C16 through F16:

1. Click cell **C16**. This will be the upper-left corner of the range to clear.

2. Position the cell pointer over cell C16. With the cell pointer the shape of ⊕, click and drag the cell pointer to F16 to select the range C16:F16.
If your pointer changes to a crosshair + *, or an arrow* ↖ *, do not drag the cell pointer to F16, until pointer changes to* ⊕ *.* Note that when you select a range, the first cell in that range, cell C16 in this example, remains white and the other cells in the range are highlighted. See Figure 1-27.

Figure 1-27
Highlighted cell
range

highlighted range ————

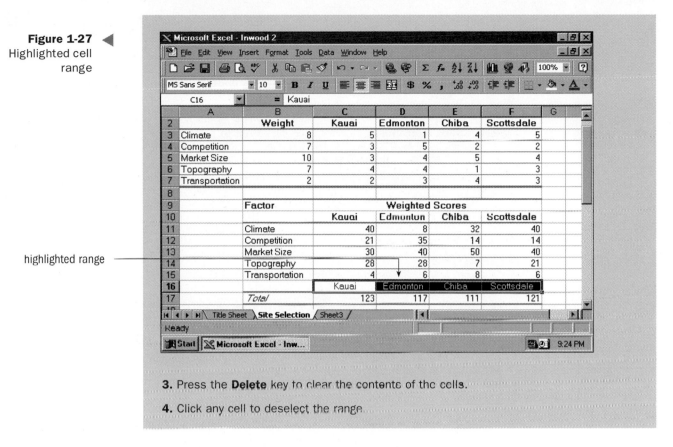

3. Press the **Delete** key to clear the contents of the cells.

4. Click any cell to deselect the range.

Now that you have cleared the unwanted labels from the cells, Mike wants you to print the site selection worksheet.

Printing the Worksheet

You can print an Excel worksheet using either the Print command on the File menu or the Print button on the Standard toolbar. If you use the Print command, Excel displays a dialog box where you can specify which worksheet pages you want to print, the number of copies you want to print, and the print quality (resolution). If you use the Print button, you do not have these options; Excel prints one copy of the entire worksheet using the current print settings.

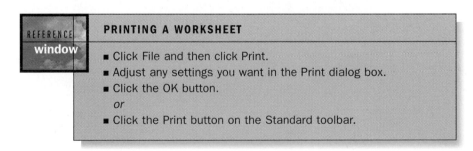

REFERENCE
window

PRINTING A WORKSHEET

- Click File and then click Print.
- Adjust any settings you want in the Print dialog box.
- Click the OK button.
  or
- Click the Print button on the Standard toolbar.

Mike wants a printout of the entire Site Selection worksheet. You decide to select the Print command from the File menu instead of using the Print button so you can check the Print dialog box settings.

To check the print settings and then print the worksheet:

1. Make sure your printer is turned on and contains paper.

2. Click **File** on the menu bar, and then click **Print** to display the Print dialog box. See Figure 1-28.

Figure 1-28 ◀
Print dialog box

identifies printer (your entry may be different)

prints selected range in worksheet

prints active sheet

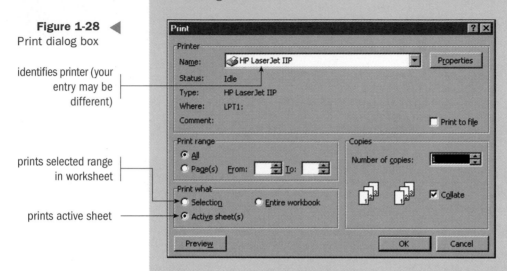

Now you need to select what to print. You could print the complete workbook, which would be the Title Sheet and the Site Selection sheet. To do this, you would click the Entire workbook option button. You could also choose to print just a portion of a worksheet. For example, to print only the weighted scores data of the Site Selection worksheet, first select this range with your mouse pointer, and then select the Selection option button in the Print dialog box. In this case, Mike needs just the Site Selection worksheet.

3. If necessary, click the **Active sheet(s)** option button in the Print what section of the dialog box to print just the Site Selection worksheet, and not the Title Sheet.

4. Make sure "1" appears in the Number of copies text box, as Mike only needs to print one copy of the worksheet.

5. Click the **OK** button to print the worksheet. See Figure 1-29.

TROUBLE? If the worksheet does not print, see your technical support person for help.

Figure 1-29 ◀
Printed
worksheet

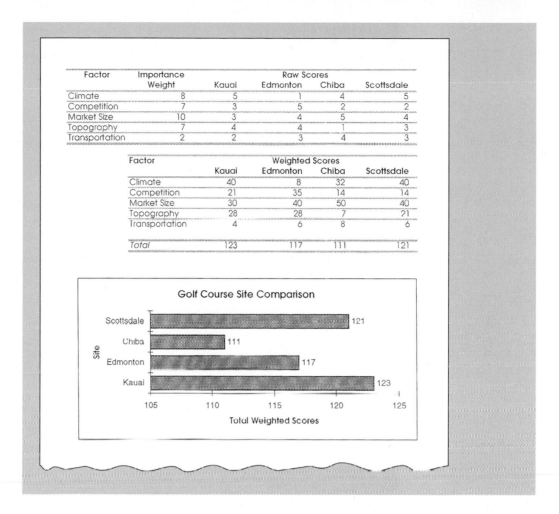

Factor	Importance Weight	Raw Scores			
		Kauai	Edmonton	Chiba	Scottsdale
Climate	8	5	1	4	5
Competition	7	3	5	2	2
Market Size	10	3	4	5	4
Topography	7	4	4	1	3
Transportation	2	2	3	4	3

Factor	Weighted Scores			
	Kauai	Edmonton	Chiba	Scottsdale
Climate	40	8	32	40
Competition	21	35	14	14
Market Size	30	40	50	40
Topography	28	28	7	21
Transportation	4	6	8	6
Total	123	117	111	121

Golf Course Site Comparison

Site
Scottsdale 121
Chiba 111
Edmonton 117
Kauai 123

105   110   115   120   125
Total Weighted Scores

Mike volunteers to put together the report with the team's final recommendation, and the meeting adjourns. You and Mike are finished working with the worksheet and are ready to close the workbook.

Closing the Workbook

Closing a workbook removes it from the screen. If a workbook contains changes that have not been saved, Excel asks if you want to save your modified worksheet before closing the workbook. You can now close the workbook.

To close the Inwood 2 workbook:

1. Click **File** on the menu bar, and then click **Close**. A dialog box displays the message "Do you want to save the changes you made to 'INWOOD 2'?"

2. Click the **Yes** button to save the Inwood 2 workbook before closing it.

The Excel window stays open so you can open or create another workbook. You do not want to, so your next step is to exit Excel.

Exiting Excel

To exit Excel, you can click the Close button on the title bar, or you can use the Exit command on the File menu.

To exit Excel:

1. Click the Close button ☒ on the title bar. Excel closes and you return to the Windows desktop.

Quick Check

1. The formula =SUM(D1:K1) adds how many cells? Write an equivalent formula without using the SUM function.
2. What cells are included in the range B4:D6?
3. Indicate whether Excel treats the following cell entries as a value, text, or a formula:
   a. Profit
   b. 11/09/95
   c. 123
   d. =B9*225
   e. 1-800-227-1240
   f. =SUM(C1:C10)
   g. 123 N. First St.
4. To print the entire worksheet, you select the _____ option button from the _____ dialog box.
5. To print a copy of your worksheet, you use the _____ command on the _____ menu.
6. You can get Excel Help in any of the following ways except:
   a. clicking Help on the menu bar
   b. clicking the Help button on the Standard toolbar
   c. closing the program window
   d. pressing the F1 key
7. Why do you need to save a worksheet? What command do you use to save the worksheet?
8. What key do you press to clear the contents of a cell from a worksheet?
9. Explain the term *what-if analysis*.

The Inwood site selection team has completed its work. Mike's worksheet helped the team analyze the data and recommend Kauai as the best site for Inwood's next golf course. Although the Japanese market was a strong factor in favor of locating the course in Japan's Chiba Prefecture, the mountainous terrain and competition from nearby courses reduced the site's desirability.

Tutorial Assignments

The other company that had planned a golf course in Chiba, Japan, has run into financial difficulties. Rumors are that the project may be canceled. A copy of the final Inwood Design team workbook is on your Student Disk. Do the Tutorial Assignments to change this worksheet to show the effect of the other project's cancellation on your site selection.

1. If necessary, start Excel and make sure your Student Disk is in the appropriate disk drive.
   Open the Inwood 3 file in the TAssign folder for Tutorial 1 on your Student Disk.
2. Use the Save As command to save the workbook as Inwood4 in the TAssign folder for Tutorial 1. That way you won't change the original workbook.
3. In the Inwood4 worksheet, change the competition raw score for Chiba from 2 to 3. What site is ranked first?

4. The label "Transportation" in cell A9 was entered incorrectly as "Transportion." Use Edit mode to insert "ta" into the label.

5. Save the worksheet.

6. Print the worksheet.

7. Use the Contents and Index command on the Help menu to access the Help Topics dialog box. From the Contents tab, learn how to insert an additional worksheet into your workbook. (*Hint*: Choose Working with workbook and worksheets topic, then managing worksheets.) Write the steps to insert a worksheet.

8. Use the Office Assistant to learn how to delete a sheet from a workbook. Write the steps to delete a sheet.

9. Enter the text "Scores if the competing project in Chiba, Japan, is canceled" in cell A1.

10. Remove the raw scores for Chiba, cells E5 through E9. Print the worksheet.

11. Use the Index command on the Help menu to learn about the AutoCalculate feature. Write a brief explanation of this feature.

12. You are considering dropping transportation as a factor in the site selection decision. Use AutoCalculate to arrive at a revised total weighted score for each of the three remaining sites. Write the response.

13. Print the worksheet data without the chart. (*Hint*: Select the worksheet data before checking out the options in the Print dialog box.)

14. Use the What's This button ⓐ. Learn more about the following Excel window components:
    a. Name box
    b. Sheet tabs
    c. Tip Wizard
    (*Hint*: Click ⓐ, then click each item with the Help pointer.)

15. Close the workbook and exit Excel without saving the changes.

Case Problems

1. Market Share Analysis at Aldon Industries Helen Shalala is assistant to the regional director for Aldon Industries, a manufacturer of corporate voice mail systems. Helen has analyzed the market share of the top vendors with installations in the region. She's on her way to a meeting with the marketing staff where she will use her worksheet to plan a new marketing campaign. Help Helen and her team evaluate the options and plan the best advertising campaign for Aldon Industries. Write your responses to questions 4 through 10.

1. If necessary, start Excel and make sure your Student Disk is in the appropriate disk drive.

2. Open the workbook Aldon in the Case folder for Tutorial 1.

3. Use the Save As command to save the workbook as Aldon 2 in the Case folder for Tutorial 1. That way you won't change the original workbook for this case.

4. Take a moment to look over the Market Share worksheet. Do the following ranges contain text, values, or formulas?
   a. B13:G13
   b. C3:C10
   c. A3:A10
   d. G3:G10

5. What is Aldon Industries' overall market share?

6. Examine the worksheet to determine in which state Aldon Industries has the highest market share.

7. Which company leads the overall market?

8. What is Aldon Industries' overall ranking in total market share (1st, 2nd, 3rd, etc.)?

9. Which companies rank ahead of Aldon Industries in total market share?

10. What formula was used to calculate Total Installations in Illinois? Develop an alternative formula to calculate Total Installations in Illinois without using the SUM function.

11. Save and print the worksheet.

2. Selecting a Hospital Laboratory Computer System for Bridgeport Medical Center David Choi is on the Laboratory Computer Selection Committee for the Bridgeport Medical Center. After an extensive search, the committee has identified three vendors whose products appear to meet its needs. The Selection Committee has prepared an Excel worksheet to help evaluate the three potential vendors' strengths and weaknesses. The raw scores for two of the vendors, LabStar and Health Systems, have already been entered. Now raw scores must be entered for the third vendor, MedTech. Which vendor's system is best for the Bridgeport Medical Center? Complete these steps to find out:

1. If necessary, start Excel and make sure your Student Disk is in the appropriate disk drive.

2. Open the workbook Medical in the Case folder for Tutorial 1.

3. Use the Save As command to save the workbook as Medical 2 in the Case folder for Tutorial 1. That way you won't change the original workbook for this case.

4. Examine the Evaluation Scores worksheet, and type the following raw scores for MedTech: Cost = 6, Compatibility = 5, Vendor Reliability = 5, Size of Installed Base = 4, User Satisfaction = 5, Critical Functionality = 9, Additional Functionality = 8.

5. Use the Save command to save the modified worksheet.

6. Print the worksheet.

7. Based on the data in the worksheet, which vendor would you recommend? Why?

8. Assume you can adjust the value for only one importance weight (cells B6 through B12). Which factor would you change and what would its new weight be in order for LabStar to have the highest weighted score? (*Hint*: Remember that the value assigned to any importance weight cannot be higher then 10.)

9. Save and print the modified worksheet.

3. Enrollments in the College of Business You work 10 hours a week in the Dean's office at your college. The Assistant Dean has a number of meetings today and has asked you to complete a worksheet she needs for a meeting with Department Chairs this afternoon.

1. Open the workbook Enroll in the Case folder for Tutorial 1 on your Student Disk.

2. Use the Save As command to save the workbook as Enrollment.

3. Complete the workbook by performing the following tasks:

a. Enter the title "Enrollment Data for College of Business" in cell A1.

b. Enter the label "Total" in cell A8.

c. Calculate the total enrollment in the College of Business for 1999 in cell B8.

d. Calculate the total enrollment in the College of Business for 1998 in cell C8.

e. Calculate the change in enrollments from 1998 to 1999. Place the results in column D. Label the column heading "Change" and use the following formula:
Change = 1999 enrollment – 1998 enrollment

4. Save the workbook.

5. Print the worksheet.

4. Krier Marine Services Vince DiOrio is an Information Systems major at a local college. To help pay for tuition, he works part-time three days a week at a nearby marina, Krier Marine Services. Vince works in the business office, and his responsibilities range from making coffee to keeping the company's books.

Recently, Jim Krier, the owner of the marina, asked Vince if he could help computerize the payroll for their part-time employees. He explained that the employees work a different number of hours each week for different rates of pay. Jim does the payroll manually now and finds it time-consuming. Moreover, whenever he makes an error, he is embarrassed and annoyed at having to take the additional time to correct it. Jim was hoping Vince could help him.

Vince immediately agrees to help. He tells Jim that he knows how to use Excel and that he can build a spreadsheet that will save him time and reduce errors. Jim and Vince meet. They review the present payroll process and discuss the desired outcomes of the payroll spreadsheet. Figure 1-30 is a sketch of the output Jim wants to get.

Figure 1-30 ◀
Sketch of
worksheet

Krier Marine Services Weekly Payroll
Week Ending 10/15

Employee	Hours	Pay Rate	Gross Pay
Bramble	15	7	formula
Juarez	28	5	"
Smith	30	7	"
DiOrio	22	6	"
Total			formula

1. Open the workbook Payroll in the Cases folder for Tutorial 1 on your Student Disk.
2. Use the Save As command to save the workbook as Payroll 2.
3. Complete the worksheet by performing the following tasks:
   a. Enter the employee hours in column B.
   b. Enter the employee pay rate in column C.
   c. In column D, enter the formulas to compute gross pay for each employee (*Hint:* Use Hours times Pay Rate.)
   d. In cell D9, enter the SUM function to calculate total gross pay.
4. Save the workbook.
5. Print the worksheet.
6. Remove the hours for the four employees.
7. Enter the following hours: 18 for Bramble, 25 for Juarez, 35 for Smith, and 20 for DiOrio.
8. Print the new worksheet.

Lab Assignments

Spreadsheets

These Lab Assignments are designed to accompany the interactive Course Lab called Spreadsheets. To start the Spreadsheets Lab, click the Start button on the Windows 95 taskbar, point to Programs, point to Course Labs, point to New Perspectives Applications, and click Spreadsheets. If you do not see Course Labs on your Programs menu, see your instructor or technical support person.

Spreadsheets Spreadsheet software is used extensively in business, education, science, and the humanities to simplify tasks that involve calculations. In this Lab you will learn how spreadsheet software works. You will use spreadsheet software to examine and modify worksheets, as well as to create your own worksheets.

1. Click the Steps button to learn how spreadsheet software works. As you proceed through the Steps, answer all of the Quick Check questions that appear. After you complete the Steps, you will see a Quick Check Summary report. Follow the instructions on the screen to print this report.
2. Click the Explore button. Click OK to display a new worksheet. Click File, and then click Open to display the Open dialog box. Click the file Income, then press the Enter key to open the Income and Expense Summary worksheet. Notice that the worksheet contains labels and values for income from consulting and training. It also contains labels and values for expenses such as rent

and salaries. The worksheet does not, however, contain formulas to calculate Total Income, Total Expenses, or Profit. Do the following:

a. Calculate the Total Income by entering the formula =SUM(C4:C5) in cell C6.

b. Calculate the Total Expenses by entering the formula =SUM(C9:C12) in cell C13.

c. Calculate Profit by entering the formula =C6-C13 in cell C15.

d. Manually check the results to make sure you entered the formulas correctly.

e. Print your completed worksheet that shows your results.

3. You can use a spreadsheet to keep track of your grade in a class. Click the Explore button to display a blank worksheet. Click File and then click Open to display the Open dialog box. Click the file Grades to open the Grades worksheet. This worksheet contains all the labels and formulas necessary to calculate your grade based on four test scores.

Suppose you receive a score of 88 out of 100 on the first test. On the second test, you score 42 out of 48. On the third test, you score 92 out of 100. You have not taken the fourth test yet. Enter the appropriate data on the Grade worksheet to determine your grade after taking three tests. Print out your worksheet.

4. Worksheets are handy for answering "what if" questions. For example, suppose you decide to open a lemonade stand. You're interested in how much profit you can make each day. What if you sell 20 cups of lemonade? What if you sell 100? What if the cost of lemons increases?

In Explore, open the file Lemons and use the worksheet to answer questions a through d, then print the worksheet for item e:

a. What is your profit if you sell 20 cups a day?

b. What is your profit if you sell 100 cups a day?

c. What is your profit if the price of lemons increases to $.07 and you sell 100 cups?

d. What is your profit if you raise the price of a cup of lemonade to $.30? (Lemons still cost $.07 and you assume you will sell 100 cups.)

e. Suppose your competitor boasts that she sold 50 cups of lemonade in one day and made exactly $12.00. On your worksheet, adjust the cost of cups, water, lemons, and sugar, and the price per cup to show a profit of exactly $12.00 for 50 cups sold. Print this worksheet.

5. It is important to make sure the formulas in your worksheet are accurate. An easy way to test this is to enter 1s for all the values on your worksheet, and then check the calculations manually. In Explore, open the worksheet Receipt, which calculates sales receipts. Enter 1 as the value for Item 1, Item 2, and Item 3. Enter .01 for the Sales Tax rate. Now, manually calculate what you would pay for three items that cost $1.00 each in a state where sales tax is 1% (.01). Do your manual calculations match those of the worksheet? If not, correct the formulas in the worksheet and print out a formula report of your revised worksheet.

6. In Explore, create your own worksheet showing your household budget for one month. Make sure you put a title on the worksheet. Use formulas to calculate your total income and your total expenses for the month. Add another formula to calculate how much money you were able to save. Print a formula report of your worksheet. Also, print your worksheet, showing realistic values for one month.

Creating a Worksheet

Producing a Sales Comparison Report for MSI

OBJECTIVES

In this tutorial you will:

- Plan, build, test, document, preview, and print a worksheet

- Enter labels, values, and formulas

- Calculate a total using the AutoSum button

- Copy formulas using the fill handle and Clipboard

- Learn about relative, absolute, and mixed references

- Use the AVERAGE, MAX, and MIN functions to calculate values in the worksheet

- Spell check the worksheet

- Insert a row

- Reverse an action using the Undo button

- Move a range of cells

- Format the worksheet using AutoFormat

- Center printouts on a page

- Customize worksheet headers

Motorcycle Specialties Incorporated

CASE Motorcycle Specialties Incorporated (MSI), a motorcycle helmet and accessories company, provides a wide range of specialty items to motorcycle enthusiasts throughout the world. MSI has its headquarters in Atlanta, Georgia, but it markets its products in North America, South America, Australia, and Europe.

The company's Marketing and Sales Director, Sally Caneval, meets regularly with the regional sales managers who oversee global sales in each of the four regions in which MSI does business. This month, Sally intends to review overall sales in each region for the last two fiscal years and present her findings at her next meeting with the regional sales managers. She has asked you to help her put together a report that summarizes this sales information.

Specifically, Sally wants the report to show total sales for each region of the world for the two most recent fiscal years. Additionally, she wants to see the percentage change between the two years. She also wants the report to include the percentage each region contributed to the total sales of the company in 1999. Finally, she wants to include summary statistics on the average, maximum, and minimum sales for 1999.

SESSION

2.1

In this session you will learn how to plan and build a worksheet; enter labels, numbers, and formulas; and copy formulas to other cells.

Developing Worksheets

Effective worksheets are well planned and carefully designed. A well-designed worksheet should clearly identify its overall goal. It should present information in a clear, well-organized format, and include all the data necessary to produce the results that address the goal of the application.

Further, the process of developing a good worksheet includes the following planning and execution steps:

- Determine the worksheet's purpose, what it will include, and how it will be organized

- Enter the data and formulas into the worksheet

- Test the worksheet

- Edit the worksheet to correct any errors or make modifications

- Document the worksheet

- Improve the appearance of the worksheet

- Save and print the completed worksheet

Planning the Worksheet

Sally begins developing a worksheet that compares global sales by region over two years by first creating a planning analysis sheet. Her **planning analysis sheet** helps her answer the following questions:

1. What is the goal of the worksheet? This helps to define the problem to solve.

2. What are the desired results? This information describes the **output**—the information required to help solve the problem.

3. What data is needed to calculate the results you want to see? This information is the **input**—data that must be entered.

4. What calculations are needed to produce the desired output? These calculations specify the formulas used in the worksheet.

Sally's completed planning analysis sheet is shown in Figure 2-1.

Excel

Figure 2-1 ◀
Planning
analysis sheet

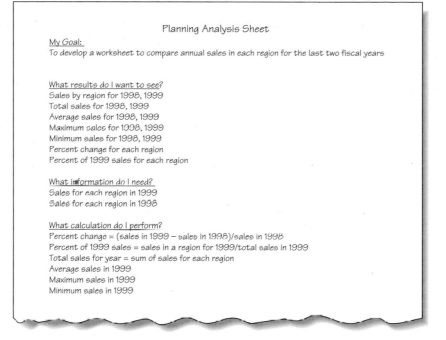

Planning Analysis Sheet

My Goal:
To develop a worksheet to compare annual sales in each region for the last two fiscal years

What results do I want to see?
Sales by region for 1998, 1999
Total sales for 1998, 1999
Average sales for 1998, 1999
Maximum sales for 1998, 1999
Minimum sales for 1998, 1999
Percent change for each region
Percent of 1999 sales for each region

What information do I need?
Sales for each region in 1999
Sales for each region in 1998

What calculation do I perform?
Percent change = (sales in 1999 – sales in 1998)/sales in 1998
Percent of 1999 sales = sales in a region for 1999/total sales in 1999
Total sales for year = sum of sales for each region
Average sales in 1999
Maximum sales in 1999
Minimum sales in 1999

Next, Sally makes a rough sketch of her design, including titles, column headings, row labels, and where data values and totals should be placed. Figure 2-2 shows Sally's sketch. With these two planning tools, Sally is now ready to enter the data into Excel and build the worksheet.

Figure 2-2 ◀
Sketch of
worksheet

Motorcycle Specialties Incorporated
Sales Comparison 1999 with 1998

Region	Year 1999	Year 1998	% Change	% of 1999 Sales
North America	365000	314330	0.16	0.28
South America	354250	292120	0.21	0.28
Australia	251140	262000	-0.04	0.19
Europe	310440	279996	0.11	0.24
Total	1280830	1148446	0.12	

Average	320207.5
Maximum	365000
Minimum	251140

Building the Worksheet

You will use Sally's planning analysis sheet, Figure 2-1, and the rough sketch shown in Figure 2-2 to guide you in preparing the sales comparison worksheet. You will begin by establishing the layout of the worksheet by entering titles and column headings. Next you will work on inputting the data and formulas that will calculate the results Sally needs.

To start Excel and organize your desktop:

1. Start Excel as usual.

2. Make sure your Student Disk is in the appropriate disk drive.

3. Make sure the Microsoft Excel and Book1 windows are maximized.

Entering Labels

When you build a worksheet, it's a good practice to enter the labels before entering any other data. These labels will help you identify the cells where you will enter data and formulas in your worksheet. As you type a label in a cell, Excel aligns the label at the left side of the cell. Labels that are too long to fit in a cell spill over into the cell or cells to the right, if those cells are empty. If the cells to the right are not empty, Excel displays only as much of the label as fits in the cell. Begin creating the sales comparison worksheet for Sally by entering the two-line title.

To enter the worksheet title:

1. If necessary, click cell **A1** to make it the active cell.

2. Type **Motorcycle Specialties Incorporated** and press the **Enter** key. Since cell A1 is empty, the title appears in cell A1 and spills over into cells B1, C1, and D1. Cell A2 is now the active cell.

   TROUBLE? If you make a mistake while typing, remember that you can correct errors with the Backspace key. If you notice the error only after you have pressed the Enter key, then double-click the cell to activate Edit mode, and use the edit keys on your keyboard to correct the error.

3. In cell A2 type **Sales Comparison 1999 with 1998** and press the **Enter** key.

Next, you will enter the column headings defined on the worksheet sketch in Figure 2-2.

To enter labels for the column headings:

1. If necessary, click cell **A3** to make it the active cell.

2. Type **Region** and press the → key to complete the entry. Cell B3 is the active cell.

3. In cell **B3** type **Year 1999** and press the → key.

   Sally's sketch shows that three more column heads are needed for the worksheet. Enter those next.

4. Enter the remaining column heads as follows:
   Cell C3: **Year 1998**
   Cell D3: **% Change**
   Cell E3: **% of 1999 Sales**
   See Figure 2-3.

   TROUBLE? If any cell does not contain the correct label, either edit the cell or retype the entry.

Figure 2-3
Worksheet
after titles and
column
headings
entered

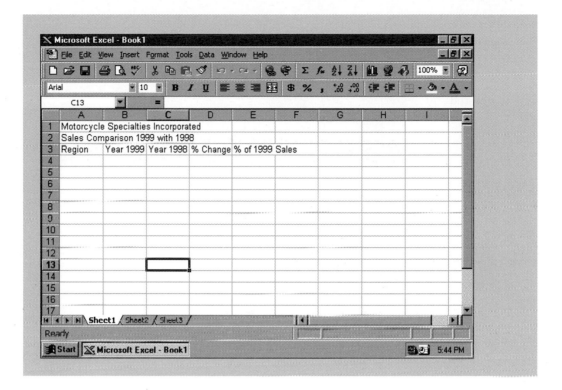

Recall that MSI conducts business in four different regions of the world, and the spreadsheet needs to track the sales information for each region. So Sally wants labels reflecting the regions entered into the worksheet. Enter these labels next.

To enter the regions:

1. Click cell **A4**, type **North America,** and press the **Enter** key.

2. In cell A5 type **South America,** and press the **Enter** key.

3. Type **Australia** in cell A6, and **Europe** in cell A7.

The last set of labels to be entered identify the summary information that will be included in the report.

To enter the summary labels:

1. In cell A8 type **Total** and press the **Enter** key.

2. Type the following labels into the specified cells:
   Cell A9: **Average**
   Cell A10: **Maximum**
   Cell A11: **Minimum**
   See Figure 2-4.

Figure 2-4 ◄
Worksheet
after all labels
have been
entered

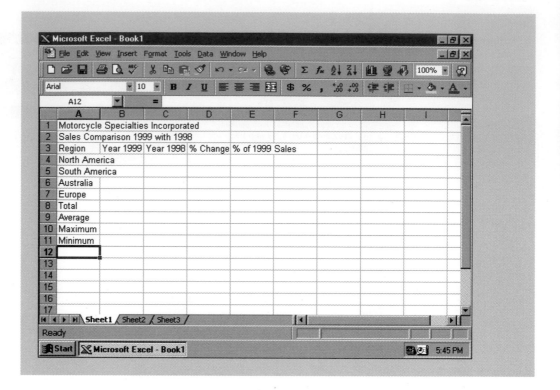

The labels that you just entered into the worksheet will help to identify where the data and formulas need to be placed.

Entering Data

Recall that values can be numbers, formulas, or functions. The next step in building the worksheet is to enter the data, which in this case is the numbers representing sales in each region during 1998 and 1999.

To enter the sales values for 1998 and 1999:

1. Click cell **B4** to make it the active cell. Type **365000** and press the **Enter** key. See Figure 2-5. Notice that the region name, North America, is no longer completely displayed in cell A4 because cell B4 is no longer empty. Later in the tutorial you will learn how to increase the width of a column in order to display the complete contents of cells.

Figure 2-5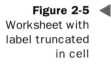
Worksheet with
label truncated
in cell

label truncated ───

label spills over
to cell B5

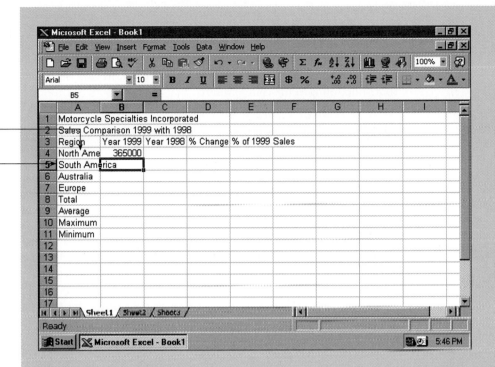

2. In cell B5 type **354250** and press the **Enter** key.

3. Enter the values for cells B6, **251140**, and B7, **310440**.

   Next, type the values for sales during 1998.

4. Click cell **C4**, type **314330**, and press the **Enter** key.

5. Enter the remaining values in the specified cells as follows:
   Cell C5: **292120**
   Cell C6: **262000**
   Cell C7: **279996**
   Your screen should now look like Figure 2-6.

Figure 2-6 ◀
Worksheet
after sales for
1998 and 1999
entered

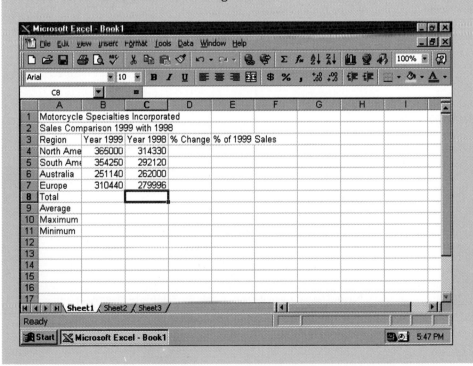

Now that you have entered the labels and data, you need to enter the formulas that will calculate the data to produce the output, or the results. The first calculation Sally wants to see is the total sales for each year. To determine total sales for 1999, you would simply sum the sales from each region for that year. In the previous tutorial you used the SUM function to calculate the weighted total score for the Scottsdale golf site by typing that function into the cell. Similarly, you can use the SUM function to calculate total sales for each year for MSI's comparison report.

Using the AutoSum Button

Since the SUM function is used more often than any other function, Excel includes the AutoSum button on the Standard toolbar. This button automatically creates a formula that contains the SUM function. To do this, Excel looks at the cells adjacent to the active cell, makes an assumption as to which cells you want to sum, and displays a formula based on its best determination about the range you want to sum. You can press the Enter key to accept the formula, or you can select a different range of cells to change the range in the formula. You will use the AutoSum button to calculate the total sales for each year.

To calculate total sales in 1999 using the AutoSum button:

1. Click cell **B8** because this is where you want to display the total sales for 1999.

2. Click the **AutoSum** button Σ on the Standard toolbar. Excel enters a SUM function in the selected cell and determines that the range of cells to sum is B4:B7, the range directly above the selected cell. See Figure 2-7. In this case, that's exactly what you want to do.

Figure 2-7 ◄
Using the
AutoSum tool

outline of cells
to be summed

range of cells
to be summed

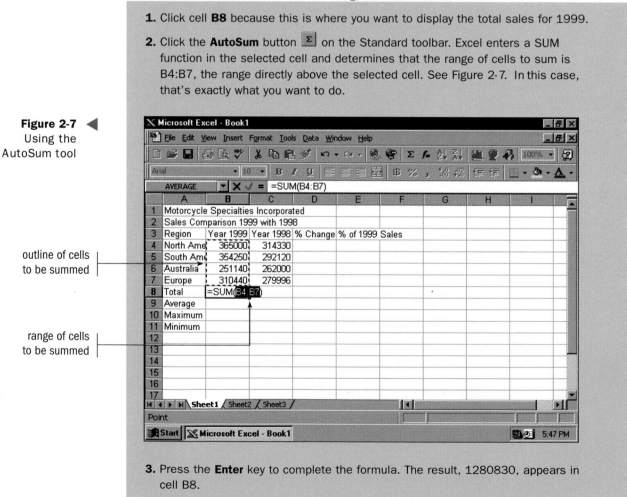

3. Press the **Enter** key to complete the formula. The result, 1280830, appears in cell B8.

Now use the same approach to calculate the total sales for 1998.

To calculate total sales in 1998 using the AutoSum button:

1. Click cell **C8** to make it the active cell.

2. Click the **AutoSum** button Σ on the Standard toolbar.

3. Press the **Enter** key to complete the formula. The result, 1148446, appears in cell C8.

Next, you need to enter the formula to calculate the percent change in sales for North America between 1999 and 1998.

Entering Formulas

Recall that a formula is an equation that performs calculations in a cell. By entering an equal sign (=) as the first entry in the cell, you are telling Excel that the numbers or symbols that follow constitute a formula, not just data. Reviewing Sally's worksheet plan, you note that you need to calculate the percent change in sales in North America. The formula is:

percent change in sales for North America =

(1999 sales in North America - 1998 sales in North America)/1998 sales in North America

So, in looking at the worksheet, the formula in Excel would be:

(B4-C4)/C4

If a formula contains more than one arithmetic operator, Excel performs the calculations in the standard order of precedence of operators shown in Figure 2-8. The **order of precedence** is a set of predefined rules that Excel uses to calculate a formula unambiguously by determining which part of the formula to calculate first, which part second, and so on.

Figure 2-8 ◄
Order of
precedence
operations

Order	Operator	Description
1	^	Exponentiation
2	* or /	Multiplication or division
3	+ or −	Addition or subtraction

Exponentiation has the highest rank, followed by multiplication and division, and finally addition and subtraction. For example, because multiplication has precedence over addition, in the formula =3+4*5 the result of the formula is 23.

When a formula contains more than one operator with the same order of precedence, Excel performs the operation from left to right. Thus, in the formula =4*10/8, Excel multiplies 4 by 10 before dividing the product by 8. The result of the calculation is 5. You can enter parentheses in a formula to make it easier to understand or to change the order of operations. Excel always performs any calculations contained in parentheses first. In the formula =3+4*5, the multiplication is performed before the addition. If instead you wanted the formula to add 3+4 and then multiply the sum by 5, you would enter the formula =(3+4)*5. The result of the calculation is 35.

Now enter the percent change formula as specified in Sally's planning sheet.

To enter the formula for the percent change in sales for North America:

1. Click cell **D4** to make it the active cell.

2. Type **=(B4-C4)/C4** and press the **Enter** key. Excel performs the calculations and displays the value 0.1612 in cell D4. The formula is no longer visible in the cell. If you select the cell, the result of the formula appears in the cell, and the formula you entered appears in the formula bar.

Next, you need to enter the percent change formulas for the other regions, as well as the percent change for the total company sales. You could type the formula =(B5-C5)/C5 in cell D5, the formula =(B6-C6)/C6 in cell D6, the formula =(B7-C7)/C7 in cell D7, and the formula =(B8-C8)/C8 in cell D8. However, this approach is time-consuming and error prone. Instead, you can copy the formula you entered in cell C4 (percent change in North American sales) into cells D5, D6, D7, and D8. **Copying** duplicates the underlying formula in a cell into other cells, automatically adjusting cell references to reflect the new cell address. Copying formulas from one cell to another saves time and reduces the chances of entering incorrect formulas when building worksheets.

Copying a Formula Using the Fill Handle

You can copy formulas using menu commands, toolbar buttons, or the fill handle. The **fill handle** is a small black square located in the lower-right corner of the selected cell, as shown in Figure 2-9. In this section you will use the fill handle to copy the formulas. In other situations you can also use the fill handle for copying values and labels from one cell or a group of cells.

Figure 2-9 ◄
Fill handle

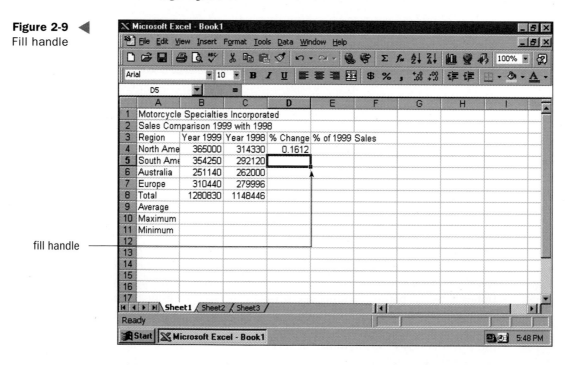

fill handle

REFERENCE window

COPYING CELL CONTENTS WITH THE FILL HANDLE

- Click the cell that contains the label, value, or formula you want to copy. If you want to copy the contents of more than one cell, select the range of cells you want to copy.
- To copy to adjacent cells, click and drag the fill handle to outline the cells where you want the copy or copies to appear, and then release the mouse button.

You want to copy the formula from cell D4 to cells D5, D6, D7, and D8.

To copy the formula from cell D4 to cells D5, D6, D7, and D8:

1. Click cell **D4** to make it the active cell.

2. Position the pointer over the fill handle (in the lower-right corner of cell D4) until the pointer changes to $+$.

3. Click and drag the pointer down the worksheet to outline cells D5 through D8. See Figure 2-10.

Figure 2-10 ◀
Copying a
formula

outline of cells
formula will
be copied to

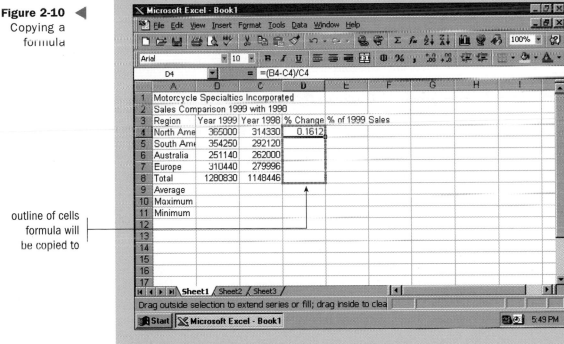

4. Release the mouse button. Excel copies the formula from D4 to cells D5 to D8. Values now appear in cells D5 through D8.

5. Click any cell to deselect the range. See Figure 2-11.

Figure 2-11 ◀
Worksheet
after formula
copied

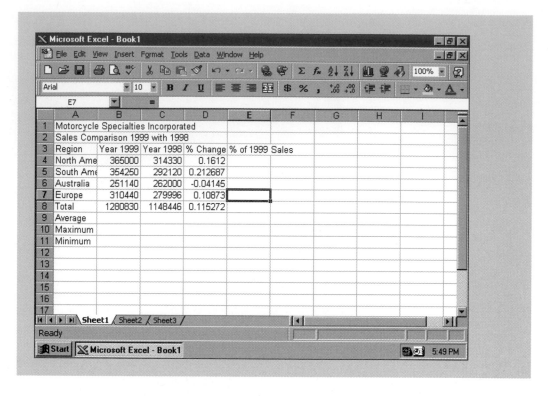

Notice that Excel didn't copy the formula =(B4-C4)/C4 exactly. Rather, it automatically adjusted the cell references for each new formula location. Why did that happen?

Copying a Formula Using Relative References

When you copy a formula that contains cell references, Excel automatically adjusts the cell references for the new locations. For example, when Excel copied the formula from cell D4, =(B4-C4)/C4, it automatically changed the cell references in the formula to reflect the formula's new position in the worksheet. So in cell D5 the cell references adjust to =(B5-C5)/C5. Cell references that change when copied are called **relative cell references**.

Take a moment to look at the formulas in cells D5, D6, D7, and D8.

To examine the formulas in cells D5, D6, D7, and D8:

1. Click cell **D5**. The formula =(B5-C5)/C5 appears in the formula bar.

When Excel copied the formula from cell D4 to cell D5, the cell references changed. The formula =(B4-C4)/C4 became =(B5-C5)/C5 when Excel copied the formula down one row to row 5.

2. Examine the formulas in cells D6, D7, and D8. Notice that the cell references were adjusted for the new locations.

Copying a Formula Using an Absolute Reference

According to Sally's plan, in the worksheet you need to display the percent that each region contributed to the total sales in 1999. For example, if the company's total sales were $100,000 and sales in North America were $25,000, then sales in North America would be 25% of total sales. To complete this calculation for each region you need to divide each region's sales by the total company sales, as shown in the following formulas:

Contribution by North America	=B4/B8
Contribution by South America	=B5/B8
Contribution by Australia	=B6/B8
Contribution by Europe	=B7/B8

First, enter the formula to calculate the percent North America contributed to total sales.

To calculate North America's percent of total 1999 sales:

1. Click cell **E4** to make it the active cell.

2. Type =**B4/B8** and press the **Enter** key to display the value .284971 in cell E4.

Cell E4 displays the correct result. Sales in North America for 1999 were 365,000, which is approximately .28 of the 1,280,830 in total sales in 1999. Next, you decide to copy the formula in cell E4 to cells E5, E6, and E7.

To copy the percent formula in cell E4 to cells E5 through E7:

1. Click cell **E4**, and then move the pointer over the fill handle in cell E4 until it changes to +.

2. Click and drag the pointer to cell E7 and release the mouse button.

3. Click any blank cell to deselect the range. The message "#DIV/0!" appears in cells E5 through E7. See Figure 2-12.

Figure 2-12 ◀
Error message displayed in worksheet after copying formula

error message ——

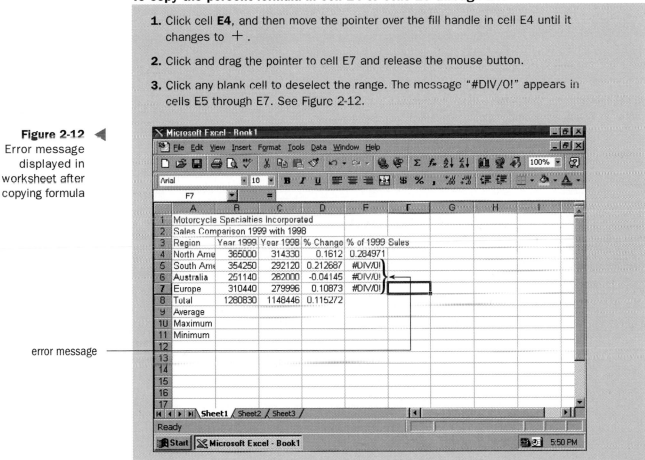

Something is wrong. Cells E5 through E7 display "#DIV/0!," a message that means that Excel was instructed to divide by zero. Take a moment to look at the formulas you copied into cells E5, E6, and E7.

To examine the formulas in cells E5 through E7:

1. Click cell **E5** and look at the formula displayed in the formula bar, =B5/B9. The first cell reference changed from B4 in the original formula to B5 in the copied formula. That's correct because the sales data for South America is entered in cell B5. The second cell reference changed from B8, in the original formula to B9, which is not correct. The correct formula should be =B5/B8 because the total sales are in cell B8, not cell B9.

2. Look at the formulas in cells E6 and E7 and see how the cell references changed in each formula.

As you observed, the cell reference to total company sales (B8) in the original formula was changed to B9, B10, and B11 in the copied formulas. The problem with the copied formulas is that Excel adjusted *all* the cell references relative to their new location.

Absolute Versus Relative References

Sometimes when you copy a formula, you don't want Excel to change all cell references automatically to reflect their new positions in the worksheet. If you want a cell reference to point to the same location in the worksheet when you copy it, you must use an absolute reference. An **absolute reference** is a cell reference in a formula that does not change when copied to another cell.

To create an absolute reference, you insert a dollar sign ($) before the column and row of the cell reference. For example, the cell reference $B$8 is an absolute reference, whereas the cell reference B8 is a relative reference. If you copy a formula that contains the absolute reference $B$8 to another cell, the cell reference to $B$8 does not change. On the other hand, if you copy a formula containing the relative reference B8 to another cell, the reference to B8 changes. In some situations, a cell might have a **mixed reference**, such as $B8; in this case, when the formula is copied, the row number changes but the column letter does not.

To include an absolute reference in a formula, you can type a dollar sign when you type the cell reference, or you can use the F4 key to change the cell reference type while in Edit mode.

REFERENCE window	**EDITING CELL REFERENCE TYPES**
	■ Double-click the cell that contains the formula you want to edit.
	■ Use the arrow keys to move the insertion point to the part of the cell reference you want to change.
	■ Press the F4 key until the reference is correct.
	■ Press the Enter key to complete the edit.

To correct the problem in your worksheet, you need to use an absolute reference, instead of a relative reference, to indicate the location of total sales in 1999. That is, you need to change the formula from =B4/B8 to =B4/$B$8. The easiest way to make this change is in Edit mode.

To change a cell reference to an absolute reference:

1. Click cell **E4** to move to the cell that contains the formula you want to edit.

2. Double-click the mouse button to edit the formula in the cell. Notice that each cell reference in the formula in cell E4 appears in a different color and the corresponding cells referred to in the formula are outlined in the same color. This feature is called Range Finder and is designed to make it easier for you to check the accuracy of your formula.

3. Make sure the insertion point is to the right of the division (/) operator, anywhere in the cell reference B8.

4. Press the **F4** key to change the reference to $B$8.

> **TROUBLE?** If your reference shows the **mixed reference** B$8 or $B8, continue to press the F4 key until you see $B$8.

5. Press the **Enter** key to update the formula in cell E4.

Cell E4 still displays .284971, which is the formula's correct result. But remember, the problem in your original formula did not surface until you copied it to cells E5 through E7. To correct the error, you need to copy the revised formula and then check the results. Although you can again use the fill handle to copy the formula, you can also copy the formula using the Clipboard and the Copy and Paste buttons on the Standard toolbar.

Copying Cell Contents Using the Copy and Paste Method

You can duplicate the contents of a cell or range by making a copy of the cell or range and then pasting the copy into one or more locations in the same worksheet, another worksheet, or another workbook.

When you copy a cell or range of cells, the copied material is placed on the Clipboard. You can copy labels, numbers, dates, or formulas.

REFERENCE window	**COPYING AND PASTING A CELL OR RANGE OF CELLS**
	■ Select the cell or range of cells to be copied. ■ Click the Copy button on the Standard toolbar. ■ Select the range into which you want to copy the formula. ■ Click the Paste button on the Standard toolbar. ■ Press the Enter key.

You need to copy the formula in cell E4 to the Clipboard and then paste that formula into cells E5 through E7.

To copy the revised formula from cell E4 to cells E5 through E7:

1. Click cell **E4** because it contains the revised formula that you want to copy.

2. Click the **Copy** button on the Standard toolbar. A moving dashed line surrounds cell E4, indicating that the formula has been copied and is available to be pasted into other cells.

3. Click and drag to select cells **E5** through **E7**.

4. Click the **Paste** button ⬚ on the Standard toolbar. Excel adjusts the formula and pastes it into cells E5 through E7.

5. Click any cell to deselect the range and view the formulas' results. Press the **Escape** key to clear the Clipboard and remove the dashed line surrounding cell E4. See Figure 2-13.

Figure 2-13 ◄
Results of
copying the
formula with
an absolute
reference

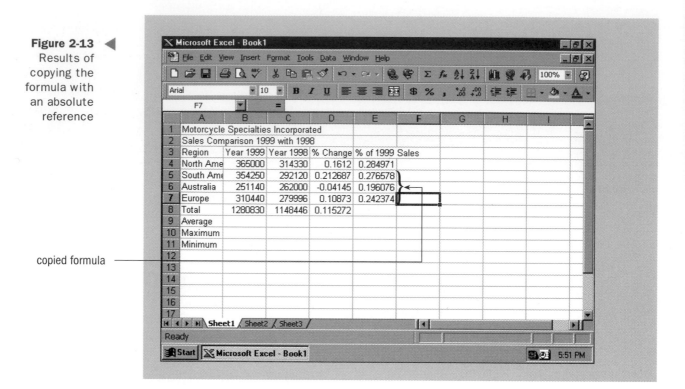

copied formula ——————

Copying this formula worked. When you pasted the formula from cell E4 into the range E5:E7, Excel automatically adjusted the relative reference (B4), while using the cell reference ($B$8) for all absolute references. You have now implemented most of the design as specified in the planning analysis sheet. Now rename the worksheet to accurately describe its contents, then save the workbook to your Student Disk before entering the formulas to compute the summary statistics.

Renaming the Worksheet

Before saving the workbook, look at the sheet tab in the lower-left corner of the worksheet window: the sheet is currently named Sheet1—the name Excel automatically uses when it opens a new workbook. Now that your worksheet is taking shape, you want to give it a more descriptive name that better indicates its contents. Change the worksheet name to Sales Comparison.

To change a worksheet name:

1. Double-click the **Sheet1** sheet tab to select it.

2. Type the new name, **Sales Comparison**, over the current name, Sheet1. Click any cell in the worksheet. The sheet tab displays the name "Sales Comparison."

Saving the New Workbook

Now you want to save the workbook. Because this is the first time you have saved this workbook, you will use the Save As command and name the file MSI Sales Report.

To save the workbook as MSI Sales Report:

1. Click **File** on the menu bar, and then click **Save As** to display the Save As dialog box.

2. In the File name text box, type **MSI Sales Report** but don't press the Enter key yet. You still need to check some other settings.

3. Click the **Save in** list arrow, and then click the drive containing your Student Disk.

4. In the folder list, double-click the **Tutorial.02** folder to select the folder into which you want to save the workbook. Your Save As dialog box should look like the dialog box in Figure 2-14.

Figure 2-14 ◀
Saving the
worksheet as
MSI Sales
Report

enter name of
worksheet here

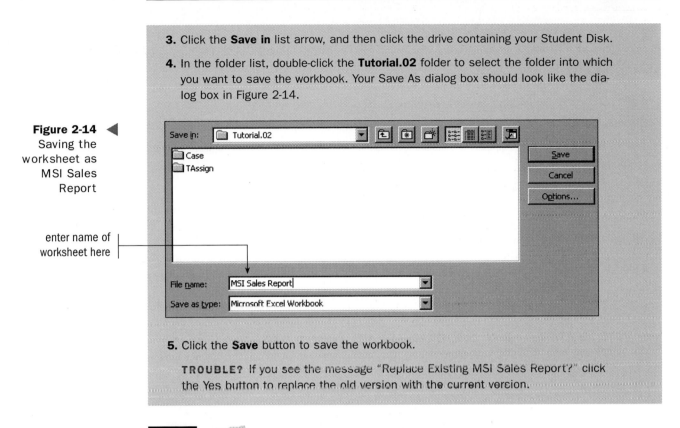

5. Click the **Save** button to save the workbook.

TROUBLE? If you see the message "Replace Existing MSI Sales Report?" click the Yes button to replace the old version with the current version.

Quick Check

1. Describe how AutoSum works.

2. In cell C5 you have the formula =A5+B5. After you copy this formula to cell C6, the formula in cell C6 would appear in the formula bar as _____.

3. In the formula =A5+B5, A5 and B5 are examples of _____ references.

4. In the formula =A8+(1+$C$1), $C$1 is an example of a(n) _____.

5. When you copy a formula using the Copy ▣ and Paste ▣ buttons on the Standard toolbar, Excel uses the _____ to temporarily store the formula.

6. The _____ is a small black square located in the lower-right corner of a selected cell.

7. Describe the steps you take to change the name of the sheet tab.

8. List the steps to follow to create a worksheet.

Now that you have planned and built the Sales Comparison worksheet by entering labels, values, and formulas, you need to complete the worksheet by entering some functions and format the worksheet. You will do this in Session 2.2.

In this session you will finish the worksheet as you learn how to enter several statistical functions, increase the column width, insert a row between the titles and column headings, move the contents of a range to another location, and apply one of the Excel predefined formats to the report. You will also spell check the worksheet, and preview and print it.

Excel Functions

According to Sally's planning analysis sheet, you still need to enter the formulas for the summary statistics. To enter these statistics you'll use three Excel functions, AVERAGE, MAX, and MIN. The many Excel functions help you enter formulas for calculations and other specialized tasks, even if you don't know the mathematical details of the calculations. As you recall, a function is a calculation tool that performs a predefined operation. You are already familiar with the SUM function, which adds the values in a range of cells. Excel provides hundreds of functions, including a function to calculate the average of a list of numbers, a function to find a number's square root, a function to calculate loan payments, and a function to calculate the number of days between two dates. Figure 2-15 shows how Excel organizes these functions into categories.

Figure 2-15 ◄
Excel function
categories

Function Category	Examples of Functions in This Category
Financial	Calculate loan payments, depreciation, interest rate, internal rate of return
Date & Time	Display today's date and/or time; calculate the number of days between two dates
Math & Trig	Round off numbers; calculate sums, logs, and least common multiple; generate random numbers
Statistical	Calculate average, standard deviation, and frequencies; find minimum, maximum; count how many numbers are in a list
Lookup & Reference	Look for a value in a range of cells; find the row or column location of a reference
Database	Perform crosstabs, averages, counts, and standard deviation for an Excel database
Text	Convert numbers to text; compare two text entries; find the length of a text entry
Logical	Perform conditional calculations
Information	Return information about the formatting, location, or contents of a range

Each function has a **syntax**, which specifies the order in which you must type the parts of the function and where to put commas, parentheses, and other punctuation. The general syntax of an Excel function is:

NAME(*argument1,argument2,...*)

The syntax of most functions requires you to type the function name followed by one or more arguments in parentheses. Function **arguments** specify the values that Excel must use in the calculation, or the cell references that Excel must include in the calculation. For example, in the function SUM(A1:A20) the function name is SUM and the argument is A1:A20, which is the range of cells you want to total.

You can use a function in a simple formula such as =SUM(A1:A20), or a more complex formula such as =SUM(A1:A20)*52. As with all formulas, you enter the formula that contains a function in the cell where you want to display the results. The easiest way to enter a function in a cell is to use the Paste Function button on the Standard toolbar, which leads you step-by-step through the process of entering a formula containing a function.

If you prefer, you can type the function directly into the cell. Although the function name is always shown in uppercase, you can type it in either uppercase or lowercase. Also, even though parentheses enclose the arguments, you need not type the closing parenthesis if the function ends the formula. Excel automatically adds the closing parenthesis when you press the Enter key to complete the formula.

According to Sally's planning analysis sheet, the next step is to calculate the average regional sales for 1999.

AVERAGE Function

AVERAGE is a statistical function that calculates the average, or the arithmetic mean. The syntax for the AVERAGE function is:

AVERAGE(*number1,number2,...*)

Generally, when you use the AVERAGE function, *number* is a range of cells. To calculate the average of a range of cells, Excel sums the values in the range, then divides by the number of non-blank cells in the range.

REFERENCE window

USING THE PASTE FUNCTION BUTTON

- Click the cell where you want to display the results of the function. Then click the Paste Function button on the Standard toolbar to open the Paste Function dialog box.
- Click the type of function you want in the Function category list box.
- Click the function you want in the Function name list box.
- Click the OK button to open a second dialog box.
- Accept the default information or enter the information you want the function to use in its calculations.
- Click the OK button to close the dialog box and display the results of the function in the cell.

Sally wants you to calculate the average sales in 1999. You'll use the Paste Function button to enter the AVERAGE function, which is one of the statistical functions.

To enter the AVERAGE function using the Paste Function button:

1. Click cell **B9** to select the cell where you want to enter the AVERAGE function.

2. Click the **Paste Function** button ![fx] on the Standard toolbar to display the Paste Function dialog box.

   TROUBLE? If the Office Assistant opens and offers help on this feature, click the No option button.

3. Click **Statistical** in the Function category list box.

4. Click **AVERAGE** in the Function name list box. See Figure 2-16. The syntax for the AVERAGE function, AVERAGE(*number1,number2,...*), is displayed beneath the Function category box.

Figure 2-16 ◀
Paste Function
dialog box

syntax for
AVERAGE Function →

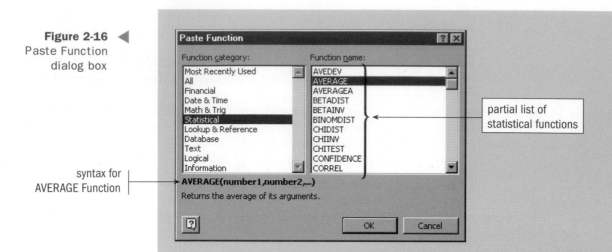

partial list of
statistical functions

5. Click the **OK** button to open the AVERAGE dialog box. Notice that the range B4:B8 appears in the Number1 text box, and =AVERAGE(B4:B8) appears in the formula bar. See Figure 2-17.

Figure 2-17 ◀
AVERAGE
dialog box

range includes
cell B8 →

Collapse Dialog
Box button

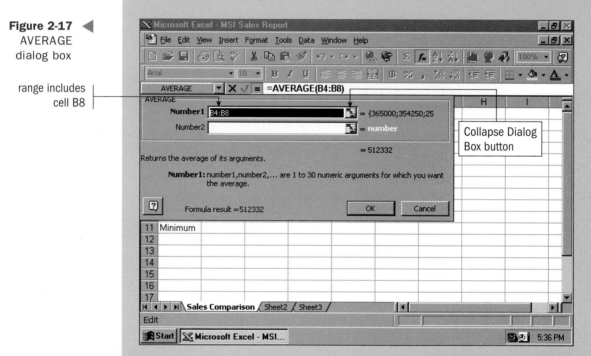

Excel has incorrectly included the total sales for 1999 (cell B8) in the range to calculate the average. The correct range is B4:B7.

6. Click the **Collapse Dialog Box** button to the right of the Number1 text box to collapse the dialog box to the size of one row. This makes it easier for you to identify and select the correct range.

7. Position the cell pointer over cell **B4**, click and drag to select the range **B4:B7**, and then click the **Collapse Dialog Box** button. The collapsed dialog box is restored and the correct range, B4:B7, is displayed in the Number1 text box. The formula =AVERAGE(B4:B7) is displayed in the formula bar.

8. Click the **OK** button to close the dialog box and return to the worksheet. The average, 320207.5, now appears in cell B9.

According to your plan, you need to enter a formula to find the largest regional sales amount in 1999. To do this, you'll use the MAX function.

MAX Function

MAX is a statistical function that finds the largest number. The syntax of the MAX function is:

$$MAX(number1,number2,...)$$

In the MAX function, *number* can be a constant number such as 345, a cell reference such as B6, or a range of cells such as B5:B16. You can use the MAX function to simply display the largest number or to use the largest number in a calculation. Although you can use the Paste Function to enter the MAX function, this time you'll type the MAX function directly into cell B10.

To enter the MAX function by typing directly into a cell:

1. If necessary, click cell **B10** to select it as the cell into which you want to type the formula that uses the MAX function.

2. Type **=MAX(B4:B7)** and press the **Enter** key. Cell B10 displays 365000, the largest regional sales amount in 1999.

Next, you need to find the smallest regional sales amount in 1999. For that, you'll use the MIN function.

MIN Function

MIN is a statistical function that finds the smallest number. The syntax of the MIN function is:

$$MIN(number1,number2,...)$$

You can use the MIN function to display the smallest number or to use the smallest number in a calculation.

You'll enter the MIN function directly into cell B11, using the pointing method.

Building Formulas by Pointing

Excel provides several ways to enter cell references into a formula. One is to type the cell references directly, as you have done so far in all the formulas you've entered. Another way to put a cell reference in a formula is to **point** to the cell reference you want to include while creating the formula. To use the pointing method to enter the formula, you click the cell or range of cells whose cell references you want to include in the formula. You may prefer to use this method to enter formulas, because it minimizes typing errors.

Now enter the formula to calculate the minimum sales by using the pointing method.

To enter the MIN function using the pointing method:

1. If necessary, click cell **B11** to move to the cell where you want to enter the formula that uses the MIN function.

2. Type **=MIN(** to begin the formula.

3. Position the cell pointer in cell **B4**, and then click and drag to select cells **B4** through **B7**. As you drag the mouse over the range, notice that the message "4Rx1C" appears in a ScreenTip, informing you that four rows and one column have been selected. Release the mouse button, and then press the **Enter** key. Cell B11 displays 251140, the smallest regional sales amount for 1999. See Figure 2-18.

Figure 2-18 ◄
Worksheet
after labels,
numbers,
formulas, and
functions
entered

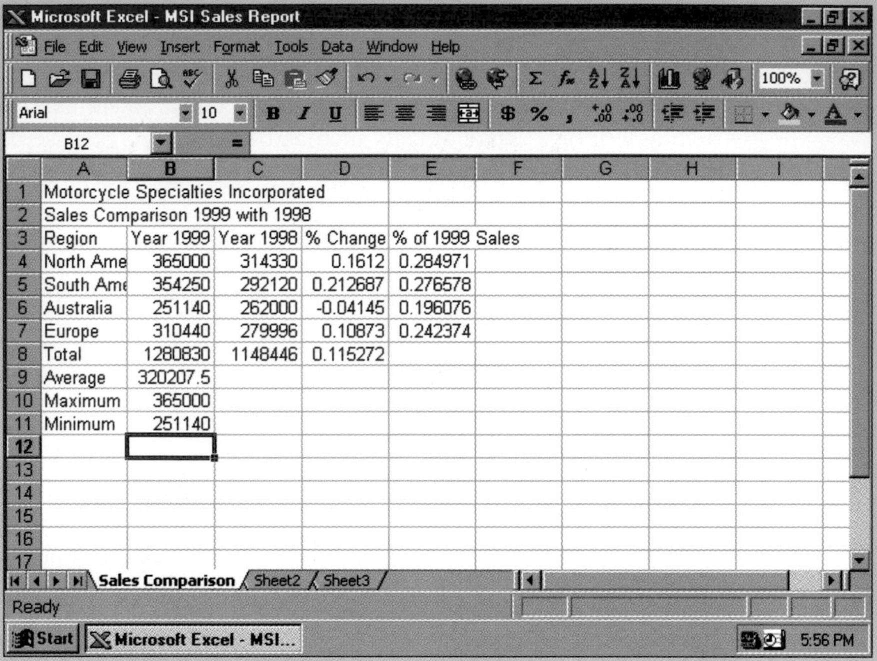

	A	B	C	D	E	F	G	H	I
1	Motorcycle Specialties Incorporated								
2	Sales Comparison 1999 with 1998								
3	Region	Year 1999	Year 1998	% Change	% of 1999 Sales				
4	North Ame	365000	314330	0.1612	0.284971				
5	South Ame	354250	292120	0.212687	0.276578				
6	Australia	251140	262000	-0.04145	0.196076				
7	Europe	310440	279996	0.10873	0.242374				
8	Total	1280830	1148446	0.115272					
9	Average	320207.5							
10	Maximum	365000							
11	Minimum	251140							
12									
13									
14									
15									
16									
17									

Now that the worksheet labels, values, formulas, and functions have been entered, Sally reviews the worksheet.

Testing the Worksheet

Before trusting a worksheet and its results, you should test it to make sure you entered the correct formulas. You want the worksheet to produce accurate results.

Beginners often expect their Excel worksheets to work correctly the first time. Sometimes they do work correctly the first time, but even well-planned and well-designed worksheets can contain errors. It's best to assume that a worksheet has errors and test it to make sure it is correct. While there are no rules for testing a worksheet, here are some approaches:

■ Entering **test values**, numbers that generate a known result, to determine whether your worksheet formulas are accurate. For example, try entering a 1 into each cell. After you enter the test values, you compare the results in your worksheet with the known results. If the results on your worksheet don't match the known results, you probably made an error.

■ Entering **extreme values**, such as very large or very small numbers, and observing their effect on cells with formulas.

■ Working out the numbers ahead of time with pencil, paper, and calculator, and comparing these results with the output from the computer.

Sally used the third approach to test her worksheet. She had calculated her results using a calculator (Figure 2-2) and then compared them with the results on the screen (Figure 2-18). The numbers agree, so she feels confident that the worksheet she created contains accurate results.

Spell Checking the Worksheet

You can use the Excel spell check feature to help identify and correct spelling and typing errors. Excel compares the words in your worksheet to the words in its dictionary. If Excel finds a word in your worksheet not in its dictionary, it shows you the word and some suggested corrections, and you decide whether to correct it or leave it as is.

REFERENCE window	CHECKING THE SPELLING IN A WORKSHEET
	■ Click cell A1 to begin the spell check from the top of the worksheet.
	■ Click the Spelling button on the Standard toolbar.
	■ Change the spelling or ignore the spell check's suggestion for each identified word.
	■ Click the OK button when the spell check is complete.

You have tested your numbers and formulas for accuracy. Now you can check the spelling of all text entries in the worksheet.

To check the spelling in a worksheet:

1. Click cell **A1** to begin spell checking in the first cell of the worksheet.

2. Click the **Spelling** button 🗹 on the Standard toolbar to check the spelling of the text in the worksheet. A message box indicates that Excel has finished spell checking the entire worksheet. No errors were found.

   TROUBLE? If the spell check does find a spelling error in your worksheet, use the Spelling dialog box options to correct the spelling mistake and continue checking the worksheet.

Improving the Worksheet Layout

Although the numbers are correct, Sally does not want to present a worksheet without a more polished appearance. She feels that there are a number of simple changes you can make to the worksheet that will improve its layout and make the data more readable. Specifically, she asks you to increase the width of column A so that the entire region names are displayed, insert a blank row between the titles and column headings, move the summary statistics down three rows from their current location, and apply one of the predefined Excel formats to the worksheet.

Changing Column Width

Changing the column width is one way to improve the appearance of the worksheet, making it easier to read and interpret data. In Sally's worksheet, you need to increase the width of column A so that the entire labels for North America and South America appear in their cells.

Excel provides several methods for changing column width. For example, you can click a column heading or click and drag the pointer to select a series of column headings and then use the Format menu. You can also use the dividing line between column headings in the column header row. When you move the pointer over the dividing line between two column headings, the pointer changes to ✛. You can then use the pointer to drag the dividing line to a new location. You can also double-click the dividing line to make the column as wide as the longest text label or number in the column.

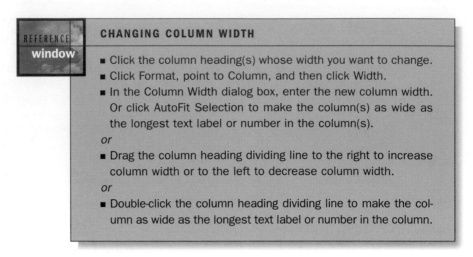

Sally has asked you to change column A's width so that the complete region name is displayed.

To change the width of column A:

1. Position the pointer ✛ on the A in the column heading area.

2. Move the pointer to the right edge of the column heading dividing columns A and B. Notice that the pointer changes to the resize arrow ↔.

3. Click and drag the resize arrow to the right, increasing the column width 12 characters or more, as indicated in the ScreenTip that pops up on the screen.

4. Release the mouse button. See Figure 2-19.

Figure 2-19 ◀
Worksheet
after width of
column A
increased

now entire contents
of cell displayed

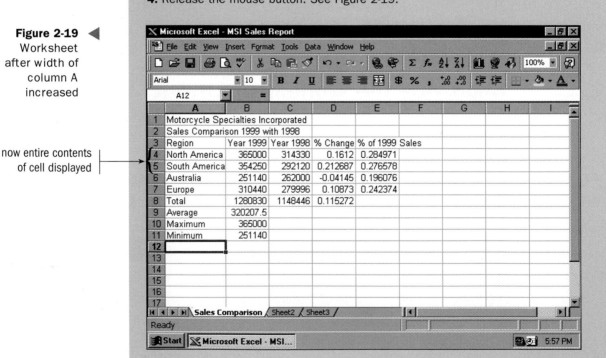

Next, you need to insert a row between the title and the column heading.

Inserting a Row into a Worksheet

At times, you may need to add one or more rows or columns to a worksheet to make room for new data or to make the worksheet easier to read. The process of inserting columns and rows is similar; you select the number of columns or rows you want to insert and then use the Insert command to insert the columns or rows. When you insert rows or columns, Excel repositions other rows and columns in the worksheet and automatically adjusts cell references in formulas to reflect the new location of values used in calculations.

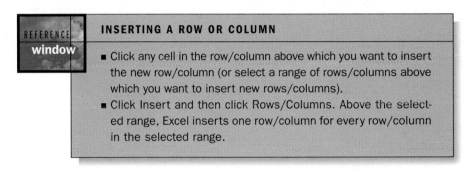

REFERENCE
window

INSERTING A ROW OR COLUMN

- Click any cell in the row/column above which you want to insert the new row/column (or select a range of rows/columns above which you want to insert new rows/columns).
- Click Insert and then click Rows/Columns. Above the selected range, Excel inserts one row/column for every row/column in the selected range.

Sally wants one blank row between the titles and column headings in her worksheet.

To insert a row into a worksheet:

1. Click cell **A2**.

2. Click **Insert** on the menu bar, and then click **Rows**. Excel inserts a blank row above the original row 2. All other rows shift down one row. See Figure 2-20.

Figure 2-20
Worksheet after one row inserted above original row 2

row inserted in wrong position

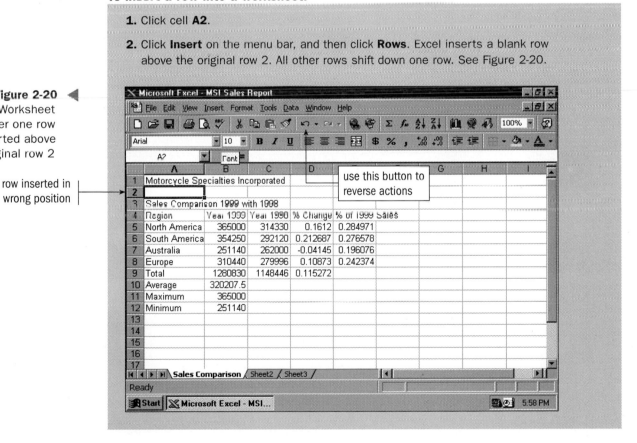

The blank row isn't really where you wanted it. You inserted a row between the two lines of the title instead of between the title and the column heading. To correct this error you can either delete the row or use the Undo button. If you need to delete a row or column, select the row(s) or column(s) you want to delete, then click Delete on the Edit menu, or press the Delete key on your keyboard. You use the Undo button because it is a feature you find valuable in many situations.

Using the Undo Button

The Excel Undo button lets you cancel recent actions one at a time. Click the Undo button to reverse the last command or delete the last entry you typed. To reverse more than one action, click the arrow next to the Undo button and click the action you want to undo on the drop-down list.

Now use the Undo button to reverse the row insertion.

To reverse the row insertion:

1. Click the **Undo** button 🔙 on the Standard toolbar to restore the worksheet to its status before the row was inserted.

Now you can insert the blank row in the correct place—between the second line of the worksheet title and the column heads.

To insert a row into a worksheet:

1. Click cell **A3** because you want to insert one row above row 3. If you wanted to insert several rows, you would select as many rows as you wanted to insert before using the Insert command.

2. Click **Insert** on the menu bar, and then click **Rows**. Excel inserts a blank row above the original row 3. All other rows shift down one row. See Figure 2-21.

Figure 2-21 ◀
Worksheet after one row inserted

row inserted in desired location

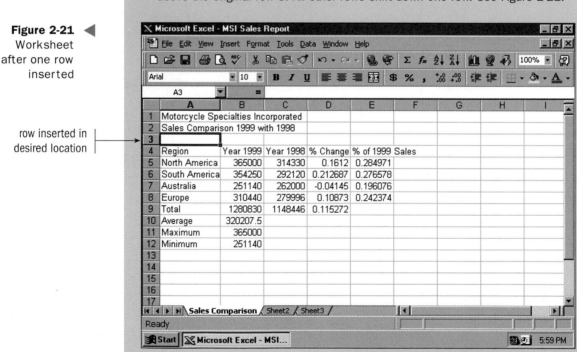

Adding a row changed the location of the data in the worksheet. For example, the percent change in North American sales, originally in cell D4, is now in cell D5. Did Excel adjust the formulas to compensate for the new row? Check cell D5 and any other cells you want to view to verify that the cell references were adjusted.

To examine the formula in cell D5 and other cells:

1. Click cell **D5**. The formula =(B5-C5)/C5 appears in the formula bar. You originally entered the formula =(B4-C4)/C4 in cell D4 to calculate percent change in North America. Excel automatically adjusted the cell reference to reflect the new location of the data.

2. Inspect other cells below row 3 to verify that their cell references were automatically adjusted when the new row was inserted.

Sally has also suggested moving the summary statistics down three rows from the present location to make the report easier to read. So, you will need to move the range of cells containing the average, minimum, and maximum sales to a different location in the worksheet.

Moving a Range Using the Mouse

To place the summary statistics three rows below the other data in the report, you could use the Insert command to insert three blank rows between the total and average sales. Alternatively, you could use the mouse to move the summary statistics to a new location. Since you already know how to insert a row, try using the mouse to move the summary statistics to a new location. This technique is called **drag-and-drop**. You simply select the cell range you want to move and use the pointer ⬚ to drag the cells' contents to the desired location.

REFERENCE
window

MOVING A RANGE USING THE MOUSE

- Select the cell or range of cells you want to move.
- Place the mouse pointer over any edge of the selected range until the pointer changes to an arrow.
- Click and drag the outline of the range to the new worksheet location.
- Release the mouse button.

Sally has asked you to move the range A10 through B12 to the new destination area A13 through B15.

To move a range of cells using the drag-and-drop technique:

1. Select the range of cells **A10:B12**, which contains the sales summary statistics you want to move.

2. Place the mouse pointer over any edge of the selected range until the pointer changes to an arrow . See Figure 2-22.

Figure 2-22 ◀
Range to
be moved

pointer shape
indicates you can
move selected range

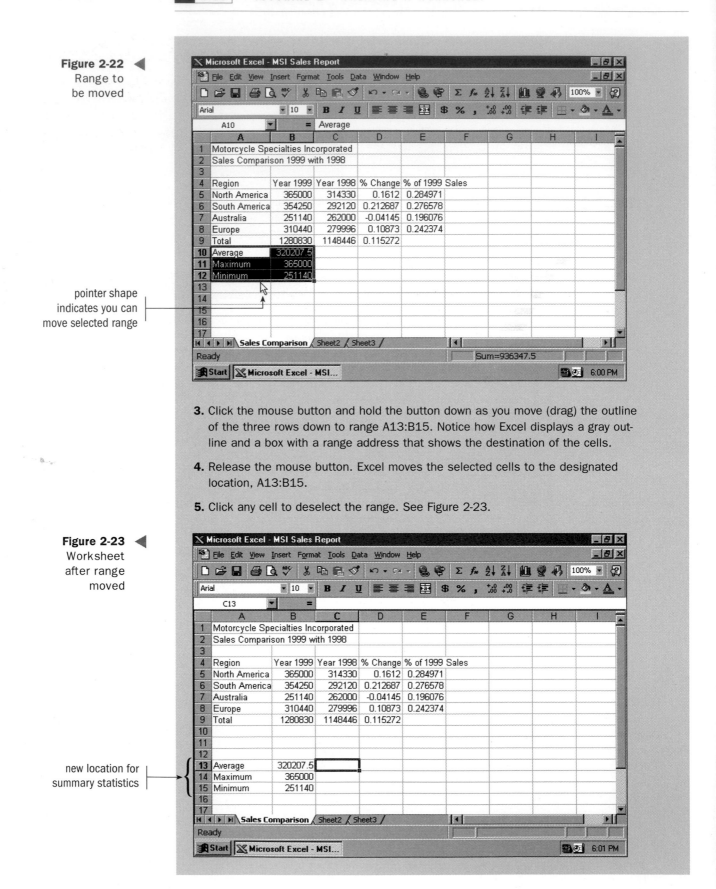

3. Click the mouse button and hold the button down as you move (drag) the outline of the three rows down to range A13:B15. Notice how Excel displays a gray outline and a box with a range address that shows the destination of the cells.

4. Release the mouse button. Excel moves the selected cells to the designated location, A13:B15.

5. Click any cell to deselect the range. See Figure 2-23.

Figure 2-23 ◀
Worksheet
after range
moved

new location for
summary statistics

Next, Sally wants you to use the Excel AutoFormat feature to improve the worksheet's appearance by emphasizing the titles and aligning numbers in cells.

Using AutoFormat

The **AutoFormat** feature lets you change your worksheet's appearance by selecting from a collection of predesigned worksheet formats. Each worksheet format in the AutoFormat collection gives your worksheet a more professional appearance by applying attractive fonts, borders, colors, and shading to a range of data. AutoFormat also adjusts column widths, row heights, and the alignment of text in cells to improve the worksheet's appearance.

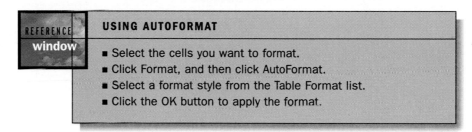

REFERENCE window	USING AUTOFORMAT
	■ Select the cells you want to format.
	■ Click Format, and then click AutoFormat.
	■ Select a format style from the Table Format list.
	■ Click the OK button to apply the format.

Now you'll use AutoFormat's Simple format to improve the worksheet's appearance.

To apply AutoFormat's Simple format:

1. Select cells **A1:E9** as the range you want to format using AutoFormat.

2. Click **Format** on the menu bar, and then click **AutoFormat** The AutoFormat dialog box opens. See Figure 2-24.

Figure 2-24 ◀
AutoFormat
dialog box

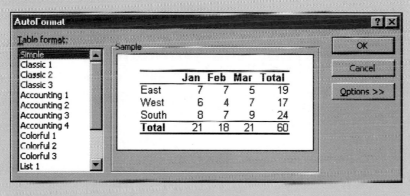

3. The Table format box lists the available formats. The format called "Simple" is selected and the Sample box shows how the Simple format looks when applied to a worksheet.

4. Click each of the formats from Simple down to Accounting 1. Notice the different font styles and colors of each format shown in the Sample box.

5. Click the **Simple** format, and then click the **OK** button to apply this format.

6. Click any cell to deselect the range. Figure 2-25 shows the newly formatted worksheet.

Figure 2-25
Worksheet
after using the
Simple
AutoFormat

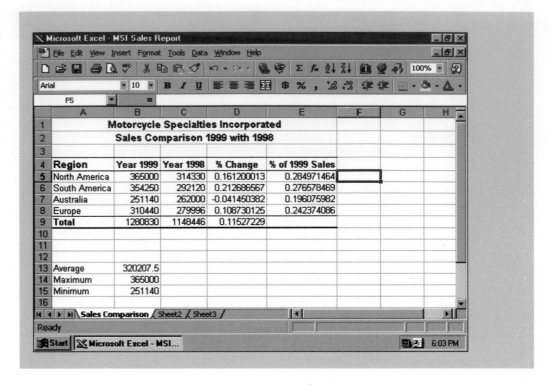

You show the worksheet to Sally. She's impressed with the improved appearance and decides to hand it out to the regional sales managers at their next meeting. She asks you to print it so she can make copies.

Previewing the Worksheet Using Print Preview

Before you print a worksheet, you can use the Excel Print Preview window to see how it will look when printed. The **Print Preview window** shows you margins, page breaks, headers, and footers that are not always visible on the screen. If the preview isn't what you want, you can close the Print Preview window and change the worksheet before printing it.

To preview the worksheet before you print it:

1. Click the **Print Preview** button on the Standard toolbar. After a moment Excel displays the worksheet in the Print Preview window. See Figure 2-26.

Figure 2-26 ◀
Print preview of
sales
comparison
worksheet

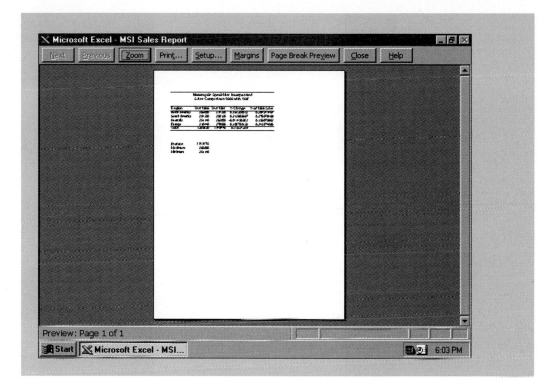

When Excel displays a full page in the Print Preview window, you might have difficulty seeing the text of the worksheet because it is so small. Don't worry if the preview isn't completely readable. One purpose of the Print Preview window is to see the overall layout of the worksheet and how it will fit on the printed page. If you want a better view of the text, you can use the Zoom button.

To display an enlarged section of the Print Preview window:

1. Click the **Zoom** button to display an enlarged section of the Print Preview.

2. Click the **Zoom** button again to return to the full-page view.

Notice that the Print Preview window contains several other buttons. Figure 2-27 describes each of these buttons.

Figure 2-27 ◀
Description of
Print Preview
buttons

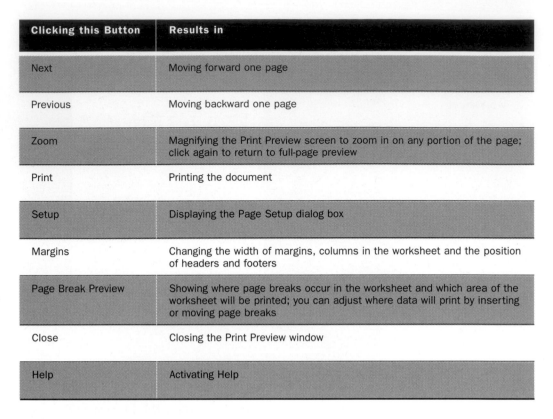

Clicking this Button	Results in
Next	Moving forward one page
Previous	Moving backward one page
Zoom	Magnifying the Print Preview screen to zoom in on any portion of the page; click again to return to full-page preview
Print	Printing the document
Setup	Displaying the Page Setup dialog box
Margins	Changing the width of margins, columns in the worksheet and the position of headers and footers
Page Break Preview	Showing where page breaks occur in the worksheet and which area of the worksheet will be printed; you can adjust where data will print by inserting or moving page breaks
Close	Closing the Print Preview window
Help	Activating Help

Looking at the worksheet in Print Preview, you observe that it is not centered on the page. By default, Excel prints a worksheet at the upper left of the page's print area. You can specify that the worksheet be centered vertically, horizontally, or both.

Centering the Printout

Worksheet printouts generally look more professional centered on the printed page. You decide that Sally would want you to center the sales comparison worksheet both horizontally and vertically on the printed page.

To center the printout:

1. Click the **Setup** button to display the Page Setup dialog box.

2. Click the **Margins** tab. See Figure 2-28. Notice that the preview box displays a worksheet positioned at the upper-left edge of the page.

Excel

Figure 2-28 ◀
Margins tab of
Page Setup
dialog box

indicates that
worksheet will be
displayed in upper-
left corner of page

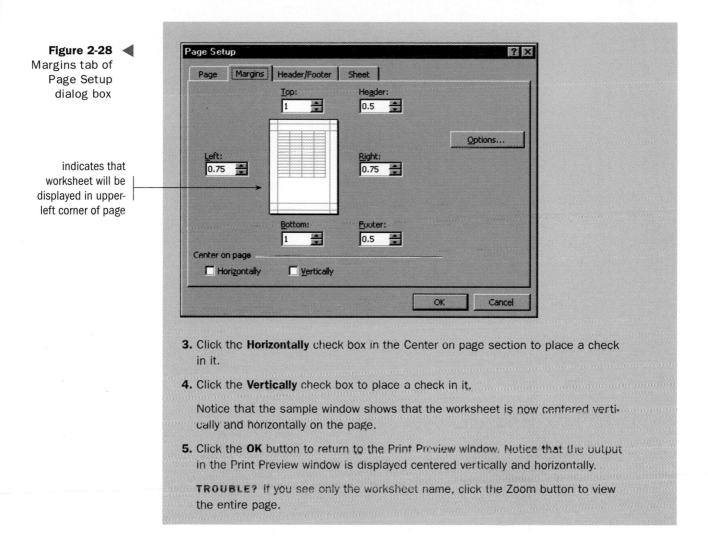

3. Click the **Horizontally** check box in the Center on page section to place a check in it.

4. Click the **Vertically** check box to place a check in it.

   Notice that the sample window shows that the worksheet is now centered vertically and horizontally on the page.

5. Click the **OK** button to return to the Print Preview window. Notice that the output in the Print Preview window is displayed centered vertically and horizontally.

   TROUBLE? If you see only the worksheet name, click the Zoom button to view the entire page.

Adding Headers and Footers

Headers and footers can provide you with useful documentation on your printed worksheet, such as the name of the person who created the worksheet, the date it was printed, and its filename. The **header** is text printed in the top margin of every worksheet page. A **footer** is text printed in the bottom margin of every page. Headers and footers are not displayed in the worksheet window. To see them, you must preview or print the worksheet.

Excel uses formatting codes in headers and footers to represent the items you want to print. Formatting codes produce dates, times, and filenames that you might want a header or footer to include. You can type these codes, or you can click a formatting code button to insert the code. Figure 2-29 shows the formatting codes and the buttons for inserting them.

Figure 2-29 ◀
Header
and footer
formatting
buttons

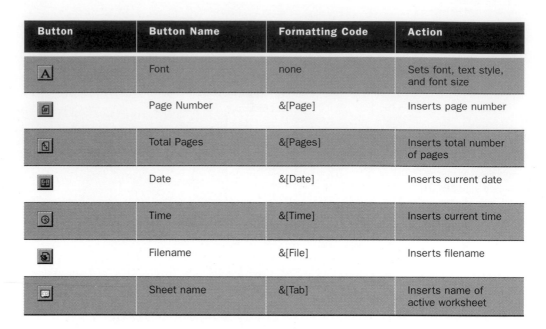

Button	Button Name	Formatting Code	Action
A	Font	none	Sets font, text style, and font size
#	Page Number	&[Page]	Inserts page number
⊞	Total Pages	&[Pages]	Inserts total number of pages
▦	Date	&[Date]	Inserts current date
⊕	Time	&[Time]	Inserts current time
▤	Filename	&[File]	Inserts filename
▦	Sheet name	&[Tab]	Inserts name of active worksheet

Sally asks you to add a header that includes the filename and today's date. She also wants you to add a footer that displays the page number.

To add a header and a footer to your worksheet:

1. In the Print Preview window, click the **Setup** button to open the Page Setup dialog box, and then click the **Header/Footer** tab.

2. Click the **Custom Header** button to display the Header dialog box.

3. With the insertion point in the Left section box, click the **Filename** button ▤. The code &[File] appears in the Left section box.

TROUBLE? If you clicked the wrong code, double-click the code, press the Delete key, then repeat Steps 2 and 3.

4. Click the **Right section** box to move the insertion point to the Right section box.

5. Click the **Date** button ▦. The code &[Date] appears in the Right section box. See Figure 2-30.

Figure 2-30 ◀
Inserting
formatting
codes into
the Header
dialog box

formatting code to
display workbook
filename

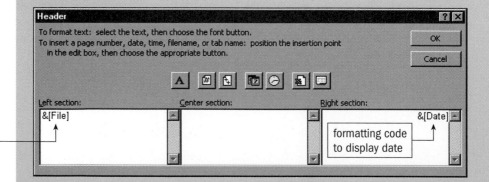

TROUBLE? If you clicked the wrong code, double-click the code, press the Delete key, then repeat Step 5.

6. Click the **OK** button to complete the header and return to the Page Setup dialog box. Notice that the header shows the filename on the left and the date on the right.

7. Click the **Custom Footer** button to display the Footer dialog box.

8. Click the **Center section** box to move the insertion point to the Center Section box.

9. Click the **Page Number** button 🔳. The code &[Page] appears in the Center section box.

10. Click the **OK** button to complete the footer and return to the Page Setup dialog box. Notice that the footer shows the page number in the bottom center of the page.

11. Click the **OK** button to return to the Print Preview window. The changed header appears in the Print Preview window.

12. Click the **Close** button to exit the Print Preview window and return to the worksheet.

You'll use the Print button on the Standard toolbar to print one copy of the worksheet with the current settings. First, save the worksheet before printing it.

To save your page setup settings:

1. Click the **Save** button 🔳 on the Standard toolbar.

2. Click the **Print** button 🔳 on the Standard toolbar. See Figure 2-31.

TROUBLE? If you see a message that indicates that you have a printer problem, click the Cancel button to cancel printing. Check your printer to make sure it is turned on and is online; also make sure it has paper. Then go back and try Step 2 again. If you have no printer available, click the Cancel button.

Figure 2-31 ◀
Printed
worksheet

Motorcycle Specialties Incorporated
Sales Comparison 1999 with 1998

Region	Year 1999	Year 1998	% Change	% of 1999 Sales
North America	365000	314330	0.161200013	0.284971464
South America	354250	292120	0.212686567	0.276578469
Australia	251140	262000	-0.041450382	0.196075982
Europe	310440	279996	0.108730125	0.242374086
Total	1280830	1148446	0.11527229	

Average	320207.5		
Maximum	365000		
Minimum	251140		

Sally reviews the printed worksheet and is satisfied with its appearance. She will make four copies to be distributed to the regional managers at the next meeting.

Documenting the Workbook

Documenting the workbook provides valuable information to those using the workbook. Documentation includes external documentation as well as notes and instructions within the workbook. This information could be as basic as who created the worksheet and the date it was created, or it could be more detailed, summarizing formulas and layout.

Depending on the use of the workbook, the required amount of documentation varies. Sally's planning analysis sheet and sketch for the sales comparison worksheet are one form of external documentation. This information can be useful to someone who would need to modify the worksheet in any way because it states the goals, required input, output, and the calculations used.

One source of internal documentation would be a worksheet that is placed as the first worksheet in the workbook, such as the Title Sheet worksheet in the workbook you worked with in Tutorial 1 to determine the best location for the new Inwood golf course. In more complex workbooks, this sheet may also include an index of all worksheets in the workbook, instructions on how to use the worksheets, where to enter data, how to save the workbook, and how to print reports. This documentation method is useful because the information is contained directly in the workbook and can easily be viewed upon opening the workbook, or printed if necessary. Another source of internal documentation is the **Property dialog box**. This dialog box enables you to electronically capture information such as the name of the workbook's creator, the creation date, the number of revisions, and other information related to the workbook.

If you prefer, you can include documentation in each sheet of the workbook. One way is to attach notes to cells by using the Comments command to explain complex formulas and assumptions.

The worksheet itself can be used as documentation. Once a worksheet is completed, it is a good practice to print and file a "hard" copy of your work as documentation. This hard copy file should include a printout of each worksheet with the values displayed and another printout of the worksheet displaying the cell formulas.

Displaying and Printing Worksheet Formulas

You can document the formulas you entered in a worksheet by displaying and printing them. When you display formulas, Excel shows the formulas you entered in each cell instead of showing the results of the calculations. You want a printout of the formulas in your worksheet for documentation.

To display worksheet formulas:

1. Click **Tools** on the menu bar, and then click **Options** to open the Options dialog box.

2. Click the **View** tab, and then click the **Formulas** check box in the Window options section to place a check in it.

3. Click the **OK** button to return to the worksheet. The width of each column nearly doubles to accommodate the underlying formulas. See Figure 2-32.

Figure 2-32 ◀
Displaying formulas in a worksheet

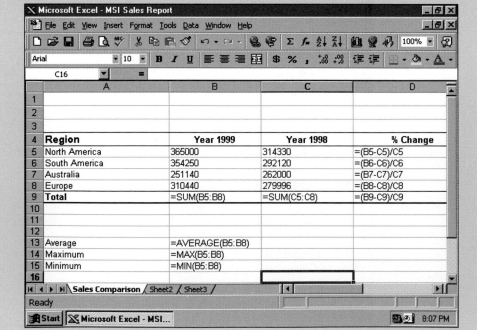

	A	B	C	D
1				
2				
3				
4	**Region**	**Year 1999**	**Year 1998**	**% Change**
5	North America	365000	314330	=(B5-C5)/C5
6	South America	354250	292120	=(B6-C6)/C6
7	Australia	251140	262000	=(B7-C7)/C7
8	Europe	310440	279996	=(B8-C8)/C8
9	**Total**	=SUM(B5:B8)	=SUM(C5:C8)	=(B9-C9)/C9
10				
11				
12				
13	Average	=AVERAGE(B5:B8)		
14	Maximum	=MAX(B5:B8)		
15	Minimum	=MIN(B5:B8)		
16				

Now print the worksheet with the formulas displayed. Before printing the formulas you need to change the appropriate settings in the Page Setup dialog box to show the gridlines and the row/column headings, center the worksheet on the page, and fit the printout on a single page.

To adjust the print setups to display formulas:

1. Click **File** on the menu bar, and then click **Page Setup** to display the Page Setup dialog box.

2. Click the **Sheet** tab to view the sheet options. Click the **Row and Column Headings** check box to print the row numbers and column letters along with the worksheet results.

3. Click the **Gridlines** check box to place a check in it and select that option.

4. Click the **Page** tab, and then click the **Landscape** option button. This option prints the worksheet with the paper position so it is wider than it is tall.

5. Click the **Fit to** option button in the Scaling section of the Page tab. This option reduces the worksheet when you print it, so it fits on the specific number of pages in the Fit to check box. The default is 1.

6. Click the **Print Preview** button to open the Print Preview window.

7. Click the **Print** button. See Figure 2-33.

Figure 2-33 ◀
Printout of
worksheet
formulas

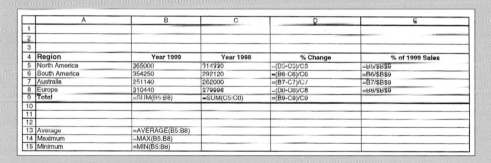

	A	B	C	D	E
1					
2					
3					
4	Region	Year 1999	Year 1998	% Change	% of 1999 Sales
5	North America	365000	314220	=(B5-C5)/C5	=B5/$B$9
6	South America	354250	292120	=(B6-C6)/C6	=B6/$B$9
7	Australia	251140	262000	=(B7-C7)/C7	=B7/$B$9
8	Europe	310440	279998	=(B8-C8)/C8	=B8/$B$9
9	Total	=SUM(B5:B8)	=SUM(C5:C8)	=(B9-C9)/C9	
10					
11					
12					
13	Average	=AVERAGE(B5:B8)			
14	Maximum	=MAX(B5:B8)			
15	Minimum	=MIN(B5:B8)			

After printing the formulas, return the worksheet so it displays the worksheet values.

To turn off the formulas display:

1. Click **Tools** on the menu bar, and then click **Options** to open the Options dialog box.

2. Click the **View** tab if necessary, and then click **Formulas** to remove the check mark next to that option to deselect it.

3. Click the **OK** button to return to the worksheet. The formulas are no longer displayed.

4. Close the workbook and exit Excel.

Quick Check

1. To move a range of cells, you must _____ the range first.

2. A _____ is text that is printed in the top margin of every worksheet page.

3. _____ is a command that lets you change your worksheet's appearance by selecting a collection of predesigned worksheet formats.

4. Describe how to insert a row or a column.

5. To reverse your most recent action, which button should you click?
   a. [icon]
   b. [icon]
   c. [icon]

6. Describe how you use the pointing method to create a formula.

7. To display formulas instead of values in your worksheet, you choose what command?

8. If your worksheet has too many columns to fit on one printed page, you should try _____ orientation.

You have planned, built, formatted, and documented Sally's sales comparison worksheet. It is ready for her to present to the regional sales managers at their next meeting.

Tutorial Assignments

After Sally meets with the regional sales managers for MSI, she decides it would be a good idea to provide the managers with their own copy of the sales comparison worksheet, so they can update the report with next year's sales data, and also modify it to use for their own sales tracking purposes. Before passing it on to them, she wants to provide more documentation, and add some additional information that the managers thought would be useful to them. Complete the following for Sally:

1. Start Windows and Excel, if necessary. Insert your Student Disk into the appropriate disk drive. Make sure the Excel and Book1 windows are maximized.

2. Open the workbook MSI1 in the TAssign folder for Tutorial 2 on your Student Disk.

3. Save your workbook as MSI Sales Report 2 in the TAssign folder for Tutorial 2 on your Student Disk.

4. Make Sheet2 the active sheet. Use Sheet2 to include information about the workbook. Insert the information in Figure 2-34 into Sheet2. Increase the width of column A as necessary.

Excel

Figure 2-34 ◀

Cell	Text Entry
A1	Motorcycle Specialties Incorporated
A3	Created By:
A4	Date created:
A6	Purpose:
B3	enter your name
B4	enter today's date
B6	Sales report comparing sales by region for 1999 with 1998

5. Change the name of the worksheet from Sheet2 to Title Sheet.

6. Print the Title Sheet sheet.

7. Make Sales Comparison the active sheet.

 8. Open the Office Assistant and enter the search phrase "Insert a column" to obtain instruction on inserting a new column into a worksheet. Insert a new column between columns C and D.

9. In cell D4 enter the heading "Change."

10. In cell D5 enter the formula to calculate the change in sales for North America from 1998 to 1999. (*Hint*: Check that the figure in cell D5 is 50670.)

11. Copy the formula in D5 to the other regions and total (D6 through D9) using the fill handle.

12. Calculate summary statistics for 1998. In cell C13 display the average sales, in cell C14 display the maximum, and in cell C15 display the minimum.

13. Save the workbook.

14. Print the sales comparison worksheet.

 15. a. Use the Office Assistant to learn how to attach comments to a cell. List the steps.
  b. Insert the following comment into cell F4: "Divide 1999 sales in each region by total sales in 1999."

 16. Open the MSI3 workbook and save it as MSI Report 4.
  a. Use the AutoSum button to compute the totals for 1998 and 1999. Print the worksheet. Are the results correct?
  b. Replace the values in the range B5:C8 with "1". Print the worksheet. Are the results correct? Why do you think this problem occurred?
  c. Use the pointing method to correct the formula. Print the worksheet.

17. a. Use the Office Assistant to learn how to use row and column headers in your formulas to create formulas (enter the search phrase "labels as formulas").
    b. Open the MSI5 workbook and save it as MSI Report 6.
    c. In cell D5, calculate the change in sales in North America from 1998 to 1999 using the labels in columns B and C.
    d. Copy the formula in D5 to the other regions and total (D6 through D9) using the fill handle.
    e. Print the worksheet.
    f. Print the formulas.
    g. Save the worksheet.

18. Open the MSI7 workbook and save it as MSI Report 8.
    a. Activate the Sales Comparison sheet and select the range A1:E9. Copy the selected range to the Clipboard. Activate Sheet2 and paste the selected range to the corresponding cells in Sheet2. Apply the Classic 1 AutoFormat to this range. Print Sheet2.
    b. Insert a new sheet using the Worksheet command from the Insert menu. Return to the Sales Comparison sheet and copy the range A1:E9 to the corresponding cells in the new sheet. Apply the 3D Effects 2 AutoFormat to this range. Print this sheet.
    c. Use the Delete Sheet command from the Edit menu to delete the Title Sheet sheet.
    d. Move the Sales Comparison sheet so it is the third sheet in the workbook.
    e. Save the workbook.

Case Problems

1. Magazine Circulation Report You are a research analyst in the marketing department of a large magazine publisher. You have been assigned the task of compiling circulation data on the company's competition. Circulation statistics for the top six magazines appear in Figure 2-35.

Figure 2-35 ◀

Magazine	Prior Year	Current Year
Better Homes & Gardens	8000	8002
Family Circle	5138	5108
Good Housekeeping	4975	5101
National Geographic	9925	9787
Reader's Digest	16300	16256
TV Guide	15337	14920

1. Open a new workbook and enter the data from Figure 2-35 in a worksheet.

2. Use the AutoSum button to compute total circulation for all six magazines listed for both the current year and the prior year.

3. Use the Paste Function dialog box to compute the average circulation for all six magazines for both the current and the prior year.

4. For each magazine, create and enter a formula to compute the increase/decrease in circulation compared to the prior year.

5. Use AutoFormat to improve the appearance of the worksheet. Use Classic 1 as the format.

6. Rename the sheet Total Circulation.

7. Use a sheet in the workbook to enter your name, the date created, and the purpose of this sheet. Rename the sheet Title Sheet.

8. Save the worksheet as Magazine in the Case folder for Tutorial 2.

9. Print both the worksheets.

2. Compiling Data on the U.S. Airline Industry The editor of *Aviation Week and Space Technology* has asked you to research the current status of the U.S. airline industry. You collect information on the revenue-miles and passenger-miles for each major U.S. airline (Figure 2-36).

Figure 2-36 ◄

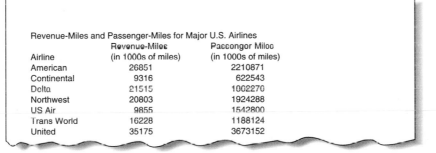

Revenue-Miles and Passenger-Miles for Major U.S. Airlines		
	Revenue-Miles	Passenger Miles
Airline	(in 1000s of miles)	(in 1000s of miles)
American	26851	2210871
Continental	9316	622543
Delta	21515	1002270
Northwest	20803	1924288
US Air	9855	1542800
Trans World	16228	1188124
United	35175	3673152

You want to calculate the following summary information to use in the article:

- total revenue-miles for the U.S. airline industry
- total passenger-miles for the U.S. airline industry
- each airline's share of the total revenue-miles
- each airline's share of the total passenger-miles
- average revenue-miles for U.S. airlines
- average passenger-miles for U.S. airlines

Complete these steps:

1. Open a new workbook and enter the labels and data from Figure 2-36.

2. In cell A2, insert a second line to the title that reads:

    Compiled by: *XXXX*

    where *XXXX* is your name.

3. Enter the formulas to compute the total and average revenue-miles and passenger-miles. Use the SUM and AVERAGE functions where appropriate. Remember to include row labels to describe each statistic.

4. Add a column to display each airline's share of the total revenue-miles. Remember to include a column heading. You decide the appropriate location for this data.

5. Add a column to display each airline's share of the total passenger-miles. Remember to include a column heading. You decide the appropriate location for this data.

6. Name the worksheet Mileage Data.

7. Save the worksheet as Airline in the Case folder for Tutorial 2.

8. Print the worksheet. Center the report, no gridlines, and place the date in the upper-right corner of the header.

9. Select an AutoFormat to improve the appearance of your output.

10. Save your workbook.

11. Print the worksheet, centered on the page, no gridlines or row and column headings.

12. Print the formulas for the worksheet. Include row and column headings in the output.

3. Fresh Air Sales Incentive Program Carl Stambaugh is assistant sales manager at Fresh Air Inc., a manufacturer of outdoor and expedition clothing. Fresh Air sales representatives contact retail chains and individual retail outlets to sell the Fresh Air line.

This year, to spur sales, Carl has decided to run a sales incentive program for sales representatives. Each sales representative has been assigned a sales goal 15% higher than his or her total sales last year. All sales representatives who reach this new goal will be awarded an all-expenses-paid trip for two to Cozumel, Mexico.

Carl wants to track the results of the sales incentive program with an Excel worksheet. He has asked you to complete the worksheet by adding the formulas to compute:

- actual sales in 1999 for each sales representative

- sales goal in 1999 for each sales representative

- percent of goal reached for each sales representative

He also wants a printout before he presents the worksheet at the next sales meeting. Complete these steps:

1. Open the workbook Fresh (in the Case folder for Tutorial 2 on your Student Disk). Maximize the worksheet window and save the workbook as Fresh Air Sales Incentives in the Case folder for Tutorial 2.

2. Complete the worksheet by adding the following formulas:
   a. 1999 Actual for each employee = Sum of Actual Sales for each quarter
   b. Goal 1999 for each employee = 1998 Sales X (1 + Goal % increase)
   c. % Goal reached for each employee = 1999 Actual / 1999 Goal

   (*Hint:* Use the Copy command. Review relative versus absolute references.)

3. Make the formatting changes using an AutoFormat to improve the appearance of the worksheet.

4. Print the worksheet, centered horizontally and vertically, and add an appropriate header. Add your name and date in the footer.

5. At the bottom of the worksheet (three rows after the last sales rep) add the average, maximum, and minimum statistics for columns C through I.

6. Save the workbook.

7. Print the worksheet.

8. As you scroll down the worksheet, the column headings no longer appear on the screen, making it difficult to know what each column represents. Use the Help system to look up "Freezing Panes." Implement this feature in your worksheet. Save the workbook. Explain the steps you take to freeze the panes.

4. Stock Portfolio for Juan Cortez Your close friend, Juan Cortez, works as an accountant at a local manufacturing company. While in college, with a double major in accounting and finance, Juan dabbled in the stock market and expressed an interest in becoming a financial planner and running his own firm. To that end, he has continued his professional studies in the evenings with the aim of becoming a certified financial planner. He has already begun to provide financial planning services to a few clients. Because of his hectic schedule as a full-time accountant, part-time student taking evening classes, and part-time financial planner with client visits on the weekends, Juan finds it difficult to keep up with the data processing needs for his clients. You have offered to assist him until he completes his studies for the certified financial planner exams.

Juan asks you to set up a worksheet to keep track of a stock portfolio for one of his clients.

Open a new workbook and do the following:

1. Figure 2-37 shows the data you will enter into the workbook. For each stock, you will enter the name, number of shares purchased, and purchase price. Periodically, you will also enter the current price of each stock so Juan can review the changes with his clients.

2. In addition to entering the data, you need to make the following calculations:
   a. Cost = No of shares * Purchase price
   b. Current Value = No of shares * Current price
   c. Gains/Losses = Current value minus Cost
   d. Totals for Cost, Current value, and Gains/Losses

   Enter the formulas to calculate the Cost, Current Value, Gains/Losses, and Totals.

3. Save the workbook as Portfolio in the Case folder for Tutorial 2.

Figure 2-37

Stock	No. Of Shares	Purchase Price	Cost	Current Price	Current Value	Gains/ Losses
PepsiC	100	50.25		52.50		
FordM	250	31		30		
AT&T	50	60		61.25		
IBM	100	90.25		95.75		
Xerox	50	138		134		
Total						

4. Print the worksheet. Center the worksheet horizontally and vertically. Add an appropriate header.

5. Apply an AutoFormat that improves the appearance of the worksheet. Save the worksheet as Portfolio 2. Print the worksheet.

6. Print the formulas for the worksheet. Include row and column headings in the printed output.

7. Clear the prices in the Current price column of the worksheet.

8. Enter the following prices:

   PepsiC   55

   FordM   29.5

   AT&T   64

   IBM   91.25

   Xerox   125

   Print the worksheet.

9. From the financial section of your newspaper, look up the current price of each stock (all these stocks are listed on the New York Stock Exchange). Enter these prices in the worksheet. Print the worksheet.

Developing a Professional-Looking Worksheet

Producing a Projected Sales Report for the Pronto Salsa Company

In this tutorial you will:

- Format data using the Number, Currency, and Percentage formats

- Align cell contents

- Center text across columns

- Change fonts, font style, and font size

- Use borders and color for emphasis

- Add comments and graphics to a worksheet using the Drawing toolbar

- Remove gridlines from the worksheet

- Print in landscape orientation

Pronto Salsa Company

CASE

Anne Castelar owns the Pronto Salsa Company, a successful business located in the heart of Tex-Mex country. She is working on a plan to add a new product, de Chili Guero Medium, to Pronto's gourmet salsa line.

Anne wants to take out a bank loan to purchase additional food-processing equipment to handle the production increase the new salsa requires. She has an appointment with her bank loan officer at 2:00 this afternoon. To prepare for the meeting, Anne creates a worksheet to show the projected sales of the new salsa and the expected effect on profits. Although the numbers and formulas are in place on the worksheet, Anne has no time to format the worksheet for the best impact. She planned to do that now, but an unexpected problem with today's produce shipment requires her to leave the office for a few hours. Anne asks you to complete the worksheet. She shows you a printout of the unformatted worksheet and explains that she wants the finished worksheet to look very professional—like those you see in business magazines. She also asks you to make sure that the worksheet emphasizes the profits expected from sales of the new salsa.

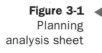

SESSION

3.1

In this session you will learn how to make your worksheets easier to understand through various formatting techniques. You will format values using Currency formats, Number formats, and Percentage formats. You will also change font styles and font sizes, and change the alignment of data within cells and across columns. As you perform all these tasks, you'll find the Format Painter button an extremely useful tool.

Opening the Workbook

After Anne leaves, you develop the worksheet plan in Figure 3-1 and the worksheet format plan in Figure 3-2.

Figure 3-1 ◀
Planning
analysis sheet

Planning Analysis For Projected Sales Report

My Goal
To format the worksheet so it produces a professional-looking printout

What results do I want to see?
The profits that are expected from sales of the new salsa product

What information do I need?
The unformatted worksheet

What calculations will I perform?
None; formulas have already been entered

Figure 3-2 ◀
Format plan

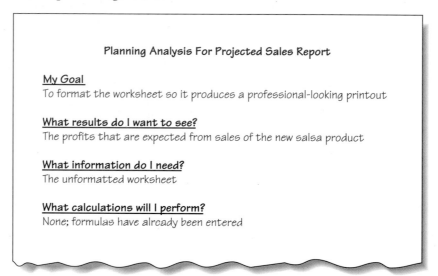

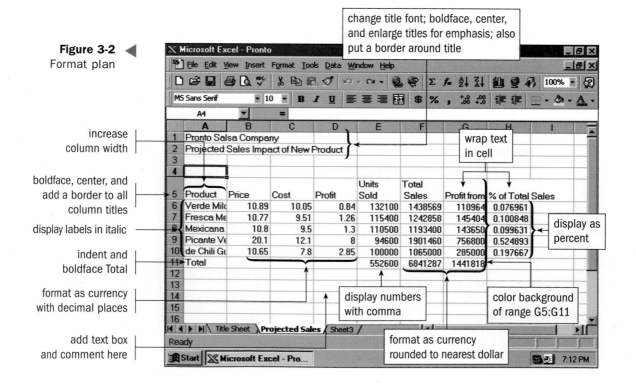

Anne has already entered all the formulas, numbers, and labels. Your main task is to format this information so it is easy to read and understand, and appears professional. This can be accomplished on two levels—by formatting the detailed data in the worksheet and by enhancing the appearance of the worksheet as a whole.

On the data level, you decide that the numbers should be formatted according to their use. For example, the product prices need to appear as dollar values. Secondly, the column and row labels need to fit within their cells. Also, the labels need to stand out more. To enhance the worksheet as a whole, you need to structure it so that related information is visually grouped together using lines and borders. Anne also wants certain areas of the worksheet that contain key information to stand out, and color may be a useful tool for this.

With all that needs to be done before Anne's 2:00 meeting, you decide that the best place to begin is with formatting the data within the worksheet. Once that is done, you will work to improve the worksheet's overall organization and appearance.

Now that the planning is done, you are ready to start Excel and open the workbook of unformatted data that Anne created.

To start Excel and organize your desktop:

1. Start Excel as usual.

2. Make sure your Student Disk is in the appropriate disk drive.

3. Make sure the Microsoft Excel and Book1 windows are maximized.

Now you need to open Anne's file and begin formatting the worksheet. Anne stored the workbook as Pronto, but before you begin to change the workbook, save it using the filename Pronto Salsa Company. This way, the original workbook, Pronto, remains unchanged in case you want to work through this tutorial again.

To open the Pronto workbook and save the workbook as Pronto Salsa Company:

1. Click the **Open** button 🖼 on the Standard toolbar to display the Open dialog box.

2. Open the **Pronto** workbook in the Tutorial.03 folder on your Student Disk.

3. Click **File** on the menu bar, and then click **Save As** to display the Save As dialog box.

4. In the File name text box, change the filename to **Pronto Salsa Company**.

5. Click the **Save** button to save the workbook under the new filename. The new filename, Pronto Salsa Company, appears in the title bar.

   TROUBLE? If you see the message "Replace existing file?" click the Yes button to replace the old version of Pronto Salsa Company with your new version.

6. Click the **Projected Sales** sheet tab. See Figure 3-3.

Figure 3-3 ◄
Pronto Salsa
Company
workbook

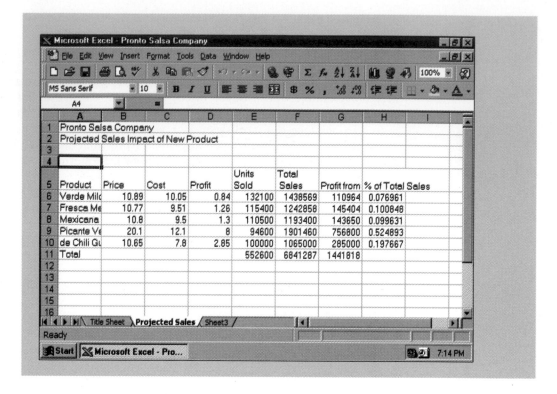

Studying the worksheet, you notice that the salsa names do not fit in column A. It is easy to widen column A, but if you do, some of the worksheet will scroll off the screen. Other formatting tasks are easier if you can see the entire worksheet, so you decide to do these tasks first.

Formatting Worksheet Data

Formatting is the process of changing the appearance of the data in worksheet cells. Formatting can make your worksheets easier to understand, and draw attention to important points.

In the previous tutorial you used AutoFormat to improve the appearance of your worksheet. AutoFormat applies a predefined format to your entire workbook. AutoFormat is easy to use, but its predefined format might not suit every worksheet. If you decide to customize a workbook's format, you can use the extensive Excel formatting options. When you select your own formats, you can format an individual cell or a range of cells.

Formatting changes only the appearance of the worksheet; it does not change the text or numbers stored in the cells. For example, if you format the number .123653 using a Percentage format that displays only one decimal place, the number appears in the worksheet as 12.4%; however, the original number, .123653, remains stored in the cell. When you enter data into cells, Excel applies an automatic format, referred to as the General format. The **General format** aligns numbers at the right side of the cell, uses a minus sign for negative values, and displays numbers without trailing zeros to the right of the decimal point. You can change the General format by using AutoFormat, the Format menu, the Shortcut menu, or toolbar buttons.

There are many ways to access the Excel formatting options. The Format menu provides access to all formatting commands. See Figure 3-4.

Figure 3-4 ◀
Format menu

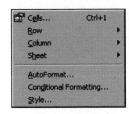

The Shortcut menu provides quick access to the Format dialog box. See Figure 3-5. To display the Shortcut menu, make sure the pointer is positioned within the range you have selected to format, and then click the right mouse button.

Figure 3-5 ◀
Shortcut menu

The Formatting toolbar contains formatting buttons, including the style and alignment buttons, and the Font Style and Font Size boxes. See Figure 3-6.

Figure 3-6 ◀
Formatting
toolbar buttons

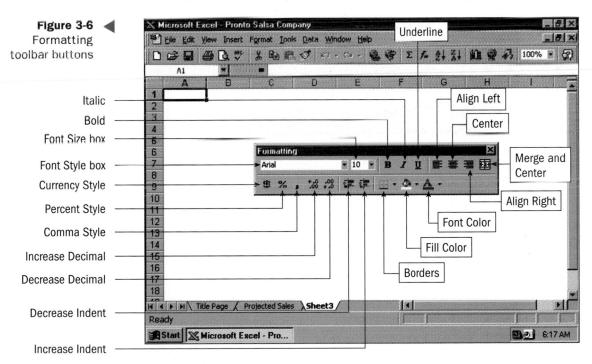

Most experienced Excel users develop a preference for which menu or buttons they use to access the Excel formatting options; however, most beginners find it easy to remember that all formatting options are available from the Format menu.

Looking at Anne's worksheet, you decide to change the appearance of the data first.

Changing the Appearance of Numbers

When the data in the worksheet appears as numbers, you want each number to appear in a style appropriate for what it is representing. The Excel default General format is often not the most appropriate style. For example, dollar values may require the dollar symbol ($) and thousand markers, and these can be applied to numerical data simply by changing the data's format. You can also standardize the number of decimal places displayed in a cell through formatting. Excel has a variety of predefined number formats. Figure 3-7 describes some of the most commonly used formats.

Figure 3-7 ◀
Commonly used
number formats

Category	Display Option
General	Excel default Number format; displays numbers without dollar signs, commas, or trailing decimal places
Number	Sets decimal places, negative number display, and comma separator
Currency	Sets decimal places and negative number display, and inserts dollar signs and comma separators
Accounting	Specialized monetary value format used to align dollar signs, decimal places, and comma separators
Date	Sets date or date and time display
Percentage	Inserts percent sign to the right of a number with a set number of decimal places

To change the number formatting, you select the cell or range of cells to be reformatted, and then use the Format Cells command or the Formatting toolbar button to apply a different format.

Currency Formats

In reviewing Anne's unformatted worksheet, you recognize that there are several columns of data that reflect currency. You decide to apply the Currency format to the Cost, Price, and Profit columns.

You have several options when formatting values as currency. You need to decide the number of decimal places you want displayed; whether or not you want to see the dollar sign; and how you want negative numbers to look. Keep in mind that if you want the currency symbols and decimal places to line up within a column, you should choose the Accounting format, rather than the Currency format.

In the Pronto Salsa Company worksheet, you want to apply the Currency format to the values in columns B, C, and D. The numbers will be formatted to include a dollar sign with two decimal places. You also decide to display negative numbers in the worksheet in parentheses.

To format columns B, C, and D using the Currency format:

1. Select the range **B6:D10**.

2. Click **Format** on the menu bar, and then click **Cells** to display the Format Cells dialog box.

3. If necessary, click the **Number** tab. See Figure 3-8.

Figure 3-8
Number tab of
Format Cells
dialog box

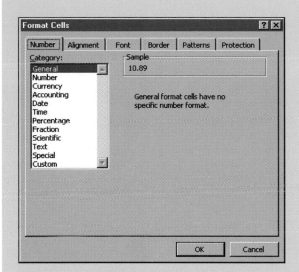

4. Click **Currency** in the Category list box. The Number tab changes to display the Currency formatting options, as shown in Figure 3-9. Notice that a sample of the selected format appears near the top of the dialog box. As you make further selections, the sample automatically changes to reflect your choices.

Figure 3-9
Selecting a
Currency
format

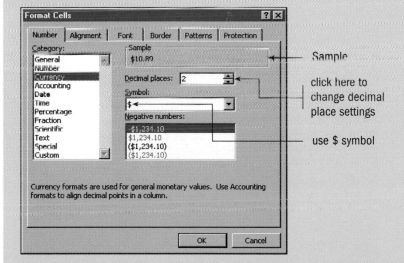

Notice that 2 decimal places is the default setting. A dollar sign ($) appears in the Symbol list box, indicating that the dollar sign will be displayed. If you are using a different currency, click the down arrow in the Symbol list box to select the currency symbol you want to display. Given the current options selected, you only need to select a format for negative numbers.

5. Click the third option **($1,234.10)** in the Negative numbers list box.

6. Click the **OK** button to format the selected range.

7. Click any cell to deselect the range and view the new formatting. See Figure 3-10.

Figure 3-10
Currency
formats in
columns B, C,
and D

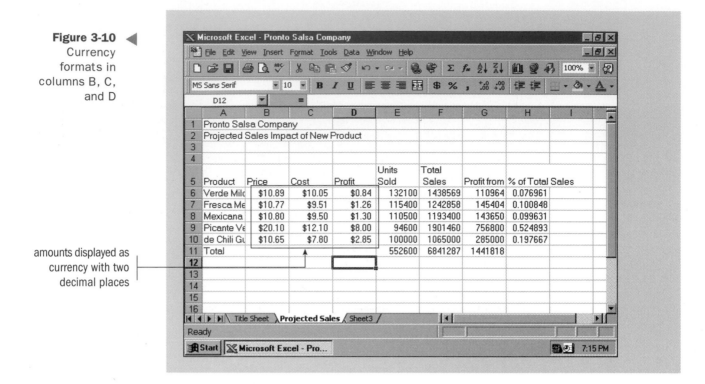

amounts displayed as
currency with two
decimal places

When your worksheet has large dollar amounts, you might want to use a Currency format that does not display any decimal places. To do this you use the Decrease Decimal button on the Formatting toolbar, or change the decimal places setting in the Format Cells dialog box. Currency values displayed with no decimal places are rounded to the nearest dollar: $15,612.56 becomes $15,613; $16,507.49 becomes $16,507; and so on.

You decide to format the Total Sales column as currency rounded to the nearest dollar.

To format cells F6 through F11 as currency rounded to the nearest dollar:

1. Select the range **F6:F11**.

2. Click **Format** on the menu bar, and then click **Cells** to display the Format Cells dialog box.

3. If necessary, click the **Number** tab.

4. Click **Currency** in the Category list box.

5. Click the **Decimal places** spin box down arrow twice to change the setting to 0 decimal places. Notice that the sample format changes to reflect the new settings.

6. Click the **OK** button to apply the format. Notice that Excel automatically increased the column width to display the formatted numbers.

7. Click any cell to deselect the range.

After formatting the Total Sales figures in column F, you realize you should have used the same format for the numbers in column G. To save time, you simply copy the formatting from column F to column G.

The Format Painter Button

The Format Painter button on the Standard toolbar lets you copy formats quickly from one cell or range to another. You simply click a cell containing the formats you want to copy, click the Format Painter button, and then use the click-drag technique to select the range to which you want to apply the copied formats.

To copy the format from cell F6:

1. Click cell **F6** because it contains the format you want to copy.

2. Click the **Format Painter** button 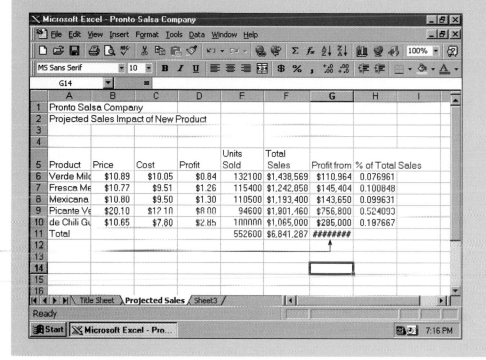 on the Standard toolbar. As you move the pointer over the worksheet cells, notice that the pointer turns to ⊹⛏.

3. Position ⊹⛏ over cell G6, and then click and drag to select cells **G6:G11**. When you release the mouse button, the cells appear in the Currency format, rounded to the nearest dollar—the same format used in cells F6 through F11.

4. Click any cell to deselect the range and view the formatted Profit from Sales column. See Figure 3-11.

Figure 3-11 ◀
Worksheet after Format Painter used to copy formats

number symbols indicate column width needs to increase

As you review the changes on the screen, you notice that cell G11 contains number symbols (######) instead of values. This is because the formatting change has caused the data to exceed the width of the cell.

Number Symbol (###) Replacement

If a number is too long to fit within a cell's boundaries, Excel displays a series of number symbols (###) in the cell. The number symbols indicate that the number of digits in the value exceeds the cell's width. The number or formula is still stored in the cell, but the current cell width is not large enough to display the value. To display the value, you just need to increase the column width. One way you can do this is to use the Shortcut menu.

To replace the number symbols by increasing the column width:

1. Position the pointer on the column heading for column G.

2. Right-click the mouse button to display the Shortcut menu.

3. Click **Column Width** to display the Column Width dialog box.

4. Type **9** in the Column Width box.

5. Click the **OK** button to view the total sales, $1,441,818.

6. Click any cell to view the formatted data.

Now the cells containing price, cost, profit, total sales, and profit from sales are formatted as currency. Next, you want to apply formats to the numbers in columns E and H so that they are easier to read.

Number Formats

Like Currency formats, the Excel Number formats offer many options. You can select Number formats to specify

- the number of decimal places displayed
- whether to display a comma to delimit thousands, millions, and billions
- whether to display negative numbers with a minus sign, parentheses, or red numerals

REFERENCE window	**FORMATTING NUMBERS**
	■ Select the cells you want the new format applied to.
	■ Click Format, click Cells, and then click the Numbers tab in the Format Cells dialog box.
	■ Select a format category from the Category list box.
	■ Select the desired options for the selected format.
	■ Click the OK button.

To access all Excel Number formats, you can use the Number tab in the Format Cells dialog box. You can also use the Comma Style button, the Increase Decimal button, and the Decrease Decimal button on the Formatting toolbar to select some Number formats.

Looking at your planning sheet and sketch, you can see that the numbers in column E need to be made easier to read by changing the format to include commas.

To format the contents in column E with a comma and no decimal places:

1. Select the range **E6:E11**.

2. Click the **Comma Style** button ⌐'⌐ on the Formatting toolbar to apply the Comma Style. The default for the Comma Style is to display numbers with two places to the right of the decimal. Use the Decrease Decimal button ⌐.00→.0⌐ on the Formatting toolbar to decrease the number of decimal places displayed in cells formatted with the Comma Style to zero.

3. Click the **Decrease Decimal** button ⌐.00→.0⌐ on the Formatting toolbar twice to display the number with no decimal places.

4. Click any cell to deselect the range and view the formatted Units Sold column. See Figure 3-12.

Figure 3-12
Cells formatted
with Number
format

Number format —

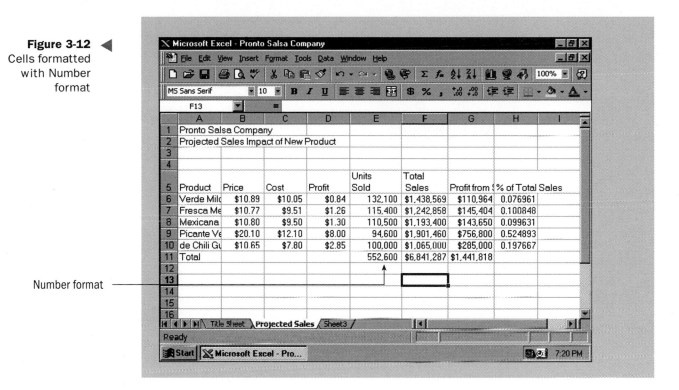

Looking at the numbers in column H, you realize that they are difficult to interpret and decide that you do not need to display so many decimal places. What are your options for displaying percentages?

Percentage Format

When formatting values as percentages, you need to select how many decimal places you want displayed. The Percentage format with no decimal places displays the number 0.18037 as 18%. The Percentage format with two decimal places displays the same number as 18.04%. If you want to use the Percentage format with two decimal places, you select this option using the Number tab in the Format Cells dialog box. You can also use the Percent Style button on the Formatting toolbar, and then click the Increase Decimal button twice to add two decimal places.

Your format sketch specifies a Percentage format with no decimal places for the values in column H. You could use the Number tab to choose this format. But it's faster to use the Percent Style button on the Formatting toolbar.

To format the values in column H as a percentage with no decimal places:

1. Select the range **H6:H10.**

2. Click the **Percent Style** button ![%] on the Formatting toolbar.

3. Click any cell to deselect the range and view the Percent Style. See Figure 3-13.

Figure 3-13 ◀
Percent of total
sales formatted
with Percent
Style

Percent Style —

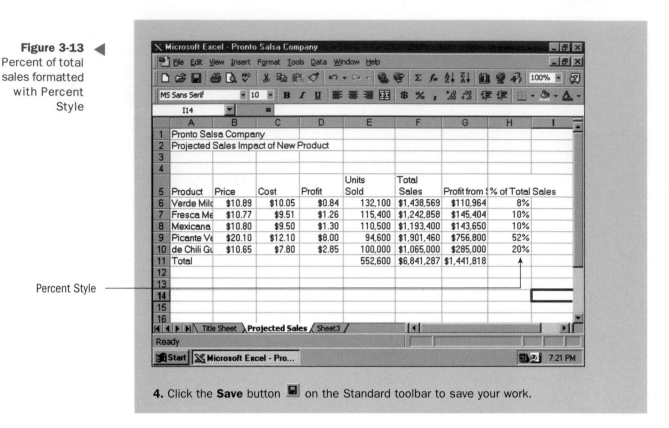

4. Click the **Save** button 🔲 on the Standard toolbar to save your work.

You review the worksheet. You have now formatted all the numbers in the worksheet appropriately. The next step in formatting Anne's worksheet is to improve the alignment of the data in the cells.

Aligning Cell Contents

The **alignment** of data in a cell is the position of the data relative to the right and left edges of the cell. Cell contents can be aligned on the left or right side of the cell, or centered in the cell. When you enter numbers and formulas, Excel automatically aligns them on the cell's right side. Excel automatically aligns text entries on the cell's left side. The default Excel alignment does not always create the most readable worksheet. Figure 3-14 shows a worksheet with the column titles left-aligned and the numbers in the columns right-aligned.

Figure 3-14 ◀
Poorly
formatted
worksheet

column titles
left-aligned

numbers
right-aligned

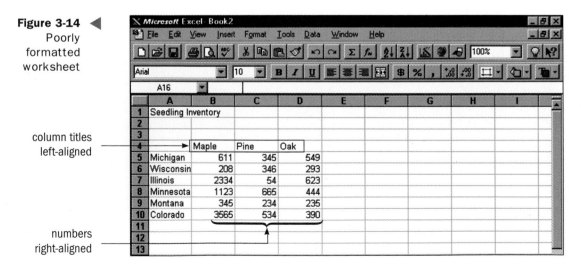

Notice how difficult it is to figure out which numbers go with each column title. Centering or right-aligning column titles would improve the readability of the worksheet in Figure 3-14. As a general rule, you should center column titles, format columns of numbers so that the decimal places are in line, and leave columns of text aligned on the left. You can change the alignment of cell data using the four alignment tools on the Formatting toolbar, or you can access additional alignment options by selecting the Alignment tab in the Format Cells dialog box.

To center the column titles:

1. Select the range **A5:H5**.

2. Click the **Center** button on the Formatting toolbar to center the cell contents.

3. Click any cell to deselect the range and view the centered titles. See Figure 3-15.

Figure 3-15 ◀
Worksheet with
centered
column titles

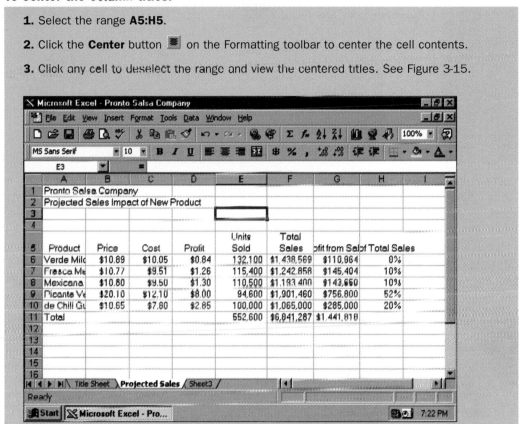

Notice that the column titles in columns G and H are not fully displayed. Although you could widen the column widths of these two columns to display the entire text, the Excel Wrap Text option enables you to display a label within a cell.

Wrapping Text in a Cell

As you know, if you enter a label that's too wide for the active cell, Excel extends the label past the cell border and into the adjacent cells—provided those cells are empty. If you select the Wrap Text option, Excel will display your label entirely within the active cell. To accommodate the label, the height of the row in which the cell is located is increased, and the text is "wrapped" onto the additional lines.

Now wrap the column titles in columns G and H.

To wrap text within a cell:

1. Select the range **G5:H5**.

2. Click **Format** on the menu bar, and then click **Cells** to display the Format Cells dialog box.

3. Click the **Alignment** tab. See Figure 3-16.

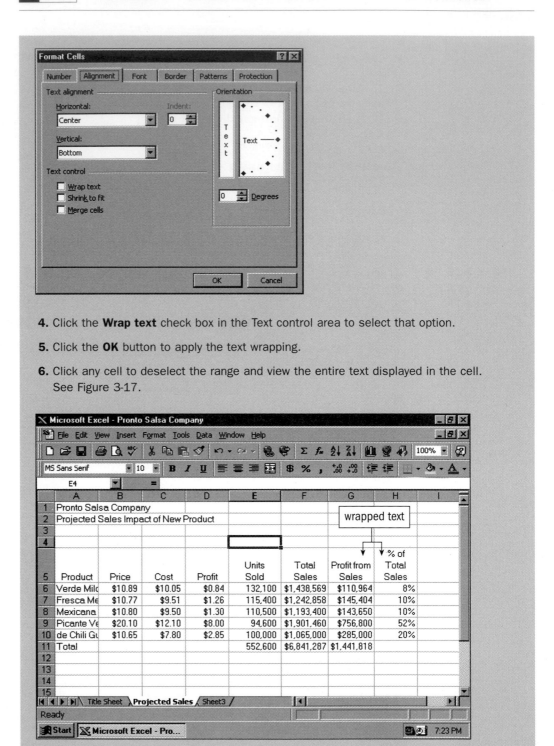

Figure 3-16 ◄
Alignment tab
of Format Cells
dialog box

4. Click the **Wrap text** check box in the Text control area to select that option.

5. Click the **OK** button to apply the text wrapping.

6. Click any cell to deselect the range and view the entire text displayed in the cell.
See Figure 3-17.

Figure 3-17 ◄
Wrapping text
in a cell

Now you will center the main worksheet titles.

Centering Text Across Columns

Sometimes you might want to center a cell's contents across more than one column. This
is particularly useful for centering titles at the top of a worksheet. Now you will use the
Center Across Selections option from the Format Cells dialog box to center the worksheet
titles in cells A1 and A2 across columns A through H.

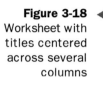

Excel

To center the worksheet titles across columns A through H:

1. Select the range **A1:H2**.

2. Click **Format**, click **Cells**, and if necessary click the **Alignment** tab in the Format Cells dialog box.

3. Click the arrow next to the Horizontal text alignment list box to display the horizontal text alignment options.

4. Click the **Center Across Selection** option to center the title lines across columns A through H.

5. Click the **OK** button.

6. Click any cell to deselect the range. See Figure 3-18.

Figure 3-18 ◀
Worksheet with
titles centered
across several
columns

cell contents centered
across columns
A through H

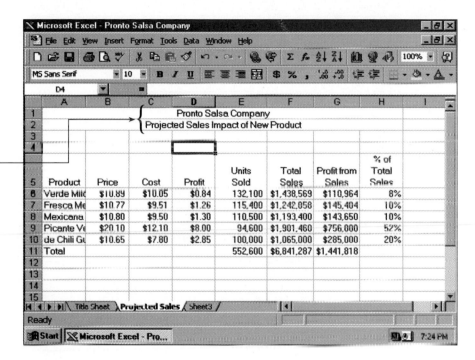

Indenting Text Within a Cell

When you type text in a cell it is left-aligned. You can indent text from the left edge by using the Increase Indent button on the Formatting toolbar or the Index spinner button in the Alignment tab of the Format Cells dialog box. You decide to indent the word "Total" to provide a visual cue of the change from detail to summary information.

To indent text within a cell:

1. Click cell **A11** to make it the active cell.

2. Click the **Increase Indent** button 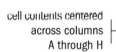 on the Formatting toolbar to indent the word "Total" within the cell.

3. Click the **Save** button ▣ on the Standard toolbar to save the worksheet.

You check your plan and confirm that you selected formats for all worksheet cells containing data, and that the data within the cells is aligned properly. The formatting of the worksheet contents is almost complete. Your next task is to improve the appearance of the labels by changing the font style of the title and the column headings.

You decide to use the Bold button on the Formatting toolbar to change some titles in the worksheet to boldface.

Changing the Font, Font Style, and Font Size

A **font** is a set of letters, numbers, punctuation marks, and symbols with a specific size and design. Figure 3-19 shows some examples. A font can have one or more of the following **font styles**: regular, italic, bold, and bold italic.

Figure 3-19
Selected fonts

Font	Regular Style	Italic Style	Bold Style	Bold Italic Style
Times	AaBbCc	*AaBbCc*	**AaBbCc**	***AaBbCc***
Courier	AaBbCc	*AaBbCc*	**AaBbCc**	***AaBbCc***
Garamond	AaBbCc	*AaBbCc*	**AaBbCc**	***AaBbCc***
Helvetica Condensed	AaBbCc	*AaBbCc*	**AaBbCc**	***AaBbCc***

Most fonts are available in many sizes, and you can also select font effects, such as strikeout, underline, and color. The Formatting toolbar provides tools for changing font style by applying boldface, italics, underline, and increasing or decreasing font size. To access other font effects, you can open the Format Cells dialog box from the Format menu.

REFERENCE window	CHANGING FONT, FONT STYLE, AND FONT SIZE
	■ Select the cells you want the new format to apply to. ■ Click Format, click Cells, and then click the Font tab in the Format Cells dialog box. ■ Select a typeface from the Font list box. ■ Select a font style from the Font style list box. ■ Select a type size from the Size list box. ■ the OK button. or ■ Select the cells you want the new format to apply to. ■ Select the font, font size, and font style using the buttons on the Formatting toolbar.

You begin by formatting the word "Total" in cell A11 in boldface letters.

To apply the boldface font style:

1. If necessary, click cell **A11**.

2. Click the **Bold** button on the Formatting toolbar to set the font style to bold-face. Notice that when a style like bold is applied to a cell's content, the toolbar button appears depressed to indicate that the style is applied to the active cell.

You also want to display the column titles in boldface. To do this, first select the range you want to format, and then click the Bold button to apply the format.

To display the column titles in boldface:

1. Select the range **A5:H5**.

2. Click the **Bold** button 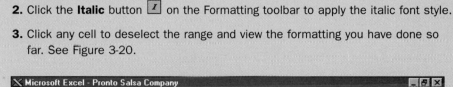 on the Formatting toolbar to apply the boldface font style.

3. Click any cell to deselect the range.

Next, you decide to display the salsa products' names in italics.

To italicize the row labels:

1. Select the range **A6:A10.**

2. Click the **Italic** button ⌐I⌐ on the Formatting toolbar to apply the italic font style.

3. Click any cell to deselect the range and view the formatting you have done so far. See Figure 3-20.

Figure 3-20 ◄
Bold and Italic
formats applied

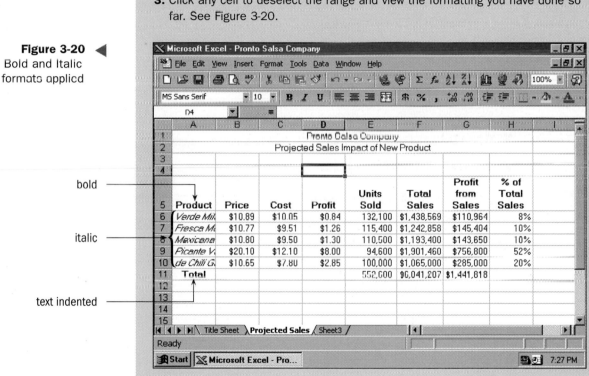

bold

italic

text indented

Next, you want to change the font and size of the worksheet titles for emphasis. You use the Font dialog box (instead of the toolbar) so you can preview your changes. Remember, although the worksheet titles appear to be in columns A through F, they are just spilling over from column A. To format the titles, you need to select only cells A1 and A2—the cells where the titles were originally entered.

To change the font and font size of the worksheet titles:

1. Select the range **A1:A2**.

2. Click **Format** on the menu bar, and then click **Cells** to display the Format Cells dialog box.

3. Click the **Font** tab. See Figure 3-21.

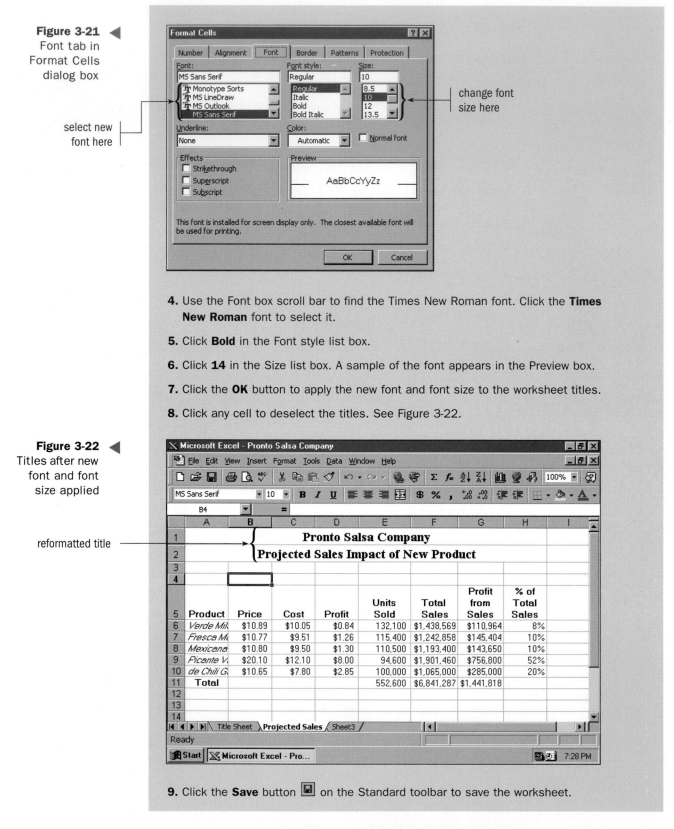

Figure 3-21 ◄
Font tab in
Format Cells
dialog box

select new
font here

change font
size here

4. Use the Font box scroll bar to find the Times New Roman font. Click the **Times New Roman** font to select it.

5. Click **Bold** in the Font style list box.

6. Click **14** in the Size list box. A sample of the font appears in the Preview box.

7. Click the **OK** button to apply the new font and font size to the worksheet titles.

8. Click any cell to deselect the titles. See Figure 3-22.

Figure 3-22 ◄
Titles after new
font and font
size applied

reformatted title

	Product	Price	Cost	Profit	Units Sold	Total Sales	Profit from Sales	% of Total Sales
1				Pronto Salsa Company				
2				Projected Sales Impact of New Product				
3								
4								
5	Product	Price	Cost	Profit	Units Sold	Total Sales	Profit from Sales	% of Total Sales
6	Verde Mi	$10.89	$10.05	$0.84	132,100	$1,438,569	$110,964	8%
7	Fresca M	$10.77	$9.51	$1.26	115,400	$1,242,858	$145,404	10%
8	Mexicana	$10.80	$9.50	$1.30	110,500	$1,193,400	$143,650	10%
9	Picante V	$20.10	$12.10	$8.00	94,600	$1,901,460	$756,800	52%
10	de Chili G	$10.65	$7.80	$2.85	100,000	$1,065,000	$285,000	20%
11	Total				552,600	$6,841,287	$1,441,818	
12								
13								
14								

9. Click the **Save** button 🖫 on the Standard toolbar to save the worksheet.

You hope Anne will approve of the Times New Roman font—it looks like the font on the Pronto salsa jar labels.

Quick Check

1 If the number .128912 is in a cell, what will Excel display if you:
  a. Format the number using the Percentage format with no decimal places
  b. Format the number using the Currency format with 2 decimal places and the dollar sign

2 List three ways you can access formatting commands, options, and tools.

3 Explain why Excel might display 3,045.39 in a cell, but 3045.38672 in the formula bar.

4 List the options available on the Formatting toolbar for aligning data.

5 What are the general rules you should follow for aligning column headings, numbers, and text labels?

6 Explain two ways to completely display a label that currently is not entirely displayed.

7 The _____ copies formats quickly from one cell or range to another.

8 A series of ######## in a cell indicates _____.

Now that you have finished formatting the data in the worksheet, you need to enhance the worksheet's appearance and readability as a whole. You will do this in Session 3.2 by applying borders, colors, and a text box.

SESSION

3.2

In this session you learn how to enhance a worksheet's overall appearance by adding borders and color. You will use the Drawing toolbar to add a text box and graphic to the worksheet, and use landscape orientation to print the worksheet.

Adding and Removing Borders

A well-constructed worksheet is clearly divided into zones that visually group related information. Figure 3-23 shows the zones on your worksheet. Lines, called **borders**, can help to distinguish different zones of the worksheet and add visual interest.

Figure 3-23 ◀
Information
zones

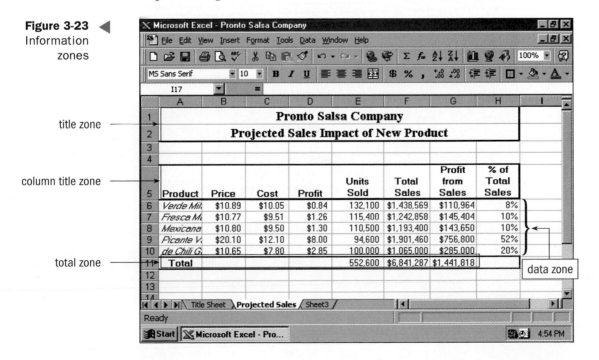

You can create lines and borders using either the Borders button on the Formatting toolbar, or the Border tab in the Format Cells dialog box. You can place a border around a single cell or a group of cells using the Outline option. To create a horizontal line, you place a border at the top or bottom of a cell. To create a vertical line, you place a border on the right or left side of a cell.

The Border tab lets you choose from numerous border styles, including different line thicknesses, double lines, dashed lines, and colored lines. With the Borders button, your choice of border styles is more limited.

To remove a border from a cell or group of cells, you can use the Border tab in the Format Cells dialog box. To remove all borders from a selected range of cells, select the None button in the Presets area.

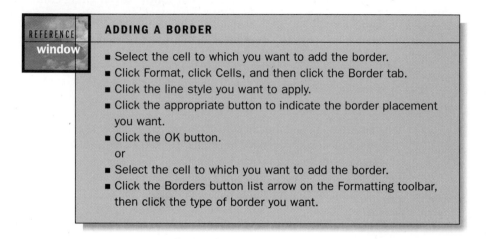

REFERENCE window

ADDING A BORDER

- Select the cell to which you want to add the border.
- Click Format, click Cells, and then click the Border tab.
- Click the line style you want to apply.
- Click the appropriate button to indicate the border placement you want.
- Click the OK button.
  or
- Select the cell to which you want to add the border.
- Click the Borders button list arrow on the Formatting toolbar, then click the type of border you want.

You decide that a thick line under all column titles will separate them from the data in the columns. To do this, you use the Borders button on the Formatting toolbar.

To underline column titles:

1. If you took a break after the last session, make sure Excel is running and the Projected Sales worksheet of the Pronto Salsa Company workbook is open.

2. Select the range **A5:H5**.

3. Click the **Borders** button list arrow on the Formatting toolbar. The Borders palette appears. See Figure 3-24.

Figure 3-24 ◀
Borders palette

medium thick underline

double-ruled line

thick outline

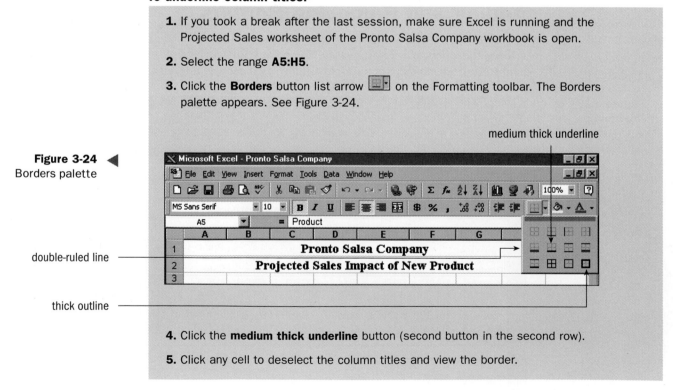

4. Click the **medium thick underline** button (second button in the second row).

5. Click any cell to deselect the column titles and view the border.

You also want a line to separate the data from the totals in row 11, and a double-ruled line below the totals. This time you use the Border tab in the Format Cells dialog box to apply borders to cells.

To add a line separating the data and the totals and a double-ruled line below the totals:

1. Select the range **A11:H11**.

2. Click **Format** on the menu bar, click **Cells**, and then click the **Border** tab in the Format Cells dialog box. See Figure 3-25.

Figure 3-25 ◀
Border tab from
Format Cells
dialog box

applies selected line
style to top border

applies selected line
style to bottom border

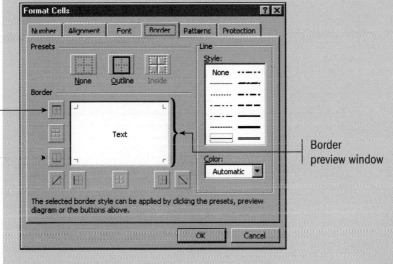

Border
preview window

3. Click the **medium thick line** in the Line Style box (third from the bottom in the second column).

4. Click the **top border** button. A thick line appears at the top of the Border preview window.

5. Click the **double-ruled line** in the Line Style box.

6. Click the **bottom border** button. A double-ruled line appears at the bottom of the Border preview window.

7. Click the **OK** button to apply the borders.

8. Click any cell to deselect the range and view the borders. See Figure 3-26.

Figure 3-26 ◀
Borders applied
to worksheet

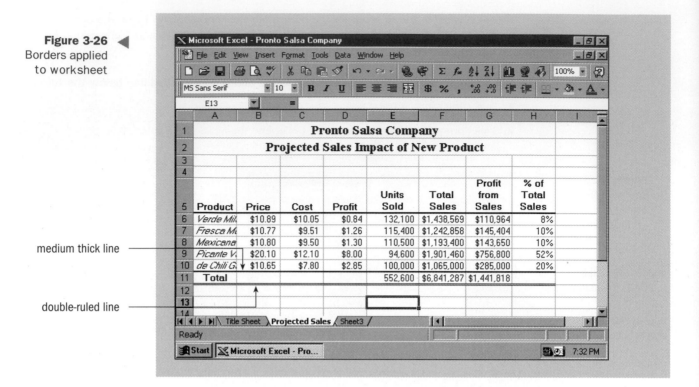

medium thick line ⎯⎯⎯

double-ruled line ⎯⎯⎯

You consult your format sketch and see that you planned a border around the title zone to add a professional touch. You decide to add this border next.

To place an outline border around the title zone:

1. Select the range **A1:H2**.

2. Click the **Borders** button list arrow ▦ on the Formatting toolbar to display the Borders palette.

3. Click the **thick outline** button in the last row.

4. Click any cell to deselect the titles and view the border.

5. Click the **Save** button 🖫 on the Standard toolbar to save the worksheet.

In addition to a border around the title zone, you want to add color to emphasize the Profit from Sales column.

Using Color for Emphasis

Patterns and colors provide visual interest, emphasize worksheet zones, or indicate data-entry areas. You should base the use of patterns or colors on the way you intend to use the worksheet. If you print the worksheet in color and distribute a hard copy of it, or if you plan to use a color projection device to display your worksheet on screen, you can take advantage of the Excel color formatting options. If you do not have a color printer, you can use patterns. It is difficult to predict how colors you see on your screen will be translated into gray shades on your printout.

Excel

REFERENCE window

APPLYING PATTERNS AND COLOR

- Select the cells you want to fill with a pattern or color.
- Click Format, click Cells, and then click the Patterns tab in the Format Cells dialog box.
- Select a pattern from the Pattern drop-down list. If you want the pattern to appear in a color, select a color from the Pattern palette, too.
- If you want a colored background, select it from the Cell shading color palette. You can also select colors by clicking the Color button on the Formatting toolbar and then clicking the color you want.

You want your worksheet to look good when you print it in black and white on the office laser printer, but you also want it to look good on the screen when you show it to Anne. You decide that a yellow background will enable the Profit from Sales column to stand out and looks fairly good on the screen and the printout. You apply this format using the Patterns tab in the Format Cells dialog box.

To apply a color to the Profit from Sales column:

1. Select the range **G5:G11**.

2. Click **Format** on the menu bar, click **Cells**, and then click the **Patterns** tab in the Format Cells dialog box. See Figure 3-27.

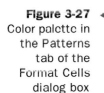

Figure 3-27
Color palette in the Patterns tab of the Format Cells dialog box

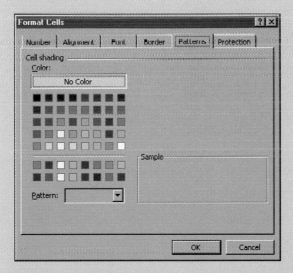

3. Click the **yellow square** in the fourth row (third square from the left) of the Cell shading Color palette.

4. Click the **OK** button to apply the color.

5. Click any cell to deselect the range and view the color in the Profit from Sales column. See Figure 3-28.

Figure 3-28 ◄
Worksheet
after applying
color to
a column

yellow background —

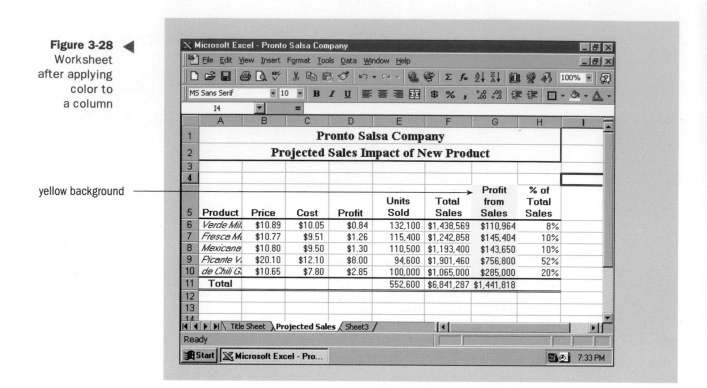

You delayed changing the width of column A because you knew that doing so would cause some columns to scroll off the screen, forcing you to scroll around the worksheet to format all the labels and values. Now that you have finished formatting labels and values, you can change the width of column A to best display the information in that column. To do this, you can use the Shortcut menu to change the column width.

To change the column width using the Shortcut menu:

1. Position the pointer on the column heading for column A.

2. Right-click the mouse button to display the Shortcut menu.

3. Click **Column Width** to display the Column Width dialog box.

4. Type **25** in the Column Width text box.

5. Click the **OK** button.

6. Click any cell to deselect the column and view the results of the column width change. See Figure 3-29.

Figure 3-29
Results of
changing
column width

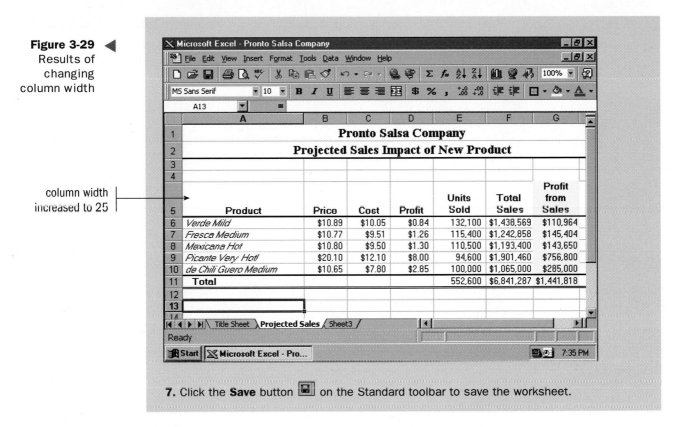

column width
increased to 25

7. Click the **Save** button 🔲 on the Standard toolbar to save the worksheet.

Adding Comments to the Worksheet

The Excel Text Box feature lets you display a comment in a worksheet. A comment is like an electronic Post-It note that you paste inside a rectangular text box in the worksheet.

To add a comment to your worksheet, you first create a text box, then you simply type the text in the box. You create a text box using the Text Box button, which is located on the Drawing toolbar.

Activating a Toolbar

Excel provides many toolbars. You have been using two: the Standard toolbar and the Formatting toolbar. Some of the other toolbars include the Chart toolbar, the Drawing toolbar, and the Visual Basic toolbar. To activate a toolbar, it's usually easiest to use the toolbar Shortcut menu, but to activate the Drawing toolbar you can simply click the Drawing button on the Standard toolbar. When you finish using a toolbar, you can easily remove it from the worksheet.

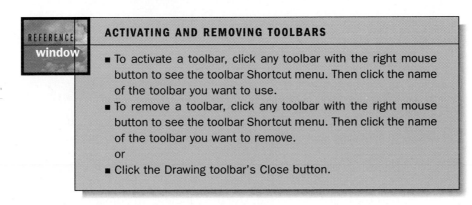

REFERENCE
window

ACTIVATING AND REMOVING TOOLBARS

■ To activate a toolbar, click any toolbar with the right mouse button to see the toolbar Shortcut menu. Then click the name of the toolbar you want to use.

■ To remove a toolbar, click any toolbar with the right mouse button to see the toolbar Shortcut menu. Then click the name of the toolbar you want to remove.
or

■ Click the Drawing toolbar's Close button.

You need the Drawing toolbar to accomplish your next formatting task. (If your Drawing toolbar is already displayed, skip the following step.)

To display the Drawing toolbar:

1. Click the **Drawing** button 🖋 on the Standard toolbar.

The toolbar might appear in any location in the worksheet window; this is called a **floating toolbar**. You don't want the toolbar obstructing your view of the worksheet, so drag it to the bottom of the worksheet window, to **anchor** it there. (If your toolbar is already anchored at the bottom of the worksheet window, or at the top, skip the next set of steps.)

To anchor the Drawing toolbar to the bottom of the worksheet window:

1. Position the pointer on the title bar of the Drawing toolbar.

2. Click and drag the toolbar to the bottom of the screen.

3. Release the mouse button to attach the Drawing toolbar to the bottom of the worksheet window. See Figure 3-30.

Figure 3-30 ◀
Drawing toolbar
attached
to bottom
of window

Drawing toolbar

Text Box tool

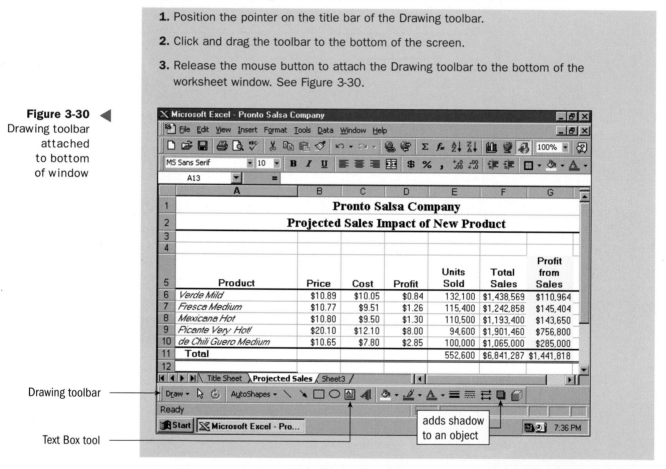

Now that the Drawing toolbar is where you want it, you proceed with your plan to add a comment to the worksheet.

Adding a Text Box

A **text box** is a block of text that sits in the worksheet. It is useful for adding comments to worksheets and charts. The text box is one example of a graphic object. With Excel you can create a variety of graphic objects, such as boxes, lines, circles, arrows, and text boxes. To move, modify, or delete an object, you first select it by moving the pointer over the object until the pointer changes to ⬚, then clicking. Small square handles indicate that the object is selected. Use these handles to adjust the object's size, change its location, or delete it.

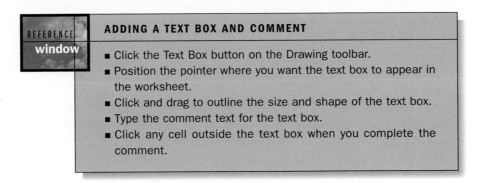

REFERENCE
window

ADDING A TEXT BOX AND COMMENT

■ Click the Text Box button on the Drawing toolbar.
■ Position the pointer where you want the text box to appear in the worksheet.
■ Click and drag to outline the size and shape of the text box.
■ Type the comment text for the text box.
■ Click any cell outside the text box when you complete the comment.

You want to draw attention to the new salsa product's low price and high profit margin. To do this, you plan to add a text box to the bottom of the worksheet that contains a comment about expected profits.

To add a comment in a text box:

1. Scroll the worksheet so you can see rows 7 through 21.

2. Click the **Text Box** button on the Drawing toolbar. As you move the pointer inside the worksheet area, the pointer changes to ↓. Position the crosshair of the pointer at the top of cell **A13** to mark the upper-left corner of the text box.

3. Click and drag + to cell **C18**, and then release the mouse button to mark the lower-right corner of the text box. See Figure 3-31.

   You are ready to type the text into the text box.

Figure 3-31 ◀
Creating a
text box

text box ──────→

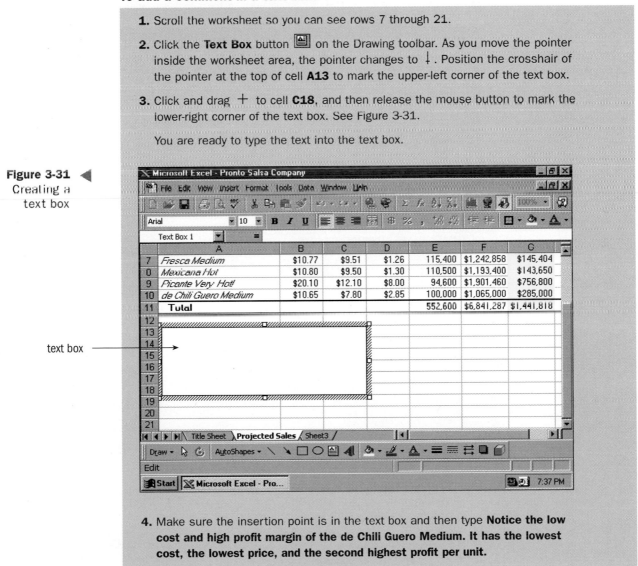

4. Make sure the insertion point is in the text box and then type **Notice the low cost and high profit margin of the de Chili Guero Medium. It has the lowest cost, the lowest price, and the second highest profit per unit.**

You want to use a different font style to emphasize the name of the new salsa product in the text box.

To italicize the name of the new salsa product:

1. Position I in the text box just before the word "de Chili."

2. Click and drag I to the end of the word "Medium", and then release the mouse button.

   TROUBLE? Don't worry if the text in your text box is not arranged exactly like the text in the figure. If the size of your text box differs slightly from the one in the figure, the lines of text might break differently.

3. Click the **Italic** button [I] on the Formatting toolbar.

4. Click any cell to deselect the product name, which now appears italicized. See Figure 3-32.

Figure 3-32 ◀
Italicizing text
in the text box

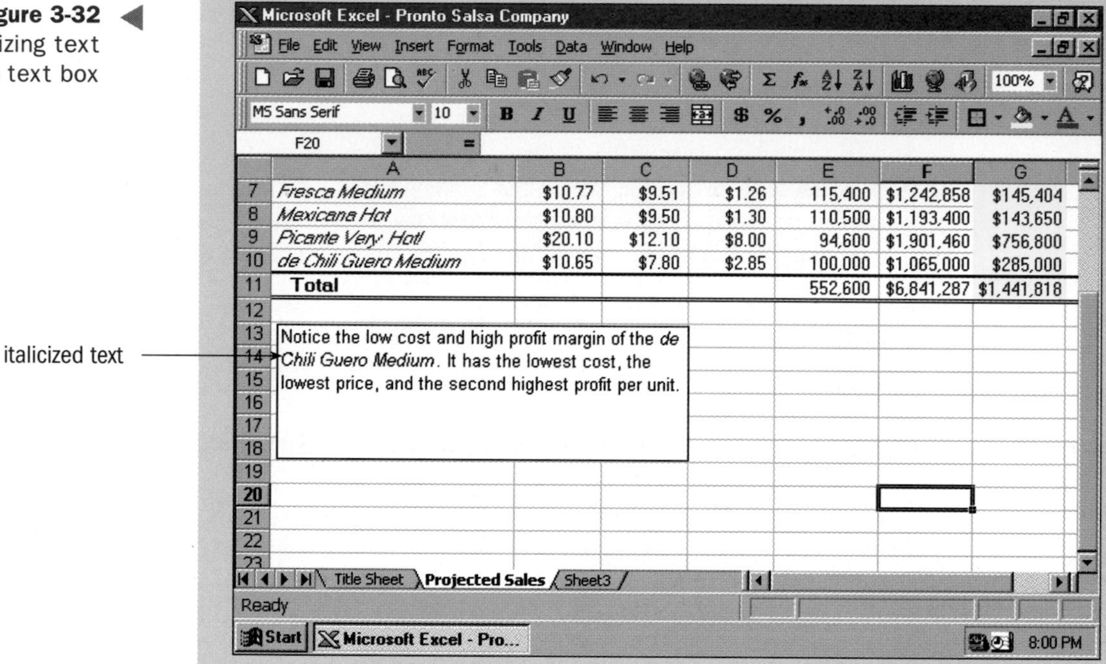

italicized text ——

You decide to change the text box size so that there is no empty space at the bottom.

To change the text box size:

1. Click the **text box** to select it and display the patterned border with handles.

2. Position the pointer on the center handle at the bottom of the text box. The pointer changes to $\updownarrow$.

3. Click and drag $\updownarrow$ up to shorten the box, and then release the mouse button.

You want to change the text box a bit more by adding a drop shadow to it.

To add a shadow to the text box:

1. Make sure the text box is still selected. (Look for the patterned border and handles.)

2. Click the **Shadow** button [▢] on the Drawing toolbar to display the gallery of Shadow options. See Figure 3-33.

Figure 3-33 ◀
Shadow
style options

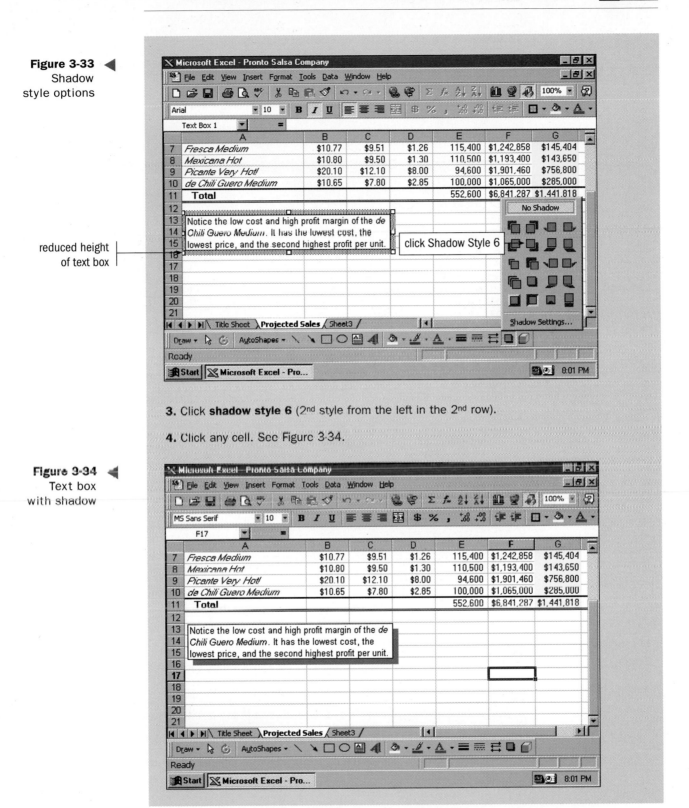

reduced height
of text box

3. Click **shadow style 6** (2nd style from the left in the 2nd row).

4. Click any cell. See Figure 3-34.

Figure 3-34 ◀
Text box
with shadow

Adding an Arrow

You decide to add an arrow pointing from the text box to the row with information on
the new salsa.

To add an arrow:

1. Click the **Arrow** button ![arrow icon] on the Drawing toolbar. As you move the mouse pointer inside the worksheet, the pointer changes to $+$.

2. Position $+$ on the top edge of the text box in cell **B12**. To ensure a straight line, press and hold the **Shift** key as you drag $+$ to cell **B10**, and then release the mouse button. See Figure 3-35.

Figure 3-35 ◄
Creating
an arrow

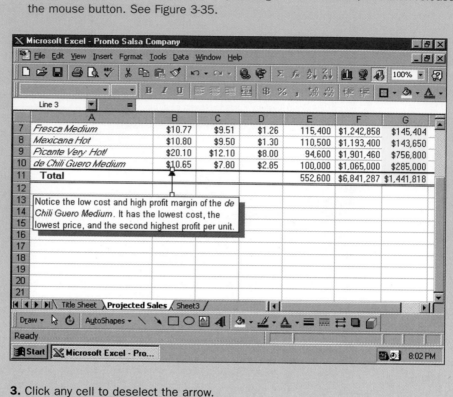

3. Click any cell to deselect the arrow.

You want the arrow to point to cell D10 instead of B10, so you need to reposition it.

Like a text box, an arrow is an Excel object. To modify the arrow object, you must select it. When you do so, two small square handles appear on it. You can reposition either end of the arrow by dragging one of the handles.

To reposition the arrow:

1. Scroll the worksheet until row 5 appears as the first visible row in the window.

2. Move the pointer over the arrow object until the pointer changes to ✛.

3. Click the **arrow**. Handles appear at each end of the arrow.

4. Move the pointer to the top handle on the arrowhead until the pointer changes to ↖.

5. Click and drag $+$ to cell **D10**, and then release the mouse button.

6. Click any cell to deselect the arrow object. See Figure 3-36.

Figure 3-36 ◄
Moving
the arrow

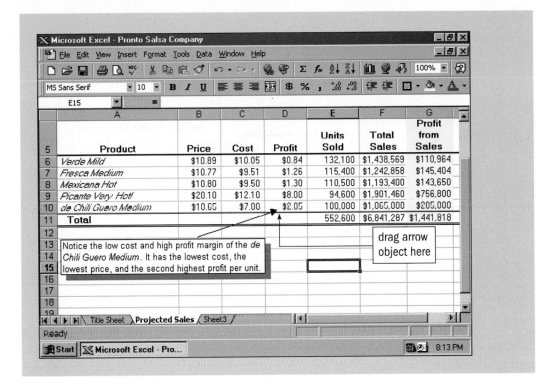

Now that the text box is finished, you can remove the Drawing toolbar from the worksheet.

To remove the Drawing toolbar:

1. Click the **Drawing** button 🔲 on the Standard toolbar. The Drawing toolbar is removed from the window, and the Drawing button 🔲 no longer appears depressed (selected).

2. Press **Ctrl + Home** to make cell A1 the active cell.

3. Click the **Save** button 🔲 on the Standard toolbar to save your work.

You have now made all the formatting changes and enhancements to Anne's worksheet. She has just returned to the office, and you show her the completed worksheet. She is very pleased with how professional the worksheet looks, but she thinks of one more way to improve the appearance of the worksheet. She asks you to remove the gridlines from the worksheet display.

Controlling the Display of Gridlines

Although normally the boundaries of each cell are outlined in black, Anne has decided that the appearance of your worksheet will be more effective if you remove the display of gridlines. To remove the gridline display, you deselect the Gridlines option in the View tab of the Options dialog box.

To remove the display of gridlines in the worksheet:

1. Click **Tools** on the menu bar, click **Options**, and if necessary, click the **View** tab in the Options dialog box.

2. Click the **Gridlines** check box in the Window option to remove the check and deselect the option.

3. Click the **OK** button to display the worksheet without gridlines. See Figure 3-37.

Figure 3-37 ◄
Worksheet
without
gridlines

no gridlines ──────

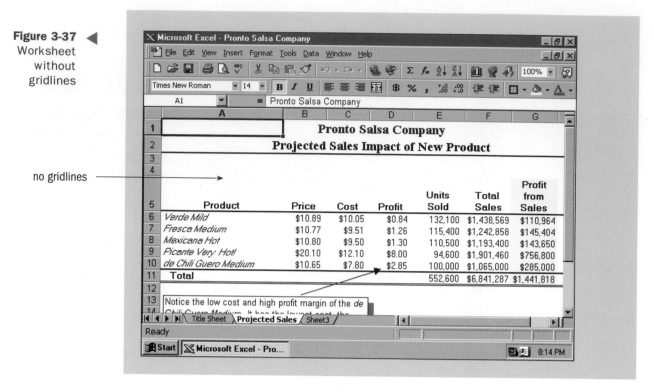

Now you are ready to print the worksheet.

Printing the Worksheet

Before you print a worksheet, you can use the Excel Print Preview window to see how it will look when printed. Recall that the Print Preview window shows you margins, page breaks, headers, and footers that are not always visible on the screen.

To preview the worksheet before you print it:

1. Click the **Print Preview** button on the Standard toolbar to display the first worksheet page in the Print Preview window. See Figure 3-38.

Figure 3-38 ◄
Print Preview

active Next button
indicates more pages

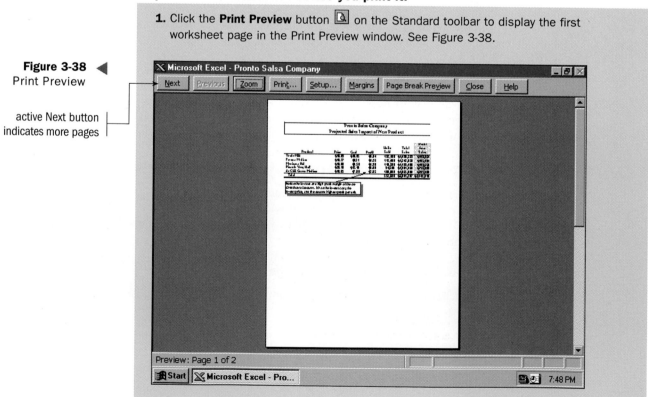

2. Click the **Next** button to preview the second worksheet page. Only one column appears on this page.

3. Click the **Previous** button to preview the first page again.

Looking at the Print Preview, you see that the worksheet is too wide to fit on a single page. You realize that if you print the worksheet lengthwise, however, it will fit on a single sheet of paper.

Portrait and Landscape Orientations

Excel provides two print orientations, portrait and landscape. **Portrait orientation** prints the worksheet with the paper positioned so it is taller than it is wide. **Landscape orientation** prints the worksheet with the paper positioned so it is wider than it is tall. Because some worksheets are wider than they are tall, landscape orientation is very useful.

You can specify print orientation using the Page Setup command on the File menu or using the Setup button in the Print Preview window. Use the landscape orientation for the Projected Sales worksheet.

To change the print orientation to landscape:

1. In the Print Preview window, click the **Setup** button to display the Page Setup dialog box. If necessary, click the **Page** tab.

2. Click the **Landscape** option button in the Orientation section to select this option.

3. Click the **OK** button to return to the Print Preview window. See Figure 3-39. Notice the Landscape orientation; that is, the page is wider than it is tall.

Figure 3-39 ◀
Landscape orientation

Next button no longer active

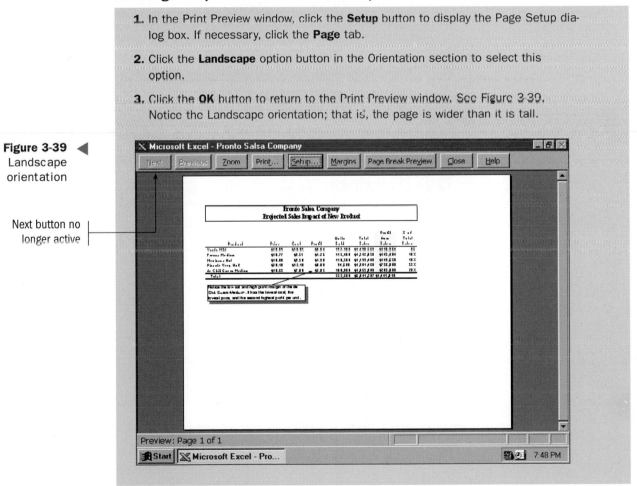

Before printing the worksheet, center the output on the page, and use the header/footer tab to document the printed worksheet.

To center the printed output:

1. Click the **Setup** button to display the Page Setup dialog box. Click the **Margins** tab.

2. Click the **Center on page Horizontally** check box to place a check in it and select that option.

Next, modify the printed footer by adding the date in the left section, and Anne's name in the right section.

To change the worksheet footer:

1. Click the **Header/Footer** tab, and then click the **Custom footer** to display the Footer dialog box.

2. In the Left section box, click the **Date** button to display &Date in the Left section box.

3. Click the **Right section** box, then type **Prepared by Anne Castelar.**

4. Click the **OK** button to complete the footer and return to the Page Setup dialog box. See Figure 3-40.

Figure 3-40
Page Setup after changing the footer

from right section of Custom Footer dialog box

from left section of Custom Footer dialog box

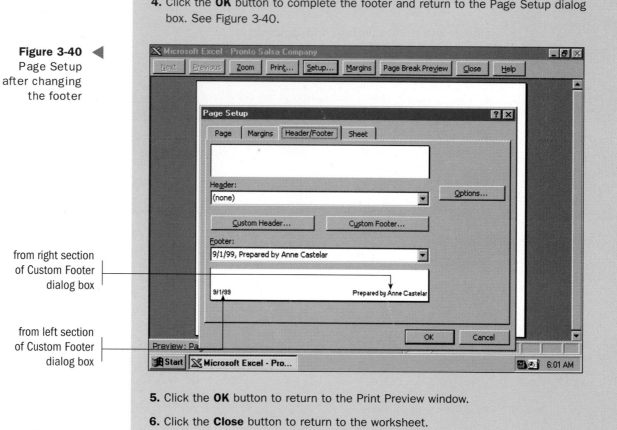

5. Click the **OK** button to return to the Print Preview window.

6. Click the **Close** button to return to the worksheet.

The worksheet is ready to print, but you always save your work before printing.

To save your page setup settings and print the worksheet:

1. Click the **Save** button on the Standard toolbar.

2. Click the **Print** button on the Standard toolbar. The worksheet prints. See Figure 3-41.

TROUBLE? If you see a message that indicates that you have a printer problem, click the Cancel button to cancel the printout. Check your printer to make sure it is turned on and is online; also make sure it has paper. Then go back and try Step 2 again. If you have no printer available, click the Cancel button.

Figure 3-41 ◀
Printed
worksheet

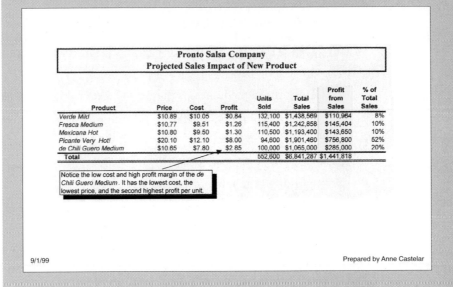

TROUBLE? If the title for the last two columns didn't print completely, you need to increase the row height for row 5. Select row 5. Drag the border below row 5 until the row height is 42.75 or greater (check the reference area of the formula bar). Click the Print button.

Now that you are done formatting the worksheet, close the workbook and exit Excel.

3. Close the workbook and exit Excel.

Quick Check

1. List two ways you can place a double-ruled line at the bottom of a range of cells.

2. Describe how to activate the Drawing toolbar.

3. To move, modify, or delete an object, you must _____ it first.

4. A _____ is a block of text that is placed in the worksheet.

5. _____ orientation prints the worksheet with the paper positioned so it is taller than it is wide.

6. If you are asked to remove the gridlines from the worksheet display, you will do what to the worksheet?

7. An arrow is an example of a _____.

You have completed formatting the Projected Sales worksheet and are ready to give it to Anne to check over before she presents it at her meeting with the bank loan officer.

Tutorial Assignments

After you show Anne the Projected Sales worksheet, the two of you discuss alternative ways to improve the worksheet's appearance. You decide to make some of these changes and give Anne the choice between two formatted worksheets. Do the following:

1. Start Windows and Excel, if necessary. Insert your Student Disk into the appropriate disk drive. Make sure the Excel and Book1 windows are maximized. Open the workbook Pronto2 in the TAssign folder for Tutorial 3 and save as Pronto3.

2. Center the percentages displayed in column H.

3. Make the contents of cells A10 through H10 bold to emphasize the new product. Make any necessary column-width adjustments.

4. Apply the color yellow to cells A1 through H2.

5. Right-align the label in cell A11.

6. Draw a vertical line to separate the product names from the rest of the data (the line begins in row 6 and continues to row 10).

7. Enter your name in the footer so that it appears on the printout of the worksheet. Make sure the footer also prints the date and filename. Remove any other information from the header and footer.

8. Make sure the Page Setup menu settings are set for centered horizontally and vertically, no row/column headings, and no cell gridlines.

9. Preview the printout to make sure it fits on one page. Save and print the worksheet.

10. Fill the text box with the color yellow so that it appears as a "yellow sticky note."

11. Change the color of the two-line title to red (the text, not the background color).

12. In step 4 you applied the color yellow to the cells A1 through H2. Remove the yellow color so that the background is the same as the rest of your worksheet.

13. If you answered steps 10, 11, or 12, save the worksheet as Pronto4.

14. a. Study the worksheet shown in Figure 3-42. Then open the Office Assistant and inquire about rotating and merging text in a cell.

Figure 3-42 ◀

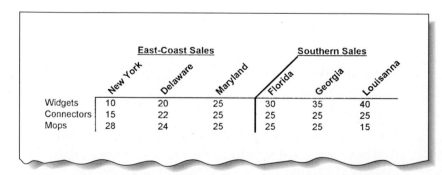

b. Open the workbook Explore3 and save it as Explore3 Solution.
c. Use the Rotate Text formatting feature to change the worksheet so it is similar to Figure 3-42. Make any other changes to make the worksheet as similar as possible to the one shown in Figure 3-42.
d. Save and print the worksheet.

Case Problems

1. Jenson Sports Wear Quarterly Sales Carl is the national sales manager for Jenson Sports Wear, a company that sells sports wear to major department stores. He has been using an Excel worksheet to track the results of a sales incentive program in which his sales staff has been participating. He has asked you to format the worksheet so it looks professional. He also wants a printout before he presents the worksheet at the next sales meeting. Complete these steps to format and print the worksheet:

1. Start Windows and Excel, if necessary. Insert your Student Disk into the appropriate disk drive. Make sure the Excel and Book1 windows are maximized. Open the workbook Running in the Case folder for Tutorial 3 on your Student Disk. Maximize the worksheet window and save the workbook as Running2 in the Case folder for Tutorial 3.

2. Complete the worksheet by doing the following:

   a. Calculating totals for each product
   b. Calculating quarterly subtotals for the Shoes and Shirts departments
   c. Calculating totals for each quarter and an overall total

3. Modify the worksheet so it is formatted as shown in Figure 3-43.

4. Use the Page Setup dialog box to center the output both horizontally and vertically.

5. Add the filename, your name, and the date in the footer section and delete the formatting code &[File] from the Center section of the header.

6. Save the worksheet.

7. Preview the worksheet and adjust the page setup as necessary for the printed results you want.

8. Print the worksheet.

9. Place the comment "Leading product" in a text box. Remove the border from the text box. (*Hint*: Use the Format Object dialog box.) Draw an oval object around the comment. (*Hint*: Use the Oval tool on the Drawing toolbar.) Draw an arrow from the edge of the oval to the number in the worksheet representing the leading product. Save and print the worksheet. Your printout should fit on one page.

Figure 3-43 ◀

Jenson Sports Wear
Quarterly Sales by Product

Shoes	Qtr 1	Qtr 2	Qtr 3	Qtr 4	Total
Running	1,750	2,050	2,125	2,200	8,125
Tennis	2,450	2,000	2,200	2,400	9,050
Basketball	1,150	1,300	1,450	1,500	5,400
Subtotal	5,350	5,350	5,775	6,100	22,575

Shirts	Qtr 1	Qtr 2	Qtr 3	Qtr 4	Total
Tee	900	1,100	1,000	1,050	4,050
Polo	2,000	2,100	2,200	2,300	8,600
Sweat	250	250	275	300	1,075
Subtotal	3,150	3,450	3,475	3,650	13,725
Total	8,500	8,800	9,250	9,750	36,300

2. Age Group Changes in the U.S. Population Rick Stephanopolous works for the U.S. Census Bureau and has been asked by his manager to prepare a report on changes in the U.S. population. Part of his report focuses on age group changes in the population from 1970 through 1980. Rick has created a worksheet that contains information from the U.S. Census reports from these years, and he is ready to format it. Complete these steps to format the worksheet:

1. Start Windows and Excel, if necessary. Insert your Student Disk into the appropriate disk drive. Make sure the Excel and Book1 windows are maximized. Open the workbook Census in the Case folder for Tutorial 3, and then save the workbook as US Population in the Case folder for Tutorial 3.

2. Make the formatting changes shown in Figure 3-44, adjusting column widths as necessary.

3. Use the Page Setup dialog box to modify the header so that the Right section consists of your name, a space, the current date, and the filename. Delete the contents of the Center section of the header.

4. Save the workbook.

5. Preview and print the worksheet. Your printout should fit on one page.

Figure 3-44

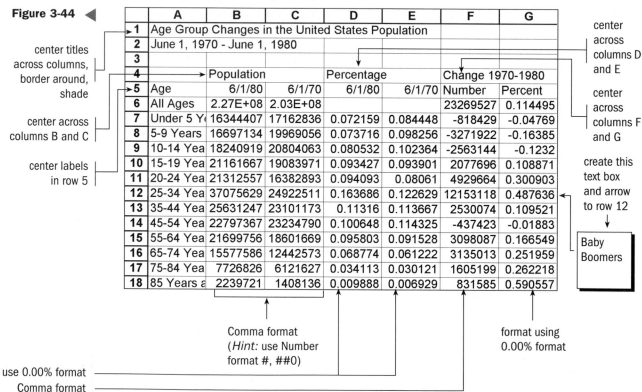

6. Change the border color of the text box from black to red. Change the color of the arrow to red. Save the workbook as US Population2. If you have access to a color printer, print the worksheet.

3. State Recycling Campaign Fred Birnbaum is working as an intern in the state's Waste Disposal Department. They have a pilot project on recycling for three counties (Seacoast, Metro, and Pioneer Valley). You have been asked to complete the worksheet and format it for presentation to their board of directors.

1. Start Windows and Excel, if necessary. Insert your Student Disk into the appropriate disk drive. Make sure the Excel and Book1 windows are maximized. Open the workbook Recycle in the Case folder on your Student Disk and save it as Recycle2.

2. Add two columns to calculate yearly totals for tons and a dollar value for each material in each county.

3. Insert three rows at the top of the worksheet to include:

   State Recycling Project
   Material Reclamation 1999
   <blank row>

4. Format the worksheet until you feel confident that the board of directors will be impressed with the appearance of the report.

5. Rename the worksheet Recycle Data.

6. Save the worksheet.

7. Print the worksheet centered horizontally and vertically on the page, using landscape orientation.

8. Remove the gridlines from the display. Use the Border tab of the Format Cells dialog box to place the recycle data, cells A6 to K20, in a grid. Save the workbook as Recycle3.

9. Change the magnification of the sheet so you can view the recycle data on the screen without having to scroll. (*Hint:* Use the Zoom control on the Standard toolbar.)

4. Cash Budgeting at Halpern's Appliances Fran Valence, the business manager for Halpern's Appliances, a small retail appliance store, is in the process of preparing a cash budget for January. The store has a loan that must be paid the first week in February. Fran wants to determine whether the business will have enough cash to make the loan payment to the bank.

Fran sketches the projected budget so that it will have the format shown in Figure 3-45.

Figure 3-45 ◄

```
             Halpern's Appliances Cash Budget
          Projected Cash Receipts and Disbursements
          January 1, 1999
          Cash balance, January 1, 1999               xxxx
          Projected receipts during January:
                Cash sales during month         xxxx
                Collections from credit sales    xxxx
                      Total cash receipts              xxxx
          Projected disbursements during January:
                Payments for goods purchased     xxxx
                Salaries                         xxxx
                Rent                             xxxx
                Utilities                        xxxx
                      Total cash disbursements        xxxx
          Cash balance, January 31, 1999              xxxx
```

Do the following:

1. Start Windows and Excel, if necessary. Insert your Student Disk into the appropriate disk drive. Make sure the Excel and Book1 windows are maximized.

2. Use only columns A, B, and C to create the worksheet sketched in Figure 3-45.

3. Use the following formulas in your worksheet:

   a. Total cash receipts = Cash sales during month + Collections from credit sales
   b. Total cash disbursements = Payments for goods purchased + Salaries + Rent + Utilities
   c. Cash Balance, January 31, 1999 = Cash Balance, January 1, 1999 + Total cash receipts - Total cash disbursements

Figure 3-46 ◀

Budget Item	Amount
Cash balance at beginning of month	32000
Cash sales during month	9000
Collections from credit sales	17500
Payments for goods purchased	15000
Salaries	4800
Rent	1500
Utilities	800

4. Enter the data in Figure 3-46 into the worksheet.

5. Use the formatting techniques you learned in this tutorial to create a professional-looking worksheet.

6. Save the worksheet as Budget in the Case folder for Tutorial 3 on your Student Disk.

7. Print the projected cash budget.

8. After printing the budget Fran remembers that starting in January the monthly rent increases by $150. Modify the projected cash budget accordingly. Print the revised cash budget.

9. Add a footnote to the title Halpern's Appliances Cash Budget title line so it appears as

   Halpern's Appliances Cash Budget[1]
   Add the line
   [1]Prepared by <insert your name>

two rows after the last row. (*Hint*: Check out Superscript in the Font tab of the Format Cells dialog box.) Save the workbook as Budget1. Print the revised budget.

Creating Charts

Charting Sales Information for Cast Iron Concepts

Cast Iron Concepts

CASE

The regional sales manager of Cast Iron Concepts (CIC), a distributor of cast iron stoves, Andrea Puest, is required to present information on how well the company's products are selling within her territory. Andrea sells in the New England region, which currently includes Massachusetts, Maine, and Vermont. She sells four major models—Star Windsor, Box Windsor, West Windsor, and Circle Windsor. The Circle Windsor is CIC's latest entry in the cast iron stove market. Due to production problems it was only available for sale the last four months of the year.

Andrea will make a presentation before the Director of Sales for CIC and the other regional managers next week when the entire group meets at corporate headquarters. Andrea gives you the basic data on sales in her territory for the past year. She must report on how well each model is moving in total for the region as well as within each state she covers. She knows that this kind of information is often understood best when it is presented in graphical form. So, she thinks she would like to show this information in a column chart as well as in a pie chart. You will help her prepare for her presentation by creating the charts she needs.

SESSION

4.1

In this session you will learn about the variety of Excel chart types and learn to identify the elements of a chart. You will learn how to create a column chart and learn a number of techniques for improving your chart, including moving and resizing it, adding and editing chart text, enhancing a chart title by adding a border, and using color for emphasis.

Excel Charts

Andrea's sales data is saved in a workbook named Concepts. You will generate the charts from the data in this workbook.

To start Excel, open the Concepts workbook, and rename it:

1. Start Excel as usual.

2. Open the **Concepts** workbook in the Tutorial.04 folder on your Student Disk.

The Title Sheet sheet appears as the first sheet in the workbook. You can type your name and the current date and then save the workbook under a new name.

3. Type your name and the current date in the appropriate cells in the Title Sheet sheet.

4. Save the workbook as **Cast Iron Concepts**. After you do so, the new filename appears in the title bar.

5. Click the **Sales Data** tab to move to that sheet. See Figure 4-1.

Figure 4-1 ◀
Sales Data
worksheet in
Cast Iron
Concepts
workbook

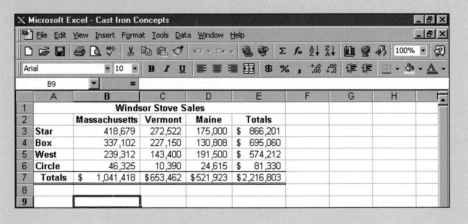

The worksheet shows the annual sales in dollars for each Windsor stove model by state. The total sales during the year for each model are in column E, and the total sales for each state appear in row 7.

It is easy to visually represent this kind of worksheet data. You might think of these graphical representations as "graphs"; however, in Excel they are referred to as **charts**. Figure 4-2 shows the 14 chart types within Excel that you can use to represent worksheet data.

Each chart type has two or more subtypes that provide various alternative charts for the selected chart type. For example, the Column chart type has seven subtypes, as shown in Figure 4-3. You can find more information on chart types and formats in the *Microsoft Excel User's Guide*, in the Excel Help facility, and in the Excel Chart Wizard.

Excel

Figure 4-2 ◀
Excel chart
types

Icon	Chart Type	Purpose
	Area	Shows magnitude of change over a period of time
	Column	Shows comparisons between the data represented by each column
	Bar	Shows comparisons between the data represented by each bar
	Line	Shows trends or changes over time
	Pie	Shows the proportion of parts to a whole
	XY (Scatter)	Shows the pattern or relationship between sets of (x,y) data points
	Radar	Shows change in data relative to a center point
	Surface chart	Shows the interrelationships between large amounts of data
	Bubble	A special type of XY (Scatter) that shows the pattern or relationship between sets of data points; compares three sets of data
	Stock	Compares high, low, open, and close prices of a stock
	Cylinder	Shows comparisons between the data represented by each cylinder
	Cone	Shows comparisons between the data represented by each cone
	Pyramid	Shows comparisons between the data represented by each pyramid
	Doughnut	Shows the proportion of parts to a whole

Figure 4-3 ◀
Chart subtypes
for Column
chart type

Chart Subtype Icon	Description
	Clustered column
	Stacked column
	100% Stacked column
	Clustered column with 3-D visual effect
	Stacked column with 3-D visual effect
	100% Stacked column with 3-D visual effect
	3-D column

Figure 4-4 shows the elements of a typical Excel chart. Understanding the Excel chart terminology is particularly important so you can successfully construct and edit charts.

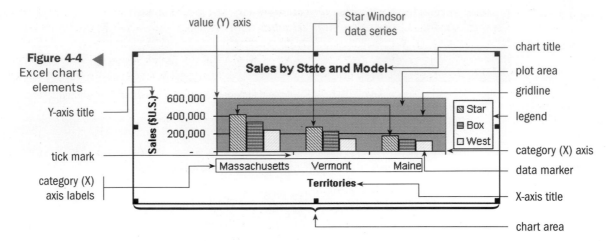

Figure 4-4
Excel chart elements

The entire chart and all its elements are contained in the **chart area**. The **plot area** is the rectangular area defined by the axis, with the Y-axis forming the left side and the X-axis forming the base; in Figure 4-4 the plot area is in gray. The **axis** is a line that borders one side of the plot area, providing a frame for measurement or comparison in a chart. Data values are plotted along the **value** or **Y-axis**, which is typically vertical. Categories are plotted along the **category** or **X-axis**, which is usually horizontal. Each axis in a chart can have a title that identifies the scale or categories of the chart data; in Figure 4-4 the **X-axis title** is "Territories" and the **Y-axis title** is "Sales ($U.S.)." The **chart title** identifies the chart.

A **tick mark label** identifies the categories, values, or series in the chart. **Tick marks** are small lines that intersect an axis like divisions on a ruler, and represent the scale used for measuring values in the chart. Excel automatically generates this scale based on the values selected for the chart. **Gridlines** extend the tick marks on a chart axis to make it easier to see the values associated with the data markers. The **category names** or **category labels**, usually displayed on the X-axis, correspond to the labels you use for the worksheet data.

A **data point** is a single value originating from a worksheet cell. A **data marker** is a graphic representing a data point in a chart; depending on the type of chart, a data marker can be a bar, column, area, slice, or other symbol. For example, sales of the Star Windsor stove in Massachusetts (value 418,679 in cell B3 of the worksheet on your screen) is a data point. Each column in the chart in Figure 4-4 that shows the sales of Windsor stoves is a data marker. A **data series** is a group of related data points, such as the Star Windsor sales shown as red column markers in the chart.

When you have more than one data series, your chart will contain more than one set of data markers. For example, Figure 4-4 has three data series, one for each Windsor stove. When you show more than one data series in a chart, it is a good idea to use a **legend** to identify which data markers represent each data series.

Charts can be placed in the same worksheet as the data; this type of chart is called an **embedded chart**, and enables you to place the chart next to the data so it can easily be reviewed and printed on one page. You can also place a chart in a separate sheet, called a **chart sheet**, which contains only one chart and doesn't have rows and columns. In this tutorial you will create both an embedded chart and a chart that resides in a separate chart sheet.

Planning a Chart

Before you begin creating a chart you should plan it. Planning a chart includes the following steps:

- identifying the data points to be plotted, as well as the labels representing each data series and categories for the X-axis

- choosing an appropriate chart type

- sketching the chart, including data markers, axes, titles, labels, and legend

- deciding on the location of the chart within the workbook

Remember, Andrea wants to compare sales for each model in each state in which she sells. She thinks that a column chart is the best way to provide her audience with an accurate comparison of sales of Windsor stoves in her New England territory. She also needs to show how total sales in her territory are broken down by stove model. When showing parts of a whole, a pie chart is most effective, so she will create a pie chart to use in her presentation as well.

Andrea sketched the column chart and pie chart shown in Figure 4-5.

Figure 4-5 ◀
Sketch of
column and
pie charts

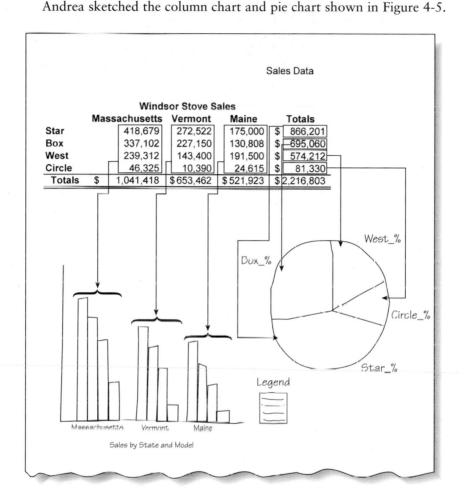

The sketches show roughly how Andrea wants the charts to look. It is difficult to envision exactly how a chart will look until you know how the data series looks when plotted; therefore, you don't need to incorporate every detail in the chart sketch. As you construct the charts, you can take advantage of Excel previewing capabilities to try different formatting options until your charts look just the way you want.

Create the column chart first. In looking at the sketch for this chart, note that Andrea wants to group the data by states; that is, the four models are shown for each of the three states. The names of the states in cells B2:D2 of the worksheet will be used as category labels. The names of each stove model, in cells A3:A6, will represent the legend text. The data series for the chart are in rows B3:D3, B4:D4, B5:D5, and B6:D6.

Creating a Column Chart

After studying Andrea's sketch for the column chart, you are ready to create it, using the Sales Data worksheet. When you create a chart, you first select the cells that contain the data you want to appear in the chart and then you click the Chart Wizard button on the Standard toolbar. The Chart Wizard consists of four dialog boxes that guide you through the steps required to create a chart. Figure 4-6 identifies the tasks you perform in each of the Chart Wizard dialog boxes.

Figure 4-6 ◀
Tasks
performed in
each step of
the Chart
Wizard

Dialog Box	Tasks Performed
Chart Type	Select the type of chart you want to create—displays a list of chart types available in Excel; for each chart type, presents you with several chart subtypes from which you can choose
Chart Source Data	Specify the worksheet cells that contain the data and labels that will appear in the chart
Chart Options	Change the look of the chart by changing options that affect the titles, axes, gridlines, legends, data labels, and data tables
Chart Location	Specify where to place the chart: embedded in a work-sheet along with the worksheet data, or in a separate sheet called a chart sheet

You know that Andrea intends to create a handout of the worksheet and chart, so you want to embed the column chart in the same worksheet as the sales data, making it easier for her to create a one-page handout.

REFERENCE window

CREATING A CHART

- Select the data you want to chart.
- Click the Chart Wizard button on the Standard toolbar.
- Follow the series of steps in the Chart Wizard dialog boxes.

Before activating the Chart Wizard you will need to select the cells containing the data the chart will display. If you want the column and row labels to appear in the chart, include the cells that contain them in your selection as well. For this chart, select the range A2 through D6, which includes the sales of each Windsor stove model in the three states as well as names of the stove models and states.

To create the column chart using the Chart Wizard:

1. Select cells **A2:D6**, making sure no cells are highlighted in column E or row 7.

   Now that you have selected the chart range, you use the Chart Wizard to create the column chart.

2. Click the **Chart Wizard** button 📊 on the Standard toolbar to display the Chart Wizard - Step 1 of 4 - Chart Type dialog box. See Figure 4-7.

   TROUBLE? If the Office Assistant appears on your screen, click the button next to the message "No, don't provide help now" to close the Office Assistant.

   This first dialog box asks you to select the type of chart you want to create. The Chart type list box displays each of the 14 chart types available in Excel. The default chart type is the Column chart type. To the right of the Chart type list box is a gallery of chart subtypes for the selected chart. Select the chart type you want to create.

Excel

Figure 4-7 ◄
Chart Wizard -
Step 1 of 4 -
Chart Type
dialog box

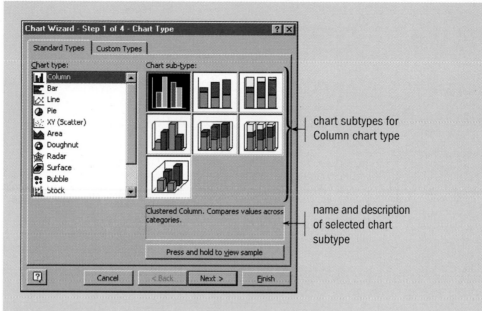

chart subtypes for
Column chart type

name and description
of selected chart
subtype

You want to create a column chart.

3. If necessary, click the **Column** chart type (the default) to select it. Seven Column chart subtypes are displayed. The Clustered Column chart subtype is the default subtype for the Column chart type. Click and hold the **Press and hold to view sample** button to display a preview of the Clustered Column chart subtype. See Figure 4-8. Release the mouse button.

To view any other Column chart subtype, select another subtype option and click the Press and hold to view sample button.

Figure 4-8 ◄
Preview of
Clustered
Column chart
type

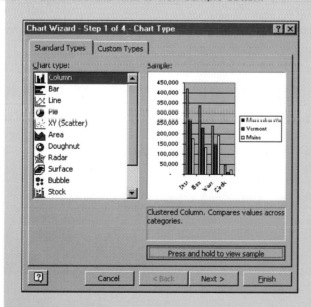

You decide to use the Clustered Column chart type, the default selection.

4. Click the **Next** button to display the Chart Wizard - Step 2 of 4 - Chart Source Data dialog box. See Figure 4-9. In this step you confirm or specify the worksheet cells that contain the data and labels to appear in the chart.

Figure 4-9 ◄
Chart Wizard -
Step 2 of 4 -
Chart Source
Data dialog box

current appearance
of chart

Andrea wants states
as category labels

Excel treating
columns in worksheet
as the data series

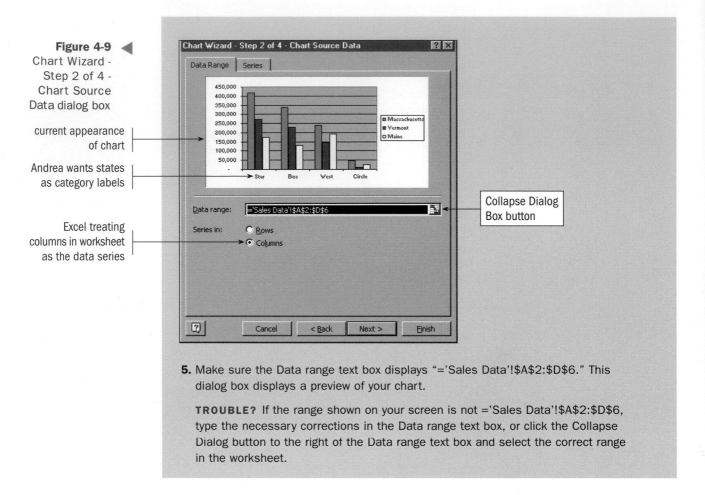

Collapse Dialog
Box button

5. Make sure the Data range text box displays "='Sales Data'!$A$2:$D$6." This dialog box displays a preview of your chart.

TROUBLE? If the range shown on your screen is not ='Sales Data'!$A$2:$D$6, type the necessary corrections in the Data range text box, or click the Collapse Dialog button to the right of the Data range text box and select the correct range in the worksheet.

In Step 2, you can also modify how the data series is organized—by rows or by columns—using the **Series in** option. In Figure 4-9, the chart uses the columns in the worksheet as the data series. To see how the chart would look if the rows in the worksheet were used as the data series, you can modify the settings in this dialog box.

Does the sample chart shown on your screen and in Figure 4-9 look like the sketch Andrea prepared (Figure 4-5)? Not exactly. The problem is that the Chart Wizard assumes that if the range to plot has more rows than columns (which is true in this case), then the data in the columns (states) becomes the data series. Andrea wants the stove models (rows) as the data series, so you need to make this change in the dialog box.

To change the data series and continue the steps in the Chart Wizard:

1. Click the **Rows** option button in the Series in area of the dialog box. The sample chart now shows the stove models as the data series and the states as category labels. See Figure 4-10.

Figure 4-10 ◄
Rows as data
series

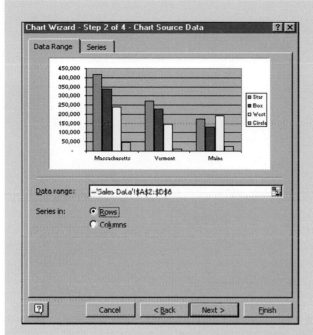

2. Click the **Next** button to display the Chart Wizard - Step 3 of 4 - Chart Options dialog box. See Figure 4-11. A preview area displays the current appearance of the chart. This tabbed dialog box enables you to change various chart options, such as titles, axes, gridlines, legends, data labels, and data tables. As you change these settings, check the preview chart in this dialog box to make sure you get the look you want.

Now add a title for the chart.

Figure 4-11 ◄
Chart Wizard -
Step 3 of 4 -
Chart Options
dialog box

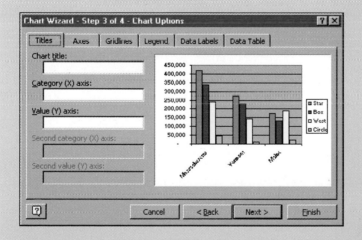

3. If necessary click the **Titles** tab, click the **Chart title** text box, and then type **Sales by State** for the chart title. Notice that the title appears in the preview area.

4. Click the **Next** button to display the Chart Wizard - Step 4 of 4 - Chart Location dialog box. See Figure 4-12. In this fourth dialog box you decide where to place the chart. You can place a chart in a worksheet, an embedded chart, or place it in its own chart sheet. You want to embed this chart in the Sales Data worksheet, which is the default option.

Figure 4-12 ◄
Chart Wizard -
Step 4 of 4 -
Chart Location
dialog box

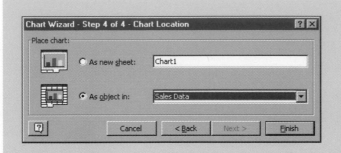

You have finished the steps in the Chart Wizard.

5. Click the **Finish** button to complete the chart and display it in the Sales Data worksheet. See Figure 4-13. Notice the selection handles around the chart; these handles indicate that the chart is selected. The Chart toolbar is automatically displayed when the chart is selected. Also, notice that the data and labels for the chart are outlined in blue, green, and purple in the worksheet. This enables you to quickly see which cells make up the chart.

TROUBLE? If you don't see the Chart toolbar, click View on the menu bar, click Toolbars, and then click the Chart check box to select that option.

Figure 4-13 ◄
Completed
column chart

indicates selected
chart element; click
list arrow to select
different element

Chart Type button;
click list arrow to
select chart type

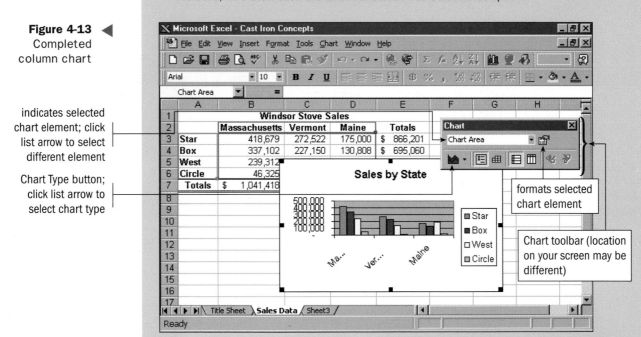

formats selected
chart element

Chart toolbar (location
on your screen may be
different)

6. Click anywhere outside the chart to deselect it. Notice that the selection handles no longer surround the chart, indicating that the chart is no longer selected, and the Chart toolbar is no longer displayed. The Chart toolbar only appears when the chart is selected.

After reviewing the column chart, you think that the area outlined for the chart is too small to highlight the comparison between models. You also note that you need to move the chart so that it does not cover the worksheet data.

Excel

Moving and Resizing a Chart

When you use the Chart Wizard to create an embedded chart, Excel displays the chart in the worksheet. The size of the chart may not be large enough to accentuate relationships between data points or display the labels correctly. Since a chart is an object, you can move, resize, or copy it like any object in the Windows environment. However, before you can move, resize, or copy a chart, you must select, or **activate** it. You select a chart by clicking anywhere within the chart area. Small black squares, called **selection handles** or **sizing handles**, appear on the boundaries of the chart, indicating that it is selected. You will also notice that some of the items on the menu bar change to enable you to modify the chart instead of the worksheet.

You decide to move and resize the chart before showing it to Andrea.

To change the size and position of the chart:

1. Scroll the worksheet until row 8 appears as the first row in the window.

2. Click anywhere within the white area of the chart border to select the chart. Selection handles appear on the chart border. See Figure 4-14.

Figure 4-14 ◀
Selected chart

menu bar has changed because chart is activated

Name box indicates selected object

selection handles

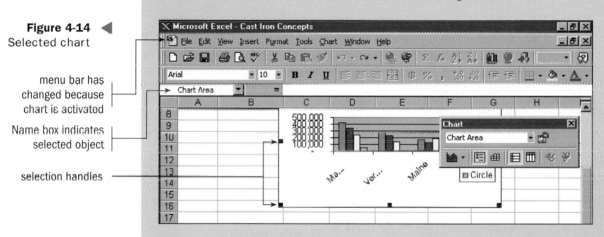

TROUBLE? If the Name box does not display the name "Chart Area," click the Chart Objects list box arrow on the Chart toolbar to display the list of chart objects. Select Chart Area.

TROUBLE? If the Chart toolbar is in the way, click and drag it to the bottom of the window to anchor it there.

3. Position the pointer anywhere on the chart border. The pointer changes to ⬚. Click and hold down the mouse button as you drag the chart down and to the left until you see the upper-left corner of the dashed outline in column A of row 8. Release the mouse button to view the chart in its new position.

Now increase the width of the chart.

4. Position the pointer on the right center selection handle. When the pointer changes to ↔, hold down the mouse button and drag the selection handle to the right until the chart outline reaches the right edge of column G. Release the mouse button to view the resized chart. See Figure 4-15.

Figure 4-15 ◀
Chart after
being moved
and resized

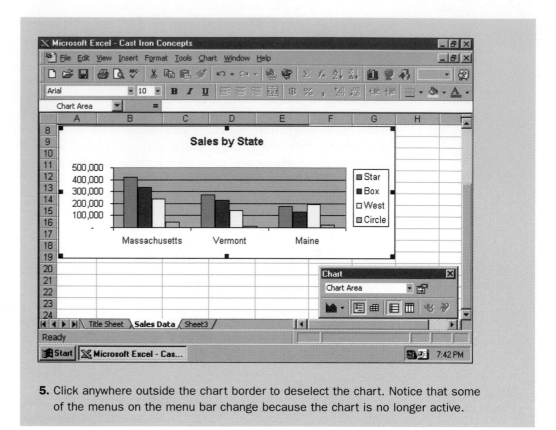

5. Click anywhere outside the chart border to deselect the chart. Notice that some of the menus on the menu bar change because the chart is no longer active.

The chart is repositioned and resized. You show Andrea the chart embedded in her Sales Data worksheet. As she reviews the chart, Andrea notices an error in the value entered for West Windsor stoves sold in Maine.

Updating a Chart

Every chart you create is linked to the worksheet data. As a result, if you change the data in a worksheet, Excel automatically updates the chart to reflect the new values. Andrea noticed that sales of West Windsor in Maine were entered incorrectly. She accidentally entered sales as 191,500, when the correct entry should have been 119,500. Correct this data entry error and observe how it changes the column chart.

To change the worksheet data and observe changes to the column chart:

1. Observe the height of the data marker for the West model in Maine (yellow data marker) in the column chart.

2. Scroll the worksheet until row 2 appears as the first row of the worksheet window.

3. Click cell **D5**, and then type **119500** and press the **Enter** key. See Figure 4-16. The total West sales (cell E5) and total sales for Maine (cell D7) automatically change. In addition, Excel automatically updates the chart to reflect the new source value. Now the data marker for the West Windsor sales in Maine is shorter.

Figure 4-16
Modified
column chart
after chart's
source data
changed

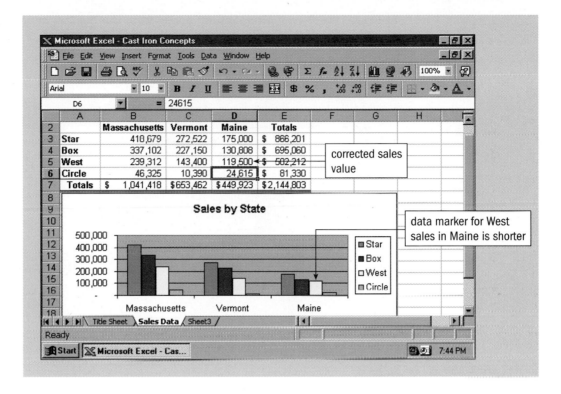

Now that the data for the West stove sales in Maine is corrected, you review the chart with Andrea for ways you can improve the presentation of the chart data.

Modifying an Excel Chart

You can make many modifications to a chart, including changing the type of chart, the text, the labels, the gridlines, and the titles. To make these modifications, you need to activate the chart. Selecting, or activating, a chart, as mentioned earlier, allows you to move and resize it. It also gives you access to the Chart commands on the menu bar and displays the Chart toolbar to use as you alter the chart.

After reviewing the column chart, Andrea believes that the Circle Windsor will distract the audience from the three products that were actually available during the entire period. Recall that the Circle Windsor was only on the market for four months and even then there were production problems. She wants to compare sales only for the three models sold during the entire year.

Revising the Chart Data Series

After you create a chart, you might discover that you specified the wrong data range, or you might decide that your chart should display different data series. Whatever your reason, you do not need to start over in order to revise the chart's data series.

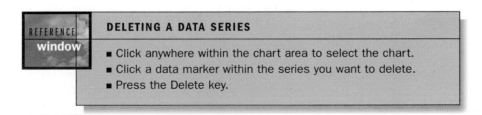

REFERENCE window	**DELETING A DATA SERIES**
	▪ Click anywhere within the chart area to select the chart.
	▪ Click a data marker within the series you want to delete.
	▪ Press the Delete key.

Andrea asks you to remove the data series representing the Circle Windsor model from the column chart.

To delete the Circle Windsor data series from the column chart:

1. Click anywhere within the chart border to select the chart.

2. Click any data marker representing the Circle data series (any light blue data marker). Selection handles appear on each column of the Circle Windsor data series and a ScreenTip is displayed identifying the selected chart item. See Figure 4-17.

Figure 4-17 ◀
Chart with
Circle data
series selected

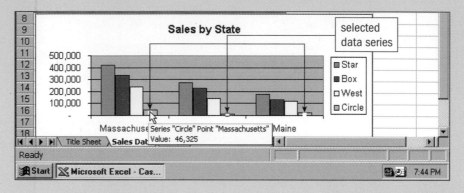

3. Press the **Delete** key. See Figure 4-18. Notice that the Circle Windsor data series is removed from the chart.

Figure 4-18 ◀
Column chart
after data
series removed

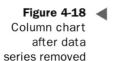

TROUBLE? If you deleted the wrong data series, click the Undo button and repeat Steps 2 and 3.

Andrea reviews her sketch and notices that the chart title is incomplete; the intended title was "Sales by State and Model." She asks you to make this change to the chart.

Editing Chart Text

Excel classifies the text in your charts in three categories: label text, attached text, and unattached text. **Label text** includes the category names, the tick mark labels, the X-axis labels, and the legend. Label text often derives from the cells in the worksheet; you usually specify it using the Chart Wizard.

Attached text includes the chart title, X-axis title, and Y-axis title. Although attached text appears in a predefined position, you can edit it, and move it using the click-drag technique.

Unattached text includes text boxes or comments that you type in the chart after it is created. You can position unattached text anywhere in the chart. To add unattached text to a chart, you use the Text Box tool on the Drawing toolbar.

As noted earlier, you need to change the chart title to "Sales by State and Model." To do this you must select the chart, select the chart title, and then add "and Model" to the title.

To revise the chart title:

1. If the chart is not selected, click the **chart** to select it.

2. Click the **chart title** object to select it. Notice that the object name Chart Title appears in the Name box and as a ScreenTip; also, selection handles surround the Chart Title object.

3. Position the pointer in the chart title text box at the end of the title and click to remove the selection handles from the Chart Title object. The pointer changes to an insertion point I.

   TROUBLE? If the insertion point is not at the end of the title, press the End key to move it to the end.

4. Press the **spacebar** and type **and Model**, and then click anywhere within the chart border to complete the change in the title and deselect it.

Checking Andrea's sketch, you notice that the Y-axis title was not included. To help clarify what the data values in the chart represent, you decide to add "Sales ($U.S.)" as a Y-axis title. You use the Chart Option command on the Chart menu to add this title.

To add the Y-axis title:

1. Make sure that the chart is still selected.

2. Click **Chart** on the menu bar, and then click **Chart Options** to display the Chart Options dialog box. If necessary, click the **Titles** tab.

3. Click the **Value (Y) axis** text box, and then type **Sales ($U.S.)**

4. Click the **OK** button to close the Chart Options dialog box.

5. If necessary, scroll the worksheet so that the entire chart is displayed.

6. Click anywhere within the chart border to deselect the Y-axis title. See Figure 4-19.

Figure 4-19
Chart after title modified and value axis label inserted

Value axis title

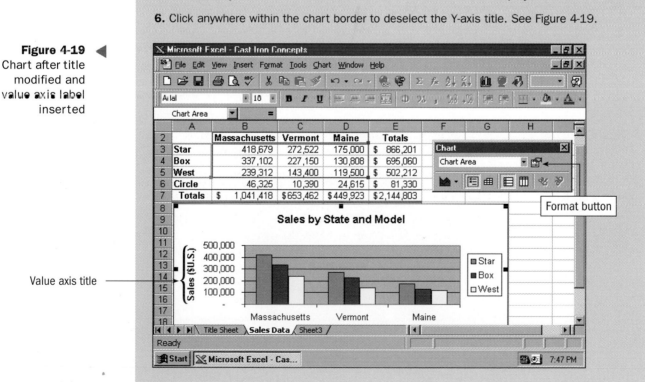

Now that the titles accurately describe the chart data, Andrea asks you to add data labels to show the exact values of the Star Windsor data series—CIC's leading model.

Adding Data Labels

A **data label** provides additional information about a data marker. Depending on the type of chart, data labels can show values, names of data series (or categories), or percentages. You can apply a label to a single data point, an entire data series, or all data markers in a chart.

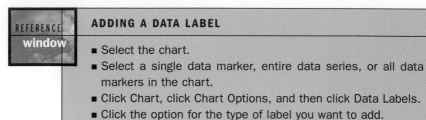

REFERENCE
window

ADDING A DATA LABEL

- Select the chart.
- Select a single data marker, entire data series, or all data markers in the chart.
- Click Chart, click Chart Options, and then click Data Labels.
- Click the option for the type of label you want to add.
- Click OK.

In this case, Andrea wants to add data labels to the Star model data series.

To apply data labels to a data series:

1. If the column chart is not selected, click anywhere within the chart border to select it.

2. Click any **Star Windsor data marker** (blue data marker) within the chart. Selection handles appear on all columns in the Star Windsor data series.

   To format any chart element, you can use the Format button on the Chart toolbar. The Format button's ToolTip name and function change depending on what chart element is selected for formatting. The list box that appears to the left of the Format button on the toolbar also displays the name of the currently selected chart element. In this case, the Star Windsor data series marker is selected, so the Format button on the Chart toolbar appears as the Format Data Series button, and when selected, opens the Format Data Series dialog box.

3. Click the **Format Data Series** button on the Chart toolbar to display the Format Data Series dialog box. Click the **Data Labels** tab if necessary. See Figure 4-20.

Figure 4-20 ◀
Active Data
Labels tab in
Format Data
Series dialog
box

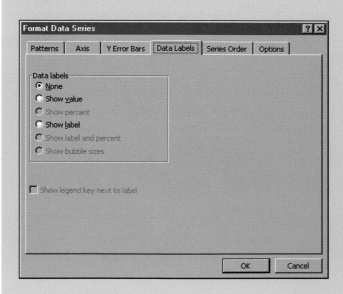

4. Click the **Show value** option button.

5. Click the **OK** button to display the column chart with data labels. See Figure 4-21.

Figure 4-21 ◄
Chart with data
labels

data labels

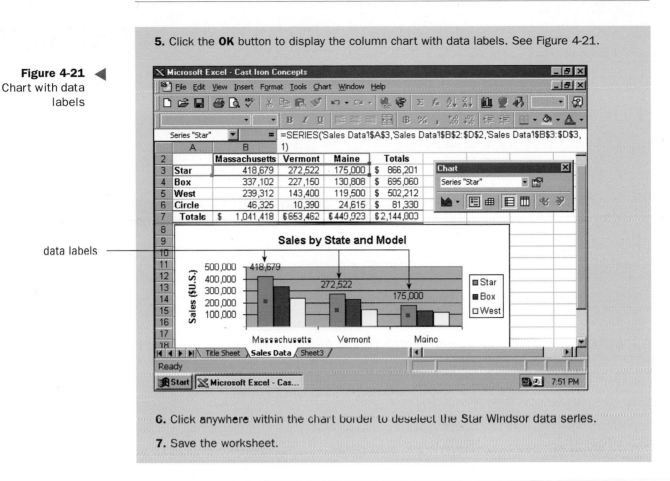

6. Click anywhere within the chart border to deselect the Star Windsor data series.

7. Save the worksheet.

Andrea is pleased with the changes in the chart's appearance. Now, she wants to add visual interest to the chart, making it look more polished.

Enhancing the Chart's Appearance

There are many ways to give charts a more professional look. The use of different font styles, types, and sizes can make chart labels and titles stand out. Also, using colors, borders, and patterns can make a chart more interesting to view.

Andrea thinks that a border and some color could accentuate the title of the chart.

Emphasizing the Title with Border and Color

The chart title is an object that you can select and format using the menu options or the toolbar buttons. Now make the changes to the chart title.

To display the title with border and color:

1. Click the **chart title** to select it and display selection handles. Now that the chart title is selected, notice that the Format button 🔲 on the Chart toolbar becomes the Format Chart Title button, and the Format button list box displays "Chart Title."

2. Click the **Format Chart Title** button 🔲 on the Chart toolbar to display the Format Chart Title dialog box, and then, if necessary, click the **Patterns** tab.

3. Click the **Weight** list arrow in the Border section to display a list of border weights.

4. Click the **second line** in the list.

5. Click the **gray** square in the Color palette (fourth row, last column) in the Area section.

6. Click the **OK** button to apply the format changes to the chart title, and then click anywhere within the chart area to deselect the title.

Andrea thinks that the chart looks better with its title emphasized. Now she wants you to work on making the data markers more distinctive. They certainly stand out on her computer's color monitor, but she is concerned that this will not be the case when she prints the chart on the office's black and white printer.

Changing Colors and Patterns

Patterns add visual interest to a chart and they can be useful when your printer has no color capability. Although your charts appear in color on a color monitor, if your printer does not have color capability, Excel translates colors to gray shades when printing. It's difficult to distinguish some colors, particularly darker ones, from one another when Excel translates them to gray shades and then prints them. To solve this potential problem, you can make your charts more readable by selecting a different pattern for each data marker.

To apply a different pattern to each data series you use the Patterns dialog box.

REFERENCE window

SELECTING A PATTERN FOR A DATA MARKER

■ Make sure the chart is selected.
■ Select the data marker or markers to which you want to apply a pattern.
■ Click the Format Data Series button on the Chart toolbar to display the Format Data Series dialog box.
■ Click the Patterns tab, click the Fill Effects button, and then click the Pattern tab to display a list of patterns.
■ Click the pattern you want to apply, and then click the OK button twice to close the dialog boxes.

You want to apply a different pattern to each data series.

To apply a pattern to a data series:

1. Make sure the chart is selected.

2. Click any data marker for the Star data series (blue data marker) to display selection handles for all three data markers for that data series.

3. Click the **Format Data Series** button 📄 on the Chart toolbar to display the Format Data Series dialog box.

4. If necessary, click the **Patterns** tab, and then click the **Fill Effects** button to display the Fill Effects dialog box. Click the **Pattern** tab to display the Pattern palette. See Figure 4-22.

Excel

Figure 4-22 ◄
Pattern options
in Fill Effects
dialog box

dark downward
diagonal pattern

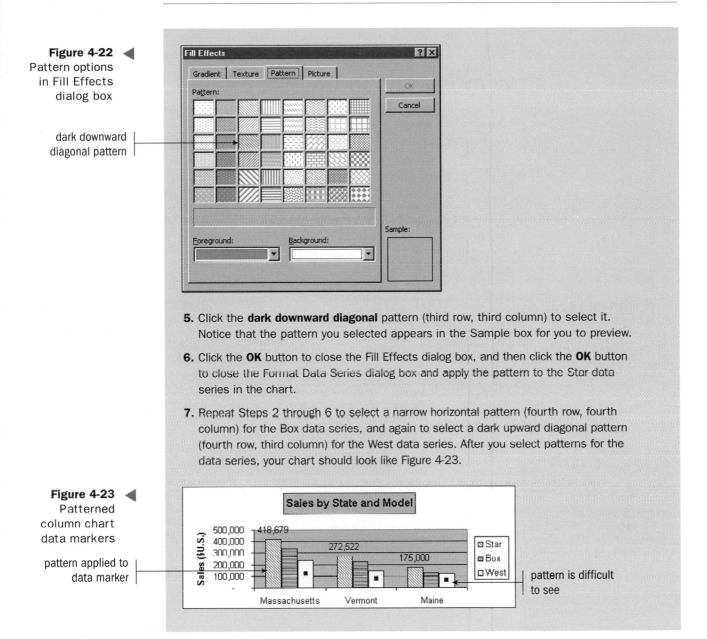

5. Click the **dark downward diagonal** pattern (third row, third column) to select it. Notice that the pattern you selected appears in the Sample box for you to preview.

6. Click the **OK** button to close the Fill Effects dialog box, and then click the **OK** button to close the Format Data Series dialog box and apply the pattern to the Star data series in the chart.

7. Repeat Steps 2 through 6 to select a narrow horizontal pattern (fourth row, fourth column) for the Box data series, and again to select a dark upward diagonal pattern (fourth row, third column) for the West data series. After you select patterns for the data series, your chart should look like Figure 4-23.

Figure 4-23 ◄
Patterned
column chart
data markers

pattern applied to
data marker

pattern is difficult
to see

You notice that the West markers appear to have no pattern applied because the pattern is very difficult to see when applied against the yellow color. You decide to change the color of the West markers to a darker color—green, so the pattern will be more visible.

To change the color of data markers:

1. If the West data markers are not selected, click any one of them to select the data markers for that data series.

2. Click the **Format Data Series** button on the Chart toolbar to display the Format Data Series dialog box.

3. If necessary, click the **Patterns** tab, click the **Fill Effects** button, and then click the **Pattern** tab in the Fill Effects dialog box to display the patterns palette.

4. In the Pattern tab, click the **Background** list arrow to display a color palette. Click the **green** square in the third row, third column, and click the **OK** button to close the Fill Effects dialog box and return to the Format Data Series dialog box.

5. Click the **OK** button to close the Format Data Series dialog box, and then click anywhere outside the chart border to deselect the chart.

You show the chart to Andrea, and she decides that it is ready to be printed and duplicated for distribution at the meeting.

Previewing and Printing the Chart

Before you print you should preview the worksheet to see how it will appear on the printed page. Remember, Andrea wants the embedded chart and the worksheet data to print on one page that she can use as a handout at the meeting.

To save and print an embedded chart:

1. Click the **Save** button 🖫 on the Standard toolbar to save the workbook.

2. Click the **Print Preview** button 🔳 on the Standard toolbar to display the Print Preview window.

3. Click the **Print** button to display the Print dialog box, and then click the **OK** button. See Figure 4-24.

Figure 4-24
Printout of worksheet with embedded column chart

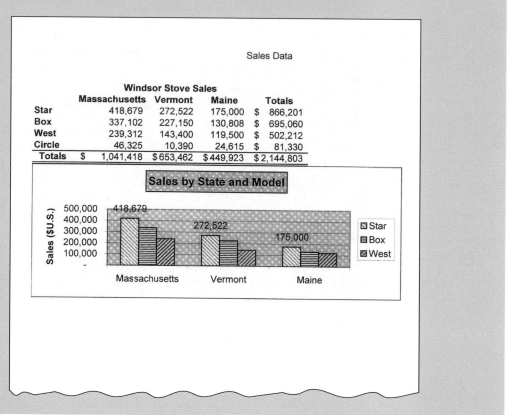

Quick Check

1. A column chart is used to show _____.

2. When you click an embedded chart, it is _____

3. Explain how to revise a chart's data series.

4. How do you move an embedded chart to a new location using the mouse?

5. Describe the action you're likely to take before beginning Step 1 of the Chart Wizard.

6. What happens when you change a value in a worksheet that is the source of data for a chart?

7 What is the purpose of a legend?

8 Explain the difference between a data point and a data marker.

You have finished creating the column chart showing stove sales by state and model for Andrea. Next, you need to create the pie chart showing total stove sales by model. You will do this in Session 4.2.

SESSION

4.2

In this session you will create a pie chart. You will also learn how to select nonadjacent ranges, how to change a 2-D pie chart to a 3-D pie chart, and how to "explode" a slice from a pie chart. You will also learn how to use chart sheets and how to add a border to a chart.

Creating a Chart in a Chart Sheet

Now Andrea wants to show the contribution of each Windsor model to the total stove sales. Recall from the planning sketch she did (Figure 4-5) that she wants to use a pie chart to show this relationship.

A pie chart shows the relationship, or proportions, of parts to a whole. The size of each slice is determined by the value of that data point in relation to the total of all values. A pie chart contains only one data series. When you create a pie chart, you generally specify two ranges. Excel uses the first range for the category labels and the second range for the data series. Excel automatically calculates the percentage for each slice, draws the slice to reflect the percentage of the whole, and gives you the option of displaying the percentage as a label in the completed chart.

Andrea's sketch (see Figure 4-5) shows estimates of each stove's contribution and how she wants the pie chart to look. The pie chart will have four slices, one for each stove model. She wants each slice labeled with the stove model's name and its percentage of total sales. Because she doesn't know the exact percentages until Excel calculates and displays them in the chart, she put "__%" on her sketch to show where she wants the percentages to appear.

Creating a Pie Chart

You begin creating a pie chart by selecting the data to be represented from the worksheet. You refer to your worksheet and note in the sketch that the data labels for the pie slices are in cells A3 through A6 and the data points representing the pie slices are in cells E3 through E6. You must select these two ranges to tell the Chart Wizard the data that you want to chart, but you realize that these ranges are not located next to each other in the worksheet. You know how to select a series of adjacent cells; now you need to learn how to select two separate ranges at once.

Selecting Nonadjacent Ranges

A **nonadjacent range** is a group of individual cells or ranges that are not next to each other. Selecting nonadjacent ranges is particularly useful when you construct charts because the cells that contain the data series and these that contain the data labels are often not side by side in the worksheet. When you select nonadjacent ranges, the selected cells in each range are highlighted. You can then format the cells, clear them, or use them to construct a chart.

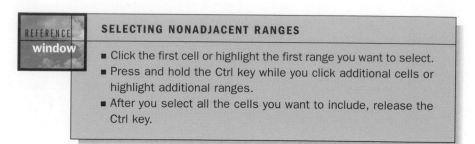

REFERENCE
window

SELECTING NONADJACENT RANGES

- Click the first cell or highlight the first range you want to select.
- Press and hold the Ctrl key while you click additional cells or highlight additional ranges.
- After you select all the cells you want to include, release the Ctrl key.

Now select the nonadjacent ranges to be used to create the pie chart.

To select range A3:A6 and range E3:E6 in the Sales Data sheet:

1. If you took a break after the last session, make sure that Excel is running, the Cast Iron Concepts workbook is open, and the Sales Data worksheet is displayed.

2. Click anywhere outside the chart border to make sure the chart is not activated. Press **Ctrl + Home** to make cell A1 the active cell.

3. Select cells **A3** through **A6**, and then release the mouse button.

4. Press and hold the **Ctrl** key while you select cells **E3** through **E6**, and then release the mouse and the Ctrl key. The two nonadjacent ranges are now selected: A3:A6 and E3:E6. See Figure 4-25.

   TROUBLE? If you don't select the cells you want on your first try, click any cell to remove the highlighting, then go back to Step 2 and try again.

Figure 4-25 ◀
Selecting
nonadjacent
cell ranges

nonadjacent ranges
selected

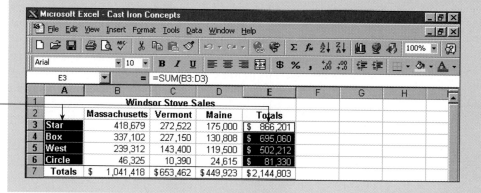

This time you'll place your new chart in a **chart sheet**, a special sheet that contains only one chart. It does not have the rows and columns of a regular worksheet. If you have many charts to create, you may want to place each chart in a separate chart sheet to avoid cluttering the worksheet. This approach also makes it easier to locate a particular chart because you can change the name on the chart sheet tab.

To create a pie chart in a chart sheet:

1. Click the **Chart Wizard** button 📊 on the Standard toolbar to display the Chart Wizard - Step 1 of 4 - Chart Type dialog box.

   TROUBLE? If the Office Assistant appears on your screen, click the button next to the message "No, don't provide help now" to close the Office Assistant.

   You want to create a pie chart.

2. Click the **Pie** chart type to select it. Six Pie chart subtypes are displayed. The Two-dimensional Pie chart subtype is the default subtype for the Pie chart type. Click the **Press and hold to view sample** button to display a preview of the Pie chart type.

You decide to use the default chart subtype.

3. Click the **Next** button to display the Chart Wizard - Step 2 of 4 - Chart Source Data dialog box. Make sure the Data range text box displays "='Sales Data'!$A$3:$A$6,'Sales Data'!$E$3:$E$6." This dialog box also displays a preview of your chart.

   TROUBLE? If the range shown on your screen is not "='Sales Data'!$A$3:$A$6, 'Sales Data'!$E$3:$E$6," type the necessary corrections in the Data range text box, or click the Collapse Dialog button located to the right of the Data range text box and select the correct range in the worksheet.

4. Click the **Next** button to display the Chart Wizard - Step 3 of 4 - Chart Options dialog box.

   Add a title for the chart.

5. If necessary, click the **Titles** tab, click the **Chart title** text box, and then type **Sales by Model** for the chart title. Notice that the title appears in the preview area.

6. Click the **Data Labels** tab, and then click the **Show label and percent** option button to place the label and percent next to each slice.

   Now remove the legend because it is no longer needed.

7. Click the **Legend** tab, and then click the **Show legend** check box to remove the check and deselect that option.

8. Click the **Next** button to display the Chart Wizard - Step 4 of 4 - Chart Location dialog box. Recall that in the fourth dialog box you decide where to place the chart. You can place a chart in a worksheet, or place it in its own chart sheet. You want to place this chart in a chart sheet.

9. Click the **As new sheet** option button to place the chart in the Chart1 chart sheet.

   You have finished the steps in the Chart Wizard.

10. Click the **Finish** button to complete the chart. The new chart, along with the Chart toolbar, appears in the chart sheet named Chart1. The chart sheet is inserted into the workbook before the worksheet on which it is based. If necessary, click the white portion of chart area to select the chart. See Figure 4-26.

Figure 4-26 ◀
Pie chart in a
chart sheet

default name for
first chart sheet

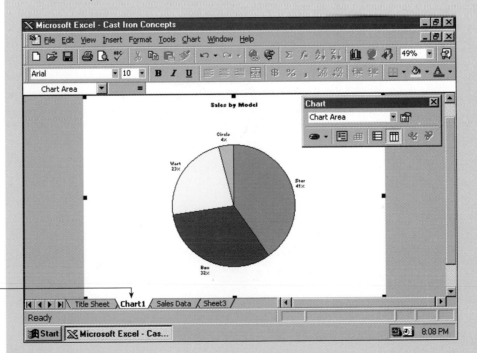

After reviewing the pie chart, Andrea asks you to change the current pie chart to a three-dimensional design to give the chart a more professional look.

Changing the Chart Type from 2-D to 3-D

As you recall, Excel provides 14 different chart types that you can choose from as you create a chart. You can also access these chart types after the chart is created and change from one type to another. To change the chart type, you can use the Chart Type command on the Chart menu or the Chart Type button on the Chart toolbar to make this change. You'll use the Chart toolbar to change this 2-D pie chart to a 3-D pie chart.

To change the pie chart to a 3-D pie chart:

1. Make sure the chart area is selected, and then click the **Chart Type** arrow on the Chart toolbar to display a palette of chart types. See Figure 4-27.

   TROUBLE? If the Chart toolbar is not displayed on the screen, click View on the menu bar, point to Toolbars, and click the Chart check box to display the Chart toolbar.

Figure 4-27 ◀
Palette of
chart types

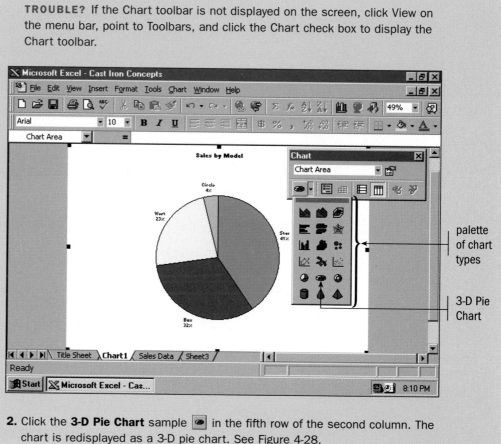

palette of chart types

3-D Pie Chart

2. Click the **3-D Pie Chart** sample in the fifth row of the second column. The chart is redisplayed as a 3-D pie chart. See Figure 4-28.

Figure 4-28 ◀
3-D pie chart

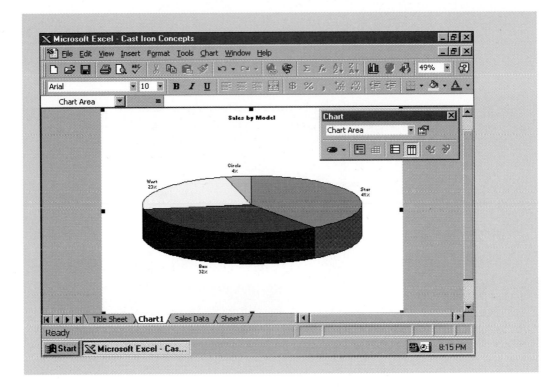

In her presentation, Andrea plans to emphasize the importance of the Star model because it is her best-selling model in the New England territory. She decides to "explode" the Star slice.

Exploding a Slice of a Pie Chart

When you create a pie chart, you may want to focus attention on a particular slice in the chart. You can present the data so a viewer can easily see which slice is larger or smaller—for example, which product sold the most. One method of emphasizing a particular slice over others is by separating the slice from the rest of the pie. The *cut* slice is more distinct because it is not connected to the other slices. A pie chart with one or more slices separated from the whole is referred to as an **exploded pie chart**.

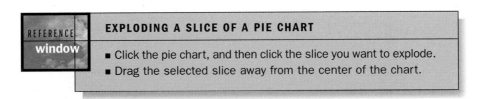

REFERENCE window

EXPLODING A SLICE OF A PIE CHART

- Click the pie chart, and then click the slice you want to explode.
- Drag the selected slice away from the center of the chart.

Andrea asks you to explode the slice that represents sales for the Star model.

To explode the slice that represents the Star model sales:

1. Click anywhere in the pie chart to select it. One selection handle appears on each pie slice and the Name box indicates that Series 1 is the selected chart object.

2. Now that you have selected the entire pie, you can select one part of it, the Star slice. Position the pointer over the slice that represents Star model sales. As you move the pointer over this slice, the ScreenTip "Series 1 Point: "Star" Value: $866,201 (41%)" is displayed. Click to select the slice. Selection handles now appear on only this slice.

3. With the pointer on the selected slice, click and hold down the mouse button while dragging the slice to the right, away from the center of the pie chart. As you drag the slice, an outline of the slice marks your progress.

4. Release the mouse button to leave the slice in the new position. See Figure 4-29.

Figure 4-29 ◀
Pie chart with
exploded slice

exploded slice

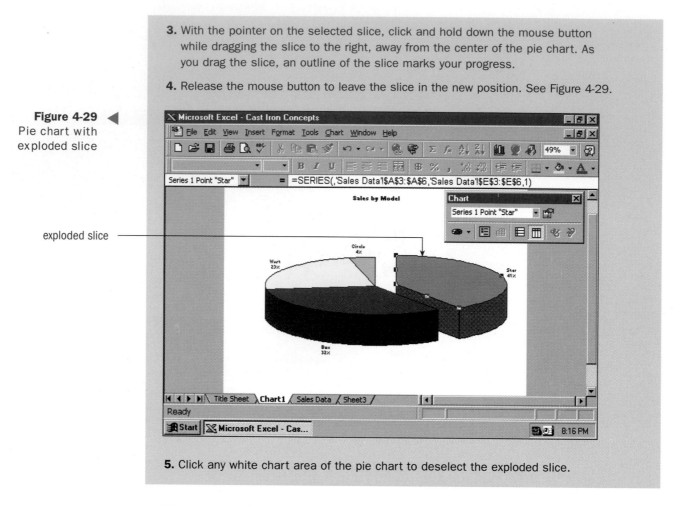

5. Click any white chart area of the pie chart to deselect the exploded slice.

The Star model now is exploded in the pie chart, but Andrea still isn't satisfied. You suggest moving the slice to the front of the pie.

Rotating a 3-D Chart

When working with a 3-D chart, you can modify the view of your chart to change its perspective, elevation, or rotation. You can change the elevation to look down on the chart or up from the bottom. You can also rotate the chart to adjust the placement of objects on the chart. Now rotate the chart so that the Star slice appears at the front of the chart.

To change the 3-D view of the chart:

1. Click **Chart** on the menu bar, and then click **3-D View** to display the 3-D View dialog box. See Figure 4-30.

Figure 4-30 ◀
3-D View dialog
box

clockwise rotation
arrow button

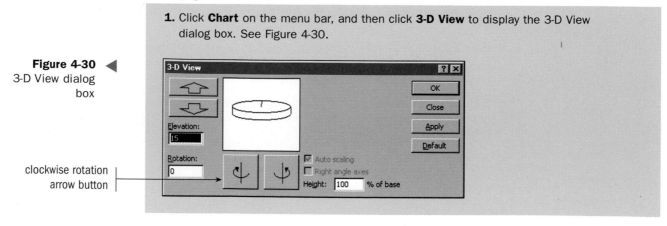

2. Click the **clockwise rotation arrow** button until the Rotation box shows 90; as you do this, notice that the pie chart sketch rotates to show the new position.

3. Click the **OK** button to apply the changes. See Figure 4-31.

Figure 4-31 ◀
3-D pie chart after view rotated to display cut slice in front

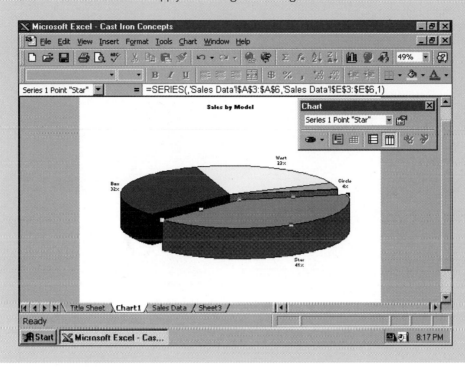

After looking over the chart, you decide to increase the size of the chart labels so that they are easier to read.

Formatting Chart Labels

You can change the font type, size, style, and the color of text in a chart using the Formatting toolbar buttons.

You look at the chart and decide that it will look better if you increase the size of the data labels from 10 to 14 points.

To change the font size of the chart labels:

1. Click any one of the four data labels to select all the data labels. Selection handles appear around all four labels, and the Name box displays "Series 1 Data Labels."

2. Click the **Font Size** list arrow on the Formatting toolbar, and then click **14**.

Now increase the font size of the title to 20 points.

To change the font size of the chart title:

1. Click the **chart title** to select it. Selection handles appear around the title.

2. Click the **Font Size** list arrow on the Formatting toolbar, and then click **20**.

3. Click any white area of the pie chart to deselect the title. See Figure 4-32.

Figure 4-32 ◀
3-D pie chart
after font size
of data labels
and title
increased

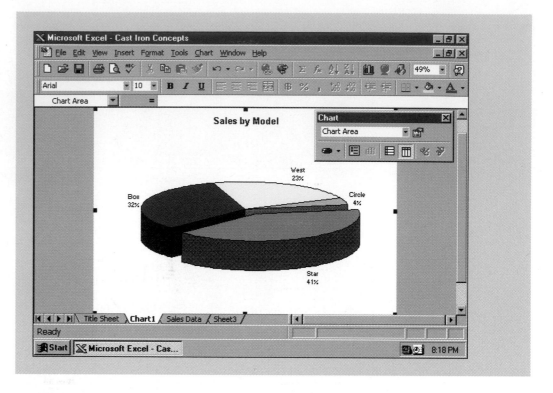

The pie chart looks good but Andrea has one last request. She asks you to apply a blue texture to the chart background.

Applying a Texture Fill Effect to the Chart Background

You can apply texture or gradient fill effects to chart walls, floors, bars, columns, and chart and plot background areas. These fill effects provide a professional look. You want to change the white chart area of the pie chart to a blue texture.

To apply a texture fill effect to the chart background:

1. Make sure the chart area is selected. If it is not, click the white area around the pie chart.

2. Click the **Format Chart Area** button 🖼 on the Chart toolbar to display the Format Chart Area dialog box.

3. If necessary, click the **Patterns** tab, click the **Fill Effects** button to display the Fill Effects dialog box, and then click the **Texture** tab. See Figure 4-33.

Figure 4-33 ◀
Texture options
in Fill Effects
dialog box

blue tissue
paper texture

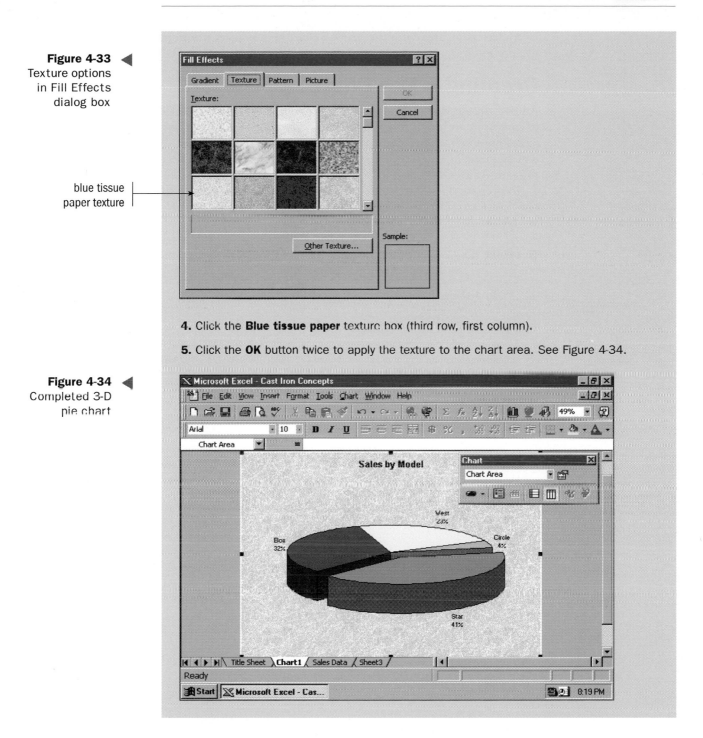

4. Click the **Blue tissue paper** texture box (third row, first column).

5. Click the **OK** button twice to apply the texture to the chart area. See Figure 4-34.

Figure 4-34 ◀
Completed 3-D
pie chart

The chart is now complete. You decide to print it and show it to Andrea.

Printing the Chart from the Chart Sheet

When you create a chart in a separate sheet, you can print that sheet separately. If necessary, you can make page setup decisions for the chart sheet alone. In this case, the chart in the chart sheet is ready for printing. You don't need to change any setup options. Now that the 3-D pie chart is complete, save the workbook and print a copy of the chart.

To save the workbook and print the chart:

1. Click the **Save** button 🖫 on the Standard toolbar to save the workbook.

2. Click the **Print** button 🖨 on the Standard toolbar to print the chart.

Andrea is pleased with the printed chart and believes it will help her when she makes her presentation next week.

Creating a Bar Chart

Andrea decides to spend some time during her presentation reviewing sales of all stoves in each state in her territory. She recalls from one of her college classes that both the bar and column chart are useful for comparing data by categories. The bar chart may have an advantage if you have long labels, because the category labels in bar charts are easier to read. Andrea asks you to prepare a bar chart comparing sales of all stoves by state.

To prepare this chart, you will first select the cells containing the chart you will display. For this chart, select the range B2 through D2 for the category axis (states) and B7 through D7 for the data series (total sales in each state).

To select range B2:D2 and range B7:D7 in the Sales Data sheet:

1. Click the **Sales Data** tab to activate the Sales Data worksheet, and then press **Ctrl + Home** to make cell A1 the active cell.

2. Select cells **B2:D2**, and then release the mouse button.

3. Press and hold the **Ctrl** key while you select cells **B7:D7**, and then release the mouse and the Ctrl key. The two nonadjacent ranges are now selected: B2:D2 and B7:D7.

   TROUBLE? If you don't select the cells you want on your first try, click any cell to remove the highlighting, and then go back to Step 2 and try again.

Place the bar chart in a separate chart sheet so that Andrea can easily locate it.

To create a bar chart in a chart sheet:

1. Click the **Chart Wizard** button 📊 on the Standard toolbar to display the Chart Wizard - Step 1 of 4 - Chart Type dialog box.

   You want to create a bar chart.

2. Click the **Bar** chart type to select it. Six Bar chart subtypes are displayed. The Clustered Bar chart is the default subtype for the Bar chart. Click the **Press and hold to view sample** button to display a preview of the Clustered Bar chart subtype.

   You decide to use the Clustered Bar chart type.

3. Click the **Next** button to display the Chart Wizard - Step 2 of 4 - Chart Source Data dialog box. Make sure the Data range box displays "='Sales data'!$B$2:$D$2,'Sales Data'!$B$7:$D$7." This dialog box also displays a preview of your chart.

   TROUBLE? If the range shown on your screen is not "='Sales data'!$B$2:$D$2, 'Sales Data'!$B$7:$D$7," type the necessary corrections in the Data range text box, or click the Collapse Dialog button and select the correct range in the worksheet.

4. Click the **Next** button to display the Chart Wizard - Step 3 of 4 - Chart Options dialog box.

   Add a title for the chart.

5. If necessary, click the **Titles** tab, and then click the **Chart title** text box. Type **Sales by State** for the chart title. Notice that the title appears in the preview area. Click the **Category (X) axis** title box, and then type **Territories**. Click the **Value (Y) axis** title box, and then type **Sales ($U.S.)**.

   Since there is only one data series, remove the legend.

6. Click the **Legend** tab and then click the **Show legend** check box to remove the check and deselect that option.

7. Click the **Next** button to display the Chart Wizard - Step 4 of 4 - Chart Location dialog box. You want this chart to be placed in a chart sheet.

8. Click the **As new sheet** option button to place this chart in a chart sheet, and then type **Bar Chart** in the As new sheet text box to rename the chart sheet.

   You have finished the steps in the Chart Wizard.

9. Click the **Finish** button to complete the chart. The new chart, along with the Chart toolbar, appears in the chart sheet named Bar Chart. The chart sheet is inserted into the workbook before the worksheet on which it is based. See Figure 4-35.

Figure 4-35 ◀
Bar chart in a
chart sheet

categories are
organized vertically

values are displayed
horizontally

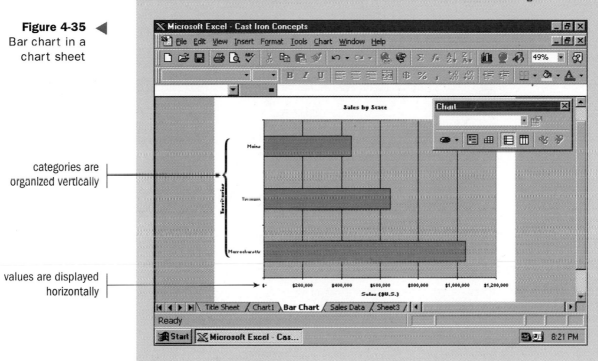

Andrea reviews the bar chart and believes it will focus the audience's attention on sales in each state.

Using Pictures in a Bar Chart

When making a presentation, an interesting way to enhance a bar or column chart is to replace the data markers with graphic images, thereby creating a picture chart. Any graphic image that can be copied to the Clipboard can serve as the basis for a picture chart. Andrea wants you to use a picture of the Windsor stove from CIC's latest catalog as the data marker in your bar chart.

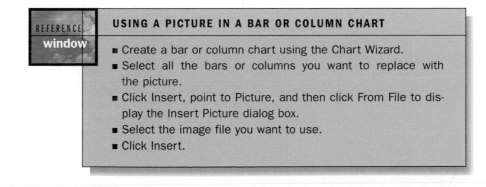

REFERENCE
window

USING A PICTURE IN A BAR OR COLUMN CHART

- Create a bar or column chart using the Chart Wizard.
- Select all the bars or columns you want to replace with the picture.
- Click Insert, point to Picture, and then click From File to display the Insert Picture dialog box.
- Select the image file you want to use.
- Click Insert.

The graphic image of the Windsor stove is located in the Tutorial.04 folder on your Student Disk. The file is named Stove. To replace the plain bars with the graphic image, you need to select one bar or column of the chart and use the Picture command on the Insert menu.

To insert the picture into the bar chart:

1. Click any column in the chart so that all three data markers are selected.

2. Click **Insert** on the menu bar, point to **Picture,** and then click **From File** to display the Insert Picture dialog box.

3. Make sure Tutorial.04 is the folder shown in the Look In list box, and then click **Stove.**

4. Click the **Insert** button to insert the picture into the chart. The three bars are each filled by the picture of the stove. See Figure 4-36. Notice that each picture is "stretched" to fit the bar it fills.

Figure 4-36 ◀
Picture chart with stretched graphic

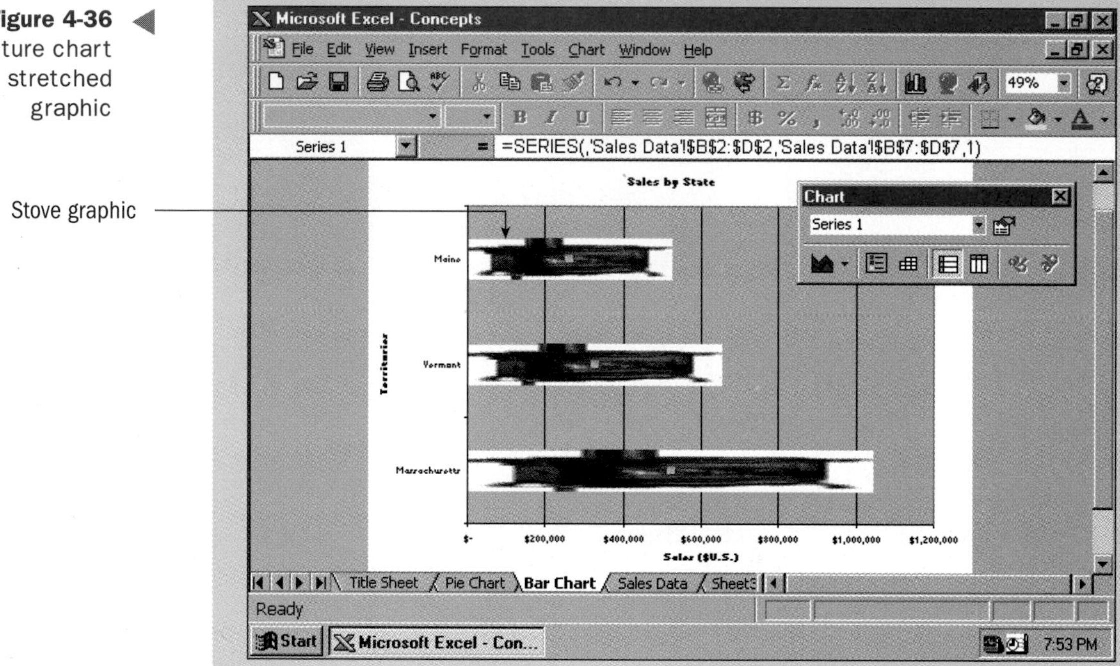

Stove graphic ────

When you insert a picture into a bar or column chart, Excel automatically stretches the picture to fill the space formerly occupied by the marker. Some pictures stretch well, but others become distorted, and detract from, rather than add to, the chart's impact.

Stretching and Stacking Pictures

As an alternative to stretching a picture, you can stack the picture so that it appears repeatedly in the bar, reaching the height of the original bar in the chart. You'll stack the Windsor stove picture in your chart to improve its appearance.

The value axis has tick mark labels at 200000, 400000, 600000, and so on. To match the axis labels, you'll stack one stove each 200000 units.

To stack the picture:

1. If the handles have disappeared from the bars, click any bar in the chart to select all the bars.

2. Click the **Format Data Series** button 🖼 on the Chart toolbar to display the Format Data Series dialog box, and if necessary, click the **Patterns** tab.

3. Click the **Fill Effects** button to display the Fill Effects dialog box, and then click the **Picture** tab.

4. Click the **Stack and scale to** option button. Accept the Units/Picture value.

5. Click the **OK** button to close the Fill Effects dialog box, and then click the **OK** button to close the Format Data Series dialog box and return to the chart sheet and display the data markers as stacked stoves.

6. Click the white area of the chart to deselect the data markers. See Figure 4-37.

Figure 4-37 ◀
Picture chart
with stacked
graphic

stacked graphic
image

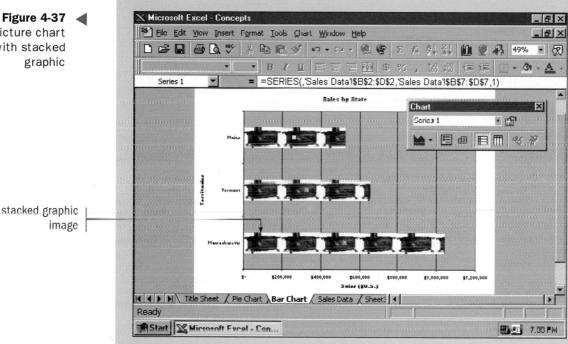

Andrea likes the picture chart, but is not sure how her audience will react to this type of chart. She wants to think about it. She asks you to save the workbook with the picture chart included and will let you know in the morning whether to print the picture chart or return to the bar chart. If Andrea asks you to remove the pictures and return to the original bars for the data markers, you will select the data series, click Edit, click Clear, and then click Formats.

Now save the workbook.

To save the workbook:

1. Click the **Title Sheet** tab to make it the active worksheet.

2. Click the **Save** button 🖫 on the Standard toolbar.

3. Close the workbook and exit Excel.

Quick Check

1. Define the following terms in relation to a pie chart:
   a. data point
   b. data marker
   c. data series

2. Explain how to select cells A1, C5, and D10 at the same time.

3. What type of chart shows the proportion of parts to a whole?

4. When creating charts, why is it important to know how to select nonadjacent ranges?

5. Explain the difference between an embedded chart and a chart placed in a chart sheet.

6. Explain how to rotate a 3-D pie chart.

7. Explain how to explode a slice from a pie chart.

8. When you change a two-dimensional pie chart to a 3-D pie chart, you change the _____.

You have finished creating the column chart, pie chart, and bar chart that Andrea needs for her presentation.

Tutorial Assignments

After having the night to think about it, Andrea comes to work the next morning and asks you to create one more chart for her presentation. Do the following:

1. Start Windows and Excel, if necessary. Insert your Student Disk into the disk drive. Make sure that the Excel and Book1 windows are maximized. Open the file Concept2 in the TAssign folder for Tutorial 4.

2. Save the file under the new name Cast Iron Concepts 2 in the TAssign folder.

3. Type your name and the current date in the Title Sheet sheet.

4. In the Sales Data sheet select the nonadjacent ranges that contain the models (A3:A6) and the total sales for each model (E3:E6).

5. Use the Chart Wizard to create a clustered column chart with 3-D visual effect. Place the completed chart in a chart sheet.

6. As you are creating the chart, remove the legend and add "Total Stove Sales by State" as the chart title.

7. Rename the chart sheet "3D Column."

8. After the chart is completed, increase the font size of the title and axis labels so that they are easier to read.

9. Put a box around the chart's title, using a thick line for a border. Add a drop shadow to the border.

10. Save the workbook. Print the chart. Include your name, the filename, and the date in the footer for the printed chart.

11. Select the walls chart element and apply a 1-color gradient fill effect. You select an appropriate color.

12. Select the value axis and change its scale so that the major unit is 150000.

13. Open the Office Assistant and learn how you can show the worksheet data in a data table, which is a grid at the bottom of the chart. (*Hint*: Search on "add data table to a chart.") Add a data table to your chart. Increase the font size associated with the data table.

14. Save the workbook, and then print the chart.

15. Switch to the Sales Data worksheet and do the following:

   a. Change the color of the West Windsor pattern to brown.

   b. Move the legend to the bottom of the chart. Increase the height of the chart, so it has a more professional look.

   c. Annotate the column chart with the note "Star model—best seller in Massachusetts!" by adding a text box and arrow using the tools on the Drawing toolbar.

   d. Save the workbook, and then print the Sales Data sheet with the embedded chart.

Case Problems

1. Illustrating Production Data at TekStar Electronics You are executive assistant to the President of TekStar Electronics, a manufacturer of consumer electronics. You are compiling the yearly manufacturing reports and have collected production totals for each of TekStar's four U.S. manufacturing plants. The workbook TekStar contains these totals. Now you need to create a 3-D pie chart showing the relative percentage of CD players each plant produced.

1. Open the workbook Tekstar in the Case folder for Tutorial 4 and add the necessary information to the Title Sheet sheet to create a summary of the workbook. Save the workbook as TekStar Electronics in the Case folder for Tutorial 4.

2. Activate the Units Sold sheet. Use the Chart Wizard to create a 3-D pie chart in a chart sheet that shows the percentage of CD players produced at each plant location. Use the Pie with 3-D Visual Effect subtype.

3. Enter "Production of CD Players" as the chart title. Show "Label" and "Percent" as the data labels. Remove the legend.

4. Pull out the slice representing the Chicago plant's CD player production.

5. Increase the font size of the title and data labels so that they are easier to read.

6. Name the chart sheet 3D Pie Chart.

7. Preview and print the chart sheet. Save your work.

8. Create an embedded chart comparing sales of all the products by city. Select the appropriate range and then use the Chart Wizard to create a clustered bar chart. Use the products as the data series and the cities as the X-axis (category) labels. Enter "Production by Product and Plant Location" as the title.

9. Move the bar chart under the table, and then enhance the chart in any way you think appropriate.

10. Preview and print the embedded bar chart. Save your work.

11. Create a clustered column chart with 3-D visual effect comparing the production of VCRs by city. Remove the legend. Place the chart in a chart sheet named "VCRs."

   a. Add a data table (a grid in a chart that contains the numeric data used to create the chart) to the chart. (*Hint*: Use the Office Assistant to find out how to add a data table to a chart.)
   b. Save the workbook, and then print the chart.

2. Dow Jones Charting You are working for a stock analyst who is planning to publish a weekly newsletter. One regular component of the newsletter will be a 15-week chart tracking the Dow Jones average. Create the chart that can be used for the newsletter.

   1. Open the workbook DowJones in the Case folder for Tutorial 4. Save the workbook as Dow Jones 8-2-96 in the Case folder for Tutorial 4.

   2. Use the Chart Wizard to create an embedded line chart (Line subtype) in the Data worksheet. Specify "Dow Jones Average" as the chart title and "Index" as the title for the Y-axis. Do not add a legend or X-axis title.

   3. Place the chart to the right of the present worksheet data and resize it until you are satisfied with its appearance.

   4. Edit the chart as follows:

      a. Change the line marker to a thick line.
      b. Apply a texture fill effect to the chart area. You decide the texture.
      c. Change the color of the plot area to a shade of yellow.
      d. Angle the text upward for the dates on the category axis.

   5. Save your workbook. Preview and print the embedded chart.

   6. Add the text box "Inflation Worries Wall Street" pointing to 7-26-96.

   7. Save your workbook. Print the chart.

   8. The Dow Jones average for the week ending 8-9-96 was 5500.

      a. Add this data to the last row of the worksheet.
      b. Modify the chart by plotting the 15-week period beginning 5-3-96 and ending 8-9-96.
      c. Save the workbook as Dow Jones 8-9-96. Preview your work and print only the chart. Center the chart vertically and horizontally on the page.

3. *New York Chronicle* You are working as an intern for Jeff Sindle, business economist, of the *New York Chronicle*—a New York newspaper with circulation in New York City and Long Island. The paper is planning to publish an economic profile of the region and you are assisting in this project.

   1. Open the workbook NewYork in the Case folder for Tutorial 4. Save the workbook as New York Economic Data. Create three charts, each in its own chart sheet.

   2. First, create a 3-D pie chart that compares the population of the six geographic areas in the study. Title the chart and enhance it as you think appropriate. Rename the chart sheet to reflect the chart it contains.

   3. Create a clustered column chart that compares the number of establishments in retail and services by the six geographic areas. (*Hint*: Categorize by type of establishment; each geographic area is a data series.) Title the chart and enhance it as you think appropriate. Rename the chart sheet to reflect the chart it contains.

4. Create a clustered bar chart comparing sales/receipts by geographic area (categorize by geographic area; the data series is sales/receipts). Title the chart and enhance it as you think appropriate. Rename the chart sheet to reflect the chart it contains.

5. Add a title sheet that includes your name, date created, purpose, and a brief description of each sheet in the workbook.

6. Save the workbook.

7. Print the entire workbook (title and data worksheet and the three chart sheets).

4. Duplicating a Printed Chart Look through books, business magazines, or textbooks for your other courses to find an attractive chart. Select one, photocopy it, and create a worksheet that contains the data displayed in the chart. You can estimate the data values plotted in the chart. Do your best to duplicate the chart you found. You might not be able to duplicate the chart fonts or colors exactly, but choose the closest available substitutes. When your work is complete, save it as Duplicate Chart in the Case folder for Tutorial 4, preview it, and print it. Submit the photocopy of the original as well as the printout of the chart you created.

Answers to Quick Check Questions

SESSION 1.1

1 cell

2 open

3 D2

4 b

5 click the "Sheet2" sheet tab

6 press Ctrl + Home

SESSION 1.2

1 8; D1 + E1 + F1 + G1+ H1 + I1 + J1 + K1

2 B4, B5, B6, C4, C5, C6, D4, D5, D6

3 a. text
b. value
c. value
d. formula
e. text
f. formula
g. text

4 Active sheet(s), Print

5 Print, File

6 c

7 When you exit Excel, the workbook is erased from RAM. So if you want to use the workbook again you need to save it to disk. Click File, then click Save As.

8 press the Delete key

9 revising the contents of one or more cells in a worksheet and observing the effect this change has on all other cells in the worksheet

SESSION 2.1

1 Select the cell where you want the sum to appear. Click the AutoSum button. Excel suggests a formula which includes the SUM function. To accept the formula press the Enter key.

2 =A6+B6

3 cell references. If you were to copy the formula to other cells, these cells are relative references

4 absolute reference

5 Windows clipboard

6 fill-handle

7   double-click the sheet tab, then type the new name, then press the Enter key or click any cell in the worksheet to accept the entry

8   determine the purpose of the worksheet, enter the data and formulas, test the worksheet; correct errors, improve the appearance, document the worksheet, save and print

SESSION 2.2

1   select

2   header

3   Autoformat

4   Click any cell in the row above which you want to insert a row. Click Insert, then click Row

5   c

6   Assuming you are entering a formula with a function, first select the cell where you want to place a formula, type =, the function name and a left parenthesis, then click and drag over the range of cells to be used in the formula. Press the Enter key.

7   click Tools, click Options, then in the View tab, click the Formula check box

8   Landscape

SESSION 3.1

1   a. 13%; b. $0.13

2   Click Format, click Cells; right-click mouse in cell you want to format; use buttons on the Formatting toolbar

3   the data in the cell is formatted with the Comma style using two decimal places

4   Left Align button, Center button, Right Align button, and Merge and Center button

5   Center column headings, right-align numbers, and left-align text

6   Position the mouse pointer over the column header, right-click the mouse and click Column Width. Enter the new column width in the Column Width dialog box. Position the mouse pointer over the right edge of the column you want to modify, then click and drag to increase the column width.

7   Format Painter button

8   The column width of a cell is not wide enough to display the numbers, and you need to increase the column width

SESSION 3.2

1   use the Borders Tab on the Format Cells dialog box, or the Borders button on the Formatting toolbar

2   Click the Drawing button on the Standard toolbar

3   select

4   text box

5   Portrait

6   Click Tools, click View tab, then click the Gridlines check box to remove the check from the check box

7   Excel (graphic) object

SESSION 4.1

1 comparisons among items or changes in data over a period of time

2 selected; also referred to as activated

3 Select the appropriate chart, click Chart Menu, then click Source Data. Click the Collapse dialog box button, then select values to be included in the chart, press the Enter key, then click the OK button

4 Select the chart, move the pointer over the chart area until the pointer changes to an arrow then click and drag to another location on the worksheet

5 select the range of cells to be used as the source of data for the chart

6 the data marker that represents that data point will change to reflect the new value

7 identifies the pattern or colors assigned to the data series in a chart

8 A data point is a value in the worksheet, while the data marker is the symbol (pie slice, column, bar, and so on) that represents the data point in the chart

SESSION 4.2

1 a. a value that originates from a worksheet cell
b. a slice in a pie chart that represents a single point
c. a group of related data points plotted in a pie chart that originate from rows or columns in a worksheet

2 Select the A1, then press and hold down the CTRL key and select cells C5 and D10

3 pie chart

4 often, the data you want to plot is not in adjacent cells

5 an embedded chart is a chart object placed in a worksheet and saved with the worksheet when the workbook is saved; a chart sheet is a sheet in a workbook that contains only a chart

6 Select the pie chart you want to rotate, click Chart on the menu bar then click 3-D View to display the 3-D View dialog box. Click either rotate button to rotate the chart.

7 Select the slice you want to "explode," then click and drag the slice away from the center.

8 chart type

Integrating Microsoft®
Office 97 Professional

TUTORIAL 1

Read This **Before You Begin**

STUDENT DISK

To complete Integration Tutorial 1, you need one Student Disk. Your instructor will either provide you with a Student Disk or ask you to make your own.

If you are supposed to make your own Student Disk, you will need one blank, formatted high-density disk. You will need to copy a folder from a file server or standalone computer onto your disk. Your instructor will tell you which computer, drive letter, and folder contains the files you need. The following table shows you which folder goes on your disk:

Student Disk	Write this on the disk label	Put these folders on the disk
1	Student Disk 1: Integration Tutorial 1	Tutorial.01

When you begin the tutorial, be sure you are using the correct Student Disk. See the inside front or inside back cover of this book for more information on Student Disk files, or ask your instructor or technical support person for assistance.

USING YOUR OWN COMPUTER

If you are going to work through this book using your own computer, you need:

■ **Computer System** Microsoft Windows 95 or Microsoft Windows NT Workstation 4.0 (or a later version) and Microsoft Office 97 Professional must be installed on your computer. This book assumes a typical installation of Microsoft Office 97 Professional.

■ **Student Disk** Ask your instructor or lab manager for details on how to get the Student Disk. You will not be able to complete the tutorials or end-of-tutorial assignments in this book using your own computer until you have a Student Disk. The Student Files may also be obtained electronically over the Internet. See the inside front or inside back cover of this book for more details.

TO THE INSTRUCTOR

To complete Integration Tutorial 1, your students must use a set of files on one Student Disk. These files are included in the Instructor's Resource Kit, and they may also be obtained electronically over the Internet. See the inside front or inside back cover of this book for more details. Follow the instructions in the Readme file to copy the files to your server or standalone computer. You can view the Readme file using WordPad. Once the files are copied, you can make Student Disks for the students yourself, or you can tell students where to find the files so they can make their own Student Disks.

COURSE TECHNOLOGY STUDENT FILES

You are granted a license to copy the Student Files to any computer or computer network used by students who have purchased this book.

Integrating Word and Excel

Creating a Customer Letter that Includes a Chart and Table for Country Gardens

OBJECTIVES

In this tutorial you will:

- Learn about Object Linking and Embedding (OLE)

- Embed an Excel chart in a Word document

- Edit an embedded Excel chart in Word

- Link an Excel worksheet to a Word document

- Test, break, and reestablish links

CASE

Country Gardens

Just over ten years ago, Sue Dickinson began selling plants and herbs cultivated on her 15-acre farm in Bristol, New Hampshire. She soon developed a reputation for producing high-quality, hardy plants. At the urging of her customers, she opened a small shop, The Country Gardener, in her barn. Today Sue's business, renamed Country Gardens, has grown to include three shops, which she manages with the help of several family members, in Derry, New Hampshire, Dunstable, Massachusetts, and the newest one in Burlington, Vermont.

Country Gardens specializes in perennials, annuals, and herbs. Sue's customer base began as local townspeople and neighbors, and has since grown to include garden centers and landscape companies throughout the northeast that purchase products in bulk to stock their own greenhouses. This year, Country Gardens has attained the much prized recognition as the largest grower and greens supplier in New England, a title established by the New England Growers and Horticultural Association (NEGHA).

In an effort to further her company's growth and to help herself and her customers better plan and strategize for the upcoming growing season, Sue has decided to offer her products through a mail-order catalog. This will enable her to introduce customers to new products without requiring them to come into the stores to view the plants. Also, it will allow her to better monitor market trends and customer needs by tracking order amounts and order timing. Finally, the catalog will give Sue's customers an opportunity to better plan their own stock and gardening needs by previewing the available products, prices, and quantities a few months before the products are needed.

Sue wants to send a letter to her customers to announce the new mail-order catalog. She has drafted the body of the letter, which highlights the company's recent recognition by the NEGHA, introduces the mail-order catalog, and previews ten new plants that will be available through the catalog. She also wants the letter to include a chart the NEGHA has supplied depicting the company's status as the top grower in the area, and a table outlining the ten new products to be offered in the catalog.

You'll complete the letter for Sue using Microsoft Office 97 Professional (or, simply, Office), which allows you to create integrated documents easily. The Office programs—Microsoft Word, Microsoft Excel, Microsoft Access, and Microsoft PowerPoint—can all share information, which saves time and ensures consistency. Sue created her letter in Word. In this tutorial, you'll open the letter and then add the chart and table, both of which were created in Excel.

Planning the Integration

Sue's letter requires the NEGHA chart and the new products table. The letter is a Word document, and both the chart and table are Excel files, as shown in Figure 1-1.

Figure 1-1 ◀
Country Gardens
documents to
integrate

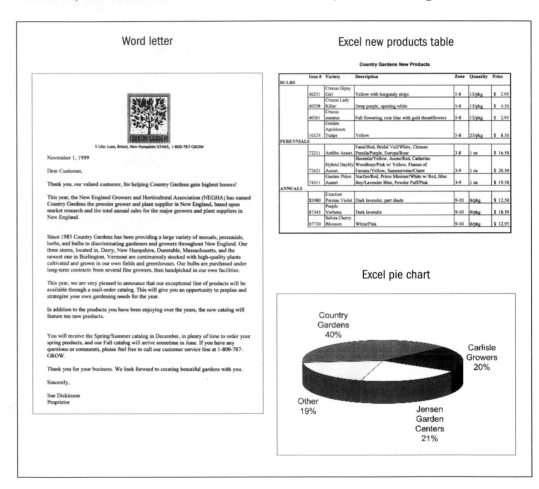

Putting all these pieces together into one Word document can be accomplished in a number of ways. For example, you could use the copy-and-paste method to integrate data from one program to another. You are familiar with the copy-and-paste method from the work you have done with Word and Excel.

Notice that the customer letter includes the company logo, which Sue copied and pasted from another file. Recall that when you use the copy-and-paste method to copy information or an object, such as the Country Gardens logo, into a document such as the customer letter, you can modify the logo once it is pasted into the letter. For example, you could resize it to fit just above the company name and address in the letterhead, and the original logo and the copied logo would remain independent of one another. Any changes made to the copy would not affect the original, and vice versa.

The copy-and-paste method worked fine for the logo, but what about the new products table? Sue created this table, which includes product specifications and pricing, in Excel. The pricing information is subject to change. Therefore, after including the table in Word, Sue might need to make changes to the Excel table. Sue doesn't want to have to keep track of these types of changes in two documents. It would be much better to simply make the change in one document and the other document would be automatically updated as well.

Object Linking and Embedding

When you need to maintain a connection between information in two places, you can use the linking or embedding methods instead of the copy-and-paste method. **Object Linking and Embedding** (OLE) allows Windows 95 programs to exchange and update data among other programs. Unlike copy-and-paste, the processes of linking and embedding retain a connection between two files from different programs, allowing you to work more efficiently.

The program containing the original information, or **object**, is called the **source** program, and the program in which you place the same information is called the **destination** program. In the case of Sue's letter, Excel is the source program for the table containing the product and pricing information and the NEGHA pie chart, and Word is the destination program. Figure 1-2 provides a description of the three integration methods and examples of when each method would be appropriate.

Figure 1-2 ◀
Comparing methods for integrating information

Method	Description	Use When
Copying-and-pasting	Places a copy of the information in a document	You will be exchanging the data between the two documents only once, and it doesn't matter if the data changes.
Embedding	Displays and stores an object in the destination document	You want the source object to become a permanent part of the destination document, and any changes you make to the object in either the destination document or the source document will not affect the other.
Linking	Displays an object in the destination document but doesn't store it there—only the location of the source document is stored in the destination document	You use the same data in more than one document, and you need to ensure that the data will be current and identical in each document. Any changes you make to the object in either the destination document or the source document will be reflected in the other.

If the object is **embedded**, it exists as a separate object in the destination program, which means that changes to the source object are not updated in the destination object, and vice versa. The advantage of embedding an object over the copy-and-paste method is that the menu and toolbar in the destination program change to those of the source program when you edit the object.

You can also link an object from one program to another. A linked object does not exist as a separate object in the destination file. Instead, OLE creates a direct connection, or **link**, between the source and destination programs so that the object exists in only one place—the source file—but the link displays the object in the destination file as well. You can manipulate and edit the object in either program. The link ensures that any changes to the object, initiated from either the source or destination program, are reflected in both files. Figure 1-3 illustrates the differences between embedding and linking.

Figure 1-3 ◀
Embedding
contrasted
with linking

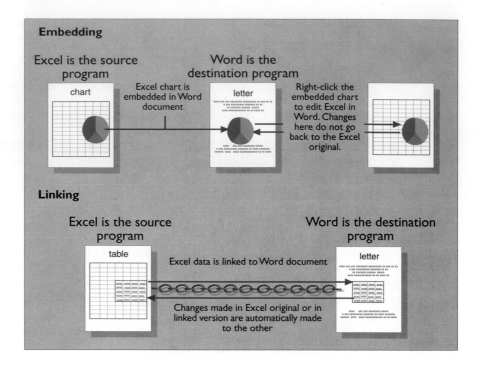

In the case of the Country Gardens customer letter, the NEGHA pie chart needs to be integrated into the customer letter first. Sue knows the data in the chart will not change, but she might need to modify the chart's size and appearance once it is integrated into the letter. To do this, Sue will want to use the Excel commands for modifying a chart; therefore, she decides to embed the chart, as shown in Figure 1-4. However, the Excel new products table must be linked between the Word document and the Excel workbook, as shown in Figure 1-4, because the prices of some of the products might change and both files would need to show the latest prices.

Figure 1-4 ◀
Integrating
Excel objects
into Word

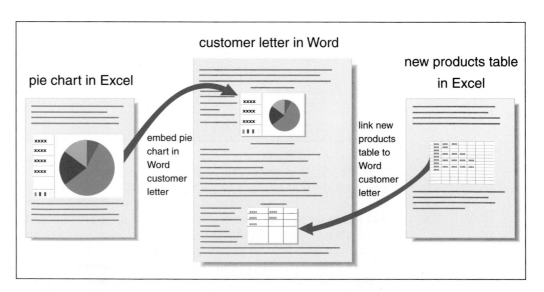

Sue has given you the Word file containing her letter. The first thing you need to do is embed the NEGHA pie chart. To do this, you need to start Word, and then open the letter document.

Integration

To start Word and open the letter document:

1. Start Word as usual.

2. Make sure your Student Disk is in the appropriate drive, and then open the document named **Letter**, which is located in the Tutorial.01 folder on your Student Disk. The letter is displayed in the document window in page layout view. See Figure 1-5.

Figure 1-5 ◀
Country
Gardens
customer letter

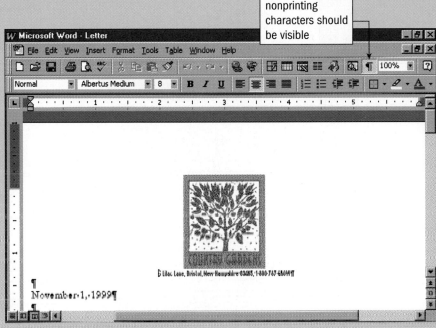

> nonprinting
> characters should
> be visible

TROUBLE? If your document does not show the nonprinting characters, click the Show/Hide button ¶ on the Standard toolbar.

Next you'll save the file with a new name. That way, the original letter remains intact on your Student Disk, in case you want to restart the tutorial.

3. Click **File** on the menu bar, and then click **Save As** to display the Save As dialog box.

4. Save the file as **Customer Letter** in the Tutorial.01 folder on your Student Disk.

You are ready to embed the Excel chart provided by the NEGHA depicting Country Gardens as the top grower in New England. To do this, you need to have access to both Word and Excel. The customer letter is already open, so now you need to start Excel and open the file containing the pie chart.

To open the chart in Excel:

1. Start Excel as usual.

2. Open the workbook named **NEGHA**, which is located in the Tutorial.01 folder on your Student Disk. The workbook is displayed in the document window. See Figure 1-6.

Figure 1-6 ◀
NEGHA
pie chart

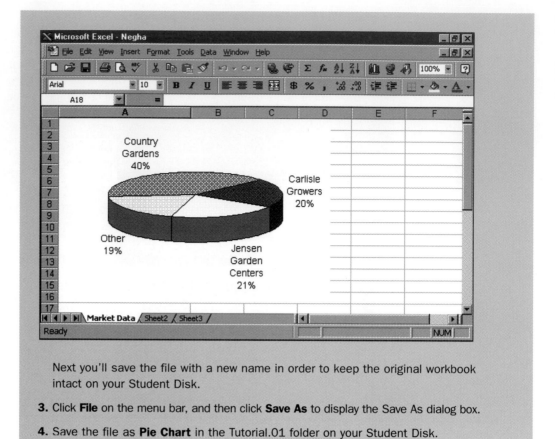

Next you'll save the file with a new name in order to keep the original workbook intact on your Student Disk.

3. Click **File** on the menu bar, and then click **Save As** to display the Save As dialog box.

4. Save the file as **Pie Chart** in the Tutorial.01 folder on your Student Disk.

Embedding an Excel Chart in a Word Document

Sue wants her letter to include the pie chart from the NEGHA showing Country Gardens as the top grower in the area for 1999. Sue knows the data for the chart will not change, so there is no need for her to link the pie chart in her Word letter to the source file. Therefore, she decides to embed it. That way, if the pie chart needs to be resized or moved once it is in the customer letter, she can make these changes using Excel chart commands. (Recall that when you embed an object, you automatically have access to the object's source program's commands and features to manipulate the embedded object in the destination program.)

REFERENCE
window

EMBEDDING AN OBJECT

- Start the source program, open the file containing the object to be embedded, select the object or information you want to embed in the destination program, and then click the Copy button on the toolbar.
- Start the destination program, open the file that will contain the embedded object, position the insertion point where you want to place the object, click Edit on the menu bar, and then click Paste Special.
- Click the Paste option button, select the option you want in the As list box, and then click the OK button.

Now you can embed the pie chart in the customer letter.

To embed the Excel chart in the Word document:

1. The pie chart should be displayed on your screen. If necessary, click the chart area (the white area around the pie) to select the chart. When the chart is selected, handles appear around the chart area.

2. Click the **Copy** button 🖻 on the Excel Standard toolbar to copy the chart to the Clipboard. The chart now appears with a rotating dashed line around its frame, indicating it has been copied.

3. Click the **Microsoft Word** button on the taskbar to return to the Customer Letter document.

4. Click to the left of the paragraph mark immediately above the paragraph that begins "Since 1985 Country Gardens..." to position the insertion point where you need to embed the pie chart. See Figure 1-7.

Figure 1-7 ◀
Placement for the pie chart in the customer letter

position insertion point here

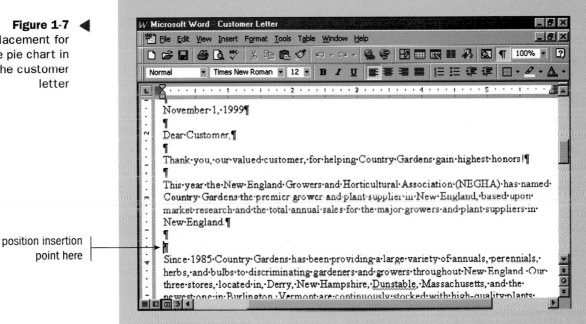

5. Click **Edit** on the menu bar, and then click **Paste Special**. The Paste Special dialog box opens. See Figure 1-8.

Figure 1-8 ◀
Paste Special dialog box

make sure this option is selected

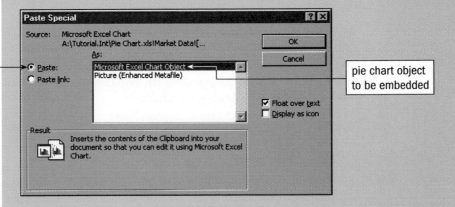

pie chart object to be embedded

6. In the As list box, click **Microsoft Excel Chart Object** to select the chart as the object to be embedded.

TROUBLE? If the Microsoft Excel Chart Object option does not appear in the As list box, you might not have selected and copied the chart correctly. Click the Cancel button, and then repeat Steps 1 through 5, making sure that when you select the chart, handles appear around the chart area, and that when you copy the chart, a rotating dashed line appears around the chart area.

7. Make sure the **Paste** option button is selected. This option will embed the chart. If you wanted to link the chart, you would choose the Paste link option.

8. Click the **OK** button. The Paste Special dialog box closes, and after a few moments, the Excel pie chart appears embedded in the letter. See Figure 1-9.

Figure 1-9 ◀
Pie chart embedded in the customer letter

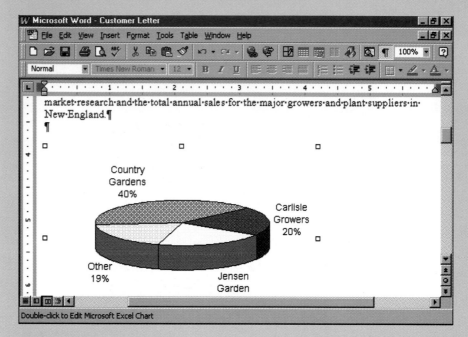

9. Click the **Save** button 🖫 on the Word Standard toolbar to save the letter with the embedded chart.

10. Click the **Microsoft Excel** button on the taskbar, click any cell outside of the chart area to deselect the chart, and then close the Pie Chart workbook.

TROUBLE? If a dialog box opens asking if you would like to save changes to the file before closing it, click the No button.

After reviewing the letter with the embedded pie chart, Sue decides that the pie chart would be more impressive if it was rotated so that the slice of pie showing Country Gardens' percentage of the market appears in front. Because you embedded the chart (as opposed to just copying and pasting it), you can use Excel chart commands from within the Word document to modify the chart.

Modifying an Embedded Object

When you make changes to an embedded object within the destination program, the changes are made to the embedded object only; the original object in the source program is not affected. When you select an embedded object, the menu commands on the destination program's menu bar change to include the menu commands of the embedded object's source program. You can then use these commands to modify the embedded object.

Now that you have embedded the pie chart in Word, you can modify it by changing the rotation of the chart so that the Country Gardens pie wedge appears in front.

To edit the pie chart from within Word:

1. Click the **Microsoft Word** button on the taskbar.

2. Double-click the **chart** to select it. After a moment, a thick border appears around the chart, and the Excel Chart menu is displayed at the top of the Word window. See Figure 1-10.

Figure 1-10 ◀
Selected Excel chart in the customer letter

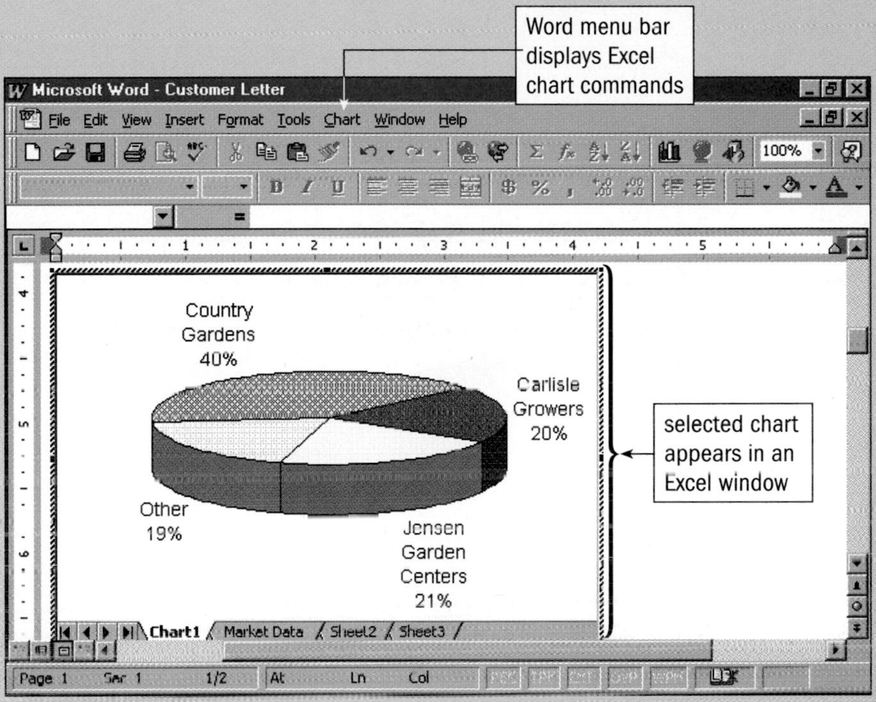

Word menu bar displays Excel chart commands

selected chart appears in an Excel window

TROUBLE? If the floating Chart toolbar appears, click its Close button to close it.

Now you can modify the chart. The chart is a 3-D pie chart, and you want to rotate it so that the Country Gardens pie wedge appears in front. You do this using the 3-D View dialog box.

3. Click **Chart** on the menu bar, and then click **3-D View**. The 3-D View dialog box opens. See Figure 1-11.

Figure 1-11 ◀
3-D View dialog box

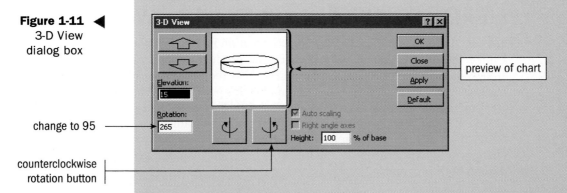

change to 95

preview of chart

counterclockwise rotation button

The Rotation text box shows the current value of 265, and the preview of the chart shows the median line pointing to the left. You want to move the Country Gardens wedge from the back of the pie to the front of the pie, so you need to move the median line counterclockwise, from the left to the right.

4. Click the **counterclockwise rotation** button until the Rotation text box shows the value **95**, and then click the **OK** button. As you click the counterclockwise rotation button, you can preview the rotation of the pie chart in the preview area of the dialog box.

The Country Gardens pie wedge is now positioned at the front of the pie chart. See Figure 1-12.

Figure 1-12 ◀
Revised
embedded
pie chart

repositioned
pie wedge

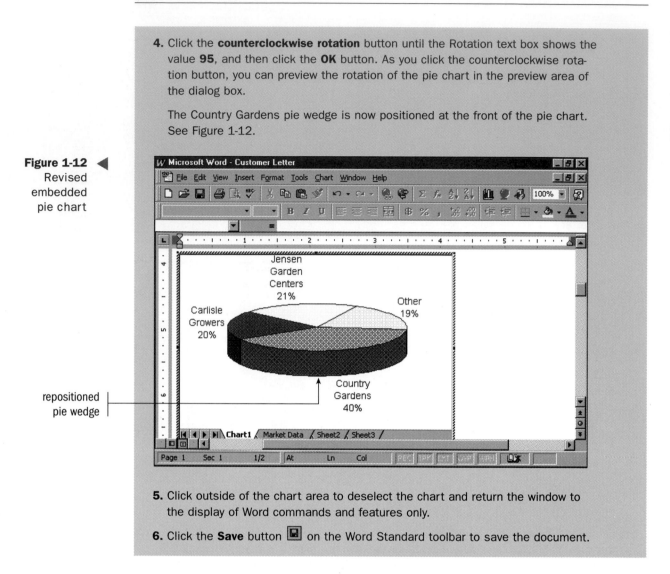

5. Click outside of the chart area to deselect the chart and return the window to the display of Word commands and features only.

6. Click the **Save** button 🖫 on the Word Standard toolbar to save the document.

Your final task is to include the table of new products in the letter. To do this, you will link the table from Excel to Word.

Linking an Object from Excel to Word

Sue maintains her product and pricing information in an Excel workbook named Products. Unlike the information in the pie chart, the product and pricing information is always subject to change. For example, Sue believes that the price of bulbs will most likely change once she gets a signed quote from her supplier. It's possible that she won't receive this quote until right before she plans to send out the letter. Therefore, instead of embedding the table as you did the chart, you'll link the table from the Products workbook to the Customer Letter document so that you can make changes from either Excel or Word and have the changes automatically reflected in the other program. This will keep the information up-to-date in both programs.

> REFERENCE
> **window**
>
> ### LINKING AN OBJECT
>
> - Start the source program, open the file containing the object to be linked, select the object or information you want to link to the destination program, and then click the Copy button on the toolbar.
> - Start the destination program, open the file that will contain the link to the copied object, position the insertion point where you want the linked object to appear, click Edit on the menu bar, and then click Paste Special.
> - Click the Paste link option button, select the option you want in the As list box, and then click the OK button.

Now you will link the product table to the letter. You first need to open the Products workbook, and then select the table object for linking.

To link the product table to the customer letter:

1. Click the **Microsoft Excel** button on the taskbar to switch to the Excel window.

2. Open the Excel workbook named **Products** in the Tutorial.01 folder on your Student Disk. Use the Save As command to save the file as **New Products**.

3. Highlight cells **A1** through **H17** to select the product table, and then click the **Copy** button 🖺 on the Excel Standard toolbar to copy the data to the Clipboard.

4. Click the **Microsoft Word** button on the taskbar to return to the customer letter.

5. Scroll the document and position the insertion point to the left of the paragraph mark above the paragraph that begins, "You will receive... ." This is where you want the product and pricing data to appear. See Figure 1-13.

Figure 1-13 ◀
Placement for
linking the
Excel
worksheet to
the customer
letter

position insertion
point here

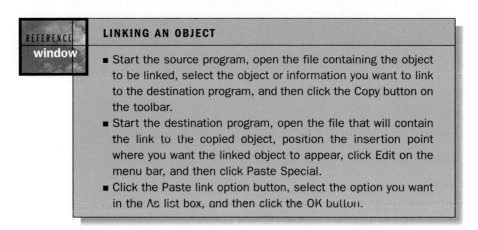

6. Click **Edit** on the Word menu bar, and then click **Paste Special**. The Paste Special dialog box opens.

7. In the Paste Special dialog box, click the **Paste link** option button to select this option, and then click **Microsoft Excel Worksheet Object** in the As section.

The Paste link option specifies that the table will be linked.

8. Click the **OK** button to close the Paste Special dialog box and to link the Excel worksheet to the customer letter. See Figure 1-14.

Figure 1-14 ◄
Linked new
products table

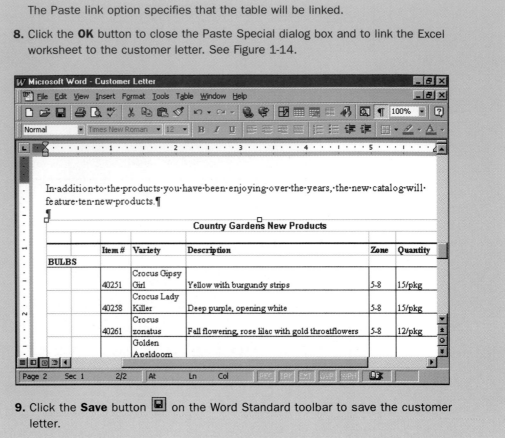

9. Click the **Save** button 🖫 on the Word Standard toolbar to save the customer letter.

Sue has just received the signed quote from her bulb supplier. As she expected, some of the prices have changed. She now would like you to update the product table.

Updating Linked Objects

Now that you have linked the product table from Excel to the customer letter, you can update the information from either the source program (Excel) or the destination program (Word), and the changes will automatically be reflected in the other program. When making changes, you can have one or both files open.

To update the product table in Excel:

1. Click the **Microsoft Excel** button on the taskbar to switch to the New Products workbook in Excel.

2. Click any cell to deselect the table.

   The price of Crocus Gipsy Girl bulbs has changed from $2.95 to $3.95 each.

3. In cell H5, enter **3.95**.

   Now check to see if this change is reflected in the customer letter.

4. Click the **Microsoft Word** button on the taskbar to switch to the customer letter. Because you linked the table from Excel to Word, the change you just made to the price of product 40251, Crocus Gipsy Girl bulbs, also appears here in the destination document. See Figure 1-15.

Figure 1-15
Observing
changes
between linked
documents

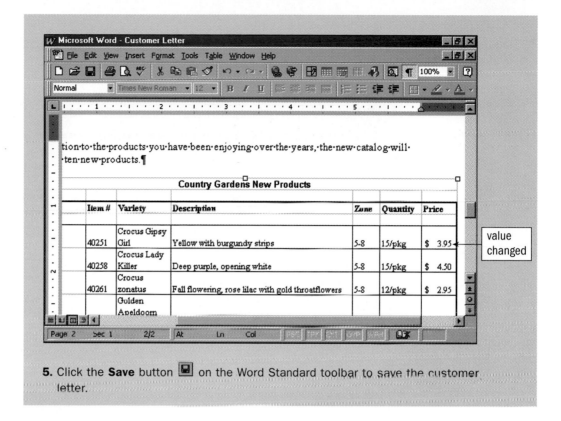

value
changed

5. Click the **Save** button 🖫 on the Word Standard toolbar to save the customer letter.

What would happen if you were working on the new product table in Excel without the Word document open? Would the information still be updated in the customer letter? To find out, make the remaining changes to the prices for bulbs with the customer letter closed. You can then reopen the customer letter to ensure that the changes appear there as well.

To change the linked object with the Word document closed:

1. Close the customer letter.

2. Click the **Microsoft Excel** button on the taskbar to switch to the New Products workbook.

3. Enter **4.95** in cell H6, and then enter **3.25** in cell H7.

4. Click the **Save** button 🖫 on the Excel Standard toolbar.

5. Click the **Microsoft Word** button on the taskbar, click **File** on the Word menu bar, and then click **1 Customer Letter** to open the letter document.

   TROUBLE? If the customer letter is not listed as 1 Customer Letter, it might be listed with the drive and filename preceding it. If you still cannot find it, use the Open command from the File menu to open the Customer Letter document.

6. Scroll the document to view the linked table. Notice that the new bulb prices appear in the linked table in Word. See Figure 1-16.

Figure 1-16 ◀
Values updated
in linked
document

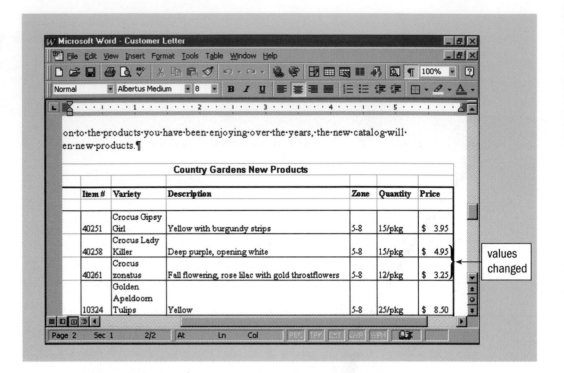

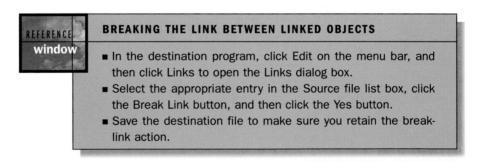

Breaking and Reestablishing Links

Once you are done working with linked documents, you can choose to break the link between the two documents. You do this by using the Links command on the Edit menu. Once you break a link, you cannot change the object in the destination file, but you can resize, move, or delete it. Also, any changes you make to the object in the source file are not reflected in the destination file once the link is broken.

REFERENCE window

BREAKING THE LINK BETWEEN LINKED OBJECTS

- In the destination program, click Edit on the menu bar, and then click Links to open the Links dialog box.
- Select the appropriate entry in the Source file list box, click the Break Link button, and then click the Yes button.
- Save the destination file to make sure you retain the break-link action.

You are done updating the new product prices and are ready to give Sue the finished letter to send to her customers. Sue believes the prices for the bulbs are final, so you can break the link between the Customer Letter document and the New Products workbook.

To break the link for the linked object:

1. In the Word window, click **Edit** on the menu bar, and then click **Links** to open the Links dialog box. There should be just one entry in the Source file list box, and it should be selected. If not, click the entry to select it.

2. Click the **Break Link** button. Word opens a dialog box asking you to confirm that you want to break the link. See Figure 1-17.

Figure 1-17 ◀
Breaking a link
between
documents

link to be broken

message box
confirming break-link

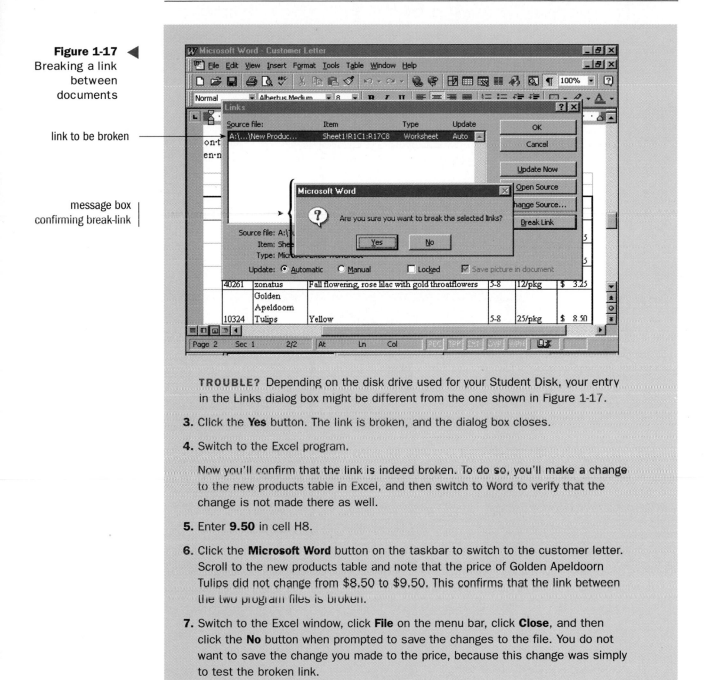

TROUBLE? Depending on the disk drive used for your Student Disk, your entry in the Links dialog box might be different from the one shown in Figure 1-17.

3. Click the **Yes** button. The link is broken, and the dialog box closes.

4. Switch to the Excel program.

    Now you'll confirm that the link is indeed broken. To do so, you'll make a change to the new products table in Excel, and then switch to Word to verify that the change is not made there as well.

5. Enter **9.50** in cell H8.

6. Click the **Microsoft Word** button on the taskbar to switch to the customer letter. Scroll to the new products table and note that the price of Golden Apeldoorn Tulips did not change from $8.50 to $9.50. This confirms that the link between the two program files is broken.

7. Switch to the Excel window, click **File** on the menu bar, click **Close**, and then click the **No** button when prompted to save the changes to the file. You do not want to save the change you made to the price, because this change was simply to test the broken link.

If you now saved the Customer Letter document, the link to the Excel object would remain broken. However, if you closed the Customer Letter document without saving it, the break-link action would not be saved, and the link between the two files would still be intact.

Sue informs you that she just finished renegotiating prices for the bulbs with her supplier—some of the prices just seemed too high. She is expecting a new quote sheet within the hour. Given this information, you decide not to break the link between the Customer Letter document and the New Products workbook.

To cancel the break-link action:

1. In the Word window, click **File** on the menu bar, click **Close**, and then click the **No** button when prompted to save the changes to the file. You don't want to save

the file because you don't want to break the link with the New Products work-book. The Customer Letter document and the New Products workbook continue to be linked.

2. Reopen the Customer Letter document, and then scroll the document to view the linked product table.

Sue asks you to print a copy of the letter so that she can review it before mailing out any letters.

To preview and print the letter:

1. Click the **Print Preview** button 🔍 on the Standard toolbar to preview the letter. If necessary, click the **Multiple Pages** button ⊞ on the Print Preview toolbar to view both pages of the letter. See Figure 1-18.

Figure 1-18 ◀
Preview of
completed
customer letter

embedded chart

linked table

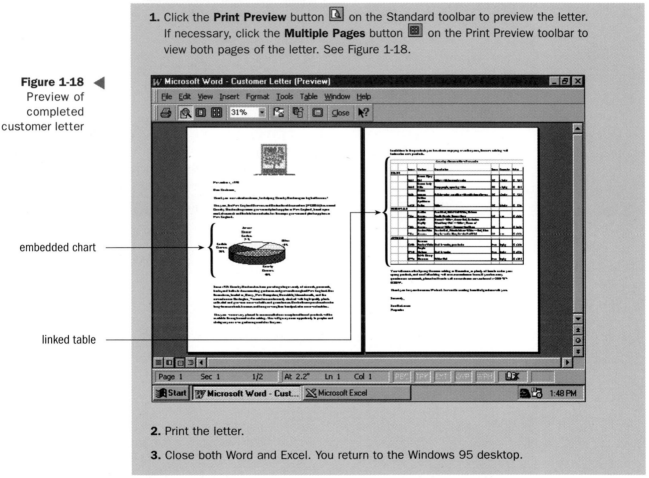

2. Print the letter.

3. Close both Word and Excel. You return to the Windows 95 desktop.

Quick Check

1 What are the three methods for integrating information from one program to another?

2 What is the difference between copying-and-pasting an object and embedding an object?

3 If an Excel chart is embedded in a Word document, which program is the source program and which is the destination program?

4 When an object is linked between two programs, how many copies of the object exist?

5 If you break the link for an object, what operations can you perform on the object in the destination program?

6 How can you reestablish a broken link?

You have integrated the NEGHA pie chart and the new products table from Excel into the customer letter Sue created in Word. She is pleased with the finished customer letter and is ready to send it to her customers.

Tutorial Assignments

Sue would like a memo to go to all Country Gardens employees introducing the plans for the catalog, the new products, and Country Gardens' status as the top grower in New England.

To create the memo:

1. Start Word, and then open the document named Memo in the TAssign folder of the Tutorial.01 folder on your Student Disk.
2. Save the document as Employee Memo in the TAssign folder.
3. Start Excel, and then open the PieChart workbook in the TAssign folder of the Tutorial.01 folder on your Student Disk.
4. Save the workbook as PieChart2 in the TAssign folder.
5. Embed the chart from Excel to Word. Place the chart between the first and second paragraphs of the memo.
6. Double-click the chart. Describe what happens. Why does this occur?

7. Explode the Country Gardens wedge of the pie. (*Hint*: With the chart selected, click the pie itself, and then click the Country Gardens wedge to select only that wedge. Then, click and drag to explode the wedge.)
8. Switch to Excel, and then close the PieChart2 file without saving it.
9. Open the Products workbook in the TAssign folder of the Tutorial.01 folder on your Student Disk, and then save it as New Products2 in the TAssign folder.
10. Link the new products table to the employee memo, and place it in the blank paragraph mark above the paragraph that begins, "Once again . . . ."

11. Double-click the new products table, and then change the price of Crocus Gipsy Girl to $4.95 and the price of Golden Apeldoorn Tulips to $9.50.
12. Switch back to the Word document. Notice that the changes are reflected there as well.
13. Save the memo, and then preview and print it.
14. Break the link between the employee memo and the table.
15. Test that the link is broken by changing the price of the Astilbe Assortment from $16.50 to $15.50 in the table in the Excel window.

16. If you now saved the Excel file with this price change, and then closed the Word file *without* saving changes when prompted, would the price of the Astilbe Assortment be $16.50 (its original price) or $15.50 (the price you changed it to in step 15)? Why?
17. Exit Word and Excel. If prompted to save any files, click the Yes button.

Case Problems

1. Electro-Lease Company John Rivers is the sales supervisor for the Electro-Lease Company in Washington, DC. Electro-Lease leases mainframe computer cables and wiring. The company just recently changed its customer relations policy to allow leasing quotes to be given over the phone. To ensure that the quotes are clearly understood by both parties, John wants all salespeople to follow up each telephone quote with a confirmation letter that provides a written quotation. The quotation will be calculated in an Excel workbook. If the customer subsequently decides to change the specifications for the quote, John wants to be able to update the confirmation letter easily. However, he also wants to control when the letter is updated so that changes aren't reflected until the customer confirms the order. To accomplish this, you'll link the quote from the Excel workbook into the confirmation letter, and then use the Office Assistant to find out about manually updating links.

1. Start Word, and then open the document named Price in the Cases folder of the Tutorial.01 folder on your Student Disk.
2. Save the document as Quote in the Cases folder.
3. Position the insertion point in the blank paragraph between paragraphs one and three of the text of the letter.
4. Start Excel, and then open the workbook named Costs in the Cases folder of the Tutorial.01 folder on your Student Disk.
5. Save the workbook as Charges in the Cases folder.
6. Maximize the Excel window, select cells A1 through G6, and then copy the selection to the Clipboard.
7. Switch to Word.
8. Link the Excel worksheet object into the Word document.
9. Save the changes, and then print the document.
10. Switch to Excel.
11. Change the quantity ordered for all three items to 2.
12. Save the changes to Charges, switch to Word, and then print the document.

13. Switch to Excel, display the Office Assistant, and then type "How do I manually update links?" in the Search text box.
    a. Click the Search button, and then select the topic "Control how linked information is updated in Microsoft Excel."
    b. In the section "What do you want to do?" click the topic "Update a linked object manually."
    c. Read the Help topic, and then close the Help window and the Office Assistant.

14. Change the type of link for the Excel worksheet object to manual.
15. Save the Word document as Confirm in the Cases folder of the Tutorial.01 folder on your Student Disk.
16. Switch to Excel, and then change the quantity ordered for Item 1 to 3.
17. Save the change to the workbook, and then exit Excel. Note that the change you just made in the previous step is not reflected in the Word document.

18. Based on what you learned from the Office Assistant in Step 13, manually update the link to the Excel worksheet object.
19. Save and print the Confirm document, and then exit Word. Note that the change you made to Item 1 is now reflected in the Word document.

2. Admissions at the University of Maine Jennifer Dolloff, a senior at the University of Maine, works in the Admissions office. She has been asked to help gather useful information for a packet to be sent to new freshmen students and their parents. Along with information on housing, meal plans, course selection, campus facilities, and so on, she needs to provide summary information on typical student expenditures (separate from tuition expenses). She decides to use Word and Excel to create a letter that includes a chart showing how student expenditures at the University of Maine for the average student have either remained the same or increased only slightly over the last few years, and also a table of the typical expenditures students can expect. The information she needs is shown in Figures 1-19 and 1-20.

Figure 1-19 ◀

Expenditures	1996	1997	1998
Books	$625.00	$650.00	$665.00
Dorm fees	$185.00	$190.00	$190.00
Lab fees	$40.00	$40.00	$40.00
Supplies	$95.00	$105.00	$110.00
Library fees	$60.00	$60.00	$75.00
TOTAL:	$1005.00	$1045.00	$1080.00

Figure 1-20 ◀

Expenditures	Estimated Amounts
Books	$680.00
Dorm fees	$200.00
Lab fees	$45.00
Supplies	$115.00
Library fees	$75.00

You'll use Word and Excel to create the letter for Jennifer.

1. Start Word and start a new document. Write a letter to parents of incoming freshmen of the University of Maine. Briefly outline the purpose of the letter, which is to provide the new students with an idea of typical student expenditures separate from tuition fees. State that the university realizes these expenditures can be difficult to meet given the cost of tuition, and that over the last three years, the school and faculty have worked to keep increases to these expenses at a minimum. Remember to include a proper salutation and closing.
2. Save the file as Expenditure Letter in the Cases folder of the Tutorial.01 folder on your Student Disk.
3. Start Excel and start a new worksheet. Rename Sheet1 as Line Chart, and then enter the data shown in Figure 1-19.
4. Create a line chart based on the data, showing how minor the increases are in expenses over the last three years.
5. Save the workbook as Estimated Expenses in the Cases folder of the Tutorial.01 folder on your Student Disk.

6. Link the line chart to the letter, selecting an appropriate placement.
7. Change the Books amount for 1998 from $665.00 to $675.00.
8. On sheet2 of the Estimated Expenses workbook, create a worksheet that shows the information in Figure 1-20. Rename the worksheet as Expenses.
9. Embed the Expenses worksheet in the Expenditure Letter document in an appropriate place.
10. Insert a row into the embedded expenses worksheet that totals the expense amounts.
11. Save, preview, and then print the letter.
12. Close Word and Excel.

Answers to Quick Check Questions

1 copying-and-pasting, embedding, linking

2 A copied-and-pasted object cannot be edited; an embedded object can be edited and modified using the commands and features of its source program.

3 Excel is the source program and Word is the destination program.

4 One copy exists in the source program; the destination program contains just the link to the original object as stored in the source program.

5 resize, move, or delete

6 Cancel the break-link action by not saving the change.

Integrating Microsoft Office 97 **Index**

C

charts
    embedding in Word documents, I 1.6–1.12
    linking to Word documents, I 1.12–1.19
copying and pasting, I 1.4, I 1.5

D

destination program, I 1.5
documents
    embedding Excel objects, I 1.6–1.12
    linking Excel objects, I 1.12–1.19

E

editing
    embedded objects, I 1.10–1.12
    linked objects, I 1.14–1.16
embedding objects, I 1.5
    Excel objects in Word documents, I 1.6–1.12
    linking compared, I 1.6
    modifying embedded objects, I 1.10–1.12
Excel
    embedding objects in Word documents,
        I 1.6–1.12
    linking objects to Word documents,
        I 1.12–1.19

I

integrating data
    comparison of methods, I 1.5
    copy-and-paste method, I 1.4, I 1.5
    object linking and embedding. *See* embed-
        ding objects; linking objects; Object
        Linking and Embedding (OLE)
    planning, I 1.4–1.8

L

linking objects, I 1.5
    breaking links, I 1.16–1.17

canceling break-link action, I 1.17–1.18
embedding compared, I 1.6
Excel objects to Word documents,
    I 1.12–1.19
updating linked objects, I 1.14–1.16

O

Object Linking and Embedding (OLE),
    I 1.5–1.19
objects, I 1.5
    embedding. *See* embedding objects
    linking. *See* linking objects
OLE. *See* embedding objects; linking objects;
    Object Linking and Embedding (OLE)

P

Paste Special dialog box, I 1.9–1.10
pasting, I 1.4, I 1.5
planning, integrations, I 1.4–1.8
programs
    destination, I 1.5
    source, I 1.5

S

source program, I 1.5

T

3-D View dialog box, I 1.11–1.12

W

Word
    embedding Excel objects in documents,
        I 1.6–1.12
    linking Excel objects to documents,
        I 1.12–1.19

Integrating Microsoft Office 97 **Task Reference**

TASK	PAGE #	RECOMMENDED METHOD
Embedded object, edit	I 1.11	Double-click the object to select it, and then edit it using appropriate commands
Embedded object, establish	I 1.8	See Reference Window: Embedding an Object
Linked object, break the link	I 1.16	See Reference Window: Breaking the Link Between Linked Objects
Linked object, establish	I 1.13	See Reference Window: Linking an Object
Linked object, reestablish the link	I 1.17	Close the destination program without saving changes by clicking File, Close, and then click No
Linked object, update	I 1.14	Make changes in the source program, or double-click the linked object to make changes in the destination file

Microsoft® Access 97

LEVEL I

TUTORIALS

Read This **Before You Begin**

TUTORIAL 1

Introduction to Microsoft Access 97

Viewing and Working with a Table Containing Customer Data

OBJECTIVES

In this tutorial you will:

- Define the terms field, record, table, relational database, primary key, and foreign key

- Start and exit Access

- Open an existing database

- Identify the components of the Access and Database windows

- Open, navigate, and print a table

- Create, run, and print a query

- Create and print a form

- Use the Access Help system

- Create, preview, and print a report

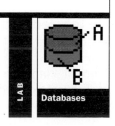

LAB

Databases

Valle Coffee

CASE

Ten years ago Leonard Valle became the president of Algoman Imports, a small distributor of inexpensive coffee beans to supermarkets in western Michigan. At that time the company's growth had leveled off, so during his first three years Leonard took several dramatic, risky steps in an attempt to increase sales and profits. First, he changed the inexpensive coffee bean varieties that Algoman Imports had been distributing to a selection of gourmet varieties from Central and South America, Africa, and several island nations. Second, he purchased facilities and equipment so that the company could roast, grind, flavor, and package the coffee beans instead of buying them already roasted and packaged whole. Because the company could now control the quality of the finest gourmet coffees, Leonard stopped distributing to supermarkets and shifted sales to restaurants and offices throughout the area.

Within two years, company sales and profits soared; consequently, Leonard took over ownership of the company. He changed the company name to Valle Coffee, continued expanding into other markets and geographic areas (specifically, Ohio and Indiana), and expanded the company's line of coffee flavors and blends.

Part of Valle Coffee's success can be credited to its use of computers in all aspects of its business, including financial management, inventory control, shipping, receiving, production, and sales. Several months ago the company upgraded to Microsoft Windows 95 and **Microsoft Access 97** (or simply **Access**), a computer program used to enter, maintain, and retrieve related data in a format known as a database. Barbara Hennessey, office manager at Valle Coffee, and her staff use Access to maintain company data such as customer orders and billing, coffee supplier orders and payments, and advertising placements and payments. Barbara recently created a database named Restaurant to track the company's restaurant customers, their orders, and related data such as the products they order. She asks for your help in completing and maintaining this database.

Using the Tutorials Effectively

These tutorials are designed to be used at a computer. Each tutorial is divided into sessions. Watch for the session headings, such as "Session 1.1" and "Session 1.2." Each session is designed to be completed in about 45 minutes, but take as much time as you need. When you've completed a session, it's a good idea to exit the program and take a break. You can exit Microsoft Access by clicking the Close button in the top-right corner of the program window.

Before you begin, read the following questions and answers. They are designed to help you use the tutorials effectively.

Where do I start?

Each tutorial begins with a case, which sets the scene for the tutorial and gives you background information to help you understand what you will be doing in the tutorial. Read the case before you go to the lab. In the lab, begin with the first session of the tutorial.

How do I know what to do on the computer?

Each session contains steps that you will perform on the computer to learn how to use Microsoft Access. The steps are numbered and are set against a colored background. Read the text that introduces each series of steps, and read each step carefully and completely before you try it.

How do I know if I did the step correctly?

As you work, compare your computer screen with the corresponding figure in the tutorial. Don't worry if your screen display is somewhat different from the figure. The important parts of the screen display are labeled in each figure. Check to make sure these parts are on your screen.

What if I make a mistake?

Don't worry about making mistakes—they are part of the learning process. Paragraphs labeled **"TROUBLE?"** identify common problems and explain how to get back on track. Follow the steps in a **"TROUBLE?"** paragraph *only* if you are having the problem described. If you run into other problems, carefully consider the current state of your system, the position of the pointer, and any messages on the screen.

How do I use the Reference Windows?

Reference Windows summarize the procedures you learn in the tutorial steps. Do not complete the actions in the Reference Windows when you are working through the tutorial. Instead, refer to the Reference Windows while you are working on the assignments at the end of the tutorial.

How can I test my understanding of the material I learned in the tutorial?

At the end of each session, you can answer the Quick Check questions. If necessary, refer to the Answers to Quick Check Questions to check your work.

After you have completed the entire tutorial, you should complete the Tutorial Assignments and Case Problems. These exercises are carefully structured so you will review what you have learned and then apply your knowledge to new situations.

What if I can't remember how to do something?

You should refer to the Task Reference at the end of the book; it summarizes how to accomplish commonly performed tasks.

What is the Databases Course Lab, and how should I use it?

This interactive Lab helps you review database concepts and practice skills that you learn in Tutorial 1. The Lab Assignments section at the end of Tutorial 1 includes instructions for using the Lab.

Now that you've seen how to use the tutorials effectively, you are ready to begin.

SESSION

1.1

In this session you will define key database terms and concepts, start Access and open an existing database, identify components of the Access and Database windows, open and navigate a table, print a table, and exit Access.

Databases

Introduction to Database Concepts

Before you begin working on Barbara's database and using Access, you need to understand a few key terms and concepts associated with databases.

Organizing Data

Data is a valuable resource to any business. At Valle Coffee, for example, important data includes customers' names and addresses, and order dates and amounts. Organizing, storing, maintaining, retrieving, and sorting this type of data are critical activities that enable a business to find and use information effectively. Before storing data on a computer, however, you first must organize the data.

Your first step in organizing data is to identify the individual fields. A **field** is a single characteristic or attribute of a person, place, object, event, or idea. For example, some of the many fields that Valle Coffee tracks are customer number, customer name, customer address, customer phone number, order number, billing date, and invoice amount.

Next, you group related fields together into tables. A **table** is a collection of fields that describe a person, place, object, event, or idea. Figure 1-1 shows an example of a Customer table consisting of four fields: Customer Number, Customer Name, Customer Address, and Phone Number.

Figure 1-1 ◀
Data organization for a table of customers

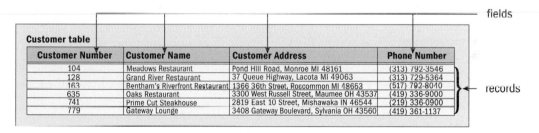

fields

records

Customer table

Customer Number	Customer Name	Customer Address	Phone Number
104	Meadows Restaurant	Pond Hill Road, Monroe MI 48161	(313) 792-3546
128	Grand River Restaurant	37 Queue Highway, Lacota MI 49063	(313) 729-5364
163	Bentham's Riverfront Restaurant	1366 36th Street, Roscommon MI 48653	(517) 792-8040
635	Oaks Restaurant	3300 West Russell Street, Maumee OH 43537	(419) 336-9000
741	Prime Cut Steakhouse	2819 East 10 Street, Mishawaka IN 46544	(219) 336-0900
779	Gateway Lounge	3408 Gateway Boulevard, Sylvania OH 43560	(419) 361-1137

The specific value, or content, of a field is called the **field value**. In Figure 1-1, the first set of field values for Customer Number, Customer Name, Customer Address, and Phone Number are, respectively, 104; Meadows Restaurant; Pond Hill Road, Monroe MI 48161; and (313) 792-3546. This set of field values is called a **record**. In the Customer table, the data for each customer is stored as a separate record. Six records are shown in Figure 1-1; each row of field values is a record.

Databases and Relationships

A collection of related tables is called a **database**, or **relational database**. Valle Coffee's Restaurant database will contain two related tables: the Customer table, which Barbara has already created, and the Order table, which you will create in Tutorial 2. Sometimes you might want information about customers and the orders they placed. To obtain this information you must have a way to connect records in the Customer table to records in the Order table. You connect the records in the separate tables through a **common field** that appears in both tables. In the sample database shown in Figure 1-2, each record in the Customer table has a field named Customer Number, which is also a field in the Order table. For example, Oaks Restaurant is the fourth customer in the Customer table and has a Customer Number of 635. This same Customer Number field value, 635, appears in three records in the Order table. Therefore, Oaks Restaurant is the customer that placed these three orders.

Figure 1-2 ◀
Database
relationship
between tables
for customers
and orders

primary keys

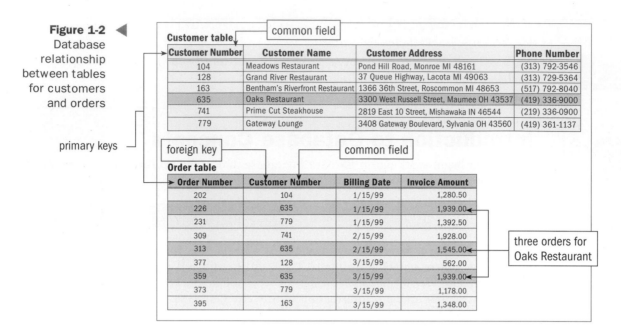

Each Customer Number in the Customer table must be unique, so that you can distinguish one customer from another and identify the customer's specific orders in the Order table. The Customer Number field is referred to as the primary key of the Customer table. A **primary key** is a field, or a collection of fields, whose values uniquely identify each record in a table. In the Order table, Order Number is the primary key.

When you include the primary key from one table as a field in a second table to form a relationship between the two tables, it is called a **foreign key** in the second table, as shown in Figure 1-2. For example, Customer Number is the primary key in the Customer table and a foreign key in the Order table. Although the primary key Customer Number has unique values in the Customer table, the same field as a foreign key in the Order table does not have unique values. The Customer Number value 635, for example, appears three times in the Order table, because the Oaks Restaurant placed three orders. Each foreign key value, however, must match one of the field values for the primary key in the other table. In the example in Figure 1-2, each Customer Number value in the Order table must match a Customer Number value in the Customer table. The two tables are related, enabling users to tie together the facts about customers with the facts about orders.

Relational Database Management Systems

To manage its databases, a company purchases a database management system. A **database management system** (**DBMS**) is a software program that lets you create databases and then manipulate data in the databases. Most of today's database management systems, including Access, are called relational database management systems. In a **relational database management system**, data is organized as a collection of tables. As stated earlier, a relationship between two tables in a relational DBMS is formed through a common field.

A relational DBMS controls the storage of databases on disk by carrying out data creation and manipulation requests. Specifically, a relational DBMS provides the following functions, which are illustrated in Figure 1-3:

- It allows you to create database structures containing fields, tables, and table relationships.

- It lets you easily add new records, change field values in existing records, and delete records.

- It contains a built-in query language, which lets you obtain immediate answers to the questions you ask about your data.

■ It contains a built-in report generator, which lets you produce professional-looking, formatted reports from your data.

■ It provides protection of databases through security, control, and recovery facilities.

Figure 1-3
A relational
database
management
system

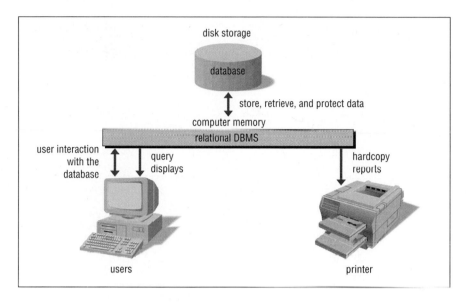

A company like Valle Coffee benefits from a relational DBMS because it allows several users working in different departments to share the same data. More than one user can enter data into a database, and more than one user can retrieve and analyze data that was entered by others. For example, Valle Coffee will keep only one copy of the Customer table, and all employees will be able to use it to meet their specific needs for customer information.

Finally, unlike other software programs, such as spreadsheets, a DBMS can handle massive amounts of data and can easily form relationships among multiple tables. Each Access database, for example, can be up to 1 gigabyte in size and can contain up to 32,768 objects (tables, queries, and so on).

Now that you've learned some database terms and concepts, you're ready to start Access and open the Restaurant database.

Starting Access

You start Access in the same way that you start other Windows 95 programs—using the Start button on the taskbar.

To start Access:

1. Make sure Windows 95 is running on your computer and the Windows 95 desktop appears on your screen.

   TROUBLE? If you're running Windows NT Workstation 4.0 (or a later version) on your computer or network, don't worry. Although the figures in this book were created while running Windows 95, Windows NT 4.0 and Windows 95 share the same interface, and Access 97 runs equally well under either operating system.

2. Click the **Start** button on the taskbar to display the Start menu, and then point to **Programs** to display the Programs menu.

3. Point to **Microsoft Access** on the Programs menu. See Figure 1-4.

Figure 1-4 ◀
Starting
Microsoft
Access

Programs menu
option

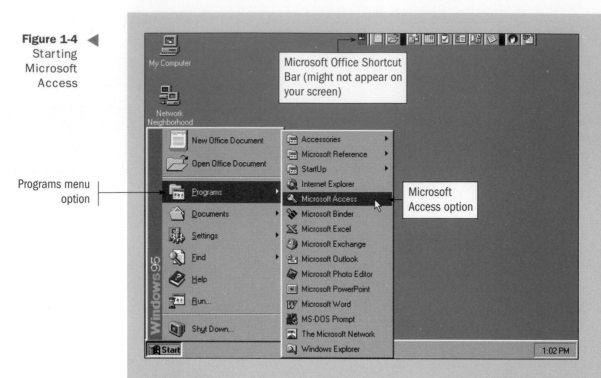

TROUBLE? If you don't see the Microsoft Access option on the Programs menu, ask your instructor or technical support person for help.

TROUBLE? The Office Shortcut Bar, which appears along the top of the desktop in Figure 1-4, might look different on your screen or it might not appear at all, depending on how your system is set up. The steps in these tutorials do not require that you use the Office Shortcut Bar; therefore, the remaining figures do not display the Office Shortcut Bar.

4. Click **Microsoft Access** to start Access. After a short pause, the Access copyright information appears in a message box and remains on the screen until the Access window is displayed. See Figure 1-5.

Figure 1-5 ◀
The Microsoft
Access window

toolbar

initial dialog box

status bar

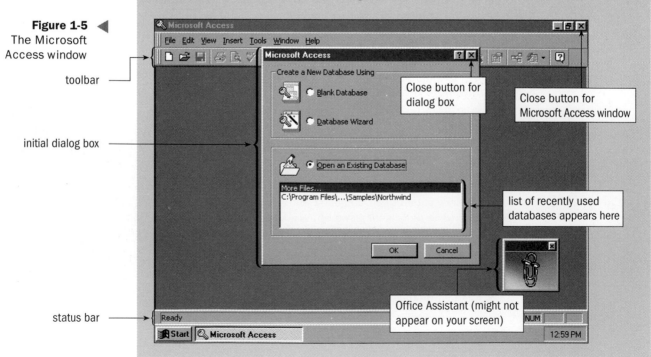

TROUBLE? Depending on how your system is set up, the Office Assistant (see Figure 1-5) might open when you start Access. For now, click the Close button [X] on the Office Assistant window to close it; you'll learn more about this feature later in this tutorial. If you've started Access immediately after installing it, you'll need to click the Start Using Microsoft Access option, which the Office Assistant displays, before closing the Office Assistant window.

When you start Access, the Access window contains a dialog box that allows you to create a new database or open an existing database. You can choose either the Blank Database option to create a new database on your own, or you can choose the Database Wizard option and let the wizard guide you through the steps for creating a database. In this case, you need to open an existing database.

Opening an Existing Database

To open an existing database, you can select the name of a database in the list of recently opened databases (if the list appears), or you can choose the More Files option to open a database not listed. You need to open an existing database—the Restaurant database on your Student Disk.

To open the Restaurant database:

1. Make sure you have created your copy of the Access Student Disk, and then place your Student Disk in the appropriate disk drive.

   TROUBLE? If you don't have a Student Disk, you need to get one before you can proceed. Your instructor will either give you one or ask you to make your own. (See your instructor for information.) In either case, be sure you have made a copy of your Student Disk before you begin; in this way, the original Student Disk files will be available on the copied disk in case you need to start over because of an error or problem.

2. In the Microsoft Access dialog box, make sure the **Open an Existing Database** option button is selected. Also, if your dialog box contains a list of files, make sure the **More Files** option is selected.

3. Click the **OK** button to display the Open dialog box. See Figure 1-6.

Figure 1-6 ◀
Open dialog
box

Look in list box

list of folders and
database files in
current folder

click to display the list
of available drives
and folders

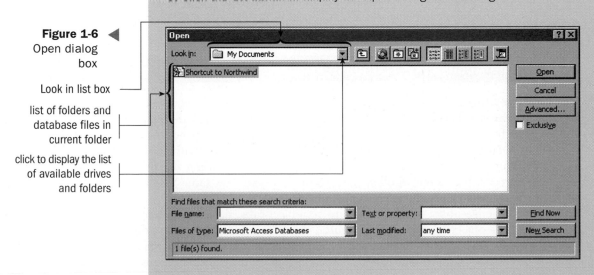

TROUBLE? The list of folders and files on your screen might be different from the list in Figure 1-6.

4. Click the **Look in** list arrow, and then click the drive that contains your Student Disk.

5. Click **Tutorial** in the list box (if necessary), and then click the **Open** button to display a list of the files in the Tutorial folder.

6. Click **Restaurant** in the list box, and then click the **Open** button. The Restaurant database is displayed in the Access window. See Figure 1-7.

Figure 1-7 ◄
Access and
Database
windows

Access window
title bar

Database window
menu bar

Database toolbar

Tables list box

Database window

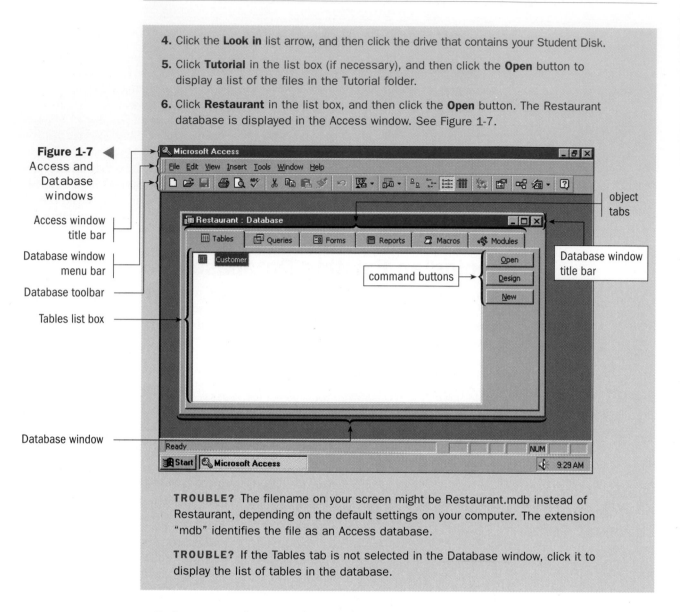

TROUBLE? The filename on your screen might be Restaurant.mdb instead of Restaurant, depending on the default settings on your computer. The extension "mdb" identifies the file as an Access database.

TROUBLE? If the Tables tab is not selected in the Database window, click it to display the list of tables in the database.

Before you can begin working with the database, you need to become familiar with the components of the Access and Database windows.

The Access and Database Windows

The **Access window** is the program window that appears when you start the program. The **Database window** appears when you open a database; this window is the main control center for working with an open Access database. Except for the Access window title bar, all screen components now on your screen are associated with the Database window (see Figure 1-7). Most of these screen components—including the title bars, window sizing buttons, menu bar, toolbar, and status bar—are the same as the components in other Windows 95 programs.

The Database window contains six object tabs. Each **object tab** controls one of the six major object groups, such as tables, in an Access database. (In addition to tables, you'll work with queries, forms, and reports later in this book; macros and modules are used for more complex database design and programming and, therefore, are outside the scope of this text.)

Barbara has already created the Customer table in the Restaurant database. She suggests that you open the Customer table and view its contents.

Opening an Access Table

As noted earlier, tables contain all the data in a database. Tables are the fundamental objects for your work in Access. To view, add, change, or delete data in a table, you first must open the table. You can open any Access object by using the Open button in the Database window.

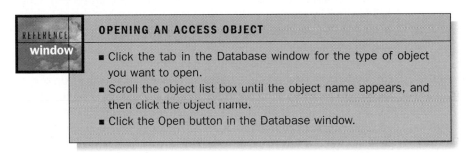

REFERENCE window

OPENING AN ACCESS OBJECT

- Click the tab in the Database window for the type of object you want to open.
- Scroll the object list box until the object name appears, and then click the object name.
- Click the Open button in the Database window.

You need to open the Customer table, which is the only table currently in the Restaurant database.

To open the Customer table:

1. If the Customer table is not highlighted, click **Customer** to select it.

2. Click the **Open** button in the Database window. The Customer table opens in Datasheet view on top of the Database and Access windows. See Figure 1-8.

Figure 1-8
Table displayed in Datasheet view

field selector for CustomerName field

table name

current record symbol

record selector for second record

field name

total number of records in the table

Specific Record box

navigation buttons

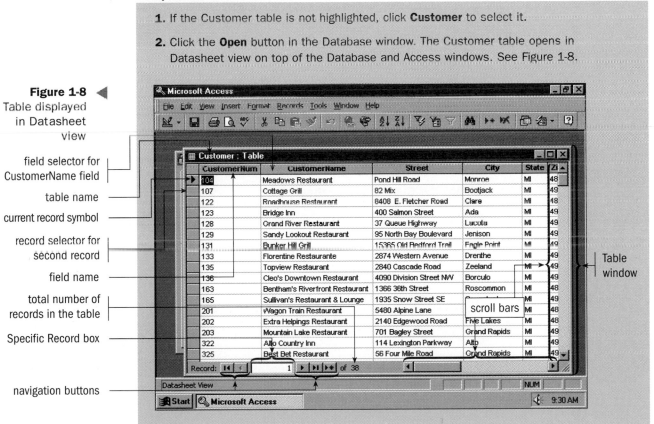

Table window

scroll bars

Datasheet view shows a table's contents as a **datasheet** in rows and columns, similar to a table or spreadsheet. Each row is a separate record in the table, and each column contains the field values for one field in the table. Each column is headed by a field name inside a field selector, and each row has a record selector to its left. Clicking a **field selector** or a **record selector** selects that entire column or row (respectively), which you can then manipulate. A field selector is also called a **column selector**, and a record selector is also called a **row selector**.

Navigating an Access Datasheet

When you first open a datasheet, Access selects the first field value in the first record. Notice that this field value is highlighted and that a darkened triangle symbol, called the current record symbol, appears in the record selector to the left of the first record. The **current record symbol** identifies the currently selected record. Clicking a record selector or field value in another row moves the current record symbol to that row. You can also move the pointer over the data on the screen and click one of the field values to position the insertion point.

The Customer table currently has nine fields and 38 records. To view fields or records not currently visible in the datasheet, you can use the horizontal and vertical scroll bars shown in Figure 1-8 to navigate through the data. The **navigation buttons**, also shown in Figure 1-8, provide another way to move vertically through the records. Figure 1-9 shows which record becomes the current record when you click each navigation button. The **Specific Record box**, which appears between the two sets of navigation buttons, displays the current record number; and the total number of records in the table appears to the right of the navigation buttons.

Figure 1-9 ◀
Navigation
buttons

Navigation Button	Record Selected	Navigation Button	Record Selected
 ⏮	First Record	 ⏭	Last Record
◀	Previous Record	▶✱	New Record
 ▶	Next Record		

Barbara suggests that you use the various navigation techniques to move through the Customer table and become familiar with its contents.

To navigate the Customer datasheet:

1. Click the right arrow button in the horizontal scroll bar a few times to scroll to the right and view the remaining fields in the Customer table.

2. Drag the scroll box in the horizontal scroll bar back to the left to return to the previous display of the datasheet.

3. Click the **Next Record** navigation button ▶. The second record is now the current record, as indicated by the current record symbol in the second record selector. Also, notice that the second record's value for the CustomerNum field is highlighted, and "2" (for record number 2) appears in the Specific Record box.

4. Click the **Last Record** navigation button ⏭. The last record in the table, record 38, is now the current record.

5. Click the **Previous Record** navigation button ◀. Record 37 is now the current record.

6. Click the **First Record** navigation button ⏮. The first record is now the current record.

Next, Barbara asks you to print the Customer table so that you can refer to it as you continue working with the Restaurant database.

Printing a Table

In Access you can print a table using either the Print command on the File menu or the Print button on the toolbar. The Print command displays a dialog box in which you can specify print settings. The Print button prints the table using the current settings. You'll use the Print button to print the Customer table.

To print the Customer table:

1. Click the **Print** button 🖨 on the Table Datasheet toolbar. Because all of the fields can't fit across one page, the table prints on two pages. You'll learn how to specify different print settings in later tutorials.

Now that you've viewed and printed the Customer table, you can exit Access.

Exiting Access

To exit Access, you simply click the Close button on the Access window title bar. When exiting, Access closes any open tables and the open database before closing the program.

To exit Access:

1. Click the **Close** button ☒ on the Access window title bar. The Customer table and the Restaurant database close, Access closes, and you return to the Windows 95 desktop.

Quick Check

1 A(n) _____ is a single characteristic of a person, place, object, event, or idea.

2 You connect the records in two separate tables through a(n) _____ that appears in both tables.

3 The _____, whose values uniquely identify each record in a table, is called a _____ when it is placed in a second table to form a relationship between the two tables.

4 In a table, the rows are called _____ and the columns are called _____.

5 The _____ identifies the selected record in an Access table.

6 Describe the two methods for navigating through a table.

Now that you've become familiar with Access and the Restaurant database, you're ready to work with the data stored in the database.

SESSION

1.2

In this session you will create and print a query; create and print a form; use the Help system; and create, preview, and print a report.

Kim Carpenter, the director of marketing at Valle Coffee, wants a list of all restaurant customers so that her staff can call customers to check on their satisfaction with Valle

Coffee's services and products. She doesn't want the list to include all the fields in the Customer table (such as Street and ZipCode). To produce this list for Kim, you need to create a query using the Customer table.

Creating and Printing a Query

A **query** is a question you ask about the data stored in a database. In response to a query, Access displays the specific records and fields that answer your question. When you create a query, you tell Access which fields you need and what criteria Access should use to select the records. Access then displays only the information you want, so you don't have to scan through the entire database for the information.

You can design your own queries or use an Access **Query Wizard**, which guides you through the steps to create a query. The Simple Query Wizard allows you to select records and fields quickly, and is an appropriate choice for producing the customer list Kim wants.

To start the Simple Query Wizard:

1. Insert your Student Disk in the appropriate disk drive.

2. Start Access, make sure the **Open an Existing Database** option button is selected and the **More Files** option is selected, and then click the **OK** button to display the Open dialog box.

3. Click the **Look in** list arrow, click the drive that contains your Student Disk, click **Tutorial** in the list box, and then click the **Open** button to display the list of files in the Tutorial folder.

4. Click **Restaurant** in the list box, and then click the **Open** button.

5. Click the **Queries** tab in the Database window to display the Queries list. The Queries list box is empty because you haven't defined any queries yet.

6. Click the **New** button to open the New Query dialog box.

7. Click **Simple Query Wizard** and then click the **OK** button. The first Simple Query Wizard dialog box opens. See Figure 1-10.

Figure 1-10 ◀
First Simple
Query Wizard
dialog box

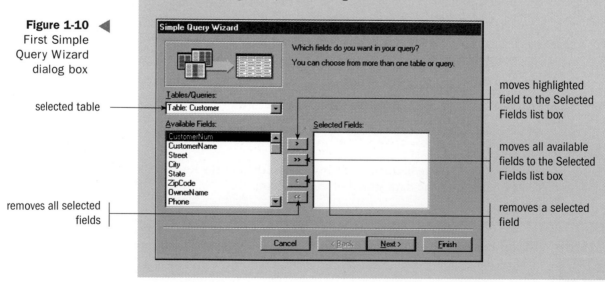

selected table —

removes all selected
fields

moves highlighted
field to the Selected
Fields list box

moves all available
fields to the Selected
Fields list box

removes a selected
field

Because Customer is the only object currently in the Restaurant database, it is listed in the Tables/Queries box. You could click the Tables/Queries list arrow to choose another table or a query on which to base the query you're creating. The Available Fields box lists the fields in the selected table (in this case, Customer). You need to select fields from this list to include them in the query. To select fields one at a time, click a field and then click the [>] button. The selected field moves from the Available Fields list box on the left to the Selected Fields list box on the right. To select all the fields, click the >> button. If you change your mind or make a mistake, you can remove a field by clicking it in the Selected Fields list box and then clicking the < button. To remove all selected fields, click the << button.

Each wizard dialog box contains buttons on the bottom that allow you to move to the previous dialog box (Back button), the next dialog box (Next button), or to cancel the creation process (Cancel button) and return to the Database window. You can also finish creating the object (Finish button) and accept the wizard's defaults for the remaining options.

Kim wants her list to include data from only the following fields: CustomerNum, CustomerName, City, State, OwnerName, and Phone. You need to select these fields to be included in the query.

To create the query using the Simple Query Wizard:

1. Click **CustomerNum** in the Available Fields list box (if necessary), and then click the > button. The CustomerNum field moves to the Selected Fields list box.
2. Repeat Step 1 for the fields **CustomerName**, **City**, **State**, **OwnerName**, and **Phone**, and then click the **Next** button. The second, and final, Simple Query Wizard dialog box opens and asks you to choose a name for your query. This name will appear in the Queries list in the Database window. You'll change the suggested name (Customer Query) to "Customer List."
3. Click at the end of the highlighted name, use the Backspace key to delete the word "Query," and then type **List**. You can now view the query results.
4. Click the **Finish** button to complete the query. Access displays the query results in Datasheet view.
5. Click the **Maximize** button on the Query window to maximize the window. See Figure 1-11.

Figure 1-11
Query results

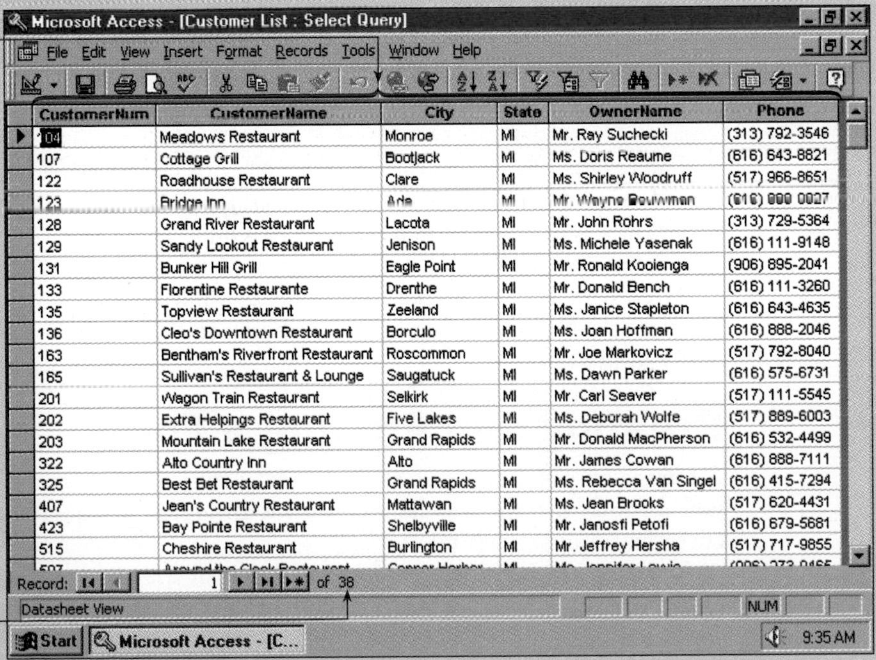

CustomerNum	CustomerName	City	State	OwnerName	Phone
104	Meadows Restaurant	Monroe	MI	Mr. Ray Suchecki	(313) 792-3546
107	Cottage Grill	Bootjack	MI	Ms. Doris Reaume	(616) 643-8821
122	Roadhouse Restaurant	Clare	MI	Ms. Shirley Woodruff	(517) 966-8651
123	Bridge Inn	Ada	MI	Mr. Wayne Bouwman	[illegible]
128	Grand River Restaurant	Lacota	MI	Mr. John Rohrs	(313) 729-5364
129	Sandy Lookout Restaurant	Jenison	MI	Ms. Michele Yasenak	(616) 111-9148
131	Bunker Hill Grill	Eagle Point	MI	Mr. Ronald Kooienga	(906) 895-2041
133	Florentine Restaurante	Drenthe	MI	Mr. Donald Bench	(616) 111-3260
135	Topview Restaurant	Zeeland	MI	Ms. Janice Stapleton	(616) 643-4635
136	Cleo's Downtown Restaurant	Borculo	MI	Ms. Joan Hoffman	(616) 888-2046
163	Bentham's Riverfront Restaurant	Roscommon	MI	Mr. Joe Markovicz	(517) 792-8040
165	Sullivan's Restaurant & Lounge	Saugatuck	MI	Ms. Dawn Parker	(616) 575-6731
201	Wagon Train Restaurant	Selkirk	MI	Mr. Carl Seaver	(517) 111-5545
202	Extra Helpings Restaurant	Five Lakes	MI	Ms. Deborah Wolfe	(517) 889-6003
203	Mountain Lake Restaurant	Grand Rapids	MI	Mr. Donald MacPherson	(616) 532-4499
322	Alto Country Inn	Alto	MI	Mr. James Cowan	(616) 888-7111
325	Best Bet Restaurant	Grand Rapids	MI	Ms. Rebecca Van Singel	(616) 415-7294
407	Jean's Country Restaurant	Mattawan	MI	Ms. Jean Brooks	(517) 620-4431
423	Bay Pointe Restaurant	Shelbyville	MI	Mr. Janosfi Petofi	(616) 679-5681
515	Cheshire Restaurant	Burlington	MI	Mr. Jeffrey Hersha	(517) 717-9855

selected fields displayed

all 38 records are included in the results

The datasheet displays the six selected fields for each record in the Customer table. The fields are shown in the order you selected them, from left to right.

The records are currently listed in order by the primary key field (CustomerNum). Kim prefers the records to be listed in order by state so that her staff members can focus on all the customers in a particular state. To display the records in the order Kim wants, you need to sort the query results by the State field.

To sort the query results:

1. Click to position the insertion point anywhere in the State column. This establishes the State column as the current field.

2. Click the **Sort Ascending** button ⌖ on the Query Datasheet toolbar. The records are now sorted in ascending alphabetical order by the values in the State field. All the records for Indiana are listed first, followed by the records for Michigan and then Ohio.

Kim asks for a printed copy of the query results so that she can bring the customer list to a meeting with her staff members. To print the query results, you can use the Print button on the Query Datasheet toolbar.

To print the query results:

1. Click the **Print** button 🖨 on the Query Datasheet toolbar to print one copy of the query results with the current settings.

2. Click the **Close** button ✕ on the menu bar to close the query.

   A dialog box opens asking if you want to save changes to the design of the query. This box appears because you changed the sort order of the query results.

3. Click the **Yes** button to save the changed query design and return to the Database window. Notice that the Customer List query is now shown in the Queries list box. In addition, because you had maximized the Query window, the Database window is also now maximized. You need to restore the window.

4. Click the **Restore** button ⧉ on the menu bar to restore the Database window.

The results of the query are not stored with the database; however, the query design is stored as part of the database with the name you specify. You can then re-create the query results at any time by running the query again. You'll learn more about creating and running queries in Tutorial 3.

After Kim leaves for her staff meeting, Barbara asks you to create a form for the Customer table so that her staff members can use the form to enter and work with data easily in the table.

Creating and Printing a Form

A **form** is an object you use to maintain, view, and print records in a database. Although you can perform these same functions with tables and queries, forms can present data in customized and useful ways.

In Access, you can design your own forms or use a Form Wizard to create forms for you automatically. A **Form Wizard** is an Access tool that asks you a series of questions, then creates a form based on your answers. The quickest way to create a form is to use an **AutoForm Wizard**, which places all the fields from a selected table (or query) on a form automatically, without asking you any questions, and then displays the form on the screen.

Barbara wants a form for the Customer table that will show all the fields for one record at a time, with fields listed one below another. This type of form will make it easier for her staff to focus on all the data for a particular customer. You'll use the AutoForm: Columnar Wizard to create the form.

To create the form using an AutoForm Wizard:

1. Click the **Forms** tab in the Database window to display the Forms list. The Forms list box is currently empty because you haven't created any forms yet.

2. Click the **New** button to open the New Form dialog box. See Figure 1-12.

Figure 1-12 ◀
New Form
dialog box

click to design your
own form

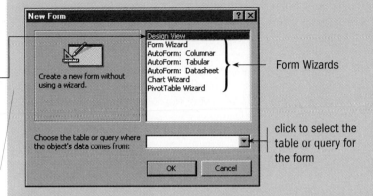

Form Wizards

click to select the
table or query for
the form

The top list box provides options for designing your own form or creating a form using one of the Form Wizards. In the bottom list box, you choose the table or query that will supply the data for the form.

3. Click **AutoForm: Columnar** to select this AutoForm Wizard.

4. Click the list arrow for choosing the table or query on which to base the form, and then click **Customer**.

5. Click the **OK** button. The AutoForm Wizard creates the form and displays it in Form view. See Figure 1-13.

Figure 1-13 ◀
Form created
by the
AutoForm:
Columnar
Wizard

The form displays one record at a time in the Customer table. Access displays the field values for the first record in the table and selects the first field value (CustomerNum). Each field name appears on a separate line and on the same line as its field value, which appears in a box. The widths of the boxes are different to accommodate the different sizes of the displayed field values; for example, compare the small box for the State field's value with the larger box for the CustomerName field's value. The AutoForm: Columnar Wizard automatically placed the field names and values on the form and supplied the background style.

Also, notice that the Form window contains navigation buttons, similar to those available in Datasheet view, which you can use to move to different records in the table.

Barbara asks you to print the data for the Embers Restaurant, which is the last record in the table. After printing this record in the form, you'll save the form with the name "Customer Data" in the Restaurant database. The form will then be available for later use. You'll learn more about creating and customizing forms in Tutorial 4.

To print the form with data for the last record, and then save and close the form:

1. Click the **Last Record** navigation button. The last record in the table, record 38 for Embers Restaurant, is now the current record.

2. Click **File** on the menu bar, and then click **Print**. The Print dialog box opens.

3. Click the **Selected Record(s)** option button, and then click the **OK** button to print only the current record in the form.

4. Click the **Save** button on the Form View toolbar. The Save As dialog box opens.

5. In the Form Name text box, click at the end of the highlighted word "Customer," press the **spacebar**, type **Data**, and then press the **Enter** key. Access saves the form as Customer Data in your Restaurant database and closes the dialog box.

6. Click the **Close** button on the Form window title bar to close the form and return to the Database window. Note that the Customer Data form is now listed in the Forms list box.

Kim returns from her staff meeting with another request. She wants the same customer list you produced earlier when you created the Customer List query, but she'd like the information presented in a more readable format. She suggests you use the Access Help system to learn about formatting data in reports.

Getting Help

The Access Help system provides the same options as the Help system in other Windows programs—the Help Contents, the Help Index, and the Find Feature, which are available on the Help menu. The Access Help system also provides additional ways to get help as you work—the Office Assistant and the What's This? command. You'll learn how to use the Office Assistant next in this section. The What's This? command provides context-sensitive Help information. When you choose this command from the Help menu, the pointer changes to the Help pointer, which you can then use to click any object or option on the screen to see a description of the object.

Finding Information with the Office Assistant

The Office Assistant is an interactive guide to finding information in the Help system. You can ask the Office Assistant a question, and it will look through the Help system to find an answer.

REFERENCE window

USING THE OFFICE ASSISTANT

- Click the Office Assistant button on any toolbar (or choose Microsoft Access Help from the Help menu).
- Click in the text box, type your question, and then click the Search button.
- Choose a topic from the list of topics displayed by the Office Assistant. Click additional topics, as necessary.
- When finished, close the Help window and the Office Assistant.

You'll use the Office Assistant to get Help about creating reports in Access.

To get Help about reports:

1. Click the **Office Assistant** button on the Database toolbar. The Office Assistant appears and displays a dialog box with several options. See Figure 1-14.

Figure 1-14 ◀
Office
Assistant

list of topics

type your question
in this text box

click to have Office
Assistant search
for an answer

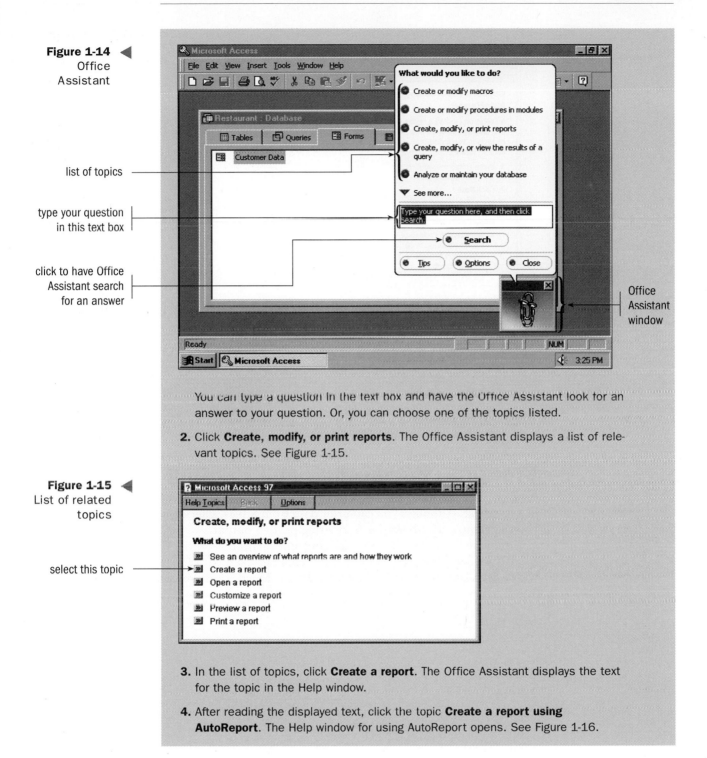

Office
Assistant
window

You can type a question in the text box and have the Office Assistant look for an answer to your question. Or, you can choose one of the topics listed.

2. Click **Create, modify, or print reports**. The Office Assistant displays a list of relevant topics. See Figure 1-15.

Figure 1-15 ◀
List of related
topics

select this topic

3. In the list of topics, click **Create a report**. The Office Assistant displays the text for the topic in the Help window.

4. After reading the displayed text, click the topic **Create a report using AutoReport**. The Help window for using AutoReport opens. See Figure 1-16.

Figure 1-16 ◀
Help
information on
AutoReport

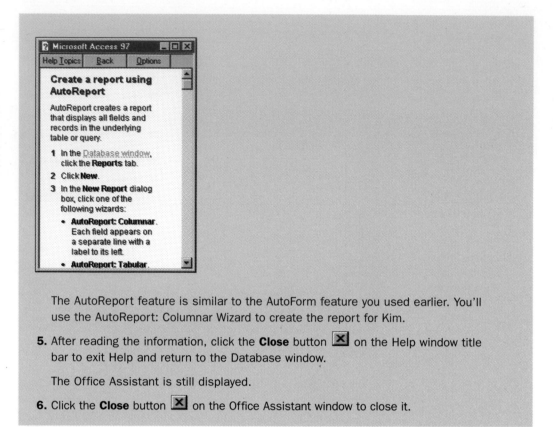

The AutoReport feature is similar to the AutoForm feature you used earlier. You'll use the AutoReport: Columnar Wizard to create the report for Kim.

5. After reading the information, click the **Close** button ⊠ on the Help window title bar to exit Help and return to the Database window.

The Office Assistant is still displayed.

6. Click the **Close** button ⊠ on the Office Assistant window to close it.

Creating, Previewing, and Printing a Report

A **report** is a formatted printout (or screen display) of the contents of one or more tables in a database. Although you can print data from tables, queries, and forms, reports allow you the greatest flexibility for formatting printed output.

Kim wants a report showing the same information as in the Customer List query you created earlier. However, she'd like the data for each customer to be grouped together, with one customer record below another, as shown in the report sketch in Figure 1-17. You'll use the AutoReport: Columnar Wizard to produce the report for Kim.

Figure 1-17 ◀
Sketch of
Kim's report

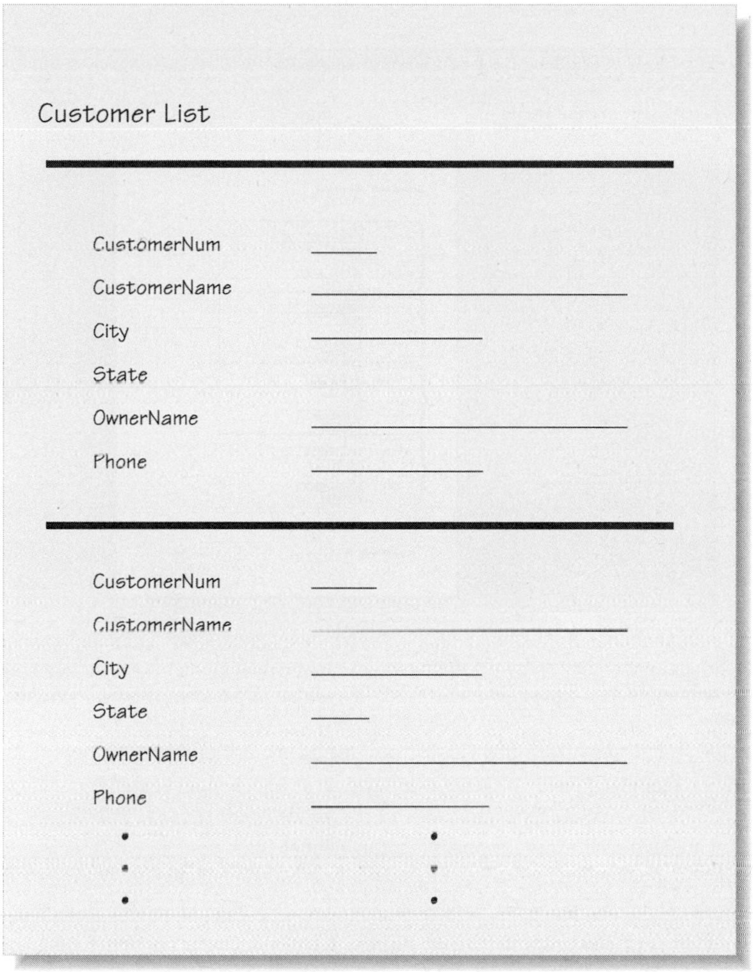

Customer List

━━━━━━━━━━━━━━━━━━━━━━━━

    CustomerNum   _____

    CustomerName   _____

    City   _____

    State

    OwnerName   _____

    Phone   _____

━━━━━━━━━━━━━━━━━━━━━━━━

    CustomerNum   _____

    CustomerName   _____

    City   _____

    State   _____

    OwnerName   _____

    Phone   _____

       •   •

       •   •

       •   •

To create the report using the AutoReport: Columnar Wizard:

1. Click the **Reports** tab in the Database window, and then click the **New** button to open the New Report dialog box. This dialog box is similar to the New Form dialog box you saw earlier.

2. Click **AutoReport: Columnar** to select this wizard for creating the report.

   Because Kim wants the same data as in the Customer List query, you need to choose that query as the basis for the report.

3. Click the list arrow for choosing the table or query on which to base the report, and then click **Customer List**.

4. Click the **OK** button. The AutoReport Wizard creates the report and displays it in Print Preview, which shows exactly how the report will look when printed.

   To better view the report, you'll maximize the window and change the Zoom setting so that you can see the entire page.

5. Click the **Maximize** button 🔲 on the Report window, click the **Zoom** list arrow (next to the value 100%) on the Print Preview toolbar, and then click **Fit**. The entire first page of the report is displayed in the window. See Figure 1-18.

Access

Figure 1-18 ◀
First page of
the report in
Print Preview

report title taken from
query name

fields grouped for
each record

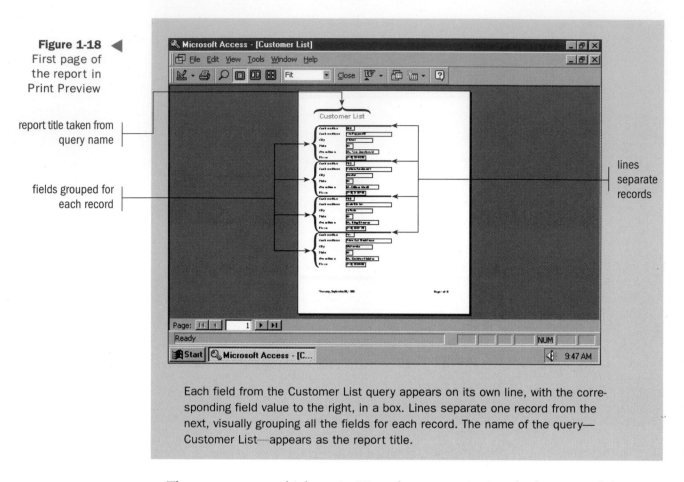

lines
separate
records

Each field from the Customer List query appears on its own line, with the corresponding field value to the right, in a box. Lines separate one record from the next, visually grouping all the fields for each record. The name of the query—Customer List—appears as the report title.

The report spans multiple pages. Kim asks you to print just the first page of the report so that she can review its format. After printing the report page, you'll close the report without saving it, because you can easily re-create it at any time. In general, it's best to save an object—report, form, or query—only if you anticipate using the object frequently or if it is time-consuming to create, because these objects can take up considerable storage space on your disk. You'll learn more about creating and customizing reports in Tutorial 4.

To print the first report page, and then close the report and exit Access:

1. Click **File** on the menu bar, and then click **Print**. The Print dialog box opens. You need to change the print settings so that only the first page of the report is printed.

2. In the Print Range section, click the **Pages** option button, type **1** in the From text box, press the **Tab** key, and then type **1** in the To text box.

3. Click the **OK** button to print the first page of the report. Now you can close the report.

4. Click the **Close** button ⊠ on the menu bar. *Do not* click the Close button on the Print Preview toolbar.

   TROUBLE? If you clicked the Close button on the Print Preview toolbar, you switched to Design view. Simply click the Close button ⊠ on the menu bar, and then continue with the tutorial.

   A dialog box opens asking if you want to save the changes to the report design.

5. Click the **No** button to close the report without saving it. Now you can exit Access.

6. Click the **Close** button ⊠ on the Access window title bar to exit Access.

Quick Check

1 A(n) _____ is a question you ask about the data stored in a database.

2 Unless you specify otherwise, the records resulting from a query are listed in order by the _____.

3 The quickest way to create a form is to use a(n) _____.

4 Describe the form created by the AutoForm: Columnar Wizard.

5 Describe how you use the Office Assistant to get Help.

6 After creating a report, the AutoReport Wizard displays the report in _____.

With the Customer table in place, Barbara can continue to build the Restaurant database and use it to store, manipulate, and retrieve important data for Valle Coffee. In the following tutorials, you'll help Barbara complete and maintain the database, and you'll use it to meet the specific information needs of other Valle Coffee employees.

Tutorial Assignments

In the Tutorial Assignments, you'll work with the Customer database, which is similar to the database you worked with in the tutorial. Complete the following:

1. Make sure your Student Disk is in the disk drive.

2. Start Access and open the Customer database, which is located in the TAssign folder on your Student Disk.

3. Choose the Contents and Index command from the Help menu, and then select the Contents tab. Open the topic "Introduction to Microsoft Access 97" and then open the topic "Databases: What they are and how they work." Read the displayed information, and then click the >> button at the top of the window to move through the remaining screens for the topic. When finished, click the Help Topics button at the top of the window to return to the Contents tab. Repeat this procedure for the similarly worded topics for tables, queries, forms, and reports. On any screen that contains boxed items, click each item and read the information displayed in the pop-up window. When finished reading all the topics, close the Help window.

4. Use the Office Assistant to ask the following question: "How do I rename a table?" Choose the topic "Rename a table, query, form, report, macro, or module" and read the displayed information. Close the Help window and the Office Assistant. Then, in the Customer database, rename the Table1 table as Customers.

5. Open the Customers table.

6. Choose the Contents and Index command from the Help menu, and then select the Index tab. Look up the word "landscape," and then choose the topic "landscape page orientation." Choose the subtopic "Set margins, page orientation, and other page setup options." Read the displayed information, and then close the Help window. Print the Customers table datasheet in landscape orientation. Close the Customers table.

7. Use the Simple Query Wizard to create a query that includes the CustomerName, OwnerName, and Phone fields from the Customers table. Name the query Customer Phone List. Sort the query results in ascending order by CustomerName. Print the query results, and then close and save the query.

8. Use the AutoForm: Columnar Wizard to create a form for the Customers table.

9. Use context-sensitive Help to find out how to move to a particular record and display it in the form. Choose the What's This? command from the Help menu, and then use the Help pointer to click the number 1 in the Specific Record box at the bottom of the form. Read the displayed information. Click to close the Help box, and then use the Specific Record box to move to record 20 (for Cheshire Restaurant) in the Customers table.

10. Print the form for the current record (20), save the form as Customer Info, and then close the form.

11. Use the AutoReport: Tabular Wizard to create a report based on the Customers table. Print the first page of the report, and then close the report without saving it.

12. Exit Access.

Case Problems

1. Ashbrook Mall Information Desk Ashbrook Mall is a large, modern mall located in Phoenix, Arizona. The Mall Operations Office is responsible for everything that happens within the mall and anything that affects the mall's operation. Among the independent operations that report to the Mall Operations Office are the Maintenance Group, the Mall Security Office, and the Information Desk. You will be helping the personnel at the Information Desk.

One important service provided by the Information Desk is to maintain a catalog of current job openings at stores within the mall. Sam Bullard, the director of the Mall Operations Office, recently created an Access database named MallJobs to store this information. You'll help Sam complete and maintain this database. Complete the following:

1. Make sure your Student Disk is in the disk drive.

2. Start Access and open the MallJobs database, which is located in the Cases folder on your Student Disk.

3. Open the Store table, print the table datasheet, and then close the table.

4. Use the Simple Query Wizard to create a query that includes the StoreName, Contact, and Extension fields from the Store table. Name the query Contact Phone List. Print the query results, and then close the query.

5. Use the AutoForm: Tabular Wizard to create a form for the Store table. Print the form, and then close it without saving it.

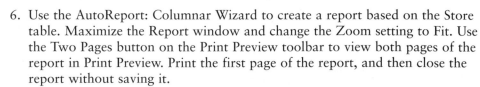

6. Use the AutoReport: Columnar Wizard to create a report based on the Store table. Maximize the Report window and change the Zoom setting to Fit. Use the Two Pages button on the Print Preview toolbar to view both pages of the report in Print Preview. Print the first page of the report, and then close the report without saving it.

7. Exit Access.

2. Professional Litigation User Services Professional Litigation User Services (PLUS) is a company that creates all types of visual aids for judicial proceedings. Clients are usually private law firms, although the District Attorney's office has occasionally contracted for their services. PLUS creates graphs, maps, timetables, and charts, both for computerized presentations and in large-size form for presentation to juries. PLUS also creates videos, animations, presentation packages, slide shows—in short, anything of a visual nature that can be used in a judicial proceeding to make, clarify, or support a point.

Raj Jawahir, a new employee at PLUS, is responsible for tracking the daily payments received from the firm's clients. He created an Access database named Payments, and needs your help in working with this database. Complete the following:

1. Make sure your Student Disk is in the disk drive.

2. Start Access and open the Payments database, which is located in the Cases folder on your Student Disk.

3. Open the Firm table, print the table datasheet, and then close the table.

4. Use the Simple Query Wizard to create a query that includes the FirmName, PLUSAcctRep, and Extension fields from the Firm table. Name the query Rep List. Sort the results in ascending order by the PLUSAcctRep field.

5. Use the Office Assistant to ask the following question: "How do I select multiple records?" Choose the topic "Selecting fields and records in Datasheet view," read the displayed information, and then close the Help window and the Office Assistant. Then select the first 11 records in the datasheet (all the records with the value "Abelson, David" in the PLUSAcctRep field), and then print just the selected records. Close the query, saving the changes to the design.

6. Use the AutoForm: Columnar Wizard to create a form for the Firm table. Move to record 31, and then print the form for the current record only. Close the form without saving it.

7. Use the AutoReport. Columnar Wizard to create a report based on the Firm table. Maximize the Report window and change the Zoom setting to Fit.

8. Use the View menu to view all eight pages of the report at the same time in Print Preview.

9. Print just the first page of the report, and then close the report without saving it.

10. Exit Access.

3. Best Friends Best Friends is a not-for-profit organization that trains hearing and service dogs for people with disabilities. Established in 1989 in Boise, Idaho, by Noah and Sheila Warnick, Best Friends is modeled after Paws With A Cause®, the original and largest provider of hearing and service dogs in the United States. Like Paws With A Cause® and other such organizations, Best Friends strives to provide "Dignity Through Independence."

To raise funds for Best Friends, Noah and Sheila periodically conduct Walk-A-Thons. The events have become so popular, Noah and Sheila created an Access database named Walks to track walker and pledge data. You'll help them complete and maintain the Walks database. Complete the following:

1. Make sure your Student Disk is in the disk drive.

2. Start Access and open the Walks database, which is located in the Cases folder on your Student Disk.

3. Open the Walker table, print the table datasheet, and then close the table.

4. Use the Simple Query Wizard to create a query that includes all the fields in the Walker table *except* the Phone field. (*Hint:* Use the >> and < buttons to select the necessary fields.) In the second Simple Query Wizard dialog box, make sure the Detail option button is selected. (This second dialog box appears because the table contains numeric values.) Name the query "Walker Distance." Sort the results in ascending order by the LastName field. Print the query results, and then close and save the query.

5. Use the AutoForm: Columnar Wizard to create a form for the Walker table. Move to record 25, and then print the form for the current record only. Close the form without saving it.

6. Use the AutoReport: Columnar Wizard to create a report based on the Walker table. Maximize the Report window and change the Zoom setting to Fit.

7. Use the View menu to view all six pages of the report at the same time in Print Preview.

8. Print just the first page of the report, and then close the report without saving it.

9. Exit Access.

4. Lopez Lexus Dealerships Maria and Hector Lopez own a chain of Lexus dealerships throughout Texas. They have used a computer in their business for several years to handle payroll and typical accounting functions. Because of their phenomenal expansion, both in the number of car locations and the number of cars handled, they created an Access database named Lexus to track their car inventory. You'll help them work with and maintain this database. Complete the following:

1. Make sure your Student Disk is in the disk drive.

2. Start Access and open the Lexus database, which is located in the Cases folder on your Student Disk.

3. Open the Cars table.

4. Print the Cars table datasheet in landscape orientation, and then close the table.

5. Use the Simple Query Wizard to create a query that includes the Model, Year, LocationCode, Cost, and SellingPrice fields from the Cars table. In the second Simple Query Wizard dialog box, make sure the Detail option button is selected. (This second dialog box appears because the table contains numeric values.) Name the query "Cost vs Selling."

6. Sort the query results in descending order by SellingPrice. (*Hint:* Use a toolbar button.)

7. Print the query results, and then close and save the query.

8. Use the AutoForm: Columnar Wizard to create a form for the Cars table. Move to record 11, and then print the form for the current record only. Close the form without saving it.

9. Use the AutoReport: Tabular Wizard to create a report based on the Cars table. Maximize the Report window and change the Zoom setting to Fit. Use the Two Pages button on the Print Preview toolbar to view both pages of the report in Print Preview. Print the first page of the report, and then close the report without saving it.

10. Exit Access.

Lab Assignments

These Lab Assignments are designed to accompany the interactive Course Lab called Databases. To start the Databases Lab, click the Start button on the Windows 95 taskbar, point to Programs, point to Course Labs, point to New Perspectives Applications, and click Databases. If you do not see Course Labs on your Programs menu, see your instructor or technical support person.

Databases

Databases This Databases Lab demonstrates the essential concepts of file and database management systems. You will use the Lab to search, sort, and report the data contained in a file of classic books.

1. Click the Steps button to review basic database terminology and to learn how to manipulate the classic books database. As you proceed through the Steps, answer all of the Quick Check questions that appear. After you complete the Steps, you will see a Quick Check summary report. Follow the instructions on the screen to print this report.

2. Click the Explore button. Make sure you can apply basic database terminology to describe the classic books database by answering the following questions:
   a. How many records does the file contain?
   b. How many fields does each record contain?
   c. What are the contents of the Catalog # field for the book written by Margaret Mitchell?
   d. What are the contents of the Title field for the record with Thoreau in the Author field?
   e. Which field has been used to sort the records?

3. In Explore, manipulate the database as necessary to answer the following questions:
   a. When the books are sorted by title, what is the first record in the file?
   b. Use the Search button to search for all the books in the West location. How many do you find?
   c. Use the Search button to search for all the books in the Main location that are checked in. What do you find?

4. Use the Report button to print out a report that groups the books by Status and sorts them by Title. On your report, circle the four field names. Draw a box around the summary statistics showing which books are currently checked in and which books are currently checked out.

Maintaining a Database

Creating, Modifying, and Updating an Order Table

OBJECTIVES

In this tutorial you will:

- Learn the guidelines for designing databases and Access tables

- Create and save a table

- Define fields and specify the primary key

- Add records to a table

- Modify the structure of a table

- Delete, move, and add fields

- Change field properties

- Copy records from another Access database

- Delete and change records

Valle Coffee

CASE

The Restaurant database currently contains only one table—the Customer table—which stores data about Valle Coffee's restaurant customers. Barbara also wants to track information about each order placed by each restaurant customer. This information includes the order's billing date and invoice amount. Barbara asks you to create a second table in the Restaurant database, named Order, in which to store the order data.

Some of the order data Barbara needs is already stored in another Valle Coffee database. After creating the Order table and adding some records to it, you'll copy the records from the other database into the Order table. Then you'll maintain the Order table by modifying it and updating it to meet Barbara's specific data requirements.

In this session you will learn the guidelines for designing databases and Access tables. You'll also learn how to create a table, define the fields for a table, select the primary key for a table, save the table structure, and add records to a table datasheet.

Guidelines for Designing Databases

A database management system can be a useful tool, but only if you first carefully design the database so that it meets the needs of those who will use it. In database design, you determine the fields, tables, and relationships needed to satisfy the data and processing requirements. When you design a database, you should follow these guidelines:

■ **Identify all the fields needed to produce the required information.** For example, Barbara needs information about customers and orders. Figure 2-1 shows the fields that satisfy those information requirements.

Figure 2-1 ◀
Barbara's data
requirements

CustomerName	BillingDate
OrderNum	OwnerName
Street	InvoiceAmt
City	PlacedBy
State	Phone
ZipCode	FirstContact
CustomerNum	

■ **Group related fields into tables.** For example, Barbara grouped the fields relating to customers into the Customer table. The other fields are grouped logically into the Order table, which you will create, as shown in Figure 2-2.

Figure 2-2 ◀
Barbara's fields
grouped into
Customer and
Order tables

Customer table	Order table
CustomerNum	OrderNum
CustomerName	BillingDate
Street	PlacedBy
City	InvoiceAmt
State	
ZipCode	
OwnerName	
Phone	
FirstContact	

■ **Determine each table's primary key.** Recall that a primary key uniquely identifies each record in a table. Although a primary key is not mandatory in Access, it's usually a good idea to include one in each table. Without a primary key, selecting the exact record you want can be a problem. For some tables, one of the fields, such as a Social Security number or credit card number, naturally serves the function of a primary key. For other tables, two or more fields might be needed to function as the primary key. In these cases, the primary key is referred to as a **composite key**. For example, a school grade table would use a combination of student number and course code to serve as the primary key. For a third category of tables, no single field or combination of fields can uniquely identify a record in a table. In these cases, you need to add a field whose sole purpose is to serve as the primary key.

For Barbara's tables, CustomerNum is the primary key for the Customer table, and OrderNum will be the primary key for the Order table.

- **Include a common field in related tables.** You use the common field to connect one table logically with another table. For example, Barbara's Customer and Order tables will include the CustomerNum field as a common field. Recall that when you include the primary key from one table as a field in a second table to form a relationship, the field is called a foreign key in the second table; therefore, the CustomerNum field will be a foreign key in the Order table. With this common field, Barbara can find all orders placed by a customer; she can use the CustomerNum value for a customer and search the Order table for all orders with that CustomerNum value. Likewise, she can determine which customer placed a particular order by searching the Customer table to find the one record with the same CustomerNum value as the corresponding value in the Order table.

- **Avoid data redundancy.** Data redundancy occurs when you store the same data in more than one place. With the exception of common fields to connect tables, you should avoid redundancy because it wastes storage space and can cause inconsistencies, if, for instance, you type a field value one way in one table and a different way in the same table or in a second table. Figure 2-3 shows an example of incorrect database design that illustrates data redundancy in the Order table; the Customer Name field is redundant and one value was entered incorrectly, in three different ways.

Figure 2-3 ◀
Incorrect
database
design with
data
redundancy

inconsistent data —

Customer table

Customer Number	Customer Name	Customer Address	Phone Number
104	Meadows Restaurant	Pond Hill Road, Monroe MI 48161	(313) 792-3546
128	Grand River Restaurant	37 Queue Highway, Lacota MI 49063	(313) 729-5364
163	Bentham's Riverfront Restaurant	1366 36th Street, Roscommon MI 48653	(517) 792-8040
635	Oaks Restaurant	3300 West Russell Street, Maumee OH 43537	(419) 336-9000
741	Prime Cut Steakhouse	2819 East 10 Street, Mishawaka IN 46544	(219) 336-0900
779	Gateway Lounge	3408 Gateway Boulevard, Sylvania OH 43560	(419) 361-1137

data redundancy

Order table

Order Number	Customer Number	Customer Name	Billing Date	Invoice Amount
202	104	Meadows Restaurant	1/15/00	1,280.50
226	635	Oakes Restaurant	1/15/99	1,939.00
231	779	Gateway Lounge	1/15/99	1,392.50
309	741	Prime Cut Steakhouse	2/15/99	1,928.00
313	635	Stokes Inn	2/15/99	1,545.00
377	128	Grand River Restaurant	3/15/99	562.00
359	635	Raks Restaurant	3/15/99	1,939.00
373	779	Gateway Lounge	3/15/99	1,178.00
395	163	Bentham's Riverfront Restaurant	3/15/99	1,348.00

- **Determine the properties of each field.** You need to identify the **properties**, or characteristics, of each field so that the DBMS knows how to store, display, and process the field. These properties include the field name, the field's maximum number of characters or digits, the field's description, the field's valid values, and other field characteristics. You will learn more about field properties later in this tutorial.

The Order table you need to create will contain the fields shown in Figure 2-2. Before you create the table, you first need to learn some guidelines for designing Access tables.

Guidelines for Designing Access Tables

As just noted, the last step of database design is to determine the properties, such as the name and data type, of each field. Access has rules for naming fields, choosing data types, and defining other properties for fields.

Naming Fields and Objects

You must name each field, table, and other object in an Access database. Access then stores these items in the database using the names you supply. It's best to choose a field or object name that describes the purpose or contents of the field or object, so that later you can easily remember what the name represents. For example, the two tables in the Restaurant database will be named Customer and Order, because these names suggest their contents.

The following rules apply to naming fields and objects:

- A name can be up to 64 characters long.

- A name can contain letters, numbers, spaces, and special characters except a period (.), exclamation mark (!), accent grave (`), and square brackets ([ ]).

- A name cannot start with a space.

- A table or query name must be unique within a database. A field name must be unique within a table, but it can be used again in another table.

In addition, experienced users of databases have the following tips for naming fields and objects:

- Capitalize the first letter of each word in the name.

- Avoid extremely long names because they are difficult to remember and refer to.

- Use standard abbreviations such as Num for Number, Amt for Amount, and Qty for Quantity.

- Do not use spaces in field names because these names will appear in column headings on datasheets and labels on forms and reports. By not using spaces you'll be able to show more fields on these objects at one time.

Assigning Field Data Types

You must assign a data type for each field. The **data type** determines what field values you can enter for the field and what other properties the field will have. For example, the Order table will include a BillingDate field, so you will assign the date/time data type to this field because it will store date values. Access will allow you to enter only dates or times as values for the field and will allow you to manipulate a value only as a date or time.

Figure 2-4 lists the ten data types available in Access, describes the field values allowed with each data type, explains when each data type should be used, and indicates the field size of each data type.

Access

Figure 2-4 ◀
Data types
for fields

Data Type	Description	Field Size
Text	Allows field values containing letters, digits, spaces, and special characters. Use for names, addresses, descriptions, and fields containing digits that are not used in calculations.	1 to 255 characters; 50 characters default
Memo	Allows field values containing letters, digits, spaces, and special characters. Use for long comments and explanations.	1 to 64,000 characters; exact size is determined by entry
Number	Allows positive and negative numbers as field values. Numbers can contain digits, a decimal point, commas, a plus sign, and a minus sign. Use for fields that you will use in calculations, except calculations involving money.	1 to 15 digits
Date/Time	Allows field values containing valid dates and times from January 1, 100 to December 31, 9999. Dates can be entered in mm/dd/yy (month, day, year) format, several other date formats, or a variety of time formats such as 10:35 PM. You can perform calculations on dates and times and you can sort them. For example, you can determine the number of days between two dates.	8 digits
Currency	Allows field values similar to those for the number data type. Unlike calculations with number data type decimal values, calculations performed using the currency data type are not subject to round-off error.	15 digits
AutoNumber	Consists of integers with values controlled by Access. Access automatically inserts a value in the field as each new record is created. You can specify sequential numbering or random numbering. This guarantees a unique field value, so that such a field can serve as a table's primary key.	9 digits
Yes/No	Limits field values to yes and no, or true and false. Use for fields that indicate the presence or absence of a condition, such as whether an order has been filled, or if an employee is eligible for the company dental plan.	1 character
OLE Object	Allows field values that are created in other programs as objects, such as photographs, video images, graphics, drawings, sound recordings, voice-mail messages, spreadsheets, and word-processing documents. These objects can be linked or embedded.	1 gigabyte maximum; exact size depends on object size
Hyperlink	Consists of text or combinations of text and numbers stored as text and used as a hyperlink address. A hyperlink address can have up to three parts: the text that appears in a field or control; the path to a file or page; and a location within the file or page. Hyperlinks help you to connect your application easily to the Internet or an intranet.	Up to 2048 characters for each of the three parts of a hyperlink data type
Lookup Wizard	Creates a field that lets you look up a value in another table or in a predefined list of values.	Same size as the primary key field used to perform the lookup

Assigning Field Sizes

The **field size** property defines a field value's maximum storage size for text and number fields only. The other data types have no field size property, because their storage size is either a fixed, predetermined amount or is determined automatically by the field value itself, as shown in Figure 2-4. A text field has a default field size of 50 characters. You set its field size by entering a number in the range 1 to 255. For example, the OrderNum and CustomerNum fields in the Order table will be text fields with sizes of 3 each.

Barbara documented the design for the Order table by listing each field's name, data type, size (if applicable), and description, as shown in Figure 2-5. OrderNum, the table's primary key, CustomerNum, a foreign key to the Customer table, and PlacedBy will each be assigned the text data type. BillingDate will have the date/time data type, and InvoiceAmt will have the currency data type.

Figure 2-5 ◄
Design for the
Order table

Field Name	Data Type	Field Size	Description
OrderNum	Text	3	primary key
CustomerNum	Text	3	foreign key
BillingDate	Date/Time		
PlacedBy	Text	25	person who placed order
InvoiceAmt	Currency		

With Barbara's design, you are ready to create the Order table.

Creating a Table

Creating a table consists of naming the fields and defining the properties for the fields, specifying a primary key (and a foreign key, if applicable) for the table, and then saving the table structure. You will use Barbara's design (Figure 2-5) as a guide to creating the Order table. First, you need to open the Restaurant database.

To open the Restaurant database:

1. Place your Student Disk in the appropriate disk drive.

2. Start Access. The Access window opens with the initial dialog box.

3. Make sure the **Open an Existing Database** option button and the **More Files** option are selected, and then click the **OK** button to display the Open dialog box.

4. Click the **Look in** list arrow, and then click the drive that contains your Student Disk.

5. Click **Tutorial** in the list box, and then click the **Open** button to display a list of the files in the Tutorial folder.

6. Click **Restaurant** in the list box, and then click the **Open** button. The Restaurant database is displayed in the Access window.

7. Make sure the Tables tab is selected in the Database window.

The Customer table is listed in the Tables list box. Now you'll create the Order table in the Restaurant database.

To begin creating the Order table:

1. Click the **New** button in the Database window. The New Table dialog box opens. See Figure 2-6.

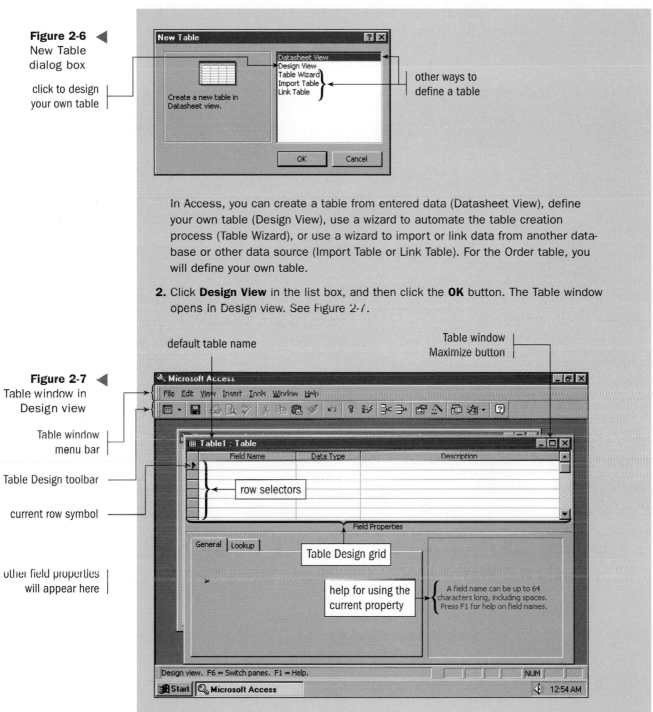

Figure 2-6
New Table
dialog box

click to design
your own table

other ways to
define a table

In Access, you can create a table from entered data (Datasheet View), define your own table (Design View), use a wizard to automate the table creation process (Table Wizard), or use a wizard to import or link data from another database or other data source (Import Table or Link Table). For the Order table, you will define your own table.

2. Click **Design View** in the list box, and then click the **OK** button. The Table window opens in Design view. See Figure 2-7.

default table name

Table window
Maximize button

Figure 2-7
Table window in
Design view

Table window
menu bar

Table Design toolbar

current row symbol

row selectors

other field properties
will appear here

Field Properties

General | Lookup

Table Design grid

help for using the
current property

A field name can be up to 64
characters long, including spaces.
Press F1 for help on field names.

You use Design view to define or modify a table structure or the properties of the fields in a table. If you create a table without using a wizard, you enter the fields and their properties for your table directly in this window.

Defining Fields

Initially, the default table name, Table1, appears in the Table window title bar, the current row symbol is positioned in the first row selector of the Table Design grid, and the insertion point is located in the first row's Field Name box. The purpose or characteristics of the current property (Field Name, in this case) appear in the lower-right of the Table window. You can display more complete information about the current property by pressing the F1 key.

You enter values for the Field Name, Data Type, and Description field properties in the upper-half of the Table window. You select values for all other field properties, most of which are optional, in the lower-half of the window. These other properties will appear when you move to the first row's Data Type text box.

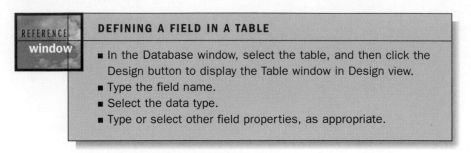

REFERENCE window

DEFINING A FIELD IN A TABLE

- In the Database window, select the table, and then click the Design button to display the Table window in Design view.
- Type the field name.
- Select the data type.
- Type or select other field properties, as appropriate.

The first field you need to define is OrderNum.

To define the OrderNum field:

1. Type **OrderNum** in the first row's Field Name text box, and then press the **Tab** key (or press the **Enter** key) to advance to the Data Type text box. The default data type, Text, appears highlighted in the Data Type text box, which now also contains a list arrow, and field properties for a text field appear in the lower-half of the window. See Figure 2-8.

Figure 2-8 ◀
Table window
after entering
the first
field name

field name

default data type

properties for
a text field

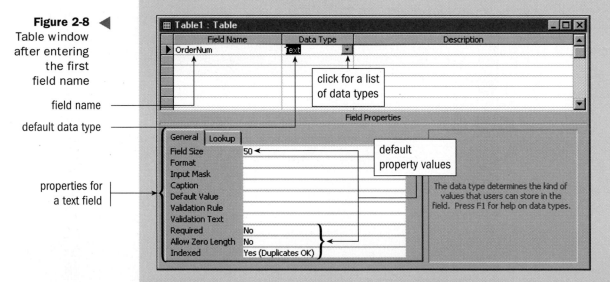

Notice that the lower-right of the window now provides an explanation for the current property, Data Type.

TROUBLE? If you make a typing error, you can correct it by clicking the mouse to position the insertion point, and then using either the Backspace key to delete characters to the left of the insertion point or the Delete key to delete characters to the right of the insertion point. Then type the correct text.

Because order numbers will not be used for calculations, you will assign the text data type to it instead of the number data type, and then enter the Description property value as "primary key." You can use the Description property to enter an optional description for a field to explain its purpose or usage. A field's Description property can be up to 255 characters long, and its value appears in the status bar when you view the table datasheet.

2. Press the **Tab** key to accept Text as the field's data type and move to the Description text box, and then type **primary key** in the Description text box.

The Field Size property has a default value of 50, which you will change to a value of 3, because order numbers at Valle Coffee contain 3 digits. The Required property has a default value of No, which means that a value does not need to be entered for the field. Because Barbara doesn't want an order entered without an order number, you will change the Required property to Yes. The Allow Zero Length property has a value of No, meaning that a value *must* be entered for the field, as is appropriate for the OrderNum field. Finally, the Indexed property has a value of "Yes (Duplicates OK)," which means that a list of index entries will be created to speed up operations using the OrderNum field.

3. Select **50** in the Field Size text box either by dragging the pointer or double-clicking the mouse, and then type **3**.

4. Click the **Required** text box to position the insertion point there. A list arrow appears on the right side of the Required text box.

5. Click the **Required** list arrow. Access displays the Required list box. See Figure 2-9.

Figure 2-9 ◄
Defining the
OrderNum field

changed from
default value of 50

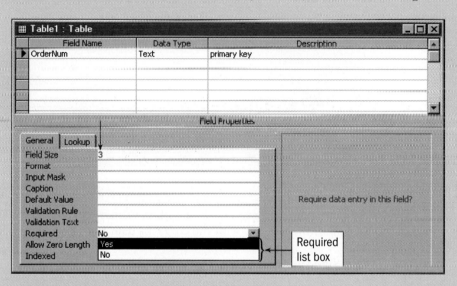

When you position the insertion point or select text in many Access text boxes, Access displays a list arrow, which you can click to display a list box with options. You can display the list arrow *and* the list box simultaneously if you click the text box near its right side.

6. Click **Yes** in the list box. The list box closes, and Yes is now the value for the Required property. The definition of the first field is complete.

Barbara's Order table design shows CustomerNum as the second field. You will define CustomerNum as a text field with a Description of "foreign key" and a Field Size of 3, because customer numbers at Valle Coffee contain 3 digits. Because it's possible that a record for an order might need to be entered for a customer not yet added to the database, Barbara asks you to leave the Required property at its default value of No and to change the Allow Zero Length property value to Yes.

To define the CustomerNum field:

1. Place the insertion point in the second row's Field Name text box, type **CustomerNum** in the text box, and then press the **Tab** key to advance to the Data Type text box.

Customer numbers are not used in calculations, so you'll assign the text data type to the field, and then enter its Description value as "foreign key."

2. Press the **Tab** key to accept Text as the field's data type and move to the Description text box, and then type **foreign key** in the Description text box.

Finally, change the Field Size property to 3 and the Allow Zero Length property to Yes.

3. Select **50** in the Field Size text box, type **3**, click the right side of the Allow Zero Length text box, and then click **Yes**. You have completed the definition of the second field. See Figure 2-10.

Figure 2-10 ◄
Table window
after defining
the first
two fields

current field

property values for
the current field

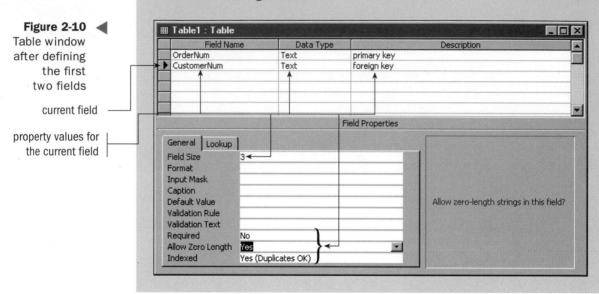

Using Barbara's Order table design in Figure 2-5, you can now complete the remaining field definitions: BillingDate with the date/time data type, PlacedBy with the text data type, and InvoiceAmt with the currency data type.

To define the BillingDate, PlacedBy, and InvoiceAmt fields:

1. Place the insertion point in the third row's Field Name text box, type **BillingDate** in the text box, and then press the **Tab** key to advance to the Data Type text box.

2. Click the **Data Type** list arrow, click **Date/Time** in the list box, and then press the **Tab** key to advance to the Description text box.

If you've assigned a descriptive field name and the field does not fulfill a special function (for example, primary key), you usually do not enter a value for the optional Description property. BillingDate is a field that does not require a value for its Description property.

Barbara does not want to require that a value be entered for the BillingDate field, nor does she want an index for the field. So, you do not need to change any of the default property values for the BillingDate field. Neither do you need to enter any new property values. Because you have finished defining the BillingDate field, you can now define the PlacedBy field.

3. Press the **Tab** key to advance to the fourth row's Field Name text box.

4. Type **PlacedBy** in the Field Name text box, and then press the **Tab** key to advance to the Data Type text box.

This field will contain names, so you'll assign the text data type to it. Also, Barbara wants to include the description "person who placed order" to clarify the contents of the field.

5. Press the **Tab** key to accept Text as the field's data type and move to the Description text box, and then type **person who placed order** in the Description text box.

   Next, you'll change the Field Size property's default value of 50 to 25, which should be long enough to accommodate all names. Also, Barbara does not want to require that a value be entered for the field.

6. Select **50** in the Field Size text box, type **25**, click the right side of the Allow Zero Length text box, and then click **Yes**.

   The definition of the PlacedBy field is complete. Next, you'll define the fifth and final field, InvoiceAmt. This field will contain dollar amounts so you'll assign the currency data type to it.

7. Place the insertion point in the fifth row's Field Name text box.

8. Type **InvoiceAmt** in the Field Name text box, and then press the **Tab** key to advance to the Data Type text box.

   You can select a value from the Data Type list box as you did for the BillingDate field. Alternatively, you can type the property value in the text box or type just the first character of the property value.

9. Type **c**. The value in the fifth row's Data Type text box changes to "currency," with the letters "urrency" highlighted. See Figure 2-11.

Figure 2-11 ◄
Selecting a
value for the
Data Type
property

"c" typed ──────────

"urrency"
automatically added
and highlighted

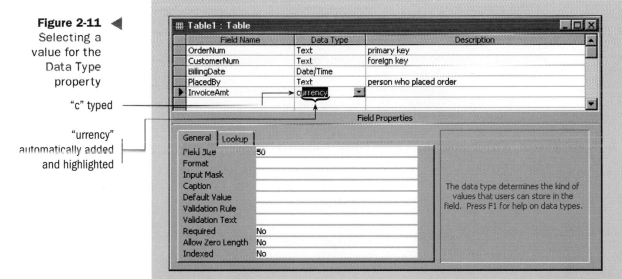

10. Press the **Tab** key to advance to the Description text box. Access changes the value for the Data Type property to Currency.

    In the Field Properties section, notice the default values for the Format and Decimal Places properties. For a field with a Format property value of Currency, two decimal places are provided when the Decimal Places property value is Auto. This is the format Barbara wants for the InvoiceAmt field, so you have finished defining the fields for the Order table.

Next, you need to specify the primary key for the Order table.

Specifying the Primary Key

Although Access does not require a table to have a primary key, including a primary key offers several advantages:

- A primary key uniquely identifies each record in a table.

- Access does not allow duplicate values in the primary key field. If a record already exists with an OrderNum value of 143, for example, Access prevents you from adding another record with this same value in the OrderNum field. Preventing duplicate values ensures the uniqueness of the primary key field and helps to avoid data redundancy.

- Access forces you to enter a value for the primary key field in every record in the table. This is known as **entity integrity**. If you do not enter a value for a field, you have actually given the field what is known as a **null value**. You cannot give a null value to the primary key field because entity integrity prevents Access from accepting and processing that record.

- Access stores records on disk in the same order as you enter them but displays them in order by the field values of the primary key. If you enter records in no specific order, you are ensured that you will later be able to work with them in a more meaningful, primary key sequence.

- Access responds faster to your requests for specific records based on the primary key.

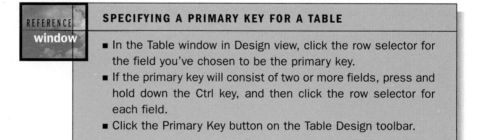

REFERENCE window	**SPECIFYING A PRIMARY KEY FOR A TABLE**
	■ In the Table window in Design view, click the row selector for the field you've chosen to be the primary key.
	■ If the primary key will consist of two or more fields, press and hold down the Ctrl key, and then click the row selector for each field.
	■ Click the Primary Key button on the Table Design toolbar.

According to Barbara's design, you need to specify OrderNum as the primary key for the Order table.

To specify OrderNum as the primary key:

1. Position the pointer on the row selector for the OrderNum field until the pointer changes to ➡. See Figure 2-12.

Primary Key button

Figure 2-12
Specifying
OrderNum as
the primary key

pointer

row selector

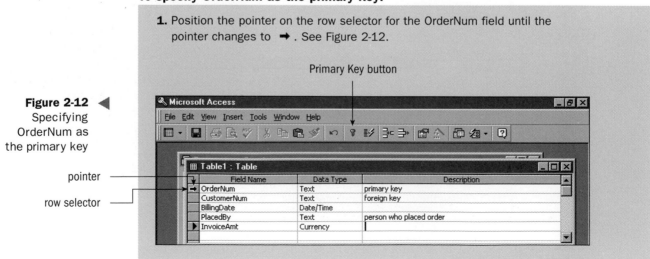

Access

2. Click the mouse button. The entire first row of the Table Design grid is highlighted.

3. Click the **Primary Key** button 🔑 on the Table Design toolbar, and then click to the right of InvoiceAmt in the fifth row's Field Name text box to deselect the first row. A key symbol appears in the row selector for the first row, indicating that the OrderNum field is the table's primary key. See Figure 2-13.

Figure 2-13 ◀
OrderNum selected as the primary key

key symbol indicating the primary key

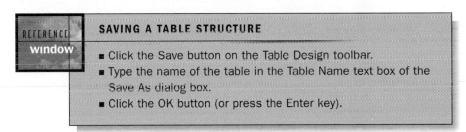

Field Name	Data Type	Description
OrderNum	Text	primary key
CustomerNum	Text	foreign key
BillingDate	Date/Time	
PlacedBy	Text	person who placed order
InvoiceAmt	Currency	

Table1 : Table

You've defined the fields for the Order table and specified its primary key, so you can now save the table structure.

Saving the Table Structure

The last step in creating a table is to name the table and save the table's structure on disk. Once the table is saved, you can use it to enter data in the table.

REFERENCE
window

SAVING A TABLE STRUCTURE

- Click the Save button on the Table Design toolbar.
- Type the name of the table in the Table Name text box of the Save As dialog box.
- Click the OK button (or press the Enter key).

You need to save the table you've defined as "Order."

To name and save the Order table:

1. Click the **Save** button 💾 on the Table Design toolbar. The Save As dialog box opens.

2. Type **Order** in the Table Name text box, and then press the **Enter** key. Access saves the table with the name Order in the Restaurant database on your Student Disk. Notice that Order appears instead of Table1 in the Table window title bar.

Next, Barbara asks you to add two records, shown in Figure 2-14, to the Order table. These two records contain data for orders that were recently placed with Valle Coffee.

Figure 2-14 ◀
Records to be added to the Order table

OrderNum	CustomerNum	BillingDate	PlacedBy	InvoiceAmt
323	624	2/15/99	Isabelle Rouy	$1,986.00
201	107	1/15/99	Matt Gellman	$854.00

Adding Records to a Table

You can add records to an Access table in several ways. A table datasheet provides a simple way for you to add records. As you learned in Tutorial 1, a datasheet shows a table's contents in rows and columns, similar to a table or worksheet. Each row is a separate record in the table, and each column contains the field values for one field in the table. To view a table datasheet, you first must change from Design view to Datasheet view.

You'll switch to Datasheet view and add the two records in the Order table datasheet.

To add the records in the Order table datasheet:

1. Click the **View** button for Datasheet view 🗔 on the Table Design toolbar. The Table window opens in Datasheet view. See Figure 2-15.

Figure 2-15 ◀
Table window in Datasheet view

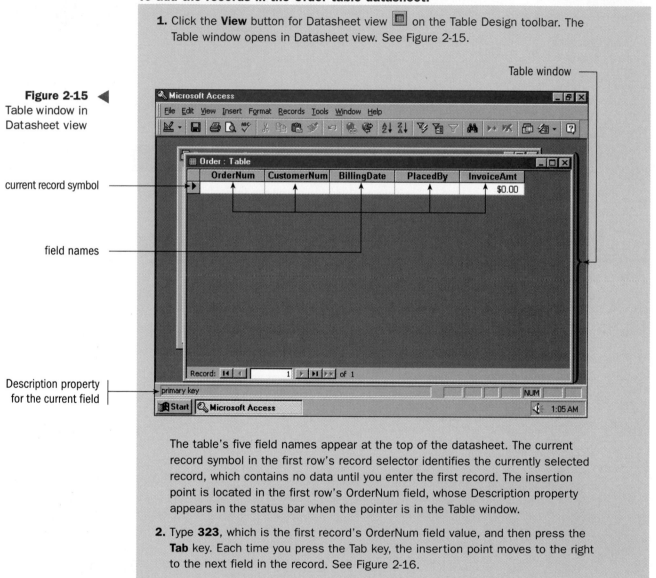

Table window

current record symbol

field names

Description property
for the current field

The table's five field names appear at the top of the datasheet. The current record symbol in the first row's record selector identifies the currently selected record, which contains no data until you enter the first record. The insertion point is located in the first row's OrderNum field, whose Description property appears in the status bar when the pointer is in the Table window.

2. Type **323**, which is the first record's OrderNum field value, and then press the **Tab** key. Each time you press the Tab key, the insertion point moves to the right to the next field in the record. See Figure 2-16.

Figure 2-16
Datasheet for
Order table
after entering
the first
field value

symbol for the
record being edited

next new
record symbol

field value entered

current record

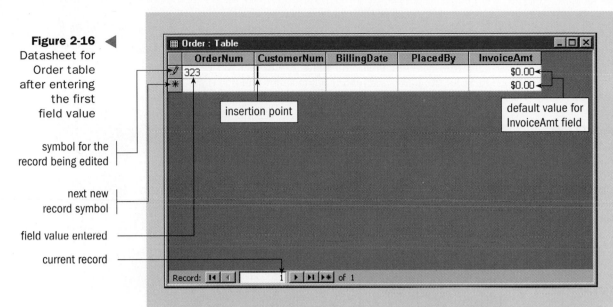

insertion point

default value for
InvoiceAmt field

TROUBLE? If you make a mistake when typing a value, use the Backspace key to delete characters to the left of the insertion point or the Delete key to delete characters to the right of the insertion point. Then type the correct text. If you want to correct a value by replacing it entirely, double-click the value to select it, and then type the correct value.

The pencil symbol in the first row's record selector indicates that the record is being edited. The star symbol in the second row's record selector identifies the second row as the next one available for a new record. The InvoiceAmt column displays "$0.00," the default value for the field.

3. Type **624** and then press the **Tab** key. The insertion point moves to the right side of the BillingDate field.

4. Type **2/15/99** and then press the **Tab** key. The insertion point moves to the PlacedBy field.

5. Type **Isabelle Rouy** and then press the **Tab** key. The insertion point moves to the InvoiceAmt field, whose field value is highlighted.

Notice that field values for text fields are left-aligned in their boxes and field values for date/time and currency fields are right-aligned in their boxes. If the default value of $0.00 is correct for the InvoiceAmt field, you can press the Tab key to accept the value and advance to the beginning of the next record. Otherwise, type the field value for the InvoiceAmt field. You do not need to type the dollar sign, commas, or decimal point (for whole dollar amounts) because Access adds these symbols automatically for you.

6. Type **1986** and then press the **Tab** key. Access displays $1,986.00 for the InvoiceAmt field, stores the first completed record in the Order table, removes the pencil symbol from the first row's record selector, advances the insertion point to the second row's OrderNum text box, and places the current record symbol in the second row's record selector.

Now you can enter the values for the second record.

7. Type **201** in the OrderNum field, press the **Tab** key to move to the CustomerNum field, type **107** in the CustomerNum field, and then press the **Tab** key. The insertion point moves to the right side of the BillingDate field.

8. Type **1/15/99** and then press the **Tab** key. The insertion point moves to the PlacedBy field.

9. Type **Matt Gellman** and then press the **Tab** key. The value in the InvoiceAmt field is now highlighted.

10. Type **854** and then press the **Tab** key. Access changes the InvoiceAmt field value to $854.00, saves the record in the Order table, and moves the insertion point to the beginning of the third row. See Figure 2-17.

Figure 2-17 ◄
Order table
datasheet after
entering the
second record

two added records ─┐

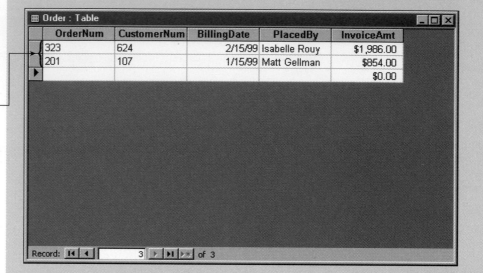

Notice that "Record 3 of 3" appears around the navigation buttons even though the table contains only two records. Access is anticipating that you will enter a new record, which would be the third of three records in the table. If you move the insertion point to the second record, the display would change to "Record 2 of 2."

Even though the Order table contains only two records, Barbara asks you to print the table datasheet so that she can bring it with her to a staff meeting. She wants to show the table design to her staff members to make sure that it will meet their needs for tracking order data.

You'll use the Print button on the Table Datasheet toolbar to print one copy of the Order table with the current settings.

To print the Order table:

1. Click the **Print** button 🖨 on the Table Datasheet toolbar.

   Notice that the two records are currently listed in the order in which you entered them. However, once you close the table or change to another view, and then redisplay the table datasheet, the records will be listed in primary key order by the values in the OrderNum field.

You have created the Order table in the Restaurant database and added two records to the table, which Access saved automatically to the database on your Student Disk.

Saving a Database

Notice the Save button on the Table Datasheet toolbar. This Save button, unlike the Save buttons in other Windows programs, does not save the active document (database) to your disk. Instead, you use the Save button to save the design of a table, query, form, or report, or to save datasheet format changes. Access does not have a button or option you can use to save the active database.

Access saves the active database to your disk automatically, both on a periodic basis and whenever you close the database. This means that if your database is stored on a disk in drive A or drive B, you should never remove the disk while the database file is open. If you do remove the disk, Access will encounter problems when it tries to save the database; this might damage the database.

Quick Check

1. What guidelines should you follow when you design a database?

2. What is the purpose of the data type property for a field?

3. For which two types of fields do you assign a field size?

4. Why did you define the OrderNum field as a text field instead of a number field?

5. A(n) _____ value, which results when you do not enter a value for a field, is not permitted for a primary key.

6. What does a pencil symbol in a datasheet's row selector represent? A star symbol?

The Order table is now complete. In Session 2.2, you'll continue to work with the Order table by modifying its structure and entering and maintaining data in the table.

SESSION
2.2

In this session you will modify the structure of a table by deleting, moving, and adding fields and changing field properties; copy records from another Access database; and update a database by deleting and changing records.

Modifying the Structure of an Access Table

Even a well-designed table might need to be modified. For example, the government at all levels and the competition place demands on a company to track more data and to modify the data it already tracks. Access allows you to modify a table's structure in Design view: you can add and delete fields, change the order of fields, and change the properties of the fields.

After meeting with her staff members and reviewing the structure of the Order table and the format of the field values in the datasheet, Barbara has several changes she wants you to make to the table. First, she has decided that it's not necessary to keep track of the name of the person who placed a particular order, so she wants you to delete the PlacedBy field. Also, she thinks that the InvoiceAmt field should remain a currency field, but she wants the dollar signs removed from the displayed field values in the datasheet. She also wants the BillingDate field moved to the end of the table. Finally, she wants you to add a yes/no field, named Paid, to the table to indicate whether the invoice has been paid for the order. The Paid field will be inserted between the CustomerNum and InvoiceAmt fields. Figure 2-18 shows Barbara's modified design for the Order table.

Figure 2-18 ◄
Modified design for the Order table

Field Name	Data Type	Field Size	Description
OrderNum	Text	3	primary key
CustomerNum	Text	3	foreign key
Paid	Yes/No		
InvoiceAmt	Currency		
BillingDate	Date/Time		

You'll begin modifying the table by deleting the PlacedBy field.

Deleting a Field

After you've defined a table structure and added records to the table, you can delete a field from the table structure. When you delete a field, you also delete all the values for the field from the table. Therefore, you should make sure that you need to delete a field and that you delete the correct field.

REFERENCE window	**DELETING A FIELD FROM A TABLE STRUCTURE**
	■ In the Table window in Design view, right-click the row selector for the field you want to delete to select the field and display the shortcut menu.
	■ Click Delete Rows on the shortcut menu.

You need to delete the PlacedBy field from the Order table structure.

To delete the PlacedBy field:

1. If you took a break after the previous session, make sure that Access is running and that the Order table of the Restaurant database is open.

2. Click the **View** button for Design view 🔲 on the Table Datasheet toolbar. The Table window for the Order table opens in Design view.

3. Position the pointer on the row selector for the PlacedBy field until the pointer changes to ➡ .

4. Right-click to select the entire row for the field and display the shortcut menu, and then click **Delete Rows**.

   A dialog box opens asking you to confirm the deletion.

5. Click the **Yes** button to close the dialog box and to delete the field and its values from the table. See Figure 2-19.

Figure 2-19 ◄
Table structure
after deleting
PlacedBy field

field deleted here ────

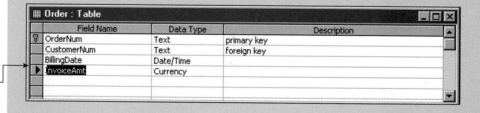

You have deleted the PlacedBy field in the Table window, but the change doesn't take place in the table on disk until you save the table structure. Because you have other modifications to make to the table, you'll wait until you finish them all before saving the modified table structure to disk.

Moving a Field

To move a field, you use the mouse to drag it to a new location in the Table window in Design view. Your next modification to the Order table structure is to move the BillingDate field to the end of the table, as Barbara requested.

To move the BillingDate field:

1. Click the **row selector** for the BillingDate field to select the entire row.

2. Place the pointer in the row selector for the BillingDate field, click the pointer ⬐ , and then drag the pointer ⬐ to the row selector below the InvoiceAmt row selector. See Figure 2-20.

Figure 2-20 ◀
Moving a field
in the table
structure

selected field

position the move
pointer in this
row selector

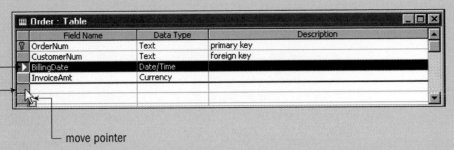

move pointer

3. Release the mouse button. Access moves the BillingDate field below the InvoiceAmt field in the table structure.

   TROUBLE? If the BillingDate field did not move, repeat Steps 1 through 3, making sure you firmly hold down the mouse button during the drag operation.

Adding a Field

Next, you need to add the Paid field to the table structure between the CustomerNum and InvoiceAmt fields. To add a new field between existing fields, you must insert a row. You begin by selecting the field that will be below the new field you want to insert.

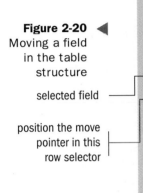

REFERENCE
window

ADDING A FIELD BETWEEN TWO EXISTING FIELDS

- In the Table window in Design view, right-click the row selector for the row above which you want to add a new field to select the field and display the shortcut menu.
- Click Insert Rows on the shortcut menu.
- Define the new field by entering the field name, data type, description (optional), and any property specifications.

To add the Paid field to the Order table:

1. Right-click the **row selector** for the InvoiceAmt field to select this field and display the shortcut menu, and then click **Insert Rows**. Access adds a new, blank row between the CustomerNum and InvoiceAmt fields. See Figure 2-21.

Figure 2-21 ◀
After inserting
a row in the
table structure

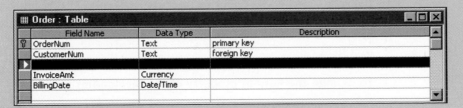

You'll define the Paid field in the new row for the Order table. Access will add this new field to the Order table structure between the CustomerNum and InvoiceAmt fields.

2. Click the **Field Name** text box for the new row, type **Paid**, and then press the **Tab** key.

The Paid field will be a yes/no field that will specify whether an invoice has been paid.

3. Type **y**. Access completes the data type as "yes/No."

4. Press the **Tab** key to select the yes/no data type and move to the Description text box.

Notice that Access changes the value in the Data Type text box from "yes/No" to "Yes/No." Barbara wants the Paid field to have a Default Value property value of "no." When you select or enter a value for a property, you *set* the property.

5. In the Field Properties section, click the **Default Value** text box, type **no**, and then click the **Description** text box for the Paid field. Notice that Access changes the Default Value property value from "no" to "No." See Figure 2-22.

Figure 2-22 ◀
Paid field
added to the
Order table

new field ——

Default Value
property set to "No"

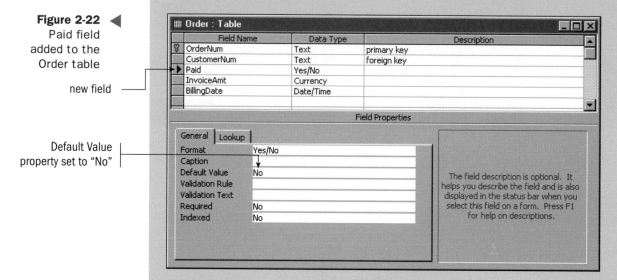

Because its field name clearly indicates its purpose, you do not need to enter a description for the Paid field.

You've completed adding the Paid field to the Order table in Design view. As with the other changes you've made, however, the Paid field is not added to the Order table in the Restaurant database until you save the changes to the table structure.

Changing Field Properties

Barbara's last modification to the table structure is to remove the dollar signs from the InvoiceAmt field values displayed in the datasheet, because repeated dollar signs are unnecessary and clutter the datasheet. You use the **Format property** to control the display of a field value.

To change the Format property of the InvoiceAmt field:

1. Click the **Description** text box for the InvoiceAmt field. The InvoiceAmt field is now the current field.

2. Click the **Format** text box in the Field Properties section, and then click the **Format** list arrow to display the Format list box. See Figure 2-23.

Figure 2-23 ◀
Format list box

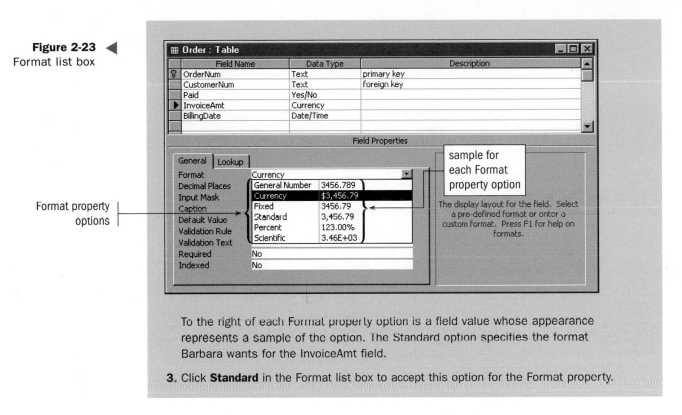

Format property
options

To the right of each Format property option is a field value whose appearance represents a sample of the option. The Standard option specifies the format Barbara wants for the InvoiceAmt field.

3. Click **Standard** in the Format list box to accept this option for the Format property.

Barbara wants you to add a third record to the Order table datasheet. Before you can add the record, you must save the modified table structure, and then switch to the Order table datasheet.

To save the modified table structure, and then switch to the datasheet:

1. Click the **Save** button 🖫 on the Table Design toolbar. The modified table structure for the Order table is stored in the Restaurant database.

2. Click the **View** button for Datasheet view 🖽 on the Table Design toolbar. The Order table datasheet opens. See Figure 2-24.

Figure 2-24 ◀
Datasheet for
the modified
Order table

records in primary
key order

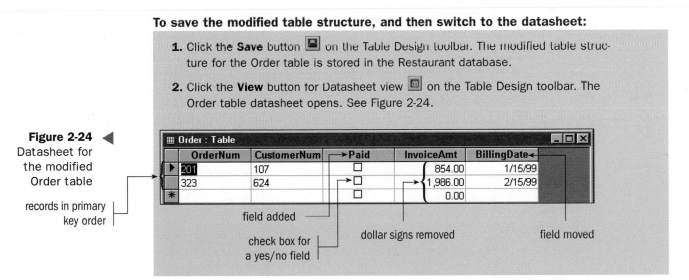

field added

check box for
a yes/no field

dollar signs removed

field moved

Notice that the PlacedBy field no longer appears in the datasheet, the BillingDate field is now the rightmost column, the InvoiceAmt field values do not contain dollar signs, and the Paid field appears between the CustomerNum and InvoiceAmt fields. The Paid column contains check boxes to represent the yes/no field values. Empty check boxes signify "No," which is the default value you assigned to the Paid field. A "Yes" value is indicated by a check mark in the check box. Also notice that the records appear in ascending order based on the value in the OrderNum field, the Order table's primary key, even though you did not enter the records in this order.

Barbara asks you to add a third record to the table. This record is for an order that has been paid.

To add the record to the modified Order table:

1. Click the **New Record** button ▶* on the Table Datasheet toolbar. The insertion point is located in the OrderNum field for the third row, which is the next row available for a new record.

2. Type **211**. The pencil symbol appears in the row selector for the third row, and the star appears in the row selector for the fourth row. Recall that these symbols represent a record being edited and the next available record, respectively.

3. Press the **Tab** key. The insertion point moves to the CustomerNum field.

4. Type **201** and then press the **Tab** key. The insertion point moves to the Paid field.

   Recall that the default value for this field is "No," which means the check box is initially empty. For yes/no fields with check boxes, you press the Tab key to leave the check box unchecked; you press the spacebar or click the check box to add or remove a check mark in the check box. Because the invoice for this order has been paid, you need to insert a check mark in the check box.

5. Press the **spacebar**. A check mark appears in the check box.

6. Press the **Tab** key. The value in the InvoiceAmt field is now highlighted.

7. Type **703.5** and then press the **Tab** key. The insertion point moves to the BillingDate field.

8. Type **1/15/99** and then press the **Tab** key. Access saves the record in the Order table and moves the insertion point to the beginning of the fourth row. See Figure 2-25.

Figure 2-25 ◀
Order table
datasheet
with third
record added

record added ———

"Yes" value ———

"No" values ———

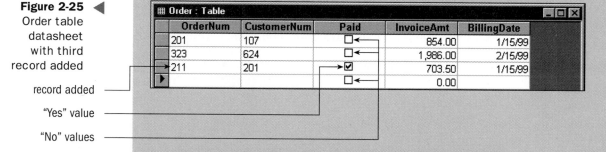

As you add records, Access places them at the end of the datasheet. If you switch to Design view then return to the datasheet or if you close the table then open the datasheet, Access will display the records in primary key sequence.

You have modified the Order table structure and added one record. Instead of typing the remaining records in the Order table, Barbara suggests that you copy them from a table that already exists in another database, and then paste them into the Order table.

Copying Records from Another Access Database

You can copy and paste records from a table in the same database or in a different database, but only if the tables have the same table structure. Barbara's Valle database in the Tutorial folder on your Student Disk has a table named Restaurant Order, which has the same table structure as the Order table. The records in the Restaurant Order table are the records Barbara wants you to copy into the Order table.

Other programs, such as Microsoft Word and Microsoft Excel, allow you to have two or more documents open at a time. However, you can have only one Access database open at a time. Therefore, you need to close the Restaurant database, open the Restaurant Order table in the Valle database, select and copy the table records, close the Valle database, reopen the Order table in the Restaurant database, and then paste the copied records.

To copy the records from the Restaurant Order table:

1. Click the **Close** button ⊠ on the Table window title bar to close the Order table, and then click the **Close** button ⊠ on the Database window title bar to close the Restaurant database.

2. Click the **Open Database** button 🗁 on the Database toolbar. The Open dialog box opens.

3. If necessary, display the list of files on your Student Disk, and then open the **Tutorial** folder.

4. Open the file named **Valle**. The Database window opens, showing the tables for the Valle database.

   Notice that the Valle database contains two tables: the Restaurant Customer table and the Restaurant Order table. The Restaurant Order table contains the records you need to copy.

5. Click **Restaurant Order** in the Tables list box, and then click the **Open** button. The datasheet for the Restaurant Order table opens. See Figure 2-26. Note that this table contains a total of 102 records.

Figure 2-26 ◀
Datasheet for
the Valle
database's
Restaurant
Order table

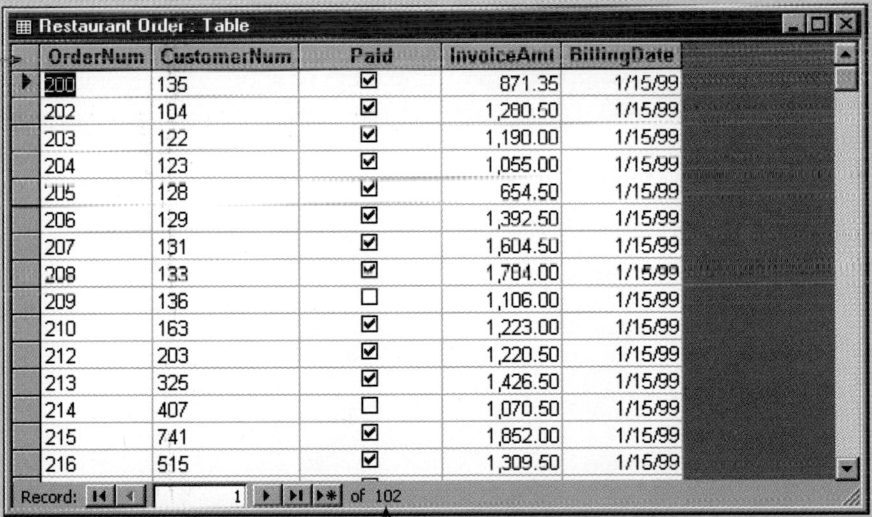

click here to
select all records

OrderNum	CustomerNum	Paid	InvoiceAmt	BillingDate
200	135	☑	871.35	1/15/99
202	104	☑	1,280.50	1/15/99
203	122	☑	1,190.00	1/15/99
204	123	☑	1,055.00	1/15/99
205	128	☑	654.50	1/15/99
206	129	☑	1,392.50	1/15/99
207	131	☑	1,604.50	1/15/99
208	133	☑	1,784.00	1/15/99
209	136	☐	1,106.00	1/15/99
210	163	☑	1,223.00	1/15/99
212	203	☑	1,220.50	1/15/99
213	325	☑	1,426.50	1/15/99
214	407	☐	1,070.50	1/15/99
215	741	☑	1,852.00	1/15/99
216	515	☑	1,309.50	1/15/99

Record: ⅠⅠ ◀ [1   ] ▶ ▶Ⅰ ▶* of 102

total number of
records in the table

Barbara wants you to copy all the records in the Restaurant Order table. You can select all records by clicking the row selector for the field name row.

6. Click the **row selector** for the field name row (see Figure 2-26). All the records in the table are now highlighted, which means that Access has selected all of them.

7. Click the **Copy** button 📋 on the Table Datasheet toolbar. All the records are copied to the Clipboard.

8. Click the **Close** button ⊠ on the Table window title bar. A dialog box opens asking if you want to save the data you copied on the Clipboard.

9. Click the **Yes** button in the dialog box. The dialog box closes and then the table closes.

10. Click the **Close** button ☒ on the Database window title bar to close the Valle database.

To finish copying and pasting the records, you must open the Order table and paste the copied records into the table.

To paste the copied records into the Order table:

1. Click **File** on the menu bar, and then click **Restaurant** in the list of recently opened databases. The Database window opens, showing the tables for the Restaurant database.

2. In the Tables list box, click **Order** and then click the **Open** button. The datasheet for the Order table opens.

You must paste the records at the end of the table.

3. Click the **row selector** for row four, which is the next row available for a new record.

4. Click the **Paste** button 🖺 on the Table Datasheet toolbar. All the records are pasted from the Clipboard, and a dialog box appears, asking if you are sure you want to paste the records.

5. Click the **Yes** button. The pasted records remain highlighted. See Figure 2-27. Notice that the table now contains a total of 105 records—the three original records plus the 102 copied records.

Figure 2-27 ◀
Table after
copying and
pasting records

original records (3)

pasted records (102)

table now contains a
total of 105 records

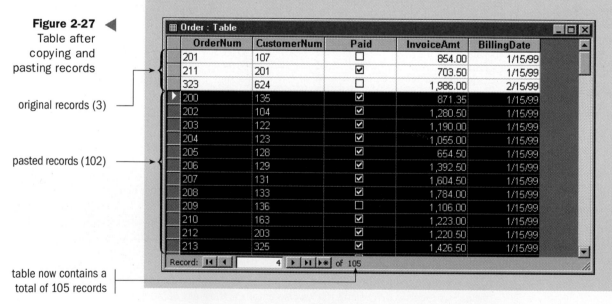

You've completed copying and pasting the records between the two tables. Now that you have all the records in the Order table, Barbara examines the records to make sure they are correct. She finds one record that she wants you to delete and another record that needs changes to its field values.

Updating a Database

Updating, or **maintaining**, a database is the process of adding, changing, and deleting records in database tables to keep them current and accurate. You've already added records to the Order table. Now Barbara wants you to delete and change records.

Deleting Records

To delete a record, you need to select the record in Datasheet view, and then delete it using the Delete Record button on the Table Datasheet toolbar or the Delete Record option on the shortcut menu.

REFERENCE window

DELETING A RECORD

- In the Table window in Datasheet view, click the row selector for the record you want to delete and then click the Delete Record button on the Table Datasheet toolbar (or right-click the row selector for the record, and then click Delete Record on the shortcut menu).
- In the dialog box asking you to confirm the deletion, click the Yes button.

Barbara asks you to delete the record whose OrderNum is 200 because this record was entered in error; it represents an order from an office customer, not a restaurant customer, and therefore does not belong in the Restaurant database. The fourth record in the table has an OrderNum value of 200. This is the record you need to delete.

To delete the record:

1. Right-click the **row selector** for row four. Access selects the fourth record and displays the shortcut menu. See Figure 2-28.

Figure 2-28 ◄
Deleting
a record

selected record —

click to delete the
selected record

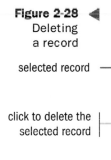

OrderNum	CustomerNum	Paid	InvoiceAmt	BillingDate
201	107	☐	854.00	1/15/99
211	201	☑	703.50	1/15/99
323	624	☐	1,986.00	2/15/99
200	135	☑	871.35	1/15/99
	04	☑	1,280.50	1/15/99
	22	☑	1,190.00	1/15/99
	23	☑	1,055.00	1/15/99
	28	☑	654.50	1/15/99
	29	☑	1,392.50	1/15/99
	31	☑	1,604.50	1/15/99
	33	☑	1,784.00	1/15/99
209	136	☐	1,106.00	1/15/99
210	163	☑	1,223.00	1/15/99
212	203	☑	1,220.50	1/15/99
213	325	☑	1,426.50	1/15/99

(Shortcut menu options shown: New Record, Delete Record, Cut, Copy, Paste, Row Height...)

Record: |◄ ◄ 4 ► ►| ►* of 105

☰ Order : Table

2. Click **Delete Record** on the shortcut menu. Access deletes the record and opens a dialog box asking you to confirm the deletion.

   TROUBLE? If you selected the wrong record for deletion, click the No button. Access ends the deletion process and redisplays the deleted record. Repeat Steps 1 and 2 to delete the correct record.

3. Click the **Yes** button to confirm the deletion and close the dialog box.

Barbara's final update to the Order table involves changes to field values in one of the records.

Changing Records

To change the field values in a record, you first must make the record the current record. Then you position the insertion point in the field value to make minor changes or select the field value to replace it entirely. In Tutorial 1, you used the mouse with the scroll bars and the navigation buttons to navigate through the records in a datasheet. You can also use keystroke combinations and the F2 key to navigate a datasheet and to select field values.

The **F2 key** is a toggle that you use to switch between navigation mode and editing mode:

- In **navigation mode**, Access selects an entire field value. If you type while you are in navigation mode, your typed entry replaces the highlighted field value.

- In **editing mode**, you can insert or delete characters in a field value based on the location of the insertion point.

The navigation mode and editing mode keystroke techniques are shown in Figure 2-29.

Figure 2-29 ◄
Navigation
mode and
editing mode
keystroke
techniques

Press	To Move the Selection in Navigation Mode	To Move the Insertion Point in Editing Mode
←	Left one field value at a time	Left one character at a time
→	Right one field value at a time	Right one character at a time
Home	Left to the first field value in the record	To the left of the first character in the field value
End	Right to the last field value in the record	To the right of the last character in the field value
↑ or ↓	Up or down one record at a time	Up or down one record at a time and switch to navigation mode
Tab or Enter	Right one field value at a time	Right one field value at a time and switch to navigation mode
Ctrl + Home	To the first field value in the first record	To the left of the first character in the field value
Ctrl + End	To the last field value in the last record	To the right of the last character in the field value

The record Barbara wants you to change has an OrderNum field value of 397. Some of the values were entered incorrectly for this record, and you need to enter the correct values.

To modify the record:

1. Make sure the OrderNum field value for the fourth record is still highlighted, indicating that the table is in navigation mode.

2. Press **Ctrl + End**. Access displays records from the end of the table and selects the last field value in the last record. This field value is for the BillingDate field.

3. Press the **Home** key. The first field value in the record is now selected. This field value is for the OrderNum field.

4. Press the ↑ key. The OrderNum field value for the previous record is selected. This is the record you need to change.

Barbara wants you to change these field values in the record: OrderNum to 398, CustomerNum to 165, Paid to "Yes" (checked), and InvoiceAmt to 1426.50. The BillingDate does not need to be changed.

5. Type **398**, press the **Tab** key, type **165**, press the **Tab** key, press the **spacebar** to insert a check mark in the Paid check box, press the **Tab** key, and then type **1426.5**. This completes the changes to the record.

6. Press the ↓ key to save the changes to the record and make the next record the current record. See Figure 2-30.

Figure 2-30
Table after changing field values in a record

field values changed

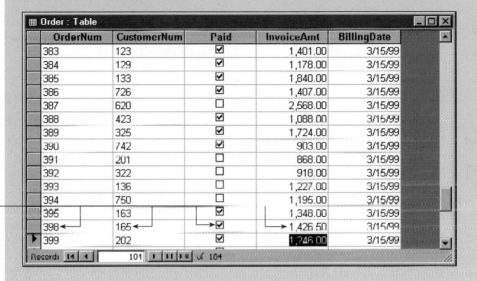

OrderNum	CustomerNum	Paid	InvoiceAmt	BillingDate
383	123	☑	1,401.00	3/15/99
384	129	☑	1,178.00	3/15/99
385	133	☑	1,840.00	3/15/99
386	726	☑	1,407.00	3/15/99
387	620	☐	2,568.00	3/15/99
388	423	☑	1,088.00	3/15/99
389	325	☑	1,724.00	3/15/99
390	742	☑	903.00	3/15/99
391	201	☐	868.00	3/15/99
392	322	☐	918.00	3/15/99
393	136	☐	1,227.00	3/15/99
394	750	☐	1,195.00	3/15/99
395	163	☑	1,348.00	3/15/99
398	165	☑	1,426.50	3/15/99
399	202	☑	1,246.00	3/15/99

Record: 14 ◀ 101 ▶ ▶I ▶* of 104

You've completed all of Barbara's updates to the Order table. Barbara asks you to print just the first page of data from the Order table datasheet so that she can show the revised table structure to her staff members. After you print the page, you can exit Access.

To print the first page of Order table data, and then exit Access:

1. Click **File** on the menu bar, and then click **Print** to display the Print dialog box.

2. In the Print Range section, click the **Pages** option button, type **1** in the From text box, press the **Tab** key, and then type **1** in the To text box.

3. Click the **OK** button to print the first page of data.

Now you can exit Access.

4. Click the **Close** button ☒ on the Access window title bar to close the Order table and the Restaurant database and to exit Access.

Quick Check

1 What is the effect of deleting a field from a table structure?

2 How do you insert a field between existing fields in a table structure?

3 A field with the _____ data type can appear in the table datasheet as a check box.

4 Which property do you use to control the display appearance of a field value?

5 Why must you close an open database when you want to copy records to it from a table in another database?

6 What is the difference between navigation mode and editing mode?

Barbara and her staff members approve of the revised table structure for the Order table. They are confident that the table will allow them to easily track order data for Valle Coffee's restaurant customers.

Tutorial Assignments

Barbara needs a database to track the coffee products offered by Valle Coffee. She asks you to create the database by completing the following:

1. Make sure your Student Disk is in the disk drive, and then start Access.

2. In the initial Access dialog box, click the Blank Database option button, and then click the OK button. In the File New Database dialog box, select the TAssign folder on your Student Disk, and then enter the filename Valle Products for the database. Click the Create button to create the new database.

3. Create a table using the table design shown in Figure 2-31.

Figure 2-31 ◀

Field Name	Data Type	Description	Field Size	Other Properties
ProductCode	Text	primary key	4	
CoffeeCode	Text	foreign key	4	
Price	Currency	price for this product		Format: Fixed Decimal Places: 2
Decaf	Text	D if decaf, Null if regular	1	Default Value: D
BackOrdered	Yes/No	back-ordered from supplier?		

4. Specify ProductCode as the primary key, and then save the table as Product.

5. Add the product records shown in Figure 2-32 to the Product table.

Figure 2-32 ◀

ProductCode	CoffeeCode	Price	Decaf	BackOrdered
2316	JRUM	8.99		Yes
9754	HAZL	40.00	D	No
9309	COCO	9.99	D	No

6. Make the following changes to the structure of the Product table:
   a. Add a new field between the CoffeeCode and Price fields, using these properties:
      Field Name: WeightCode
      Data Type: Text
      Description: foreign key
      Field Size: 1
   b. Move the BackOrdered field so that it appears between the WeightCode and Price fields.
   c. Save the revised table structure.

7. Use the Product datasheet to update the database as follows:
   a. Enter these WeightCode values for the three records: A for ProductCode 2316, A for ProductCode 9309, and E for ProductCode 9754.

   b. Add a record to the Product datasheet with these field values:

ProductCode:	9729
CoffeeCode:	COLS
WeightCode:	E
BackOrdered:	No
Price:	37.50
Decaf:	D

8. Barbara created a database with her name as the database name. The Coffee Product table in that database has the same format as the Product table you created. Copy all the records from the Coffee Product table in the Barbara database (located in the TAssign folder on your Student Disk) to the end of your Product table.

9. Close the Product table, and then reopen it so that the records are displayed in primary key order by ProductCode. Then delete the record with the ProductCode 2333 from the Product table.

10. Delete the BackOrdered field from the Product table structure.

11. Use the Access Help system to learn how to resize datasheet columns to fit the data, and then resize all columns in the datasheet for the Product table so that each column fits its data. Scroll the datasheet to make sure all field values are fully displayed. For any field values that are not fully displayed, make sure the field values are visible on the screen, and then resize the appropriate columns again.

12. Print the first page of data from the Product table datasheet, and then save and close the table.

13. Create a table named Weight based on the data shown in Figure 2-33.

Figure 2-33 ◀

WeightCode	Weight/Size
A	1 lb pkg
B	6 lb case
C	24 ct 1.5 oz pkg
D	44 ct 1.25 oz pkg
E	44 ct 1.5 oz pkg
F	88 ct 1.25 oz pkg
G	88 ct 1.5 oz pkg

   a. Select the Datasheet View option in the New Table dialog box.

   b. Enter the seven records shown in Figure 2-33. (Do *not* enter the field names at this point.)

   c. Switch to Design view, supply the table name, and then answer No if asked if you want to create a primary key.

   d. Type the following field names and set the following properties:

WeightCode

Description:	primary key
Field Size:	1

Weight/Size

Description:	weight in pounds or size in packages (number and weight) per case
Field Size:	17

   e. Specify the primary key, save the table structure changes, and then switch back to Datasheet view. If you receive any warning messages, answer Yes to continue.

f. Resize both datasheet columns to fit the data (use Access Help to learn how to resize datasheet columns, if necessary); then save, print, and close the datasheet.

14. Create a table named Coffee using the Import Table Wizard. The table you need to import is named Coffee.dbf and is located in the TAssign folder on your Student Disk. This table has a dBASE 5 file type. (You'll need to change the entry in the Files of type list box to display the file in the list.) After importing the table, complete the following:
   a. Change all field names to use the Valle Coffee convention of uppercase and lowercase letters, and then enter the following Description property values:
      CoffeeCode: primary key
      Decaf: Is decaf available for this coffee?
   b. Change the Format property of the Decaf field to Yes/No.
   c. Specify the primary key, and then save the table structure changes.
   d. Switch to Datasheet view, and then resize all columns in the datasheet to fit the data. (Use Access Help to learn how to resize datasheet columns, if necessary.) Be sure to scroll through the table to make sure that all field values are fully displayed.
   e. Save, print, and then close the datasheet. Close the Valle Products database.

Case Problems

1. Ashbrook Mall Information Desk Sam Bullard, the director of the Mall Operations Office at Ashbrook Mall, uses the MallJobs database to maintain information about current job openings at stores in the mall. Sam asks you to help him maintain the database by completing the following:

1. Make sure your Student Disk is in the disk drive.

2. Start Access and open the MallJobs database located in the Cases folder on your Student Disk.

3. Create a table using the table design shown in Figure 2-34.

Figure 2-34 ◀

Field Name	Data Type	Description	Field Size
Job	Text	primary key	5
Store	Text	foreign key	3
Hours/Week	Text		20
Position	Text		35
ExperienceReq	Yes/No		

4. Specify Job as the primary key, and then save the table as Job.

5. Add the job records shown in Figure 2-35 to the Job table.

Figure 2-35 ◀

Job	Store	Hours/Week	Position	ExperienceReq
10037	WT	negotiable	Salesclerk	No
10053	BR	14-24	Server Assistant	No
10022	JP	35-45	Assistant Manager	Yes

6. Sam created a database named Openings that contains a table with job data named Current Jobs. The Job table you created has the same format as the Current Jobs table. Copy all the records from the Current Jobs table in the Openings database (located in the Cases folder on your Student Disk) to the end of your Job table.

Access

7. Modify the structure of the Job table by completing the following:
   a. Delete the ExperienceReq field.
   b. Move the Hours/Week field so that it follows the Position field.

8. Use the Access Help system to learn how to resize datasheet columns to fit the data, and then switch to Datasheet view and resize all columns in the datasheet for the Job table.

9. Use the Job datasheet to update the database as follows:
   a. For Job 10046, change the Position value to Clerk, and change the Hours/Week value to 20-30.
   b. Add a record to the Job datasheet with the following field values:
      Job: 10034
      Store: JP
      Position: Salesclerk
      Hours/Week: negotiable
   c. Delete the record for Job 10029.

10. Switch to Design view, and then switch back to Datasheet view so that the records are displayed in primary key sequence by Job.

11. Print the Job table datasheet, and then save and close the table. Close the MallJobs database.

2. Professional Litigation User Services Raj Jawahir is responsible for tracking the daily payments received from PLUS clients. You'll help him maintain the Payments database by completing the following:

1. Make sure your Student Disk is in the disk drive.

2. Start Access and open the Payments database located in the Cases folder on your Student Disk.

3. Create a table named Payment using the table design shown in Figure 2-36.

Figure 2-36 ◀

Field Name	Data Type	Description	Field Size	Other Properties
Payment#	Text	primary key	5	
Firm#	Text	foreign key	4	
DatePaid	Date/Time			Format: Medium Date
AmtPaid	Currency			Format: Standard
				Decimal Places: 2
				Default Value: 0

4. Add the payment records shown in Figure 2-37 to the Payment table.

Figure 2-37 ◀

Payment#	Firm#	DatePaid	AmtPaid
10031	1147	6/3/99	2435.00
10002	1100	6/1/99	1300.00
10015	1142	6/1/99	2000.00

5. Modify the structure of the Payment table by completing the following:
   a. Add a new field between the Payment# and Firm# fields, using these properties:
      Field Name: Deposit#
      Data Type: Text
      Field Size: 3
   b. Move the DatePaid field so that it follows the AmtPaid field.

6. Use the Payment datasheet to update the database as follows:
   a. Enter these Deposit# values for the three records: 100 for Payment# 10002, 101 for Payment# 10015, and 103 for Payment# 10031.
   b. Add a record to the Payment datasheet with these field values:

   Payment#:   10105
   Deposit#:   117
   Firm#:   1103
   AmtPaid: 2,500.00
   DatePaid: 6/20/99

7. Raj created a database named PlusPays that contains recent payments in the Payment Records table. The Payment table you created has the same format as the Payment Records table. Copy all the records from the Payment Records table in the PlusPays database (located in the Cases folder on your Student Disk) to the end of your Payment table.

8. Use the Access Help system to learn how to resize datasheet columns to fit the data, and then resize all columns in the datasheet for the Payment table.

9. For Payment# 10002, change the AmtPaid value to 1100.00.

10. Delete the record for Payment# 10101.

11. Print the first page of data from the Payment table datasheet, and then save and close the table. Close the Payments database.

3. Best Friends Noah and Sheila Warnick continue to track information about participants in the Walk-A-Thons held to benefit Best Friends. Help them maintain the Walks database by completing the following:

1. Make sure your Student Disk is in the disk drive.

2. Start Access and open the Walks database located in the Cases folder on your Student Disk.

3. Create a table named Pledge using the Import Table Wizard. The table you need to import is named Pledge.dbf and is located in the Cases folder on your Student Disk. This table has a Microsoft FoxPro file type. (You'll need to change the entry in the Files of type list box to display the file in the list. Make sure you choose the Microsoft FoxPro file type, not the Microsoft FoxPro 3.0 file type.) After importing the table, complete the following:
   a. Change all field names to use uppercase and lowercase letters, as appropriate, and then enter the following Description property values:

   PledgeNo: primary key
   WalkerID: foreign key
   PerMile: amount pledged per mile

   b. Specify the primary key, and then save the table structure changes.
   c. Switch to Datasheet view, and then resize all columns in the datasheet to fit the data. (Use Access Help to learn how to resize datasheet columns, if necessary.)

4. Modify the structure of the Pledge table by completing the following:
   a. Add a new field between the PaidAmt and PerMile fields, using these properties:

   Field Name: DatePaid
   Data Type: Date/Time
   Format: Medium Date

   b. Change the Data Type of both the PledgeAmt field and the PaidAmt field to Currency. For each of these fields, choose the Fixed format.

5. Use the Pledge datasheet to update the database as follows:
   a. Enter these DatePaid values for the five records: 9/15/99 for PledgeNo 1, 9/1/99 for PledgeNo 2, 8/27/99 for PledgeNo 3, 9/20/99 for PledgeNo 4, and 8/30/99 for PledgeNo 5. Resize the DataPaid column to fit the data.
   b. Add a record to the Pledge datasheet with these field values:

   PledgeNo: 6
   Pledger: Fernando Carazana
   WalkerID: 138
   PledgeAmt: 25
   PaidAmt: 25
   DatePaid: 9/18/99
   PerMile: ()

   c. Enter the value 183 in the WalkerID field for PledgeNo 1.
   d. Change both the PledgeAmt value and the PaidAmt value for PledgeNo 3 to 10.00.
   e. Change the WalkerID value for PledgeNo 5 to 187.

6. Print the Pledge table datasheet, and then save and close the table. Close the Walks database.

4. Lopez Lexus Dealerships Maria and Hector Lopez use the Lexus database to track the car inventory in the chain of Lexus dealerships they own. You'll help them maintain the Lexus database by completing the following:

1. Make sure your Student Disk is in the disk drive.

2. Start Access and open the Lexus database located in the Cases folder on your Student Disk.

3. Use the Import Spreadsheet Wizard to create a new table named Locations. The data you need to import is contained in the Lopez workbook, which is a Microsoft Excel file located in the Cases folder on your Student Disk.
   a. Select the Import Table option in the New Table dialog box.
   b. Change the entry in the Files of type list box to display the list of Excel workbook files in the Cases folder.
   c. Select the Lopez file and then click the Import button.
   d. In the Import Spreadsheet Wizard dialog boxes, choose the option for using column headings as field names, select the option for choosing your own primary key and specify LocationCode as the primary key; and enter the table name (Locations). Otherwise, accept the wizard's choices for all other options for the imported data.

4. Use the Access Help system to learn how to resize datasheet columns to fit the data, and then open the Locations table and resize all columns in the datasheet.

5. Modify the structure of the Locations table by completing the following:
   a. For the LocationCode field, enter a Description property of "primary key," change the Field Size to 2, and change the Required property to Yes.
   b. For the LocationName field, change the Field Size to 20.
   c. For the ManagerName field, change the Field Size to 30.
   d. Save the table. If you receive any warning messages about lost data or integrity rules, click the Yes button.

6. Use the Locations datasheet to update the database as follows:
   a. For LocationCode A2, change the ManagerName value to Curran, Leo.
   b. Add a record to the Locations datasheet with these field values:
      LocationCode: H2
      LocationName: Houston
      ManagerName: Cohen, Sandra
   c. Delete the record for LocationCode L2.

7. Print the Locations table datasheet, and then close the table and the Lexus database.

Querying a Database

Retrieving Information About Restaurant Customers and Their Orders

OBJECTIVES

In this tutorial you will:

- Learn how to use the Query window in Design view
- Create, run, and save queries
- Define a relationship between two tables
- Sort data in a query
- Filter data in a query
- Specify an exact match condition in a query
- Change a datasheet's appearance
- Use a comparison operator to match a range of values
- Use the And and Or logical operators
- Perform calculations in a query using calculated fields, aggregate functions, and record group calculations

Valle Coffee

At a recent company meeting, Leonard Valle and other Valle Coffee employees discussed the importance of regularly monitoring the business activity of the company's restaurant customers. For example, Kim Carpenter and her marketing staff track customer activity to develop new strategies for promoting Valle Coffee products. Barbara Hennessey and her office staff need to track information about all the orders for which bills were sent out on a specific date so that they can determine whether the bills have been paid. In addition, Leonard is interested in analyzing the payment history of restaurant customers to determine which customers pay their invoices in a timely manner, which customers have higher invoice amounts, and so on. All of these informational needs can be satisfied by queries that retrieve information from the Restaurant database.

SESSION

3.1

In this session you will use the Query window in Design view to create, run, and save queries; define a one-to-many relationship between two tables; sort data with a toolbar button and in Design view; and filter data in a query datasheet.

Introduction to Queries

As you learned in Tutorial 1, a query is a question you ask about data stored in a database. For example, Kim might create a query to find records in the Customer table for only those customers in a specific state. When you create a query, you tell Access which fields you need and what criteria Access should use to select the records.

Access provides powerful query capabilities that allow you to:

- display selected fields and records from a table
- sort records
- perform calculations
- generate data for forms, reports, and other queries
- update data in the tables in a database
- find and display data from two or more tables

Most questions about data are generalized queries in which you specify the fields and records you want Access to select. These common requests for information, such as "Which customers have unpaid bills?" or "Which type of coffee sells best in Ohio?" are called **select queries**. The answer to a select query is returned in the form of a datasheet.

More specialized, technical queries, such as finding duplicate records in a table, are best formulated through a Query Wizard. A Query Wizard prompts you for information through a set of questions and then creates the appropriate query based on your answers. In Tutorial 1, you used the Simple Query Wizard to display only some of the fields in the Customer table; Access provides other Query Wizards for more complex queries. For common, informational queries, it is easier for you to design your own query rather than use a Query Wizard.

Kim wants you to create a query to display the customer number, customer name, city, owner name, and first contact information for each record in the Customer table. She needs this information for a market analysis her staff is completing on Valle Coffee's restaurant customers. You'll open the Query window to create the query for Kim.

The Query Window

You use the Query window in Design view to create a query. In Design view you specify the data you want to view by constructing a query by example. Using **query by example (QBE)**, you give Access an example of the information you are requesting. Access then retrieves the information that precisely matches your example.

For Kim's query, you need to display data from the Customer table. You'll begin by starting Access, opening the Restaurant database, and displaying the Query window in Design view.

To start Access, open the Restaurant database, and open the Query window in Design view:

1. Place your Student Disk in the appropriate disk drive.

2. Start Access and open the Restaurant database located in the Tutorial folder on your Student Disk. The Restaurant database is displayed in the Access window.

3. Click the **Queries** tab in the Database window, and then click the **New** button. The New Query dialog box opens. See Figure 3-1.

Figure 3-1 ◀
New Query
dialog box

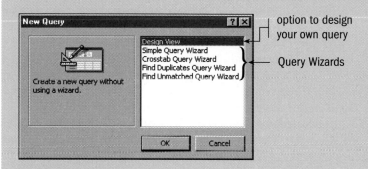

option to design
your own query

Query Wizards

You'll design your own query instead of using a Query Wizard.

4. If necessary, click **Design View** in the list box.

5. Click the **OK** button. Access opens the Show Table dialog box on top of the Query window. Notice that the title bar of the window shows that you are creating a select query.

The query you are creating will retrieve data from the Customer table, so you need to add this table to the Select Query window.

6. Click **Customer** in the Tables list box (if necessary), click the **Add** button, and then click the **Close** button. Access places the Customer table field list in the Select Query window and closes the dialog box.

To display more of the fields you'll be using for creating queries, you'll maximize the Select Query window.

7. Click the **Maximize** button on the Select Query window title bar. See Figure 3-2.

Query Type button
shows select query

Run button

Figure 3-2 ◀
Select Query
window in
Design view

View button for
Datasheet view

field list

design grid

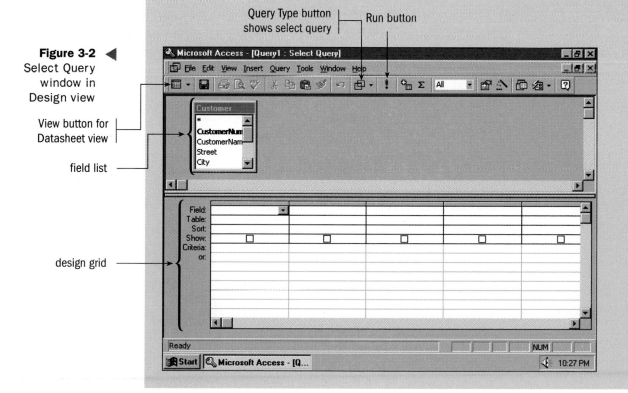

In Design view, the Select Query window contains the standard title bar, menu bar, toolbar, and status bar. On the toolbar, the Query Type button shows a select query; the icon on this button changes according to the type of query you are creating. The title bar on the Select Query window displays the query type, Select Query, and the default query name, Query1. You'll change the default query name to a more meaningful one later when you save the query.

The Select Query window in Design view contains a field list and the design grid. The **field list**, which appears in the upper-left area of the window, contains the fields for the table you are querying. The table name appears at the top of the list box, and the fields are listed in the order in which they appear in the table.

In the **design grid**, you include the fields and record selection criteria for the information you want to see. Each column in the design grid contains specifications about a field you will use in the query. You can choose a single field for your query by dragging its name from the field list to the design grid in the lower portion of the window. Alternatively, you can double-click a field name to place it in the next available column in the design grid.

When you are constructing a query, you can see the query results at any time by clicking the View button or the Run button on the Query Design toolbar. In response, Access displays the datasheet, which contains the set of fields and records that result from answering, or **running**, the query. The order of the fields in the datasheet is the same as the order of the fields in the design grid. Although the datasheet looks just like a table datasheet and appears in Datasheet view, a query datasheet is temporary and its contents are based on the criteria you establish in the design grid. In contrast, a table datasheet shows the permanent data in a table. However, you can update data while viewing a query datasheet, just as you can when working in a table datasheet or a form.

If the query you are creating includes all the fields from the specified table, you could use one of the following three methods to transfer all the fields from the field list to the design grid:

- Click and drag each field individually from the field list to the design grid. Use this method if you want the fields in your query to appear in an order that is different from the order in the field list.

- Double-click the asterisk in the field list. Access places the table name followed by a period and an asterisk (as in "Customer.*") in the design grid. This signifies that the order of the fields will be the same in the query as it is in the field list. Use this method if the query does not need to be sorted or to have conditions for the records you want to select. The advantage of using this method is that you do not need to change the query if you add or delete fields from the underlying table structure. They will all appear automatically in the query.

- Double-click the field list title bar to highlight all the fields, and then click and drag one of the highlighted fields to the design grid. Access places each field in a separate column and arranges the fields in the order in which they appear in the field list. Use this method rather than the previous one if your query needs to be sorted or to include record selection criteria.

Now you'll create and run Kim's query to display selected fields from the Customer table.

Creating and Running a Query

A table datasheet displays all the fields in the table, in the same order as they appear in the table. In contrast, a query datasheet can display selected fields from a table, and the order of the fields can be different from that of the table.

Kim wants the CustomerNum, CustomerName, City, OwnerName, and FirstContact fields to appear in the query results. You'll add each of these fields to the design grid.

To select the fields for the query, and then run the query:

1. Drag **CustomerNum** from the Customer field list to the design grid's first column Field text box, and then release the mouse button. See Figure 3-3.

Figure 3-3 ◀
Field added to
the design grid

drag field from here

release mouse
button here

indicates that the
field will appear
in the datasheet

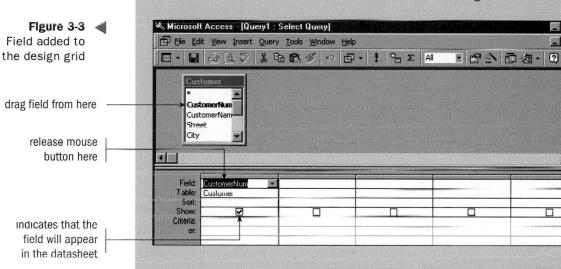

In the design grid's first column, the field name CustomerNum appears in the Field text box, the table name Customer appears in the Table text box, and the check mark in the Show check box indicates that the field will be displayed in the datasheet when you run the query. There are times when you might choose not to display a field and its values in the query results. For example, if you are creating a query to show all the customers located in Michigan, and you assign the name "Customers in Michigan" to the query, you would not need to include the State field value for each record in the query results. Even if you choose not to include a field in the display of the query results, you can still use the field as part of the query to select specific records or to specify a particular sequence for the records in the datasheet.

2. Double-click **CustomerName** in the Customer field list. Access adds this field to the second column of the design grid.

3. Scrolling the Customer field list as necessary, repeat Step 2 for the **City**, **OwnerName**, and **FirstContact** fields to add these fields to the design grid in that order.

Having selected the fields for Kim's query, you can now run the query.

4. Click the **Run** button 🔲 on the Query Design toolbar. Access runs the query and displays the results in Datasheet view. See Figure 3-4.

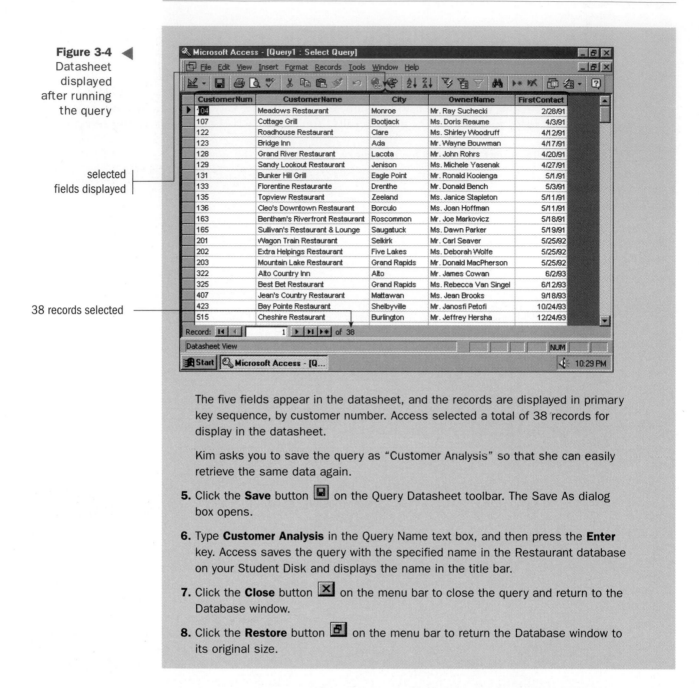

Figure 3-4 ◀
Datasheet
displayed
after running
the query

selected
fields displayed

38 records selected

The five fields appear in the datasheet, and the records are displayed in primary key sequence, by customer number. Access selected a total of 38 records for display in the datasheet.

Kim asks you to save the query as "Customer Analysis" so that she can easily retrieve the same data again.

5. Click the **Save** button 🖫 on the Query Datasheet toolbar. The Save As dialog box opens.

6. Type **Customer Analysis** in the Query Name text box, and then press the **Enter** key. Access saves the query with the specified name in the Restaurant database on your Student Disk and displays the name in the title bar.

7. Click the **Close** button ☒ on the menu bar to close the query and return to the Database window.

8. Click the **Restore** button 🗗 on the menu bar to return the Database window to its original size.

Barbara also wants to view specific information in the Restaurant database. However, she needs to see data from both the Customer table and the Order table at the same time. To accomplish this, you need to define a relationship between the two tables.

Defining Table Relationships

One of the most powerful features of a relational database management system is its ability to define relationships between tables. You use a common field to relate one table to another. The process of relating tables is often called performing a **join**. When you join tables that have a common field, you can extract data from them as if they were one larger table. For example, you can join the Customer and Order tables by using the CustomerNum field in both tables as the common field. You then can use a query, form, or report to extract selected data from each table, even though the data is contained in two separate tables, as shown in Figure 3-5. In the Orders query shown in Figure 3-5, the OrderNum, Paid, and InvoiceAmt columns are fields from the Order table; and the CustomerName and State columns are fields from the Customer table. The joining of records is based on the common field of CustomerNum. The Customer and Order tables have a type of relationship called a one-to-many relationship.

Figure 3-5 ◀
One-to-many
relationship
and sample
query

primary table

fields from Order
table

query that joins fields
from the Customer
and Order tables

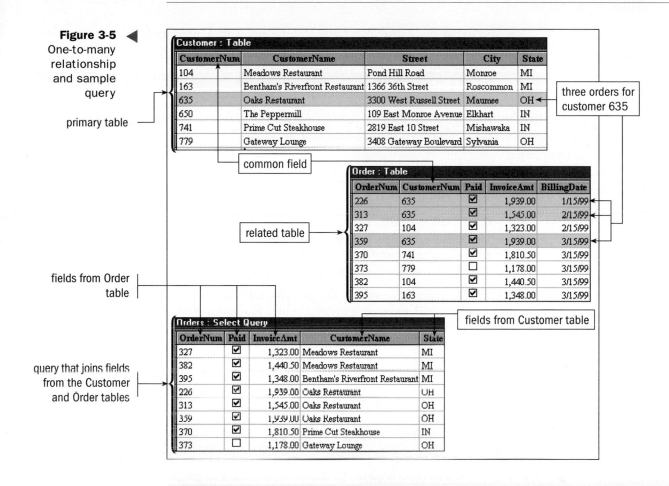

One-to-Many Relationships

A **one-to-many relationship** exists between two tables when one record in the first table matches zero, one, or many records in the second table, and when one record in the second table matches exactly one record in the first table. For example, as shown in Figure 3-5, customer 635 has three orders, customer 650 has zero orders, customers 163, 741, and 779 each have one order, and customer 104 has two orders. Every order has a single matching customer.

Access refers to the two tables that form a relationship as the primary table and the related table. The **primary table** is the "one" table in a one-to-many relationship; in Figure 3-5, the Customer table is the primary table because there is only one customer for each order. The **related table** is the "many" table; in Figure 3-5, the Order table is the related table because there can be many orders for each customer.

Because related data is stored in two tables, inconsistencies between the tables can occur. Consider the following scenarios:

- Barbara adds an order to the Order table for customer 107, Cottage Grill. This order does not have a matching record in the Customer table. The data is inconsistent, and the order record is considered to be an **orphaned** record.

- Barbara changes Oaks Restaurant from customer number 635 to 997 in the Customer table. Three orphaned records for customer 635 now exist in the Order table, and the database is inconsistent.

- Barbara deletes the record for Meadows Restaurant, customer 104, in the Customer table because this customer is no longer a Valle Coffee customer. The database is again inconsistent; two records for customer 104 in the Order table have no matching record in the Customer table.

You can avoid these problems by specifying referential integrity between tables when you define their relationships.

Referential Integrity

Referential integrity is a set of rules that Access enforces to maintain consistency between related tables when you update data in a database. Specifically, the referential integrity rules are as follows:

- When you add a record to a related table, a matching record must already exist in the primary table.

- If you attempt to change the value of the primary key in the primary table, Access prevents this change if matching records exist in a related table. However, if you choose the **cascade updates** option, Access permits the change in value to the primary key and changes the appropriate foreign key values in the related table.

- When you delete a record in the primary table, Access prevents the deletion if matching records exist in a related table. However, if you choose the **cascade deletes** option, Access deletes the record in the primary table and all records in related tables that have matching foreign key values.

Now you'll define a one-to-many relationship between the Customer and Order tables so that you can use fields from both tables to create a query that will retrieve the information Barbara wants.

Defining a Relationship Between Two Tables

When two tables have a common field, you can define a relationship between them in the Relationships window. The **Relationships window** illustrates the relationships among a database's tables. In this window you can view or change existing relationships, define new relationships between tables, and rearrange the layout of the tables.

You need to open the Relationships window and define the relationship between the Customer and Order tables. You'll define a one-to-many relationship between the two tables, with Customer as the primary table and Order as the related table, and with CustomerNum as the common field (the primary key in the Customer table and a foreign key in the Order table).

To define a one-to-many relationship between the two tables:

1. Click the **Relationships** button ⊞ on the Database toolbar. Access displays the Show Table dialog box on top of the Relationships window. See Figure 3-6.

Figure 3-6 ◀
Show Table
dialog box

add both tables

Relationships window

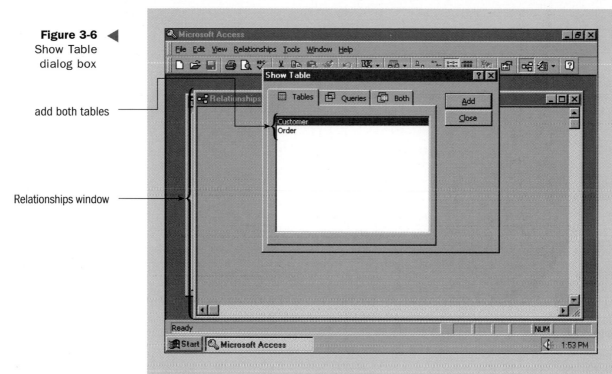

Each table participating in a relationship must be added to the Relationships window.

2. Click **Customer** (if necessary) and then click the **Add** button. The Customer table is added to the Relationships window.

3. Click **Order** and then click the **Add** button. The Order table is added to the Relationships window.

4. Click the **Close** button in the Show Table dialog box. Access closes the dialog box and reveals the entire Relationships window.

To form the relationship between the two tables, you drag the common field of CustomerNum from the primary table to the related table. Access then opens the Relationships dialog box in which you select the relationship options for the two tables.

5. Click **CustomerNum** in the Customer table list, and drag it to **CustomerNum** in the Order table list. When you release the mouse button, Access opens the Relationships dialog box. See Figure 3-7.

Figure 3-7 ◀
Relationships
dialog box

primary table

common field

referential
integrity option

cascade options

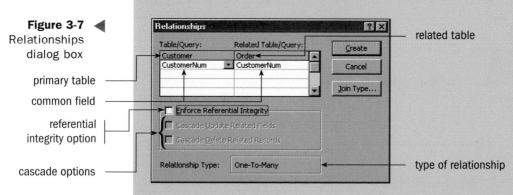

related table

type of relationship

The primary table, related table, and common field appear at the top of the dialog box. The type of relationship, one-to-many, appears at the bottom of the dialog box. When you click the Enforce Referential Integrity check box, the two cascade options become available. With the Cascade Update Related Fields option,

Access will change the appropriate foreign key values in the related table when you change a primary key value in the primary table. With the Cascade Delete Related Records option, when you delete a record in the primary table, Access will delete all records in the related table that have a matching foreign key value.

6. Click the **Enforce Referential Integrity** check box, click the **Cascade Update Related Fields** check box, and then click the **Cascade Delete Related Records** check box. You have now selected all the necessary relationship options.

7. Click the **Create** button to define the one-to-many relationship between the two tables and close the dialog box. The completed relationship appears in the Relationships window. See Figure 3-8.

Figure 3-8 ◀
Defined
relationship
in the
Relationships
window

"one" side of
the relationship

join line

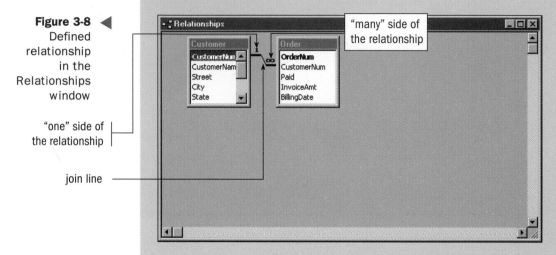

The *join line* connects the CustomerNum fields, which are common to the two tables. The common field joins the two tables, which have a one-to-many relationship. The join line is thick at both ends; this signifies that you have chosen the option to enforce referential integrity. If you do not select this option, the join line is thin at both ends. The "one" side of the relationship has the digit 1 at its end, and the "many" side of the relationship has the infinity symbol ∞ at its end. The two tables are still separate tables, but you can use the data in them as if they were one table.

8. Click the **Save** button 🖫 on the Relationship toolbar to save the layout in the Relationships window.

9. Click the **Close** button ⊠ on the Relationships window title bar. Access closes the Relationships window and returns you to the Database window.

Now that you have joined the Customer and Order tables, you can create a query to produce the information Barbara wants. As part of her tracking of payments received from restaurant customers, Barbara needs a query that displays the CustomerName, City, and State fields from the Customer table and the BillingDate, InvoiceAmt, and Paid fields from the Order table.

To create, run, and save the query using the Customer and Order tables:

1. From the Queries tab in the Database window, click the **New** button to open the New Query dialog box, click **Design View** in the dialog box, and then click the **OK** button. Access opens the Show Table dialog box on top of the Query window in Design view.

   You need to add both tables to the Query window.

2. Click **Customer** in the Tables list box (if necessary), click the **Add** button, click **Order**, click the **Add** button, and then click the **Close** button. Access places the

Customer and Order field lists in the Query window and closes the Show Table dialog box. Note that the one-to-many relationship that exists between the two tables is shown in the Query window.

You need to place the CustomerName, City, and State fields from the Customer field list into the design grid, and then place the BillingDate, InvoiceAmt, and Paid fields from the Order field list into the design grid.

3. Double-click **CustomerName** in the Customer field list. Access places CustomerName in the design grid's first column Field text box.

4. Repeat Step 3 to add the **City** and **State** fields from the Customer table, and then add the **BillingDate**, **InvoiceAmt**, and **Paid** fields (in that order) from the Order table, so that these fields are placed in the second through sixth columns of the design grid.

The query specifications are complete, so you can now run the query.

5. Click the **Run** button on the Query Design toolbar. Access runs the query and displays the results in the datasheet.

6. Click the **Maximize** button on the Query window. See Figure 3-9.

Figure 3-9
Datasheet for the query based on the Customer and Order tables

fields from the Customer table

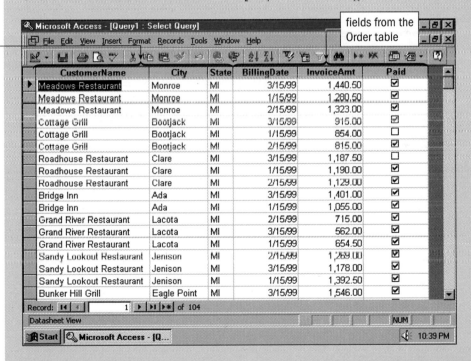

Only the six selected fields from the Customer and Order tables appear in the datasheet. The records are displayed in order according to the values in the primary key field, CustomerNum, even though this field is not included in the query datasheet.

Barbara plans on tracking the data retrieved by the query frequently, so she asks you to save the query as "Customer Orders."

7. Click the **Save** button on the Query Datasheet toolbar. The Save As dialog box opens.

8. Type **Customer Orders** in the Query Name text box, and then press the **Enter** key. Access saves the query with the specified name and displays the name in the Query window title bar.

Barbara decides she wants the records displayed in alphabetical order by customer name. Because your query displays data in order by the field value of CustomerNum, the primary key for the Customer table, you need to sort the records by CustomerName to display the data in the order Barbara wants.

Sorting Data in a Query

Sorting is the process of rearranging records in a specified order or sequence. Often you need to sort data before displaying or printing it to meet a specific request. For example, Barbara might want to review order information arranged by the Paid field because she is interested in which orders are still unpaid. On the other hand, Leonard might want to view order information arranged by the InvoiceAmt totals for each customer because he tracks company sales.

When you sort data in a database, Access does not change the sequence of the records in the underlying tables. Only the records in the query datasheet are rearranged according to your specifications.

To sort records, you must select the **sort key**, which is the field used to determine the order of records in the datasheet. In this case, Barbara wants the data sorted by the customer name, so you need to specify the CustomerName field as the sort key. Sort keys can be text, number, date/time, currency, AutoNumber, or yes/no fields, but not memo, OLE object, or hyperlink fields. You sort records in either ascending (increasing) or descending (decreasing) order. Figure 3-10 shows the results of each type of sort for different data types.

Figure 3-10 ◀
Sorting results
for different
data types

Data Type	Ascending Sort Results	Descending Sort Results
Text	A to Z	Z to A
Number	lowest to highest numeric value	highest to lowest numeric value
Date/Time	oldest to most recent date	most recent to oldest date
Currency	lowest to highest numeric value	highest to lowest numeric value
AutoNumber	lowest to highest numeric value	highest to lowest numeric value
Yes/No	yes (check mark in check box) then no values	no then yes values

Access provides several methods for sorting data in a table or query datasheet and in a form. One method, clicking the toolbar sort buttons, lets you quickly sort the displayed records.

Using a Toolbar Button to Sort Data

The **Sort Ascending** and **Sort Descending** buttons on the toolbar allow you to sort records immediately, based on the selected field. First you select the column on which you want to base the sort, and then click the appropriate sort button on the toolbar to rearrange the records in either ascending or descending order. Unless you save the datasheet or form after you've sorted the records, the rearrangement of records is temporary.

Recall that in Tutorial 1 you used the Sort Ascending button to sort query results by the State field. You'll use this same button to sort the Customer Orders query results by the CustomerName field.

To sort the records using a toolbar sort button:

1. Click any visible CustomerName field value to establish this field as the current field.

2. Click the **Sort Ascending** button on the Query Datasheet toolbar. Access rearranges the records in ascending order by customer name. See Figure 3-11.

Figure 3-11
Sorting records on a single field in a datasheet

Sort Ascending button

Sort Descending button

records sorted in ascending order by CustomerName

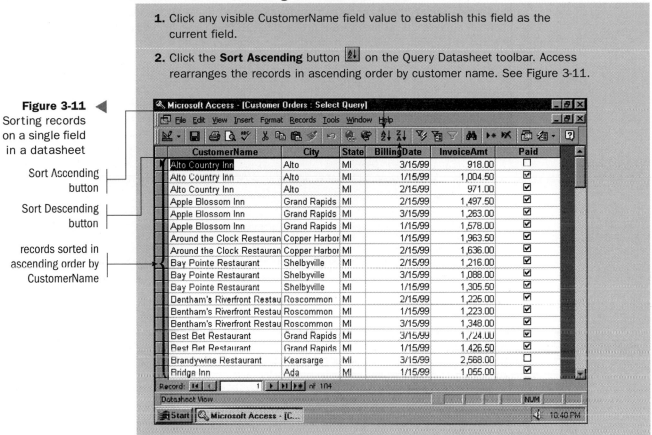

After viewing the query results, Barbara decides that she'd prefer the records to be arranged by the value in the Paid field so that she can determine more easily which invoices have been paid. She wants to view all the unpaid invoices before the paid invoices (descending order for the Paid field, which is a yes/no field); plus, she wants to display the records within each group in decreasing value of the InvoiceAmt field. To do this you need to sort using two fields.

Sorting Multiple Fields in Design View

Sort keys can be unique or nonunique. A sort key is **unique** if the value of the sort key field for each record is different. The CustomerNum field in the Customer table is an example of a unique sort key because each customer record has a different value in this field. A sort key is **nonunique** if more than one record can have the same value for the sort key field. The Paid field in the Order table is a nonunique sort key because more than one record has the same Paid value.

When the sort key is nonunique, records with the same sort key value are grouped together, but they are not in a specific order within the group. To arrange these grouped records in a specific order, you can specify a **secondary sort key**, which is a second sort key field. The first sort key field is called the **primary sort key**. Note that the primary sort key is not the same as a table's primary key field. A table has at most one primary key, which must be unique, whereas any field in a table can serve as a primary sort key.

Access lets you select up to 10 different sort keys. When you use the toolbar sort buttons, the sort key fields must be in adjacent columns in the datasheet. You highlight the columns, and Access sorts first by the first column and then by each other highlighted column in order from left to right.

Barbara wants the records sorted first by the Paid field and then by the InvoiceAmt field. Although the two fields are adjacent, they are in the wrong order. If you used a toolbar sort button, the InvoiceAmt field would be the primary sort key instead of the Paid field. When you have two or more nonadjacent sort keys or when the fields to be used for sorting are in the wrong order, you must specify the sort keys in the Query window in Design view. Access first uses the sort key that is leftmost in the design grid. Therefore, you must arrange the fields you want to sort from left to right in the design grid with the primary sort key being the leftmost sort key field.

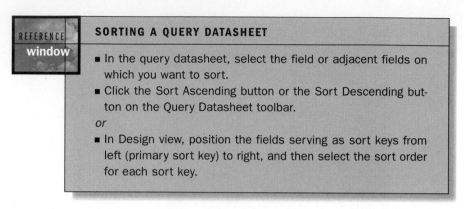

REFERENCE window

SORTING A QUERY DATASHEET

- In the query datasheet, select the field or adjacent fields on which you want to sort.
- Click the Sort Ascending button or the Sort Descending button on the Query Datasheet toolbar.

or

- In Design view, position the fields serving as sort keys from left (primary sort key) to right, and then select the sort order for each sort key.

To achieve the results Barbara wants, you need to switch to Design view, move the InvoiceAmt field to the right of the Paid field, and then specify the sort order for the two fields.

To select the two sort keys in Design view:

1. Click the **View** button for Design view ▧ on the Query Datasheet toolbar. Access closes the window and opens the query in Design view.

   First, you'll move the InvoiceAmt field to the right of the Paid field.

2. If necessary, click the right arrow in the design grid's horizontal scroll bar to scroll to the right until both the InvoiceAmt and Paid fields are visible.

3. Position the pointer above the InvoiceAmt field name until the pointer changes to ↓ , and then click to select the field. See Figure 3-12.

Figure 3-12 ◀
Selected
InvoiceAmt
field

entire column
is highlighted

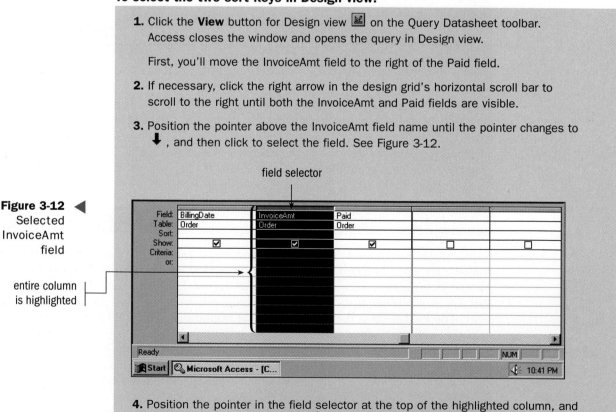

4. Position the pointer in the field selector at the top of the highlighted column, and then click and drag the pointer ⍩ to the right until the vertical line on the right of the Paid field is highlighted. See Figure 3-13.

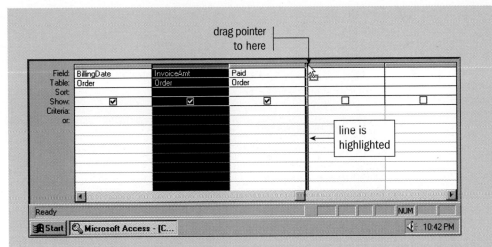

Figure 3-13 ◀
Dragging the
field in the
design grid

drag pointer
to here

line is
highlighted

5. Release the mouse button. Access places the InvoiceAmt field to the right of the Paid field.

The fields are now in the correct order for the sort. Now you need to specify a descending sort order for each of the two fields.

6. Click the **Paid Sort** text box, click the **Sort** list arrow, and then click **Descending**. You've selected a descending sort order for the Paid field, which will be the primary sort key. The Paid field is a yes/no field, and a descending sort order for this type of field displays all the no (unpaid) values before the yes (paid) values.

7. Click the **InvoiceAmt Sort** text box, click the **Sort** list arrow, click **Descending**, and then click in the Criteria text box for the InvoiceAmt field. You've selected a descending sort order for the InvoiceAmt field, which will be the secondary sort key. See Figure 3-14.

Figure 3-14 ◀
Selecting two
sort keys in
Design view

primary sort key

secondary sort key

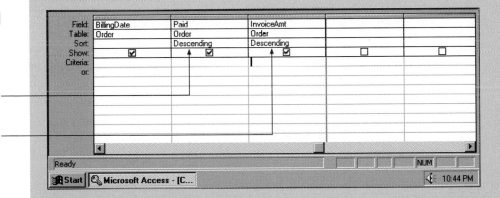

You have finished your query changes, so now you can run the query and then save the modified query with the same query name.

8. Click the **Run** button [!] on the Query Design toolbar. Access runs the query and displays the query datasheet. The records appear in descending order, based on the values of the Paid field. Within groups of records with the same Paid field value, the records appear in descending order by the values of the InvoiceAmt field. See Figure 3-15.

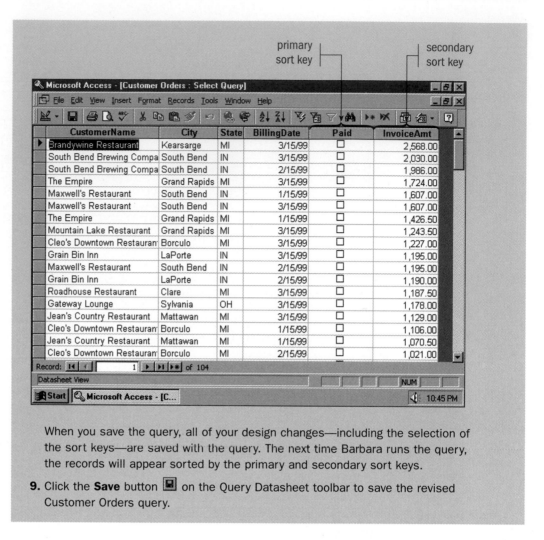

Figure 3-15 ◀
Datasheet
sorted on
two fields

When you save the query, all of your design changes—including the selection of the sort keys—are saved with the query. The next time Barbara runs the query, the records will appear sorted by the primary and secondary sort keys.

9. Click the **Save** button 🔲 on the Query Datasheet toolbar to save the revised Customer Orders query.

Barbara wants to focus her attention for a few minutes on the orders in the datasheet that are unpaid. Because selecting only the unpaid orders is a temporary change Barbara wants in the datasheet, you do not need to switch to Design view and change the query. Instead, you can apply a filter.

Filtering Data

A **filter** is a set of restrictions you place on the records in an open datasheet or form to *temporarily* isolate a subset of the records. A filter lets you view different subsets of displayed records so you can focus on only the data you need. Unless you save a query or form with a filter applied, an applied filter is not available the next time you run the query or open the form. The simplest technique for filtering records is Filter By Selection. **Filter By Selection** lets you select all or part of a field value in a datasheet or form, and then display only those records that contain the selected value in the field.

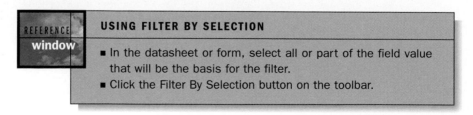

REFERENCE window

USING FILTER BY SELECTION

- In the datasheet or form, select all or part of the field value that will be the basis for the filter.
- Click the Filter By Selection button on the toolbar.

For Barbara's request, you need to select an unchecked box in the Paid field, which represents an unpaid order, and then use Filter By Selection to display only those query records with this value.

To display the records using Filter By Selection:

1. Click any check box that is unchecked in the Paid column. When you click the check box, you select the field value, but you also change the check box from unchecked to checked. Because you've changed an unpaid order to a paid order, you need to click the same check box a second time.

2. Click the same check box a second time. The field value changes back to unchecked, which is now the selected field value.

3. Click the **Filter By Selection** button [icon] on the Query Datasheet toolbar. Access displays the filtered results. Only the 25 query records that have an unchecked Paid field value appear in the datasheet; these records are the unpaid order records. Note that the status bar display and the selected Remove Filter button on the toolbar both indicate that records have been filtered. See Figure 3-16.

Figure 3-16 ◀
Using Filter
By Selection

indicates records
have been filtered

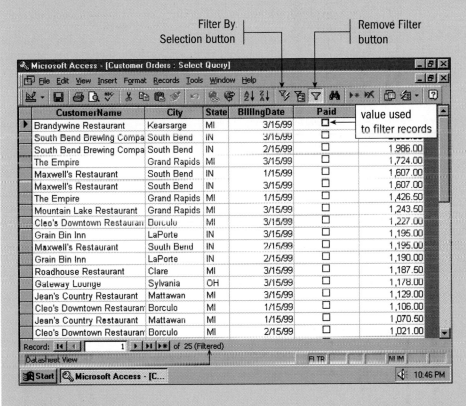

Barbara asks you to print the current datasheet so that she can give the printout to a staff member who is tracking unpaid orders.

4. Click the **Print** button [icon] on the Query Datasheet toolbar. Access prints the datasheet.

Now you can redisplay all the query records by clicking the Remove Filter button; this button works as a toggle to switch between the filtered and nonfiltered displays.

5. Click the **Remove Filter** button [icon] on the Query Datasheet toolbar. Access redisplays all the records in the query datasheet.

6. Click the **Save** button [icon] on the Query Datasheet toolbar, and then click the **Close** button [icon] on the menu bar to save and close the query and return to the Database window.

7. Click the **Restore** button [icon] on the menu bar to return the Database window to its original size.

Quick Check

[1] What is a select query?

[2] Describe the field list and the design grid in the Query window in Design view.

[3] How are a table datasheet and a query datasheet similar? How are they different?

[4] The _____ is the "one" table in a one-to-many relationship, and the _____ is the "many" table in the relationship.

[5] _____ is a set of rules that Access enforces to maintain consistency between related tables when you update data in a database.

[6] For a date/time field, what is ascending sort order?

[7] When must you define multiple sort keys in Design view instead of in the query datasheet?

[8] A(n) _____ is a set of restrictions you place on the records in an open datasheet or form to temporarily isolate a subset of records.

The queries you've created will help Valle Coffee employees retrieve just the information they want to view. In the next session, you'll continue to create queries to meet their information needs.

SESSION

3.2

In this session you will specify an exact match condition in a query, change a datasheet's appearance, use a comparison operator to match a range of values, use the And and Or logical operators to define multiple selection criteria for queries, and perform calculations in queries.

Barbara wants to display customer and order information for all orders billed on 1/15/99 so she can see which orders have been paid. For this request, you need to create a query that displays selected fields from the Order and Customer tables and selected records that satisfy a condition.

Defining Record Selection Criteria for Queries

Just as you can display selected fields from a table in a query datasheet, you can display selected records. To tell Access which records you want to select, you must specify a condition as part of the query. A **condition** is a criterion, or rule, that determines which records are selected. To define a condition for a field, you place the condition in the field's Criteria text box in the design grid.

A condition usually consists of an operator, often a comparison operator, and a value. A **comparison operator** asks Access to compare the values of a database field to the condition value and to select all the records for which the relationship is true. For example, the condition >1000.00 for the InvoiceAmt field selects all records in the Order table having InvoiceAmt field values greater than 1000.00. The Access comparison operators are shown in Figure 3-17.

Figure 3-17 ◀
Access
comparison
operators

Operator	Meaning	Example
=	equal to (optional, default operator)	="Hall"
<	less than	<#1/1/94#
<=	less than or equal to	<−100
>	greater than	>"C400"
>=	greater than or equal to	>=18.75
<>	not equal to	<>"Hall"
Between ... And...	between two values (inclusive)	Between 50 And 325
In ()	in a list of values	In ("Hall", "Seeger")
Like	matches a pattern that includes wildcards	Like "706*"

Specifying an Exact Match

For Barbara's request, you need to create a query that will display only those records in the Order table with the value 1/15/99 in the BillingDate field. This type of condition is called an **exact match** because the value in the specified field must match the condition exactly in order for the record to be included in the query results. You'll use the Simple Query Wizard to create the query, and then you'll specify the exact match condition.

To create the query using the Simple Query Wizard:

1. If you took a break after the previous session, make sure that Access is running, the Restaurant database is open, and the Queries tab is displayed in the Database window, and then click the **New** button.

2. Click **Simple Query Wizard** and then click the **OK** button. Access opens the first Simple Query Wizard dialog box, in which you select the tables and fields for the query.

3. Click the **Tables/Queries** list arrow, and then click **Table: Order**. The fields in the Order table appear in the Available Fields list box. See Figure 3-18.

Figure 3-18 ◀
First Simple
Query Wizard
dialog box

selected table ⎯⎯⎯⎯⎯

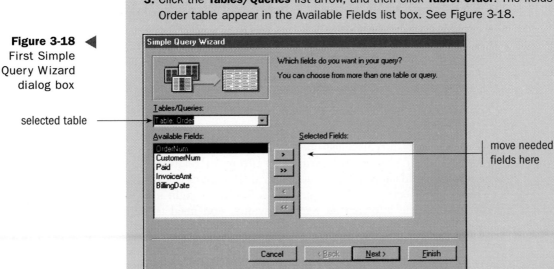

move needed
fields here

Except for the CustomerNum field, you will include all fields from the Order table in the query.

4. Click the ⟫ button. Access removes all the fields from the Available Fields list box and places them in the same order in the Selected Fields list box.

5. Click **CustomerNum** in the Selected Fields list box, click the ⟨ button to move the CustomerNum field back to the Available Fields list box, and then click **BillingDate** in the Selected Fields list box.

Barbara also wants certain information from the Customer table included in the query results.

6. Click the **Tables/Queries** list arrow, and then click **Table: Customer**. The fields in the Customer table now appear in the Available Fields list box.

7. Click **CustomerName** in the Available Fields list box, and then click the ⟩ button to move CustomerName to the Selected Fields list box.

8. Repeat Step 7 for the **State**, **OwnerName**, and **Phone** fields.

9. Click the **Next** button to open the second Simple Query Wizard dialog box, in which you choose whether the query will display records from the selected tables or a summary of those records. Barbara wants to view the details for the records, not a summary.

10. Make sure the **Detail** option button is selected, and then click the **Next** button to open the last Simple Query Wizard dialog box, in which you choose a name for the query and complete the wizard. You need to enter a condition for the query, so you'll want to modify the query's design.

11. Type **January Orders**, click the **Modify the query design** option button, and then click the **Finish** button. Access saves the query as January Orders and opens the query in Design view. See Figure 3-19.

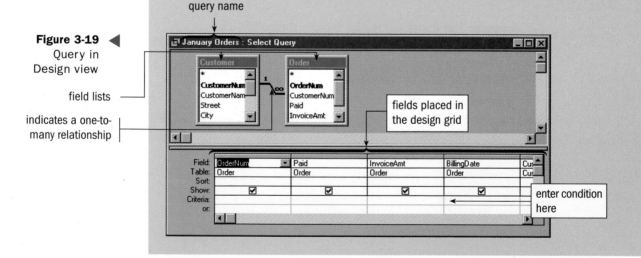

Figure 3-19
Query in Design view

field lists

indicates a one-to-many relationship

query name

fields placed in the design grid

enter condition here

The field lists for the Customer and Order tables appear in the top portion of the window, and the join line indicating a one-to-many relationship connects the two tables. The selected fields appear in the design grid. Not all of the fields are visible in the grid; to see the other selected fields, you need to scroll to the right using the horizontal scroll bar.

To display the information Barbara wants, you need to enter the condition for the BillingDate field in its Criteria text box. Barbara wants to display only those records with a billing date of 1/15/99.

To enter the exact match condition, and then run the query:

1. Click the **BillingDate Criteria** text box, type **1/15/99**, and then press the **Enter** key. Access changes the condition to #1/15/99#.

   Access automatically placed number signs (#) before and after the condition. You must place date and time values inside number signs when using these values as selection criteria. If you omit the number signs, however, Access will include them automatically.

2. Click the **Run** button 🔘 on the Query Design toolbar. Access runs the query and displays the selected field values for only those records with a BillingDate field value of 1/15/99. A total of 36 records are selected and displayed in the datasheet. See Figure 3-20.

only records with a
BillingDate value
of 1/15/99
are selected

Figure 3-20 ◄
Datasheet
displaying
selected fields
and records

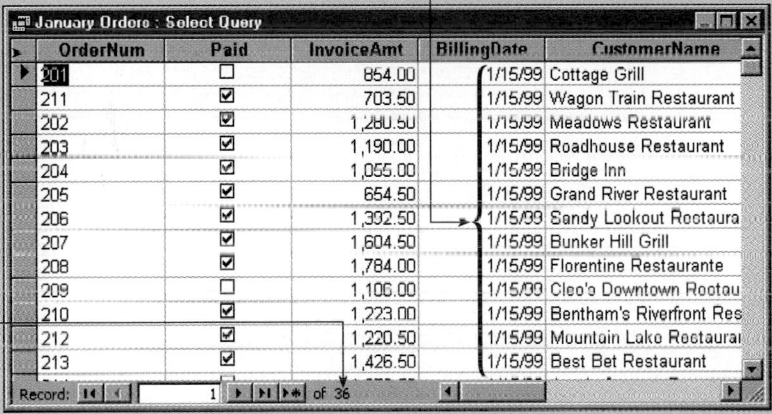

click here to
select all records

36 records selected

OrderNum	Paid	InvoiceAmt	BillingDate	CustomerName
201	☐	854.00	1/15/99	Cottage Grill
211	☑	703.50	1/15/99	Wagon Train Restaurant
202	☑	1,280.50	1/15/99	Meadows Restaurant
203	☑	1,190.00	1/15/99	Roadhouse Restaurant
204	☑	1,055.00	1/15/99	Bridge Inn
205	☑	654.50	1/15/99	Grand River Restaurant
206	☑	1,392.50	1/15/99	Sandy Lookout Restaura
207	☑	1,604.50	1/15/99	Bunker Hill Grill
208	☑	1,784.00	1/15/99	Florentine Restaurante
209	☐	1,106.00	1/15/99	Cleo's Downtown Restau
210	☑	1,223.00	1/15/99	Bentham's Riverfront Res
212	☑	1,220.50	1/15/99	Mountain Lake Restaurai
213	☑	1,426.50	1/15/99	Best Bet Restaurant

Record: I◄ ◄   1   ► ►I ►* of 36

Barbara would like to see more fields and records on the screen at one time. She asks you to maximize the datasheet, change the datasheet's font size, and resize all the columns to their best fit.

Changing a Datasheet's Appearance

You can change the characteristics of a datasheet, including the font type and size of text in the datasheet, to improve its appearance or readability. You can also resize the datasheet columns to view more columns on the screen at the same time.

You'll maximize the datasheet, change the font size from the default 10 to 8, and then resize the datasheet columns.

To change the font size and resize columns in the datasheet:

1. Click the **Maximize** button 🔲 on the Query window title bar.

2. Click the **record selector** to the left of the field names at the top of the datasheet (see Figure 3-20). The entire datasheet is selected.

3. Click **Format** on the menu bar, and then click **Font** to open the Font dialog box.

4. Scroll the Size list box, click **8**, and then click the **OK** button. The font size for the entire datasheet changes to 8.

   Next you need to resize the columns to their best fit—that is, so each column is just wide enough to fit the longest value in the column.

5. Position the pointer in the OrderNum field selector. When the pointer changes to ↓, click to select the entire column.

6. Click the horizontal scroll right arrow until the Phone field is fully visible, and position the pointer in the Phone field selector until the pointer changes to ↓.

7. Press and hold the **Shift** key, and then click the mouse button. All the columns are selected. Now you can resize all of them at once.

8. Position the pointer at the right edge of the Phone field selector until the pointer changes to ↔. See Figure 3-21.

Figure 3-21 ◀
Preparing to resize all columns to their best fit

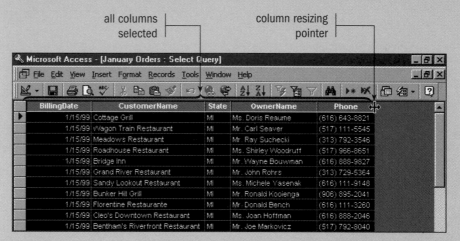

9. Double click the mouse button. All columns are resized to their best fit, which makes each column just large enough to fit the longest *visible* field value in the column, including the field name at the top of the column. Scroll through the datasheet and resize individual columns as needed to completely display all field values.

10. If necessary, scroll to the left so that the OrderNum field is visible, and then click any field value box to deselect all columns. See Figure 3-22.

Figure 3-22 ◀
Datasheet after changing font size and column widths

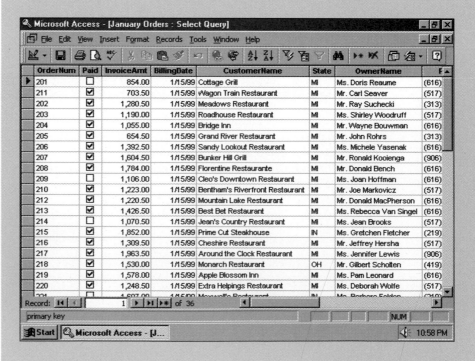

TROUBLE? Your screen might show more or fewer columns depending on the monitor you are using.

11. Click the **Save** button 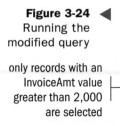 on the Query Datasheet toolbar, and then click the **Close** button ☒ on the menu bar. Access saves and closes the query, and you return to the Database window.

After viewing the query results, Barbara decides that she would like to see the same fields but only for those records whose InvoiceAmt exceeds $2,000. She wants to note this information and pass it along to her staff members so that they can contact those customers with higher outstanding invoices. To create the query needed to produce these results, you need to use a comparison operator to match a range of values—in this case, any InvoiceAmt value greater than $2,000.

Using a Comparison Operator to Match a Range of Values

Once you create and save a query, you can click the Open button to run it again, or you can click the Design button to change its design. Because the design of the query you need to create next is similar to the January Orders query, you will change its design, run the query to test it, and then save the query with a new name, keeping the January Orders query intact.

To change the January Orders query design to create a new query:

1. With the January Orders query selected in the Database window, click the **Design** button. Access opens the January Orders query in Design view.

2. Click the **InvoiceAmt Criteria** text box, type **>2000**, and then press the **Tab** key. See Figure 3-23.

Figure 3-23 ◀
Changing a
query's design
to create
a new query

new condition ⎯⎯⎯⎯⎯

condition to delete ⎯⎯⎯⎯⎯

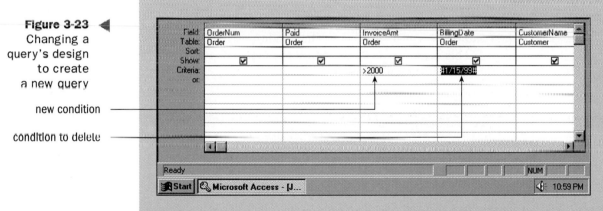

The new condition specifies that a record will be selected only if its InvoiceAmt field value exceeds 2000. Before you run the query, you need to delete the condition for the BillingDate field.

3. With the BillingDate field condition highlighted, press the **Delete** key. Access deletes the selected condition for the BillingDate field.

4. Click the **Run** button ⧉ on the Query Design toolbar. Access runs the query and displays the selected fields for only those records with an InvoiceAmt field value greater than 2000. A total of four records are selected. See Figure 3-24.

Figure 3-24 ◀
Running the
modified query

only records with an
InvoiceAmt value
greater than 2,000
are selected

Of the records retrieved, Barbara notes that order numbers 365 and 387 have not yet been paid and the amount of each. She gives this information to her staff.

So that Barbara can display this information again, as necessary, you'll save the query as High Invoice Amounts.

5. Click **File** on the menu bar, and then click **Save As/Export** to open the Save As dialog box.

6. Type **High Invoice Amounts** in the New Name text box, and then press the **Enter** key. Access saves the query using the new query name and displays the new query name in the datasheet window title bar.

7. Click the **Close** button ☒ on the menu bar. The Database window becomes the active window.

Leonard asks Barbara for a list of the orders billed on 1/15/99 that are still unpaid. He wants to know which customers are slow in paying their invoices. To produce this data, you need to create a query containing two conditions.

Defining Multiple Selection Criteria for Queries

Multiple conditions require you to use **logical operators** to combine two or more conditions. When you want a record selected only if two or more conditions are met, you need to use the **And logical operator**. In this case, Leonard wants to see only those records with a BillingDate field value of 1/15/99 *and* a Paid field value of No. If you place conditions in separate fields in the *same* Criteria row of the design grid, all the conditions in that row must be met in order for a record to be included in the query results. However, if you place conditions in *different* Criteria rows, Access selects a record if at least one of the conditions is met. If none of the conditions is met, then Access does not select the record. This is known as the **Or logical operator**. The difference between these two logical operators is illustrated in Figure 3-25.

Figure 3-25 ◀
Logical operators And and Or for multiple selection criteria

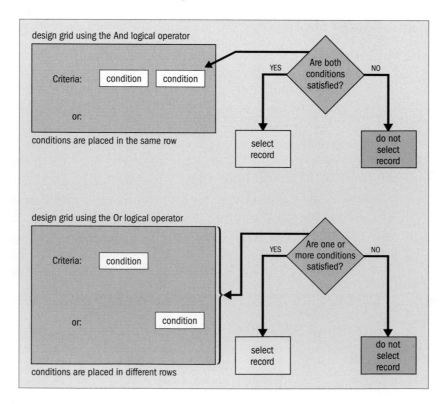

The And Logical Operator

To create the query, you need to modify the existing January Orders query to show only the unpaid orders billed on 1/15/99. For the modified query, you must add a second condition in the same Criteria row. The condition #1/15/99# for the BillingDate field finds records billed on the specified date, and the condition "No" in the Paid field finds records whose invoices have not been paid. Because the conditions appear in the same Criteria row, Access selects records only if both conditions are met.

After modifying the query, you'll save it and rename it as "Unpaid January Orders," overwriting the January Orders query, which Barbara no longer needs.

To modify the January Orders query and use the And logical operator:

1. In the Queries tab of the Database window, click **January Orders** and then click the **Design** button to open the query in Design view.

2. Click the **Paid Criteria** text box, type **no**, and then press the **Tab** key. See Figure 3-26.

Figure 3-26 ◀
Query to
find unpaid
January orders

And logical operator:
conditions entered
In the same row

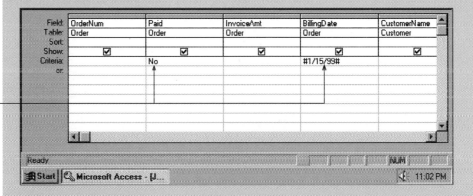

The condition for the BillingDate field is already entered, so you can run the query.

3. Click the **Run** button 🔃 on the Query Design toolbar. Access runs the query and displays in the datasheet only those records that meet both conditions: a BillingDate field value of 1/15/99 and a Paid field value of No. A total of six records are selected. See Figure 3-27.

Figure 3-27 ◀
Results of
query using the
And logical
operator

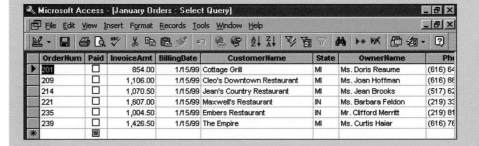

Now you can save the changes to the query and rename it.

4. Click the **Save** button 🔲 on the Query Datasheet toolbar, and then click the **Close** button ⊠ on the menu bar.

5. Right-click **January Orders** in the Queries list box, and then click **Rename** on the shortcut menu.

6. Click to position the insertion point to the left of the word "January," type **Unpaid**, press the **spacebar**, and then press the **Enter** key. The query name is now Unpaid January Orders.

Leonard also wants to determine which restaurant customers are most valuable to Valle Coffee. Specifically, he wants to see a list of those customers who have been placing orders for many years or who place orders for a substantial amount of money. He needs this information so that he can call the customers personally and thank them for their business. To create this query, you need to use the Or logical operator.

The Or Logical Operator

For Leonard's request, you need a query that selects records when either one of two conditions is satisfied or when both conditions are satisfied. That is, a record is selected if the FirstContact field value is less than 1/1/92 (to find those customers who have been doing business with Valle Coffee the longest) *or* if the InvoiceAmt field value is greater than 2000 (to find those customers who spend more money). You will enter the condition for the FirstContact field in one Criteria row and the condition for the InvoiceAmt field in another Criteria row.

To display the information Leonard wants to view, you'll create a new query containing the CustomerName, OwnerName, Phone, and FirstContact fields from the Customer table and the InvoiceAmt field from the Order table. Then you'll specify the conditions using the Or logical operator.

To create the query and use the Or logical operator:

1. From the Queries tab of the Database window, click the **New** button to open the New Query dialog box, click **Design View**, and then click the **OK** button. Access opens the Show Table dialog box on top of the Query window in Design view.

2. Click **Customer** in the Tables list box (if necessary), click the **Add** button, click **Order**, click the **Add** button, and then click the **Close** button. Access places the Customer and Order field lists in the Query window and closes the Show Table dialog box.

3. Double-click **CustomerName** in the Customer field list. Access places CustomerName in the design grid's first column Field text box.

4. Repeat Step 3 to add the **OwnerName**, **Phone**, and **FirstContact** fields from the Customer table, and then add the **InvoiceAmt** field from the Order table.

   Now you need to specify the first condition, <1/1/92, in the FirstContact field.

5. Click the **FirstContact Criteria** text box, type **<1/1/92** and then press the **Tab** key.

   Because you want records selected if either of the conditions for the FirstContact or InvoiceAmt fields is satisfied, you must enter the condition for the InvoiceAmt field in the "or" row of the design grid.

6. Press the ↓ key, and then type **>2000**. See Figure 3-28.

Figure 3-28 ◀
Query window
with the Or
logical operator

Or logical operator:
conditions entered
in different rows

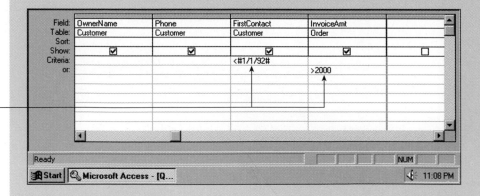

The query specifications are complete, so you can now run the query.

7. Click the **Run** button ⚡ on the Query Design toolbar. Access runs the query and displays only those records that meet either condition: a FirstContact field value less than 1/1/92 or an InvoiceAmt field value greater than 2000. A total of 35 records are selected.

    Leonard wants the list displayed in alphabetical order by CustomerName.

8. Click any visible CustomerName field value to establish this field as the current field, and then click the **Sort Ascending** button ⬇ on the Query Datasheet toolbar.

9. Resize all datasheet columns to their best fit. Be sure to scroll through the entire datasheet to make sure that all values are completely displayed. See Figure 3-29.

Figure 3-29 ◀
Results of
query using the
Or logical
operator

records with
FirstContact values
earlier than 1/1/92

records with
InvoiceAmt values
greater than 2,000

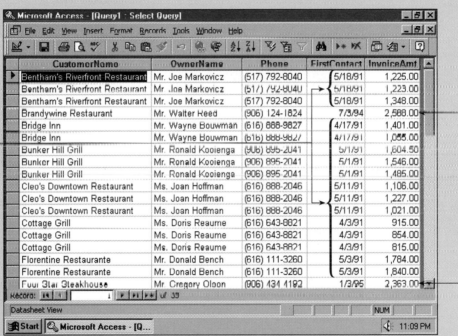

Now you'll save the query as Top Customers, print the query results, and then close the query.

10. Click the **Save** button 🖫 on the Query Datasheet toolbar, type **Top Customers** in the Query Name text box, and then press the **Enter** key. Access saves the query with the specified name in the Restaurant database.

11. Click the **Print** button 🖨 on the Query Datasheet toolbar to print the query results, and then click the **Close** button ☒ on the menu bar to close the query and return to the Database window.

Next, Leonard asks Barbara if the Restaurant database can be used to perform calculations. He is considering adding a 2% late charge to the unpaid invoices billed in January, and he wants to know exactly what these charges would be.

Performing Calculations

In addition to using queries to retrieve, sort, and filter data in a database, you can use a query to perform calculations. To perform a calculation, you define an **expression** containing a combination of database fields, constants, and operators. For numeric expressions, the data types of the database fields must be number, currency, or date/time; the constants are numbers such as .02 (for the 2% late charge); and the operators can be arithmetic operators (+ − * /) or other specialized operators. In complex expressions you can use parentheses ( ) to indicate which calculation should be performed first. In expressions without parentheses, Access calculates in the following order of precedence: multiplication and division before addition and subtraction. Access calculates operators that have equal precedence in order from left to right.

To perform a calculation in a query, you add a calculated field to the query. A **calculated field** is a field that displays the results of an expression. A calculated field appears in a query datasheet but does not exist in a database. When you run a query that contains a calculated field, Access evaluates the expression defined by the calculated field and displays the resulting value in the datasheet.

Creating a Calculated Field

To produce the information Leonard wants, you need to open the Unpaid January Orders query and create a calculated field that will multiply each InvoiceAmt field value by .02 to account for the 2% late charge Leonard is considering.

To enter an expression for a calculated field, you can type it directly in a Field text box in the design grid. Alternatively, you can open the Zoom box or Expression Builder and use either one to enter the expression. The **Zoom box** is a large text box for entering text, expressions, or other values. **Expression Builder** is an Access tool that contains an expression box for entering the expression, buttons for common operators, and one or more lists of expression elements, such as table and field names. Unlike a Field text box, which is too small to show an entire expression at one time, the Zoom box and Expression Builder are large enough to display lengthy expressions. In most cases Expression Builder provides the easiest way to enter expressions.

REFERENCE window	**USING EXPRESSION BUILDER**
	■ Display the query in Design view.
	■ In the design grid, position the insertion point in the Field text box of the field for which you want to create an expression.
	■ Click the Build button on the Query Design toolbar.
	■ Use the expression elements and common operators to build the expression.
	■ Click the OK button.

You'll begin by opening the Unpaid January Orders query in Design view and modifying it to show only the information Leonard wants to view.

To modify the Unpaid January Orders query:

1. In the Queries tab, click **Unpaid January Orders**, and then click the **Design** button.

Leonard wants to see only the OrderNum, CustomerName, and InvoiceAmt fields. So, you'll first delete the unnecessary fields, and then uncheck the Show boxes for the Paid and BillingDate fields. You need to keep these two fields in the query because they specify the conditions for the query; however, they do not have to be included in the query results.

2. Scroll the design grid to the right until the last three fields—State, OwnerName, and Phone—are visible.

3. Position the pointer on the State field until the pointer changes to ↓ , click and hold down the mouse button, drag the mouse to the right to highlight the State, OwnerName, and Phone fields, and then release the mouse button.

4. Press the **Delete** key to delete the three selected fields.

5. Scroll the design grid back to the left, click the **Show** check box for the Paid field to remove the check mark, and then click the **Show** check box for the BillingDate field to remove the check mark.

   Next, you'll move the InvoiceAmt field to the right of the CustomerName field so that the InvoiceAmt values will appear next to the calculated field values in the query results.

6. Make sure both the InvoiceAmt field and the empty field to the right of the CustomerName field are visible in the design grid.

7. Select the InvoiceAmt field, and then use the pointer ⛋ to drag the field to the right of the CustomerName field.

8. If necessary, scroll the design grid so that the empty field to the right of InvoiceAmt is visible, and then click anywhere in the design grid to deselect the InvoiceAmt field. See Figure 3-30.

Figure 3-30 ◀
Modified query
before adding
the calculated
field

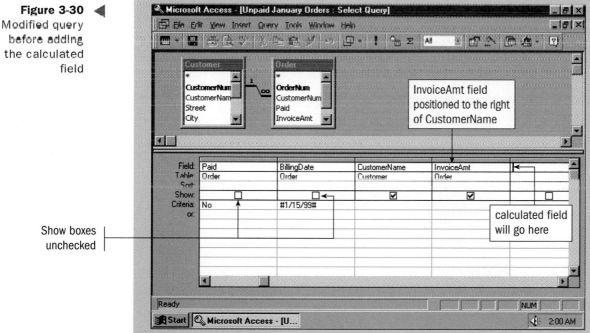

Show boxes
unchecked

Now you're ready to use Expression Builder to enter the calculated field in the Unpaid January Orders query.

To add the calculated field to the Unpaid January Orders query:

1. Position the insertion point in the Field text box to the right of the InvoiceAmt field, and then click the **Build** button ▦ on the Query Design toolbar. The Expression Builder dialog box opens. See Figure 3-31.

Figure 3-31 ◄
Initial
Expression
Builder dialog
box

expression box

expression elements

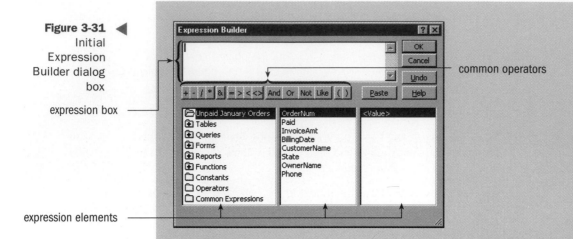

common operators

You use the common operators and expression elements to help you build an expression. Note that the Unpaid January Orders query is already selected in the list box on the bottom left; the fields included in the query are listed in the center box.

The expression for the calculated field will multiply the InvoiceAmt field values by the numeric constant .02 (which represents a 2% late charge). To include a field in the expression, you select the field and then click the Paste button. To include a numeric constant, you simply type the constant in the expression.

2. Click **InvoiceAmt** and then click the **Paste** button. Access places [InvoiceAmt] in the expression box.

To include the multiplication operator in the expression, you click the asterisk (*) button.

3. Click the * button in the row of common operators, and then type **.02**. You have completed the entry of the expression. See Figure 3-32.

Figure 3-32 ◄
Completed
expression for
the calculated
field

expression

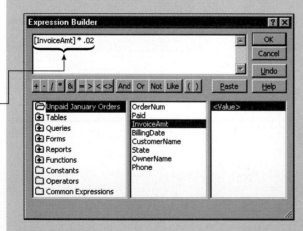

4. Click the **OK** button. Access closes the Expression Builder dialog box and adds the expression to the design grid.

Next, you need to specify a name for the calculated field as it will appear in the query results.

5. Press the **Home** key to position the insertion point to the left of the expression.

You'll enter the name LateCharge, which is descriptive of the field's contents; then you'll run the query.

6. Type **LateCharge:** Make sure you include the colon following the field name. The colon is used to separate the field name from its expression.

Now you can run the query.

7. Click the **Run** button 🔃 on the Query Design toolbar. Access runs the query and displays the query datasheet, which contains the three specified fields and the calculated field. See Figure 3-33.

Figure 3-33 ◀
Datasheet displaying the calculated field

specified name for calculated field

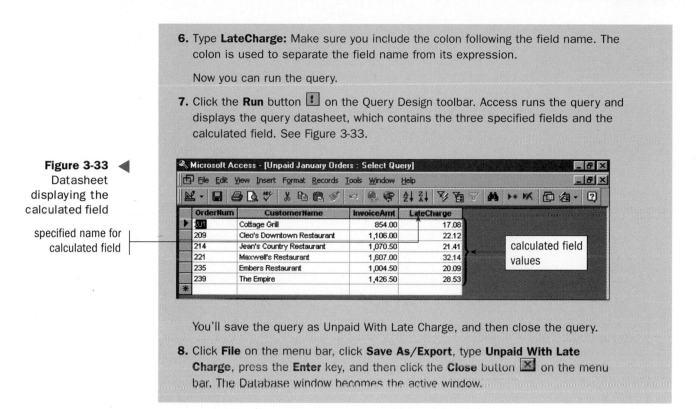

You'll save the query as Unpaid With Late Charge, and then close the query.

8. Click **File** on the menu bar, click **Save As/Export**, type **Unpaid With Late Charge**, press the **Enter** key, and then click the **Close** button ☒ on the menu bar. The Database window becomes the active window.

Barbara prepares a report of Valle Coffee's restaurant business for Leonard on a regular basis. The information in the report includes a summary of the restaurant orders. Barbara lists the total invoice amount for all orders, the average invoice amount, and the total number of orders. She asks you to create a query to determine these statistics from data in the Order table.

Using Aggregate Functions

You can calculate statistical information, such as totals and averages, on the records selected in a query. To do this, you use the Access aggregate functions. **Aggregate functions** perform arithmetic operations on selected records in a database. Figure 3-34 lists the most frequently used aggregate functions. Aggregate functions operate on the records that meet a query's selection criteria. You specify an aggregate function for a specific field, and the appropriate operation applies to that field's values for the selected records.

Figure 3-34 ◀
Frequently used aggregate functions

Aggregate Function	Determines	Data Types Supported
Avg	Average of the field values for the selected records	AutoNumber, Currency, Date/Time, Number
Count	Number of records selected	AutoNumber, Currency, Date/Time, Memo, Number, OLE Object, Text, Yes/No
Max	Highest field value for the selected records	AutoNumber, Currency, Date/Time, Number, Text
Min	Lowest field value for the selected records	AutoNumber, Currency, Date/Time, Number, Text
Sum	Total of the field values for the selected records	AutoNumber, Currency, Date/Time, Number

To display the total, average, and count of all the invoice amounts in the Order table, you will use the Sum, Avg, and Count aggregate functions for the InvoiceAmt field.

To calculate the total, average, and count of all invoice amounts:

1. Click the **New** button to open the New Query dialog box, click **Design View** (if necessary), and then click the **OK** button. Access opens the Show Table dialog box on top of the Query window in Design view.

2. Click **Order**, click the **Add** button, and then click the **Close** button. Access adds the Order field list to the top of the Query window and closes the dialog box.

   To perform the three calculations on the InvoiceAmt field, you need to add the field three times to the design grid.

3. Double-click **InvoiceAmt** in the Order field list three times to add three copies of the field to the design grid.

   You need to select an aggregate function for each InvoiceAmt field. When you click the Totals button on the Query Design toolbar, Access adds a row labeled "Total" to the design grid. The Total row provides a list of the aggregate functions that can be selected.

4. Click the **Totals** button [Σ] on the Query Design toolbar. Access inserts a row labeled "Total" between the Table and Sort rows in the design grid. See Figure 3-35.

Figure 3-35 ◀
Total row
inserted in the
design grid

Totals
button

Total row ──→

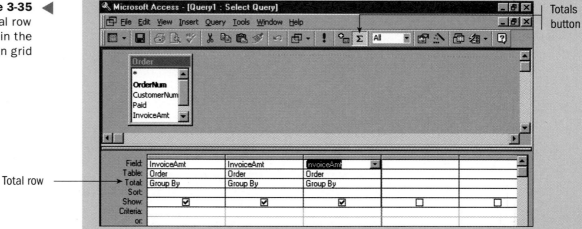

In the Total row, you specify the aggregate function you want to use for a field.

5. Click the right side of the first column's **Total** text box, and then click **Sum**. This field will calculate the total of all the InvoiceAmt field values.

   Access automatically assigns a datasheet column name of "SumOfInvoice Amount" for this field. You can change the datasheet column name to a more descriptive or readable name by entering the name you want in the Field text box. However, you must also keep InvoiceAmt in the Field text box because it identifies the field whose values will be summed. The Field text box will contain the datasheet column name you specify followed by the field name (InvoiceAmt) with a colon separating the two names.

6. Position the insertion point to the left of InvoiceAmt in the first column's Field text box, and then type **Total of Invoices:**. Be sure you include the colon at the end.

7. Click the right side of the second column's **Total** text box, and then click **Avg**. This field will calculate the average of all the InvoiceAmt field values.

8. Position the insertion point to the left of InvoiceAmt in the second column's Field text box, and then type **Average of Invoices:**.

9. Click the right side of the third column's **Total** text box, and then click **Count**. This field will calculate the total number of invoices (orders).

10. Position the insertion point to the left of InvoiceAmt in the third column's Field text box, and then type **Number of Invoices:**.

The query design is complete, so you can run the query.

11. Click the **Run** button [!] on the Query Design toolbar. Access runs the query and displays one record containing the three aggregate function values. The one row of summary statistics represents calculations based on the 104 records selected in the query.

You need to resize the three columns to their best fit to see the column names.

12. Resize each column by double-clicking the ✛ on the right edge of each column's field selector; then position the insertion point at the start of the field value in the first column. See Figure 3-36.

Figure 3-36 ◀
Results of the query using aggregate functions

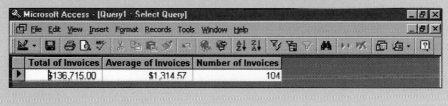

Total of Invoices	Average of Invoices	Number of Invoices
$136,715.00	$1,314.57	104

You'll save the query as Invoice Statistics.

13. Click the **Save** button [▦] on the Query Datasheet toolbar, type **Invoice Statistics**, and then press the **Enter** key.

Barbara's report to Leonard also includes the same invoice statistics (total, average, and count) for each month. Because Valle Coffee sends invoices to their restaurant customers once a month, each invoice in a month has the same billing date. Barbara asks you to display the invoice statistics for each different billing date in the Order table.

Using Record Group Calculations

In addition to calculating statistical information on all or selected records in selected tables, you can calculate statistics for groups of records. For example, you can determine the number of customers in each state or the total invoice amounts by billing date.

To create a query for Barbara's latest request, you can modify the current query by adding the BillingDate field and assigning the Group By operator to it. The **Group By operator** divides the selected records into groups based on the values in the specified field. Those records with the same value for the field are grouped together, and the datasheet displays one record for each group. Aggregate functions, which appear in the other columns of the design grid, provide statistical information for each group.

You need to modify the current query to add the Group By operator for the BillingDate field. This will display the statistical information grouped by billing date for the 104 selected records in the query.

To add the BillingDate field with the Group By operator, and then run the query:

1. Click the **View** button for Design view [▨] on the Query Datasheet toolbar to switch to Design view.

2. Scroll the Order field list, if necessary, and then double-click **BillingDate** to add the field to the design grid. Group By, which is the default option in the Total row, appears for the BillingDate field.

You've completed the query changes, so you can run the query.

3. Click the **Run** button 🔳 on the Query Design toolbar. Access runs the query and displays three records, one for each BillingDate group. Each record contains the three aggregate function values and the BillingDate field value for the group. Again, the summary statistics represent calculations based on the 104 records selected in the query. See Figure 3-37.

Figure 3-37 ◀
Aggregate
functions
grouped by
BillingDate

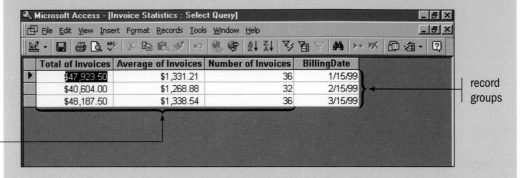

aggregate function
results

record
groups

You'll save the query as Invoice Statistics by Billing Date, and then close the query.

4. Click **File** on the menu bar, and then click **Save As/Export**.

5. Position the insertion point to the right of the last character in the New Name text box, press the **spacebar**, type **by Billing Date**, and then press the **Enter** key.

6. Click the **Close** button ⊠ on the menu bar. The Database window becomes the active window.

7. Click the **Close** button ⊠ on the Access window title bar to close the Restaurant database and to exit Access.

Quick Check

1. A(n) _____ is a criterion, or rule, that determines which records are selected for a query datasheet.

2. In the design grid, where do you place the conditions for two different fields when you use the And logical operator? The Or logical operator?

3. To perform a calculation in a query, you define a(n) _____ containing a combination of database fields, constants, and operators.

4. How does a calculated field differ from a table field?

5. What is an aggregate function?

6. The _____ operator divides selected records into groups based on the values in a field.

The queries you've created and saved will help Leonard, Barbara, Kim, and other employees monitor and analyze the business activity of Valle Coffee's restaurant customers. The queries can be run at any time, modified as needed, or used as the basis for designing new queries to meet additional information requirements.

Access

Tutorial Assignments

Barbara needs information from the Valle Products database, and she asks you to query the database by completing the following:

1. Make sure your Student Disk is in the disk drive, start Access, and then open the Valle Products database located in the TAssign folder on your Student Disk.

2. Create a select query based on the Product table. Display the ProductCode, WeightCode, and Price fields in the query results; sort in descending order based on the Price field values; and select only those records whose CoffeeCode value equals COLA. (*Hint:* Do not display the CoffeeCode field values in the query results.) Save the query as COLA Coffee, run the query, print the query datasheet, and then close the query.

3. Define a one-to-many relationship between the primary Coffee table and the related Product table, and then define a one-to-many relationship between the primary Weight table and the related Product table. (*Hint:* Add all three tables to the Relationships window, and then define the two relationships.) Select the referential integrity option and both cascade options for both relationships.

4. Create a select query based on the Coffee, Product, and Weight tables. Display the CoffeeType, CoffeeName, ProductCode, Price, and Weight/Size fields in that order. Sort in ascending order based on the CoffeeName field values. Select only those records whose CoffeeType equals "Special Import." Save the query as Special Imports, and then run the query. Resize all columns in the datasheet to fit the data. Print the datasheet and then close the query.

5. Create a query based on the Product table that shows all products that do not have a WeightCode field value of B, and whose Price field value is less than 30; display all fields except Decaf from the Product table. Save the query as Pricing, and then run the query.

6. Open the Pricing query in Design view. Create a calculated field named NewPrice that displays the results of increasing the Price values by 4%. Display the results in descending order by NewPrice. Save the query as New Prices, run the query, print the query datasheet, and then close the query.

7. Open the Special Imports query in Design view. Modify the query to display only those records with a CoffeeType field value of Special Import or with a Price field value greater than 50. Run the query, and then resize all columns in the datasheet to fit the data. Save the query as Special Imports Plus Higher Priced, print the query datasheet, and then close the query.

8. Create a new query based on the Product table. Use the Min and Max aggregate functions to find the lowest and highest values in the Price field. Name the two aggregate fields Lowest Price and Highest Price, respectively. Save the query as Lowest And Highest Prices, run the query, and then print the query datasheet.

9. Open the Lowest And Highest Prices query in Design view. Use the Show Table button on the Query Design toolbar to display the Show Table dialog box; then add the Weight table to the query. Modify the query so that the records are grouped by the Weight/Size field. Save the query as Lowest And Highest Prices By Weight/Size, run the query, print the query datasheet, and then close the query. Close the Valle Products database.

Case Problems

1. Ashbrook Mall Information Desk Sam Bullard wants to view specific information about jobs available at the Ashbrook Mall. He asks you to query the MallJobs database by completing the following:

1. Make sure your Student Disk is in the disk drive, start Access, and then open the MallJobs database located in the Cases folder on your Student Disk.

2. Define a one-to-many relationship between the primary Store table and the related Job table. Select the referential integrity option and both cascade options for the relationship.

3. Create a select query based on the Store and Job tables. Display the StoreName, Location, Position, and Hours/Week fields, in that order. Sort in ascending order based on the StoreName field values. Run the query, save the query as Store Jobs, and then print the datasheet.

4. Use Filter By Selection to temporarily display only those records with a Location field value of D1 in the Store Jobs query datasheet. Print the datasheet and then remove the filter.

5. Open the Store Jobs query in Design view. Modify the query to display only those records with a Position value of Clerk. Run the query, save the query as Clerk Jobs, and then print the datasheet.

6. Open the Clerk Jobs query in Design view. Modify the query to display only those records with a Position value of Clerk and with an Hours/Week value of 20-30. Run the query, save it with the same name, print the datasheet, and then close the query. Close the MallJobs database.

2. Professional Litigation User Services Raj Jawahir is completing an analysis of the payment history of PLUS clients. To help him find the information he needs, you'll query the Payments database by completing the following:

1. Make sure your Student Disk is in the disk drive, start Access, and then open the Payments database located in the Cases folder on your Student Disk.

2. Define a one-to-many relationship between the primary Firm table and the related Payment table. Select the referential integrity option and both cascade options for the relationship.

3. Create a select query based on the Firm and Payment tables. Display the Firm#, FirmName, AmtPaid, and DatePaid fields, in that order. Sort in descending order based on the AmtPaid field values. Select only those records whose AmtPaid is greater than 2,400.00. Save the query as Large Payments, and then run the query. Print the datasheet and then close the query.

4. For all payments on 6/2/99, display the Payment#, AmtPaid, DatePaid, and FirmName fields. Save the query as June 2 Payments, and then run the query. Switch to Design view, modify the query so that the DatePaid values do not appear in the query results, and then save the modified query. Run the query, print the query results, and then close the query.

5. For all firms that have Nancy Martinez as a PLUS account representative, display the FirmName, FirmContact, AmtPaid, and DatePaid fields. Save the query as Martinez Accounts, run the query, print the query results, and then close the query.

6. For all payments made on 6/11/99 or 6/12/99, display the DatePaid, AmtPaid, FirmName, and Firm# fields. Display the results in ascending order by DatePaid and then in descending order by AmtPaid. Save the query as Selected Dates, run the query, print the query datasheet, and then close the query.

7. Use the Payment table to display the highest, lowest, total, average, and count of the AmtPaid field for all payments. Then do the following:
   a. Specify column names of HighestPayment, LowestPayment, TotalPayments, AveragePayment, and #Payments. Save the query as Payment Statistics, and then run the query. Resize all datasheet columns to their best fit, and then print the query results.
   b. Change the query to display the same statistics by DatePaid. Save the query as Payment Statistics By Date, run the query, and then print the query results.
   c. Change the Payment Statistics By Date query to display the same statistics by DatePaid then by Deposit#. Save the query as Payment Statistics By Date By Deposit, print the query results using landscape orientation, and then close the query. Close the Payments database.

3. Best Friends Noah and Sheila Warnick want to find specific information about the Walk-A-Thons they conduct for Best Friends. You'll help them find the information in the Walks database by completing the following:

1. Make sure your Student Disk is in the disk drive, start Access, and then open the Walks database located in the Cases folder on your Student Disk.

2. Define a one-to-many relationship between the primary Walker table and the related Pledge table. Select the referential integrity option and both cascade options for the relationship.

3. For all walkers with a PledgeAmt field value of greater than 20, display the WalkerID, LastName, PledgeNo, and PledgeAmt fields. Sort the query in descending order by PledgeAmt. Save the query as Large Pledges, run the query, print the query datasheet, and then close the query.

4. For all walkers who pledged less than $10 or who pledged $5 per mile, display the Pledger, PledgeAmt, PerMile, LastName, and FirstName fields. Save the query as Pledged Or Per Mile, run the query, and then print the query datasheet. Change the query to select all walkers who pledged less than $10 and who pledged $5 per mile. Save the query as Pledged And Per Mile, and then run the query. Describe the results. Close the query.

5. For all pledges, display the Pledger, Distance, PerMile, and PledgeAmt fields. Save the query as Difference. Create a calculated field named CalcPledgeAmt that displays the results of multiplying the Distance and PerMile fields; then save the query. Create a second calculated field named Difference that displays the results of subtracting the CalcPledgeAmt field from the PledgeAmt field. Format the calculated fields as fixed with two decimal places. (*Hint:* Choose the Properties option on the shortcut menu for the selected fields.) Display the results in ascending order by PledgeAmt. Save the modified query, and then run the query. Resize all datasheet columns to their best fit, print the query results, and then close the query.

6. Use the Pledge table to display the total, average, and count of the PledgeAmt field for all pledges. Then do the following:
   a. Specify column names of TotalPledge, AveragePledge, and #Pledges.
   b. Change properties so that the values in the TotalPledge and AveragePledge columns display two decimal places and the fixed format. (*Hint:* Choose the Properties option on the shortcut menu for the selected field.)
   c. Save the query as Pledge Statistics, run the query, resize all datasheet columns to their best fit, and then print the query datasheet.
   d. Change the query to display the sum, average, and count of the PledgeAmt field for all pledges by LastName. (*Hint:* Use the Show Table button on the Query Design toolbar to add the Walker table to the query.) Save the query as Pledge Statistics By Walker, run the query, print the query datasheet, and then close the query. Close the Walks database.

4. Lopez Lexus Dealerships Maria and Hector Lopez want to analyze data about the cars and different locations for their Lexus dealerships. Help them query the Lexus database by completing the following:

1. Make sure your Student Disk is in the disk drive, start Access, and then open the Lexus database located in the Cases folder on your Student Disk.

2. Define a one-to-many relationship between the primary Locations table and the related Cars table. Select the referential integrity option and both cascade options for the relationship.

3. For all vehicles, display the Model, Year, LocationCode, and SellingPrice fields. Save the query as Car Info, and then run the query. Resize all datasheet columns to their best fit. In Datasheet view, sort the query results in ascending order by the SellingPrice field. Print the query datasheet, and then save and close the query.

4. For all vehicles manufactured in 1998, display the Model, Year, Cost, SellingPrice, and LocationName fields. Sort the query in descending order by Cost. Save the query as 1998 Cars, and then run the query. Modify the query to remove the display of the Year field values from the query results. Save the modified query, run the query, print the query datasheet, and then close the query.

5. For all vehicles located in Houston or with a transmission of A4, display the Model, Year, Cost, SellingPrice, Transmission, LocationCode, and LocationName fields. Save the query as Location Or Trans, run the query, and then print the query datasheet using landscape orientation. Change the query to select all vehicles located in Houston and with a transmission of A4. Save the query as Location And Trans, run the query, print the query datasheet in landscape orientation, and then close the query.

6. For all vehicles, display the Model, Year, Cost, and SellingPrice fields. Save the query as Profit. Then create a calculated field named Profit that displays the difference between the vehicle's selling price and cost. Display the results in descending order by Profit. Save the query, run the query, print the query datasheet, and then close the query.

7. Use the Cars table to determine the total cost, average cost, total selling price, and average selling price of all vehicles. Use the Index tab in online Help to look up the word "caption"; then choose the topic "Change a field name in a query." Read the displayed information, and then choose and read the subtopic "Display new field names by changing the Caption property." Close the Help window. Set the Caption property of the four fields to Total Cost, Average Cost, Total Selling Price, and Average Selling Price, respectively. Save the query as Car Statistics, run the query, resize all datasheet columns to their best fit, and then print the query datasheet. Revise the query to show the car statistics by LocationName. (*Hint:* Use the Show Table button on the Query Design toolbar to display the Show Table dialog box.) Set the Caption property of the LocationName field to Location. Save the revised query as Car Statistics By Location, run the query, print the query datasheet, and then close the query.

8. Use the Office Assistant to ask the following question: "How do I create a Top Values query?" Choose the topic "Display only the highest or lowest values in the query's results." Read the displayed information, and then close the Help window and the Office Assistant. Open the Profit query in Design view, and then modify the query to display only the top five values for the Profit field. Save the query as Top Profit, run the query, print the query datasheet, and then close the query. Close the Lexus database.

Creating Forms and Reports

Creating an Order Data Form, a Customer Orders Form, and a Customers and Orders Report

Access

Valle Coffee

CASE

Barbara Hennessey wants to continue to enhance the Restaurant database to make it easier for her office staff members and other Valle Coffee employees to find and maintain data. In particular, she wants the database to include a form for the Order table, similar to the Customer Data form, which is based on the Customer table. She also wants a form that shows data from both the Customer and Order tables at the same time, so that all the order information for each customer appears with the corresponding customer data, giving a complete picture of the restaurant customers and their orders.

In addition, Kim Carpenter would like a report showing customer and order data so that her marketing staff members have printed output to refer to when completing market analyses and planning strategies for selling to restaurant customers. She wants the information to be formatted attractively, perhaps including the Valle Coffee cup logo on the report for visual interest.

SESSION

4.1

In this session you will create a form using the Form Wizard, change a form's AutoFormat, navigate a form, find data using a form, print selected form records, and maintain table data using a form.

Creating a Form Using the Form Wizard

As you learned in Tutorial 1, a form is an object you use to maintain, view, and print records in a database. In Access, you can design your own forms or use Form Wizards to create them for you automatically.

Barbara asks you to create a new form her staff can use to view and maintain data in the Order table. In Tutorial 1, you used the AutoForm Wizard, which creates a form automatically using all the fields in the selected table or query, to create the Customer Data form. To create the form for the Order table, you'll use the Form Wizard. The **Form Wizard** allows you to choose some or all of the fields in the selected table or query, choose fields from other tables and queries, and display the chosen fields in any order on the form. You can also choose a style for the form.

To open the Restaurant database and activate the Form Wizard:

1. Place your Student Disk in the appropriate disk drive.

2. Start Access and open the Restaurant database located in the Tutorial folder on your Student Disk. The Restaurant database is displayed in the Access window.

3. Click the **Forms** tab in the Database window to select the tab. The Forms list includes the Customer Data form you created in Tutorial 1.

4. Click the **New** button in the Database window. The New Form dialog box opens.

5. Click **Form Wizard**, click the list arrow for choosing a table or query, click **Order** to select this table as the source for the form, and then click the **OK** button. The first Form Wizard dialog box opens. See Figure 4-1.

Figure 4-1 ◀
First Form
Wizard
dialog box

selected table ⟶

fields in the
selected table

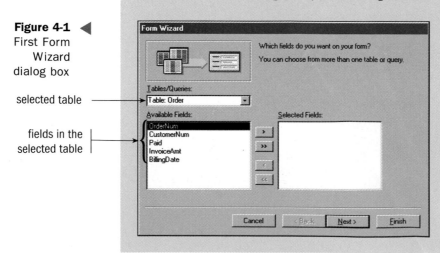

Barbara wants the form to display all the fields in the Order table, but in a different order. She would like the Paid field to be placed at the bottom of the form so that it stands out more, making it easier to determine if an order has been paid.

To finish creating the form using the Form Wizard:

1. Click **OrderNum** in the Available Fields list box (if necessary), and then click the ▸ button to move the field to the Selected Fields list box.

2. Repeat Step 1 to select the **CustomerNum**, **InvoiceAmt**, **BillingDate**, and **Paid** fields, in that order.

3. Click the **Next** button to display the second Form Wizard dialog box, in which you select a layout for the form. See Figure 4-2.

Figure 4-2 ◄
Choosing a
layout for
the form

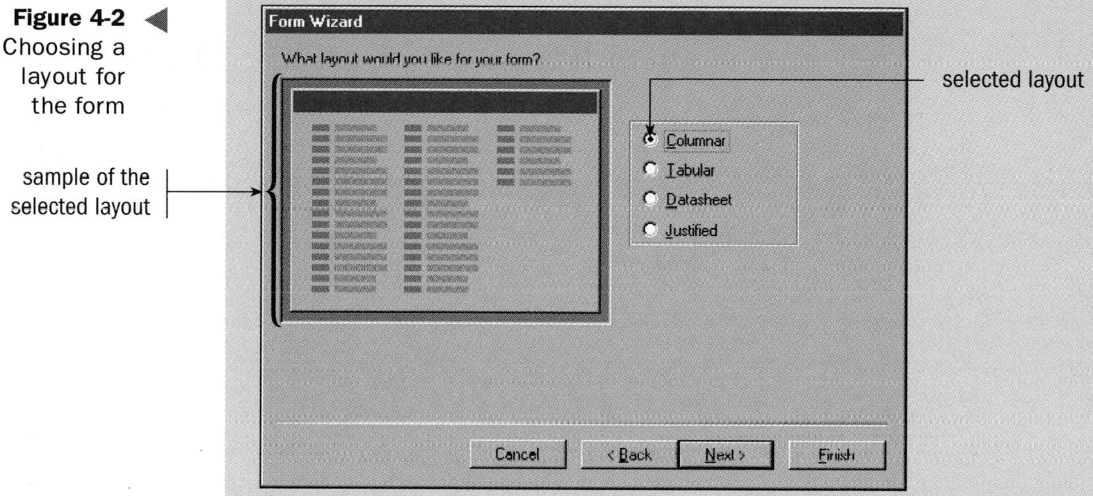

sample of the
selected layout

selected layout

The layout choices are columnar, tabular, datasheet, and justified. A sample of the selected layout appears on the left side of the dialog box.

4. Click each of the option buttons and review the corresponding sample layout.

The tabular and datasheet layouts display the fields from multiple records at one time, whereas the columnar and justified layouts display the fields from one record at a time. Barbara thinks the columnar layout is the appropriate arrangement for displaying and updating data in the table, so you'll choose this layout.

5. Click the **Columnar** option button (if necessary), and then click the **Next** button. Access displays the third Form Wizard dialog box, in which you choose a style for the form. See Figure 4-3.

Figure 4-3 ◄
Choosing a
style for
the form

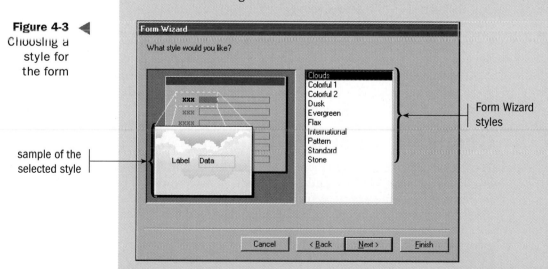

Form Wizard
styles

sample of the
selected style

A sample of the selected style appears in the box on the left. If you choose a style, which is called an *AutoFormat*, and decide you'd prefer a different one after the form is created, you can change it.

6. Click each of the styles and review the corresponding sample.

Barbara likes the Evergreen style and asks you to use it for the form.

7. Click **Evergreen** and then click the **Next** button. Access displays the final Form Wizard dialog box and shows the table name as the default for the form name and for the title that will appear in the form title bar. See Figure 4-4.

Figure 4-4 ◀
Final Form
Wizard
dialog box

option to
display the form

option to change
the form's design

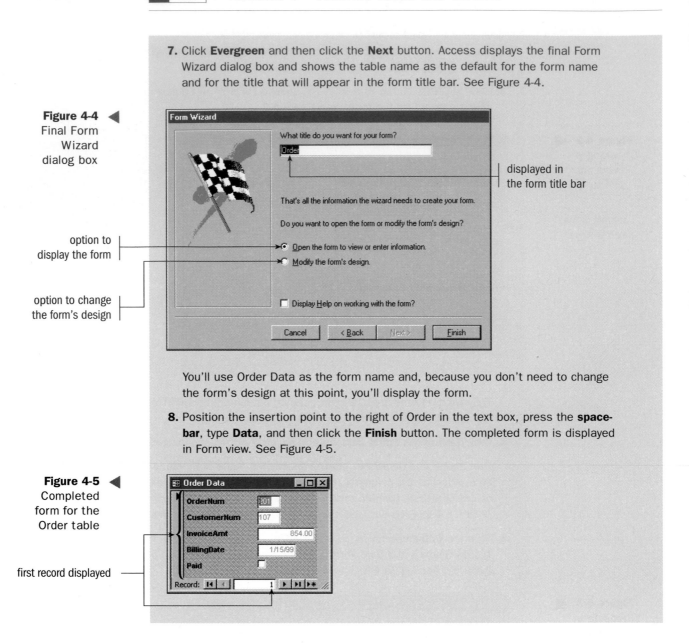

displayed in
the form title bar

You'll use Order Data as the form name and, because you don't need to change the form's design at this point, you'll display the form.

8. Position the insertion point to the right of Order in the text box, press the **space-bar**, type **Data**, and then click the **Finish** button. The completed form is displayed in Form view. See Figure 4-5.

Figure 4-5 ◀
Completed
form for the
Order table

first record displayed

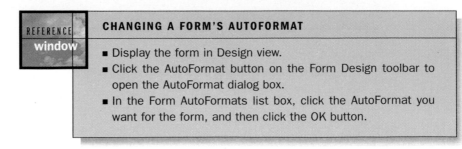

After viewing the form, Barbara decides that she doesn't like the form's style—the green background makes the field names difficult to read and the green type for the field values is too light. She asks you to change the form's style.

Changing a Form's AutoFormat

You can change a form's appearance by choosing a different AutoFormat for the form. As you learned when you created the Order Data form, an **AutoFormat** is a predefined style for a form (or report). The AutoFormats available for a form are the ones you saw when you selected the form's style using the Form Wizard. To change an AutoFormat, you must switch to Design view.

REFERENCE
window

CHANGING A FORM'S AUTOFORMAT

- Display the form in Design view.
- Click the AutoFormat button on the Form Design toolbar to open the AutoFormat dialog box.
- In the Form AutoFormats list box, click the AutoFormat you want for the form, and then click the OK button.

To change the AutoFormat for the Order Data form:

1. Click the **View** button for Design view 🔲 on the Form View toolbar. The form is displayed in Design view. See Figure 4-6.

Figure 4-6 ◄
Form displayed
in Design view

Form window

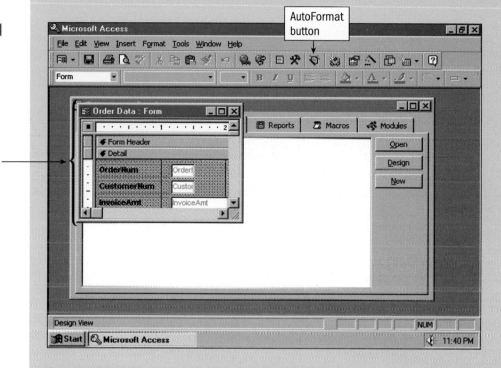

TROUBLE? If your screen displays any other windows than those shown in Figure 4-6, click the Close button 🗙 on the particular window's title bar to close it.

You use Design view to modify an existing form or to create a form from scratch. In this case, you need to change the AutoFormat for the Order Data form.

2. Click the **AutoFormat** button 🔲 on the Form Design toolbar. The AutoFormat dialog box opens.

3. Click the **Options** button to display the AutoFormat options. See Figure 4-7.

Figure 4-7 ◄
AutoFormat
dialog box

AutoFormats
for forms

AutoFormat options

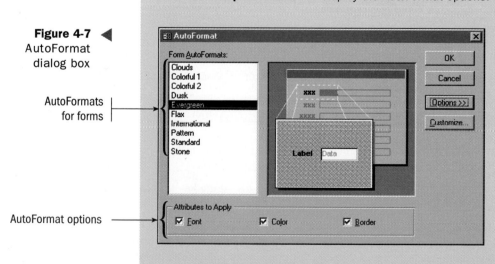

A sample of the selected AutoFormat appears to the right of the Form AutoFormats list box. The options at the bottom of the dialog box allow you to apply the selected AutoFormat or just its font, color, or border.

Barbara decides that she prefers the Standard AutoFormat, because its field names and field values are easy to read.

4. Click **Standard** in the Form AutoFormats list box, and then click the **OK** button. The AutoFormat dialog box closes, the AutoFormat is applied to the form, and the Form window in Design view becomes the active window.

5. Click the **View** button for Form view 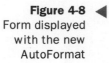 on the Form Design toolbar. The form is displayed in Form view with the new AutoFormat. See Figure 4-8.

Figure 4-8 ◀
Form displayed
with the new
AutoFormat

You have finished modifying the format of the form and can now save it.

6. Click the **Save** button 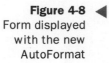 on the Form View toolbar to save the modified form.

Barbara wants to view some data in the Order table using the form. To view data, you need to navigate through the form.

Navigating a Form

To maintain and view data using a form, you must know how to move from field to field and from record to record. The mouse movement, selection, and placement techniques to navigate a form are the same techniques you've used to navigate a table datasheet and the Customer Data form you created in Tutorial 1. Also, the navigation mode and editing mode keystroke techniques are the same as those you used previously for datasheets (see Figure 2-29).

To navigate through the form:

1. Press the **Tab** key to move to the CustomerNum field value, and then press the **End** key to move to the Paid field. Because the Paid field is a yes/no field, its value is not highlighted; instead, a dashed box appears around the field name to indicate it is the current field.

2. Press the **Home** key to move back to the OrderNum field value. The first record in the Order table still appears in the form.

3. Press **Ctrl** + **End** to move to the Paid field in record 104, which is the last record in the table. The record number for the current record appears between the navigation buttons at the bottom of the form.

4. Click the **Previous Record** navigation button to move to the Paid field in record 103.

5. Press the ↑ key twice to move to the InvoiceAmt field value in record 103.

6. Position the insertion point between the numbers "2" and "6" in the InvoiceAmt field value to switch to editing mode, press the **Home** key to move the insertion point to the beginning of the field value, and then press the **End** key to move the insertion point to the end of the field value.

7. Click the **First Record** navigation button to move to the InvoiceAmt field value in the first record. The entire field value is highlighted because you have switched from editing mode to navigation mode.

8. Click the **Next Record** navigation button to move to the InvoiceAmt field value in record 2, which is the next record.

Barbara asks you to display the records for Jean's Country Restaurant, whose customer number is 407, because she wants to review the orders for this customer.

Finding Data Using a Form

The **Find** command allows you to search the data in a form and to display only those records you want to view. You choose a field to serve as the basis for the search by making that field the current field; then you enter the value you want Access to match in the Find in field dialog box. You can use the Find command for a form or datasheet, and you can activate the command from the Edit menu or by clicking the toolbar Find button.

REFERENCE
window

FINDING DATA

- On a form or datasheet, click anywhere in the field value you want to search.
- Click the Find button on the toolbar to open the Find in field dialog box.
- In the Find What text box, type the field value you want to find.
- Complete the remaining options, as necessary, to specify the type of search you want Access to perform.
- Click the Find First button to have Access begin the search at the beginning of the table, or click the Find Next button to begin the search at the current record.
- Click the Find Next button to continue the search for the next match.
- Click the Close button to stop the search operation.

You need to find all records in the Order table for Jean's Country Restaurant, whose customer number is 407.

To find the records using the Order Data form:

1. Position the insertion point in the CustomerNum field value box. This is the field for which you will find matching values.

2. Click the **Find** button 🔍 on the Form View toolbar to open the Find in field dialog box. Note that the title bar of the dialog box specifies the name of the field that Access will search, in this case, the CustomerNum field.

3. If the Find in field dialog box covers any part of the form, move the dialog box by dragging its title bar. See Figure 4-9.

Figure 4-9 ◀
Find in field
dialog box

current field

type search
value here

search options

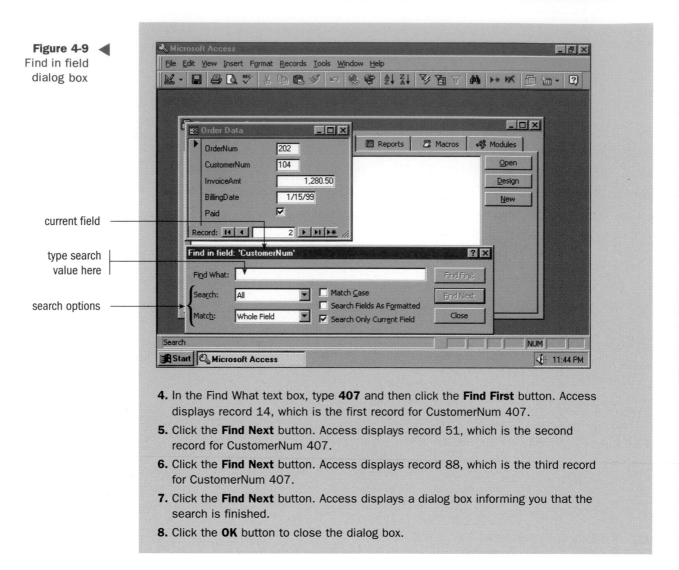

4. In the Find What text box, type **407** and then click the **Find First** button. Access displays record 14, which is the first record for CustomerNum 407.

5. Click the **Find Next** button. Access displays record 51, which is the second record for CustomerNum 407.

6. Click the **Find Next** button. Access displays record 88, which is the third record for CustomerNum 407.

7. Click the **Find Next** button. Access displays a dialog box informing you that the search is finished.

8. Click the **OK** button to close the dialog box.

The search value you enter can be an exact value, such as the customer number 407 you just entered, or it can include wildcard characters. A **wildcard character** is a placeholder you use when you know only part of a value or when you want to start or end with a specific character or match a certain pattern. Figure 4-10 shows the wildcard characters you can use when finding data.

Figure 4-10 ◀
Wildcard
characters

Wildcard Character	Purpose	Example
*	Match any number of characters. It can be used as the first and/or last character in the character string.	th* finds *the, that, this, therefore,* and so on
?	Match any single alphabetic character.	a?t finds *act, aft, ant,* and *art*
[ ]	Match any single character within the brackets.	a[fr]t finds *aft* and *art* but not *act* and *ant*
!	Match any character not within brackets.	a[!fr]t finds *act* and *ant* but not *aft* and *art*
-	Match any one of a range of characters. The range must be in ascending order (a to z, not z to a).	a[d-p]t finds aft and ant but not act and art
#	Match any single numeric character.	#72 finds *072, 172, 272, 372,* and so on

To check if their orders have been paid, Barbara wants to view the order records for two customers: Cheshire Restaurant (CustomerNum 515) and Around the Clock Restaurant (CustomerNum 597). You'll use the * wildcard character to search for these customers' orders.

To find the records using the * wildcard character:

1. Double-click **407** in the Find What text box to select the entire value, and then type **5***.

   Access will match any field value in the CustomerNum field that starts with the digit 5.

2. Click the **Find First** button. Access displays record 16, which is the first record for CustomerNum 515. Note that the Paid field value is checked, indicating that this order has been paid.

3. Click the **Find Next** button. Access displays record 17, which is the first record for CustomerNum 597.

4. Click the **Find Next** button. Access displays record 39, which is the second record for CustomerNum 597.

5. Click the **Find Next** button. Access displays record 68, which is the second record for CustomerNum 515.

6. Click the **Find Next** button. Access displays record 82, which is the third record for CustomerNum 515.

7. Click the **Find Next** button. Access displays a dialog box informing you that the search is finished.

8. Click the **OK** button to close the dialog box.

9. Click the **Close** button to close the Find in field dialog box.

All five orders have been paid, but Barbara wants to make sure Valle Coffee has a record of payment for order number 375. She asks you to print the data displayed on the form for record 82, which is for order number 375, so she can ask a staff member to look for the payment record for this order.

Previewing and Printing Selected Form Records

Access prints as many form records as can fit on a printed page. If only part of a form record fits on the bottom of a page, the remainder of the record prints on the next page. Access allows you to print all pages or a range of pages. In addition, you can print the currently selected form record.

Before printing record 82, you'll preview the form record to see how it will look when printed.

To preview the form and print the data for record 82:

1. Make sure record 82 is the current record in the Order Data form.

2. Click the **Print Preview** button on the Form View toolbar. The Print Preview window opens, showing the form records for the Order table in miniature.

3. Click the **Maximize** button on the form title bar.

4. Click the **Zoom** button on the Print Preview toolbar, and then use the vertical scroll bar to view the contents of the window. See Figure 4-11.

Figure 4-11 ◀
Print Preview
window
displaying
form records

Zoom button

form records

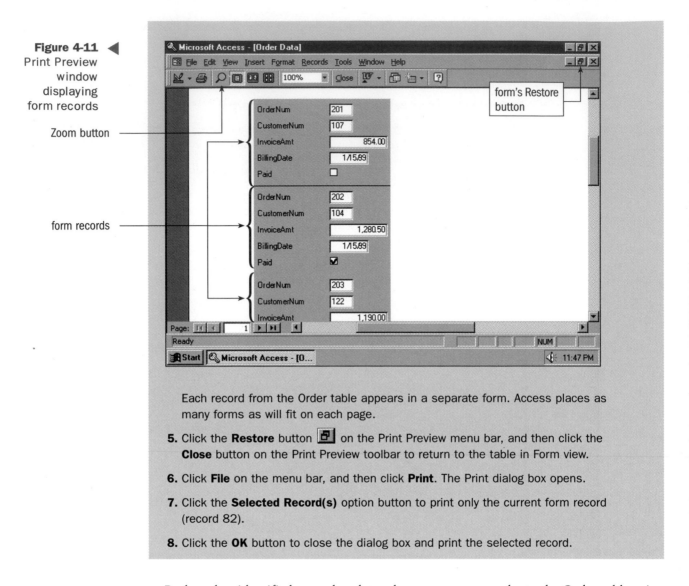

Each record from the Order table appears in a separate form. Access places as many forms as will fit on each page.

5. Click the **Restore** button 🔲 on the Print Preview menu bar, and then click the **Close** button on the Print Preview toolbar to return to the table in Form view.

6. Click **File** on the menu bar, and then click **Print**. The Print dialog box opens.

7. Click the **Selected Record(s)** option button to print only the current form record (record 82).

8. Click the **OK** button to close the dialog box and print the selected record.

Barbara has identified several updates she wants you to make to the Order table using the Order Data form, as shown in Figure 4-12.

Figure 4-12 ◀
Updates to the
Order table

Order Number	Update Action
319	Change InvoiceAmt to 1,175.00 Change Paid to Yes
392	Delete record
400	Add new record for CustomerNum 135, InvoiceAmt of 1,350.00, BillingDate of 3/15/99, and Paid status of No

Maintaining Table Data Using a Form

Maintaining data using a form is often easier than using a datasheet, because you can concentrate on all the changes required to a single record at a time. You already know how to navigate a form and find specific records. Now you'll make the changes Barbara requested to the Order table using the Order Data form.

First, you'll update the record for OrderNum 319.

To change the record using the Order Data form:

1. Make sure the Order Data form is displayed in Form view.

   The current record number appears between the sets of navigation buttons at the bottom of the form. If you know the number of the record you want to change, you can type the number and press the Enter key to go directly to the record. When she reviewed the order data to identify possible corrections, Barbara noted that 48 is the record number for order number 319.

2. Select the number 82 that appears between the navigation buttons, type **48**, and then press the **Enter** key. Record 48 is now the current record.

   You need to change the InvoiceAmt field value to 1,175.00 and the Paid field value to Yes for this record.

3. Position the insertion point between the numbers 9 and 5 in the InvoiceAmt field value, press the **Backspace** key, and then type **7**. Note that the pencil symbol appears in the top left of the form, indicating that the form is in editing mode.

4. Press the **Tab** key twice to move to the Paid field value, and then press the **spacebar** to insert a check mark in the check box. See Figure 4-13

Figure 4-13 ◀
Order record
after changing
field values

indicates
editing mode

field values changed

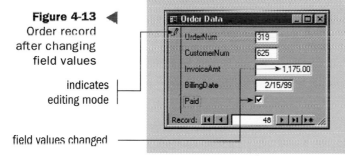

You have completed the changes for order number 319. Barbara's next update is to delete the record for order number 392. The customer who placed this order canceled it before the order was filled and processed.

To delete the record using the Order Data form:

1. Click anywhere in the OrderNum field value to make it the current field.

2. Click the **Find** button 🔍 on the Form View toolbar. The Find in field dialog box opens.

3. Type **392** in the Find What text box, click the **Find First** button, and then click the **Close** button. The record for order number 392 is now the current record.

   To delete the record, you first need to select the entire record by clicking anywhere in the large rectangular area surrounding the record selector.

4. Click the **record selector** in the top left of the form to select the entire record. See Figure 4-14.

Figure 4-14 ◀
Entire record
selected

click to select
the entire record

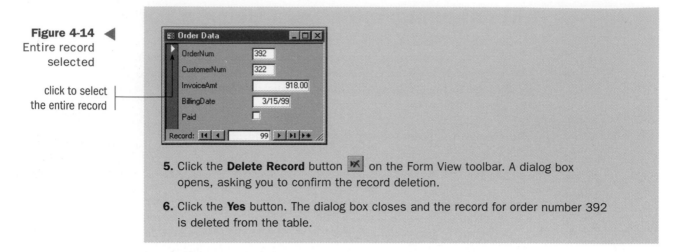

5. Click the **Delete Record** button ⊠ on the Form View toolbar. A dialog box opens, asking you to confirm the record deletion.

6. Click the **Yes** button. The dialog box closes and the record for order number 392 is deleted from the table.

Barbara's final maintenance change is to add a record for a new order placed by Topview Restaurant.

To add the new record using the Order Data form:

1. Click the **New Record** button ▶* on the Form View toolbar. Record 104, the next record available for a new record, becomes the current record. All field value boxes are empty, and the insertion point is positioned at the beginning of the field value for OrderNum.

2. Refer to Figure 4-15 and enter the value shown for each field, pressing the Tab key to move from field to field.

Figure 4-15 ◀
Completed
form for the
new record

> **TROUBLE?** Compare your screen with Figure 4-15. If any field value is wrong, correct it now using the methods described earlier for editing field values.

3. After entering the value for BillingDate, press the **Tab** key twice (if necessary). Record 105, the next record available for a new record, becomes the current record, and the record for order number 400 is saved in the Order table.

You've completed Barbara's changes to the Order table, so you can close the Order Data form.

4. Click the **Close** button ⊠ on the form title bar. The form closes and you return to the Database window. Notice that the Order Data form is listed in the Forms list box.

Quick Check

1 Describe the difference between creating a form using the AutoForm Wizard and creating a form using the Form Wizard.

2 What is an AutoFormat, and how do you change one for an existing form?

3. Which table record is displayed in a form when you press Ctrl + End?

4. You can use the Find command to search for data in a form or _____.

5. Which wildcard character matches any single alphabetic character?

6. How many form records does Access print by default on a page?

7. How do you select an entire form record?

The Order Data form will enable Barbara and her staff to enter and maintain data easily in the Order table. In the next session, you'll create another form for working with data in both the Order and Customer tables at the same time. You'll also create a report showing data from both tables.

SESSION 4.2

In this session you will create a form with a main form and a subform, create a report using the Report Wizard, insert a picture on a report, preview and print a report, and compact a database.

Barbara would like you to create a form so that she can view the data for each customer and all the orders for the customer at the same time. The type of form you need to create will include a main form and a subform.

Creating a Form with a Main Form and a Subform

To create a form based on two tables, you must first define a relationship between the two tables. In Tutorial 3, you defined a one-to-many relationship between the Customer (primary) and Order (related) tables, so you are ready to create the form based on both tables.

When you create a form containing data from two tables that have a one-to-many relationship, you actually create a main form for data from the primary table and a subform for data from the related table. Access uses the defined relationship between the tables to automatically join the tables through the common field that exists in both tables.

Barbara and her staff will use the form when contacting customers about the status of their order payments. Consequently, the main form will contain the customer number and name, owner name, and phone number; the subform will contain the order number, paid status, invoice amount, and billing date.

You'll use the Form Wizard to create the form.

To activate the Form Wizard to create the form:

1. If you took a break after the previous session, make sure that Access is running, the Restaurant database is open, and the Forms tab is displayed in the Database window, and then click the **New** button. The New Form dialog box opens.

   When creating a form based on two tables, you first choose the primary table and select the fields you want to include in the main form; then you choose the related table and select fields from it for the subform.

2. Click **Form Wizard**, click the list arrow for choosing a table or query, click **Customer** to select this table as the source for the main form, and then click the **OK** button. The first Form Wizard dialog box opens, in which you select fields in the order you want them to appear on the main form.

   Barbara wants the form to include only the CustomerNum, CustomerName, OwnerName, and Phone fields from the Customer table.

3. Click **CustomerNum** in the Available Fields list box (if necessary), and then click the [>] button to move the field to the Selected Fields list box.

4. Repeat Step 3 for the **CustomerName**, **OwnerName**, and **Phone** fields.

The CustomerNum field will appear in the main form, so you do not have to include it in the subform. Otherwise, Barbara wants the subform to include all the fields from the Order table.

5. Click the **Tables/Queries** list arrow, and then click **Table: Order**. The fields from the Order table appear in the Available Fields list box. The quickest way to add the fields you want to include is to move all the fields to the Selected Fields list box, and then remove only the field you don't want to include (CustomerNum).

6. Click the [>>] button to move all the fields from the Order table to the Selected Fields list box.

7. Click **Order.CustomerNum** in the Selected Fields list box, and then click the [<] button to move the field back to the Available Fields list box. Note that the table name (Order) is included in the field name to distinguish it from the same field (CustomerNum) in the Customer table.

8. Click the **Next** button. The next Form Wizard dialog box opens. See Figure 4-16.

Figure 4-16 ◀
Choosing a
main/subform
format

primary table ——

related table ——

option for a form
with a subform

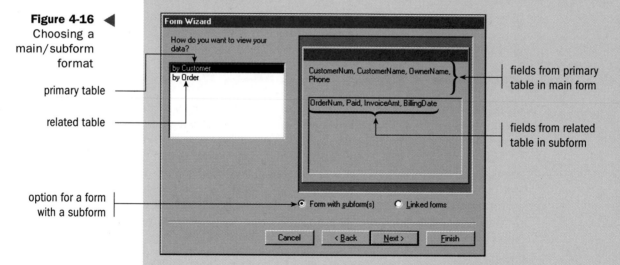

fields from primary
table in main form

fields from related
table in subform

In this dialog box, the list box on the left shows the order in which you will view the selected data: first by data from the Customer table (primary table), then by data from the Order table (related table). The form will be displayed as shown in the right side of the dialog box, with the fields from the Customer table at the top in the main form, and the fields from the Order table at the bottom in the subform. The selected option button specifies a main form with a subform.

The default options shown in Figure 4-16 are correct for creating a form with Customer data in the main form and Order data in the subform.

To finish creating the form:

1. Click the **Next** button. The next Form Wizard dialog box opens, in which you choose the subform layout.

The tabular layout displays subform fields as a table, whereas the datasheet layout displays subform fields as a table datasheet. The layout choice is a matter of personal preference. You'll use the datasheet layout.

2. Click the **Datasheet** option button (if necessary), and then click the **Next** button. The next Form Wizard dialog box opens, in which you choose the form's AutoFormat.

   Barbara wants all forms to have the same style, so you will choose the Standard AutoFormat, which is the same AutoFormat you used to create the Order Data form earlier.

3. Click **Standard** (if necessary) and then click the **Next** button. The next Form Wizard dialog box opens, in which you choose names for the main form and the subform.

   You will use Customer Orders as the main form name and Order Subform as the subform name.

4. Position the insertion point to the right of the last letter in the Form text box, press the **spacebar**, and then type **Orders**. The main form name is now Customer Orders. Note that the default subform name, Order Subform, is the name you want, so you don't need to change it.

   You have answered all the Form Wizard questions.

5. Click the **Finish** button. The completed form is displayed in Form view.

   Notice that some columns in the subform are not wide enough to display the field names entirely. You need to resize the columns to their best fit.

6. Double-click the pointer ↔ at the right edge of each column in the subform. The columns are resized to their best fit and all field names are fully displayed. See Figure 4-17.

Figure 4-17
Completed form

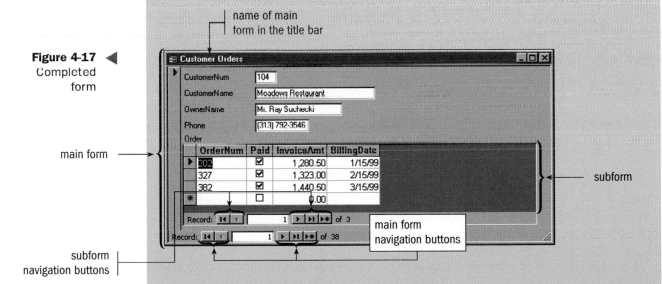

In the main form, Access displays the fields from the first record in the Customer table in columnar format. The records in the main form appear in primary key sequence by customer number. Customer 104 has three related records in the Order table; these records are shown at the bottom in a datasheet format. The form shows that Meadows Restaurant has placed three orders with Valle Coffee, and each order has been paid.

Two sets of navigation buttons appear near the bottom of the form. You use the top set of navigation buttons to select records from the related table in the subform and the bottom set to select records from the primary table in the main form.

You'll use the navigation buttons to view different records.

To navigate to different main form and subform records:

1. Click the **Last Record** navigation button ▶❘ in the main form. Record 38 in the Customer table for Embers Restaurant becomes the current record in the main form. The subform shows that this customer placed three orders with Valle Coffee, all of which are unpaid.

2. Click the **Last Record** navigation button ▶❘ in the subform. Record 3 in the Order table becomes the current record in the subform.

3. Click the **Previous Record** navigation button ◀ in the main form. Record 37 in the Customer table for The Empire becomes the current record in the main form. This customer has placed two orders, both of which are unpaid.

   You have finished your work with the form, so you can close it.

4. Click the **Close** button ✕ on the form title bar. The form closes, and you return to the Database window. Notice that both the main form, Customer Orders, and the subform, Order Subform, appear in the Forms list box.

Kim would like a report showing data from both the Customer and Order tables so that all the pertinent information about restaurant customers and their orders is available in one place.

Creating a Report Using the Report Wizard

As you learned in Tutorial 1, a report is a formatted hardcopy of the contents of one or more tables in a database. In Access, you can create your own reports or use the Report Wizard to create them for you. Like the Form Wizard, the **Report Wizard** asks you a series of questions and then creates a report based on your answers. Whether you use the Report Wizard or design your own report, you can change the report's design after you create it.

Kim wants you to create a report that includes selected customer data from the Customer table and all the orders from the Order table for each customer. Kim sketched a design of the report she wants (Figure 4-18). Like the Customer Orders form you just created, which includes a main form and a subform, the report will be based on both tables, which are joined in a one-to-many relationship through the common field of CustomerNum. As shown in the sketch in Figure 4-18, the selected customer data from the primary Customer table includes the customer number, name, city, state, owner name, and phone. Below the data for each customer, the report will include the order number, paid status, invoice amount, and billing date from the related Order table. The set of field values for each order is called a **detail record**.

Access

Figure 4-18 ◀
Report sketch
for the
Customers and
Orders report

fields from Customer
table: primary table

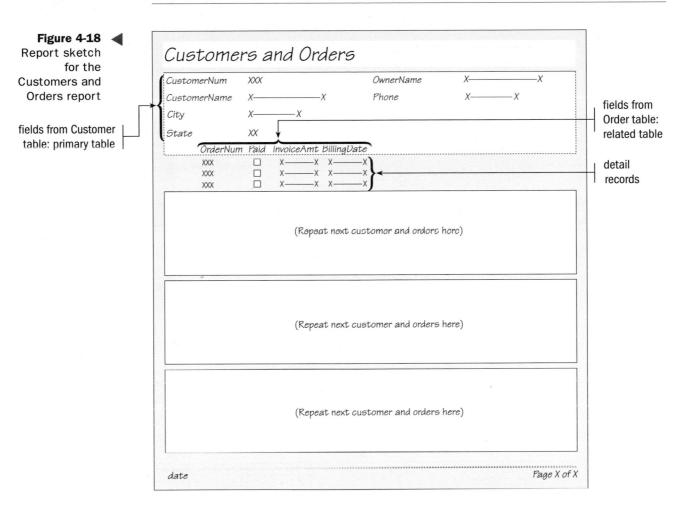

fields from
Order table:
related table

detail
records

You'll use the Report Wizard to create the report according to the design in Kim's sketch.

To activate the Report Wizard and select the fields to include in the report:

1. Click the **Reports** tab in the Database window to display the Reports list box. You have not created and saved any reports, so the list box is empty.

2. Click the **New** button in the Database window. The New Report dialog box opens.

   Although the data for the report exists in two tables (Customer and Order), you can choose only one table or query to be the data source for the report in the New Report dialog box. However, in the Report Wizard dialog boxes you can include data from other tables. You will select the primary Customer table in the New Report dialog box.

3. Click **Report Wizard**, click the list arrow for choosing a table or query, and then click **Customer**. See Figure 4-19.

Figure 4-19 ◄
Completed
New Report
dialog box

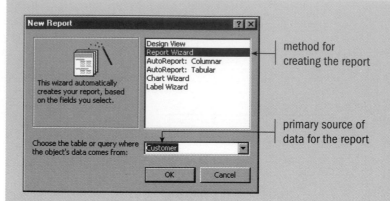

method for
creating the report

primary source of
data for the report

4. Click the **OK** button. The first Report Wizard dialog box opens.

   In the first Report Wizard dialog box, you select fields in the order you want them to appear on the report. Kim wants the CustomerNum, CustomerName, City, State, OwnerName, and Phone fields from the Customer table to appear on the report.

5. Click **CustomerNum** in the Available Fields list box, and then click the ▸ button. The field moves to the Selected Fields list box.

6. Repeat Step 5 for **CustomerName**, **City**, **State**, **OwnerName**, and **Phone**.

7. Click the **Tables/Queries** list arrow, and then click **Table: Order**. The fields from the Order table appear in the Available Fields list box.

   The CustomerNum field will appear on the report with the customer data, so you do not have to include it in the detail records for each order. Otherwise, Kim wants all the fields from the Order table to be included in the report. The easiest way to include the necessary fields is to add all the Order table fields to the Selected Fields list box and then to remove the only field you don't want to include—CustomerNum.

8. Click the ▸▸ button to move all the fields from the Available Fields list box to the Selected Fields list box.

9. Click **Order.CustomerNum** in the Selected Fields list box, click the ◂ button to move the selected field back to the Available Fields list box, and then click the **Next** button. The second Report Wizard dialog box opens. See Figure 4-20.

Figure 4-20 ◄
Choosing a
grouped or
ungrouped
report

grouped by table —

click to display
tips and examples —

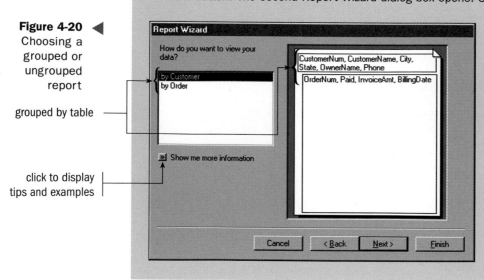

Access

You can choose to arrange the selected data grouped by table, which is the
default, or ungrouped. For a grouped report, the data from a record in the primary
table appears as a group, followed by the joined records from the related table.
For the report you are creating, data from a record in the Customer table appears
in a group, followed by the records for the customer from the Order table. An
example of an ungrouped report would be a report of records from the Customer
and Order tables in order by OrderNum. Each order and its associated customer
data would appear together; the data would not be grouped by table.

You can display tips and examples for the choices in the Report Wizard dialog box by
clicking the ⟩⟩ button ("Show me more information").

To display tips about the options in the Report Wizard dialog box:

1. Click the ⟩⟩ button. The Report Wizard Tips dialog box opens. Read the
   displayed information in the dialog box.

   You can display examples of different grouping methods by clicking the ⟩⟩ button
   ("Show me examples").

2. Click the ⟩⟩ button. The Report Wizard Examples dialog box opens. See
   Figure 4-21.

Figure 4-21 ◄
Report Wizard
Examples
dialog box

click to
display examples

click to return to
Report Wizard Tips
dialog box

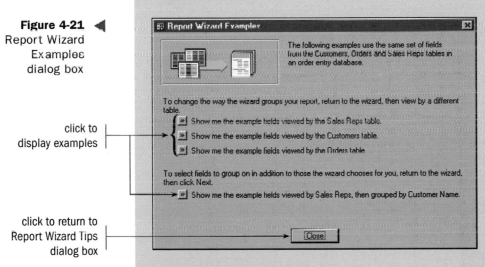

You can display examples of different grouping methods by clicking the ⟩⟩
buttons.

3. Click each ⟩⟩ button in turn, review the displayed example, and then click the
   Close button to return to the Report Wizard Examples dialog box.

4. Click the **Close** button to return to the Report Wizard Tips dialog box, and then
   click the **Close** button to return to the second Report Wizard dialog box.

The default options shown on your screen are correct for the report Kim wants, so you
can continue responding to the Report Wizard questions.

To finish creating the report using the Report Wizard:

1. Click the **Next** button. The next Report Wizard dialog box opens, in which you
   choose additional grouping levels.

Two grouping levels are shown: one for each customer's data, the other for a customer's orders. Grouping levels are useful for reports with multiple levels, such as those containing month, quarter, and annual totals; or containing city and country groups. Kim's report contains no further grouping levels, so you can accept the default options.

2. Click the **Next** button. The next Report Wizard dialog box opens, in which you choose the sort order for the detail records. See Figure 4-22.

Figure 4-22 ◀
Choosing the
sort order for
detail records

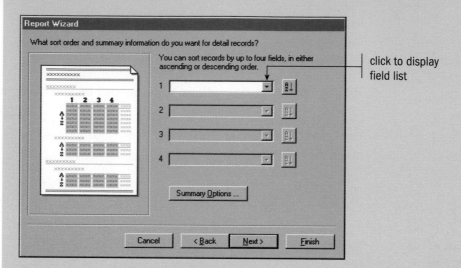

click to display
field list

The records from the Order table for a customer represent the detail records for Kim's report. She wants these records to appear in increasing, or ascending, order by the value in the OrderNum field.

3. Click the **1** list arrow, click **OrderNum**, and then click the **Next** button. The next Report Wizard dialog box opens, in which you choose a layout and page orientation for the report. See Figure 4-23.

Figure 4-23 ◀
Choosing the
report layout
and page
orientation

layout sample

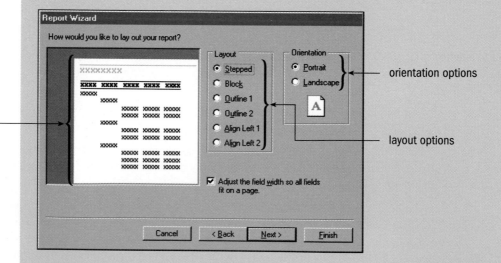

orientation options

layout options

A sample of each layout appears in the box on the left.

4. Click each layout option and examine each sample that appears. You'll use the Outline 2 layout option because it resembles the layout shown in Kim's sketch of the report.

5. Click the **Outline 2** option button, and then click the **Next** button. The next Report Wizard dialog box opens, in which you choose a style for the report.

Access

A sample of the selected style, or AutoFormat, appears in the box on the left. You can always choose a different AutoFormat after you create the report, just as you could when creating a form. Kim likes the appearance of the Corporate AutoFormat, so you'll choose this one for your report.

6. Click **Corporate** and then click the **Next** button. The last Report Wizard dialog box opens, in which you choose a report name, which also serves as the printed title on the report.

According to Kim's sketch, the report title you need to specify is "Customers and Orders."

7. Type **Customers and Orders** and then click the **Finish** button. The Report Wizard creates the report based on your answers and saves it to your Student Disk. Then Access opens the Customers and Orders report in Print Preview.

To better view the report, you need to maximize the report window.

8. Click the **Maximize** button ▣ on the Customers and Orders title bar.

To view the entire page, you need to change the Zoom setting.

9. Click the **Zoom** list arrow on the Print Preview toolbar, and then click **Fit**. The first page of the report is displayed in Print Preview. See Figure 4-24.

Figure 4-24 ◀
Report
displayed in
Print Preview

Zoom list arrow ─────────

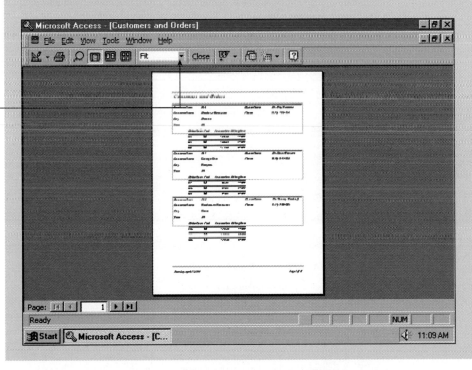

When a report is displayed in Print Preview, you can use the pointer to toggle between a full-page display and a close-up display of the report. Kim asks you to check the report to see if any adjustments need to be made. To do so, you need to view a close-up display of the report.

To view a close-up display of the report and make any necessary corrections:

1. Click the pointer ⊕ at the top center of the report. The display changes to show the report close up. See Figure 4-25.

Figure 4-25 ◀
Close-up view
of the report

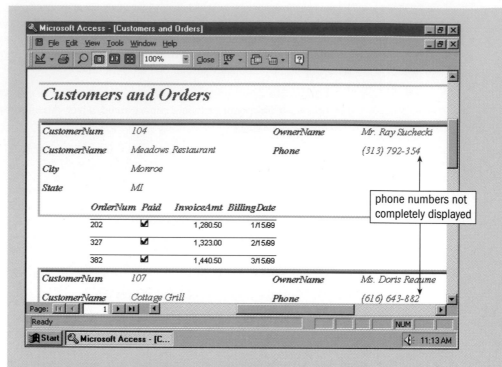

TROUBLE? Scroll your screen as necessary so that it matches the screen in Figure 4-25.

Notice that the last digit in each phone number is not visible in the report. To fix this, you need to first display the report in Design view.

2. Click the **View** button for Design view 📐 on the Print Preview toolbar. Access displays the report in Design view. See Figure 4-26.

Figure 4-26 ◀
Report
displayed in
Design view

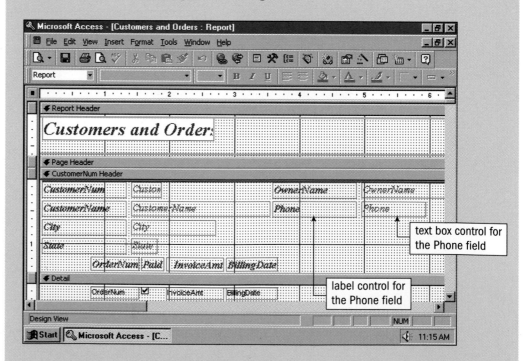

TROUBLE? If the Toolbox is displayed on your screen, close it by clicking its Close button ⊠.

You use the Report window in Design view to modify existing reports and to create custom reports.

Each item on a report in Design view is called a *control*. For example, the Phone field consists of two controls: the label "Phone," which appears on the report to identify the field value, and the Phone text box in which the actual field value appears. You need to widen the text box control for the Phone field so that the entire field value is visible in the report.

3. Click the text box control for the Phone field to select it. Notice that small black boxes appear on the border around the control. These boxes, which are called *handles*, indicate that the control is selected and can be manipulated.

4. Position the pointer on the center right handle of the Phone text box control until the pointer changes to ↔. See Figure 4-27.

Figure 4-27 ◀
Resizing the Phone text box control

drag this pointer to the right

handles indicate control is selected

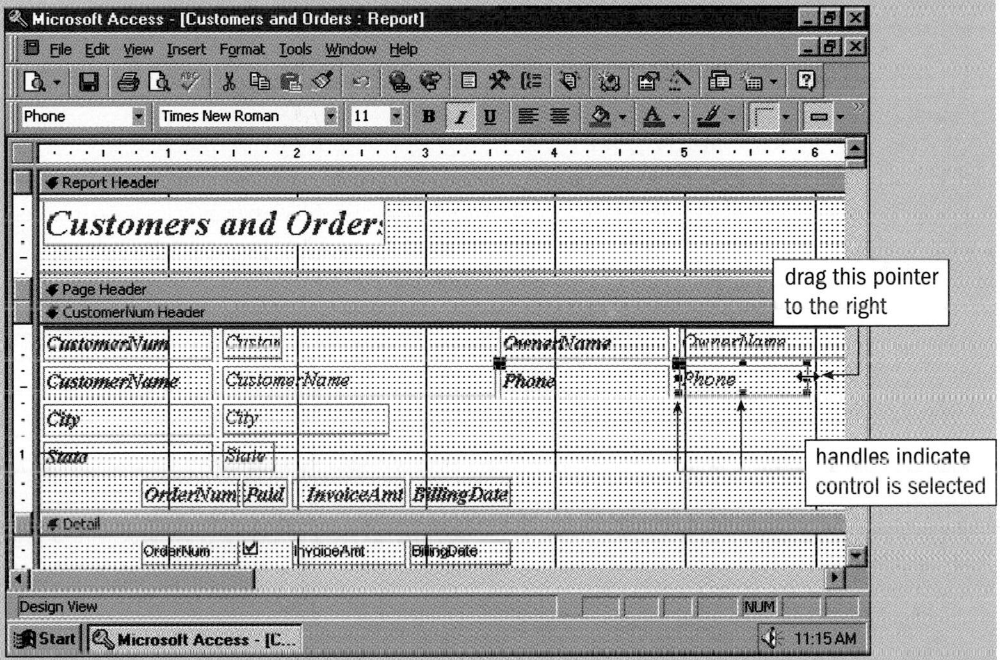

5. Click and drag the pointer to the right until the right edge of the control is aligned with the 6-inch mark on the horizontal ruler, and then release the mouse button.

   Now you need to switch back to Print Preview and make sure that the complete value for the Phone field is visible.

6. Click the **View** button for Print Preview 🔍 on the Report Design toolbar. The report appears in Print Preview. Notice that the Phone field values are now completely displayed.

7. Click **File** on the menu bar, and then click **Save** to save the modified report.

Kim decides that she wants the report to include the Valle Coffee cup logo to the right of the report title, for visual interest. You can add the logo to the report by inserting a picture of the coffee cup.

Inserting a Picture on a Report

In Access, you can insert a picture or other graphic image on a report or form to enhance the appearance of the report or form. Sources of graphic images include Microsoft Paint, other drawing programs, and scanners. The file containing the picture you need to insert is named ValleCup, and is located in the Tutorial folder on your Student Disk.

To insert the picture on the report:

1. Click the **Close** button on the Print Preview toolbar to display the report in Design view. See Figure 4-28.

click to select Report
Header section

Figure 4-28 ◀
Inserting a
picture in
Design view

Report
Header section

insert picture here

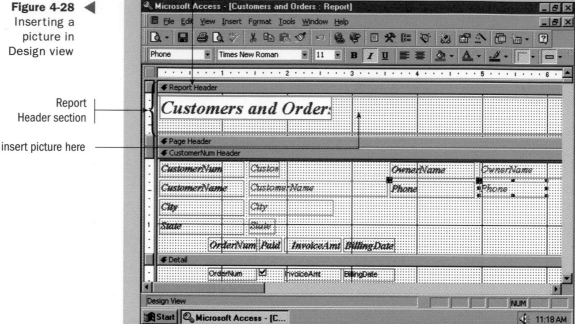

Kim wants the picture to appear on the first page of the report only; therefore, you need to insert the picture in the Report Header section (see Figure 4-28). Any text or graphics placed in this section appear once at the beginning of the report.

2. Click the **Report Header** bar to select this section of the report. The bar is highlighted to indicate the section is selected.

3. Click **Insert** on the menu bar, and then click **Picture**. The Insert Picture dialog box opens. See Figure 4-29.

Figure 4-29 ◀
Insert Picture
dialog box

selected picture file

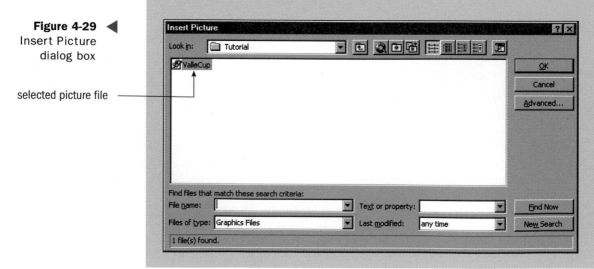

4. Make sure Tutorial appears in the Look in text box, click **ValleCup** to select the picture of the Valle Coffee cup, and then click the **OK** button. The picture is inserted at the far left of the Report Header section, covering some of the report title text. See Figure 4-30.

Figure 4-30 ◀
Picture
inserted
in report

inserted picture

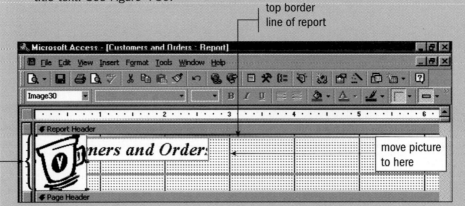

Notice that handles appear on the border around the picture, indicating that the picture is selected and can be manipulated.

Kim wants the picture to appear to the right of the report title, so you need to move the picture using the mouse.

5. Position the pointer on the picture until the pointer changes to 🖐, and then click and drag the mouse to move the picture to the right so that its left edge aligns with the 3-inch mark on the horizontal ruler and its top edge is just below the top border line above the report title (see Figure 4-30).

6. Release the mouse button. The picture appears in the new position. See Figure 4-31.

Figure 4-31 ◀
Repositioned
picture in
the report

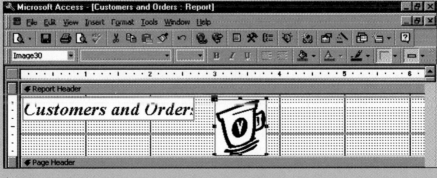

TROUBLE? If your picture is in a different location from the one shown in Figure 4-31, use the pointer 🖐 to reposition the picture until it is in approximately the same position shown in the figure. Be sure that the top edge of the picture is below the top border line of the report.

7. Click the **View** button for Print Preview 🔍 on the Report Design toolbar to view the report in Print Preview. The report now includes the inserted picture. If necessary, click the **Zoom** button 🔍 on the Print Preview toolbar to display the entire report page. See Figure 4-32.

Figure 4-32 ◀
Print Preview
of report
with picture

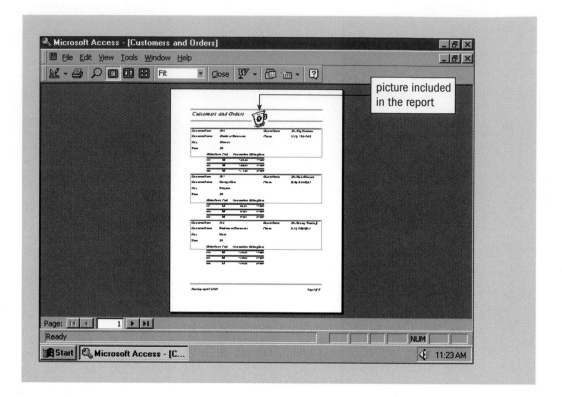

The report is now complete. You'll print a hardcopy of just the first page of the report so that Kim can review the report layout and the inserted picture.

To print page 1 of the report:

1. Click **File** on the menu bar, and then click **Print**. The Print dialog box opens.

2. In the Print Range section, click the **Pages** option button. The insertion point now appears in the From text box so that you can specify the range of pages to print.

3. Type **1** in the From text box, press the **Tab** key to move to the To text box, and then type **1**. These settings specify that only page 1 of the report will be printed.

4. Click the **OK** button. The Print dialog box closes and the first page of the report is printed. See Figure 4-33.

Figure 4-33 ◀
First page
of the
Customers and
Orders report

report title

fields from
Customer table

fields from
Order table

page footer

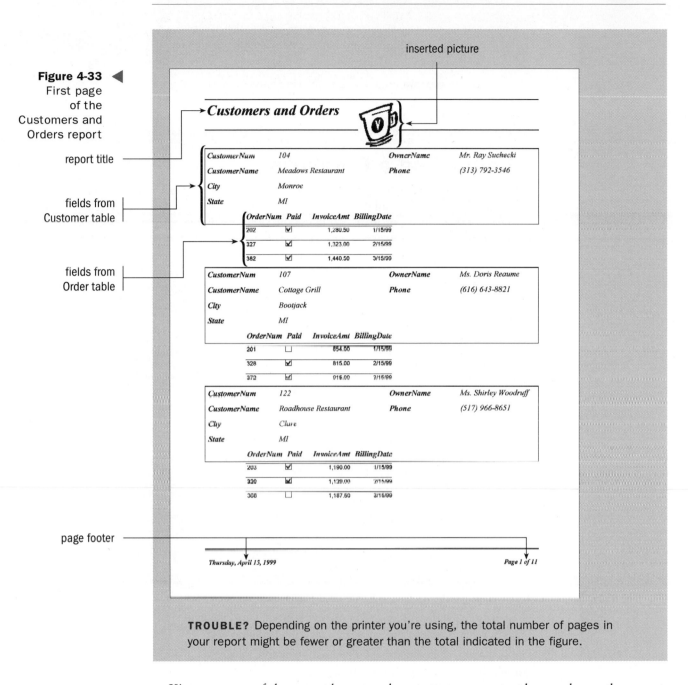

inserted picture

TROUBLE? Depending on the printer you're using, the total number of pages in your report might be fewer or greater than the total indicated in the figure.

Kim approves of the report layout and contents, so you can close and save the report.

To close and save the report:

1. Click the **Close** button ☒ on the menu bar.

   TROUBLE? If you click the Close button on the Print Preview toolbar by mistake, Access redisplays the report in Design view. Click the Close button ☒ on the menu bar.

   Access displays a dialog box asking if you want to save the changes to the design of your report.

2. Click the **Yes** button to save and close the report and return to the Database window.

You no longer need to have the Database window maximized, so you can restore it now.

3. Click the **Restore** button 🔲 on the Database window.

Before you exit Access, you'll compact the Restaurant database to free up disk space.

Compacting a Database

When you delete records in an Access table, the space occupied by the deleted records on disk does not become available for other records. The same is true if you delete an object, such as a table, query, or form. To make the space available, you must compact the database. **Compacting** a database rearranges the data and objects in a database and creates a smaller copy of the database. Unlike making a copy of a database file, which you do to protect your database against loss or damage, you compact the database to make it smaller, thereby making more space available on your disk. Before compacting a database, you must close it.

REFERENCE window	**COMPACTING A DATABASE**
	■ Make sure the database you want to compact is closed.
	■ In the Access window, click Tools on the menu bar, point to Database Utilities, and then click Compact Database to open the Database to Compact From dialog box.
	■ In the Look in box, select the drive and directory containing the database you want to compact; in the File name box, select the database you want to compact.
	■ Click the Compact button. Access opens the Compact Database Into dialog box.
	■ In the Save in box, select the drive and directory for the location of the compacted database; in the File name text box, type the name you want to assign to the compacted database.
	■ Click the Save button.

You'll compact the Restaurant database, delete the original (uncompacted) database file, and then rename the compacted file.

To compact the Restaurant database:

1. Click the **Close** button ☒ on the Database window title bar.

2. Click **Tools** on the menu bar, point to **Database Utilities**, and then click **Compact Database**. Access opens the Database to Compact From dialog box, in which you select the database you want to compact.

3. Make sure Tutorial appears in the Look in list box, click **Restaurant** in the list box, and then click the **Compact** button. Access opens the Compact Database Into dialog box, in which you enter the filename for the compacted copy of the database and select its drive and folder location.

Usually you would make a backup copy of the database as a safeguard before compacting. Here, you'll save the compacted database with a different name, delete the original database file, and then rename the compacted database to the original database name.

4. Type **Compacted Restaurant** in the File name text box, make sure Tutorial appears in the Save in list box, and then click the **Save** button. Access compacts the Restaurant database, creating the copied file named Compacted Restaurant, and returns you to the Access window.

Now you need to exit Access, delete the original Restaurant database, and then rename the compacted database as Restaurant. To delete and rename the necessary files, you'll open the Exploring window from the desktop.

To open the Exploring window and delete and rename the database files:

1. Click the **Close** button ⊠ on the Access window title bar. Access closes and you return to the Windows 95 desktop.

2. Using the right mouse button, click the **Start** button on the taskbar, and then click **Explore**. The Exploring window opens.

3. Scrolling as necessary, click the plus symbol to the left of the drive that contains your Student Disk in the All Folders list box, and then click **Tutorial**. The list of files in the Tutorial folder on your Student Disk appears in the Contents of 'Tutorial' list box. See Figure 4-34.

Figure 4-34 ◀
Original and compacted database files in Exploring window

original database file ─────

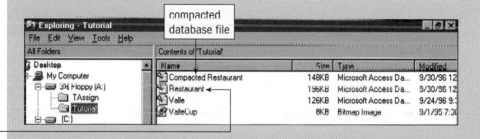

Verify that both database files—the original Restaurant database and the Compacted Restaurant database—are included in the window. Note the difference in size of the two files.

TROUBLE? The size of your files might be different from those in the figure.

Now you need to delete the original (uncompacted) database file and then rename the compacted file.

4. Click **Restaurant** in the list box, click **File** on the menu bar, and then click **Delete**. The Confirm File Delete dialog box opens and asks you to confirm the deletion.

5. Click the **Yes** button to delete the file.

6. Click **Compacted Restaurant** in the list box, click **File** on the menu bar, and then click **Rename**. The filename appears highlighted inside a box to indicate it is selected for editing.

7. Position the insertion point to the left of the word "Compacted," and then use the **Delete** key to delete the word "Compacted" and the space following it.

8. Press the **Enter** key. The filename of the compacted file is now Restaurant.

9. Click the **Close** button ⊠ on the Exploring title bar to close the Exploring window and return to the desktop.

Quick Check

1 How are a related table and a primary table associated with a form that contains a main form and a subform?

2 Describe how you use the navigation buttons to move through a form containing a main form and a subform.

3 When you use the Report Wizard, the report name is also used as the _____.

4 To insert a picture on a report, the report must be displayed in _____.

5 Any text or graphics placed in the _____ section of a report appear only on the first page of the report.

6 What is the purpose of compacting a database?

Barbara is satisfied that both forms—the Order Data form and the Customer Orders form—will make it easier to enter, view, and update data in the Restaurant database. The Customers and Orders report presents important information about Valle Coffee's restaurant customers in an attractive, professional format, which will help Kim and her staff in their sales and marketing efforts.

Tutorial Assignments

Barbara wants to enhance the Valle Products database with forms and reports, and she asks you to complete the following:

1. Make sure your Student Disk is in the disk drive, start Access, and then open the Valle Products database located in the TAssign folder on your Student Disk.

2. Use the Form Wizard to create a form based on the Product table. Select all fields for the form, the Columnar layout, the Stone style, and the title name of Product Data.

3. Using the form you created in the previous step, print the fifth form record, change the AutoFormat to Standard, save the changed form, and then print the fifth form record again.

4. Use the Product Data form to update the Product table as follows:
   a. Navigate to the record with the ProductCode 2310. Change the field values for WeightCode to A, Price to 8.99, and Decaf to Null for this record.
   b. Use the Find command to move to the record with the ProductCode 4306, and then delete the record.
   c. Add a new record with the following field values:
      ProductCode: 2306
      CoffeeCode: AMAR
      WeightCode: A
      Price: 8.99
      Decaf: Null
      Print only this form record, and then save and close the form.

5. Use the Form Wizard to create a form containing a main form and a subform. Select the CoffeeName and CoffeeType fields from the Coffee table for the main form, and select all fields except CoffeeCode from the Product table for the subform. Use the Tabular layout and the Standard style. Specify the title Coffee Products for the main form and the title Product Subform for the subform. Print the fourth main form record and its subform records.

6. Use the Report Wizard to create a report based on the primary Coffee table and the related Product table. Select all fields from the Coffee table except Decaf, and select all fields from the Product table except CoffeeCode. In the third Report Wizard dialog box, specify the CoffeeType field as an additional grouping level. Sort the detail records by ProductCode. Choose the Align Left 1 layout and the Casual style for the report. Specify the title Valle Coffee Products for the report.

7. Insert the ValleCup picture, which is located in the TAssign folder on your Student Disk, in the Report Header section of the Valle Coffee Products report. Position the picture so that its left edge aligns with the 4-inch mark on the horizontal ruler and its top edge is just below the top border line of the report.

8. Print only the first page of the report, and then close and save the modified report.

9. Compact the Valle Products database; name the copy of the database Compacted Valle Products. After the compacting process is complete, delete the original Valle Products database, and then rename the Compacted Valle Products file as Valle Products.

Case Problems

1. Ashbrook Mall Information Desk Sam Bullard wants the MallJobs database to include forms and reports that will help him track and distribute information about jobs available at the Ashbrook Mall. You'll create the necessary forms and reports by completing the following:

1. Make sure your Student Disk is in the disk drive, start Access, and then open the MallJobs database located in the Cases folder on your Student Disk.

2. Use the Form Wizard to create a form based on the Store table. Select all fields for the form, the Columnar layout, and the Clouds style. Specify the title Store Data for the form.

3. Change the AutoFormat for the Store Data form to Flax.

4. Use the Find command to move to the record with the Store value of TC, and then change the Contact field value for this record to Sarah Pedicini.

5. Use the Store Data form to add a new record with the following field values:
   Store: PW
   StoreName: Pet World
   Location: B2
   Contact: Killian McElroy
   Extension: 2750
   Print only this form record, and then save and close the form.

6. Use the Form Wizard to create a form containing a main form and a subform. Select all the fields from the Store table for the main form, and select all fields except Store from the Job table for the subform. Use the Tabular layout and the Flax style. Specify the title Jobs By Store for the main form and the title Job Subform for the subform.

7. Display the Jobs By Store form in Design view. To improve the appearance of the form, you need to reduce the width of the subform so that it does not block out the Flax background. Maximize the Form window, if necessary. Click the subform to select it; handles will appear around the subform to indicate it is selected. Position the pointer on the right middle handle until the pointer changes to ↔, click and drag the mouse to the left until the right edge

of the subform aligns with the 4-inch mark on the horizontal ruler, and then release the mouse button. Restore the Form window and then display the form in Form view.

8. Print the eighth main form record and its subform records, and then save and close the Jobs By Store form.

9. Use the Report Wizard to create a report based on the primary Store table and the related Job table. Select all fields from the Store table, and select all fields from the Job table except Store. Sort the detail records by Job. Choose the Block layout and Landscape orientation for the report. Choose the Bold style. Specify the title Available Jobs for the report, and then print and close the report.

10. Compact the MallJobs database; name the copy of the database Compacted MallJobs. After the compacting process is complete, delete the original MallJobs database, and then rename the Compacted MallJobs file as MallJobs.

2. Professional Litigation User Services Raj Jawahir continues his work with the Payments database to track and analyze the payment history of PLUS clients. To help him, you'll enhance the Payments database by completing the following:

1. Make sure your Student Disk is in the disk drive, start Access, and then open the Payments database located in the Cases folder on your Student Disk.

2. Use the Form Wizard to create a form containing a main form and a subform. Select the Firm# and FirmName fields from the Firm table for the main form, and select all fields except Firm# from the Payment table for the subform. Use the Datasheet layout and the Dusk style. Specify the title Firm Payments for the main form and the title Payment Subform for the subform. Resize all columns in the subform to their best fit. Print the first main form record and its displayed subform records.

3. For the form you just created, change the AutoFormat to Colorful 2, save the changed form, and then print the first main form record and its displayed subform records.

4. Navigate to the third record in the subform for the first main record, and then change the AmtPaid field value to 1,500.00.

5. Use the Find command to move to the record with the Firm# 1136, and delete the record. Answer Yes to any warning messages about deleting the record.

6. Use the appropriate wildcard character to find all records with the abbreviation "DA" (for District Attorney) in the firm name. (*Hint:* You must enter the wildcard character before and after the text you are searching for.) How many records did you find?

7. Use the Report Wizard to create a report based on the primary Firm table and the related Payment table. Select all fields from the Firm table except Extension, and select all fields from the Payment table except Firm#. In the third Report Wizard dialog box, specify the PLUSAcctRep field as an additional grouping level. Sort the detail records by AmtPaid in *descending* order. Choose the Outline 1 layout and the Formal style for the report. Specify the title Payments By Firms for the report.

8. Insert the Plus picture, which is located in the Cases folder on your Student Disk, in the Report Header section of the Payments By Firms report. Leave the picture in its original position at the left edge of the report header.

9. Use the Office Assistant to ask the following question: "How do I move an object behind another?" Choose the topic "Move a control in front of or behind other controls." Read the information and then close the Help window. Make sure the Plus picture is still selected, and then move it behind the Payments By Firms title.

EXPLORE

10. Use the Office Assistant to ask the following question: "How do I change the background color of an object?" Choose the topic "Change the background color of a control or section." Read the information and then close the Help window and the Office Assistant. Select the Payments By Firms title object, and then change its background color to Transparent. Select each of the two horizontal lines in the Report Header section that cut through the middle of the Plus picture, and then use the Delete key to delete each line.

11. Display the report in Print Preview. Print just the first page of the report, and then close and save the report.

12. Compact the Payments database; name the copy of the database Compacted Payments. After the compacting process is complete, delete the original Payments database, and then rename the Compacted Payments file as Payments.

3. Best Friends Noah and Sheila Warnick want to create forms and reports for the Walks database. You'll help them create these database objects by completing the following:

1. Make sure your Student Disk is in the disk drive, start Access, and then open the Walks database located in the Cases folder on your Student Disk.

2. Use the Form Wizard to create a form based on the Walker table. Select all fields for the form, the Columnar layout, and the Colorful 1 style. Specify the title Walker Data for the form.

3. Use the Walker Data form to update the Walker table as follows:
   a. For the record with the WalkerID 223, change the LastName to Hoban and the Distance to 0.
   b. Add a new record with the following values:
      WalkerID: 225
      LastName: DelFavero
      FirstName: Cindi
      Phone: 711-1275
      Distance: 2.0
      Print just this form record.
   c. Delete the record with the WalkerID field value of 123.

4. Change the AutoFormat of the Walker Data form to Pattern, save the changed form, and then use the form to print the last record in the Walker table. Close the form.

5. Use the Form Wizard to create a form containing a main form and a subform. Select all the fields from the Walker table for the main form, and select the PledgeAmt, PaidAmt, and DatePaid fields from the Pledge table for the subform. Use the Tabular layout and the Standard style. Specify the title Walkers And Pledges for the main form and the title Pledge Subform for the subform. Use the navigation buttons to find the first main form record that contains values in the subform. Print this main form record and its subform records.

6. Use the Report Wizard to create a report based on the primary Walker table and the related Pledge table. Select all fields from the Walker table, and select all fields from the Pledge table except WalkerID. Sort the detail records by PledgeNo. Choose the Align Left 2 layout and Landscape orientation for the report. Choose the Soft Gray style. Specify the title Walk-A-Thon Walkers And Pledges for the report.

7. View both pages of the report in Print Preview. (*Hint:* Use a toolbar button.) Notice that the pledge data for the third record appears at the top of the second page. You need to decrease the size of the bottom margin so that the pledge data will appear with its corresponding walker data. Use the Office Assistant to ask the question, "How do I change the margins in a report?" Choose the topic "Set margins, page orientation, and other page setup options" and then read the displayed Help information. Use the Page Setup command to change the bottom margin of the report to .5".

8. Print the entire report.

9. Compact the Walks database; name the copy of the database "Compacted Walks." After the compacting process is complete, delete the original Walks database, and then rename the Compacted Walks file as Walks.

4. Lopez Lexus Dealerships Maria and Hector Lopez want to create forms and reports that will help them track and analyze data about the cars and different locations for their Lexus dealerships. Help them enhance the Lexus database by completing the following:

1. Make sure your Student Disk is in the disk drive, start Access, and then open the Lexus database located in the Cases folder on your Student Disk.

2. Use the Form Wizard to create a form containing a main form and a subform. Select all the fields from the Locations table for the main form, and select the VehicleID, Model, Class, Year, Cost, and SellingPrice fields from the Cars table for the subform. Use the Datasheet layout and the International style. Specify the title Locations And Cars for the main form and the title Cars Subform for the subform. Resize all columns in the subform to their best fit. Print the first main form record and its displayed subform records.

3. For the form you just created, change the AutoFormat to Standard, save the changed form, and then print the first main form record and its displayed subform records.

4. Navigate to the second record in the subform for the fifth main record, and then change the SellingPrice field value to $42,175.00.

5. Use the Find command to move to the record with the LocationCode P1, and delete the record. Answer Yes to any warning messages about deleting the record.

6. Use the appropriate wildcard character to find all records with a LocationCode value that begins with the letter "A." How many records did you find?

7. Use the Report Wizard to create a report based on the primary Locations table and the related Cars table. Select all fields from the Locations table, and select all fields from the Cars table except Manufacturer and LocationCode. Specify two sort fields for the detail records: first, the VehicleID field in ascending order, then the Cost field in descending order. Choose the Align Left 1 layout and Landscape orientation for the report. Choose the Compact style. Specify the title Dealership Locations And Cars for the report, and then print just the first page of the report.

8. Compact the Lexus database; name the copy of the database Compacted Lexus. After the compacting process is complete, delete the original Lexus database, and then rename the Compacted Lexus file as Lexus.

Answers to Quick Check Questions

SESSION 1.1

1 field

2 common field

3 primary key; foreign key

4 records; fields

5 current record symbol

6 Use the horizontal and vertical scroll bars to view fields or records not currently visible in the datasheet; use the navigation buttons to move vertically through the records.

SESSION 1.2

1 query

2 primary key

3 AutoForm Wizard

4 The form displays each field name on a separate line to the left of its field value, which appears in a box; the widths of the boxes represent the size of the fields.

5 Click the Office Assistant button on any toolbar, type a question in the text box, click the Search button, and then choose a topic from the list displayed.

6 Print Preview

SESSION 2.1

1 Identify all the fields needed to produce the required information; group related fields into tables; determine each table's primary key; include a common field in related tables; avoid data redundancy; and determine the properties of each field.

2 The data type determines what field values you can enter for the field and what other properties the field will have.

3 text fields and number fields

4 Order numbers will not be used for calculations.

5 null

6 the record being edited; the next row available for a new record

SESSION 2.2

1 The field and all its values are removed from the table.

2 In Design view, right-click the row selector for the row above which you want to insert the field, click Insert Rows on the shortcut menu, and then define the new field.

3 yes/no

4 Format property

5 Access allows you to have only one database open at a time.

6 In navigation mode, the entire field value is selected and anything you type replaces the field value; in editing mode, you can insert or delete characters in a field value based on the location of the insertion point.

SESSION 3.1

1 a general query in which you specify the fields and records you want Access to select

2 The field list contains the table name at the top of the list box and the table's fields listed in the order in which they appear in the table; the design grid displays columns that contain specifications about a field you will use in the query.

3 A table datasheet and a query datasheet look the same, appearing in Datasheet view, and can be used to update data in a database. A table datasheet shows the permanent data in a table, whereas a query datasheet is temporary and its contents are based on the criteria you establish in the design grid.

4 primary table; related table

5 referential integrity

6 oldest to most recent date

7 when you have two or more nonadjacent sort keys or when the fields to be used for sorting are in the wrong order

8 filter

SESSION 3.2

1 condition

2 in the same Criteria row; in different Criteria rows

3 expression

4 A calculated field appears in a query datasheet but does not exist in a database, as does a table field.

5 a function that performs an arithmetic operation on selected records in a database

6 Group By

SESSION 4.1

1 The AutoForm Wizard creates a form automatically using all the fields in the selected table or query; the Form Wizard allows you to choose some or all of the fields in the selected table or query, choose fields from other tables and queries, and display fields in any order on the form.

2 An AutoFormat is a predefined style for a form (or report). To change a form's AutoFormat, display the form in Design view, click the AutoFormat button on the Form Design toolbar, click the new AutoFormat in the Form AutoFormats list box, and then click OK.

3 the last record in the table

4 datasheet

5 the question mark (?)

6 as many form records as can fit on a printed page

7 Click the record selector in the top left of the form.

SESSION 4.2

1 The main form displays the data from the primary table and the subform displays the data from the related table.

2 You use the top set of navigation buttons to select and move through records from the related table in the subform and the bottom set to select and move through records from the primary table in the main form.

3 report title

4 Design view

5 Report Header

6 to make the database smaller and make more space available on your disk

NEW
PERSPECTIVES
SERIES

Microsoft®
PowerPoint® 97

LEVEL I

TUTORIALS

Read This **Before You Begin**

STUDENT DISKS

To complete PowerPoint 97 Tutorials 1 and 2, you need 2 Student Disks. Your instructor will either provide you with Student Disks or ask you to make your own.

If you are supposed to make your own Student Disks, you will need 2 blank, formatted high-density disks. You will need to copy a set of folders from a file server or standalone computer onto your disks. Your instructor will tell you which computer, drive letter, and folders contain the files you need. The following table shows you which folders go on each of your disks, so that you will have enough disk space to complete all the tutorials, Tutorial Assignments, and Case Problems:

Student Disk	Write this on the disk label	Put these folders on the disk
1	Student Disk 1: PowerPoint 97 Tutorial 1	Tutorial.01
2	Student Disk 2: PowerPoint 97 Tutorial 2	Tutorial.02

When you begin each tutorial, be sure you are using the correct Student Disk. See the inside front or inside back cover of this book for more information on Student Disk files, or ask your instructor or technical support person for assistance.

USING YOUR OWN COMPUTER

If you are going to work through this book using your own computer, you need:

■ **Computer System** Microsoft Windows 95 or Microsoft Windows NT Workstation 4.0 (or a later version) and Microsoft PowerPoint 97 must be installed on your computer. This book assumes a typical installation of PowerPoint 97.

■ **Student Disks** Ask your instructor or lab manager for details on how to get the Student Disks. You will not be able to complete the tutorials or end-of-tutorial assignments in this book using your own computer until you have Student Disks. The Student Files may also be obtained electronically over the Internet. See the inside front or inside back cover of this book for more details.

To complete PowerPoint 97 Tutorials 1 and 2, your students must use a set of files on 2 Student Disks. These files are included in the Instructor's Resource Kit, and they may also be obtained electronically over the Internet. See the inside front or inside back cover of this book for more details. Follow the instructions in the Readme file to copy the files to your server or standalone computer. You can view the Readme file using WordPad. Once the files are copied, you can make Student Disks for the students yourself, or you can tell students where to find the files so they can make their own Student Disks.

COURSE TECHNOLOGY STUDENT FILES

You are granted a license to copy the Student Files to any computer or computer network used by students who have purchased this book.

Creating a PowerPoint Presentation

Presentation to Reach Potential Customers of Inca Imports International

PowerPoint

OBJECTIVES

In this tutorial you will:

- Start and exit PowerPoint

- Create an outline with the AutoContent Wizard

- Identify the components of the PowerPoint window

- Edit text of the presentation in Outline View and Slide View

- Open an existing presentation

- Insert and delete slides

- Change the design template

- Use the PowerPoint Help system

- Create speaker notes

- Preview, print, and save a presentation

CASE

Inca Imports International

Three years ago Patricia Cuevas and Angelena Cristenas began an import business called Inca Imports International. Working with suppliers in South America, particularly in Ecuador and Peru, the company imports fresh fruits and vegetables to North America during the winter and spring (which are summer and fall in South America) and sells them to small grocery stores in the Los Angeles area.

Inca Imports now has 34 employees and is healthy and growing. The company has recently made plans to construct a distribution facility in Quito, Ecuador, and to launch a marketing campaign to position itself for further expansion. Patricia (President of Inca Imports) assigned Carl Vetterli (Vice President of Sales and Marketing) the task of identifying potential customers and developing methods to reach them. Carl has scheduled a meeting with Patricia, Angelena (Vice President of Operations), Enrique Hoffmann (Director of Marketing), and other colleagues to review the results of his market research.

For his presentation Carl will use an electronic slide show that will include a demographic profile of Inca Imports' current customers, the results of a customer satisfaction survey, a vision statement of the company's future growth, a list of options for attracting new clients, and recommendations for a marketing strategy. Carl asks you to help create the slides for his presentation by using Microsoft PowerPoint 97 (or simply PowerPoint).

Using the Tutorials Effectively

These tutorials are designed to be used at a computer. Each tutorial is divided into sessions. Watch for the session headings, such as "Session 1.1" and "Session 1.2." Each session is designed to be completed in about 45 minutes, but take as much time as you need. When you've completed a session, it's a good idea to exit the program and take a break. You can exit Microsoft PowerPoint by clicking the Close button in the top-right corner of the program window.

Before you begin, read the following questions and answers. They are designed to help you use the tutorials effectively.

Where do I start?

Each tutorial begins with a case, which sets the scene for the tutorial and gives you background information to help you understand what you will be doing in the tutorial. Read the case before you go to the lab. In the lab, begin with the first session of the tutorial.

How do I know what to do on the computer?

Each session contains steps that you will perform on the computer to learn how to use Microsoft PowerPoint. The steps are numbered and are set against a colored background. Read the text that introduces each series of steps, and read each step carefully and completely before you try it.

How do I know if I did the step correctly?

As you work, compare your computer screen with the corresponding figure in the tutorial. Don't worry if your screen display is somewhat different from the figure. The important parts of the screen display are labeled in each figure. Check to make sure these parts are on your screen.

What if I make a mistake?

Don't worry about making mistakes—they are part of the learning process. Paragraphs labeled "**TROUBLE?**" identify common problems and explain how to get back on track. Follow the steps in a **TROUBLE?** paragraph *only* if you are having the problem described. If you run into other problems, carefully consider the current state of your system, the position of the pointer, and any messages on the screen.

How do I use the Reference Windows?

Reference Windows summarize the procedures you learn in the tutorial steps. Do not complete the actions in the Reference Windows when you are working through the tutorial. Instead, refer to the Reference Windows while you are working on the assignments at the end of the tutorial.

How can I test my understanding of the material I learned in the tutorial?

At the end of each session, you can answer the Quick Check questions. If necessary, refer to the Answers to Quick Check Questions to check your work.

After you have completed the entire tutorial, you should complete the Tutorial Assignments and Case Problems. These exercises are carefully structured so you will review what you have learned and then apply your knowledge to new situations.

What if I can't remember how to do something?

You should refer to the Task Reference at the end of the book; it summarizes how to accomplish commonly performed tasks.

Now that you've seen how to use the tutorials effectively, you are ready to begin.

PowerPoint

In this session you will learn how to start and exit PowerPoint, use the AutoContent Wizard to create an outline of Carl's presentation, and identify the parts of the PowerPoint window. You will also learn how to use Outline View to insert and edit text in an outline.

What Is PowerPoint?

PowerPoint is a powerful presentation graphics program that provides everything you need to produce an effective presentation in the form of black-and-white or color overheads, 35mm photographic slides, or on-screen slides. You may have already seen your instructors use PowerPoint presentations to enhance their classroom lectures.

Using PowerPoint, you can prepare each component of a presentation: individual slides, speaker notes, an outline of the presentation, and audience handouts. Carl's presentation will include slides, speaker notes, and handouts. In addition, you can easily create a consistent format for your presentation by using a slide master. A **slide master** is a slide that contains the text and graphics that will appear on every slide of a particular kind in the presentation. For example the company's name, the date, and the company's logo can be put on the slide master so this information will appear on every slide in the presentation.

As you create Carl's slides, you'll learn to use many of PowerPoint's features. Before you begin creating the slides, however, you should make sure the presentation is carefully planned.

Planning a Presentation

Planning a presentation before you create it improves the quality of your presentation, makes your presentation more effective and enjoyable, and, in the long run, saves you time and effort. As you plan your presentation, you should answer several questions: What is my purpose or objective for this presentation? What type of presentation is needed? Who is the audience? What information does that audience need? What is the physical location of my presentation? What is the best format for presenting the information contained in this presentation, given the location of the presentation?

In planning his presentation, Carl identifies the following elements of the presentation:

- **Purpose of the presentation:** To identify potential customers and ways to reach them

- **Type of presentation:** Recommend a strategy for the new marketing campaign

- **Audience for the presentation:** Patricia, Angelena, Enrique, and other key staff members in a weekly executive meeting

- **Audience needs:** To understand who our current clients are and to determine the best way to reach similar new clients

- **Location of the presentation:** Small boardroom

- **Format:** Oral presentation; electronic slide show of five to seven slides

Carl has carefully planned his presentation; you can now use PowerPoint to create it. You begin by starting PowerPoint.

Starting PowerPoint

You start PowerPoint in the same way that you start other Windows 95 programs—using the Start button on the taskbar.

To start PowerPoint:

1. Make sure Windows 95 is running on your computer and the Windows 95 desktop appears on your screen.

   TROUBLE? If you're running Windows NT Workstation 4.0 (or a later version) on your computer or network, don't worry. Although the figures in this book were created while running Windows 95, Windows NT 4.0 and Windows 95 share the same interface, and PowerPoint 97 runs equally well under either operating system.

2. Click the **Start** button on the taskbar to display the Start menu, and then point to **Programs** to display the Programs menu.

3. Point to **Microsoft PowerPoint** on the Programs menu. See Figure 1-1.

Figure 1-1 ◀
Starting
Microsoft
PowerPoint

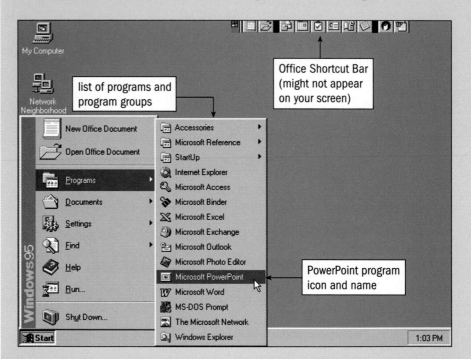

   TROUBLE? If you don't see Microsoft PowerPoint on the Programs menu, ask your instructor or technical support person for help.

   TROUBLE? The Office Shortcut Bar, which appears along the top border of the desktop in Figure 1-1, might look different on your screen or it might not appear at all, depending on how your system is set up. The steps in these tutorials do not require that you use the Office Shortcut Bar; therefore, the remaining figures do not display the Office Shortcut Bar.

4. Click **Microsoft PowerPoint**. After a short pause the PowerPoint dialog box appears on the screen. See Figure 1-2.

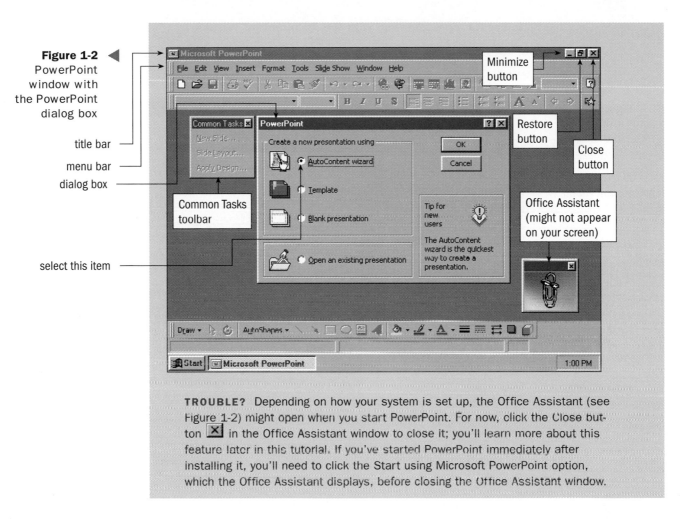

PowerPoint

Figure 1-2 ◀
PowerPoint
window with
the PowerPoint
dialog box

title bar

menu bar

dialog box

select this item

TROUBLE? Depending on how your system is set up, the Office Assistant (see Figure 1-2) might open when you start PowerPoint. For now, click the Close button [×] in the Office Assistant window to close it; you'll learn more about this feature later in this tutorial. If you've started PowerPoint immediately after installing it, you'll need to click the Start using Microsoft PowerPoint option, which the Office Assistant displays, before closing the Office Assistant window.

Now that you've started PowerPoint, you're ready to create Carl's presentation. Your first step will be using the AutoContent Wizard.

Using the AutoContent Wizard to Create an Outline

PowerPoint helps you quickly create effective presentations by using wizards, which ask you a series of questions to determine the organizational structure and style for your presentation. The **AutoContent Wizard** lets you choose a presentation category such as "Product/Services Overview," "Recommending a Strategy," or "Generic." After you have selected the type of presentation you want, the AutoContent Wizard creates a general outline for you to follow.

If you open a new presentation without using the AutoContent Wizard, you must create your own outline, one slide at a time (though creating your own outline is more efficient if it doesn't fall into one of PowerPoint's predefined types). Carl, however, asks you to use the AutoContent Wizard because his presentation topic is a common one: recommending a strategy. The AutoContent Wizard will automatically create a title slide and standard outline, which you can then edit to fit Carl's presentation.

To create a presentation with the AutoContent Wizard:

1. With the PowerPoint startup dialog box on the screen, click the **AutoContent wizard** radio button, then click the **OK** button. The first of several AutoContent Wizard dialog boxes appears. See Figure 1-3.

Figure 1-3 ◀
AutoContent
Wizard dialog
box

current topic of
AutoContent Wizard

click to go to next
AutoContent Wizard
dialog box

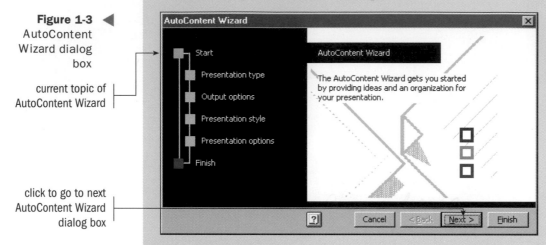

TROUBLE? If the PowerPoint startup dialog box doesn't appear on your screen, click File, then click New. When the New Presentation dialog box opens, click the Presentations tab, click the AutoContent Wizard button, and then click the OK button.

TROUBLE? If the Office Assistant opens to ask if you want help with the AutoContent Wizard, click "No, don't provide help now."

2. Read the information in the AutoContent Wizard dialog box, then click the **Next** button to display the next dialog box of the AutoContent Wizard.

This dialog box allows you to select the type of presentation that you're going to give. Carl wants you to select a general presentation on recommending a strategy.

3. Make sure the **All** button is selected, if necessary click **Recommending a Strategy** in the list box, then click the **Next** button to display the next AutoContent Wizard dialog box.

This dialog box displays the question "How will this presentation be used?"

4. Make sure the **Presentations, informal meetings, handouts** radio button is selected, because Carl's presentation will be for an informal meeting. It will not be a presentation for the Internet or for a kiosk (a stand-alone booth or demonstration). Then click the **Next** button.

The next AutoContent dialog box allows you to specify the presentation style, that is, the mode of the presentation. See Figure 1-4.

Figure 1-4 ◀
AutoContent
Wizard dialog
box to specify
presentation
style

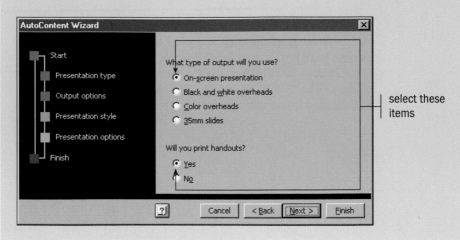

select these
items

Carl wants you to create an on-screen presentation; he will make his presentation directly from a computer screen. Carl will also want you to print handouts for his presentation.

5. If necessary click the **On-screen presentation** radio button, make sure the **Yes** radio button is selected below the question "Will you print handouts?" then click the **Next** button to display the next AutoContent dialog box.

Here you'll specify the title and author of the presentation.

6. Drag I across all the text in the Presentation title text box, type **Reaching Potential Customers**, press the **Tab** key, type **Carl Vetterli** in the Your name text box, and then press the **Tab** key. If any text in the Additional information text box is highlighted, press the **Delete** key. See Figure 1-5.

Figure 1-5 ◀
AutoContent Wizard dialog box with presentation title and author

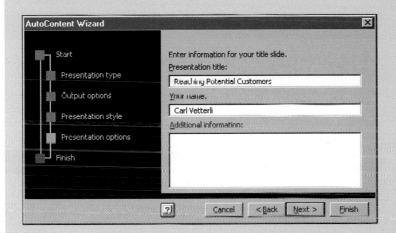

7. Click the **Next** button. The final AutoContent Wizard dialog box appears, letting you know that you have completed the AutoContent Wizard.

8. Click the **Finish** button. PowerPoint now displays the outline of the presentation that the AutoContent wizard automatically created, as well as a slide miniature of slide 1. If necessary drag the Common Tasks floating toolbar to the right side of the presentation window so it doesn't cover any text of the outline. See Figure 1-6.

Figure 1-6 ◀
PowerPoint window with outline of presentation

Standard toolbar

Formatting toolbar

presentation window

Outlining toolbar

View toolbar
status bar

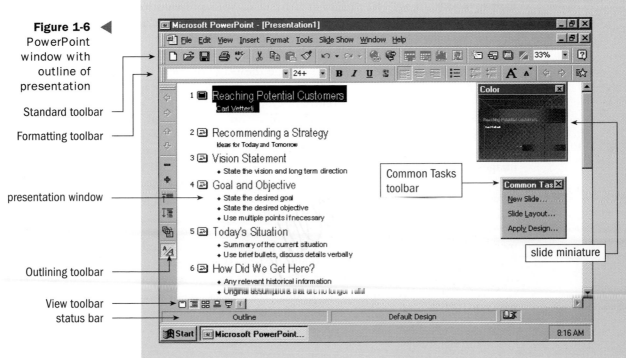

> **TROUBLE?** If the presentation window doesn't fill the entire screen as in Figure 1-6, click the Maximize button in the upper-right corner of the presentation window, and, if necessary, drag the horizontal scroll button to the far left so you can see the left edge of the outline text.

You'll need to edit the outline that the AutoContent Wizard created to fit Carl's presentation, but first you should make sure that you're familiar with the PowerPoint window.

The PowerPoint Window

The PowerPoint window contains features common to all Windows programs, as well as features specific to PowerPoint, such as the options available on the toolbars.

Common Windows Elements

Several elements of the PowerPoint window are common to other Windows 95 programs. For example, as shown in Figure 1-2, the PowerPoint window has a title bar, menu bar, and window sizing buttons. These elements function the same way in PowerPoint as they do in other Windows programs. However, the PowerPoint window also includes items that are specific to PowerPoint, such as the toolbars.

The Toolbars

Like many Windows programs, PowerPoint supplies several toolbars, as shown in Figure 1-6. A **toolbar** is a horizontal or vertical ribbon of icons that provides menu short-cuts. When you move the mouse pointer over one of the icons on the toolbar, the outline of the button appears, followed by a **ToolTip**, which is a yellow box containing the name of the button. You will learn to use the toolbars for tasks that are repeated often, such as opening or saving a file.

The toolbar immediately below the menu bar is the **Standard toolbar**, which allows you to use many of the standard Windows and PowerPoint commands, such as opening an existing presentation, saving the current presentation to disk, printing the presentation, and cutting and pasting text and graphics. Below the Standard toolbar is the **Formatting toolbar**, which allows you to format the text of your presentations. The vertical toolbar on the left edge of the PowerPoint window is the **Outlining toolbar**, which allows you to change the view of or make modifications to the outline.

Finally the small toolbar immediately above the status bar is the **View toolbar**, which contains buttons that allow you to change the way you view a slide presentation. Each way of seeing a presentation is called a **view**, and the status bar indicates which view you are in. Notice that you are currently in Outline View. Clicking the **Slide View button** allows you to see and edit text and graphics on an individual slide. In Slide View the Drawing toolbar is automatically displayed at the bottom of the screen instead of the Outlining toolbar. Clicking the **Slide Sorter View button** changes the view to miniature images of all the slides at once. You use this view to change the order of the slides or set special features for your slide show. Clicking the **Notes Page View button** changes the view so you can see and edit your presentation notes on individual slides. To present your slide show, you can click the **Slide Show button** .

As with other Windows programs, PowerPoint lets you select commands by using the menus with the keyboard or the mouse, by using shortcut keys, or by using toolbar buttons. Because the toolbar buttons are usually the easiest and fastest method of selecting commands, in these tutorials you will use the toolbars more often than the menus or keyboard.

Now that you're familiar with the PowerPoint window, you're ready to adapt PowerPoint's default outline to fit Carl's presentation.

Adapting an AutoContent Outline

After you complete the AutoContent Wizard, PowerPoint displays the outline with the title and Carl Vetterli's name in slide 1. PowerPoint also automatically includes other slides with suggested text located in placeholders. A **placeholder** is a region of a slide or a location in an outline reserved for inserting text or graphics. Furthermore, in Outline View, each main heading of the outline, or the **title** of each slide, appears to the right of the slide icon and slide number, as shown in Figure 1-6. The **main text** of each slide is indented and bulleted under the title.

To adapt the AutoContent outline to fit Carl's presentation, you must **select**, or highlight, the placeholders one at a time, and then replace them with other text.

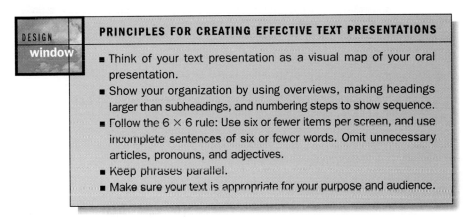

DESIGN window

PRINCIPLES FOR CREATING EFFECTIVE TEXT PRESENTATIONS

- Think of your text presentation as a visual map of your oral presentation.
- Show your organization by using overviews, making headings larger than subheadings, and numbering steps to show sequence.
- Follow the 6 × 6 rule: Use six or fewer items per screen, and use incomplete sentences of six or fewer words. Omit unnecessary articles, pronouns, and adjectives.
- Keep phrases parallel.
- Make sure your text is appropriate for your purpose and audience.

You'll now begin to replace the main text to fit Carl's presentation. Later, you'll need to edit it further to make sure it conforms with the 6 x 6 rule (see the Design Window above).

To replace the main text in a slide:

1. Position the pointer on the bullet that is located just beneath the title of slide 3. The text to the right of this bullet is "State the vision and long term direction." The pointer changes to ⊕.

2. Click ⊕ on the bullet to select the text. See Figure 1-7. By clicking a bullet, you can quickly select all the text in a bulleted item of the main text of a slide. (You could also select the text by positioning I before the "S" in the sentence "State the vision and long term direction" and dragging I over the text while holding down the mouse button.) Once the text is selected, you can begin typing to replace it.

Figure 1-7 ◄
Outline after
selecting item

slide icon ———

title of slide 3 ———

pointer on bullet ———

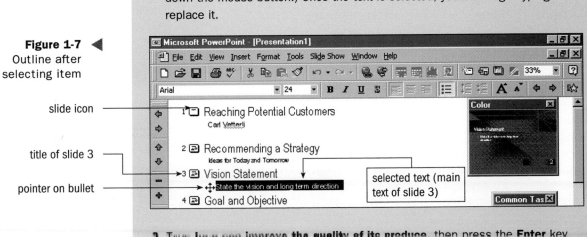

selected text (main text of slide 3)

3. Type **Inca can improve the quality of its produce**, then press the **Enter** key. Your screen should now look like Figure 1-8. Notice that as soon as you started typing, the selected text disappeared. Notice also that when you press the Enter

key, PowerPoint automatically inserts a bullet for the next item in the list, and the insertion point appears to the right of the bullet.

Figure 1-8 ◀
New text in
outline

marked word not
found in the
PowerPoint dictionary

new bulleted item

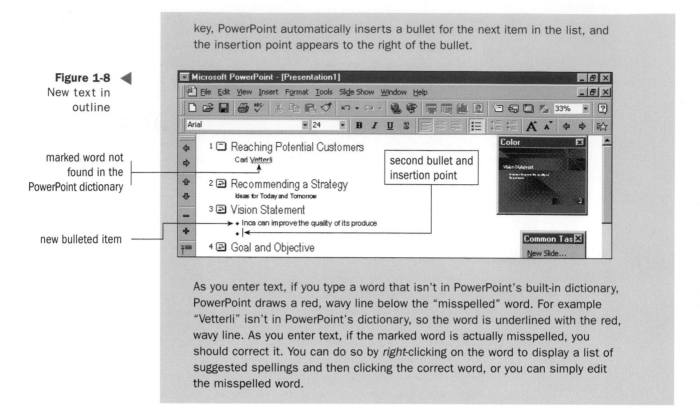

As you enter text, if you type a word that isn't in PowerPoint's built-in dictionary, PowerPoint draws a red, wavy line below the "misspelled" word. For example "Vetterli" isn't in PowerPoint's dictionary, so the word is underlined with the red, wavy line. As you enter text, if the marked word is actually misspelled, you should correct it. You can do so by *right*-clicking on the word to display a list of suggested spellings and then clicking the correct word, or you can simply edit the misspelled word.

Carl has two more bullets he wants you to add to the Vision Statement slide. You'll do that now.

To add new text to the outline:

1. Type **Inca can sell more produce to more customers**, then press the **Enter** key.

2. Type **Inca can become the clear market leader in southern California**, then press the **Enter** key. Your screen should now look like Figure 1-9.

Figure 1-9 ◀
Outline after
inserting new
text

new text

bullet to be deleted

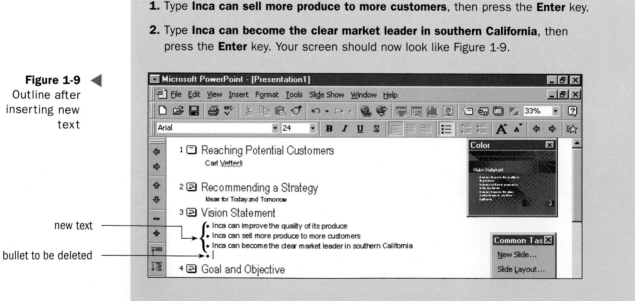

Carl realizes that he wants only three items in the list, not four, so he asks you to delete the fourth bullet.

3. Press the **Backspace** key to delete the fourth bullet and move the insertion point to the end of the preceding line.

Next Carl wants you to replace the placeholder text in slide 4, "Goal and Objective."

4. Make the changes to slide 4 using the text shown in Figure 1-10.

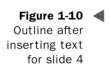

Figure 1-10 ◀
Outline after
inserting text
for slide 4

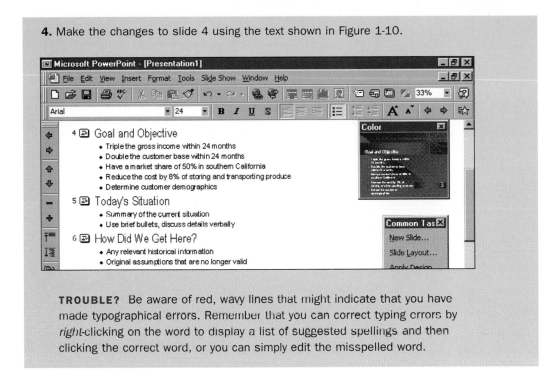

TROUBLE? Be aware of red, wavy lines that might indicate that you have made typographical errors. Remember that you can correct typing errors by *right*-clicking on the word to display a list of suggested spellings and then clicking the correct word, or you can simply edit the misspelled word.

Your presentation window should now look like Figure 1-10. You have made substantial progress on Carl's presentation but realize that you need to attend a meeting in a few minutes. Therefore you'll need to save your work and then exit PowerPoint.

Saving the Presentation and Exiting PowerPoint

In addition to saving your work before you exit PowerPoint, you should also save about every 15 minutes, so you won't lose all your work if, for example, a power failure occurs.

To save a presentation for the first time:

1. Place your Student Disk into the appropriate drive.

TROUBLE? If you don't have a Student Disk, you need to get one before you can proceed. Your instructor will either give you one or ask you to make your own by following the instructions on the "Read This Before You Begin" page before this tutorial. See your instructor or technical support person for more information.

2. Click the **Save** button 🖫 on the Standard toolbar. The Save dialog box opens.

3. Click the **Save in** list arrow, then click the drive that contains your Student Disk.

4. Double-click the **Tutorial.01** folder to open that folder.

5. Click in the **File name** text box, type **Reaching Potential Customers**, and then click the **Save** button.

PowerPoint saves the presentation to the disk using the filename Reaching Potential Customers. That name now appears in the title bar.

Having saved your work, you're now ready to exit PowerPoint.

To exit PowerPoint:

1. Click the **Close** button ☒ in the upper-right corner of the PowerPoint window. (You could also click **File** on the menu bar, then click **Exit**.)

Quick Check

1. In one to three sentences, describe the purpose of the PowerPoint program and the components of a presentation that you can create with it.

2. Why should you plan a presentation before you create it? What are some of the presentation elements that should be considered?

3. Describe the purpose of the AutoContent Wizard.

4. Define the following terms:
   a. slide master
   b. placeholder
   c. title (on a slide)
   d. main text (on a slide)

5. What is the 6 × 6 rule?

6. What does a red, wavy line indicate?

7. Why is it important to save your work frequently?

When you return from your meeting, you'll continue to edit the text of Carl's presentation, as well as create speaker notes.

SESSION

1.2

In this session you will learn how to open an existing presentation, edit and change text in Outline View and Slide View, add and delete slides, and change the design template. You will also learn how to use PowerPoint's Help system, create speaker notes, and preview and print a presentation.

Editing the Presentation in Outline View

When you return from your meeting, Carl has already looked at the text of the first four slides. Reviewing the 6 × 6 rule, he realizes that in a slide presentation, each text item should be as short as possible. It's easier for the audience to read short phrases. In addition Carl knows that he'll be conveying most of the information orally, so the main text doesn't have to be in complete sentences.

Carl decides he wants you to apply the 6 × 6 rule as much as possible. To simplify the text in slide 3, you'll omit the company name because the audience will know Carl is talking about Inca Imports. Similarly, articles (for example, the, a), many possessive pronouns (for example, your, its), and most adjectives (for example, high, clear, very) can safely be left out of titles and the main text. Therefore Carl asks you to change "Inca can improve the quality of its produce" to "Improve quality of produce." Carl also realizes that by changing the title of slide 4 from "Goal and Objective," to "Two-Year Goals," he can delete the words "within 24 months" from the bulleted list.

You'll now make Carl's changes. First you need to start PowerPoint and open the presentation you worked on in the last session.

To start PowerPoint and open an existing presentation:

1. Using the steps described in Session 1.1, start PowerPoint.

2. With the PowerPoint startup dialog box on the screen, click the **Open an existing presentation** radio button, then click the **OK** button to display the Open dialog box.

3. Click the **Look in** list arrow to display the list of available drives, then click the drive that contains your Student Disk.

4. Double-click the **Tutorial.01** folder to open that folder, click **Reaching Potential Customers** in the Name list box, then click the **Open** button. Carl's presentation should now appear on your screen. If necessary click the **Maximize** button so the presentation window fills the screen.

Now that you've opened Carl's presentation, you're ready to edit the outline.

To edit the outline:

1. Using Figure 1-11 as a guide, change the text of slides 3 and 4 of Carl's presentation by dragging I to select the text and then deleting or retyping it as necessary.

Figure 1-11
Text of slides
3 and 4

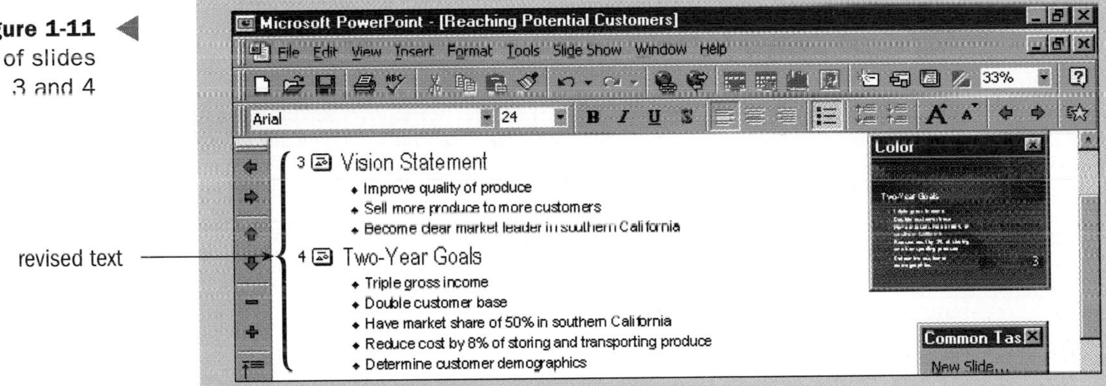

revised text

Carl reads through the text of the edited slides 3 and 4. He decides to switch the second and third items under "Two-Year Goals" (slide 4) and asks you to make this change.

Moving Text Up and Down in Outline View

In PowerPoint it's easy to switch main text items in Outline View. You'll reverse the order of the second and third items in slide 4 now.

To move an item of text in Outline View:

1. Click ✛ on the bullet to the left of the text "Have market share of 50% in southern California" in slide 4 to highlight the text.

2. Click the **Move Up** button on the Outlining toolbar. The highlighted item is now moved up one position in the list, so the second and third items are switched. See Figure 1-12.

Figure 1-12 ◀
Moving a
bulleted item

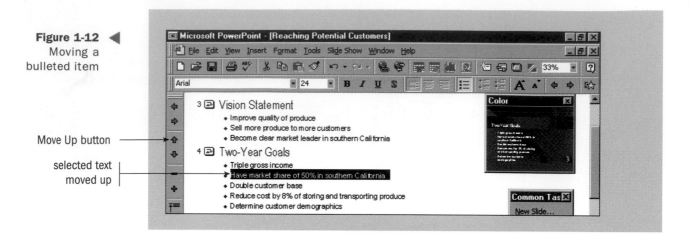

Move Up button

selected text
moved up

You can also use this same method to move entire slides. You'll have a chance to practice moving an entire slide in both Outline View and Slide Sorter View in the Tutorial Assignments and Case Problems.

Carl reviews the change you made to slide 4 and realizes that he also needs to present more information on his customer demographics study. He decides the demographic information should be a separate slide and asks you to create it. Instead of deleting the bulleted item and then retyping it as a new slide title, you can promote the item from main text to slide title.

Promoting and Demoting the Outline Text

To **promote** an item means to increase the outline level of an item, for example, to change a bulleted item into a slide title. To **demote** an item means to decrease the outline level, for example, to change a slide title into a bulleted item within another slide.

You'll now promote the item "Determine customer demographics" to create the new slide.

To promote an item:

1. Click I anywhere within the bulleted item "Determine customer demographics" in slide 4.

2. Click the **Promote** button on either the Outlining toolbar or the Formatting toolbar. "Determine customer demographics" is now the title of a new slide 5, and "Today's Situation" becomes slide 6, as shown in Figure 1-13.

Figure 1-13 ◀
Outline text
after promoting
item
Promote button
(dimmed)

Demote button

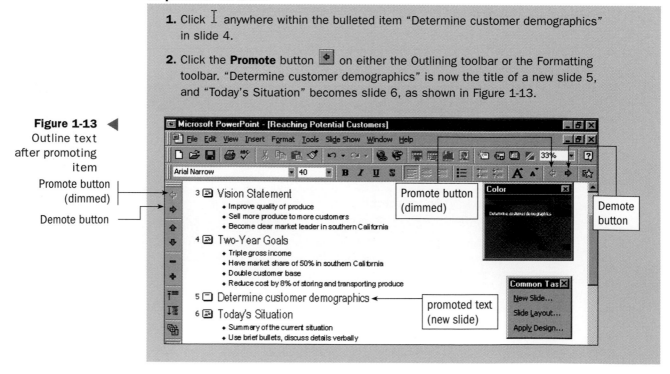

Promote button
(dimmed)

Demote
button

promoted text
(new slide)

Because the title of slide 5 is wordy, Carl asks you to edit it.

3. Change the title "Determine customer demographics" to "Customer Demographics."

You're now ready to add the bulleted items beneath the title of slide 5. However, because the current outline level is a slide title, any text that you type will be at the same outline level, that is, a slide title. To add main text, therefore, you must move down a level in the outline. You can do this by using the Demote command.

To demote an item:

1. Click ⊺ at the end of the title "Customer Demographics," then press the **Enter** key. PowerPoint creates a new slide 6.

2. Click the **Demote** button ⊞ on the Outlining or Formatting toolbar to change the outline level from slide title to main text. PowerPoint creates a bullet, with the insertion point appearing to the right of it.

3. Type the main text of slide 5, as shown in Figure 1-14. Make sure you have typed the information correctly. Watch for any words that PowerPoint marks with a red, wavy line, indicating that the word isn't in PowerPoint's built-in dictionary. Make any necessary corrections.

Figure 1-14 ◀
Outline after
inserting text

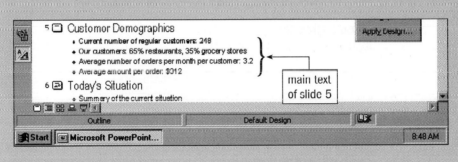

You have now created a new fifth slide for Carl's presentation. After reviewing the changes you've made to his presentation, Carl decides several slides are unnecessary. He asks you to delete these unnecessary slides that the AutoContent Wizard automatically created.

Deleting Slides

Carl decides that he doesn't need slides on "Recommending a Stategy," "Today's Situation," "How Did We Get Here?" or "Available Options." You can delete slides in any view except Slide Show View. However it's often easiest to delete slides in Outline View, which is the view you're currently in.

To delete slides in Outline View:

1. Click the **up arrow** on the vertical scroll bar until you can see all the text of slide 2 on the screen.

2. Click ✛ on the slide icon for slide 2. The title and the main text of slide 2 are selected. See Figure 1-15.

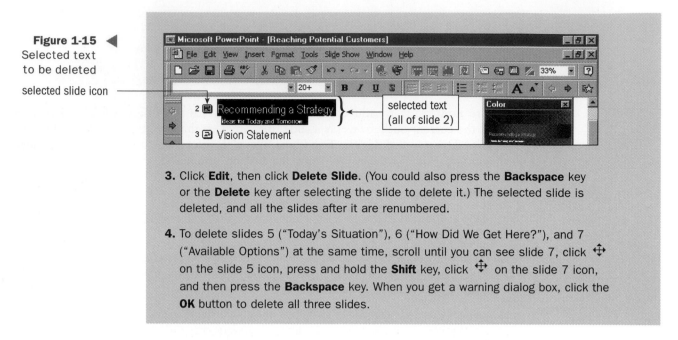

Figure 1-15 ◀
Selected text
to be deleted

selected slide icon ————

3. Click **Edit**, then click **Delete Slide**. (You could also press the **Backspace** key or the **Delete** key after selecting the slide to delete it.) The selected slide is deleted, and all the slides after it are renumbered.

4. To delete slides 5 ("Today's Situation"), 6 ("How Did We Get Here?"), and 7 ("Available Options") at the same time, scroll until you can see slide 7, click ✛ on the slide 5 icon, press and hold the **Shift** key, click ✛ on the slide 7 icon, and then press the **Backspace** key. When you get a warning dialog box, click the **OK** button to delete all three slides.

The new slide 5 in Carl's presentation is now "Recommendation." Carl asks you to edit that slide also.

To edit slide 5:

1. Edit the title of slide 5 to change "Recommendation" to "Recommendations."

2. Edit the main text of slide 5 so the bulleted items match those in Figure 1-16.

Figure 1-16 ◀
Text of slide 5

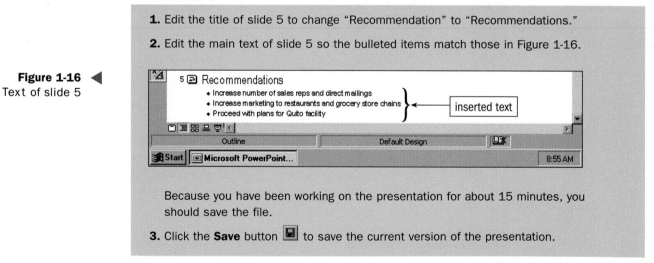

Because you have been working on the presentation for about 15 minutes, you should save the file.

3. Click the **Save** button 🖫 to save the current version of the presentation.

You have adapted and edited Carl's presentation in Outline View and completed the five slides of his presentation. Carl now wants you to use Slide View to see how his presentation looks.

Viewing Slides in Slide View

Viewing your presentation in Outline View doesn't show you how each of your slides will look during an actual presentation. You can get a better idea of how the slides will look from the Slide Miniature, but the miniature is too small to see the details and read the text. To see the slides as they will appear in a presentation, you must change to one of the other views. You'll now view the slides in Slide View.

To see slides in Slide View:

1. Scroll the presentation window so you can see the beginning of the outline, then click the pointer anywhere within the text of slide 1. This makes slide 1 the current slide, so that when you switch to Slide View, slide 1 will appear on the screen first.

2. Click the **Slide View** button 🔲 on the View toolbar to display slide 1 in the presentation window. After looking over the slide, you will view the next slide.

3. Click the **Next Slide** button ⯆ at the bottom of the vertical scroll bar to display slide 2, "Vision Statement."

4. To view slide 3, drag the scroll box down until the message by the scroll box says that you're on slide 3, then release the mouse button. See Figure 1-17.

Figure 1-17 ◀
Moving scroll
box to slide 3

presentation
window in
Slide View

Drawing toolbar

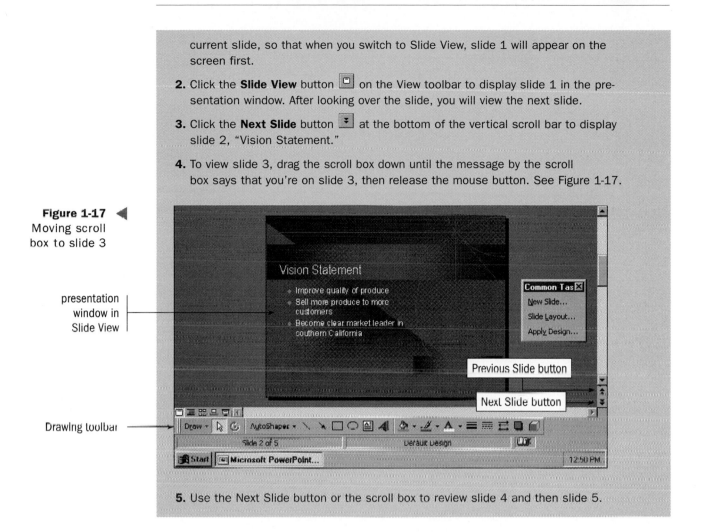

5. Use the Next Slide button or the scroll box to review slide 4 and then slide 5.

Carl has also viewed the presentation and decides further changes are necessary. He asks you to move text and add a new slide. You can make these changes in Slide View.

Editing the Presentation in Slide View

The advantage of editing in Outline View is that you can see much (or even all) of the text of your entire presentation at once. The disadvantage is that you can't see exactly how the text will appear in the completed slide show. For example in Outline View you can't see the text color, the background color, or the background graphics on the slides, but you can see these things in Slide View.

As Carl reviews slide 3 ("Two-Year Goals") of his PowerPoint presentation, he decides that the text of the fourth bullet is awkward. He wants to move the phrase "by 8%" to the end of the fourth item, so that it becomes "Reduce cost of storing and transporting produce by 8%." Carl asks you to change the text using the cut-and-paste method.

Moving Text Using Cut and Paste

Cut and paste is an important way to move text in PowerPoint. To **cut** means to remove text (or some other item) from the document and place it on the Windows Clipboard. The **Clipboard** is an area where text and graphics that have been cut or copied are stored until you act on them further. To **paste** means to transfer a copy of the text from the Clipboard into the document. To perform a cut-and-paste operation, you simply highlight the material you want to move, cut it, and then paste the material where you want it.

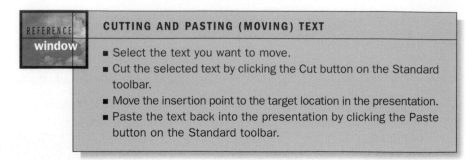

REFERENCE window

CUTTING AND PASTING (MOVING) TEXT

- Select the text you want to move.
- Cut the selected text by clicking the Cut button on the Standard toolbar.
- Move the insertion point to the target location in the presentation.
- Paste the text back into the presentation by clicking the Paste button on the Standard toolbar.

You'll now change the text using the cut-and-paste method.

To move text using cut and paste:

1. In Slide View use the Previous Slide button or the scroll box to move to slide 3.

2. Select the phrase "by 8%" in the fourth item of slide 3 by dragging I over it. See Figure 1-18.

Figure 1-18 ◀
Selecting text
for cut and
paste

Cut button ──

Paste button ──

selected text ──

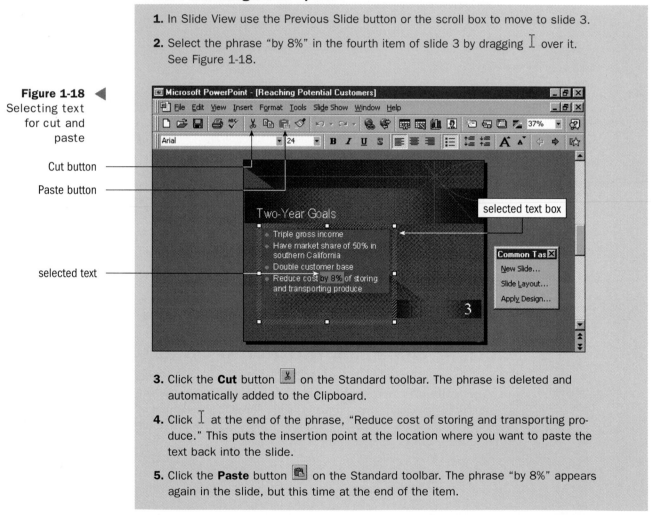

3. Click the **Cut** button 🔏 on the Standard toolbar. The phrase is deleted and automatically added to the Clipboard.

4. Click I at the end of the phrase, "Reduce cost of storing and transporting produce." This puts the insertion point at the location where you want to paste the text back into the slide.

5. Click the **Paste** button 📋 on the Standard toolbar. The phrase "by 8%" appears again in the slide, but this time at the end of the item.

You can also use the cut-and-paste method to copy selected text instead of moving it; simply click the Copy button on the Standard toolbar instead of the Cut button. Then you can paste a copy of the text anywhere in the presentation.

Furthermore, in addition to cut and paste, you can use **drag and drop** to move text in PowerPoint. You simply select the text by dragging the pointer over it, move the pointer into the selected area, press and hold down the left mouse button while you drag the text, and then release the mouse button when the selected text is positioned where you want it. You'll have a chance to use drag and drop at the end of this tutorial.

Now that you've completed the changes for slide 3, you're ready to add a new slide to Carl's presentation.

Adding a New Slide and Choosing a Layout

Carl decides his presentation needs a slide that summarizes Inca Imports' new marketing plan, so he asks you to add a new slide. You'll add the slide in Slide View now.

To add a slide in Slide View:

1. With slide 3 still in the presentation window, click **New Slide** on the Common Tasks toolbar. (You could also click the **New Slide** button on the Standard toolbar.) PowerPoint displays the New Slide dialog box. See Figure 1-19.

Figure 1-19 ◀
New Slide
dialog box

select this layout

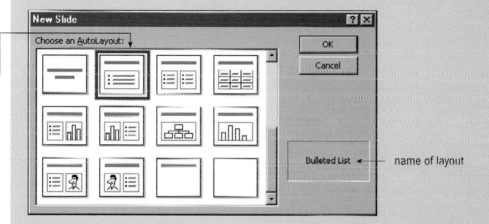

name of layout

Before adding a new slide, you must decide where you want the placeholders for titles, text, and graphics to go. PowerPoint gives you the option of selecting from a variety of AutoLayout slides, which are preformatted slides with placeholders already in them. You can also choose a Blank layout.

2. Click on a few of the AutoLayouts, and read their names in the lower-right corner of the dialog box. If you wanted to start with a blank slide, you would click the Blank layout, which is in the fourth column of the third row. However Carl wants his new slide to be a bulleted list.

3. If necessary scroll up in the Choose an AutoLayout list box, then click the second layout in the top row, titled Bulleted List. See Figure 1-19.

4. Click the **OK** button. PowerPoint inserts a new slide containing a title and main text placeholder for the bulleted list.

5. Click the title placeholder (where the slide says "Click to add title"), then type **Our New Marketing Campaign**.

6. Click the main text placeholder, then type the three bulleted items shown in Figure 1-20.

Figure 1-20 ◀
Completed new
slide 4

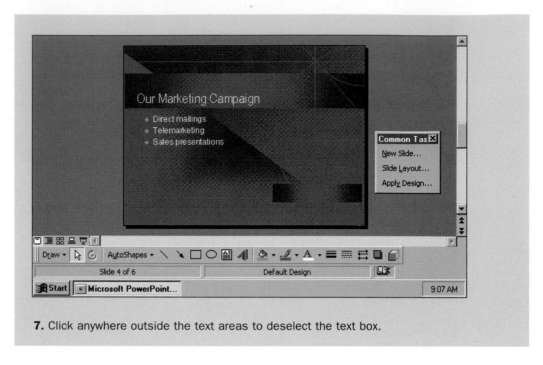

7. Click anywhere outside the text areas to deselect the text box.

You have now added a new slide, with a new layout. Carl is almost satisfied with the slides, but he thinks the design template should be changed to one that is more appropriate for his presentation.

Changing the Design Template

When you use the AutoContent Wizard or open a blank presentation, PowerPoint provides a predetermined **design template**, that is, the colors and format of the background and the type style of the titles, accents, and other text. The default design template that PowerPoint uses with the "Recommending a Strategy" option in the AutoContent Wizard is titled Default Design, with certain colors for the text, background, and graphics. You can easily change the default design template to one of many more that PowerPoint provides. To change the design template, you click the Apply Design button on the Standard toolbar.

Carl wants you to change the template for his presentation to the one titled Ribbons.

To change the template:

1. Click the **Apply Design** button 🖳 on the Standard toolbar. (You could also click **Apply Design** on the Common Tasks toolbar.) The Apply Design dialog box opens. See Figure 1-21.

PowerPoint

Figure 1-21 ◀
Apply Design
dialog box

selected design
template

view of selected
design template

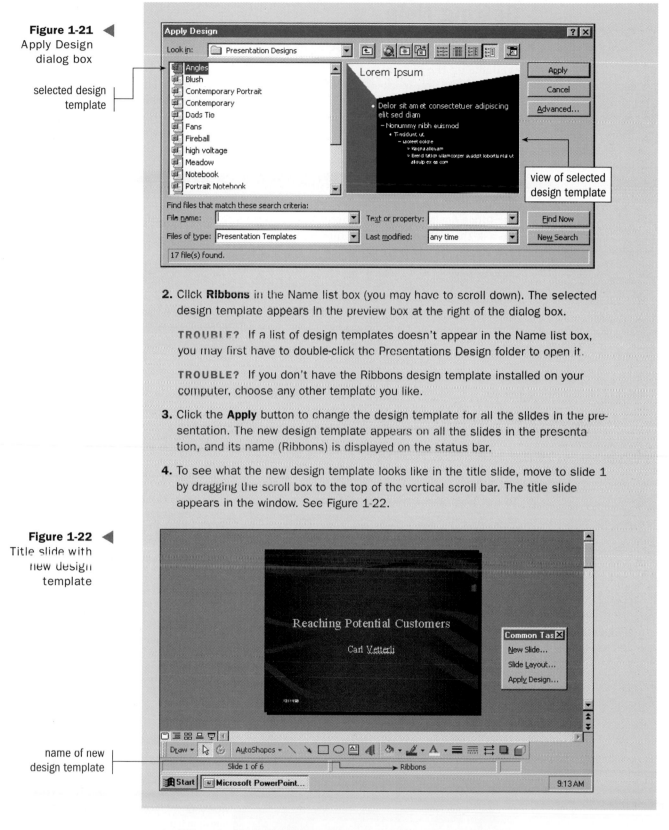

2. Click **Ribbons** in the Name list box (you may have to scroll down). The selected design template appears in the preview box at the right of the dialog box.

TROUBLE? If a list of design templates doesn't appear in the Name list box, you may first have to double-click the Presentations Design folder to open it.

TROUBLE? If you don't have the Ribbons design template installed on your computer, choose any other template you like.

3. Click the **Apply** button to change the design template for all the slides in the presentation. The new design template appears on all the slides in the presentation, and its name (Ribbons) is displayed on the status bar.

4. To see what the new design template looks like in the title slide, move to slide 1 by dragging the scroll box to the top of the vertical scroll bar. The title slide appears in the window. See Figure 1-22.

Figure 1-22 ◀
Title slide with
new design
template

name of new
design template

Carl likes the look of the new design template and is pleased with the slides you have created for his presentation. You're now ready to prepare the other parts of Carl's presentation: the speaker notes and audience handouts (which are simply a printout of the slides). **Speaker notes** are printed pages that contain a picture of and notes about each slide to help the speaker remember what to say while a particular slide is displayed during the presentation. Because you aren't sure how to create speaker notes, you consult the PowerPoint Help system.

Getting Help

The PowerPoint Help system provides the same options as the Help system in other Windows programs—the Help Contents, the Help Index, and the Find feature, which are available on the Help menu. The PowerPoint Help system also provides additional ways to get help as you work—the Office Assistant and the What's This? command.

You'll learn how to use the Office Assistant next in this section. The What's This? command provides context-sensitive help information. When you choose this command from the Help menu, the pointer changes to the Help pointer, which you can then use to click any object or option on the screen to see a description of the object.

Finding Information with the Office Assistant

The **Office Assistant** is an interactive guide to finding information in the Help system. You can ask the Office Assistant a question, and it will look through the Help system to find an answer.

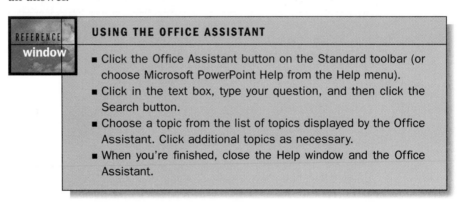

REFERENCE window

USING THE OFFICE ASSISTANT

- Click the Office Assistant button on the Standard toolbar (or choose Microsoft PowerPoint Help from the Help menu).
- Click in the text box, type your question, and then click the Search button.
- Choose a topic from the list of topics displayed by the Office Assistant. Click additional topics as necessary.
- When you're finished, close the Help window and the Office Assistant.

You'll use the Office Assistant to get help about creating speaker notes in PowerPoint.

To get help about speaker notes:

1. Click the **Office Assistant** button 🗟 on the Standard toolbar. The Office Assistant appears and displays a dialog box with several options. See Figure 1-23. The Office Assistant dialog box shown on your screen may not display all the options shown in the figure.

Figure 1-23 ◀
Office
Assistant
dialog box

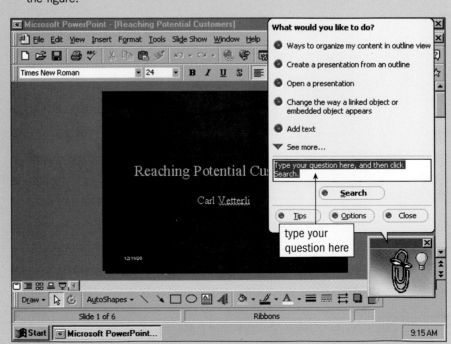

You can now type a question in the text box and have the Office Assistant look for an answer to your question.

2. Type **How do I create speaker notes?** and then click the **Search** option. The Office Assistant displays a list of relevant topics.

3. Click the topic **Create speaker notes and handouts**. The Office Assistant displays the text for the topic in the Help window. See Figure 1-24.

Figure 1-24 ◀
Help window
after clicking
topic "Create
speaker notes
and handouts"

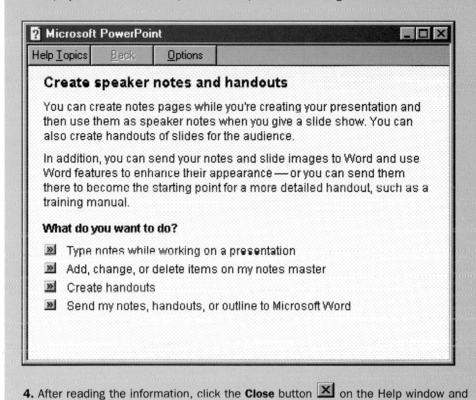

4. After reading the information, click the **Close** button ⊠ on the Help window and then on the Office Assistant window to close both windows.

After reading about speaker notes, you're now ready to create them for Carl's presentation.

Creating Speaker Notes

You'll create speaker notes for three of the slides in Carl's presentation.

To create speaker notes:

1. Make sure slide 1 still appears in the presentation window, then click the **Notes Page View** button ▣. PowerPoint now displays a page for the speaker notes for slide 1, with the placeholder "Click to add text" in a blank text box.

2. Click the **Zoom** list arrow on the Standard toolbar and click **100%** so that you can see the speaker notes at full size, and then, if necessary, scroll so you can see the "Click to add text" placeholder.

3. Click the placeholder and type **Welcome the participants**, press the **Enter** key, type **Thank them for coming**, press the **Enter** key, and type **State need for this meeting: to find ways to increase customer base**.

This completes the notes for slide 1. See Figure 1-25.

Figure 1-25 ◄
Notes Page
View of slide 1

partial view of slide

text of
speaker notes

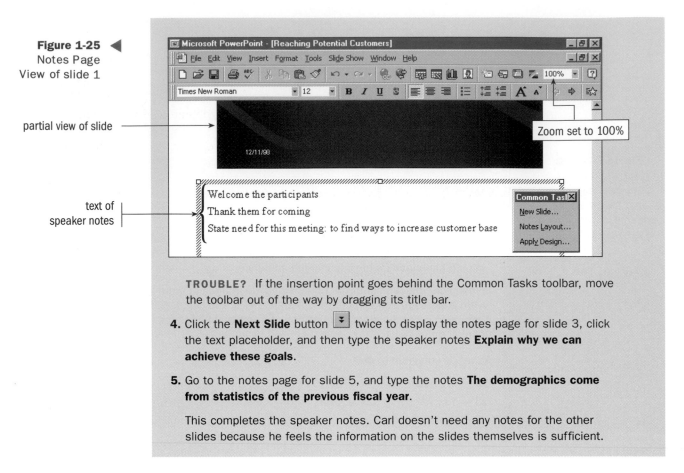

TROUBLE? If the insertion point goes behind the Common Tasks toolbar, move the toolbar out of the way by dragging its title bar.

4. Click the **Next Slide** button ▼ twice to display the notes page for slide 3, click the text placeholder, and then type the speaker notes **Explain why we can achieve these goals**.

5. Go to the notes page for slide 5, and type the notes **The demographics come from statistics of the previous fiscal year**.

This completes the speaker notes. Carl doesn't need any notes for the other slides because he feels the information on the slides themselves is sufficient.

You have made significant progress on Carl's presentation, so you should now save your work. Because you saved the presentation previously, you can simply click the Save button 🖫 to save the current version of the file over the now obsolete version.

To save a file that has been saved previously:

1. Make sure your Student Disk is still in the disk drive.

2. Click 🖫 on the Standard toolbar to save the file using its current filename, Reaching Potential Customers.

A copy of the updated presentation is now on your Student Disk.

Viewing the Completed Slide Show

You now want to look over Carl's completed presentation.

To view the completed presentation as a slide show:

1. Change to Slide View and scroll up to view slide 1, click the **Zoom** list arrow on the Standard toolbar, and then click **Fit**. Now the slide fits into the presentation window.

2. Click the **Slide Show** button 🖵 on the View toolbar.

3. After you read a slide, click the left mouse button or press the **spacebar** to advance to the next slide. Continue advancing until you have seen the entire slide show and PowerPoint returns to Slide View. You can also exit the slide show at any time by pressing the Esc key.

Carl is satisfied with the presentation; you can now print the handouts and speaker notes.

Previewing and Printing the Presentation

Usually, before you print or present a slide show, you should do a final spell check of all the slides and speaker notes by using PowerPoint's Spell Checker feature. You'll have a chance to use the spell checker in the Tutorial Assignments and Case Problems at the end of this tutorial.

Before printing on your black-and-white printer, you should preview the presentation to make sure the text is legible in black and white.

To preview the presentation in black and white:

1. Make sure slide 1, in Slide View, appears on your screen, then click the **Black and White View** button ▣ on the Standard toolbar. See Figure 1-26.

Figure 1-26 ◀
Slide in black-and-white view

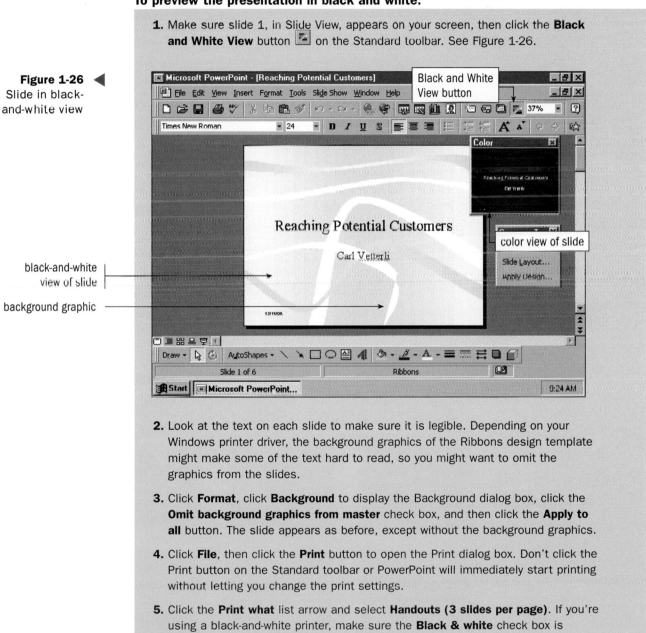

2. Look at the text on each slide to make sure it is legible. Depending on your Windows printer driver, the background graphics of the Ribbons design template might make some of the text hard to read, so you might want to omit the graphics from the slides.

3. Click **Format**, click **Background** to display the Background dialog box, click the **Omit background graphics from master** check box, and then click the **Apply to all** button. The slide appears as before, except without the background graphics.

4. Click **File**, then click the **Print** button to open the Print dialog box. Don't click the Print button on the Standard toolbar or PowerPoint will immediately start printing without letting you change the print settings.

5. Click the **Print what** list arrow and select **Handouts (3 slides per page)**. If you're using a black-and-white printer, make sure the **Black & white** check box is selected. See Figure 1-27.

Figure 1-27 ◀
Print dialog box

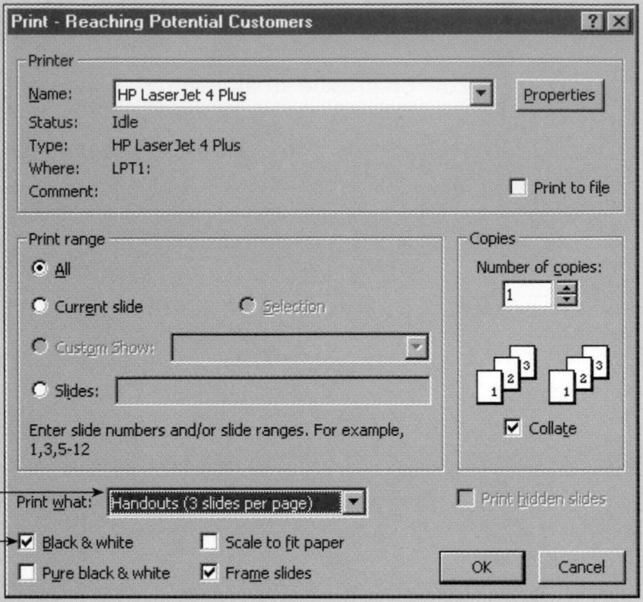

item to print ————→

select this ————→

6. Click the **OK** button to print the handouts. Be patient. Graphics usually take a long time to print, even on a fast printer. You should have two handout pages, each containing three slides.

   You're now ready to print the speaker notes.

7. Again, click the **Print what** list arrow, but this time select **Notes Pages**. Then click the **OK** button to print the speaker notes.

8. To see how the slides look as a group, first click the **Black and White View** button ▨ to return to color view, then click the **Slide Sorter View** button ▨. If necessary drag the Common Tasks toolbar so it doesn't cover any of the slides. Compare your handouts with the six slides shown in Figure 1-28.

Figure 1-28 ◀
Completed
presentation in
Slide Sorter
View

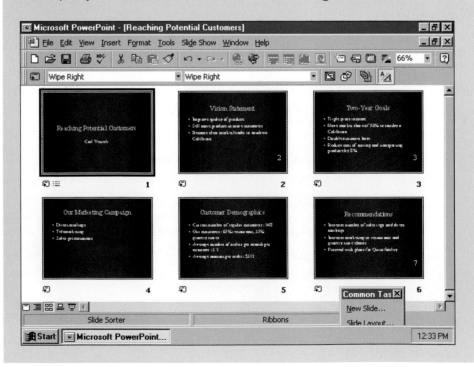

Now that you have created, edited, saved, and printed Carl's presentation, you can exit PowerPoint.

To exit PowerPoint:

1. Click ☒ in the upper-right corner of the PowerPoint window. Because you have made changes since the last time you saved the presentation, PowerPoint displays a dialog box with the message "Do you want to save the changes you made to Reaching Potential Customers?"

2. Click the **Yes** button to save the current version and exit PowerPoint.

Quick Check

1. Explain how to do the following in Outline View:
   a. move text up
   b. delete a slide
   c. change placeholder text
   d. edit text

2. What does it mean to promote a slide in Outline View? To demote a slide?

3. Explain a benefit of Outline View over Slide View and a benefit of Slide View over Outline View.

4. Explain how to do the following:
   a. move text using cut and paste in any view
   b. add a slide in Slide View

5. What is a design template? How do you change the template in a presentation?

6. How does the Office Assistant provide help?

7. What are speaker notes? How do you create them?

8. Why is it necessary to preview a presentation before printing it?

You have created a presentation using the AutoContent Wizard, edited it to fit Carl's presentation, and created and printed speaker notes and handouts. Carl thanks you for your help; he believes that your work will allow him to make an effective presentation.

Tutorial Assignments

After Carl presents his market research to his colleagues, Enrique Hoffman (Director of Marketing) decides he needs to present a new marketing campaign, based on Carl's research. Before presenting to his colleagues at Inca Imports, Enrique asks you to finalize his slides by doing the following:

1. Start PowerPoint and make sure your Student Disk is in the disk drive.

2. Click the Open an existing file radio button, open the file Campaign in the Tutorial.01 TAssign folder on your Student Disk, and save the file as New Marketing Campaign. (To save a file with a different filename, click File, click Save As, type the new filename in the File name text box, and then click the Save button.)

3. In Outline View, delete the unnecessary articles "a," "an," and "the" from each main text slide.

4. In slide 2, move (using drag and drop) the phrase "by telephone" so it immediately follows the phrase "Follow up" in the same item of the main text.
   a. Select the phrase "by telephone."

b. Move the pointer within the region of the selected text, press and hold the mouse button, drag the pointer to the right of the words "Follow up," and then release the mouse button.

c. Click anywhere outside the text area to deselect the text.

5. Move the second item in slide 3, "Will develop slide presentation," down so that it becomes the third (last) item in the main text.

6. In slide 4, the third item of the main text is "Step #2. Establishing Contact with Potential Customers." Promote that item to become a slide title (new slide 5).

7. In the new slide 6, demote the second, third, and fourth bulleted items so they appear indented beneath the first item, "Organize data for our market advantage."

8. Edit the main text of slide 8 so the phrase "Must hire" becomes simply "Hire."

9. Move the entire slide 9 ("Key Issues") up to become slide 8, so that "Becoming More Effective" is the last slide. *Hint:* Remember that to move an entire slide, you click on the slide icon and then click the Move Up button.

10. Spell check the presentation by clicking Tools, then clicking Spelling. When PowerPoint stops at a word that is misspelled, click the correctly spelled word from within the Suggestions, so that it becomes the "Change To" word, and then click the Change button. If PowerPoint stops at a word that is actually spelled correctly but that it doesn't recognize, click the Ignore button.

11. View the entire presentation in Slide Show View.

12. Use the Save command to save the presentation to your Student Disk using the default filename.

13. Use the Office Assistant to find out how to print the outline of the presentation, and then do so.

14. Close the file.

Case Problems

1. New Weave Fashions Shaunda Shao works for New Weave Fashions, a clothing supplier for specialty retail stores in the Northwest. New Weave contracts with wholesale fashion centers to supply New Weave retailers with women's shoes, sports fashions, and boutique merchandise. Shaunda's job is to provide training for New Weave's fledgling retailers. She asks you to help her finalize a presentation she'll use as part of training. Do the following:

1. Open the file Newweave in the Tutorial.01 Cases folder on your Student Disk and save the file as New Weave.

2. In the first bulleted item in slide 2, use cut and paste to move the year ("1998") from the end of the line of text to the beginning, delete the word "in" that now appears at the end of the line, and change "Sales" to "sales."

3. In the second bulleted item in slide 2, use drag and drop to move "increased only 5.5%" from the middle of the line to the end of the line of text. *Hint:* See Tutorial Assignment 4 for instructions for using drag and drop.

4. In slide 4, divide the second item into two separate items, and then revise the results so that they become "Obtaining volume discounts," and "Obtaining quick, reliable delivery."

5. Also in slide 4, move the last item ("Competing with well-known stores") so it becomes the second item in the main text of slide 2.

6. In slide 6, promote the phrase "Telephone follow-ups" so that it is on the same level as the bulleted item above it.

CREATING A POWERPOINT PRESENTATION **TUTORIAL 1** **P 1.31**

PowerPoint

7. Spell check the presentation by using the Spelling button on the Standard toolbar or by clicking Tools, then clicking Spelling. *Hint*: See Tutorial Assignment 10 for more details on spell checking the presentation.

8. View all the slides of the presentation in Slide Show View.

9. Preview the slides in Black and White View. If some of the text is illegible, change the design template to make the text readable or delete the background graphics.

10. Save the file using its default filename.

11. Use the Help Index to find out how to print only slide 5, and then do so. *Hint*: Click Help on the menu bar, click Contents and Index, click the Index tab, type "printing" in the text box labeled 1, click handouts, and then click the Display button to display the Topics Found dialog box.

12. Print handouts of all the slides (3 slides per page) in black and white, and close the file.

2. InfoTech Pratt Deitschmann is seeking venture capital in the amount of $2.5 million for his startup company, InfoTech. InfoTech provides mailroom, word processing, in-house printing, and other information-output services for large corporations and law practices. Pratt has created a presentation to give to executives at A.B. O'Dair & Company, a New York City investment banking firm, and has asked you to finalize it by doing the following:

1. Open the file Infotech in the Tutorial.01 Cases folder on your Student Disk and save the file as InfoTech Capital.

2. Use the What's This? Help feature to learn how to increase the size of the title of slide 1 from 44 to 48 points, and then do so. *Hint*: Click Help on the menu bar, click What's This? and then click the pointer on the Increase Font Size button on the Formatting toolbar.

3. Delete "and Objective" from the title of slide 2.

4. Add the following speaker notes to the notes page of slide 3: "Remind audience that we are a customer-centered company."

5. Delete the first item of the main text of slide 4.

6. In slide 4, promote the four items that are double-indented to single-indented, so that all items in the main text are at the same level.

7. In slide 5, move the second item of the main text to become the third (last) item.

8. In slide 7, use cut and paste to move the text and make other changes so that the first item becomes "Initial venture capital of $2.5 million."

9. Spell check the presentation by using the Spelling button on the Standard toolbar or by clicking Tools, and then clicking Spelling. *Hint*: See Tutorial Assignment 10 for more details on spell checking the presentation.

10. Use Slide Show View to view the entire presentation.

11. You decide to switch slides 5 and 6. Switch to Slide Sorter View, click on slide 6, press and hold the left mouse button, then drag it to the left. When a line appears to the left of slide 5, release the mouse button.

12. Save the file using the current filename.

13. Preview the slides in black and white to make sure they are all legible. If any text isn't legible, delete the background graphics from the design template.

14. Print the slides as handouts (6 slides per page).

15. Close the file.

3. Team One Facilities Management Virgil Pino works for Team One Facilities Management, an international company that manages municipal waste disposal facilities. Virgil asks you to help him to communicate the unfortunate news that escalating travel costs threaten Team One's profitability. Do the following:

1. Close any presentation that might be in the PowerPoint presentation window.

2. Begin a new presentation by clicking File, then clicking New on the menu bar. In the New Presentation dialog box, click the Presentation Designs tab, click the Whirlpool icon, and then click the OK button.

3. In the New Slide dialog box, select the Title Slide layout button, and then click the OK button.

4. In Slide View replace the slide placeholders with the presentation title, "Rescuing Our Road Warriors," and the name of the author, "Virgil Pino."

5. Virgil has already created some of the text for other slides, so insert the file Teamone into the current presentation.
   a. Click Insert and then click Slides from File to open the Slide Finder dialog box.
   b. Make sure the Find Presentation tab is selected, and then click the Browse button to locate and select the Teamone file in the Tutorial.01 Cases folder on your Student Disk.
   c. Click the Open button in the Insert Slides From File dialog box, click the Display button in the Slide Finder dialog box, click the Insert All button, and then click the Close button.

6. In slide 3, add a new bulleted item between the last and the next-to-the-last items. Type the text of the item, "Cost per trip increased by 30%."

7. Insert a new slide 4 in the Bulleted List layout (located on the first row, second column of the AutoLayout dialog box), and then click the OK button. Make the title of the slide "Alternatives Considered." Type the following four items in the main text of the slide:
   a. Decrease amount of travel
   b. Decrease travel costs
   c. Increase other means of networking
   d. Increase efficiency of each trip

8. In slide 5, delete the item, "Coordinate trips to visit more clients per trip."

9. Switch to Outline View and promote the item "Managers' Vision for the Future" so that it becomes the title of a new slide (slide 6).

10. In slide 6, move the first item in the main text so it becomes the last item.

11. In Outline View, add a new slide 7 in the Bulleted List layout, with the title "Summary" and with the bulleted items "Change to meet growth," "Overcome efficiency gap," "Manage travel time and money better," and "Rescue our road warriors."

12. Create a new slide 8 while still in Outline View. Then go into Slide View, and change the Slide Layout to Blank. *Hint:* To change a slide layout, click Format, click Slide Layout, select the Blank layout, then click the Apply button.

13. Spell check the presentation by using the Spelling button on the Standard toolbar or by clicking Tools, then clicking Spelling. *Hint:* See Tutorial Assignment 10 for more details on spell checking the presentation.

14. Save the presentation using the filename Rescuing Our Road Warriors.

15. Preview the slides in black and white, then print them as handouts (6 slides per page).

16. Close the file.

NEW
PERSPECTIVES
SERIES

Integrating Microsoft® Office 97 Professional

TUTORIAL 2

Read This **Before You Begin**

STUDENT DISK

To complete Integration Tutorial 2, you need two Student Disks. Your instructor will either provide you with Student Disks or ask you to make your own.

If you are supposed to make your own Student Disks, you will need two blank, formatted high-density disks. You will need to copy a set of folders from a file server or standalone computer onto your disks. Your instructor will tell you which computer, drive letter, and folders contain the files you need. The following table shows you which folders go on your disks, so that you will have enough disk space to complete all the tutorials, Tutorial Assignments, and Case Problems:

Student Disk	Write this on the disk label	Put these folders on the disk
2	Student Disk 2: Integration Tutorial 2 Tutorial and Tutorial Assignments	Tutorial.02 (from Disk 2 folder)
3	Student Disk 3: Integration Tutorial 2 Case Problems	Tutorial.02 (from Disk 3 folder)

When you begin the tutorial, be sure you are using the correct Student Disk. See the inside front or inside back cover of this book for more information on Student Disk files, or ask your instructor or technical support person for assistance.

USING YOUR OWN COMPUTER

If you are going to work through this book using your own computer, you need:

■ **Computer System** Microsoft Windows 95 or Microsoft Windows NT Workstation 4.0 (or later version) and Microsoft Office 97 Professional must be installed on your computer. This book assumes a Typical installation of Microsoft Office 97 Professional.

■ **Student Disks** Ask your instructor or lab manager for details on how to get the Student Disks. You will not be able to complete the tutorial or end-of-tutorial assignments using your own computer until you have the Student Disks. The Student Files may also be obtained electronically over the Internet. See the inside front or inside back cover of this book for more details.

To complete Integration Tutorial 2, your students must use a set of files on two Student Disks. These files are included in the Instructor's Resource Kit, and they may also be obtained electronically over the Internet. See the inside front or inside back cover of this book for more details. Follow the instructions in the Readme file to copy the files to your server or standalone computer. You can view the Readme file using WordPad. Once the files are copied, you can make Student Disks for the students yourself, or you can tell students where to find the files so they can make their own Student Disks.

COURSE TECHNOLOGY STUDENT FILES

You are granted a license to copy the Student Files to any computer or computer network used by students who have purchased this book.

Integrating Word, Excel, Access, and PowerPoint

Creating a Form Letter and an Integrated Presentation for Country Gardens

In this tutorial you will:

- Merge an Access query with a Word document
- View merged documents
- Preview and print a merged document
- Create a Word outline
- Convert a Word outline to PowerPoint slides
- Copy and paste an Access query in a PowerPoint presentation
- Link an Excel chart to a PowerPoint presentation

Country Gardens

CASE

Sue Dickinson is ready to expand the marketing and promotional activities of her plant supply company, Country Gardens. First, Sue wants to send out the completed promotional letter, which announces the new mail-order catalog, highlights her company's recognition by the NEGHA, and introduces its new products. Sue plans on doing separate mailings to coincide with different promotional events at each of her company's three stores. The store in Derry, New Hampshire has an open house planned for next month. So, Sue first wants to send the letter to only those customers in New Hampshire so that they receive the letter before the open house. Later, she will do a separate mailing for Vermont customers to coincide with the Burlington store's grand opening, and a separate mailing to Massachusetts customers to coincide with the Dunstable store's participation in a town fair.

Sue also needs to prepare a presentation for next month's Eastern Regional Growers Conference, which is sponsored by the NEGHA. The conference provides a good opportunity for Country Gardens and other area greens suppliers to share information and promote their companies and products. This year, Sue is particularly concerned that her presentation be successful, so that she can take full advantage of Country Gardens' recognition as the year's largest grower and greens supplier in New England.

In this tutorial, you'll complete the promotional letter for Sue by merging it, as a form letter in Word, with the names and addresses of Country Gardens' New Hampshire customers. This data is stored in an Access query. After completing the form letter, you'll use Word's outline feature to create an outline of the topics Sue wants to present at the conference. Then, you'll convert the outline to a PowerPoint presentation. The presentation will also include the Excel pie chart showing Country Gardens as the largest area grower and an Access query listing the company's ten new products. You'll use different integration methods to include these items in the presentation.

Planning the Form Letter

A **form letter** is a Word document that contains standard paragraphs of text and a minimum of variable text, usually just the names and addresses of the letter recipients. The **main document** of a form letter contains the text, punctuation, spaces, graphics, and other information you want to be the same in each letter. You then insert into the main document special instructions, called **merge fields**, that tell Word where to print the variable information. The variable information is contained in a **data source**, which can be another Word document, an Access database, or some other source. When you merge the main document with the data source, Word replaces the merge fields with the appropriate information from the data source. The process of merging the main document with the data source is called a **mail merge**.

In this case, Sue's promotional letter will be the main document and the Access database containing the names and addresses of Country Gardens' customers will be the data source. Figure 2-1 shows Sue's plan for the form letter.

Figure 2-1 ◀
Sue's plan for
the form letter

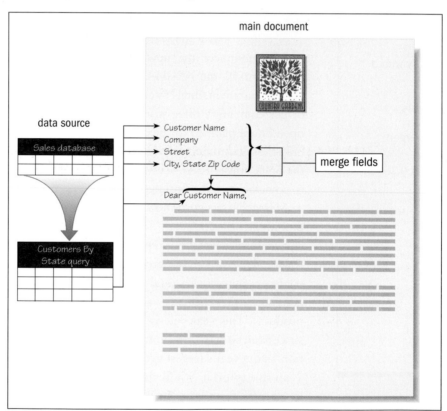

Note that the data source is actually a query in the Sales database. This query, which Sue created and saved as "Customers By State," retrieves the data for only those customers in New Hampshire.

You'll follow Sue's plan to merge the Access data with the Word document to create the form letter.

Merging Access Data with a Word Document

When specifying an Access database as the data source for a mail merge, you can select any table or query defined in the database as the actual data source. If you select a table, Word retrieves all the data in the table each time you use the data source. If you select a query, you have the option of using only the original query instructions to retrieve the data; or, if you expect the query instructions to change, you can establish a link between the Word document and the query so that it retrieves data based on the latest query instructions. Each time you use a linked query as the data source, Word carries out the current instructions of the query.

For example, Sue first wants to send her letter to only those customers in New Hampshire. So, she will use the Customers By State query she created as the data source for the mail merge. This query currently includes selection criteria for the State field so that the results show the address data for New Hampshire customers only. Sue knows that she will be changing the query instructions later when she completes the other two mailings (to Vermont customers and then to Massachusetts customers). Specifically, she will modify the selection criteria for the State field so that the query retrieves the customer data for a different state. Therefore, Sue will want to have the Word document linked to the query so that the mail merge will always use the latest query instructions. Otherwise, the mail merge would always retrieve the data based on the original query instructions and would always show the New Hampshire customer data.

When you merge Access data with a Word document, you are creating a different type of link from other links between Office 97 programs. A standard link, such as from Excel to Word, establishes a two-way connection between the source and destination programs that allows you to update information from either program and have it reflected in the other. However, in order to ensure database integrity and enforce database security, all updates to an Access database must take place from within Access. Therefore, you cannot create a two-way link between Access and another program. The mail merge between Word and Access creates a one-way link in which any changes you make to the Access data will be reflected in the mail merge results in Word, but any changes you make to the merged data in Word will not be made to the data in Access.

The first step in completing the mail merge is to specify the main document and the data source.

Specifying the Main Document and the Data Source

A mail-merge main document can be a new or existing Word document. In this case, the main document is Sue's promotional letter. The document, which is named Letter2 and is stored on your Student Disk, is a slightly modified version of the document you worked with in the first integration tutorial. You'll begin by starting Word and opening the letter document.

To start Word and open the letter document:

1. Start Word as usual.

2 Make sure your Student Disk is in the appropriate drive, and then open the document named **Letter2**, which is located in the Tutorial.02 folder on your Student Disk. The letter is displayed in the document window in page layout view.

   Next you'll save the file with a new name. That way, the original letter remains intact on your Student Disk, in case you want to restart the tutorial.

3. Click **File** on the menu bar, and then click **Save As** to display the Save As dialog box.

4. Save the file as **Main Letter** in the Tutorial.02 folder on your Student Disk.

Now you need to specify the letter as the main document and the Access query as the data source.

To specify the main document and the data source:

1. Click **Tools** on the menu bar, and then click **Mail Merge**. The Mail Merge Helper dialog box opens. See Figure 2-2.

Figure 2-2 ◀
Mail Merge
Helper
dialog box

click to choose the
type of merge
document

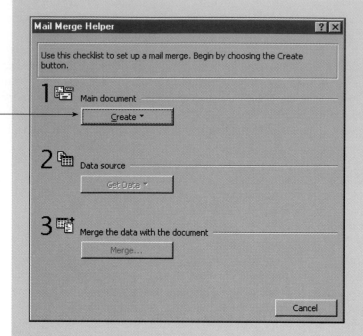

The type of merge document you need to create is a form letter.

2. Click the **Create** button, and then click **Form Letters**. Word displays a dialog box asking if you want to use the active window as the main document or create a new main document. In this case, you want to use the active window, which contains the customer letter, as the main document.

3. Click the **Active Window** button. The area below the Create button now indicates the type of mail merge (form letters) and the name of the main document (Main Letter).

Next you need to specify the data source, which is the Customers By State query in the Sales database.

4. Click the **Get Data** button, and then click **Open Data Source**. The Open Data Source dialog box opens.

The Sales database is located in the Tutorial.02 folder on your Student Disk.

5. Make sure that the **Tutorial.02** folder is displayed in the Look in list box.

Because the dialog box currently shows only the Word documents in the selected folder, you need to change the entry in the Files of type list box to show the Access database files.

6. Click the **Files of type** list arrow, and then click **MS Access Databases**. The dialog box now shows a list of all the Access database files in the Tutorial.02 folder on your Student Disk.

7. Click **Sales** and then click the **Open** button. A Microsoft Access dialog box opens, in which you can choose a table or query in the selected database as the data source. In this case, you need to specify the query Sue created—Customers By State. This query retrieves only those records with a State value of "NH."

8. Click the **Queries** tab in the dialog box, and then make sure **Customers By State** is selected. See Figure 2-3.

Figure 2-3 ◀
Selecting a
query as the
data source

selected query ⎯

specifies that the
merge will use the
latest query
instructions to
retrieve the data

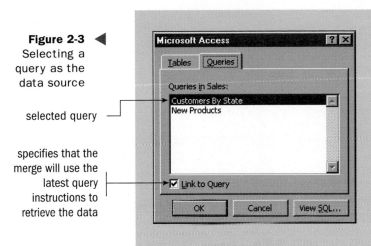

Notice the Link to Query check box on the Queries tab. If you clear this check box, the merge will always use the original query instructions to retrieve the data. If you want to maintain a link to the query so that the merge will use the latest query instructions to retrieve the data, you would leave this check box selected.

Sue knows that she will modify the query's design later by changing the instructions so that it retrieves the address information for only those customers in Vermont, and then again to retrieve the address information for only those customers in Massachusetts. Therefore, you need to maintain the link to the query.

9. Make sure the **Link to Query** check box is selected, and then click the **OK** button. After a moment, Word displays a dialog box indicating that your main document does not contain merge fields. Your next step will be to insert the merge fields, so you need to edit the main document.

10. Click the **Edit Main Document** button. The Mail Merge Helper dialog box closes, and the insertion point is positioned in the Country Gardens address at the top of the main document.

Inserting the Merge Fields

As noted earlier, a merge field is a special instruction that tells Word where to insert the variable information from the data source into a form letter.

REFERENCE
window

INSERTING MERGE FIELDS IN A MAIN DOCUMENT

- Position the insertion point where you want the merge field to appear in the main document.
- Click the Insert Merge Field button on the Mail Merge toolbar.
- Click the name of the field you want to insert.

To complete Sue's form letter, you need to insert seven merge fields, one for each of the following pieces of information: customer name, company name (if any), street, city, state, and zip code—all for the inside address—and customer name again in the salutation of the letter.

To insert the merge fields in the letter document:

1. Scroll the document window and then position the insertion point in the blank paragraph directly above the salutation ("Dear,"). This is where the customer's name and address will appear.

2. Click the **Insert Merge Field** button on the Mail Merge toolbar. A list of the available fields to merge is displayed. See Figure 2-4.

Figure 2-4 ◀
Inserting
merge fields
in the main
document

Mail Merge toolbar ─

fields available
in data source

first merge field
will go here

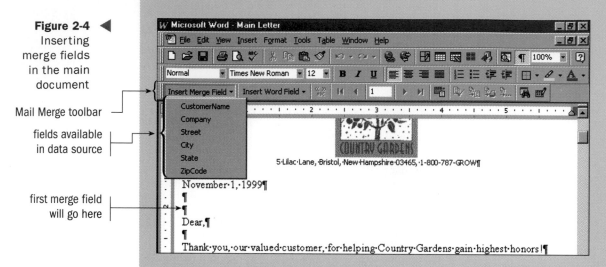

3. Click **CustomerName** to select this field. Word inserts the field name in the document, enclosed in chevrons. The chevrons identify the text as a merge field. See Figure 2-5.

Figure 2-5 ◀
First merge
field inserted

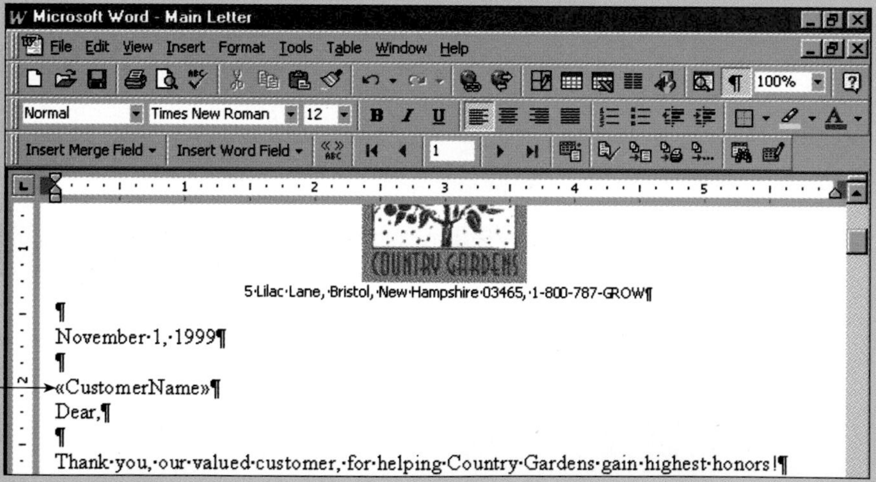

merge field
in document

The company name (if any) should appear on the line below the customer name.

4. Press the **Enter** key to move the insertion point to the next line, click the **Insert Merge Field** button on the Mail Merge toolbar, and then click **Company**. Word inserts the Company merge field in the document.

5. Repeat Step 4 to insert the **Street** field on the third line of the inside address.

6. Repeat Step 4 to insert the **City** field on the fourth line of the inside address.

The State and ZipCode fields must appear on the same line as the City field, with a comma and a space separating the city and state, and a space separating the state and zip code.

Integration

7. Type **,** (a comma), press the **spacebar**, click the **Insert Merge Field** button on the Mail Merge toolbar, and then click **State**.

8. Press the **spacebar**, click the **Insert Merge Field** button on the Mail Merge toolbar, and then click **ZipCode**.

9. Press the **Enter** key to insert a blank line between the inside address and the salutation.

The final merge field you need to insert is the CustomerName field again, after the word "Dear" in the salutation of the letter.

10. Position the insertion point between the "r" in the word "Dear" and the comma following it, press the **spacebar**, click the **Insert Merge Field** button on the Mail Merge toolbar, and then click **CustomerName**. The merge fields are now complete. See Figure 2-6.

Figure 2-6 ◀
Main document
with all merge
fields inserted

completed
merge fields

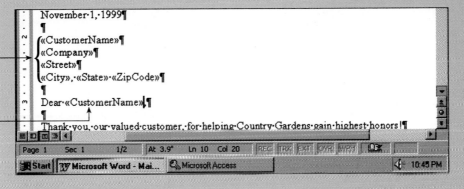

November·1,·1999¶
¶
«CustomerName»¶
«Company»¶
«Street»¶
«City»,·«State»·«ZipCode»¶
¶
Dear·«CustomerName»,¶
¶
Thank·you,·our·valued·customer,·for·helping·Country·Gardens·gain·highest·honors!¶

Page 1   Sec 1   1/2   At 3.9"   Ln 10   Col 20   REC TRK EXT OVR WPH

Start   Microsoft Word - Mai...   Microsoft Access   10:45 PM

TROUBLE? Compare your screen with Figure 2-6 and make sure there are no extra spaces or punctuation around the merge fields. If you need to delete a merge field, click and drag the mouse to select the entire field, and then press the Delete key.

11. Save the letter.

Performing the Mail Merge

With the main document and merge fields in place, you're ready to perform the mail merge. You can choose to merge the data to a new Word document, to electronic mail, or directly to the printer. In this case, Sue wants the merge results placed in a new document, so that she can check the merged form letters before printing them.

To complete the mail merge:

1. Click the **Mail Merge Helper** button on the Mail Merge toolbar. The Mail Merge Helper dialog box opens.

Notice that in the area below the Merge button, the dialog box indicates which options are in effect. Any blank lines in addresses will be suppressed so that there are no gaps (by default). For example, if an address does not include a company name, the merge will not produce a blank line in that space. Also, by default, the results will be merged to a new document.

2. Click the **Merge** button. The Merge dialog box opens. See Figure 2-7.

Figure 2-7 ◄
Merge
dialog box

destination for
merge results

blank lines in
addresses will be
suppressed

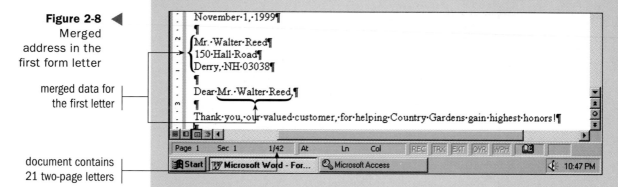

In the Merge to list box, you can choose to merge the data to a new document, to electronic mail, or directly to the printer. Sue wants to check the merged document before printing, so you do not have to change any settings in this dialog box.

3. Click the **Merge** button. The Access data is merged with the Word form letter and placed in a new document named "Form Letters1" (the default name supplied by Word). The form letter for each of the 21 recipients is contained in the merged document, separated by a section break. These 21 recipients are the customers in New Hampshire, as determined by the results of the Customers By State query.

4. Scroll the document until you can see the first merged address. Word replaced each merge field with the appropriate Access data. See Figure 2-8.

Figure 2-8 ◄
Merged
address in the
first form letter

merged data for
the first letter

document contains
21 two-page letters

```
    November·1,·1999¶
    ¶
    Mr.·Walter·Reed¶
    150·Hall·Road¶
    Derry,·NH·03038¶
    ¶
    Dear·Mr.·Walter·Reed,¶
    ¶
    Thank·you,·our·valued·customer,·for·helping·Country·Gardens·gain·highest·honors!¶
```

Page 1   Sec 1   1/42   At   Ln   Col   REC TRK EXT OVR WPH

Start Microsoft Word - For...   Microsoft Access   10:47 PM

Notice that the merged document contains 42 pages. Each letter is two pages long, and there are 21 letters in all.

5. Use the buttons in the vertical scroll bar to page through the merged document. Notice that in addresses that do not include a company name, the blank line is suppressed. Also, notice that each two-page form letter is separated from the others by a section break.

6. Save the document as **Merged Letters** in the Tutorial.02 folder on your Student Disk, and then close the document. You return to the main document.

When you're working with mail merged documents, you don't have to open the document containing the merge results in order to view them. You can view the merged documents right from the main document.

7. Click the **View Merged Data** button on the Mail Merge toolbar. Word displays the information from the first merged letter in place of the merge fields.

8. Practice using the navigation buttons on the Mail Merge toolbar to display different form letters, and then click the **First Record** button on the Mail Merge toolbar to redisplay the first form letter.

After viewing the merged documents, Sue decides to print just one of the letters to check its appearance and layout before printing all the letters.

Previewing and Printing the Merged Document

You can preview and print a merged document in the same way that you do any Word document—using the Print Preview and Print buttons on the Standard toolbar.

For the sample letter Sue wants to print, she decides that it would be best to print one that includes a company name in the address. This will allow her to make sure that the additional line for the company name does not cause a bad page break across the two pages of the letter. She asks you to preview and print the letter for Mills Gardens, which includes the company name. The record for Mills Gardens is the 16th record (in the query results), so you'll use the Go to Record text box to display the record.

To display, preview, and print the merged letter for Mills Gardens:

1. Double-click the number **1** in the Go to Record text box on the Mail Merge toolbar to select the number, type **16**, and then press the **Enter** key. Word displays the record for Mills Gardens.

2. Click the **Print Preview** button ⟨image⟩ on the Standard toolbar. Both pages of the letter are displayed in Print Preview. See Figure 2-9.

Figure 2-9 ◄
Completed
form letter in
Print Preview

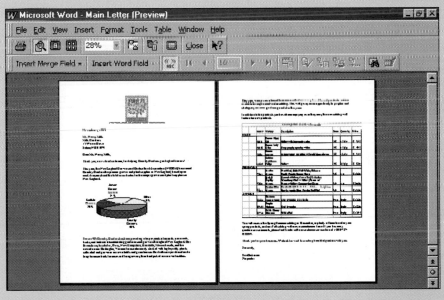

TROUBLE? If only one page is displayed, click the Multiple Pages button ⟨image⟩ on the Print Preview toolbar, and then drag to select 1 x 2 pages.

Sue approves of the letter's layout and pagination, and she asks you to print one copy of it and then close it.

3. Click the **Print** button ⟨image⟩ on the Print Preview toolbar. Word prints one copy of the current merged letter (for Mills Gardens).

4. Click the **Close** button on the Print Preview toolbar to return to the main document.

Before saving and closing the document, you need to redisplay the merge fields so that they will appear instead of the address data the next time the Main Letter document is opened.

5. Click the **View Merged Data** button ⟨image⟩ on the Mail Merge toolbar to redisplay the merge fields.

6. Save and close the main document. Notice that when you close the document, Access closes automatically.

Sue plans on reviewing the printed letter with her assistants to make sure everyone approves of it before she prints and mails all the form letters.

Next, Sue needs to prepare her presentation for the Eastern Regional Growers Conference, which will be held next month. In her presentation, Sue wants to promote her company's new products and new mail-order catalog, as well as highlight the NEGHA recognition as the area's top grower and greens supplier.

Sue has already created the PowerPoint presentation file, selected a suitable template for the presentation, and created the first slide, which shows the Country Gardens logo and slogan. One of her assistants, Judy Pon, created a Word document in which she entered the text for the remaining slides based on notes she took during a meeting with Sue about the conference. To complete the presentation, you first need to create a Word outline from Judy's document.

Creating a Word Outline

You can create an outline in Word by typing text directly in outline view in a new document. When you do, Word automatically assigns heading levels to the text to format it as an outline. You can also format the text in an existing document by displaying it in outline view and assigning each paragraph an appropriate heading level.

The document created by Sue's assistant is named Outline, and is stored on your Student Disk. You need to open this document and format it as an outline so that you can then convert it to slides 2 through 7 in Sue's PowerPoint presentation.

To open the document and display it in outline view:

1. Open the document named **Outline**, which is located in the Tutorial.02 folder on your Student Disk.

2. Save the document as **Outline For Slides** in the Tutorial.02 folder.

   To format the document's text as an outline, you first need to switch to outline view.

3. Click the **Outline View** button located to the left of the horizontal scroll bar. The document is displayed in outline view, and the Outlining toolbar is displayed. See Figure 2-10.

Figure 2-10 ◀
Document displayed in outline view

Outlining toolbar

text before formatting

Outline View button

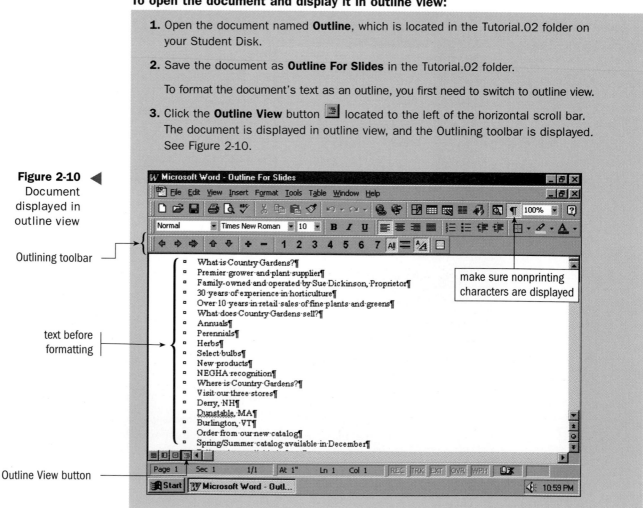

make sure nonprinting characters are displayed

Integration

To format text as an outline, you use the Promote and Demote buttons on the Outlining toolbar. The **Promote** button moves the selected paragraph to the next-higher outline level. The **Demote** button moves the selected paragraph to the next-lower outline level. (Word refers to any text marked by an end-of-paragraph mark as a paragraph, even if the text consists of only one or two words.)

The easiest way to format the text for Sue's outline is to select all of it and then promote it to the first outline level. Then you can demote text as necessary. When converted to PowerPoint slides, paragraphs at the first outline level will be converted to slide titles; paragraphs at the second outline level will be converted to first-level text on the slides; paragraphs at the third outline level will be converted to second-level text on the slides, and so on.

To format the text as a Word outline:

1. Click **Edit** on the menu bar, and then click **Select All**.

2. Click the **Promote** button on the Outlining toolbar. Word formats each paragraph as a first-level heading.

3. Click anywhere in the document to deselect the text. See Figure 2-11.

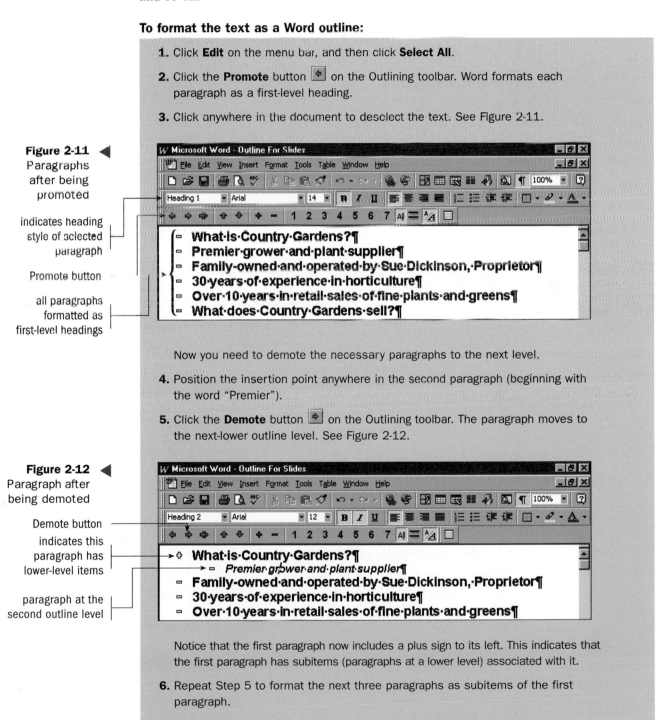

Figure 2-11
Paragraphs after being promoted

indicates heading style of selected paragraph

Promote button

all paragraphs formatted as first-level headings

Now you need to demote the necessary paragraphs to the next level.

4. Position the insertion point anywhere in the second paragraph (beginning with the word "Premier").

5. Click the **Demote** button on the Outlining toolbar. The paragraph moves to the next-lower outline level. See Figure 2-12.

Figure 2-12
Paragraph after being demoted

Demote button

indicates this paragraph has lower-level items

paragraph at the second outline level

Notice that the first paragraph now includes a plus sign to its left. This indicates that the first paragraph has subitems (paragraphs at a lower level) associated with it.

6. Repeat Step 5 to format the next three paragraphs as subitems of the first paragraph.

7. Refer to Figure 2-13 to format the next seven paragraphs as indicated.

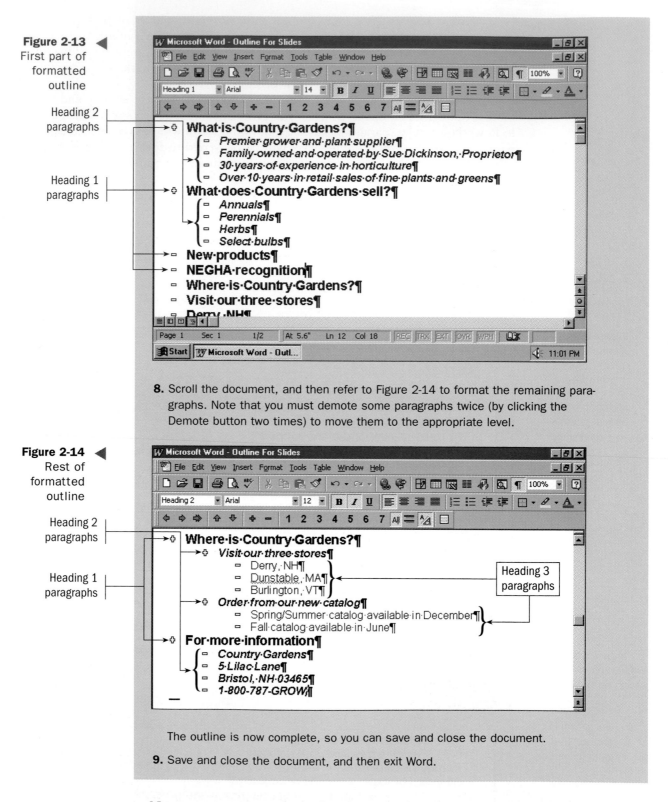

Figure 2-13
First part of
formatted
outline

Heading 2
paragraphs

Heading 1
paragraphs

8. Scroll the document, and then refer to Figure 2-14 to format the remaining paragraphs. Note that you must demote some paragraphs twice (by clicking the Demote button two times) to move them to the appropriate level.

Figure 2-14
Rest of
formatted
outline

Heading 2
paragraphs

Heading 1
paragraphs

Heading 3
paragraphs

The outline is now complete, so you can save and close the document.

9. Save and close the document, and then exit Word.

Now you can convert the outline document to slides in Sue's PowerPoint presentation.

Converting a Word Outline to PowerPoint Slides

You can convert a Word outline to a new PowerPoint presentation or include an outline as slides in an existing presentation. When converting an outline to slides, PowerPoint uses the heading styles in the Word document to determine how to format the text. For example, each paragraph formatted with the Heading 1 style becomes the title of a new slide, each Heading 2 becomes the first level of text on a slide, and so on.

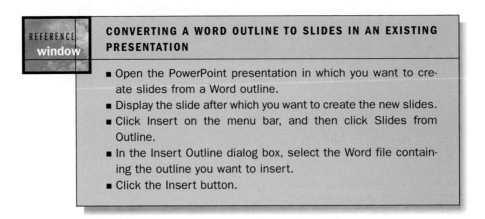

REFERENCE window

CONVERTING A WORD OUTLINE TO SLIDES IN AN EXISTING PRESENTATION

- Open the PowerPoint presentation in which you want to create slides from a Word outline.
- Display the slide after which you want to create the new slides.
- Click Insert on the menu bar, and then click Slides from Outline.
- In the Insert Outline dialog box, select the Word file containing the outline you want to insert.
- Click the Insert button.

Now you can open Sue's PowerPoint presentation and create slides from the Outline For Slides Word document.

To convert the outline to PowerPoint slides:

1. Start PowerPoint and then open the presentation named **Growers** in the Tutorial.02 folder on your Student Disk. The presentation opens and displays its first and only slide, which contains the Country Gardens logo and slogan.

   TROUBLE? If the Common Task window is displayed on your screen, click its Close button to close it.

2. Save the presentation as **Growers Conference** in the Tutorial.02 folder.

   When you insert slides from an outline (or other file), PowerPoint inserts them after the current slide.

3. Click **Insert** on the menu bar, and then click **Slides from Outline**. The Insert Outline dialog box opens.

4. Make sure the dialog box displays the list of files in the Tutorial.02 folder, click **Outline For Slides**, and then click the **Insert** button. PowerPoint inserts and formats the text of the Word outline to create slides 2 through 7, and displays the first new slide (slide 2). See Figure 2-15.

Figure 2-15 ◀
First slide inserted from outline

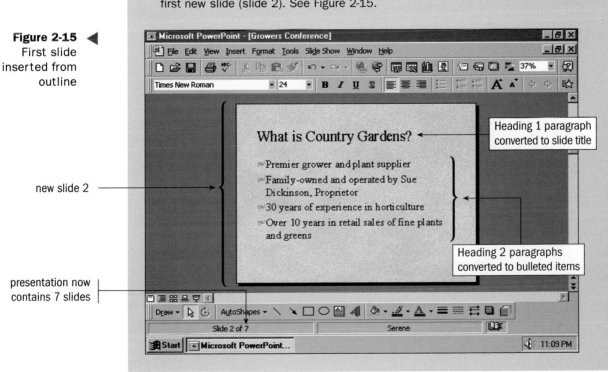

Heading 1 paragraph converted to slide title

new slide 2

Heading 2 paragraphs converted to bulleted items

presentation now contains 7 slides

5. Use the buttons in the vertical scroll bar to page through and view all the slides.

Notice that each Heading 1 paragraph in the Word outline was converted to a slide title; each Heading 2 paragraph was converted to a bulleted item; and each Heading 3 paragraph was converted to a subitem in a bulleted list. Also, note that PowerPoint automatically assigned the Bulleted List layout to each slide.

6. Save the presentation.

With the text for all the slides in place, you can now complete the presentation by integrating the new products table and the NEGHA pie chart.

Copying and Pasting an Access Query in a PowerPoint Presentation

Sue wants the "New products" slide (slide 4) to include the list of Country Gardens' ten new products being offered this year. This product data is stored as an Access query in the Sales database. Sue knows that this data will not change before the conference, so she asks you to copy and paste the query on slide 4.

To prepare to copy and paste the query:

1. Move to slide 4 in the presentation.

This slide will include only the title "New products" and the pasted Access query data. Therefore, the current layout of the slide, Bulleted List, is inappropriate. You need to change the layout of the slide to Title Only before you copy and paste the query.

2. Click the **Slide Layout** button 🔲 on the Standard toolbar. The Slide Layout dialog box opens.

3. Click the **Title Only** layout, and then click the **Apply** button. PowerPoint applies the layout to the slide.

Now you can copy and paste the Access query on the slide.

To copy and paste the New Products query on slide 4:

1. Start Access and open the **Sales** database located in the Tutorial.02 folder on your Student Disk.

2. Click the **Queries** tab to display the list of queries in the database, click **New Products,** and then click the **Open** button. Access displays the results of the query in Datasheet view. See Figure 2-16.

Figure 2-16 ◄
New Products
query results

click here to select
entire query

data for Country
Gardens' ten
new products

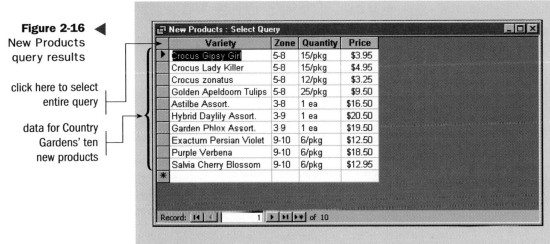

Sue wants all the data from the query to appear on the slide.

3. Click the selector to the left of the column headings (refer to Figure 2-16). Access selects the entire query.

4. Click the **Copy** button 📋 on the Query Datasheet toolbar to copy the query to the Clipboard.

5. Close the query and then exit Access. You return to the presentation.

   Now you can paste the query on slide 4.

6. Click the **Paste** button 📋 on the Standard toolbar. PowerPoint inserts the query, but it is not positioned properly on the slide.

7. Use the pointer ✛ to drag the query so that its left edge is aligned with the left edge of the slide title.

   Next you need to fix the query columns, which are misaligned.

8. Position the insertion point immediately to the left of the column heading "Zone," and then press the **Tab** key twice.

9. Use the Tab key to align the rest of the query data as shown in Figure 2-17. When finished, click in an empty area on the slide to deselect the query.

Figure 2-17 ◄
Query after
aligning
columns

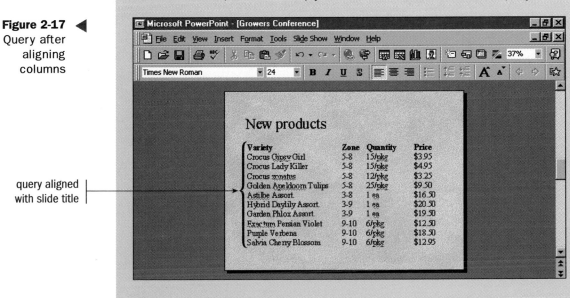

query aligned
with slide title

10. Save the presentation.

Linking an Excel Chart to a PowerPoint Presentation

Sue wants the Excel pie chart showing Country Gardens as the area's top grower to be included on the "NEGHA recognition" slide (slide 5). Recall that the chart shows sales data for the top growers. Sue has been reviewing the fourth quarter sales and she thinks that the sales figures for the year might come in even higher than the figures the NEGHA used to create the pie chart. Because Sue might need to revise the Country Gardens data series in the pie chart to reflect the new sales figures, she asks you to link the chart to the presentation.

To link the Excel pie chart to the presentation:

1. Move to slide 5 in the presentation.

   First you need to change the slide layout to Title Only, because this slide will include only the slide title and the linked pie chart.

2. Click the **Slide Layout** button 🖼 on the Standard toolbar. The Slide Layout dialog box opens.

3. Click the **Title Only** layout, and then click the **Apply** button.

4. Start Excel and then open the workbook named **NEGHA** located in the Tutorial.02 folder on your Student Disk.

5. On the Market Data worksheet, click the **pie chart** to select it (if necessary), and then click the **Copy** button 🗐 on the Standard toolbar.

6. Click the **PowerPoint** button on the taskbar to switch back to the presentation.

7. Click **Edit** on the menu bar, and then click **Paste Special**. The Paste Special dialog box opens.

8. Make sure **Microsoft Excel Chart Object** is selected, click the **Paste link** option button, and then click the **OK** button. The chart is linked to the slide. You need to resize and reposition the chart.

9. Use the corner sizing handles and the pointer to resize and reposition the chart so that it looks like the one shown in Figure 2-18. When finished, click in an empty area on the slide to deselect the chart.

Figure 2-18 ◀
Linked chart
after
repositioning
and resizing

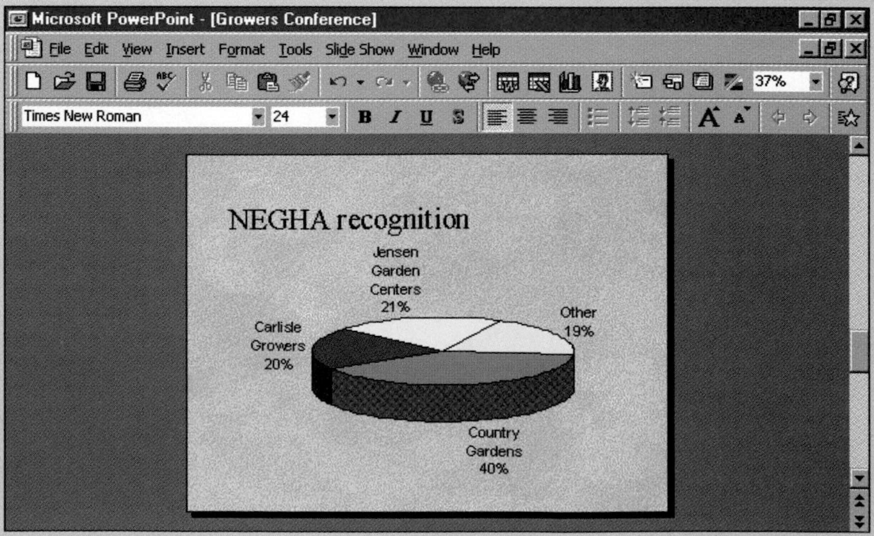

10. Save the presentation.

Sue wants to view the slides in slide sorter view to determine if she wants to rearrange the order of slides.

To view the slides in slide sorter view:

1. Click the **Slide Sorter View** button 🔲 to the left of the horizontal scroll bar. Scroll the window so that slides 1 through 6 are displayed. See Figure 2-19.

Figure 2-19 ◄
Completed
presentation in
slide sorter
view

Word outline text
converted to new
slide titles and
bulleted items

copied and pasted
Access query

linked Excel chart

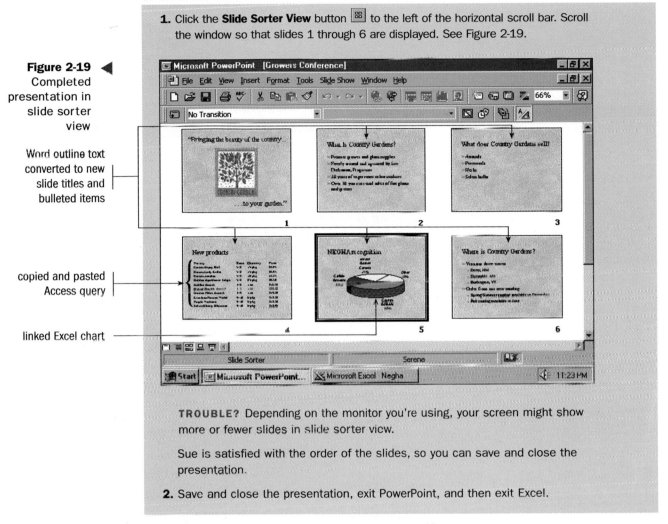

TROUBLE? Depending on the monitor you're using, your screen might show more or fewer slides in slide sorter view.

Sue is satisfied with the order of the slides, so you can save and close the presentation.

2. Save and close the presentation, exit PowerPoint, and then exit Excel.

Quick Check

1. Describe the relationship between the main document and the data source for a mail merge.

2. How do you insert merge fields in a main document?

3. Describe the results of clearing the Link to Query check box when specifying a query as the data source for a mail merge.

4. How do you view merged documents directly from the main document?

5. Describe how the Promote and Demote buttons work in outline view in Word.

6. What is the meaning of the plus sign to the left of a paragraph in outline view in Word?

7. Describe how PowerPoint interprets heading levels when converting a Word outline to presentation slides.

Sue is pleased with her finished letter and presentation, and she is confident that they will both contribute to the successful promotion of Country Gardens. The integration features of Office 97 make it easy for Sue to work with information created in different programs to produce just the results she wants.

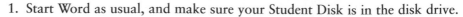

Tutorial Assignments

Now that the promotional letter is complete, Sue is ready to send it out to her customers. To do so, she wants to print the customers' names and addresses on mailing labels that can be placed on the envelopes. Also, Sue wants to prepare a brief presentation to give to her employees at the next staff meeting. The presentation will be about the upcoming Eastern Regional Growers Conference.

1. Start Word as usual, and make sure your Student Disk is in the disk drive.

2. In the active window, create a mailing labels main document, which will be merged with the address data.

3. For the data source of the mail merge, specify the Customers By State query in the Sales database, which is stored in the TAssign folder on your Student Disk.

4. Set up the main document:
   a. In the Label Options dialog box, make sure the Label products box displays "Avery standard." Scroll down and choose product number 5160 - Address. Accept all other defaults in this dialog box.
   b. Complete the Create Labels dialog box by inserting the following merge fields, as shown (be sure to include the necessary punctuation and spaces):
      CustomerName
      Company
      Street
      City, State ZipCode

5. Merge the records to a new document, and then save the document as Merged Labels in the TAssign folder on your Student Disk.

6. Preview the Merged Labels document, print just the first page, and then close the document.

7. Save the main document as Main Labels in the TAssign folder on your Student Disk, and then close the document.

8. Open the document named Topics, which is located in the TAssign folder on your Student Disk.

9. Save the document as Topics Outline in the TAssign folder.

10. Format the Topics Outline document as an outline. Format the following paragraphs as first-level headings:
    About the Conference
    Company Booth
    New Products
    Estimated Breakdown of Participants
    Assignments
    Format all other paragraphs as second-level headings, *except* the following four paragraphs, which should be formatted as third-level headings:
    Make presentation
    Attend the owners' meeting
    Manage the booth
    Lead break-out group discussion

11. Use the What's This? command on the Help menu to learn about the Move Up and Move Down buttons on the Outlining toolbar. Then use the necessary button (or buttons) to reposition the paragraph "Estimated Breakdown of Participants" as the third Heading 1 paragraph in the outline.

12. Save and close the Topics Outline document.

13. Start PowerPoint and create a new presentation using the Meadow template. Choose the Title Slide layout for the first slide.

14. On the first slide, type the title "Staff Meeting" and the subtitle "Preparing for the Eastern Regional Growers Conference."

15. Convert the Topics Outline document to slides 2 through 6 in the presentation.

16. On slide 2, use the Tab key to align the words "Durham, NH" under the words "The New England Center"; then delete the comma after the word "Center."

17. Save the presentation as Staff Meeting in the TAssign folder on your Student Disk.

18. Move to slide 4 and complete the following:
    a. Change the layout of the slide to Title Only.
    b. Open the Excel workbook named Groups, which is located in the TAssign folder on your Student Disk, and then link the pie chart in the workbook to slide 4.
    c. Resize and reposition the chart so that it is centered on the slide.

19. Move to slide 5 and complete the following:
    a. Change the layout of the slide to Title Only.
    b. Open the Access database named Sales, which is located in the TAssign folder on your Student Disk, and then copy and paste the data in the New Products query to slide 5.
    c. Resize and reposition the data so that it is centered on the slide.
    d. Fix the alignment of the columns of data on the slide.

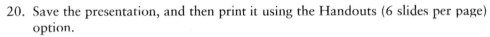 20. Save the presentation, and then print it using the Handouts (6 slides per page) option.

21. Exit all open programs.

Case Problems

1. Electro-Lease Company John Rivers, the sales supervisor for the Electro-Lease Company, has printed several follow-up letters to customers providing written quotations. Now he needs to send the letters to the customers. To help John, you'll use the mail-merge feature to produce the envelopes needed for the mailing.

1. Start Word as usual, and make sure your Student Disk is in the disk drive.

 2. In the active window, create an envelopes main document, which will be merged with the address data.

3. For the data source of the mail merge, specify the Customers table in the Leases database, which is stored in the Cases folder on your Student Disk.

 4. Set up the main document:
    a. Accept all the default settings in the Envelope Options dialog box.
    b. Complete the Envelope address dialog box by inserting the following merge fields, as shown (be sure to include the necessary punctuation and spaces):
        CustomerName
        Company
        Street
        City, State ZipCode

5. Merge the records to a new document, and then save the document as Merged Envelopes in the Cases folder on your Student Disk.

6. Preview the Merged Envelopes document, and then close the document.

7. Save the main document as Main Envelopes in the Cases folder on your Student Disk.

8. From the main document, view the data for record 19.

9. Position the insertion point to the left of the word "Boulevard" in the address on the envelope, delete the word "Boulevard," and then type "Street." Switch to Access and open the Customers table. View the data for record 19. Was the change you made in Word reflected in the Access table? Why or why not? Switch back to Word and close the Main Envelopes document without saving it.

10. In Access, change the entry in the Street field for record 17 to "25 Great Road." Close the Customers table. Switch to Word and then open the Main Envelopes document. View the data for record 17 from the main document. Was the change you made in Access reflected in the Word document? Why or why not?

11. Print the currently displayed record. (If your printer is equipped to print envelopes, you can print the data on an envelope; otherwise, print on regular paper.)

12. Exit Word. Do not save changes to the Main Envelopes document.

2. Admissions at the University of Maine Jennifer Dollof has been asked by her manager, the head of the Admissions office, to prepare a presentation to give to incoming freshmen students and their parents during orientation. You'll prepare the presentation for Jennifer by completing the following:

1. Create an outline document in Word containing the topics to present during orientation. Review Case Problem 2 in the first integration tutorial for ideas on presentation topics. Include enough topics for five or six presentation slides. Be sure to include both first-level headings and second-level headings (at least) in the outline. Save the document as Orientation Outline in the Cases folder on your Student Disk.

2. Create a PowerPoint presentation using a template of your choice. Create a title slide for the presentation using text of your choice. Save the presentation as Slides For Orientation in the Cases folder on your Student Disk.

3. Convert the Orientation Outline document you created in Step 1 to slides in your presentation.

4. In Case Problem 2 in the first integration tutorial, you created a line chart in Excel. Link this chart to an appropriate slide in your presentation.

5. Insert an appropriate piece of clip art on either an individual slide (such as the title slide) or on the slide master so that the clip art picture appears on each slide in the presentation. If necessary, use the Office Assistant to find out how to insert a clip art picture on a slide.

6. Save the presentation, and then run the slide show.

7. Print the presentation slides using the Handouts (6 slides per page) option.

8. Close any open programs.

Answers to Quick Check Questions

1 The main document contains the standard text and the merge fields for the mail merge; the data source contains the variable information that will replace the merge fields in the main document during the mail merge.

2 In the main document, position the insertion point where you want the merge field to appear, click the Insert Merge Field button on the Mail Merge toolbar, and then click the name of the field you want to insert.

3 The mail merge will always use the original query instructions to retrieve the data from the data source.

4 Click the View Merged Data button on the Mail Merge toolbar.

5 The Promote button moves the selected paragraph to the next-higher outline level; the Demote button moves the selected paragraph to the next-lower outline level.

6 The plus sign indicates that the paragraph has subitems (paragraphs at a lower level) associated with it.

7 Paragraphs at the first heading level are converted to slide titles; paragraphs at the second heading level are converted to first-level text on the slides; paragraphs at the third heading level are converted to second-level text on the slides, and so on.

Integrating Microsoft Office 97 Task Reference

TASK	PAGE #	RECOMMENDED METHOD
Access query, copy and paste into PowerPoint	I 2.16	Display the query results, click the selector to the left of the column headings to select the query, click 🖿, switch to the PowerPoint slide, click 🖿
Data source, specify for a mail merge	I 2.5	Click Tools, click Mail Merge, specify the main document, click Get Data, click Open Data Source, select the source file for the data
Main document, specify for a mail merge	I 2.5	Click Tools, click Mail Merge, click Create, specify the type of main document, specify the active window or a new document
Merge fields, insert	I 2.7	See Reference Window: Inserting Merge Fields in a Main Document
Merge results, view from the main document	I 2.10	Click 🖿 on the Mail Merge toolbar
Paragraph, move to the next-higher outline level	I 2.13	Click ⬅ on the Outlining toolbar
Paragraph, move to the next-lower outline level	I 2.13	Click ➡ on the Outlining toolbar
Word outline, convert to PowerPoint Slides	I 2.15	See Reference Window: Converting a Word Outline to Slides in an Existing Presentation

Creating Web Pages with Microsoft® Office 97 Professional

TUTORIAL

Read This **Before You Begin**

TUTORIAL

Creating Web Pages with Microsoft Office 97 Professional

Creating Hypertext Documents for Jackson Electronics

Web Pages
& HTML

Jackson Electronics

CASE You work at Jackson Electronics, a company that manufactures electronic equipment ranging from modules that control theater lighting to desktop scanners. The company has grown to employ more than 4500 people. The Jackson Electronics management team is looking for new ways to get information such as sales reports, new product information, and product schedules to employees quickly and easily. Currently, this type of information is often printed and distributed in the form of paper memos.

Eager to cut printing and paper costs, the company would like to make this information available **online**—in an electronic form over the company's network. An employee then could access the information from his or her computer. Besides saving money, online reports can be quickly updated to incorporate the latest news and distributed almost instantaneously to employees in Jackson Electronics plants across the country.

Your supervisor, Jeff Brooks, has asked you to help develop one of the first online documents as a "test case." He suggests that you compile information about a new desktop scanner, the ScanMaster. Jackson Electronics recently upgraded to Microsoft Office 97, and Jeff particularly wants you to use the tools that come with many of the Office 97 programs to develop your online document. You'll start by saving a Microsoft Word document in a format that can be placed on the Web. Then you'll create connections between that document and the other supporting documents for the ScanMaster—including a fact sheet, a sales report, and a marketing presentation.

SESSION

1

In this session, you will learn how to create a document in HTML format, the file format used by the World Wide Web (WWW). You'll learn how to create hyperlinks between and within Office documents by copying and pasting so that you can easily access other information from a single document. You'll explore how to navigate a series of hyperlinks using Office's Web toolbar.

Sharing Information Online

Web Pages & HTML

The document you'll be creating lets you take advantage of today's technology in sharing and disseminating information online. At Jackson Electronics, information about, for example, products, hiring practices, and company policies, is stored in Word documents. Sales reports and projections are stored in Excel workbooks. Raw data is often placed in Access databases. Jackson Electronics employees also use PowerPoint to create presentations for stockholders, prospective employees, and at trade shows. The number and content of these documents is constantly changing. Jackson Electronics needs a system that makes this information accessible to all employees.

One of the most popular ways to present and organize information so that it is easily accessible online is through hyperlinks. **Hyperlinks** are objects in a document that you can click to access information in other locations in that or other documents. This system of linked information is called **hypertext**, although the linked items are not limited to text. A hyperlink can be a word, a phrase, or a picture. When you click a hyperlink, your computer takes you to a new location or document, called the **target** of the hyperlink.

Hyperlinks offer a new way of making information available. Consider, for example, how Jackson Electronics has always published information before. When the company releases a new product, they create a product portfolio—a little booklet describing the product. Think of reading the product portfolio for a new product such as the ScanMaster. You turn each page to progress through the information. You might start with a market summary. The next page might be a product definition report, followed perhaps by a pricing plan. Information that is organized like a book is called a **linear document**. An online document that includes links to targets is called a **hyperlink document**. A hyperlink document differs from a linear document in that you can jump from one topic to the next in whatever order you want, using the hyperlinks available to you. Figure 1 shows how information is stored in both the linear and the hyperlink models.

Figure 1 ◀
Linear and hyperlink documents

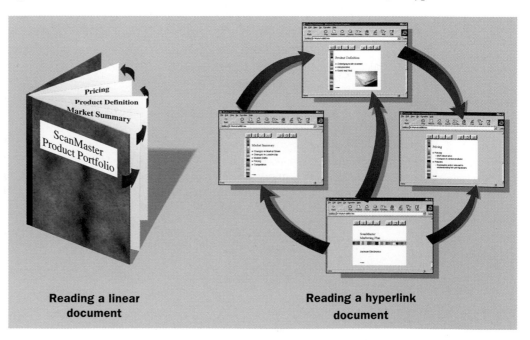

Reading a linear document

Reading a hyperlink document

As more hyperlinks are added between and within various documents, a structure emerges that you can navigate, traveling from hyperlink to hyperlink, following a path of information and ideas. You've already worked with one such structure when you accessed Microsoft Office's online Help system. By clicking a keyword or phrase, you were able to access additional helpful information. Another hypertext structure you might be familiar with is the World Wide Web (WWW), or the Web.

The **Web** is a structure of linked documents on computers all over the world. Clicking a hyperlink in one document "jumps" you to another document, which could be on a computer across the room or across the globe. Each document is identified by a unique address called its Uniform Resource Locator, or more commonly, **URL**. To view files on the Web, you need a software program called a **Web browser**. The most popular browsers are Netscape Navigator and Microsoft's Internet Explorer.

The Web has proven so useful that companies are creating the Web in miniature within their own networks. These smaller hyperlink structures are called **intranets**. Jackson Electronics has created an intranet that will be the primary vehicle for the distribution of company information. Employees can access documents on the company's intranet with the same Web browser software they use to access information on the Web. Training will be easier because employees will use the same browser tool, regardless of whether information is located within or outside the company. Figure 2 shows how the intranet at Jackson Electronics can work in conjunction with the Web.

Figure 2 ◀
The World Wide
Web (WWW)
and the
Jackson
Electronics
intranet

information is shared
within the company
over the company's
intranet

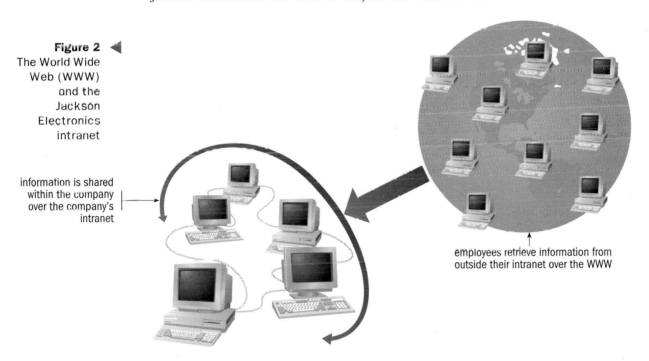

employees retrieve information from
outside their intranet over the WWW

Documents placed on the Web share a common file format called **HTML**, which stands for **Hypertext Markup Language**. A common format ensures that different Web browsers will be able to retrieve and view your document. However, HTML isn't necessary to create hyperlinks: you can use hyperlinks with your Office 97 documents in their default formats. However, many intranets use the HTML format so they can share their company documents with users outside the company, as you'll see later. Office 97 makes it easy to convert your documents to HTML format.

Converting a Word Document to HTML

Jeff has given you a Word document that contains the ScanMaster product report information, along with a few other supplementary files, including a fact sheet on the ScanMaster, a graphic image of the ScanMaster, an Excel workbook describing ScanMaster sales, and a company logo. Your task is to place this information online.

First, Jeff wants you to convert the product report from its current Word format to HTML so that it can be immediately posted on the company intranet. The Word product document is called Product and is located on your Student Disk.

To open the Product document:

1. Start Microsoft Word, and place your Student Disk in the appropriate drive.

   TROUBLE? If you don't have a Student Disk, you need to get one before you can proceed. Your instructor or technical support person will either give you one or ask you to make your own by following the instructions on the "Read This Before You Begin" page before this tutorial. See your instructor or technical support person for more information.

2. Click **File**, and then click the **Open** button.

3. Click the **Look in** drop-down arrow, and then click the drive that contains your Student Disk.

4. Click **Product**.

   TROUBLE? If the Product file appears with the "doc" extension, don't worry. This simply means your computer is set to show file extensions.

5. Click the **Open** button to open the document. Figure 3 shows the product report document as it appears within Word.

   TROUBLE? You might want to turn off Word's automatic spell checking feature (use the Spelling & Grammar tab on the Options command on the Tools menu) for the remainder of this tutorial. Otherwise, words such as "ScanMaster" will appear underlined with red wavy lines.

Figure 3 ◀
Product
document in
Word

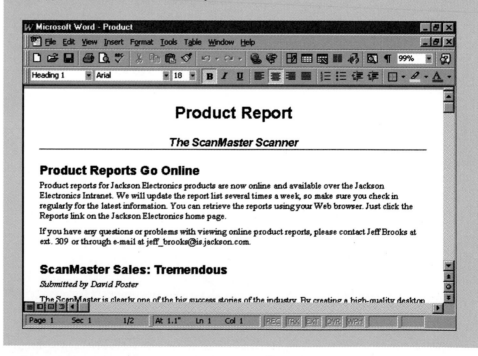

You're now ready to create your first HTML document.

Saving an Open Word Document as an HTML Document

The Office 97 programs provide the tools you need to convert Word, Excel, Access, and PowerPoint documents to HTML. However, the HTML conversion tools are different for each application. The easiest HTML tool to use is the one for Word.

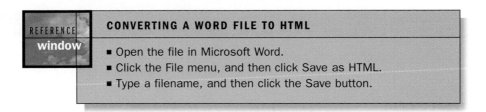

REFERENCE
window

CONVERTING A WORD FILE TO HTML

- Open the file in Microsoft Word.
- Click the File menu, and then click Save as HTML.
- Type a filename, and then click the Save button.

When you save a document in HTML format, you should use a filename without spaces—for example, Product_Report instead of Product Report—so that it is a legitimate URL. Office 97 programs automatically assign documents in HTML format the file extension "htm" or "html."

To convert the ScanMaster product report to HTML:

1. In Word, click **File**, and then click **Save as HTML**.

2. Type **ScanMaster_Report** in the File name box.

3. Verify that **HTML Document** appears in the Save as Type box.

4. Click the **Save** button. Word converts the Product document to the HTML document format. Figure 4 shows the document in HTML format.

   TROUBLE? Word might warn you that some information could be lost in converting the document to HTML format. If this warning appears, click the OK button and continue saving the document. It might take a minute on some machines to complete the conversion.

Figure 4
Product Report
document in
HTML format

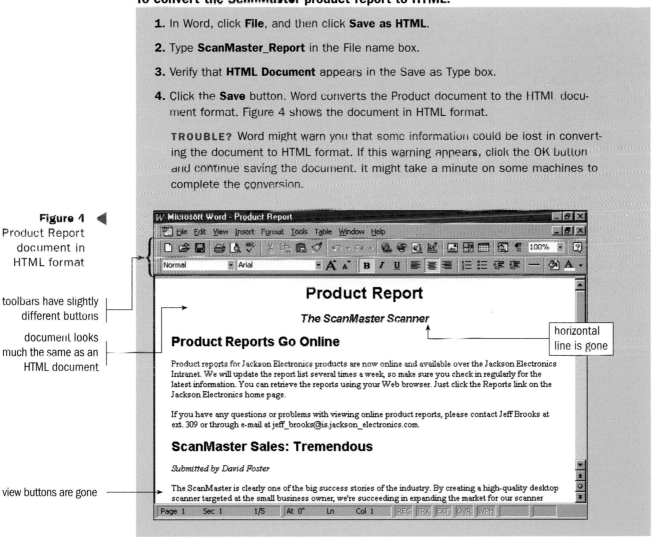

toolbars have slightly different buttons

document looks much the same as an HTML document

horizontal line is gone

view buttons are gone

When you convert a Word document to HTML, you might notice that the name in Word's title bar changes. In this example, it changes from Product to Product Report. Word documents show the filename in the title bar, while HTML documents derive the title bar name from the first line of the document. Later, you'll learn how to specify the name you want to appear in the title bar.

Previewing an HTML Document in a Browser

Sometimes, an HTML document does not appear in Word the same way as in a Web browser. To spot potential aberrations, it's a good idea to preview your document in your Web browser. The Office 97 applications include toolbar buttons that you can click to start your browser software and preview the open page.

To preview the ScanMaster product report on your Web browser:

1. Click the **Web Page Preview** button ⊞ on the Standard toolbar. The page appears in your browser's document window. See Figure 5.

   TROUBLE? If your browser window title bar does not display Internet Explorer, don't worry. You are just using a different browser.

Figure 5 ◀
HTML
document in
Web browser

HTML document in
Internet Explorer
browser; your browser
might be different

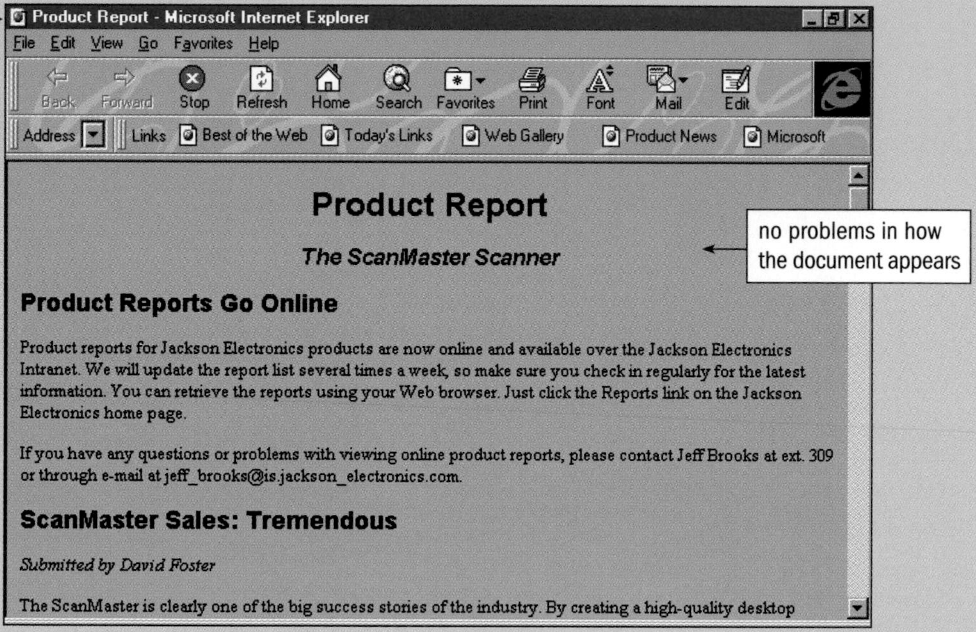

no problems in how
the document appears

2. Click the **Close** button ⊠ to close your Web browser.

3. Verify that you have returned to Microsoft Word and are viewing the ScanMaster product report in HTML format.

You're satisfied that your HTML document looks reasonable in your browser. Now you'd like to turn it into a hyperlink document.

Using Word as a Web Page Editor

Now that you have a Web document—a document in HTML format that can be accessed online—you are ready to insert hyperlinks. You can create hyperlinks that point to other locations in the document, such as to the beginning, end, or an individual section, or to another document altogether. A hyperlink within a document can be a useful navigational tool, especially if the document is long or if users need to find a specific piece of information quickly.

Initially, you decide to create a table of contents composed of hyperlinks for the product report. When a user clicks an item in the table of contents, he or she jumps to that portion of the report. The product report has three main sections: a sales summary, a description of the product, and the marketing strategy. Figure 6 shows the hyperlinks you plan to place in your table of contents and how they target the three sections of the document.

Figure 6 ◀
Hyperlinks and
their targets

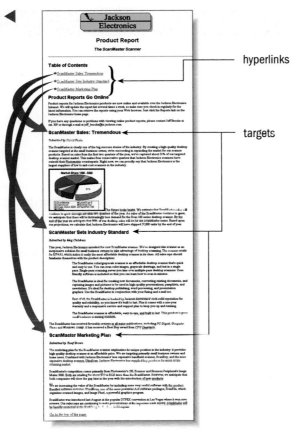

hyperlinks

targets

Entering Text into an HTML Document

Before creating your hyperlinks, you decide to enter a heading for your table of contents. You enter text in an HTML document the same way you do in a normal Word document, although, as you'll discover later, there are some differences in how you work with HTML documents versus Word documents.

To enter a heading for your table of contents:

1. Click the beginning of the line reading "Product Reports Go Online," and press the **Enter** key.

2. Press the **Up Arrow** key on your keyboard to move the insertion point to the blank line you just created.

3. Type **Table of Contents**, and then press the **Enter** key.

4. Click the **Bullets** button 🔳.

The items you want to place in the table of contents all exist as headings in later parts of the document.

Pasting a Hyperlink

You are now ready to populate the table of contents with hyperlinks to the three sections. One of the simplest ways to create a hyperlink to a specific location within a Word document is to copy the target text and then paste it as a hyperlink.

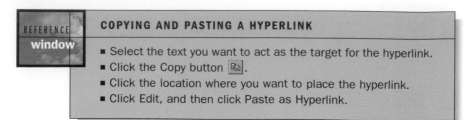

COPYING AND PASTING A HYPERLINK

- Select the text you want to act as the target for the hyperlink.
- Click the Copy button 🗐.
- Click the location where you want to place the hyperlink.
- Click Edit, and then click Paste as Hyperlink.

You decide to use the paste method to create the hyperlink to the sales section of the product report. You copy the heading for the sales section, scroll back up to the table of contents, and then paste the text in as a hyperlink. The Paste as Hyperlink command automatically creates a hyperlink that points to the text you copied.

To copy and paste a hyperlink:

1. Scroll down the document window until you reach the section with the heading "Scanner Sales: Tremendous."

2. Select the text **ScanMaster Sales: Tremendous**. This will be the target text, or the location a user will jump to when he or she clicks the hyperlink you are about to create.

3. Click the **Copy** button 🗐.

4. Scroll up the document window and click the first bulleted line of the table of contents.

5. Click **Edit**, and then click **Paste as Hyperlink**. Figure 7 shows the first hyperlink in your table of contents.

Figure 7 ◀
Pasting text as
a hyperlink

Table of Contents you
are creating

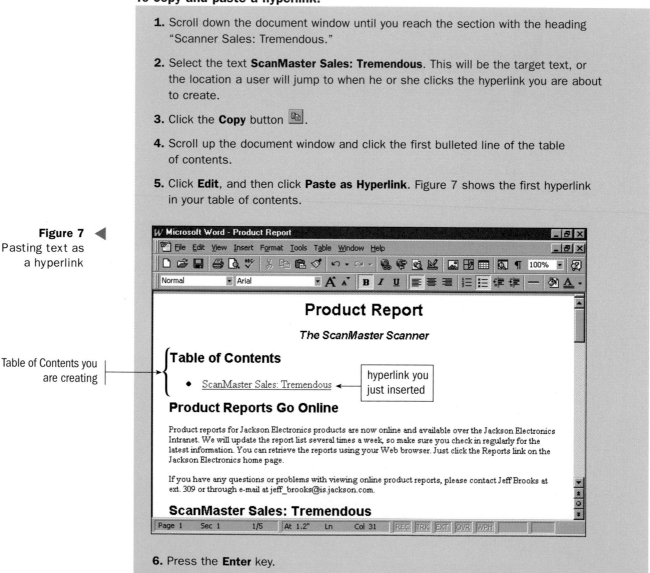

6. Press the **Enter** key.

Word displays the text you pasted as underlined blue text—a visual clue that the text is a hyperlink. A second visual clue is that your mouse pointer changes from I to 🖑 as it passes over the hyperlink.

Using the same technique, copy and paste hyperlinks for the two remaining sections of the product report.

To add the remaining hyperlinks:

1. Scroll down to each of the two remaining sections labeled "ScanMaster Sets Industry Standard" and "ScanMaster Marketing Plan."

2. For each section, select the heading text and paste it as a new item in the table of contents bulleted list using the Paste as Hypertext command. Figure 8 shows the completed table of contents.

Figure 8 ◄
Completed
hyperlinks

each hyperlink points
to a different section
of the product report

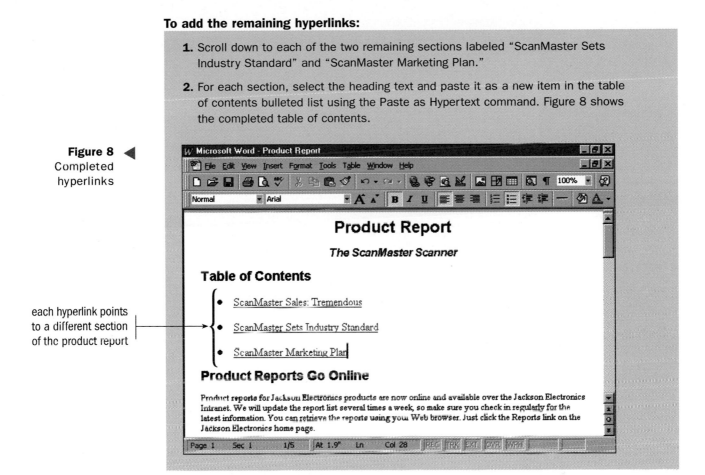

The table of contents is complete. A user ought to be able to click any of the hyperlinks and jump to the section it describes.

Navigating Hyperlinks

Now that you've created hyperlinks, you should test them to make sure they point to the correct locations in the document. You activate a hyperlink by clicking it with the mouse pointer. You decide to start by activating the last hyperlink in your list, the hyperlink to the Marketing Plan section.

To activate the Marketing Plan hyperlink:

1. Move the mouse pointer over the ScanMaster Marketing Plan entry in the table of contents until the pointer arrow changes to 🖑.

2. Click the ScanMaster Marketing Plan hyperlink. Word jumps to the bottom of the document to the beginning of the section on marketing, as shown in Figure 9.

Figure 9
Jumping to the
target of a
hyperlink

Web toolbar appears

target of third
hyperlink

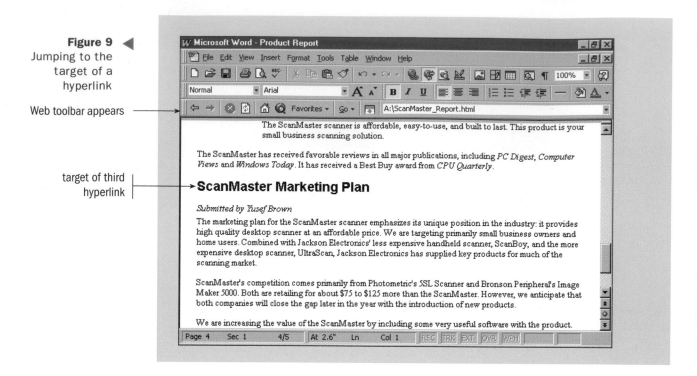

As you jump to the target, Word displays the Web toolbar above the document window. The **Web toolbar** helps you navigate your hyperlinks and work on the Web or your company's intranet.

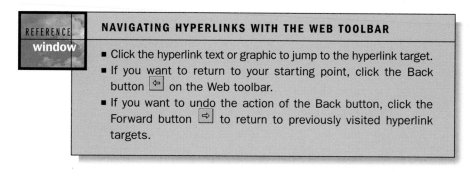

REFERENCE
window

NAVIGATING HYPERLINKS WITH THE WEB TOOLBAR

■ Click the hyperlink text or graphic to jump to the hyperlink target.
■ If you want to return to your starting point, click the Back button on the Web toolbar.
■ If you want to undo the action of the Back button, click the Forward button to return to previously visited hyperlink targets.

You use the Back button to return to the beginning of the product report.

To return to your prior location in the document:

1. Click the **Back** button on the Web toolbar. Word returns you to the table of contents at the beginning of the document. See Figure 10.

   TROUBLE? If the Web toolbar did not appear when you jumped to the marketing plan section, click the Web Toolbar button on the Standard toolbar to display it and then repeat Step 1.

Web Pages

Back button on the
Web toolbar

hyperlink you
activated has
changed color

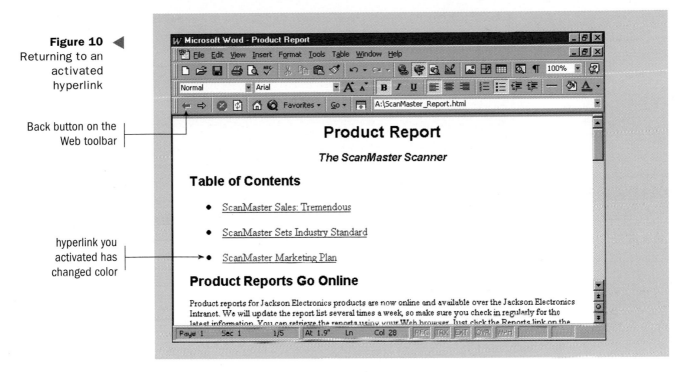

As Figure 10 indicates, the hyperlink you just activated (the marketing plan hyperlink) has changed color. This is because Word, like most Web browsers, changes the color of hyperlinks that have been previously used so that you can tell easily which hyperlinks you've followed and which you haven't.

Editing Hypertext

You also want to add a hyperlink that points from the bottom of the document to the top so that a user at the end of your document can easily return to the beginning. You decide to add the hyperlink using the same copy and paste method you used for the previous three hyperlinks, but you realize that once you insert this hyperlink, you'll want to edit the hypertext that makes up the link.

To create a hyperlink to the top of the page:

1. Scroll to the top of the document and select the text "Product Report."

2. Click the **Copy** button 📋.

3. Scroll down and add a new blank line to the bottom of the document.

4. Click **Edit**, and then click **Paste as Hyperlink**.

This hyperlink is not very descriptive. Ideally, you would like to replace the text, "Product Report" with "Go to the top of the page." How do you select hypertext to edit it? You cannot select it by clicking, since this would activate the hyperlink and send you to the hyperlink's target. Instead, you use the Hyperlink menu to select and edit it.

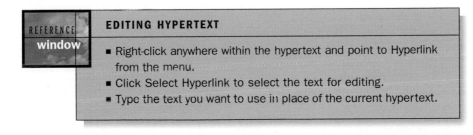

REFERENCE
window

EDITING HYPERTEXT

■ Right-click anywhere within the hypertext and point to Hyperlink from the menu.

■ Click Select Hyperlink to select the text for editing.

■ Type the text you want to use in place of the current hypertext.

You decide to make your hyperlink more descriptive.

To select and edit hyperlink text:

1. Right-click the Product Report hyperlink, point to **Hyperlink**, and then click **Select Hyperlink** from the menu. See Figure 11.

Figure 11 ◀
Hyperlink menu

hyperlink you are
trying to select

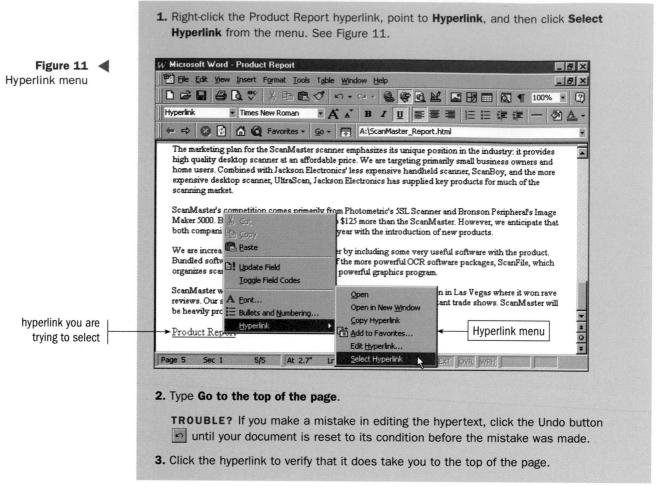

2. Type **Go to the top of the page**.

    TROUBLE? If you make a mistake in editing the hypertext, click the Undo button ↩ until your document is reset to its condition before the mistake was made.

3. Click the hyperlink to verify that it does take you to the top of the page.

The hyperlink works. Your HTML document can now be easily navigated.

Creating a Hyperlink to an HTML Document

Jeff drops by to see how you are doing on the ScanMaster product report. He's pleased that you've made the document easy to navigate. Next, he wants to you to add hyperlinks to other documents so that users who want additional information can easily get it. Specifically, he envisions links to two documents: the ScanMaster fact sheet and the Excel sales workbook. He'd also like you to improve your document by adding graphics and a design. Figure 12 shows the structure Jeff envisions.

Figure 12 ◄
Links you will
add to outside
documents

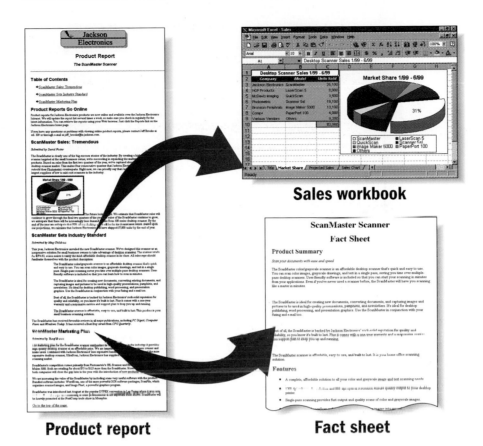

Sales workbook

Product report   **Fact sheet**

You'll start by adding the hyperlink to the fact sheet. It has already been saved in HTML format with the name "Facts" on your Student Disk. You can create a hyperlink to an HTML document using the copy and paste method, or you can convert preexisting text to hypertext if you know the location of the target.

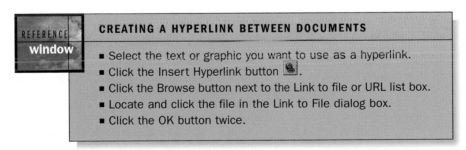

REFERENCE
window

CREATING A HYPERLINK BETWEEN DOCUMENTS

- Select the text or graphic you want to use as a hyperlink.
- Click the Insert Hyperlink button 🔲.
- Click the Browse button next to the Link to file or URL list box.
- Locate and click the file in the Link to File dialog box.
- Click the OK button twice.

Because you know that the target of the hyperlink you are creating is the Facts document, you decide to use this method to create the hyperlink.

To enter the text for the fact sheet hyperlink:

1. Scroll down the document until you reach the end of the "ScanMaster Sets Industry Standard" section.

2. Add a new line at the end of the "ScanMaster Sets Industry Standard" section.

3. Type **For more information see the product fact sheet**. Figure 13 shows the product report with the text you entered to be used as a hyperlink.

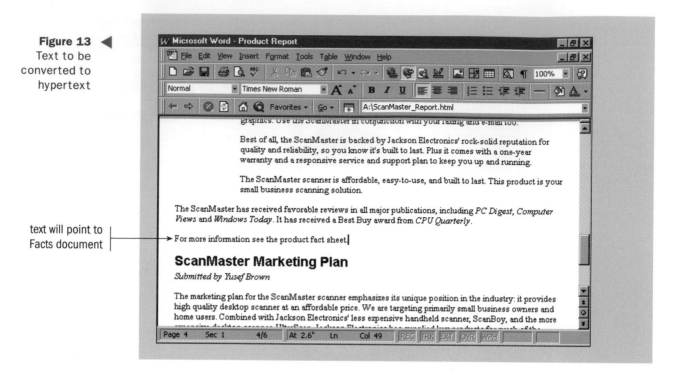

Figure 13 ◀
Text to be
converted to
hypertext

text will point to
Facts document

The next step is to convert this text to hypertext. You can do this with the Insert Hyperlink command available on the Word toolbar. Designate the Facts HTML document as the target.

To create a hyperlink to the ScanMaster fact sheet:

1. Select the text, **For more information see the product fact sheet.**

2. Click the **Insert Hyperlink** button 🖼.

3. Click the **Browse** button located next to the Link to file or URL list box.

4. Click the **Look in** drop-down arrow, and then click **3½ Floppy (A:)** (or whichever drive your student files are in.)

5. Click **Facts**.

6. Click the **OK** button twice.

You could test the hyperlink you just created in your Web browser, or you can just click it to see if it opens the correct document. Confirm that the hyperlink you created works.

To test the new hyperlink:

1. Click **For more information see the product fact sheet.** Word opens the Facts HTML document. See Figure 14.

Figure 14 ◄
Fact sheet, the
target of the
hyperlink you
added

fact sheet HTML
document

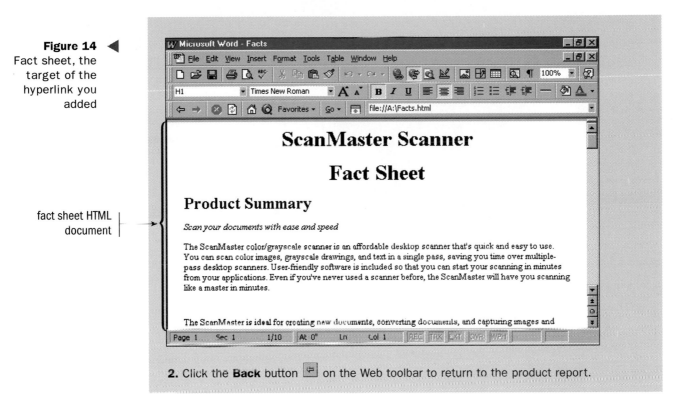

2. Click the **Back** button 📄 on the Web toolbar to return to the product report.

The hyperlink to the fact sheet HTML document works.

Creating a Hyperlink to an Office 97 Document

For most purposes, an HTML document is fine for conveying information, but sometimes it's better for users to be able to access the document in its **native format**—the format used by the program that originally created it. Office 97 allows you to create a hyperlink to almost any type of document. This is an especially useful feature for Jackson Electronics. The company has standardized operations so that almost all document processing is done in Word, all database management is done in Access, and all spreadsheet operations are done in Excel. If documents are posted on the Jackson Electronics intranet in their native formats, all employees will be able to work with those documents.

Later on, you may decide to post your Office 97 documents on the Web. In that case, you will once again have to consider whether it is better to keep them in their native format or to use the more standard HTML format.

You are now going to add the hyperlink to the Excel workbook. The workbook has not been saved in HTML format; it is an Excel file called Sales, located on your Student Disk. You can insert a hyperlink to an Office 97 document using either the paste method or the Insert Hyperlink method. You'll use the latter for the Excel hyperlink.

To create a hyperlink to the Sales workbook:

1. Scroll to the end of the "ScanMaster Sales: Tremendous" section.

2. Add a new line to the end of that section with the text: **For more information see the sales workbook.**

3. Select the text you just entered, and click the **Insert Hyperlink** button 🔗.

4. Click the **Browse** button located next to the Link to file or URL list box.

5. Click the **Look in** drop-down arrow, and then click the drive that contains your Student Disk.

6. Click **Sales.**

7. Click the **OK** button twice. Figure 15 shows the newly inserted hypertext.

Figure 15 ◄
Inserting a
hyperlink to an
Excel workbook

hyperlink to Excel
document

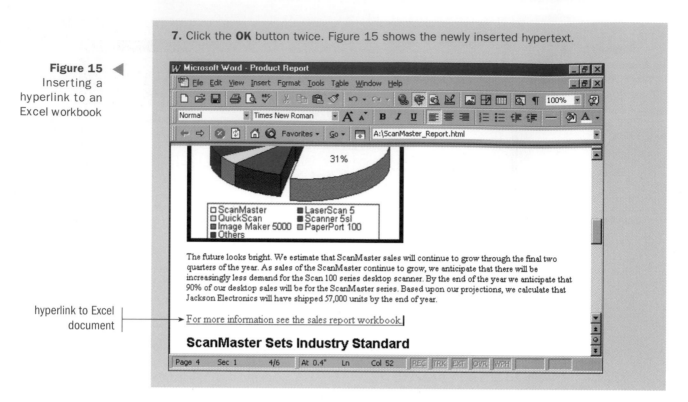

You have added the two hyperlinks: one to the fact sheet and one to the sales workbook. If you were to click, for example, the hyperlinks to the Excel workbook from within Word, Excel would automatically start with the Sales workbook open in an Excel document window. But at Jackson Electronics, all such documents will be accessed through the browser. Therefore, you decide to test your hyperlinks in your Web browser.

Testing Hyperlinks in a Browser

Web browsers that support **ActiveX**, a technology developed by Microsoft to increase the flexibility and power of Web browsers, allow you to work with Office 97 documents without ever leaving your browser. Internet Explorer 3.0 supports ActiveX, as does Netscape Navigator 3.0 when the appropriate plug-in software has been installed. If you click the Excel hyperlink with either of these browsers, your computer displays the Excel object and makes the Excel tools available. If, however, your browser does not support ActiveX and you click the Excel hyperlink, your computer might start Excel and display the workbook within an Excel document window—and you would have left your browser.

You decide to view your Web document in your browser and then test the hyperlink to the sales workbook.

To test the hyperlink to the Excel workbook in your browser:

1. Click the **Web Page Preview** button 🔍.

2. Word prompts you to save the document; click the **OK** button. The document appears in your Web browser.

3. Scroll down and then click the hyperlink **For more information see the sales workbook.** Figure 16 shows the workbook as it appears in the Internet Explorer 3.0 browser.

TROUBLE? If you are using another Web browser that supports ActiveX documents, ask your instructor how to open Office 97 files on your system. If you are using a browser that doesn't support ActiveX documents, clicking the hyperlink to an Excel workbook might start the Excel application on your desktop. In that case, exit Excel without saving the document, return to your browser window, and read through the rest of the steps without performing them.

Figure 16 ◀
Excel workbook
viewed within
Internet
Explorer 3.0

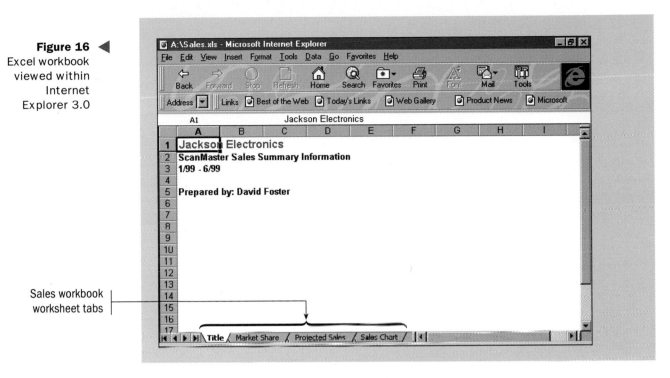

Sales workbook
worksheet tabs

Notice that the Internet Explorer menus have changed to match the Excel menus needed to work with an Excel workbook. Also note that Internet Explorer has preserved the structure of the workbook, including access to the worksheets contained within the workbook. If you want to edit the Excel object, you can display the Excel tools right in the Internet Explorer window.

To display the Excel toolbars with Internet Explorer 3.0:

1. Click the **Tools** button ⊞ on the Internet Explorer toolbar. The Excel toolbars appear within the Internet Explorer window.

   TROUBLE? If you can't see the Tools button, you might have to move one of the other Internet Explorer toolbars out of the way; or you might not be using Internet Explorer Version 3.0. Other Web browsers will have different ways of displaying Office 97 documents. Check with your instructor or the browser's Help file to learn how your browser works with ActiveX documents.

2. Now hide the Excel toolbars by clicking the **Hide Tools** button ⊞ .

3. Click the **Close** button ☒ to close your Web browser.

Satisfied that the links work, you are ready to take a break.

To save your work and exit Word:

1. Click the **Save** button 🖫 .

2. Click the **Close** button ☒ to close Word.

3. If Excel is still open, close that as well by clicking its **Close** button ☒ .

Now you can make the product report document available on the Jackson Electronics intranet. Anyone who wants to review information about the ScanMaster scanner can do so by viewing your online report.

Quick Check

1 What is hypertext?

2 What is HTML and why is it important to save your documents in HTML format if you intend to place them on the Web?

3 How do you create a hyperlink pointing from one location in a Word document to a target located in the same document?

4 What is the Web toolbar and how do you use it to navigate your hyperlinks?

5 How do you edit hypertext?

6 How do you create a hyperlink to another document?

SESSION 2

In this session, you will use some of the tools provided with Microsoft Word to enhance the appearance of your HTML product report. You'll learn to insert tables and a variety of graphical images, from bullets to horizontal lines.

Working with HTML Documents in Word

A document in HTML format is very different from a document in the native Word format. When you open an HTML document in Word, Word automatically changes its menus, removing Word features that are incompatible with the HTML format and adding new commands specific to HTML documents. Figure 17 shows, for example, how the Insert menu changes, depending upon whether you are editing a Word or an HTML document.

Figure 17 ◀
Insert menus
for Word and
HTML
documents

this menu appears
when you work with a
Word document

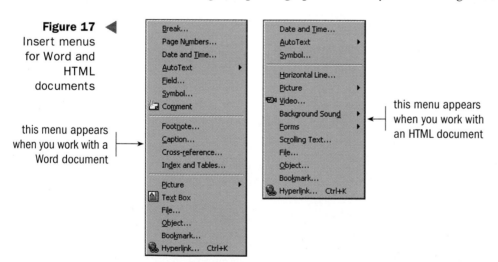

this menu appears
when you work with
an HTML document

Word lets you add a number of formatting features to your HTML documents, including:

- Horizontal lines
- Pictures, called **inline images**, that can be viewed by graphical Web browsers
- Background sound files that will be played automatically whenever a user accesses your Web page
- Forms that allow data entry for interactive Web documents
- Scrolling text that displays a marquee-style banner on your Web page
- Graphical bullets for your bulleted lists

Jeff wants you to work with some of these Word Web Page Editor features to enhance the appearance of the product report Web page you created in Session 1.

Before you begin enhancing your page, you first want to add a page title.

Specifying a Web Page Title

When you work with Word to create an HTML document, you should consider the page title. The **Web page title** is the name that appears in the Web browser's title bar when your page is accessed. It is also the name various Web search tools use to represent your page in their search results.

As the previous session showed, the Web page title is not the same as the name of the HTML document. By default, Office 97 applications select some text from the file to act as the title—usually the first line of the document or the content of the first cell in a workbook. For example, the product report page you created in the previous session had the title "Product Report," the first line of the fact sheet. This description does not convey to anyone the purpose of the document, so you decide to change it using the Properties feature of your Office application (in this case, Word).

To set the title for your Web page:

1. Start Word, and make sure your Student Disk is in the appropriate drive.

2. Click **File**, and then click the **Open** button ▣.

3. Click the **Look in** drop-down arrow, and then click the drive that contains your Student Disk.

4. Click **ScanMaster_Report**, and then click the **Open** button.

5. Click **File**, and then click **Properties**.

6. Type **ScanMaster Product Report** in the Title box of the Document Properties dialog box as displayed in Figure 18.

Figure 18 ◀
Specifying
a title

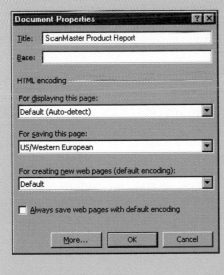

7. Click the **OK** button.

The next time a Web browser opens this page, "ScanMaster Product Report" will appear in the browser's title bar. More importantly, search tools will identify this page with that title.

Inserting a Table

Currently, your product report includes a sales chart that shows how well the scanners are selling. Jeff wants you to add a table of the actual data that make up this chart. This data is included in the Sales workbook, and you can simply paste it into your Web document. In fact, the copy and paste method works with all the Office 97 programs. For example, you can copy and paste data from an Access table or query into your HTML document using the same basic steps. You'll have an opportunity to practice this in one of the case problems later in this tutorial.

To paste the sales data into the product report:

1. Start Excel.

2. Click **File**, and then click the **Open** button 🖼️.

3. Click the **Look in** drop-down arrow, and then click the drive that contains your Student Disk.

4. Click **Sales**, and then click the **Open** button.

5. Click the **Projected Sales** tab, and select the range **A4:F7**.

6. Click the **Copy** button 🖼️.

7. Click the **Close** button ☒ to close Excel. Click the **No** button if you are prompted to save your changes.

8. Return to Word and scroll to the last line of the Sales section directly before the hyperlink you created to the sales workbook.

9. Click the end of that line so that the insertion point is at the end of the sentence "... Jackson Electronics will have shipped 57,000 units by the end of the year."

10. Click the **Paste** button 🖼️.

The sales data are now in the product report, in the form of a table.

Working with Tables

HTML tables such as the one you just inserted into your product report differ in several ways from Word tables. You do not have all the editing options with tables in HTML documents that you do with tables in Word documents. For example, you cannot use Word's AutoFormat feature to create tables based on different formats and styles. However, you do have some control over the appearance of an HTML table. For example, you can modify some of the properties of the table, the individual cells, and the table borders.

Changing Column Width

The table you just inserted would benefit from some stylistic design and formatting. You decide to begin by increasing the width of the first column. The method for changing table column width in an HTML table is the same as in a regular Word table.

To widen the table's first column:

1. Point at the border between the first and second column so that the pointer changes to ✛.

2. Drag the border to the right to increase the size of the first column just enough to remove the wrapping of the text. See Figure 19.

Figure 19 ◀
Pasting a table
from Excel

data from Excel —

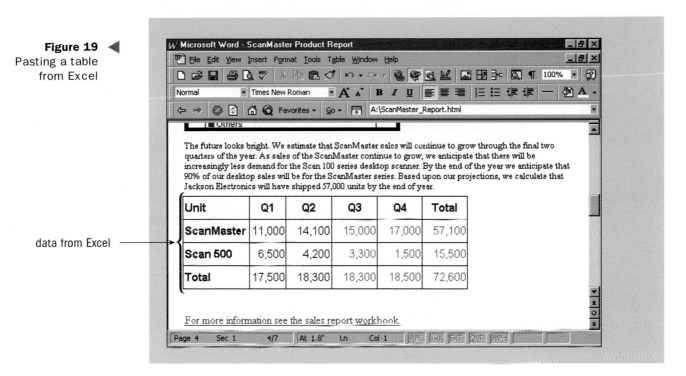

Now all the entries in the first column are on a single line, and the table looks much better.

Setting Table Properties

You can accomplish some table formatting tasks using the Table Properties dialog box. This dialog box allows you to:

- Set how the text surrounding the table wraps, to the left or the right of the table or not at all.

- Set the horizontal and vertical distance between the table and surrounding text.

- Set the table's background color.

- Set the space between the table columns.

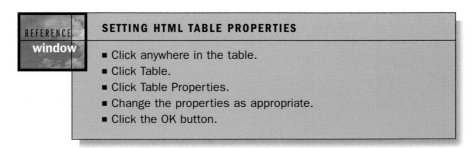

REFERENCE
window

SETTING HTML TABLE PROPERTIES

- Click anywhere in the table.
- Click Table.
- Click Table Properties.
- Change the properties as appropriate.
- Click the OK button.

You decide to revise the background color of the table, changing it to yellow to give it more emphasis.

To adjust the appearance of the table:

1. Click anywhere within the table borders.

2. Click **Table**, and then click **Table Properties**.

3. Click the **Background** drop-down arrow, and then click **Yellow**. See Figure 20.

Figure 20
Selecting a
background
color

click to create a
yellow background

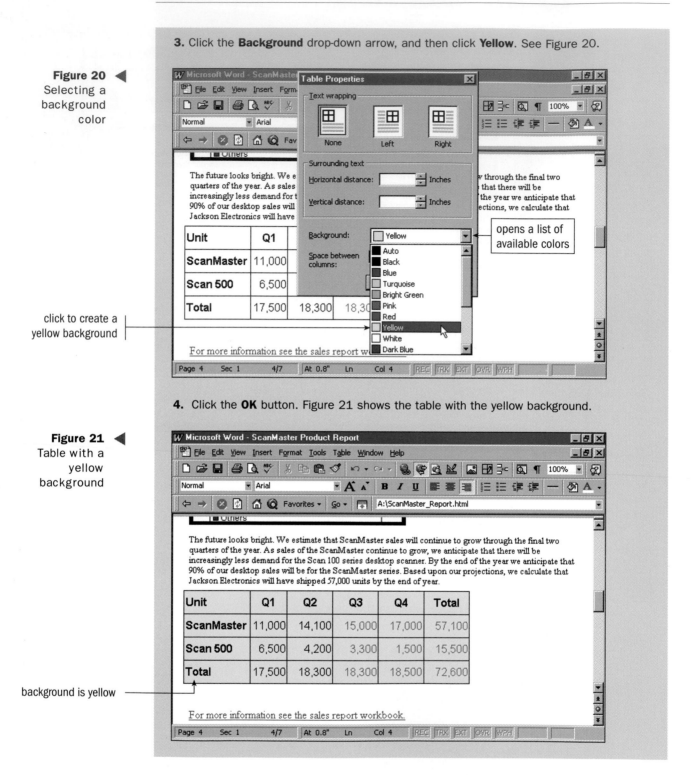

4. Click the **OK** button. Figure 21 shows the table with the yellow background.

Figure 21
Table with a
yellow
background

background is yellow

You like the look of the yellow background, but you wonder if the table wouldn't look better if you chose a different color for the first row.

Setting Cell Properties

You also can modify the appearance of individual cells within a table. With Word, you can:

- Specify whether the text in the cell is aligned with the top, middle, or bottom of the cell.
- Specify the cell's background color.
- Indicate the width and height of each individual cell.

Now you decide to format just the cells in the first row of the table (the header row) with a gray background.

To adjust the appearance of a group of cells:

1. Select all of the cells in the first row of the table.

2. Click **Table** and then click **Cell Properties**.

3. Click the **Background** drop-down arrow, and then click **Gray-25%**.

4. Click the **OK** button.

5. Click outside the table to deselect it. Figure 22 shows the revised table.

Figure 22 ◄
Formatting
individual table
cells

top cells are gray ⟶

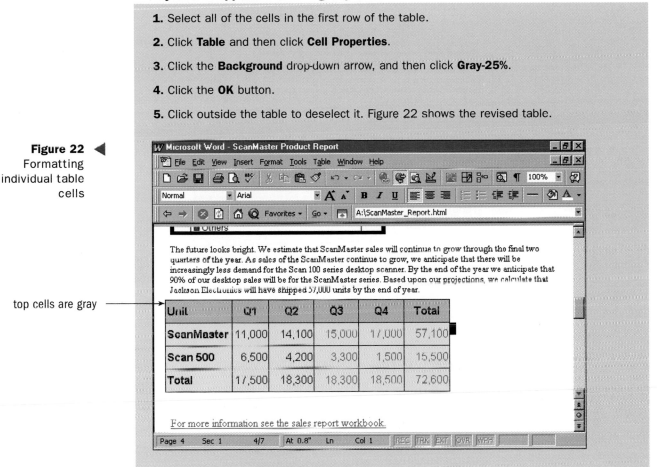

The colors gray and yellow look good together.

Defining the Table Border

The last thing you'll do with the sales information table is to modify the table borders. Unlike tables in Word documents, which you can format with a variety of table boundaries, in HTML tables you can only specify the width of the table border. You decide to increase the border width to about 1.5 points (a thick line.)

To increase the table border:

1. Click anywhere within the table.

2. Click **Table**, and then click **Borders**.

3. Click the Border Width drop-down arrow, and then click **1½ pt**.

4. Click the **OK** button.

5. Click outside the table to deselect it. Figure 23 shows the final version of the table.

Figure 23 ◀
Table with new
border

border is thicker ────▶

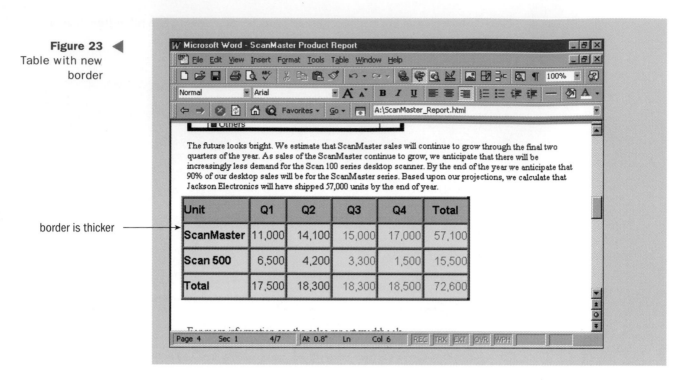

With the table entered and formatted, you decide to work on the graphical images in your report document.

Working with Inline Images

Graphics that are placed into HTML documents are called **inline images**. Unlike Word documents, HTML documents only support two kinds of graphic formats: **GIF** and **JPEG**. Of the two, the GIF format is probably the more commonly used on the World Wide Web.

Learning Image Filenames

An important difference between how a Word document and an HTML document handle graphics lies in how the two formats store graphic images. Word documents can contain graphics in many different ways: stored within the document itself, linked to external files, or shown as embedded objects. For HTML documents, inline images are always external files that the Web browser accesses when it attempts to display the Web page.

Word takes this into account when you convert a Word document to HTML format. Recall that the original Word product report contained an embedded Excel chart. When you converted it to an HTML document, Word changed the chart image to a graphic file in GIF format. Browsers that try to display this page will access the GIF file when they attempt to display the chart. Word automatically assigns a filename to the chart. To learn the filename for a specific inline image, you can view the image's properties.

To view the filename of an inline image:

1. Scroll up to the image entitled Market Share 1/99-6/99.

2. Right-click the **Market Share 1/99-6/99** image, and then click **Format Picture**.

3. Click the **Settings** tab. The filename appears in the Path box. See Figure 24.

Figure 24
Checking an
image's
filename

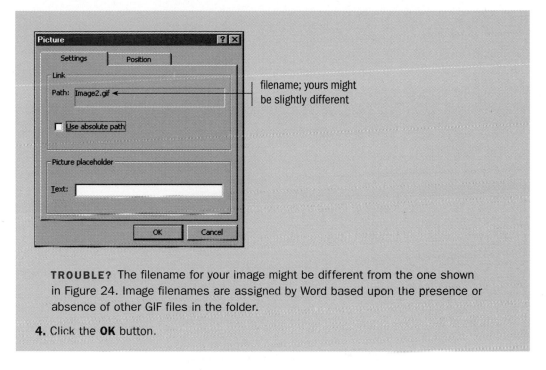

filename; yours might
be slightly different

TROUBLE? The filename for your image might be different from the one shown
in Figure 24. Image filenames are assigned by Word based upon the presence or
absence of other GIF files in the folder.

4. Click the **OK** button.

You note the filename for future reference. If you intend to share the HTML document
with other users, you will need to include this file with the HTML document.

Inserting an Image File

You can include other graphics files with your page, but you will need to convert them to
GIF or JPEG format if you intend Web browsers to be able to display them. You can do
this with any graphic file-conversion utility.

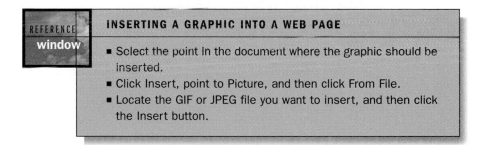

REFERENCE
window

INSERTING A GRAPHIC INTO A WEB PAGE

- Select the point in the document where the graphic should be
  inserted.
- Click Insert, point to Picture, and then click From File.
- Locate the GIF or JPEG file you want to insert, and then click
  the Insert button.

Jeff suggests that you enhance the appearance of the product report by inserting the
Jackson Electronics logo. He has already placed the company logo into a GIF file for you
to use. You decide to insert the logo at the top of the document.

To insert the Jackson Electronics logo:

1. Click the top of the document and press the **Enter** key to insert a new blank line.

2. Click the new line you created, placing the insertion point at the top of the document.

3. Click **Insert**, point to **Picture**, and then click **From File**.

4. Click the **Look in** drop-down arrow, and then click the drive containing your
Student Disk.

5. Click **Logo**, and then click the **Insert** button. Figure 25 shows the Jackson Electronics logo as it appears in the product report.

Figure 25 ◀
Inserting a
graphic image

Jackson Electronics
logo

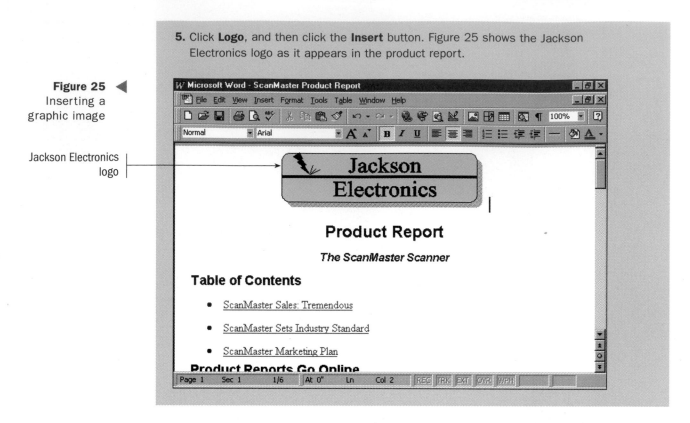

The logo adds interest to your page. Many users use graphic images on the Web to great advantage to enhance the appearance of their Web documents.

Using Picture Placeholders

Not all browsers are graphical browsers. Some browsers, like the Lynx browser, are **text-based browsers** that can only display text, not graphics or multimedia elements. For these browsers, you can include a picture placeholder with the graphic. A **picture placeholder** is text that a browser displays in place of a graphic. Picture placeholders are also displayed while users with graphical browsers are waiting to see the final image of the graphic.

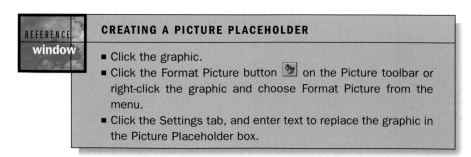

REFERENCE
window

CREATING A PICTURE PLACEHOLDER

- Click the graphic.
- Click the Format Picture button on the Picture toolbar or right-click the graphic and choose Format Picture from the menu.
- Click the Settings tab, and enter text to replace the graphic in the Picture Placeholder box.

Jeff wants to make sure that the pages you create are available to all potential users, including those with text-based browsers. You've just finished replacing the title of this page with a graphical logo. While that looks good for people using graphical browsers, it won't appear in a text-based browser. You decide to create a picture placeholder for your company logo.

To create a picture placeholder for the logo:

1. Click the **Jackson Electronics** logo.

2. Click the **Format Picture** button 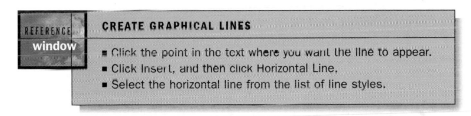 on the Picture toolbar.

> **TROUBLE?** If the Picture toolbar does not appear, right-click the Jackson Electronics logo, and click Show Picture Toolbar from the menu.

3. Click the **Settings** tab.

4. Type **Jackson Electronics** in the Picture placeholder Text box.

5. Click the **OK** button.

With text created for the picture placeholder text, users will either see the company logo or the company name at the top of the page.

Inserting Graphical Lines and Bullets

You can improve your page design by including graphical lines and bullets on your page. Word includes several graphical line styles that you can use as section dividers. These graphical lines are actually GIF files that are inserted into your document as inline images.

REFERENCE window	**CREATE GRAPHICAL LINES**
	■ Click the point in the text where you want the line to appear.
	■ Click Insert, and then click Horizontal Line.
	■ Select the horizontal line from the list of line styles.

You decide to add such a line directly after the product report title.

To insert a graphical line:

1. Click the end of the "The ScanMaster Scanner" line.

2. Click **Insert**, and then click **Horizontal Line** The Horizontal Line dialog box shown in Figure 26 displays a list of graphical lines included with Word.

Figure 26 ◀
Inserting a
horizontal line

you'll choose this
line style

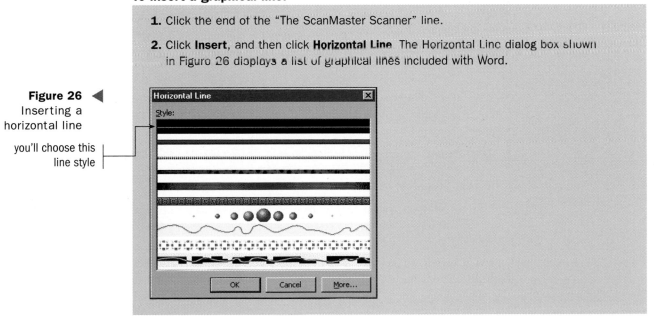

3. Click the first line in the list, and click the **OK** button. The line appears just below the Fact Sheet line as shown in Figure 27.

Figure 27 ◀
Horizontal line
in the HTML
document

horizontal line
you added

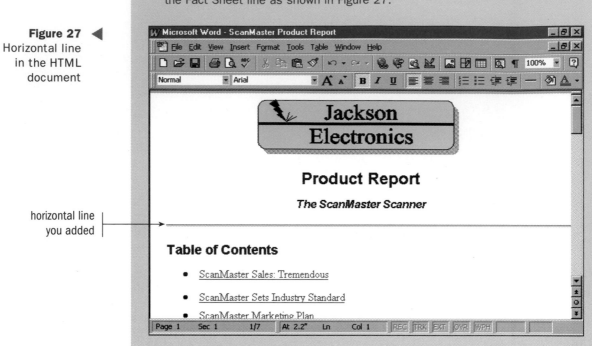

Next, you want to change the style for the bullets in the table of contents list. One of the differences between bulleted lists in HTML documents and Word documents is that you can use graphical images—not just bullet symbols—as bullets. As with graphical lines, graphical bullets are actually GIF files. So if you want to make sure the bullets appear when your file is viewed by someone's Web browser, you have to make sure that the appropriate GIF files are included.

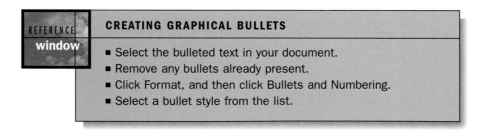

REFERENCE
window

CREATING GRAPHICAL BULLETS

- Select the bulleted text in your document.
- Remove any bullets already present.
- Click Format, and then click Bullets and Numbering.
- Select a bullet style from the list.

Before inserting graphical bullets, you must first remove the text bullets already in place.

To insert graphical bullets:

1. Select the three items in the table of contents list, and click the **Bullets** button to remove the text bullets.

2. Click **Format**, and then click **Bullets and Numbering**. The Bullets and Numbering dialog box shown in Figure 28 displays a list of graphical bullets included with Word.

Figure 28 ◀
Selecting a
different bullet

you'll choose
this bullet

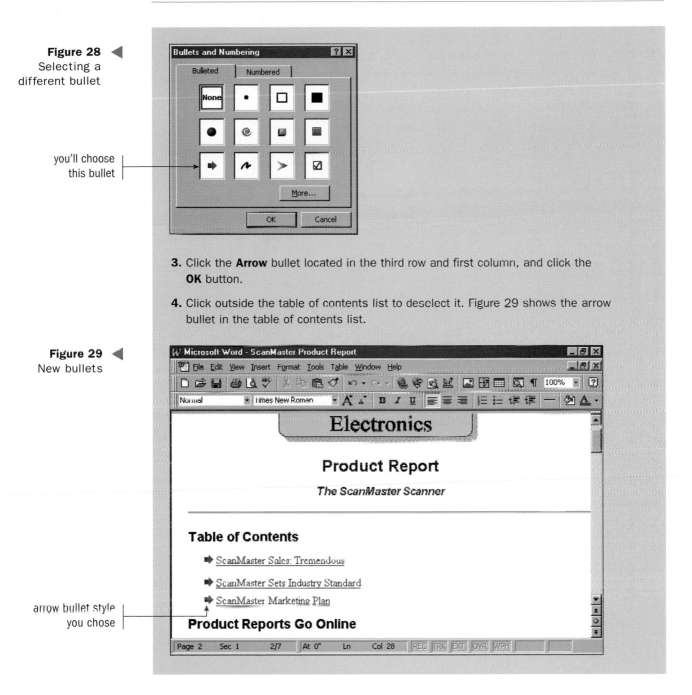

3. Click the **Arrow** bullet located in the third row and first column, and click the **OK** button.

4. Click outside the table of contents list to deselect it. Figure 29 shows the arrow bullet in the table of contents list.

Figure 29 ◀
New bullets

arrow bullet style
you chose

Setting Background Appearance

The final way in which you can enhance the appearance of the product report is by modifying the page background. Word gives you a variety of choices in creating your backgrounds. You can use the default color provided by the browser, or you can specify your own background color. Word also includes several graphical images, called **textures**, that you can insert into your background. These images can give your Web page the appearance of textured paper, marble, or wood.

As with other images in your document, a graphical background uses an external GIF file, which must be included whenever you share your Web page. You decide to explore whether using a textured background would enhance your page's appearance.

To select a background appearance:

1. Click **Format**, point to **Background**, and then click **Fill Effects**. The Fill Effects dialog box shown in Figure 30 opens to display a list of texture backgrounds.

Figure 30 ◀
Selecting
a texture

you'll choose
this texture

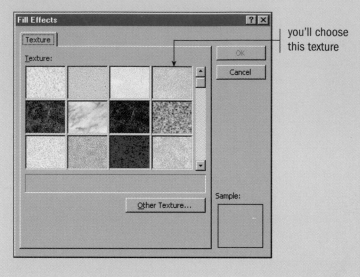

2. Click the **Stationery** texture image located in the first row and fourth column, and click the **OK** button. Figure 31 shows the Stationery background.

Figure 31 ◀
New texture

textured background ⸺

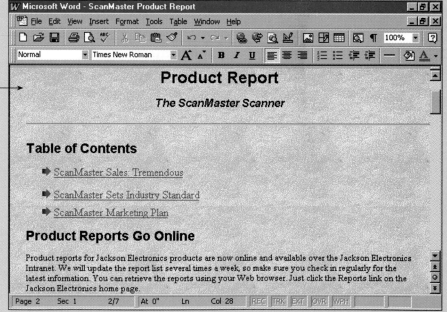

You're finished with formatting the ScanMaster product report page. Knowing that the page might appear differently in the Web browser than it does in Word document window, you decide to save it and preview it one last time.

To save and preview your Web page:

1. Click the **Save** button 🖫.

2. Click the **Web Page Preview** button 🔍. Your system's default Web browser loads and displays the image. Figure 32 shows how Internet Explorer 3.0 displays this particular page.

Figure 32 ◀
HTML
document as it
appears in
browser

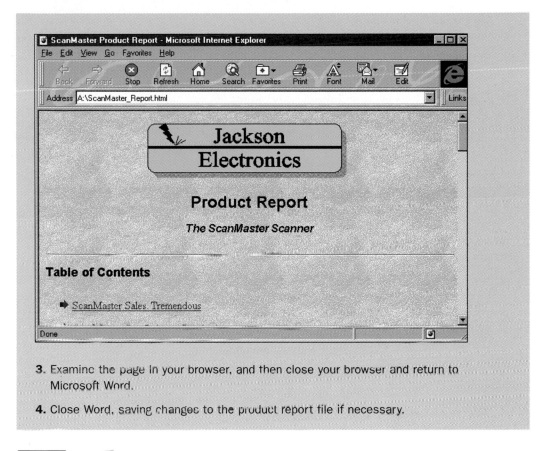

3. Examine the page in your browser, and then close your browser and return to Microsoft Word.

4. Close Word, saving changes to the product report file if necessary.

Quick Check

| 1 | What is the Web Page title, and how do you specify a title for your document with Word?

| 2 | How are Word tables different from HTML tables?

| 3 | Discuss two ways in which HTML documents handle graphics differently from Word documents.

| 4 | What are the two allowable formats for inline images?

| 5 | What are picture placeholders, and why should you include them with your Web document?

| 6 | How do bulleted lists for HTML documents differ from bulleted lists for Word documents?

SESSION

3

In this session, you will use the PowerPoint HTML Wizard to save a PowerPoint presentation as a Web document. You will explore your Web presentation in your Web browser, and will then link to it from the product report Web page.

Web Presentations

As you arrive in your office the next morning after having formatted the product report, you find an e-mail message waiting for you from Jeff. He requests that you include one more link in your product report Web page—this time, to a presentation created in PowerPoint.

Whenever Jackson Electronics promotes a new product or product line, management calls a meeting with stockholders and company officers and unveils the product with a PowerPoint marketing plan slide show. Jeff asks that you convert this marketing plan presentation so that it can be placed on the Web and linked to the product report document.

A **Web presentation** is a collection of related HTML documents on a single topic or idea that are linked. For example, an English professor could create a Web presentation of the play, *Hamlet*, in which each scene is an HTML document and contains links to the preceding and succeeding acts. Figure 33 shows how such a presentation might be diagrammed.

Figure 33 ◄
Web
presentation

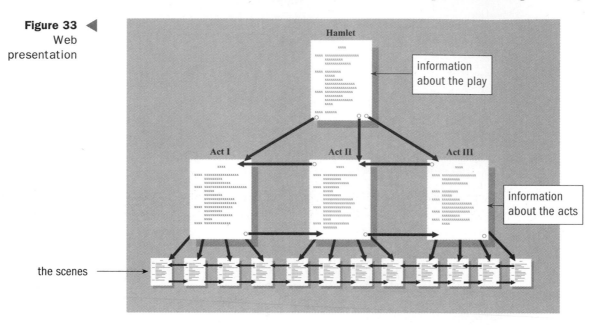

An effective Web presentation should be easy for the user to navigate. The user should always be able to move forward or backward, or at least get back to the starting point.

PowerPoint's HTML Wizard

Creating a Web presentation with Word can be a daunting task, since you have to create each HTML document individually and then insert all the necessary hyperlinks so that users can move effortlessly from one page to another. In some situations, it might be easier to create a Web presentation using PowerPoint. To do this, you first create the presentation as a PowerPoint slide show and then save the presentation in HTML format. PowerPoint's HTML Wizard saves each individual slide as a separate HTML document and creates the necessary hyperlinks between the various HTML documents.

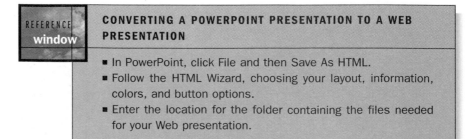

REFERENCE
window

CONVERTING A POWERPOINT PRESENTATION TO A WEB PRESENTATION

- In PowerPoint, click File and then Save As HTML.
- Follow the HTML Wizard, choosing your layout, information, colors, and button options.
- Enter the location for the folder containing the files needed for your Web presentation.

Jeff tells you that the PowerPoint presentation file you'll be working with is called Market.

To open the Market PowerPoint presentation:

1. Start Microsoft PowerPoint.

2. Click the **Open an existing presentation** option button, and then click the **OK** button.

3. Click the **Look in** drop-down arrow, and then click the drive that contains your Student Disk.

4. Click **Market**, and then click the **Open** button.

PowerPoint stores HTML documents differently than Microsoft Word. For example, PowerPoint produces several HTML documents and GIF files in the process of creating the Web presentation rather than a single document. Keeping track of the multitude of files you create can be a daunting task, so the PowerPoint Wizard creates a subfolder, named after the presentation, and places all the files within that single folder. When you create your Web presentation, you do not specify the folder where you want to place the files. Instead, specify the folder in which you want to place the *subfolder* containing the files.

The HTML Wizard gives you many page design options as you progress through it. You'll explore one set of options in creating the marketing plan, but you'll get a chance to try some other approaches in the case problems at the end of this tutorial.

Selecting a Layout

The first part of the HTML Wizard process is layout selection. You can create your own customized layouts for your presentations and then save them for use later, or you can create a new layout from scratch. You can place each slide into its own document window, or you can create a presentation that uses frames to display each presentation slide. **Frames** are a recent innovation that allows a Web browser's document window to contain several smaller windows, each displaying a different HTML document. Not all Web browsers support the use of frames, so you may want to use a standard layout for your Web presentations.

To select the layout for your Web presentation:

1. Click **File**, and then click **Save as HTML** to start PowerPoint's HTML Wizard.

   TROUBLE? If the Office Assistant appears, click the No button to continue with these steps without its help.

2. Click the **Next** button to progress to the Layout Selection dialog box.

3. Click the **New layout** option button since this is a new selection, and then click the **Next** button.

4. Click the **Standard** option button shown in Figure 34 to create a presentation without frames.

Figure 34 ◄
Save as HTML
Wizard

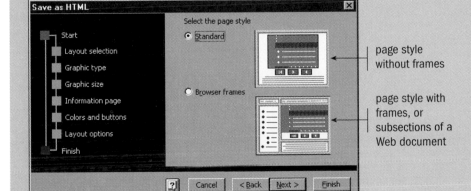

5. Click the **Next** button.

Selecting a Graphics Type

The Graphic type section of the HTML Wizard determines how your slides will be stored and displayed. You have three choices: GIF files, JPEG files, and PowerPoint animations. The first two options have been discussed earlier in this tutorial with respect to creating inline images.

If your presentation contains special effects such as animated slides, you might want to consider using PowerPoint animations for your graphics to preserve those effects for the Web. Users who want to view your special effects need a browser with a special program called a **plug-in** that supports the playing of PowerPoint animations. The PowerPoint Animation Player plug-in is available on the Office 97 CD-ROM and can be used with Internet Explorer 3.0 or Netscape 3.0.

The marketing plan does not include any special effects, so you can use GIF files to store your graphics.

You will also have to determine the size of your graphic. Size is based on the resolution of the user's monitor. A standard resolution is 640x480, so if you don't know the resolution of your audience's monitors, 640x480 is a good choice.

To select graphic type options for the marketing presentation:

1. Click the **GIF** option button, and click the **Next** button.

2. Click the **640 by 480** option button to create a graphic designed for a 640x480 monitor resolution.

3. Select ½ **width of screen** from the Width of Graphics drop-down list.

4. Click the **Next** button.

Creating an Index Page

In the next section of the HTML Wizard, you enter information about the marketing plan, the product, yourself, or the company into the presentation. This information will be placed on the presentation's index page. The **index page**, as you'll see later, is the page that summarizes the contents of your presentation. It also contains hyperlinks to each topic, or slide, in the presentation.

To enter information about the ScanMaster marketing plan:

1. Type **jeff_brooks@is.jackson_electronics.com** in the E-mail address box, and then press **Tab**.

2. Type **http://www.jackson_electronics.com/** in the Your home page box, and then press **Tab**.

3. Type **Contact Jeff Brooks at Product Development, ext. 949.** in the Other Information box, and then press **Tab**.

4. Click the **Download original presentation** check box. This gives users the option of downloading the original PowerPoint presentation file for viewing, if they are using Office 97. Figure 35 shows the completed dialog box.

Figure 35 ◄
Entering
information
about a Web
page

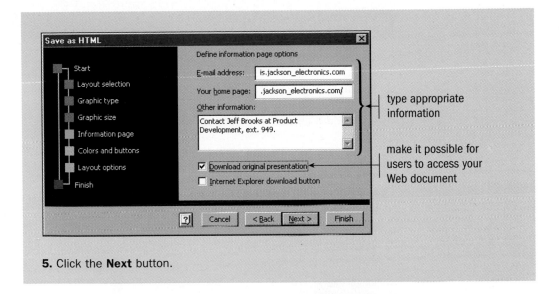

type appropriate
information

make it possible for
users to access your
Web document

5. Click the **Next** button.

Selecting Styles

The Colors and Buttons section of the HTML Wizard lets you define the text colors, background colors, and the style of navigation buttons in your Web presentation. You can use the default browser colors for your text and background or choose your own. The Wizard automatically adds navigation buttons that allow a user to move from one slide in your presentation to the next. The Wizard also lets you choose from four different button styles.

To select colors and buttons for the marketing plan presentation:

1. Click the **Use browser colors** option button to use whatever default colors the user's browser has set up.

2. Click the **Next** button.

3. Click the **Rectangle** button style shown in Figure 36 as the style for your navigation buttons.

Figure 36 ◄
Selecting a
button type

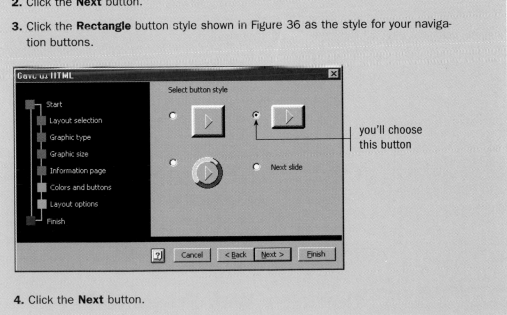

you'll choose
this button

4. Click the **Next** button.

Finalizing a Web Presentation

In the final section of the HTML Wizard, you choose where to place the navigation buttons in the document window. If your presentation includes slide notes, you can also tell the Wizard to include those notes on the Web page. Slide notes were created for this presentation, so you want to be sure to include them in the Web presentation. Finally, you choose the folder that will contain the subfolder of your HTML documents and graphics.

To finish the ScanMaster marketing presentation:

1. Click the **Navigation buttons on top** option button, and then click the **Include slide notes in pages** option button. See Figure 37.

Figure 37 ◄
Final Web page
settings

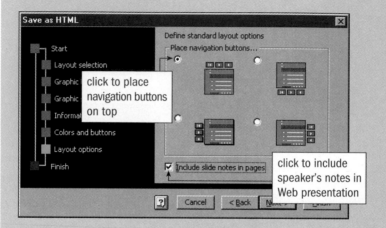

2. Click the **Next** button.

3. Click the **Browse** button, and then click the drive containing your Student Disk.

4. Click the **Select** button to return to the HTML Wizard.

5. Click the **Next** button, and then the **Finish** button.

6. Type **Marketing** when prompted to save your layout options, and then click the **Save** button.

7. Click the **OK** button when you are informed that the process was successful.

If you create another presentation, you can use the layout choices you made during this process by selecting Marketing at the very beginning of the Wizard. Now take a look at the Web presentation you just created. To do this, you need to save and close your PowerPoint presentation.

To save your changes and exit PowerPoint:

1. Click the **Save** button 🖫.

2. Click **File**, and then click **Exit**.

Viewing a Web Presentation

When viewing your Web presentation, you generally start with the index file created by the HTML Wizard.

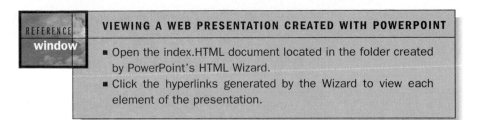

REFERENCE **window**

VIEWING A WEB PRESENTATION CREATED WITH POWERPOINT

- Open the index.HTML document located in the folder created by PowerPoint's HTML Wizard.
- Click the hyperlinks generated by the Wizard to view each element of the presentation.

The index file for the presentation you just created is located in the new folder the Wizard created—in your case, PowerPoint named the folder Market because that was the name of the original PowerPoint presentation. The index file contains links to the Web presentation and is a useful starting point for exploring your files.

To open the Web presentation:

1. Open Internet Explorer 3.0 or your Web browser.

2. Click **File**, and then click **Open**.

   TROUBLE? If you are using the Netscape browser, click File and then Open in Browser.

3. Click the Browse button and locate the index.htm file in the Market folder on drive A. Figure 38 shows the index page the HTML Wizard created for the ScanMaster marketing presentation.

Figure 38
Web presentation in browser

your date will be different

HTML Wizard automatically generates hyperlinks to each slide in your presentation

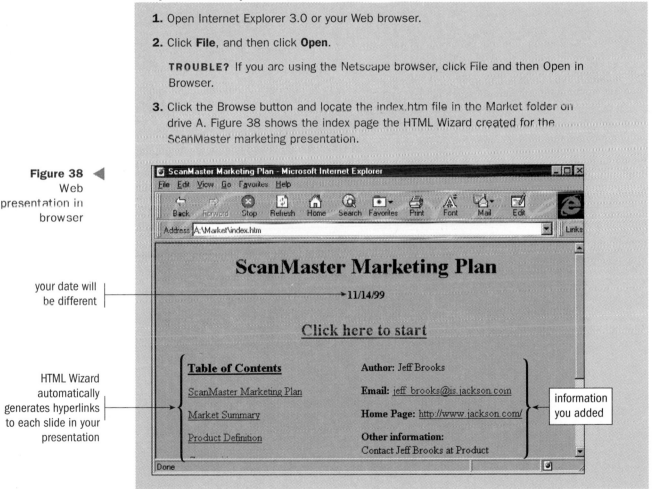

Notice that the index page lists the slide titles from the original presentation as hyperlinks to Web pages based on those slides. Next to the table of contents is the information you entered as you proceeded through the Wizard. At the bottom of the Web page is a hyperlink that users can click to download the original presentation file. You're eager to see how the marketing slides were translated onto the Web presentation.

To view the slides from the ScanMaster marketing presentation:

1. Click the **Click here to start** hyperlink. Figure 39 shows the opening page of the presentation.

Figure 39 ◀
Opening page
of Web
presentation

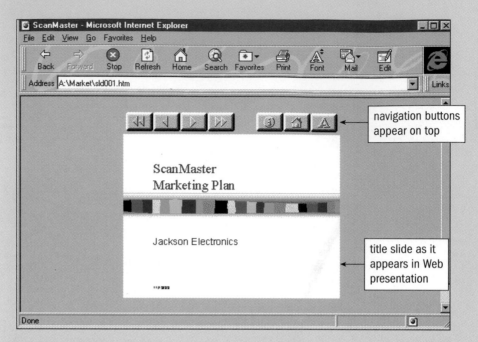

2. Click the [▶] button once to move to the "Market Summary" page displayed in Figure 40.

Figure 40 ◀
Moving to the
next slide

Next navigation button ──

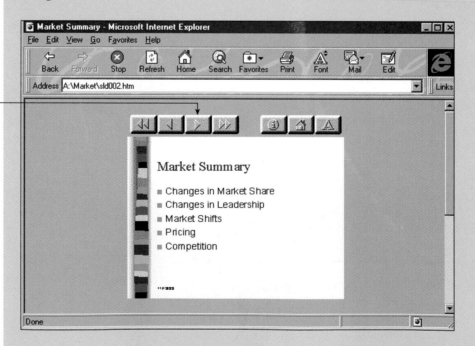

3. Scroll down the document window to view the slide notes that have been automatically attached to the page, as shown in Figure 41.

Figure 41 ◀
Notes from
PowerPoint
speaker's
notes

speaker's notes
appear at the bottom
of the Web page

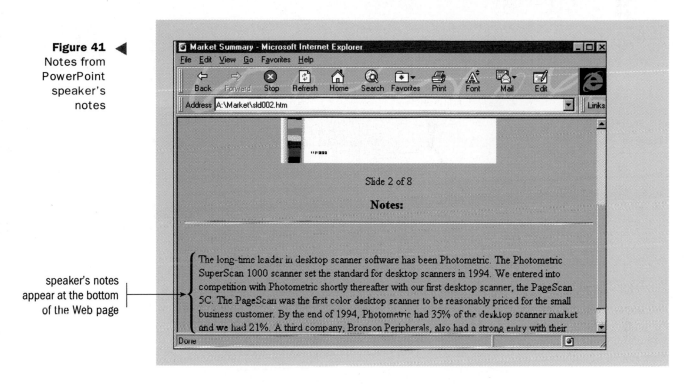

The navigation buttons that PowerPoint has created can take you to other places in the Web document. If you want to jump to either end of the presentation, you can do so with a single mouse click.

To jump to the first and last slides in the presentation:

1. Scroll up and then click the **Last** button ![Last button] to display the last slide.

2. Click the **First** button ![First button] to display the first slide.

Some people who access your Web presentation will not be using graphical browsers like Internet Explorer. For those people, the HTML Wizard has created text files of the marketing plan slides. You decide to view these files and then return to the index page.

To view text files of the ScanMaster Marketing presentation:

1. Click the **Text** button ![Text button]. The Web browser displays the page shown in Figure 42.

Figure 42 ◀
Web page in
text format

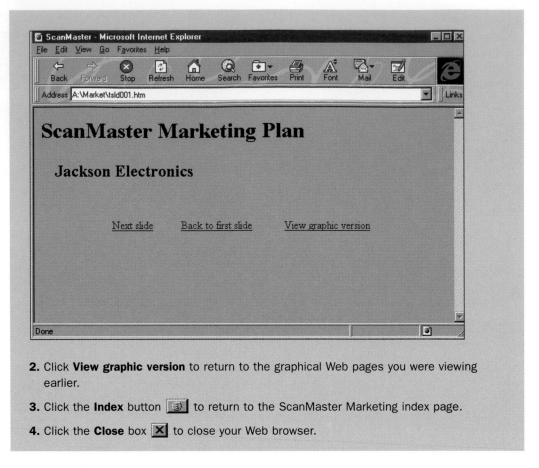

2. Click **View graphic version** to return to the graphical Web pages you were viewing earlier.

3. Click the **Index** button to return to the ScanMaster Marketing index page.

4. Click the **Close** box X to close your Web browser.

You've completed your work in converting the marketing presentation to a Web presentation. Your final task will be to add a link to the presentation into the product report document. Once you have added the link, users who access the product report will be one click away from all the major information about the ScanMaster scanner.

To add a hyperlink to the ScanMaster product report:

1. Start Word, click **File**, and then click **Open**.

2. Click the **Look in** drop-down arrow. Click the drive containing your Student Disk.

3. Click **ScanMaster_Report**, and then click **Open**. Click the **OK** button.

4. Scroll to the bottom of the ScanMaster marketing plan section of the document.

5. Type **Click here to view a marketing presentation** in a new line at the end of the marketing plan section directly before the hyperlink that takes the reader back to the top of the page.

6. Select the text you just entered and click the **Insert Hyperlink** button 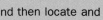.

7. Click the **Browse** button next to the Link to file or URL box, and then locate and select the **index.htm** file in the Market folder.

8. Click the **OK** button twice. Figure 43 shows the new hyperlink.

Figure 43 ◄
Hyperlink
to Web
presentation

hyperlink points to
Web presentation

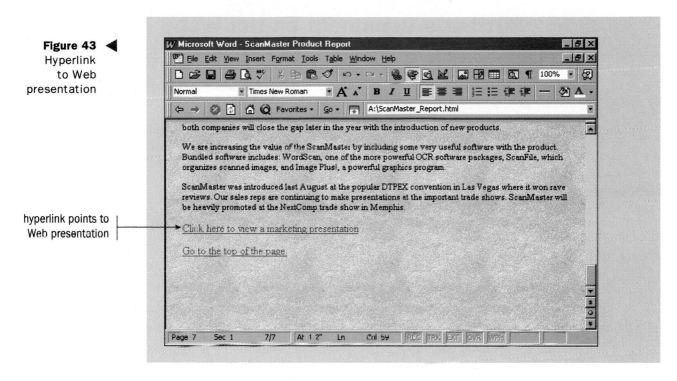

Before you release the final version of your Web page, you should make sure all the hyperlinks are working properly.

To save your changes and view the final results:

1. Click the **Save** button 🖫.

2. Click the **Close** button ☒ to close Microsoft Word.

3. Start your Web browser.

4. Click **File**, and then click **Open**.

5. Click the **Look in** drop-down arrow, and then click the drive containing your Student Disk.

6. Click **ScanMaster_Report**, and then click the **Open** button.

7. Test the hyperlinks you've created in all your Web documents.

   TROUBLE? The hyperlink that takes you to the top of the Product Report page might not be working when you open the document in your browser. If you experience any problems, please see your instructor or technical support person.

8. Once you are satisfied that your presentation is working correctly, exit the Web browser.

   TROUBLE? Unless you are using Internet Explorer 3.0 or Netscape Navigator 3.0 with support for ActiveX documents, remember that hyperlinks to Office 97 documents will not appear in the Web browser window.

Jeff is pleased with the work you've done in creating the collection of Web documents describing the ScanMaster. He collects your files and then transfers them to the company's Web server. After the files have been placed on the Web server, they will be available to everyone on the intranet at Jackson Electronics.

Putting a Document on the Web

The documents you've been working on over the course of this tutorial have been for the benefit of your company and its employees. However, more and more companies are establishing a public presence on the Web, posting documents that are designed for the general public, not just internal employees. To make a file available to the Web, you place it on a computer connected to the Web called a **Web server**.

Your **Internet Service Provider** (**ISP**)—the company or institution through which you have Internet access—usually has a Web server available for your use. Since each ISP has a different procedure for storing Web pages, you should contact your ISP to learn its policies and procedures. Generally, you should be prepared to do the following:

- If your HTML documents have a three-letter "HTM" extension, rename them with the four-letter extension "HTML." The Web requires the four-letter extension for all Web pages.

- Find out from your ISP the name of the folder into which you'll be placing your HTML documents.

- Use **FTP**, a program used on the Internet that transfers files, or e-mail to place your pages in the appropriate folder on your ISP's Web server.

- Work with your ISP to select a name for your site on the Web (such as "http://www.jackson_electronics.com"). Choose a name that will be easy for customers and interested parties to remember and return to.

- If you select a special name for your Web site, register it at http://www.internic.net. Registration is necessary to ensure that any name you give to your site is unique and not already in use by another party.

- Add your site to the indexes of search pages on the Web. This is not required, but it will make it easier for people to find your site. Each search facility has different policies regarding adding information about Web sites to their index. Be aware that some will charge a fee to include your Web site in their list.

Once you've completed these steps, your work will be available on the Web in a form that is easy for users to find and access.

Creating Web Pages with the Web Page Wizard

Jeff stops by the next day with a quick request. The company would like to have a profile page for each Jackson Electronics employee. Profiles should include contact information, details on the duties of each employee, and some additional personal interest information. Jeff wonders if you might be able to create such a profile page with Word.

One of the numerous templates that Word includes is a template for creating Web pages. Using the **Web Page Wizard**, you can create an HTML document from scratch. The Web Page Wizard offers a variety of topics and styles. Some of the types of Web pages you can create with the Wizard include:

- Two- and three-column table layouts
- Calendars
- Survey forms
- Personal pages
- Simple layout
- Table of contents

Figure 44 shows a preview of some of these page types.

Figure 44 ◄
Web Page
Wizard samples

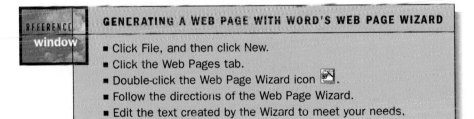

Insert Heading Here

Subheading

Contents

- Work Information
- Hot List
- Contact Information
- Current Projects
- Biographical Information
- Personal Interests

Personal Home Page

Insert Heading Here

Replace the sample text with your own words to create a Table of Contents web page. The Table of Contents page is a good way to introduce viewers to the pages in your web site. Word provides you with additional templates to create more pages. To allow navigation to other pages, select text and click Hyperlink on the Insert menu. This page uses tables to create columns. To change the way the columns look, select the cells you want to change and use the options on the Table menu.

Type some text.

New!   Add a hyperlink
        Add a hyperlink
Confidential   Add a hyperlink

Related Page 1 | Related Page 2 | Related Page 3

Table of Contents

Insert Heading Here

Month and Year

Type some text.

Sunday	Monday	Tuesday	Wednesday	Thursday	Friday	Saturday

Calendar

Insert Heading Here

- Insert a list item   - Insert a list item
- Insert a list item   - Insert a list item
- Insert a list item   - Insert a list item

Related Page 1 | Related Page 2 | Related Page 3

2 Column Layout

Within each of the topic categories, the Web Page Wizard gives you the flexibility of choosing design styles such as elegant, classical, and contemporary.

REFERENCE window

GENERATING A WEB PAGE WITH WORD'S WEB PAGE WIZARD

- Click File, and then click New.
- Click the Web Pages tab.
- Double-click the Web Page Wizard icon 🖼.
- Follow the directions of the Web Page Wizard.
- Edit the text created by the Wizard to meet your needs.

You decide to use the Web Page Wizard to create a personnel page for Jeff.

To create a personnel page with the Web Page Wizard:

1. Open Word, click **File**, and then click **New**.

2. Click the **Web Pages** tab.

3. Double-click the **Web Page Wizard** icon 🖼.

4. Click **Personal Home Page** from the Web Page list, and then click the **Next** button.

5. Click **Professional** from the visual style list, and click the **Finish** button. Figure 45 shows the Web page Word has built.

Figure 45 ◄
Web page
Wizard
document

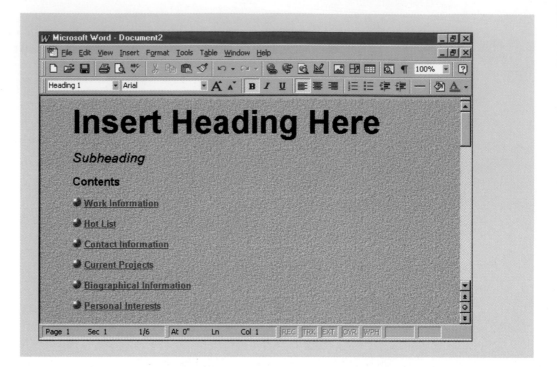

Word has created hyperlinks to six different sections of the document for you—hyperlinks to work information, a list of useful hyperlinks called a **hotlist**, contact information, current projects, biographical information, and personal interests. All that remains is for you or the individual employees to fill in the information. You place information specific to each employee in the bracketed areas. For example, for Jeff Brooks' page, you place his name and title where it currently reads "Insert Heading" and "Subheading."

To insert the new headings:

1. Select the **Insert Heading Here** line.
2. Type **Jeff Brooks**.
3. Select the **Subheading** line.
4. Type **Director of Product Development**. Figure 46 shows the Web page with the new information.

Figure 46 ◄
Document
created with
Word's Web
page Wizard

heading ———

subheading ———

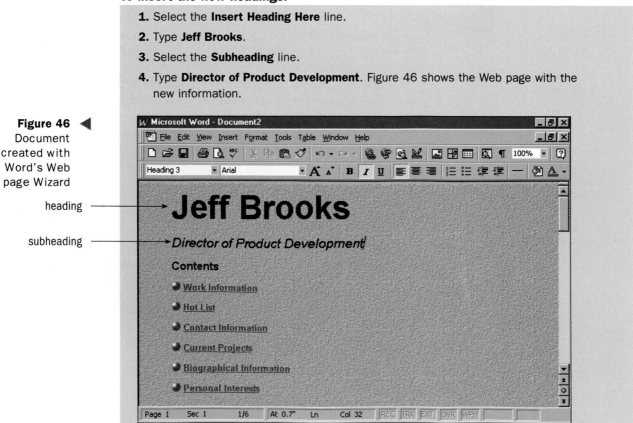

To fill out the rest of the information in this page, you should talk to Jeff Brooks. For now, save the page and exit Word. You can discuss the work you've done later with Jeff.

To save the Jeff Brooks personnel page and exit Word:

1. Click the **Save** button 🖫.

2. Click the **Save in** drop-down arrow, and then click the drive containing your Student Disk.

3. Type **Jeff_Brooks** in the File name box and verify that HTML Document is selected in the Save as Type list box.

4. Click the **Save** button.

5. Click **File**, and then click **Exit** to close Word.

Quick Check

1 What is a Web presentation?

2 What factors should you consider in creating a Web presentation?

3 How does PowerPoint differ from Word in terms of how it stores HTML documents?

4 What are the two layout options PowerPoint gives you for your Web presentations?

5 Describe the three graphic type options provided by the PowerPoint HTML Wizard.

6 What file would you first open to view a Web presentation created by the PowerPoint HTML Wizard?

7 Describe how to use Word to quickly create Web pages of different types and styles.

Tutorial Assignments

Jeff Brooks has had a few days to review your work with the product report prototype. He would like you to add a few new items to the product report Web document you created over the course of the tutorial. He hands you the following To Do list:

- Create a table of contents within the ScanMaster fact sheet made up of hyperlinks to the four main section heads of that document.
- Create hyperlinks in the fact sheet to the ScanMaster product report you've just finished working on and the ScanMaster Web presentation.
- Add the Jackson Electronics logo to the top of the fact sheet page.
- Add graphical bullets and lines to the fact sheet, and give the background a newsprint texture.

To complete Jeff's To Do list, do the following:

1. Open the TAssign folder on your Student Disk, and then open the Facts file in Word.

2. Save your document as ScanMaster_Facts.html in the TAssign folder of your Student Disk.

3. Insert a new line directly preceding the "Product Summary" line, which contains the text "Main Topics."

4. Create a bulleted list directly after this line, but do not enter any text into it.

5. Copy the four main section headings (Product Summary, Features, Specifications, and Ordering Information) and paste them into the bulleted list of main topics as hyperlinks.

6. Scroll to the bottom of the document and enter a new line at the bottom: "Click here to view the ScanMaster product report."

7. Select the text and link it to the product report HTML document that you created during the tutorial.

8. Create a new line at the bottom on the document and enter the text: "Click here to view ScanMaster Marketing Presentation."
9. Select the text and link it to the index.htm file located in the Market folder on your Student Disk.
10. Insert a blank line at the top of the page, and insert the Logo.gif file located in the TAssign folder of your Student Disk.
11. Create a picture placeholder for the logo file that says "Jackson Electronics."
12. Change the bullets in the bulleted list of main topics to graphical bullets appearing as red balls.
13. Insert a red graphical horizontal line after the second line in the document reading "Fact Sheet."
14. Format the background of the page with the Newsprint texture.
15. Give the document the page title "ScanMaster Fact Sheet."
16. Open ScanMaster_Facts.html in your Web browser, and test the hyperlinks to verify that they work properly.

Case Problems

1. Davis Books Events Page Davis Books is a popular bookstore in Lakeside, IL. Each week, the owner, John Davis, tries to schedule special events such as author signings and lectures. In order to increase the visibility of the bookstore's special events, John has asked you to put information about the bookstore and the weekly events on the World Wide Web. He has given you three Word document files: one contains information about Davis books and the other two contain information about an event in the upcoming week. John wants the pages to be linked together so that a user could go from reading an announcement about the event to a page describing it. He also would like you to enliven the pages by adding some graphical bullets and interesting textural backgrounds. To create the Davis book Web pages:

1. Open the file Davis.doc in the Cases folder of your Student Disk.
2. Save the file as Davis_Books in HTML format.
3. Open the files SD.doc and JS.doc, also located in the Cases folder of your Student Disk. These files describe two of the upcoming events.
4. Save those files as Sandy_Davis and John_Sheridan, respectively, both as HTML documents.
5. Change the descriptions of upcoming events on the Davis_Books page to hypertext, pointing to the Sandy_Davis and John_Sheridan HTML documents, respectively.
6. Create a hyperlink from the Sandy_Davis and John_Sheridan HTML documents back to the Davis_Books page, so that if a user clicks the title "Davis Books," he or she jumps back to the Davis Books page.
7. In the Davis_Books Web page, change the bulleted list to a list using graphical bullets. Choose the "red ball" graphical bullet style.
8. Format the background of all three files with the Parchment texture style.
9. In all three files, add a horizontal line beneath the title: "Davis Books." Use the thick red graphical line.
10. Save your changes, and verify that the Web pages work using Internet Explorer or your Web browser.

2. AASE Job List As an assistant to the director of communications at the American Association of Structural Engineers (AASE), it is your job to maintain a weekly job list for association members. Recently, the AASE has gone online with job information with a page on the Web. You've been asked to create a job listings page for the AASE.

The AASE places job information into an Access database. A subset of this database has been created for this task, called "Joblist." You'll place information from a table in this database into the HTML document, AASEJobs. Descriptions of the four new jobs have been placed in the Word document files: SE431, SE432, SE 433, and SE434.

Your task will be to create hyperlinks between the job list and the job descriptions.
To create the AASE job listings Web page:

1. Open the Joblist database in the Cases folder of your Student Disk in Access, and view the Jobs table in Datasheet view.
2. Copy the content of the Jobs table.
3. Open the HTML document, AASEJobs.
4. Paste the Jobs table to the end of the document.
5. Return to Access and close the Joblist database; then go back to Word.
6. Save the file as AASE_Job_List.htm.
7. Increase the width of the first row of the table by moving your pointer over the border between the first and second row until the pointer changes to a ✛, and drag the row border down until you can read the text in the header row.
8. Modify the job listing table so that the background color is white and the color of cells in the header row is yellow.
9. Format the table with a 1.5-point border.
10. Enter "AASE Job Lists" as the document's page title.
11. Open each of the job description Word documents (SE431–SE434). At the bottom of each document, change the text "Return to the AASE job listings" to a hyperlink pointing to the AASE_Job_List.htm file.
12. Save each job description document as an HTML document, and click Yes to save any possible format changes.
13. Return to the AASE_Job_List.htm file.
14. Create hyperlinks for each entry in the table that point to the corresponding job description HTML document (not the Word document).
15. Save the changes to your HTML document and close Word.
16. Open the AASE_Job_List.htm file in your Web browser.
17. Verify that the hyperlinks work and point to the appropriate targets.

3. Middle Age Arts Product Catalog Middle Age Arts sells replicas of ancient and Middle Ages artworks, ranging from wall tapestries to sculptures. In recent years, they've created a Web publication showcasing their products. Next month, they will be having a sale on items in their "Gargoyle Collection." You've been asked to create a Web publication showing items from the sale. A PowerPoint presentation has already been created by some sales reps, and you decide to adapt it to the Web.
To create the Middle Age Arts Web publication:

1. Open the Gargoyle presentation located in the Cases folder of the Student Disk in PowerPoint.
2. Save the presentation as an HTML document with the following options:
   - Use browser frames.
   - Save graphics as GIF files.
   - Format graphics for 800x600 resolutions at one-half width of the screen.
   - Include an e-mail address of sales@middle_age_arts.com.
   - Include a home page URL of http://www.middle_age_arts.com.
   - Include the following other information text:
      "Special this month! Items from the Gargoyles Collection 15–20% off. Order yours today!"
   - Do not include the original PowerPoint presentation or Internet Explorer in the Web presentation.
   - Use the standard browser colors.
   - Use the rectangle navigation button style.
   - Include slide notes on each page.
   - Name the layout options you've chosen "Sales."
3. Save the subfolder containing your HTML documents in the Cases folder of your Student Disk.
4. Open the Index.htm file in Microsoft Word. This file is located in the Gargolyes subfolder of the Cases folder on your Student Disk.

5. Replace the first two lines of the page (the page title and the date) with the GIF logo graphic, MAALogo.gif, located in the Cases folder on your Student Disk.
6. Change the hypertext from "Click here to start" to "This month's special."
7. Format the background using a Marble textured background.
8. Save your changes to the Index.htm file.
9. Open Index.htm in your Web browser, and verify that the Web publication is working properly.

4. Personal Home Page Create a home page for yourself using the Web Page Wizard in Microsoft Word. Include the following items in your page:

- Work information
- Hyperlinks to your favorite Web pages
- Information on how to contact you
- Your current projects
- Biographical information
- A list of your personal interests

To create your personal home page:

1. Start Microsoft Word.
2. Click File, and then click New from the Word menu.
3. Click the Web Pages tab and then double-click the Web Page Wizard icon.
4. Choose the Personal Home Page design type.
5. Choose a design style for your page.
6. Enter the necessary information to complete your page.
7. Save your page and view it in your Web browser.

Lab Assignments

Web Pages & HTML

It's easy to create your own Web pages. There are many software tools to help you become a Web author. In this Lab you'll experiment with a Web authoring wizard that automates the process of creating a Web page. You'll also try your hand at working directly with HTML code. To start the Lab, click the Start button on the Windows 95 Taskbar, point to Programs, point to Course Labs, point to New Perspectives Applications, and click Web Page Creation/HTML.

1. Click the Steps button to activate the Web authoring wizard and learn how to create a basic Web page. As you proceed through the Steps, answer all of the Quick Check questions. After you complete the Steps, you will see a Quick Check summary Report. Follow the instructions on the screen to print this report.

2. In Explore, click the File menu, then click New to start working on a new Web page. Use the wizard to create a Home page for a veterinarian who offers dog day-care and boarding services. After you create the page, save it and print it. Your site must have the following characteristics:
   a. Title: Dr. Dave's Dog Domain
   b. Background color: Gold
   c. Graphic: Dog.jpg
   d. Body text: Your dog will have the best care day and night at Dr. Dave's Dog Domain. Fine accommodations, good food, play time, and snacks are all provided. You can board your pet by the day or week. Grooming services also available.
   e. Text link: "Reasonable rates" links to www.cciw.com/np3/rates.htm
   f. E-mail link: "For more information:" links to **daveassist@drdave.com**

3. In Explore, use the File menu to open the HTML document called Politics.htm. After you use the HTML window (not the wizard) to make the following changes, save the revised page and print it. Refer to the table below for a list of HTML tags you can use.
   a. Change the title to Politics 2000
   b. Center the page heading
   c. Change the background color to FFE7C6 and the text color to 000000

   d. Add a line break before the sentence "What's next?"

   e. Add a bold tag to "Additional links" list.

   f. Add one more link to the "Additional links" list. The link should go to the site www.elections.ca and the clickable link should read "Elections Canada"

   g. Change the last graphic to display the image "next.gif"

HTML Tags	Meaning and location
<HTML></HTML>	States that the file is an HTML document. Opening tag begins the page; closing tag ends the page (required).
<HEAD></HEAD>	States that the enclosed text is the header of the page. Appears immediately after the opening HTML tag (required).
<TITLE></TITLE>	States that the enclosed text is the title of the page. Must appear within the opening and closing HEAD tags (required).
<BODY></BODY>	States that the enclosed material (all the text, images, and tags in the rest of the document) is the body of the document (required).
<H1></H1>	States that the enclosed text is a heading.
 	Inserts a line break. Can be used to control line spacing and breaks in lines
<UL></UL> <OL></OL>	Indicates an unordered list (list items are preceded by bullets) or an ordered list (list items are preceded by numbers or letters).
<LI>	Indicates a list item. Precedes all items in unordered or ordered lists.
<CENTER> <C/ENTER>	Indicates that the enclosed text should be centered on the width of the page.
<B></B>	Indicates that the enclosed text should appear bold face.
<I></I>	Indicates that the enclosed text should appear italic.
<A HREF=""></A>	Indicates that the enclosed text is a hypertext link; the URL of the linked material must appear within the quote marks after the equal sign.
<IMG SRC="">	Inserts an in-line image into the document. The URL of the image appears within the quote marks following the SRC+"" attribute.
<HR>	Inserts a horizontal rule.

4. In Explore, use the Web authoring wizard and the HTML window to create a Home page about yourself. You should include at least a screenful of text, a graphic, an external link, and an e-mail link. Save the page on drive A, then print the HTML code. Turn in your disk and printout.

Answers to Quick Check Questions

SESSION 1

1 Hypertext is text that contains links to other documents or information sources, called targets. The links can be activated by the reader to quickly and easily retrieve the information contained in the targets.

2 HTML stands for Hypertext Markup Language and is the universal language of the World Wide Web. All Web browsers can interpret files in HTML.

3 Copy the text that you want to link to. Paste the text at the location where you want to place the link using the Paste as Hyperlink command.

4 The Web toolbar is a toolbar found in Office 97 applications. It includes forward and backward buttons that enable you to move back and forth between your hyperlinked documents.

5 Right-click the hypertext and click Hyperlinks and Select Hyperlink from the menu. Type over the old selected hypertext and replace it with new text.

6 Select the text you want to link to another document. Click the Insert Hyperlinks button and enter the name and location of the file in the Link to File or URL box.

SESSION 2

1 The Web Page title is the title of the Web page that appears in the Web browser's title bar. You can specify the title for your Web page in the File Properties dialog box.

2 HTML tables lack several of the formatting features available with Word tables. You cannot use the AutoFormat command on HTML tables. Nor can you specify the border style or table style.

3 HTML files are limited to using only two formats: GIF and JPEG, while Word documents can display a large variety of graphic types. Also, graphic images can be stored within a Word document, while HTML files always reference graphics in external files.

4 GIF and JPEG.

5 Picture Placeholders are text descriptions that Web browsers will display in situations where they are unable to display the graphic image itself. Picture Placeholders are useful for text-based browsers.

6 HTML bulleted lists can use external graphic images to serve as bullet symbols.

SESSION 3

1 A Web presentation is a group of hyperlinked documents that provide an organized presentation of a specific topic or idea.

2 What topics will the presentation cover? How will the HTML files be linked together? How will users navigate from one point in the presentation to another?

3 PowerPoint saves several HTML files and graphic image files and places them within a separate folder.

4 Standard and Framed.

5 Graphics can be saved as GIF or JPEG files, or as animations. Animations require that the user have the Animation Player plug-in installed on the Web browser.

6 Index.htm.

7 Click File and New from the Word menu and click the Web Pages tab from the New dialog box. Double-click the Web Page Wizard and select the type and style of Web page you want to create.

Creating Web Pages **Task Reference**

TASK	PAGE #	RECOMMENDED METHOD	NOTES
Bullet, create	WP 30	Remove any bullets from the bulleted list, click Format, click Bullets and Numbering, select a bullet style of the list of bullets	See Reference Window: Creating Graphical Bullets
HTML, saving a Word document as	WP 7	Click File, click Save as HTML, enter a filename and location for the HTML file	See Reference Window: Converting a Word File to HTML
Hyperlink, create to an HTML document	WP 15	Select the text or graphic to act as a hyperlink, click [icon], enter the location of the HTML document in the Link to file or URL box	See Reference Window: Creating a Hyperlink Between Documents
Hyperlink, create to an Office 97 document	WP 17	Select the text or graphic to act as a hyperlink, click [icon], enter the location of the Office 97 document in the Link to File or URL box	
Hyperlink, navigate	WP 12	Click the hyperlink to jump to the link's target; click [icon] to return to the starting location	See Reference Window: Navigating Hyperlinks with the Web Toolbar
Hyperlink, paste a	WP 10	Copy the text you want as the hyperlink target, move to the location of the hyperlink you intend to create, click Edit, click Paste as Hyperlink	See Reference Window: Copying and Pasting a Hyperlink
Hypertext, edit	WP 13	Right-click the hypertext, click Hyperlink, click Select Hyperlink, type over the existing hypertext, replacing it with new text	See Reference Window: Editing Hypertext
Inline image, check filename	WP 27	Right-click the image, click Format Picture, click the Settings tab, view the filename in the Path box	
Inline image, insert	WP 27	Click where you want the image to appear, click Insert, point to Picture, click From File, locate the GIF or JPEG graphics file, click Insert	See Reference Window: Inserting a Graphic into a Web Page
Line, create	WP 29	Click where the line will be placed, click Insert, click Horizontal Line, select the line style from the list of horizontal lines	See Reference Window: Create Graphical Lines
Picture placeholder, create	WP 28	Right-click the inline image, click Format Picture, click the Settings tab, enter the picture placeholder text in the Picture Placeholder box	See Reference Window: Creating a Picture Placeholder
Table borders, set width	WP 25	Click anywhere within the table, click Table, click Borders, click the Border Width drop-down arrow, select a border width from the list	

Creating Web Pages **Task Reference**

TASK	PAGE #	RECOMMENDED METHOD	NOTES
Table cells, set background colors	WP 25	Select the table cells, click Table, click Cell Properties, click the Background drop-down arrow, choose the color from the list	
Table, change column width	WP 22	Point at the column border so that the pointerchanges to ⁜, drag the border to the new column width	
Table, change row height	WP 22	Point at the row border so that the pointer changes to a ⁜, drag the border to the new row height	
Table, set background colors	WP 24	Click anywhere within the table, click Table, click Table Properties, click the Background drop-down arrow, choose the color from the list	
Table, set HTML properties	WP 23	Click anywhere within the table, click Table, click Table Properties, change the properties	See Reference Window: Setting HTML Table Properties
Web page background, color	WP 32	Click Format, click Background, choose a color from the list	
Web page background, create texture	WP 32	Click Format, click Background, click Fill Effects, choose a texture from the list of textures	
Web page, create from the Web Page Wizard	WP 45	Click File, click New, click the Web Pages tab, double-click ▨, choose a design and style for your Web page	See Reference Window: Generating a Web Page with Word's Web Page Wizard
Web Page, preview	WP 32	Click ▣	
Web Page title, create	WP 21	Click File, click Properties, enter the Web Page title	
Web presentation, create from PowerPoint	WP 34	Within PowerPoint, click File, click Save as HTML, choose options for the Web presentation following steps from the HTML Wizard	See Reference Window: Converting a PowerPoint Presentation to a Web Presentation
Web presentation, view	WP 39	Open the index.htm document created by the PowerPoint HTML wizard, click the hyperlinks generated by the Wizard to view each presentation element	See Reference Window: Viewing a Web Presentation Created with PowerPoint

NEW
PERSPECTIVES
SERIES

Microsoft®
Office 97
Professional

INTERNET ASSIGNMENTS

Read This **Before You Begin**

TO THE STUDENT

STUDENT DISKS

To complete the Internet Assignments in this book, you need four Student Disks. Your instructor will either provide you with Student Disks or ask you to make your own.

If you are supposed to make your own Student Disks, you will need four blank, formatted high-density disks. You will need to copy a set of folders from a file server or standalone computer onto your disks. Your instructor will tell you which computer, drive letter, and folders contain the files you need. The following table shows you which folders go on each of your disks, so that you will have enough disk space to complete all of the Internet Assignments:

Student Disk	Write this on the disk label	Put these folders on the disk
1	Student Disk 1: Word 97 Internet Assignments	Word
2	Student Disk 2: Excel 97 Internet Assignments	Excel
3	Student Disk 3: Access 97 Internet Assignments	Access
4	Student Disk 4: PowerPoint 97 Internet Assignments	PowerPoint

When you begin each assignment, make sure you are using the correct Student Disk. See the inside front or inside back cover of this book for more information on Student Disk files, or ask your instructor or technical support person for assistance.

Please note that some of the assignments build from previous assignments in this text, which is often Case Problem 4 in the tutorial. To complete those Internet Assignments, you will use the file provided on your Internet Assignments Student Disk.

COURSE LABS

The Internet Assignments in this book feature two interactive Course Labs to help you understand Internet and E-mail concepts. The Internet: World Wide Web and E-mail Lab Assignments at the beginning of these Internet Assignments relates to these Labs. To start a Lab, click the **Start** button on the Windows 95 taskbar, point to **Programs**, point to **Course Labs**, point to **New Perspectives Applications**, and then click the name of the Lab you want to use.

USING YOUR OWN COMPUTER

If you are going to work through this book using your own computer, you need:

■ **Computer System** Microsoft Windows 95, Windows 98, or Windows NT (or a later version), a Web browser (Microsoft Internet Explorer 3.01 or higher or Netscape Navigator 3 or higher), and Microsoft Office 97 Professional must be installed on your computer. This book assumes a complete installation of Microsoft Office 97 Professional.

■ **Student Disks** Ask your instructor or lab manager for details on how to get the Student Disks. You will not be able to complete the exercises in this section using your own computer until you have Student Disks. The student files may also be obtained electronically over the Internet. See the inside front or inside back cover of this book for more details.

■ **Course Labs** See your instructor or technical support person to obtain the Course Lab software for use on your own computer.

VISIT OUR WORLD WIDE WEB SITE

Additional materials designed especially for you are available on the World Wide Web. Go to **http://www.course.com**. These Internet Assignments are also updated and maintained on your Student Online Companion page. To get to this page, go to the Course Technology home page. Click the Student Online Companions link, and then click the New Perspectives on Microsoft Office 97 Professional link to open the New Perspectives on Microsoft Office 97 home page (you might need to scroll down to see the link).

LOGGING OFF

Some browsers have a dialer application that dials the modem that does not disconnect automatically when you close the browser. Make sure that you close your Web browser and terminate the phone or server connection when you finish browsing, so as to prevent tying up phone lines in the lab. In addition, if you are working at home or outside of the lab, you should be aware that you might need to make a long distance call to connect to your server, or you might be billed for hours logged onto the Internet (depending on the Internet connection).

TO THE INSTRUCTOR

To complete the Internet Assignments in this book, your students must use a set of student files on four Student Disks. These files are included in the Instructor's Resource Kit, and they can also be obtained electronically over the Internet. See the inside front or inside back cover of this book for more details. Follow the instructions in the Readme or Help file to copy the files to your server or standalone computer. You can view the Readme file using WordPad.

Once the files are copied, you can make Student Disks for the students yourself, or you can tell students where to find the files so they can make their own Student Disks. Make sure the files get correctly copied onto the Student Disks by following the instructions in the Student Disks section above, which will ensure that students have enough disk space to complete all the Internet Assignments.

COURSE LAB SOFTWARE

These Internet Assignments feature two online, interactive Course Labs that introduce basic Internet and E-mail concepts. This Course Lab software is distributed on a CD-ROM included in the Instructor's Resource Kit. To install the Course Lab software, follow the setup instructions in the Readme file on the CD-ROM. Refer also to the Readme or Help file for essential technical notes related to running the Labs in a multiuser environment. Once you have installed the Course Lab software, your students can start the Labs from the Windows 95 desktop by clicking the **Start** button on the Windows 95 taskbar, pointing to **Programs**, pointing to **Course Labs**, pointing to **New Perspectives Applications**, and then clicking the name of the lab they want to use.

COURSE TECHNOLOGY LABS AND STUDENT FILES SOFTWARE

You are granted a license to copy the Student Files and Course Labs to any computer or computer network used by students who have purchased this book.

Internet Assignments

Using E-mail and the Internet to Increase Your Productivity

In these assignments you will learn to:

- Use Web browser software to find information

- Send and receive e-mail and learn how to use an e-mail program

- Use the Internet to find information

- Integrate information that you find on the Internet into Word, Excel, Access, and PowerPoint documents

Internet Assignments Overview

As a student you might already be familiar with the Internet and the World Wide Web. You might use the Internet to register for courses at your school, to check the status of a library book, or to send e-mail messages to your professors, friends, or family members. As you know, Microsoft Office 97 applications include a Web toolbar that makes it easy to view Web pages directly from the application. The possibilities for you as a student are endless—you can work on a term paper in Word and instantly research your topic in any library in the world, without ever leaving the computer. As a professional, you will find that e-mail and the Internet are used in many different ways to increase employee productivity, maintain communication with people around the world, and even to sell products. You have learned in this book how to use the World Wide Web as a research tool to access information that can be used to create, enhance, and update your Microsoft Office documents.

The purpose of these Internet Assignments is to challenge you to find information on the Internet that you can use to create effective documents. These open-ended case scenarios allow you to be creative as you apply the skills you have learned in the tutorials.

Please note that these assignments are updated and maintained on the Web. Specific names of links and certain steps may be slightly altered in the online version. If you ever have trouble completing the steps in these pages, follow the steps in the online version. You can get to this companion by clicking the appropiate links from **http://www.course.com**.

Lab Assignments Overview

If you do not have any prior experience working on the World Wide Web, we recommend that you complete the Internet: World Wide Web Course Lab that is included in this section and complete the Lab Assignments in the pages that follow. This Lab will give you a quick overview of the Internet and World Wide Web, and it will also give you hands-on practice with Web browsing in a simulated environment. If you are not familiar with the fundamentals of electronic mail, you should complete the E-mail Course Lab and the related assignments that follow in this section. E-mail is an important business tool in most organizations and it is important that you understand how to use an e-mail system to generate and send information.

Lab Assignments

The Internet: World Wide Web   One of the most popular services on the Internet is the World Wide Web. This Lab is a Web simulator that teaches you how to use Web browser software to find information. You can use this Lab even if your school does not provide you with Internet access.

To start the Lab, click the Start button on the Windows 95 taskbar, point to Programs, point to Course Labs, point to New Perspective Applications, and then click Internet World Wide Web. If you do not see Course Labs on your Windows 95 Programs menu, ask your instructor or technical support person for assistance.

1. Click the Steps button to learn how to use Web browser software. As you proceed through the Steps, answer all of the Quick Check questions that appear. After you complete the Steps, you will see a Quick Check summary report. Follow the instructions on the screen to print this report.

2. Click the Explore button on the Welcome screen. Use the Web browser to locate a weather map of the Caribbean Virgin Islands. What is its URL?

3. A SCUBA diver named Wadson Lachouffe has been searching for the fabled treasure of Greybeard the pirate. A link from the Adventure Travel Web site **www.atour.com** leads to Wadson's Web page called "Hidden Treasure." Locate the Hidden Treasure page, and then answer the following questions:
   a. What was the name of Greybeard's ship?
   b. What was Greybeard's favorite food?
   c. What does Wadson think happened to Greybeard's ship?

4. In the Steps, you found a graphic of Jupiter from the photo archives of the Jet Propulsion Laboratory. In the Explore section of the Lab, you can also find a graphic of Saturn. Suppose one of your friends wants a picture of Saturn for an astronomy report. Make a list of the blue, underlined links your friend must click to find the Saturn graphic. Assume that your friend begins at the Web Trainer home page.

5. Enter the URL **www.atour.com** to jump back to the Adventure Travel Web site. Write a one-page description of the information at the site, including the number of pages the site contains, and diagram the links it contains.

6. Chris Thomson, a student at UVI, has his own Web page. Use your Web browser to look at the information Chris included on his page. Suppose you could create your own Web page. What would you include? Use word processing software to design your own Web page. Make sure to indicate the graphics and links you would use.

E-Mail   E-mail that originates on a local area network with a mail gateway can travel all over the world. That's why it is so important to learn how to use it. In this Lab you will use an e-mail simulator, so even if your school's computers don't provide you with e-mail service, you will learn the basics of reading, sending, and replying to electronic mail. To start the Lab using Windows 95, click the Start button on the Windows 95 taskbar, point to Programs, point to Course Labs, point to New Perspectives Applications, and then click E-Mail.

1. Click the Steps button to learn how to work with e-mail. As you proceed through the Steps, answer all of the Quick Check questions that appear. After you complete the Steps, you will see a Quick Check summary report. Follow the instructions on the screen to print this report.

2. Click the Explore button. Write a message to re@films.org. The subject of the message is "Picks and Pans." In the body of your message, describe a movie you recently saw. Include the name of the movie, briefly summarize the plot, and then give it a thumbs up or a thumbs down. Print the message before you send it.

3. Look in your In Box for a message from jb@music.org. Read the message, and then compose a reply indicating that you will attend. Carbon copy mciccone@music.org in your message. Print your reply, including the text of JB's original message, before you send it.

4. Look in your In Box for a message from leo@sports.org. Reply to the message by adding your rating to the text of the original message as follows:

Equipment:	Your rating:
Rollerblades	2
Skis	3
Bicycle	1
Scuba gear	4
Snowmobile	5

Print your reply before you send it.

5. Go into the lab with a partner. You should each log into the E-Mail Lab on different computers. Look at the Addresses list to find the user ID for your partner. You should each send a short e-mail message to your partner. Then check your mail message from your partner. Read the message and compose a reply. Print your reply before you send it. *Note: Unlike a full-featured mail system, the e-mail simulator does not save mail in mailboxes after you log off.*

Word Internet Assignments

Tutorial 1. Mexico Vacation Letter   Your parents told you at the beginning of the school year that if you earned all As in your courses that they would pay for a Mexican vacation. Now you need to decide on a location. Based on recommendations from friends, you narrow your choices to Baja or Cabo San Lucas. You decide to use the Internet to find information about these two regions of Mexico to help make your final decision. Some important issues are lodging, recreation activities, and local tourist attractions. After finding the information you need, use Word to write a letter to your parents to tell them about your trip.

1. Log on to the Internet and use your Web browser to go to the Course Technology home page. Click the Student Online Companions link, and then click the New Perspectives on Microsoft Office 97 Professional link to open the New Perspectives on Microsoft Office 97 home page. Click the Word link, and then click the Tutorial 1 Internet Assignment link.

2. Click the ¡@migo! link to help you decide on a location. Print the pages for at least two tourist attractions that are of interest to you, and at least two hotels that you can stay at during your trip for each destination. Close your Web browser.

3. Start Word and then check your screen to make sure your settings match those in the tutorials.

4. Press the Enter key six times to add blank lines to the document, and then type today's date.

5. Insert one blank line, and then type the inside address for your parents. Insert a blank line, type an appropriate salutation, and then insert another blank line.

6. Based on the information you found on the Web, select a destination, and then use the body of your letter to describe your vacation. Include information about your destination, lodging, and any special exhibits or tourist sites that you will visit using the information you found on the Web. Include at least two paragraphs in the body of the letter.

7. Insert one blank line between the body of the letter and the salutation, and then type an appropriate salutation. Insert three blank lines for your signature, and then type your name.

8. Insert the disk labeled Student Disk 1: Word 97 Internet Assignments into the appropriate disk drive, and then save your work as Mexico Trip in the Word folder on the disk.

9. Preview the letter using the Print Preview button, and then print the letter.

10. Close the document.

Tutorial 2. Movie Review (Continued from Case Problem 4)   After submitting the movie review that you created in Case Problem 4, your student newspaper decides that you should change the article to include comments from outside sources and integrate them with your own personal opinions. You decide to use the Internet to find reviews of the four films that you featured in your article. Then you will use Word to update the Edited Movie Review document that you created in Case Problem 4 to include the new information. (*Note:* You will use the edited_movie_review file in the Word folder on your Word 97 Internet Assignments disk to complete this assignment. If you cannot locate movie reviews of the movies included in the edited_movie_review file, substitute other movies of your choice.)

1. Log on to the Internet and use your Web browser to go to the Course Technology home page. Click the Student Online Companions link, and then click the New Perspectives on Microsoft Office 97 Professional link to open the New Perspectives on Microsoft Office 97 home page. Click the Word link, and then click the Tutorial 2 Internet Assignment link.

2. Click the links to Mr. Showbiz Movie Guide, TSPNetwork, or Yahoo to find reviews of the four movies. If you cannot locate reviews of the movies you selected, use other movies of your choice. Print the pages that contain the reviews you will use.

3. Start Word and then check your screen to make sure your settings match those shown in the tutorials.

4. Open the file edited_movie_review from the Word folder on the disk labeled Student Disk 1: Word 97 Internet Assignments. Use the Save As command to save the file as Edited Movie Review 2 in the Word folder on the disk.

5. Edit your review to include the information that you found on the Web.

6. Change the paragraph alignment to left.

7. Change the title of each movie from italics to underlined.

8. Preview the document and then print it.

9. Save and close your document.

Tutorial 3. Advisory Letter on a Tuition Increase (Continued from Case Problem 3)   After your school's president received your letter, he wanted more information about tuition rates at other universities. He asks you to gather information about the tuition rates and cost of living expenses at a number of schools, including Arizona State University and The University of Florida. You need to find the rates for these schools, and then prepare a memo to give to the president. You will use the Internet to find the rates, and then create a table in Word to organize the information. Then you will use Word to prepare a brief memo explaining your findings.

1. Log on to the Internet and use your Web browser to go to the Course Technology home page. Click the Student Online Companions link, and then click the New Perspectives on Microsoft Office 97 Professional link to open the New Perspectives on Microsoft Office 97 home page. Click the Word link, and then click the Tutorial 3 Internet Assignment link.

2. Click the links to Arizona State University (fees), Arizona State University (residential), and to The University of Florida, and then search for information about undergraduate tuition and living expenses. Print the pages for the tuition rates, and then close your Web browser.

3. Start Word and then check your screen to make sure your settings match those in the tutorials.

4. Click File on the menu bar, and then click New. The New dialog box opens. Click the Memos tab, and then double-click the Contemporary Memo icon to open a new document based on the Contemporary Memo template.

5. Change the template so the memo is written to the president, from you, with a "CC" to your instructor. The subject of the memo is "Tuition Increase."

6. Type a short paragraph explaining that you have just started your research, and the table on the next page indicates undergraduate in-state tuition and living expenses for Arizona State University and The University of Florida.

7. Insert a page break after the paragraph.

8. On page two, create a table with three columns and five rows. The first cell in the first column should be blank; the second cell should indicate The University of Florida; and the third cell should indicate Arizona State University. The row headings are Tuition, Books/Supplies, and Housing. Enter the rates into the table using the data you found on the Web. (*Note:* If you could not find specific information for a category of expenses, make up some reasonable figures based on the rates at your school.) The last row of the table should be labeled "Totals." Insert a function into the correct cells to total the tuition for each school.

9. Insert the disk labeled Student Disk 1: Word 97 Internet Assignments into the appropriate disk drive, and then save the document as Tuition Rates in the Word folder on the disk.

10. Preview the document and then print it.

11. Close the document.

Tutorial 4. Student Computer Services   Michelle Starr and Andrew Geotz have started a consulting business to locate and purchase computer systems for students on their campus. They use the Internet to shop for the best prices on system components. They decide to prepare a one-page flyer to advertise their services. The general layout is to describe a new computer system and include computer-related clip-art images for interest. You will use the World Wide Web to find the information for the flyer, and then create it using Word.

1. Log on to the Internet and use your Web browser to go to the Course Technology home page. Click the Student Online Companions link, and then click the New Perspectives on Microsoft Office 97 Professional link to open the New Perspectives on Microsoft Office 97 home page. Click the Word link, and then click the Tutorial 4 Internet Assignment link.

2. Click the links to Dell Computers, PCMall, or CompUSA to find a computer system that you feel will interest your clients. Print the pages that describe the system you will include on your flyer.

3. Start Word and check your screen to make sure your settings match those in the tutorials.

4. Design your flyer using the techniques you learned in Tutorial 4. Include a clip-art image of a computer and the specifications of the computer system you found on the Web.

5. Use WordArt to present the title of your company and place the text next to the clip-art image.

6. Add a line of your choice around the page border, and then add a colored background of your choice behind the company title.

7. Insert the disk labeled Student Disk 1: Word 97 Internet Assignments in the appropriate disk drive, and then save the document as SCS Flyer in the Word folder on the disk.

8. Preview the document and then print it.

9. Close the document.

Excel Internet Assignments

Tutorial 1. Krier Marine Services (Continued from Case Problem 4)   Jim Krier is pleased with the payroll spreadsheet that Vince DiOrio prepared. Both men agree that the old computer system in the office needs to be replaced to include a CD ROM drive, modem, a larger hard drive, more RAM memory, and a faster processor. Vince volunteers to use his Internet connection at home to gather information about a new system for the office. First you will use the Internet to search for the new system, and then you will use Excel to organize and print the pricing options for Jim. (*Note:* You will use the Computer file in the Excel folder on your Excel 97 Internet Assignments disk to complete this assignment.)

1. Log on to the Internet and use your Web browser to go to the Course Technology home page. Click the Student Online Companions link, and then click the New Perspectives on Microsoft Office 97 Professional link to open the New Perspectives on Microsoft Office 97 home page. Click the Excel link, and then click the Tutorial 1 Internet Assignment link.

2. Click the links to companies that sell computers (Dell, Gateway2000, and CompUSA), and then search for a system that meets Jim's minimum requirements: Pentium 133 MHz processor, 32 megabytes RAM memory, two gigabyte hard drive, CD ROM drive, and a 33.6 modem. You will need to locate three options to present to Jim. Print the specifications of each computer selected.

3. Open the workbook Computer from Excel folder on the disk labeled Student Disk 2: Excel 97 Internet Assignments.

4. Use the Save As command to save the workbook as Computer 2 in the Excel folder on your disk.

5. Enter your name in cell B3.

6. Enter the data you found on the Web in the appropriate cells of the worksheet.

7. Select cell G8. Does this cell contain text, a value, a formula, or a function? Describe what you think the operation performed in cell G8 is supposed to do.

8. Jim realizes that price is important, but he also wants to make sure that he is getting a good deal on his new computer. Select cell E12 and change the label to "Maximum." Click cell F12 and change the function name (MIN) to MAX. Observe what happens to the asterisk in column G.

9. Save the workbook.

10. Print the worksheet and then close the file.

Tutorial 2. Stock Portfolio for Juan Cortez (Continued from Case Problem 4)   You are expecting an end-of-year bonus and want to invest it in the stock market. The workbook that you created for Juan Cortez has worked very well, so you decide to use it to track your own stock portfolio. Juan advises you to purchase the same stocks that he purchased (Pepsico Inc., Ford Motor Company, AT&T, IBM, and Xerox). (*Note:* You will use the Portfolio_2 file in the Excel folder on your Excel 97 Internet Assignment disk to complete this assignment.)

1. Open the Portfolio_2 workbook from the Excel folder on the disk labeled Student Disk 2: Excel 97 Internet Assignments, and then save it as My Portfolio in the Excel folder on your disk.

2. Log on to the Internet and use your Web browser to go to the Course Technology home page. Click the Student Online Companions link, and then click the New Perspectives on Microsoft Office 97 Professional link to open the New Perspectives on Microsoft Office 97 home page. Click the Excel link, and then click the Tutorial 2 Internet Assignment link.

3. Click the Stockmaster link or the CNN Financial Network link and search for the stocks Juan has advised you to purchase. (*Hint:* You will need to search for the stock symbols using the links on the pages.) Print the pages for your stocks.

4. Enter the current price information you found on the Web into the worksheet.

5. Change the header on the worksheet to include your name.

6. Save the worksheet.

7. Print the worksheet and then close the file.

Tutorial 3. Jenson Sports Wear (Continued from Case Problem 1)   Carl, the national sales manager for Jenson Sports Wear, was pleased with the work you did in Case Problem 1. After reviewing the sales figures, he feels that Jenson Sports Wear is financially able to open its own retail store. Carl has asked you to prepare a worksheet that will determine the profitability of this new venture. As a starting point, Carl would like to sell athletic shoes for running, tennis, and basketball. You decide to use the Internet to look for potential products. Then you will use Excel to enter the retail prices in the worksheet. (*Note:* You will use the Shoes file in the Excel folder on your Excel 97 Internet Assignment disk to complete this assignment.)

1. Log on to the Internet and use your Web browser to go to the Course Technology home page. Click the Student Online Companions link, and then click the New Perspectives on Microsoft Office 97 Professional link to open the New Perspectives on Microsoft Office 97 home page. Click the Excel link, and then click the Tutorial 3 Internet Assignment link.

2. Click the links to SneakerSource or Reebok to locate one shoe (including its price) for each of the categories: running, tennis, and basketball. Print the pages that contain the information about the shoes you locate.

3. Start Excel and open the Shoes file from the Excel folder on the disk labeled Student Disk 2: Excel 97 Internet Assignments. Save the file as Shoes 2 in the Excel folder on your disk.

4. Enter the data you located on the Internet into the appropriate cells of the Shoes 2 worksheet.

5. Enter the Mark-Up value of 200% in cell E3.

6. Place the following formulas in the appropriate cells:
   a. Revenue = Quantity * Price
   b. Cost = Revenue/(1+Mark-Up)
   c. Profit = Revenue – Cost

7. Enter the appropriate function in cells D10 through H10 to total the columns.

8. Format cells D10 through H10 to display values in the same manner as the cells in the row above them. Adjust the column widths if necessary to best fit the data.

9. Center the title of the worksheet across columns A through H, and then change the font to bold, Times New Roman, 14-point.

10. Place a medium thick line above the Total row.

11. Save the worksheet.

12. Print the worksheet.

13. Change the Mark-Up to 150%. How does this affect your profit?

14. Return the Mark-Up to 200%, and then change the quantity to order for running to 100, 20 for tennis, and 50 for basketball. How does this affect your profit?

15. Close the workbook without saving changes.

Tutorial 4. Weather Research   Next week you and your friends will leave on vacation for Rome, Italy. Your friends have asked you to find out the current weather conditions so they will know what type of clothing to pack for the trip. You decide to use the Internet to find a weather site. Then you will use Excel to create professional-looking graphs that you can give to your friends.

1. Log on to the Internet and use your Web browser to go to the Course Technology home page. Click the Student Online Companions link, and then click the New Perspectives on Microsoft Office 97 Professional link to open the New Perspectives on Microsoft Office 97 home page. Click the Excel link, and then click the Tutorial 4 Internet Assignment link.

2. Click the CNN link to do your research. Print the page that shows the four-day forecast for Rome, Italy.

3. Create a worksheet and enter the high temperature and low temperature for each of the four days. Use standard abbreviations for the days of the week (Sun, Mon, Tues, etc.). Use the table design below as a model for your worksheet.

Day	High	Low

4. Insert the disk labeled Student Disk 2: Excel 97 Internet Assignments into the appropriate disk drive, and then save the workbook as Weather Graphs in the Excel folder on the disk.

5. Double-click the Sheet1 tab and then change its name to Weather Data.

6. Create a clustered 3-D column chart with bars for the high and low temperatures. The chart title is Rome's Four-Day Forecast. The Category (X) axis is Day, and the Value (Z) axis is Temp.

7. Move the chart to Sheet2, and then change the name of the sheet to Column Chart.

8. Create another chart of your choice for the four-day forecast. You choose the chart title, and then add the correct labels for the different data series. Move the graph to Sheet3, and then rename the sheet with an appropriate name.

9. Add a title sheet that includes your name, date created, purpose, and a brief description of each sheet in the workbook. (*Hint:* Select the first sheet, click Insert on the menu bar, and then click Worksheet.) Rename the sheet as Title Sheet, and then add your name, date created, purpose, and a brief description of each sheet.

10. Save the workbook.

11. Print the entire workbook, and then close the file.

Access Internet Assignments

Tutorial 1. Lopez Lexus Dealerships (Continued from Case Problem 4) Maria and Hector Lopez are pleased with how well Access tracks their car inventory. Maria and Hector are considering expanding their Houston dealership to include pre-owned Lexus automobiles. They would like for you to use the Internet to search for pre-owned Lexus automobiles for the models that are currently in stock at the dealership to compare selling prices and overall availability. First you will use Access to determine the models in stock, and then you will search the Internet for model information. (*Note:* You will use the Lexus file in the Access folder on your Access 97 Internet Assignments disk to complete this assignment.)

1. Open the Lexus database from the Access folder the disk labeled Student Disk 3: Access 97 Internet Assignments, click the Queries tab, and then click the New button.

2. Click Simple Query Wizard and then click the OK button. Click the Tables/Queries list arrow, and then click Table: Cars. Use the Simple Query Wizard to include the Manufacturer, Model, and Year fields in your new query. In the second Simple Query Wizard dialog box, click the Summary option button, and then click the Summary Options button. Click the Count records in Cars check box in the Summary Options dialog box to count the number of cars currently in stock. Finish the query and save it as Models list.

3. Sort the query results in ascending order on the Count of Cars field using the Sort Ascending button on the toolbar, and then save and print the query results and close Access. You will search for the models with two or less cars in stock.

4. Log on to the Internet and use your Web browser to go to the Course Technology home page. Click the Student Online Companions link, and then click the New Perspectives on Microsoft Office 97 Professional link to open the New Perspectives on Microsoft Office 97 home page. Click the Access link, and then click the Tutorial 1 Internet Assignment link.

5. Explore the links to vehicle services, such as Classifieds2000, Lexus, or Automobiles.com, to find at least four pre-owned Lexus cars located in Texas and manufactured in the past five years that are the same models you found in your Models list query. (If you cannot locate any cars in Texas, search in another state.) Print the page for each car you research. When you are done searching, close your Web browser.

6. Open a new document in Word to write a brief memo to the Lopez Lexus Dealership discussing the pricing and availability of pre-owned cars that would

fit into their dealership using the information you found on the Internet. Save the document in the Access folder on the disk labeled Student Disk 3: Access 97 Internet Assignments as Lexus memo.

7. Print the memo and then close Word.

8. Submit your memo and the printed Web pages to your instructor.

Tutorial 2. Lopez Lexus Dealerships (Continued from Case Problem 4)   Based on the memo you prepared in Tutorial 1, Maria and Hector Lopez decide to expand their Houston dealership to include pre-owned Lexus automobiles. They ask you to return to the Web sites that you located previously to find pre-owned Lexus vehicles to add to their inventory. First you will search the Internet to find the information, and then you will create a new table in the Lexus database to keep track of the pre-owned vehicle inventory. (*Note:* You will use the Lexus file in the Access folder on your Access 97 Internet Assignments disk to complete this assignment.)

1. Log on to the Internet and use your Web browser to go to the Course Technology home page. Click the Student Online Companions link, and then click the New Perspectives on Microsoft Office 97 Professional link to open the New Perspectives on Microsoft Office 97 home page. Click the Access link, and then click the Tutorial 2 Internet Assignment link.

2. Use the links to the vehicle services (Classifieds2000, Lexus, or Automobiles.com) to find at least four pre-owned Lexus cars located in Houston and manufactured in the past five years. Make sure that your search discovers the model, year, selling price, mileage, and vehicle ID (or stock number) for each car. (If you do not have each of these items, continue your search or make up the information based on the entries in the Cars table.) Print the page for each car you research. When you are done searching, close your Web browser.

3. Start Access and then open the Lexus database from the Access folder on the disk labeled Student Disk 3: Access 97 Internet Assignments.

4. Create a table named Used Cars using the table design shown below.

Field Name	Data Type	Description	Field Size
VehicleID	Text	primary key	50
Manufacturer	Text		13
Model	Text		15
Year	Number		
SellingPrice	Currency		
Mileage	Number	current mileage	

5. Add the records for the cars you located on the Web to the Used Cars table.

6. Print the Used Cars table datasheet, and then save and close the table. Close the Lexus database and then close Access.

7. Submit your printed datasheet and the printed Web pages to your instructor.

Tutorial 3. Lopez Lexus Dealerships (Continued from Case Problem 4)   Jim Sweeny is the manager of the Lopez Lexus Dealership in Laredo, Texas. Jim wants to determine the cost per pound of each Lexus model so he can use the information as a promotional gimmick in his next advertising campaign. Jim contacts Maria and Hector Lopez and requests the curb weights for each of the models available at the Laredo dealership. First you need to create a query to determine which models are in stock at the Laredo dealership. Next you will use the Internet to find the weight information for each model, and then you will use Access to calculate the cost per pound. (*Note:* You will use the Lexus file in the Access folder on your Access 97 Internet Assignments disk to complete this assignment.)

1. Start Access and then open the Lexus database from the Access folder on the disk labeled Student Disk 3: Access 97 Internet Assignments.

2. Create a query to determine the models that are in stock at the Laredo dealership. Print the query datasheet, save it as Laredo stock, and then close the query.

3. Log on to the Internet and use your Web browser to go to the Course Technology home page. Click the Student Online Companions link, and then click the New Perspectives on Microsoft Office 97 Professional link to open the New Perspectives on Microsoft Office 97 home page. Click the Access link, and then click the Tutorial 3 Internet Assignment link.

4. Click the link to the Lexus home page. The weight specifications that you need are located on the Model Gallery Vehicle Profiles page. (*Note:* Lexus refers to the SC300 and SC400 models as "coupe.") Print the specifications pages that you will need for Jim, and then close your Web browser.

5. Return to Access and make sure the Lexus database is open. Create a new table named Specifications using the table design shown below.

Field Name	Data Type	Description	Field Size
Model	Text	primary key	50
Weight	Number	curb weight	

6. Add the model and curb weight information that you found on the Web to the Specifications table.

7. Create a query that will display the Model, Weight, SellingPrice, and Cost per Pound fields for the automobiles that are located in Laredo. Use the Expression Builder to create the Cost per Pound field, which is calculated by dividing the Selling Price by the Weight. To format the Cost per Pound field to display as currency, right-click the calculated field column in the query design grid, click Properties on the shortcut menu, and then change the Format setting to Currency on the property sheet.

8. Save the query as Cost per Pound, run the query, print the query datasheet, and then close the query. Close Access.

9. Submit your printed datasheet and the printed Web pages to your instructor.

Tutorial 4. Lopez Lexus Dealerships (Continued from Case Problem 4)   Maria and Hector Lopez like the report that you created in Case Problem 4. They would like you to prepare a second report that shows the Location Name, Selling Price, Vehicle ID, Year, and Average Selling Price for each model. Because they will distribute the report to employees, it must look professional. You decide to create the report using Access, and then copy an appropriate image from the Internet to insert into the report. (*Note:* You will use the Lexus file in the Access folder on your Access 97 Internet Assignments disk to complete this assignment.)

1. Log on to the Internet and use your Web browser to go to the Course Technology home page. Click the Student Online Companions link, and then click the New Perspectives on Microsoft Office 97 Professional link to open the New Perspectives on Microsoft Office 97 home page. Click the Access link, and then click the Tutorial 4 Internet Assignment link.

2. Insert the disk labeled Student Disk 3: Access 97 Internet Assignments in the appropriate disk drive, and then click the Lopez Logo link. Right-click the image, click Save Picture as on the shortcut menu, and then save the image as Lopez Logo in the Access folder on your disk. Close your Web browser.

3. Start Access and open the Lexus database from the Access folder on the disk labeled Student Disk 3: Access 97 Internet Assignments.

4. Use the Report Wizard to create a report based on the Cars and Locations tables. Add the VehicleID, Model, Year, and SellingPrice fields from the Cars table, and then add the LocationName field from the Locations table. View your data by the Cars table and add a grouping level on the Model field. Sort the data by LocationName, and then by SellingPrice. Click the Summary Options button, and then click the Avg SellingPrice check box to calculate a summary value based on this field. Choose the Align Left 1 layout and the Soft Gray style. The title of the report is "Lopez Lexus Dealership Models."

5. Open the report in Design view. Insert the image you copied from the Internet and saved on your Internet Assignments disk under the title in the Report Header section. Center and move the picture as needed.

6. Change the Avg SellingPrice calculated field to display values as currency. To do this, right-click the =Avg([SellingPrice]) field in the Model Footer in Design view, click Properties on the shortcut menu, and then type Currency in the Format property setting. Close the window.

7. Preview the report.

8. Save the report design and then print it.

9. Close Access.

PowerPoint Internet Assignments

Tutorial 1. Presentation on Selling an Idea (Continued from Case Problem 4) The "Majoring in" presentation that you created in Case Problem 4 was very successful and generated a lot of enthusiasm from the audience to major in your subject area. The public relations department of your college has asked you to prepare a 20-minute presentation addressed to a larger group of high school students on the advantages of attending your college. This time your job is to "sell" your college. You will use the Internet to gather information about your college, such as admission requirements, housing arrangements, financial aid, sporting events, or other areas of interest. Then you will add this information to the PowerPoint presentation that you created in Case Problem 4. (*Note:* You will use the Majoring in Advertising file in the PowerPoint folder on your PowerPoint 97 Internet Assignments disk to complete this assignment.)

1. Log on to the Internet and use your Web browser to go to the Course Technology home page. Click the Student Online Companions link, and then click the New Perspectives on Microsoft Office 97 Professional link to open the New Perspectives on Microsoft Office 97 home page. Click the PowerPoint link, and then click the Internet Assignment link for Tutorial 1.

2. If you do not know the URL of your college, you can use a search engine, such as Yahoo, to help you find it. Click the Yahoo link to open the Yahoo home page, type the name of your college in the Search text box, and then click the Search button. You also may want to click the Education link below the Search text box to limit the search to educational institutions, type the name of your college in the Search text box, click the Search only in Education option button, and then click the Search button. A list of matching searches will appear (you may need to scroll down the page to see the matches). Explore your college's information and look for advantages that make your school a better choice in education over other local or statewide schools. If you cannot locate a Web site for your college using Yahoo, try another search engine link (such as AltaVista or InfoSeek) to find it. If you can't find the Web site for your college, use another college of your choice.

3. Print any pages from your college's Web site that lists admission requirements, housing arrangements, financial aid, sporting events, or other areas that may interest your audience. Once you have gathered all the information you need, close your Web browser.

4. Start PowerPoint, and then open the Majoring in Advertising file from the PowerPoint folder on the disk labeled Student Disk 4: PowerPoint 97 Internet Assignments.

5. Use the Save As command to save the presentation as College Presentation in the PowerPoint folder on your disk.

6. Change the title on slide 1 to "Attending (name of your college)."

7. Alter the objectives on slide 2 to reflect the points you wish to make in your presentation.

8. Change the title of slide 3 to a title that describes the admission requirements, financial aid information, or another important area of interest for your college. Then change the slide's contents using the information you found on the Internet.

9. Change the title of slide 4 to "Meeting Your Needs at (name of your college)." Use the information you found on the Internet and decide why your college would be a good choice for a freshman. You may want to discuss housing arrangements, financial aid, sporting events, or other areas of interest. Make sure you include why your college meets students' needs.

10. Look at slide 5 and add any new strength(s) you have discovered on your college's home page.

11. Modify slide 6 to summarize the changes you made to your presentation.

12. Spell check the presentation by clicking the Spelling button on the Standard toolbar or by clicking Tools, and then clicking Spelling.

13. Preview the presentation in Slide Show View and Black and White View.

14. Save the presentation by clicking the Save button on the Standard toolbar.

15. Print your presentation as handouts with three slides per page, and then close the file and PowerPoint.

Tutorial 2. Presentation on Past Employment or Service (Continued from Case Problem 4) Your "My Job" presentation from Case Problem 4 was well received, but you feel it could be improved by including information on future opportunities in the field you discussed. You decide to browse the World Wide Web to learn more about employment or volunteer opportunities for your area of experience, and then add that information to the presentation that you created in Case Problem 4. (*Note:* You will use the My job file in the PowerPoint folder on your PowerPoint 97 Internet Assignments disk to complete this assignment.)

1. Log on to the Internet and use your Web browser to go to the Course Technology home page. Click the Student Online Companions link, and then click the New Perspectives on Microsoft Office 97 Professional link to open the New Perspectives on Microsoft Office 97 home page. Click the PowerPoint link, and then click the Internet Assignment link for Tutorial 2.

2. Explore the links to career resources, such as Career Mosaic, jobfind, or Monster to find more information about employment or volunteer opportunities in your area of expertise. Or, you can use a search engine, such as Yahoo, AltaVista, or InfoSeek, to search for the information you need using key terms such as "Careers" or "Volunteer."

3. Print the pages about any employment opportunities or other information that may be relevant to your presentation, and then close your Web browser.

4. Start PowerPoint, and then open the My job file from the PowerPoint folder on the disk labeled Student Disk 4: PowerPoint 97 Internet Assignments.

5. Save the presentation as My Job Future in the PowerPoint folder on the disk.

6. Add a new slide 6 titled "Prospective Employment (or Volunteer) Opportunities," and then add bullets to the slide using the information you found on the Internet.

7. Spell check your presentation by clicking the Spelling button on the Standard toolbar or by clicking Tools, and then clicking Spelling.

8. Save your presentation by clicking the Save button on the Standard toolbar.

9. Print your presentation slides, as three slides per page, making sure the slides are legible in black and white if you have a monochrome printer, and then close the file and PowerPoint.

Microsoft Office 97 Professional-Enhanced **Index**

Microsoft Windows 95 Brief **Task Reference**

TASK	PAGE #	RECOMMENDED METHOD	NOTES
Character, delete	WIN95 33	Press Backspace	
Check box, de-select	WIN95 21	Click the check box again	Tab to option, press Spacebar
Check box, select	WIN95 21	Click the checkbox	Tab to option, press Spacebar
Detailed file list, view	WIN95 45	From My Computer, click View, Details	
Disk, copy your	WIN95 50	Place disk in drive A:, from My Computer click ⬛ , click File, Copy Disk, Start	See Making a Backup of Your Floppy Disk
Disk, format	WIN95 30	Click ⬛ My Computer , click ⬛ 3½ Floppy (A:) , press Enter, click File, click Format, click Start	
Drop-down list, display	WIN95 20	Click ▼	
File, copy		From My Computer, right-click the file, drag to the new location, press C	
File, delete	WIN95 49	From My Computer, click the file, press Delete, click Yes	See Deleting a File
File, move	WIN95 48	From My Computer, use the left mouse button to drag the file to the desired folder or drive	See Moving a File
File, open	WIN95 37	Click ⬛	
File, print	WIN95 39	Click ⬛ Print	
File, print preview	WIN95 39	Click ⬛	
File, rename	WIN95 49	From My Computer, click the file, click File, click Rename, type new name, press Enter	See Renaming a File
File, save	WIN95 35	Click ⬛	
Folder, create	WIN95 46	From My Computer, click File, New, Folder	See Creating a New Folder
Help topic, display	WIN95 23	From the Help Contents window, click the topic, then click Open	
Help topic, open	WIN95 23	From the Help Contents window, click the book, then click Display	
Help, start	WIN95 21	Click ⬛ Start , then click Help	F1, See Starting Windows 95 Help
Icon, open	WIN95 43	Click the icon, then press Enter or double-click the icon	See Opening an Icon
Icons, view large	WIN95 45	From My Computer, click View, Large Icons	
Insertion point, move	WIN95 34	Click the desired location in the document, use arrow keys	

Microsoft Windows 95 Brief **Task Reference**

TASK	PAGE #	RECOMMENDED METHOD	NOTES
List box, scroll	WIN95 20	Click ▲ or ▼, or drag the scroll box	
Menu option, select	WIN95 17	Click the menu option	
Menu, open		Click the menu option	Alt-underlined letter
Program, quit	WIN95 10	Click ✕	Alt-F4
Program, start	WIN95 9	Click the Start button, point to Programs, point to the program option, click the program	See Starting a Program
Radio button, de-select	WIN95 21	Click a different radio button	Tab to option, press Spacebar
Radio button, select	WIN95 21	Click the radio button	Tab to option, press Spacebar
Start menu, display			Ctrl-Esc
Student data disk, create	WIN95 41	Click ▦Start, click Programs, CTI Win95, Windows 95 Brief, Make Windows 95 Student Disk, press Enter	
Text, select	WIN95 34	Drag the pointer over the text	
Tooltip, display	WIN95 19	Position pointer over the tool	
Window, change size	WIN95 17	Drag ▨	
Window, close	WIN95 10	Click ✕	Ctrl-F4
Window, maximize	WIN95 17	Click ▢	
Window, minimize	WIN95 15	Click ▬	
Window, move	WIN95 17	Drag the title bar	
Window, redisplay	WIN95 16	Click the taskbar button	
Window, restore	WIN95 16	Click ▣	
Window, switch	WIN95 12	Click the taskbar button of the program	Alt-Tab, See Switching Between Programs
Windows 95, shut down	WIN95 12	Click ▦Start, click Shut Down, Click Yes	
Windows 95, start	WIN95 5	Turn on the computer	

Microsoft Internet Explorer **Task Reference**

TASK	PAGE #	RECOMMENDED METHOD
Explorer bar, hide	IE 19	Doesn't apply to Internet Explorer 3. In Internet Explorer 4, click View, point to Explorer Bar, then click None
Help, access	IE 39	In Internet Explorer 3, click Help, click Help Topics. In Internet Explorer 4, click Help, click Contents and Index
Images, load automatically	IE 35	See "Viewing Images on Demand"
Image, view individually	IE 36	Right-click image icon ▨, click Show Picture
Link, abort	IE 25	Click ⊗
Link, activate	IE 23	Click the link
Internet Explorer, exit	IE 29	Click ✕
Internet Explorer, start	IE 12	In Internet Explorer 3, click 🏁Start, point to Programs, click Internet Explorer. In Internet Explorer 4, click 🏁Start, point to Programs, point to Internet Explorer, click Internet Explorer
Toolbar, view or hide	IE 17	In Internet Explorer 3, click View, click Options, click General tab, click check box for toolbar you want to view or hide, click OK. Make sure Toolbar is selected on View menu. In Internet Explorer 4, click View, point to Toolbars, click toolbar you want to view or hide
Toolbar, move	IE 19	Drag toolbar up, down, left, or right
Toolbar, resize	IE 19	Point at vertical bar preceding toolbar and drag left or right
URL, connect to	IE 31	See "Opening a Location"
Web page, open in Internet Explorer	IE 20	See "Opening a Web Page into the Internet Explorer Browser"
Web page, print	IE 39	Click File, click Print, click OK
Web page, view in full screen	IE 28	Doesn't apply to Internet Explorer 3. In Internet Explorer 4, click ⬒
Web pages, navigate	IE 33	Click ⬅ to move to previous page, ➡ to revisit page, 🏠 to return to home page

Microsoft Word 97 **Task Reference**

TASK	PAGE #	RECOMMENDED METHOD
Border, draw around page	W 4.21	Click Format, click Borders and Shading; on Page Border tab, click Box, apply to Whole Document; see also Rectangle, draw
Bullets, add to paragraphs	W 2.19	Select paragraphs, click [icon]
Clip art, add	W 4.13	Click Insert, click Picture, click Clip Art; click category and image, click Insert
Column break, insert	W 3.4	Click Insert, click Break, select Column Break, click OK
Columns, balance	W 4.20	Click end-of-column marker, click Insert, click Break, click Continuous option button, click OK
Columns, format text in	W 4.10	Select text, click [icon], drag to indicate to number of columns
Date, insert	W 1.13	Click Insert, click Date and Time, click desired format, click OK
Document, create new	W 1.13	Click [icon]
Document, open	W 2.3	Click [icon], select drive and folder, click the filename, click OK
Document, preview	W 2.24	Click [icon]
Document, print	W 1.22	Click [icon], or click File, click Print to specify pages or copies
Document, save	W 1.16	Click [icon], or click File, click Save As, select drive and folder, enter new filename, click Save
Document window, close	W 1.26	Click [icon] on the document window menu bar
Drop cap, insert	W 4.17	Position insertion point in paragraph, click Format, click Drop Cap, select desired features, click OK
Envelope, print	W 1.25	Click Tools, click Envelopes and Labels, click Envelopes tab, type name and address, click Print
Font size, change	W 2.21	Select text, click Font Size list arrow, click a font size
Font style, change	W 2.23	Select text, click **B**, *I*, or U
Font, change	W 2.21	Select text, click Font list arrow, click new font
Footer, insert	W 3.30	Click View, click Header and Footer, click [icon], type footer text, click Close
Format Painter, format paragraph with	W 2.18	Select text with desired format, click [icon], click in target paragraph
Graphic, crop	W 4.15	Click graphic, click [icon], drag resize handle
Graphic, resize	W 4.14	Click graphic, drag resize handle
Header, insert	W 3.7	Click View, click Header and Footer, type header text, click Close
Help, get	W 1.23	Click [icon] and type a question, click Search, click topic
Line spacing, change	W 2.29	Click Format, click Paragraph, click Indents and Spacing tab, click Line spacing list arrow, click desired line spacing option, click OK

Microsoft Word 97 **Task Reference**

TASK	PAGE #	RECOMMENDED METHOD
Margins, change	W 2.14	Click File, click Page Setup, click Margins tab, enter margin values, click OK
Nonprinting characters, display	W 1.10	Click ¶
Normal view, change to	W 1.9	Click [icon]
Numbering, add to paragraphs	W 2.20	Select paragraphs, click [icon]
Office Assistant, open	W 1.24	Click [icon]
Page, move to top of next	W 3.9	Click [icon]
Page, move to top of previous	W 3.9	Click [icon]
Page, view whole	W 4.11	Click Zoom Control list arrow, click Whole Page
Page layout view, change to	W 3.8	Click [icon]
Page number, insert	W 3.9	Click Insert, click Page Numbers, select location of numbers, click OK
Paragraph, change indent	W 2.17	Select paragraph, drag left or first-line indent marker on ruler; click [icon] or [icon]
Rectangle, draw	W 4.22	Click [icon], click [icon], drag pointer to draw rectangle
Ruler, display	W 1.9	Click View, click Ruler
Section break, create	W 3.4	Position insertion point at break location, click Insert, click Break, click an option button in Section Breaks section, click OK
Section, vertically align	W 3.5	Move insertion point into section, click File, click Page Setup, click Layout tab, click Apply to list arrow, click This section, click OK
Shading, insert	W 3.27	Click Format, click Borders and Shading, click Shading tab, select Fill and Pattern options, click OK
Spelling, correct	W 1.18	Right-click misspelled word with red, wavy line under it, click correctly spelled word
Style, apply manually	W 3.12	Select text, click Style list arrow, click style name
Style, apply with AutoFormat	W 3.35	Select text, click Format, click AutoFormat, accept or reject proposed changes
Symbol, insert	W 4.18	Click Insert, click Symbol, click desired symbol, click Insert, click Close
Table column width, change	W 3.24	Drag gridline marker on horizontal ruler
Table gridlines, display		Select table, click Table, click Show Gridlines

Microsoft Word 97 **Task Reference**

TASK	PAGE #	RECOMMENDED METHOD
Table, sum cells of	W 3.23	Click sum cell, click Σ on Tables and Borders toolbar
Table row, align text horizontally in	W 3.26	Select a cell or range, click ▤, ▤, ▤, or ▤
Table row, align text vertically in	W 3.27	Select row, click ▤, ▤, or ▤
Table row height, change	W 3.25	Click ▤, drag lower row border
Table row, add or delete borders		Select row, click ▤, ▦, or ▦; to delete click ▦
Table row, delete	W 3.22	Select row, click right-click row, click Delete Rows
Table row, insert at end of table	W 3.22	Position insertion point to lower-right cell at end of table, press Tab
Table row, insert within table	W 3.22	Select row below, right-click row, click Insert Rows
Table, center on page	W 3.32	Select the table, click ▤
Table, insert	W 3.17	Click ▦, drag to indicate number of columns and rows
Table, shade	W 3.27	Select table area, select ▤ on Tables and Borders toolbar
Table, sort		Click Table, click Sort, click Sort by list arrow and select sort column, click sort option button, click OK
Template, attach	W 3.11	Click Format, click Style Gallery, click template name, click OK
Text, align	W 2.16	Click ▤, ▤, or ▤
Text, copy by copy and paste	W 2.11	Select text, click ▤, move to target location, click ▤
Text, copy by drag and drop	W 2.9	Select text, press and hold down Ctrl and drag selected text to target location, release mouse button and Ctrl key
Text, delete	W 1.20	Press Backspace key to delete character to left of insertion point; press the Delete key to delete character to right; press Ctrl + Backspace to delete to beginning of word; press Ctrl + Delete to delete to end of word
Text, find	W 2.12	Click ▤, click ▤, type search text, click Find Next
Text, find and replace	W 2.12	Click ▤, click ▤, click Replace tab, type search text, press Tab, type replacement text, click Find Next
Text, format	W 2.22	See Font Style, change
Text, format automatically	W 3.30	Click Format, click AutoFormat, click OK
Text, justify	W 2.16	Click text, click ▤

Microsoft Word 97 **Task Reference**

TASK	PAGE #	RECOMMENDED METHOD
Text, move by cut and paste	W 2.11	Select text, click ✂, move to target location, click 📋
Text, move by drag and drop	W 2.9	Select text, drag selected text to target location; release mouse button
Text, select a block of	W 2.7	Click at beginning of block, press and hold down Shift and click at end of block
Text, select a paragraph of	W 2.9	Double-click in selection bar next to paragraph
Text, select a sentence of	W 2.6	Press Ctrl and click within sentence
Text, select entire document of	W 2.6	Press Ctrl and click in selection bar
Text, select multiple lines of	W 2.6	Click and drag in selection bar
Text, select multiple paragraphs of	W 2.6	Double-click and drag in selection bar
Toolbar, display	W 1.7	Right-click any visible toolbar, click name of desired toolbar
Word, start	W 1.4	Click Start, point to Programs, click Microsoft Word
Word, exit	W 1.26	Click File, click Exit
WordArt object, insert	W 4.4	Click ◢, click desired WordArt style, type WordArt text, select font, size, and style, click OK

Microsoft Excel 97 **Task Reference**

Microsoft Excel 97 **Task Reference**

TASK	PAGE #	RECOMMENDED METHOD
Chart, move	E 4.11	Select the chart and drag it to a new location.
Chart, rotate a 3-D chart	E 4.26	Select a 3-D chart. Click Chart, then click 3-D View. Type the values you want in the Rotation and Elevation boxes.
Chart, select	E 4.11	Click anywhere within the chart border. Same as activating.
Chart, update	E 4.12	Enter new values in worksheet. Chart link to data is automatically updated.
Chart Wizard, start	E 4.6	Click ▦.
Clipboard contents, paste into a range	E 2.15	Click ▣.
Colors, apply to a range of cells	E 3.23	See Reference Window: Applying Patterns and Color.
Column width, change	E 2.24	See Reference Window: Changing Column Width.
Copy formula, use copy-and-paste method	E 2.15	Select the cell with the formula to be copied, click ▣, click the cell you want the formula copied to, then click ▣.
Excel, exit	E 1.32	Click File, then click Exit, or click Excel Close button.
Excel, start	E 1.5	Click the Start button, then point to Programs, if necessary click Microsoft Office, and then click Microsoft Excel.
Font, select	E 3.17	Select the cell or range you want to format. Click Format, click Cells, and then click the Font tab. Select the desired Font from the Font list box.
Font, select size	E 3.17	Select the cell or range you want to format. Click Format, click Cells, and then click the Font tab. Click the Font Size list arrow, then click the desired font size.
Footer, add	E 2.34	In the Print Preview window, click Setup, then click the Header/Footer tab in the Page Setup dialog box. Click the Footer list arrow to choose a preset footer, or click Custom Footer and edit the existing footer in the Footer dialog box.
Format, bold	E 3.16	Select the cell or range you want to format, then click **B**, which toggles on and off.
Format, center text across columns	E 3.15	Select the cell or range with text to center. Click Format, click Cells, then click the Alignment tab. Click the Horizontal Text alignment arrow and select Center Across Selection.
Format, comma	E 3.10	Select the cell or range of cells you want to format, then click ▸.
Format, copy	E 3.9	Select the cell or range of cells with the format you want to copy. Click ▧, then select the cell or the range of cells you want to format.
Format, currency	E 3.6	Select the cell or range of cells you want to format. Click Format, then click Cells. Click the Number tab, click Currency in the Category box, then click the desired options.
Format, italic	E 3.17	Select the cell or range you want to format, then click *I* which toggles on and off.

Microsoft Excel 97 **Task Reference**

TASK	PAGE #	RECOMMENDED METHOD
Format, indent text	E 3.15	Select the cell or range you want to indent. Click .
Format, center in cell	E 3.13	Select the cell or range you want to format. Click , which toggles on and off.
Format, font	E 3.16	Select the cell or range you want to format. Click the Font arrow and select the desired font.
Format, percent	E 3.11	Select the cell or range of cells you want to format, then click .
Format, wrap text	E 3.13	Select the cell or cells you want to format. Click Format, click Cells, then click the Alignment tab. Click Wrap Text check box.
Formula, enter	E 1.17	Click the cell where you want the result to appear. Type = and then type the rest of the formula. For formulas that include cell references, type the cell reference or select each cell using the mouse or arrow keys. When the formula is complete, press Enter.
Formulas, display	E 2.37	Click Tools, then click Options. Click the View tab, then click the Formulas check box.
Function, enter	E 2.21	Type = to begin the function. Type the name of the function in either uppercase or lowercase letters, followed by an opening parenthesis (. Type the range of cells you want to calculate using the function, separating the first and last cells in the range with a colon, as in B9:B15, or drag the pointer to outline the cells you want to calculate. See also Paste Function button, activate.
Gridlines, add or remove	E 3.31	Click Tools, click Options, then click View. Click Gridlines check box.
Header, add	E 2.34	In the Print Preview window, click Setup, then click the Header/Footer tab in the Page Setup dialog box. Click the Header list arrow to select a preset header, or click the Custom Header button to edit the existing header in the Header dialog box.
Help, activate	E 1.26	See Reference Window: Using the Office Assistant, and Figure 1-23.
Labels, enter	E 1.15	Select cell, then type text you want in cell.
Non-adjacent ranges, select	E 4.22	Click the first cell or range of cells to select, then press and hold the Ctrl key as you select the other cell or range of cells to be selected. Release the Ctrl key when all non-adjacent ranges are highlighted.
Numbers, enter	E 1.16	Select the cell, then type the number.
Paste Function button, activate	E 2.19	See Reference Window: Using the Paste Function button.
Patterns, apply to a range of cells	E 3.23	See Reference Window: Applying Patterns and Color.
Print Preview window, open	E 2.30	Click .
Printout, center	E 2.32	In the Print Preview dialog box, click the Setup button. Then click the Margins tab, then click the Horizontally and/or Vertically check boxes.

Microsoft Excel 97 **Task Reference**

TASK	PAGE #	RECOMMENDED METHOD
Printout, landscape orientation	E 3.33	In the Print Preview window, click the Setup button. Then click the Page tab in the Page Setup dialog box, then click the Landscape option button in the Orientation box.
Range, highlight	E 1.18 E 1.28	Position pointer on the first cell of the range. Press and hold the mouse button and drag the mouse through the cells you want, then release the mouse button.
Range, move	E 2.27	Select the cell or range of cells you want to move. Place the mouse pointer over any edge of the selected range until the pointer changes to an arrow. Click and drag the outline of the range to the new worksheet location.
Range, nonadjacent	E 4.22	See Non-adjacent ranges, select.
Range, select	E 1.18 E 1.28	See Range, highlight.
Row or column, delete	E 2.25	Click the heading(s) of the row(s) or column(s) you want to delete, click Edit, then click Delete.
Row or column, insert	E 2.25	Click any cell in the row/column above which you want to insert the new row/column. Click Insert and then click Rows/Columns. Above the selected range, Excel inserts one row/column for every row/column in the highlighted range.
Sheet tab, rename	E 2.16	Double-click the sheet tab then type the new sheet name.
Sheet, activate	E 1.11	Click the sheet tab for the desired sheet.
Shortcut menu, activate	E 3.24	Select the cells or objects to which you want to apply the command, click the right mouse button, then select the command you want.
Spell check	E 2.23	Click cell A1, then click 🔲.
Text box, add	E 3.27	Click 🔲 on the Drawing toolbar. Position pointer where text box is to appear, then click and drag to outline desired size and shape. Type comment in text box.
Toolbar, add or remove	E 3.25	Click any toolbar with right mouse button. Click the name of the toolbar you want to use/remove from the shortcut menu.
Undo button, activate	E 2.26	Click 🔲.
Workbook, open	E 1.11	Click 🔲 (or click File, then click Open). Make sure the Look in box displays the name of the folder containing the workbook you want to open. Click the name of the workbook you want to open, then click Open.
Workbook, save with a new name	E 1.21	Click File then click Save As. Change the workbook name as necessary. Specify the folder in which to save workbook in the Save in box. Click Save.
Workbook, save with same name	E 1.21	Click 🔲.
Worksheet, close	E 1.31	Click File, then click Close, or click the worksheet Close button.
Worksheet, print	E 1.29	Click 🔲 to print without adjusting any print options. Use the Print command on the File menu to adjust options.

Microsoft Access 97 **Task Reference**

Microsoft Access 97 **Task Reference**

TASK	PAGE #	RECOMMENDED METHOD
Record, add a new one	A 1.12	Click ▶*
Record, delete	A 2.25	Right-click the record's row selector, click Delete Record, click Yes
Record, move to first	A 1.12	Click ◄
Record, move to last	A 1.12	Click ►|
Record, move to next	A 1.12	Click ►
Record, move to previous	A 1.12	Click ◄
Record, move to a specific one	A 1.12	Type the record number in the Specific Record box, press Enter
Records, redisplay all after filter	A 3.17	Click
Relationship, define between two tables	A 3.8	Click
Report Wizard, activate	A 4.17	Click the Reports tab, click New, click Report Wizard, choose the table or query for the report, click OK
Sort, specify ascending	A 3.12	Click
Sort, specify descending	A 3.12	Click
Table, create	A 2.6	Click the Tables tab, click New, click Design View, click OK
Table, open	A 1.11	Click the Tables tab, click the table name, click Open
Table, print	A 1.13	Click
Table structure, save	A 2.13	See Reference Window: Saving a Table Structure

Microsoft PowerPoint 97 **Task Reference**

TASK	PAGE #	RECOMMENDED METHOD
AutoContent Wizard, use	P 1.8	Click AutoContent wizard radio button on PowerPoint startup dialog box; or click File, click New, click Presentations tab, click AutoContent Wizard, click OK
Background graphic, remove	P 1.27	Click Format, click Background, click Omit background graphics from master check box, click Apply or Apply to all
Black & White, view	P 1.27	Click ▣
Clip art, insert	P 2.11	Click ▣, click desired clip-art layout, click Apply, double-click clip-art placeholder, click desired clip-art category, click desired clip-art image, click OK
Design template, change	P 1.22	Click ▣, click name of desired template file, click Apply
Next or previous slide, go to	P 1.19	In Slide View, click ▾ or click ▴
Notes Page View	P 1.25	Click ▣
Organization chart, add co-worker	P 2.16	Click ▣ Co-worker or Co-worker ▣, click existing box
Organization chart, add subordinate	P 2.15	Click Subordinate: ▣, click existing box
Organization chart, insert	P 2.14	Change slide layout to Organization Chart; double-click organization chart placeholder; type names, positions, etc.; add subordinates and co-workers
Outline text, demote	P 1.17	Place insertion point in text of slide title or bulleted item, click ▣
Outline text, move	P 1.15	Position ✛ on slide icon or bullet, click ▲ or ▼
Outline text, promote	P 1.16	Place insertion point in text of slide title or bulleted item, click ▣
Outline View	P 1.10	Click ▣
Picture(s), group or ungroup	P 2.12	Select picture(s), click Draw list arrow, click Group or click Ungroup
Picture, insert	P 2.7	Click Insert, click Picture, select disk and folder, click name of picture file, click OK
Presentation, open	P 1.15	Click ▣, select disk and folder, click filename in Name list box, click Open
Presentation, print	P 1.27	Click File, click Print
Presentation, save	P 1.13	Click ▣; if necessary, select disk and folder, type name in File name text box, click Save
Presentation, save with a new filename	P 2.3	Click File, click Save As, enter new filename in File name text box, click Save
Shape, create	P 2.17	Click AutoShapes list arrow, click desired shape, drag ✛ to draw and size shape

Microsoft PowerPoint 97 **Task Reference**

TASK	PAGE #	RECOMMENDED METHOD
Shape, flip	P 2.18	Select shape, click Draw list arrow, point to Rotate or Flip, click Flip Vertical or Flip Horizontal
Slide layout, change	P 2.8	Click Format, click Slide Layout, click desired layout, click Apply or Reapply
Slide Show, exit	P 1.26	Press Esc
Slide Show, view	P 1.26	Click 🖳; press spacebar or click left mouse button to advance; press Backspace or click right mouse button to go back
Slide Sorter View	P 1.28	Click 🈁
Slide View	P 1.19	Click ▢
Slide, delete	P 1.17	In Outline View, click slide icon, press Delete. In Slide View, click slide icon, click Edit, click Delete
Spelling, check	P 1.27	Click ✓
Text boxes, align	P 2.6	Click to select first text box, press and hold Shift, click to select other text box(es), click Draw list arrow, point to Align or Distribute, click alignment position
Text box, create	P 2.19	Click ▣, click pointer on slide, type text
Text box, resize	P 2.4	Click text box to select it, drag a resize handle
Text box, rotate	P 2.20	Select text box, click ↻, drag a resize handle

Integrating Microsoft Office 97 **Task Reference**

TASK	PAGE #	RECOMMENDED METHOD
Access query, copy and paste into PowerPoint	I 2.16	Display the query results, click the selector to the left of the column headings to select the query, click 🖿, switch to the PowerPoint slide, click 🖺
Data source, specify for a mail merge	I 2.5	Click Tools, click Mail Merge, specify the main document, click Get Data, click Open Data Source, select the source file for the data
Embedded object, edit	I 1.11	Double-click the object to select it, and then edit it using appropriate commands
Embedded object, establish	I 1.8	See Reference Window: Embedding an Object
Linked object, break the link	I 1.16	See Reference Window: Breaking the Link Between Linked Objects
Linked object, establish	I 1.13	See Reference Window: Linking an Object
Linked object, reestablish the link	I 1.17	Close the destination program without saving changes by clicking File, Close, and then click No
Linked object, update	I 1.14	Make changes in the source program, or double-click the linked object to make changes in the destination file
Main document, specify for a mail merge	I 2.5	Click Tools, click Mail Merge, click Create, specify the type of main document, specify the active window or a new document
Merge fields, insert	I 2.7	See Reference Window: Inserting Merge Fields in a Main Document
Merge results, view from the main document	I 2.10	Click ⟪»⟫ on the Mail Merge toolbar
Paragraph, move to the next-higher outline level	I 2.13	Click ⬅ on the Outlining toolbar
Paragraph, move to the next-lower outline level	I 2.13	Click ➡ on the Outlining toolbar
Word outline, convert to PowerPoint Slides	I 2.15	See Reference Window: Converting a Word Outline to Slides in an Existing Presentation

Creating Web Pages **Task Reference**

TASK	PAGE #	RECOMMENDED METHOD
Bullet, create	WP 30	Remove any bullets from the bulleted list, click Format, click Bullets and Numbering, select a bullet style of the list of bullets
HTML, saving a Word document as	WP 7	Click File, click Save as HTML, enter a filename and location for the HTML file
Hyperlink, create to an HTML document	WP 15	Select the text or graphic to act as a hyperlink, click ▧, enter the location the HTML document in the Link to file or URL box
Hyperlink, paste a	WP 10	Copy the text you want as the hyperlink target, move to the location of the hyperlink you intend to create, click Edit, click Paste as Hyperlink
Hypertext, edit	WP 13	Right-click the hypertext, click Hyperlink, click Select Hyperlink, type over the existing hypertext, replacing it with new text
Inline image, insert	WP 27	Click where you want the image to appear, click Insert, point to Picture, click From File, locate the GIF or JPEG graphics file, click Insert
Line, create	WP 29	Click where the line will be placed, click Insert, click Horizontal Line, select the line style from the list of horizontal lines
Picture placeholder, create	WP 28	Right-click the inline image, click Format Picture, click the Settings tab, enter the picture placeholder text in the Picture Placeholder box
Table borders, set width	WP 25	Click anywhere within the table, click Table, click Borders, click the Border Width drop-down arrow, select a border width from the list
Table cells, set background colors	WP 25	Select the table cells, click Table, click Cell Properties, click the Background drop-down arrow, choose the color from the list
Table, change column width	WP 22	Point at the column border so that the pointer changes to ✛, drag the border to the new column width
Table, set background colors	WP 24	Click anywhere within the table, click Table, click Table Properties, click the Background drop-down arrow, choose the color from the list
Web page background, create texture	WP 32	Click Format, click Background, click Fill effects, choose a texture from the list of textures
Web page, create from the Web Page Wizard	WP 45	Click File, click New, click the Web Pages tab, double-click ▨, choose a design and style for your Web page
Web Page title, create	WP 21	Click File, click Properties, enter the Web Page title
Web presentation, create from PowerPoint	WP 34	Within PowerPoint, click File, click Save as HTML, choose options for the Web presentation following steps from theHTML Wizard
Web presentation, view	WP 39	Open the index.htm document created by the PowerPoint HTML wizard, click the hyperlinks generated by the Wizard to view each presentation element